Crammed with cutting-edge information on materials and techniques, formulas, suppliers, how-to's, and more, this is a book I wish I had when I first started!

—Christopher Tucker, BAFTA winner for Best Makeup Artist, Quest for Fire [La Guerre du feu] (1981), BAFTA nominee for Best Special Visual Effects and Best Makeup Artist, The Company of Wolves (1984), and Emmy nominee for Outstanding Achievement in Makeup for a Miniseries or Special, War and Remembrance (1988)

Todd's book is always the first thing I recommend to people that want to learn special effects. From the hobbyist, to beginner, to expert, there is always great information and new things to learn on every page!

—Frank Ippolito, Makeup effects artist

In an age of information overload Todd distills the art and science of special effects makeup, providing insights into the reasons behind specific techniques.

—Kazuhiro Tsuji, Oscar nominated makeup artist for *Click* (2006) and *Norbit* (2007); BAFTA winner for *How the Grinch Stole Christmas* (2000) and BAFTA nominee for *Planet of the Apes* (2001)

The most relevant, up-to-date, and useful information that is out there right now, peppered with keen insights from the author. Highly recommended!

—Thom Floutz, Oscar nominated makeup effects artist for *Hellboy II: The Golden Army* (2008); Emmy winner for *Six Feet Under* (2001)

I purchased the first edition of Todd's book for all the producers of the show 'Face-Off,' so they could truly understand the current state of the art. From silicone prosthetics, to 'bondo' transfers, this book has it all!

—Matt Singer, Inventor of 3rd Degree and Dermaflage

Right now, I think if you ask any of the older, successful and well known spfx makeup artists what helped and inspired them early on, they'd say, 'Richard Corson and Dick Smith's Monster Makeup Handbook'. But I think if you could somehow go into the future 20-30 years or more and ask the same question of spfx artists in that day, they'd say, 'the Debreceni books.' Heck, everybody's saying that now…

—Bob Brown, makeup effects artist and designer

With so many new techniques and materials developing these days in the makeup FX world, this is one book I find myself referring to regularly.

—Steve Wang, makeup effects artist, creature designer

Special Makeup Effects for Stage and Screen: Making and Applying Prosthetics

Special Makeup Effects for Stage and Screen: Making and Applying Prosthetics

Todd Debreceni

Second Edition

NEW YORK AND LONDON

First published 2013
by Focal Press
70 Blanchard Rd Suite 402
Burlington, MA 01803

Simultaneously published in the UK
by Focal Press
2 Park Square, Milton Park, Abingdon, Oxon OX14 4RN

Focal Press is an imprint of the Taylor & Francis Group, an Informa business

Library of Congress Cataloging-in-Publication Data
Debreceni, Todd.
Special makeup effects for stage and screen: making and applying prosthetics/Todd Debreceni. —2nd ed.
p. cm.
Includes bibliographical references and index.
ISBN 978-0-240-81696-8 (pbk. : alk. paper)—ISBN 978-0-240-81697-5 (eBook)
1. Theatrical prosthetic makeup. I. Title.
PN2068.D43 2012
792.02'7—dc23

2012035620

ISBN: 978-0-240-81696-8 (pbk)
ISBN: 978-0-240-81697-5 (ebk)
Printed in the United States of America by Courier, Kendallville, Indiana
Typeset in ITC Giovanni Book
Project Managed and Typeset by: diacriTech.

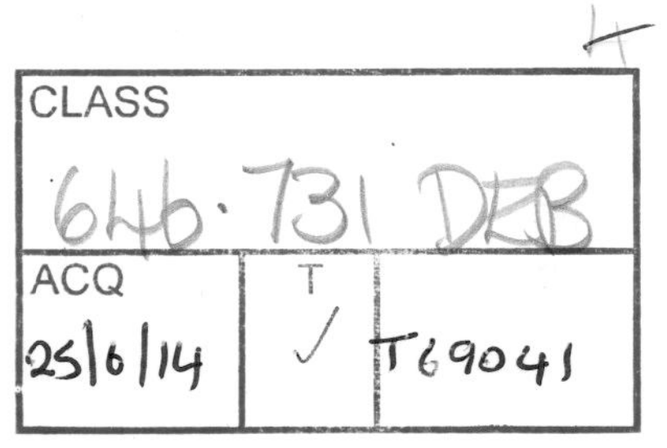

Contents

FOREWORD xv
ACKNOWLEDGMENTS xvii
PREFACE xix

CHAPTER 1 • The Industry

Introduction 1
Stage vs. Screen 8
Contributions From Medicine 14
The Workspace 18
Safety and Health 19
Professionalism 24
Your Portfolio 28
Your Kit 29
Chapter Summary 29
Endnotes 30

CHAPTER 2 • Anatomy and Design

Introduction 31
Using Computer as a Makeup Design Tool 33
Elements of Design 40
  Body Types 41
Human Body 43
  Skeletal System 44
  Skeletomuscular System 47
Surface Anatomy 52
  Eyes, Ears, and Nose 53
  Mouth 59
  Skin 61
Symmetry and Proportion 66
  Anatomical Planes 66
  Facial Ratios and Phi 68
  Ratios and Body Proportions 69

Geometric Analysis 71
Distinctions of Gender, Age, and Ancestry 74
Distinctions of Gender 74
Distinctions of Age 75
Distinctions of Ancestry 81
Chapter Summary 86
Endnotes 86

CHAPTER 3 • Lifecasting

Introduction 89
Safety Risks 90
The Materials 94
The Process 96
Overview 96
Teeth 101
Face and Neck 107
Bust: Head and Shoulders 121
Hands, Arms, Legs, Feet, and Ears 129
Hands and Arms 129
Legs and Feet 129
Ears 130
Full Body 132
Full Body: Prone 133
Full Body: Standing 138
Chapter Summary 140

CHAPTER 4 • Sculpting the Makeup

Introduction 141
Materials 141
Preparing the Positive 143
Tools 143
Clay 145
Reference Photos 147
Teeth 147
Materials 148
Sculpting the Face 149
Blocking the Sculpture 151
Refining the Sculpture 153

Sculpting the Face, Head, and Neck 158
Blocking the Sculpture 160
Sculpting Hands 162
  Blocking the Sculpture 163
Sculpting Ears 164
Blocking the Sculpture 164
Chapter Summary 167
Endnotes 167

CHAPTER 5 • Breakdown of the Sculpture

Introduction 169
Tools and Materials 171
Release Agents and Sealers 171
Making the Negative Mold 172
Keys, Flashing, and Cutting Edges 174
  Building the Clay Wall 175
  Building a Different Clay Wall 177
Stone (Gypsum) Molds 178
Other Types of Molds 180
Silicone Rubber Molds 186
Matrix Molds 200
Fiberglass Molds 209
Fillers 211
Resin Molds 212
Epoxy Molds 212
Syntactic Dough 212
Urethane Molds 213
Chapter Summary 222
Endnotes 223

CHAPTER 6 • Casting the Appliances

Introduction 225
Silicone: Platinum and Tin 228
Coloration 228
  Materials 230
  De-airing/Degassing Silicone 231
Gel-Filled Silicone Appliances 231
  Filling the Mold 232
  Injection Filling 232

Hand Filling ... 234
Removing the Appliance ... 234
Foam Latex ... 238
Materials ... 239
Quirks ... 239
Running Foam Latex ... 242
Prepping the Mold ... 243
Filling the Mold ... 244
Heat-Curing Foam ... 245
Removing the Appliance ... 246
Cold Foam (Urethane) ... 247
Materials ... 248
Quirks ... 248
Prepping the Mold ... 248
Filling the Mold ... 249
Removing the Appliance ... 250
Gelatin and Foamed Gelatin ... 250
Materials ... 251
Quirks ... 252
Filling the Mold ... 253
Removing the Appliance ... 255
Dental Acrylic ... 257
Materials ... 257
Filling the Mold and Removing the Appliance ... 258
Seaming and Painting Silicone Appliances ... 263
Seaming and Patching ... 263
Painting the Appliance ... 265
Painting Teeth ... 276
Chapter Summary ... 279

CHAPTER 7 • Applying the Makeup Appliance

Introduction ... 281
Skin Types ... 284
Adhesives ... 285
Application Techniques ... 287
Attaching the Appliance ... 288
Conforming Molds ... 299
Blending the Edges ... 301
Applying the Makeup ... 302

Foam Latex 302
Gelatin 304
Cold Foam 305
Silicone 305
Removing the Appliance 305
Materials 306
Removers 306
Technique 306
Skin Care 307
Cleaning and Storing the Appliance 308
Chapter Summary 308

CHAPTER 8 • Hair and Wigs

Introduction 309
Types and Varieties of Hair 310
Tools and Materials for Postiche 310
Wigs 312
Weft Wigs 313
Knotted Wigs 314
Hair Attachment 315
Preparation for a Wig 315
How to Put on a Wig 316
How to Put on a Lace Wig 317
Beards, Mustaches, and Eyebrows 319
Laid-On Facial Hair 319
Crepe Wool (Hair) 320
Ventilating Hair 329
Preparation 334
Technique 335
Punching Hair 338
Technique 338
Chapter Summary 342
Endnotes 342

CHAPTER 9 • Animatronic

Introduction 343
Technology 349
Mechanical 349

Electronic ... 357
Structural ... 362
Surface ... 364
Chapter Summary ... 370
Endnotes ... 370

CHAPTER 10 • Other Makeup Effects

Introduction ... 374
Resin Eyes ... 387
Bondo ... 389
Cap Material ... 389
Bald Caps ... 390
Making a Bald Cap ... 390
Applying a Bald Cap ... 393
Building Up Ears and Nose ... 397
Tuplast ... 397
Nose and Scar Wax ... 398
Materials ... 398
Rigid Collodion ... 399
Stencils ... 400
Tattoos and Character/Creature Textures ... 400
Airbrush ... 409
Spatter and Stipple ... 410
3D Prosthetic Transfers ... 412
Making 3D Transfers ... 412
3D Prosthetic Bondo, Pros-Aide Transfers or TPA Transfers ... 414
Materials ... 414
Electrostatic Flocking ... 418
Wrinkle (Age) Stipple ... 420
Trauma, Wounds, and Bruises ... 422
Bruises ... 423
The Baseball Stitch ... 423
Nosebleed on Demand ... 423
Burns and Blisters ... 424
Other Skin Conditions ... 425
Skin-Safe Silicone and Gelatin ... 425
Chapter Summary ... 427

Appendix A 429

Appendix B 433

Appendix C 447

Appendix D 467

Appendix E 475

Glossary 479

Index 493

Foreword

25 years ago, I would have loved to have stumbled upon this book.

In 1987, I started special effects makeup as a high-school hobby in Kyoto, Japan.

There was no Internet then and the only source of information was a lone Kyoto bookstore selling foreign books and magazines.

At that time, the few Japanese books published about special effects makeup were technically primitive and without the detail needed to manifest what I was seeing in my mind's eye. I found some books based on American and English movies and their artists, but these didn't have the precise technical information of this book you are reading now.

On weekends, I would spend half the day at the bookstore, exploring shelf to shelf, seeking magazines with new information. I was thirsty for knowledge about materials and technique. But most books were expensive overly technical manuals written for chemists, manufacturers, or dentists. Because I would rather spend money buying materials, I carried a small notebook to copy information. There were no cell phones with cameras to snap pictures of pages back then.

Actually, these challenges provoked me to figure out many things by myself. Lacking information, I was driven to experimentation. Out of the crucible of trial and error came new innovations. But I often wished how nice it would be to have a visionary makeup manual at my finger tips, all in one book. It would have saved me time and money and jump started my career a lot faster.

Well now that book has arrived. In an age of information overload Todd distills the art and science of special effects makeup, providing insights into the reasons behind specific techniques. Which ones are good and which ones lead you up the wrong path. Hands-on knowledge from Todd himself and many other top artists in the industry guarantee an authenticity rarely found in journals and magazines.

The most important way to learn a technique is to make it your own. I meet people who use techniques without any reason, just because they were told to do it that way. Professional artists understand why they use certain processes and adapt them to their own ways because they know what they are best at and are able to tune in to their creative flow.

Todd illustrates the reasoning behind why he picks a particular way to do something and explains what not to do. Sometimes those reasons are more important than technique by itself.

Technology and materials are constantly evolving. Once you digest this book, you will be able to grow your skills with each project. In other words, Todd teaches you to use your mind as a tool as well as your hands.

This book provides a great start for the beginner with correct and most detailed easy to understand information. It provides valuable information for professionals too.

For people aspiring to become special effects makeup artists, an obstacle is that they often cannot figure out where and how to start. They have passion growing in their hearts while imagining awesome creations. This book is your road map, a guide filled with in-depth information. But above all, it will fuel you with great inspiration.

I recommend *Special Makeup Effects for Stage and Screen* very highly to artists at any level.

Kazuhiro Tsuji

Acknowledgments

Wow! The 2nd Edition! Special makeup effects are the most fun I've ever had professionally, in large part, because of the incredible artists and craftsmen (both male and female) who work in this astonishing, ever-evolving field. I have never met or gotten to know more amazing, open, sharing, and supportive artists, and I want to express my deepest gratitude and appreciation to them as well as family and friends who supported, encouraged, contributed to, and assisted with this book. In my thinking, there are no secrets in this field, a sentiment widely attributed to the undisputed Godfather of special makeup effects, Dick Smith. I fully intend to carry on that tradition. Dick has been and will always be an inspiration to me.

Acknowledgments, gratitude, and appreciation to Neill Gorton; Dave Parvin; Matthew Mungle; Guy Louis-XVI and FuseFX; Mark Alfrey; Olivia Wegner; Bob Brown; Kazuhiro Tsuji; Josh Turi; Cristina Patterson; Jane O'Kane; Chris Clarke; John Lyons, Justin Neill, and Mould Life; Matt Singer; Kato DeStefan; Christopher Tucker; Ve Neill; Dave and Lou Elsey; Rebecca Hunt; Thomas E. Surprenant; Miles Teves; Bill Forsche; Thom Floutz; Jordu Schell; Gina Ortiz-Sodano; Steve Wang; Destiny McKeever; Tami Lane; Greg Nicotero, Howard Berger and KNB EFX Group; Alison and Will Chilen; TomLauten, Siobhan Lauten, and Nimba Creations; Vincent Van Dyke; Carl Lyon; Diane Woodhouse Lewis; Dominie Till; Stan Edmunds; Christien Tinsley, Jason Hamer and Tinsley Transfers; David Mosher; John Wilbanks; Mari Matson; Ian Jowett and Darren Grassby of 2Baldies FX; Robert Hubbard; Pixologic, Inc.; Brian Adams; Elliot Summons; Esteban Mendoza; Kris Martins Costa; Jamie Salmon; John Schoonraad; Brian Landis Folkins; Stuart Bray; Brian Wade; Rob Riffey; Aeni Domme and Stephen Sinek; Nicole Feil; Kelly Rooney Pearsall; Russell Pearsall; Kevin Kirkpatrick; Mark Garbarino; Toby Sells; Naomi Lynch; Vittorio Sodano; Eva Marie Denst; Thea and FX Warehouse; Suzanne Patterson; Dr. Eugene F. Fairbanks MD; Ed McCormick and EnvironMolds; Phyllis Brownbridge-Somers and WM Creations; Sharon Britt and Whip Mix Corporation; Diana Ben-Kiki; Rob Whitehead; Matt Pilley; Chris Guarino; Brad Frikkars and Jason Reese at Smooth-On—I'd be toast without you guys; Mike Fuller and Brooke Wheeler at Reynolds Advanced Materials; Tom Savini; Claire Greene; Raquel Bianchini; Pete Tindall; Ron Root; Bill Barto, Joe Lester, and the FX Lab; Martha Ruskai and Allison Lowrey; Jordan McDonald; Karen Spencer; Tess Fondie; Karen Taylor; Nick Sugar; Brian Walker Smith; Frank Ippolito; Marcel Banks; Chase Heilman; Mike Sisbarro and Silicones Inc.; Conor McCullagh; Gil Mosko and GM Foam; Meredith Faragosa and Price-Driscoll; Luke Pammant; Derek Lawrey; Brandon McMenamin; Janelle D'Ambrosio; Kelsey Rich; Phil Martin; Terry Milligan;

Don & Ellen Long; Tom Flanagan; Lisa DiMichelle; John Dunsmoor; Sara Seidman Vance; Richard Takash; Rinat Alony; Gary Willett; Daniele Tirinnanzi; Harry Lapping; Robert VanDeest; last but not least—Cryssie Bender, Ted, Lois, Amy, and Donna Debreceni.

I also want to thank my *many* students over the years who taught me while I was teaching them that no matter how good you get, you can still learn from others. *Fact:* You *can* teach an old dog new tricks!

Preface

FIGURE 1
Livvy Wegner.
Image reproduced by permission of Bob Brown.

I've been fascinated by the trappings of the entertainment industry since I was a child. The sets, wardrobe, props, miniatures, makeup, acting, etc for *Movie Magic*. Watching Ghoulardi and *Shock Theatre* in Cleveland, Ohio, as a kid was almost a ritual. I remember watching, mesmerized, as Lon Chaney, Jr., changed from Larry Talbot into *The Wolf Man* right before my eyes. How'd they *do* that?! And Claude Raines as *The Invisible Man* was *invisible!* I watched footprints appear in the snow and no one was making them. I had to learn how to do that! Playing make believe and getting *paid* for it. How cool would that be?!

Of course, many years later, after countless issues of *Famous Monsters of Filmland, Fangoria*, and now *Cinefex* and *Makeup Artist Magazine*, everybody knows how they do it. But it doesn't matter! Its still way cool and a heck of a lot more fun way to make a living than working 9 to 5 in the corporate world. Anyway, for me it is. It's the *doing* that floats my boat. If anything, since the first edition I'm even more into creating makeup effects than before. It just keeps getting better!

Was this always my chosen path? No, but the defining moment for me came in 2002. I had begun teaching animation and visual effects part time at an art school in Denver just a few years earlier and our department director asked me if I'd like to teach a new "special topics" class; it could be just about anything as long as it was industry related. My immediate reply was, "I'd like to do a class on prosthetic makeup."

Ironically, I had just begun to teach myself this craft using a few books I'd found: one by Lee Baygan, a couple by Tom Savini, and Vincent Kehoe's *Special Makeup Effects*. I was also doing some research online and was devouring behind-the-scenes footage on DVD releases such as Tim Burton's remake of *Planet of the Apes*, which was good but didn't really provide anything terribly enlightening in the way of techniques I could use. I still had rather limited hands-on experience. Well, somebody once told me that the best way to learn how to do something is to teach it to somebody else. So I did. And I found that adage is true.

The books offered pretty good step-by-step training: Baygan's *Techniques of Three-Dimensional Makeup* and Tom Savini's *Grand Illusions* and *Grand Illusions II*, for example; great stuff, but nothing had been written less than 10 or 15 years earlier than this book, and no book was only about creating prosthetic makeup (although Paul Thompson wrote a very good makeup textbook, *Character Make-up*, that was published in 2005 by Makeup Designory).

As I started exploring, I found great retrospectives of various artists' work. I found some outstanding "how-to" DVDs, videos, and myriad online tutorials. In fact, many of the artists whose work has inspired me and from whom I have learned contributed a great deal to this textbook. I learned a lot of valuable, helpful, and insightful stuff, most of it *really* good, but it still wasn't enough for me. To me, some of it felt incomplete, merely an appetizer.

I felt there were steps missing from some process descriptions, or the "how" was presented clearly but not the "why." I'd see somebody do something that looked like it was important, but there'd be no explanation of what it was I had just seen. The "why" is as important as the "how." Teaching the special topics class was an incredible learning experience for me and for my students, and my techniques and skill evolved with each subsequent class. I experimented, tested, and got better. I discovered *Makeup Artist Magazine* and the International Makeup Artist Trade Show (IMATS). Then, I met Dave Parvin, Neill Gorton, Matthew Mungle, Mark Alfrey, and a host of others. My chops improved dramatically.

There is encyclopedic information available out there in hardback, on the Internet, and elsewhere if you know where to look, what to look for, and are willing to pay for (some of) it. But there was no real textbook for creating special makeup effects. Well, there are textbooks, but not like this one. Even since the first edition. But make no mistake: this is not a traditional stage makeup book. There are plenty of terrific books on the market already that can show you how to do that. If that's what you want to learn, I can recommend several books that will help you. This book will help teach you how to design and create three-dimensional prosthetic makeup.

I started thinking about this book in 2002 when I couldn't find the answers to my many questions. The thing is, the more I learn, the more questions I have, and I think that's good. I believe that no matter how good you get at doing something, there will always be someone who can teach you something new. It has certainly been true for me. I also believe that anything worth doing is worth doing well, and I hope this book will continue to evolve as the craft, and my knowledge, evolves. I'm still growing as an artist, and I imagine I'll keep learning as long as I'm working in this field. I certainly hope so! Of all the crafts in the entertainment industry, I have never met a group of professionals who are more open and sharing than the artists who work in special makeup effects. This book was written in that spirit.

For the most part, makeup for film, television, and theater can be separated into three categories: *straight*, or *basic*, makeup, which is designed to alleviate discernable visual changes in appearance that can occur as a result of the film, television, or theater process; *corrective* makeup, akin to beauty makeup, which is designed to enhance an actor's positive features and downplay or disguise others; and *character* makeup or *transformational* makeup, which includes not only ethnic and age makeup but fantasy/whimsical, science fiction, and monster/horror makeup. This book concentrates primarily on the transformational aspects of prosthetic makeup appliances. Although monster, zombie, and horror/gore makeup is undeniably fun, the focus of this book is not gore; however, the information contained here most definitely applies to creating monster, zombie, and horror/gore-related makeups as well.

The emphasis of this book is on getting from Point A ("before") to Point B ("after") and the myriad routes one can take to get there; from concept to "Action!" The subject of special makeup effects is vast, as those of you who've been immersed in it already know, but those of you who are not yet seasoned veterans needn't be discouraged by the range of information about to be opened up before you. There are many hats worn by the creative professionals working in the field of special makeup effects, and not all of them are worn on the same head.

It's difficult to tell someone how to sculpt a face for a character makeup or how to sculpt anything for that matter. That is, someone can *tell* you; someone can *show* you pictures in a step-by-step manner, just like the ones presented in this book, but you still have to *do* it yourself. The very nature of everything you do as a makeup effects artist is physical. You can read every article, book, or description ever written about a particular technique, or watch every videotape, DVD, or streaming tutorial ever produced, but it will never take the place of actually *doing the work*.

My intention is that you will read this book and look at the images to gain an understanding of the concepts and steps to achieve the intended results, then go back to read it again while actually doing the work yourself. This book is not only for your instruction but also for your reference. It is to be used in its entirety or for only those sections that are less familiar and unclear to you. This book will never replace face-to-face training with someone who can provide immediate feedback on the physical work you are creating. This book will be best utilized in conjunction with face-to-face interaction with a makeup effects expert.

In many ways, this is a cookbook. Inside are "recipes" you can follow (or modify and adapt to suit your own tastes) to whip up a creative makeup effects masterpiece of your own. There are plenty of accompanying images to offer inspiration. Something that you might want to consider is taking this book to your local FedEx/Kinko's and have them cut off the binding and coil bind it so you can lay it flat and it won't flip shut. That way, you can refer to it continually as you work and follow along with many of the procedures presented in these pages.

The field of special makeup effects has evolved well beyond the application of straight makeup and into a realm bounded by gray areas of industry specialization. Let's say, for instance, that you have a script that calls for a newborn infant. Does the need for this newborn infant—a preemie in a neonatal incubator—fall to the props folks, or is it a makeup effect? Hmm... good question. Certainly prop fabricators have the skill and technology to mold and cast such objects when the need for them arises, but how do you get to the mold-making stage in the first place? Can a full-body lifecast of a newborn be made? Not likely. *Don't even try!* You probably won't get to use a real newborn for the shot, either; what responsible parent or guardian would even let you? It's a bit too risky for most people. So, how do you get from script to screen with your preemie? Sculpt it? Absolutely.

Enter today's makeup effects artist. The prop guys can sculpt, but traditionally, prop sculpture needs have leaned more in the direction of industrial design—futuristic/fantasy weapons and the like—than in the human or animal anatomy direction. "But, Todd," you might be saying to yourself, "aren't you talking about special effects, then, and not special *makeup* effects?" I did say that there are *gray areas* of industry specialization. You say "tomato," I say "tomato." But I digress.

Many of the advances in materials used in makeup effects have their origins in the field of medicine, and you almost need to be a chemist to understand the inherent properties and uses of materials such as foam latex, platinum silicone, tin silicone, urethane rubber, polymers, resins, wax, gelatin, etc *bondo*. In his excellent book, *Special Makeup Effects* (Focal Press, 1991), celebrated makeup artist Vincent Kehoe noted that special makeup effects can be as rudimentary as cuts, bruises, scars, burns, and tattoos. Every makeup artist needs to know how to create these, but the demands made today on a well-versed makeup artist—a makeup *effects* artist—are often to create much, much more, and often spontaneously on the spot. This book addresses that "much, much more" in a way that I hope will be beneficial to aspiring makeup effects artists as well as to makeup artists who already have some experience with the effects side of the business but want to learn even more.

With tips, tricks, techniques, and now detailed tutorials from many of our industry's most gifted artists, plus a new page format with more, larger color photos, may this cookbook of special makeup effects become dog-eared from use and its pages lovingly stained by the fruits of your labor. I hope this book does for others what the astonishing artists who have contributed to this book have done for me. I hope this second edition of the book will feel even more complete than the first edition, but with room still for even further improvement in yet a subsequent edition well down the road. Now clear off some workspace and get cookin'!

—Todd Debreceni

Note: The information and techniques described in this text are presented in good faith; no warranty is expressed or implied, and the author, Back Porch F/X, and Focal Press assume no liability for the use of the information or techniques. Use the techniques and materials presented in this text at your own risk.

CHAPTER 1

The Industry

Key Points

- Differences between working on stage and on screen
- Contributions from medicine
- Workspace necessities
- Workplace safety
- Professionalism
- Your portfolio
- Your makeup kit

INTRODUCTION

"Plus ça change, plus c'est la même chose." The more things change, the more they remain the same. These words, attributed to French journalist and novelist Alphonse Karr from *Les Gruêpes* in 1849, could hardly be more accurate in describing the business of special makeup effects today. Despite enormous advances in computer-generated imagery (CGI) technology (take a look at the makeup effects in *The Exorcism of Emily Rose*, for example, extensive digital makeup effects, very little of it is practical), the majority of makeup effects work in motion pictures is still very physical. Makeup effects for theater are practical by necessity; there can be no digital enhancement before a live audience. In fact, once a practical effect becomes digital, it is referred to as a *visual effect*, not a special effect. However, a great deal of design is being done digitally, which we discuss in Chapter 2. In motion pictures and television, a significant amount of work is beginning to be done through the use of digitally compositing elements of CGI with live-action footage. It can be a very effective combination, especially when you realize you

can only add, not take away, with makeup appliances. An outstanding example of practical makeup effects with digital accompaniment can be seen in *The Mummy* (1999) as the High Priest Imhotep, played by Arnold Vosloo, begins to regenerate.

It certainly hasn't always been that way, but inventive, innovative, creative people have been fooling the eye with special effects and special makeup effects since before the advent of moving pictures in the 1890s. There are scads of books and Web sites in which you can find ample history of film, theater, stage craft, special effects, and special makeup effects, so this chapter doesn't present a history lesson. But a few pioneers are worth at least mentioning; their contributions to our industry and our craft have been monumental.

Arguably the first great master of special makeup effects was actor Lon Chaney, who designed and applied his own makeup in the horror classics *The Phantom of the Opera* (1925), *The Unknown* (1927), and *The Hunchback of Notre Dame* (1923).

Many years later, Academy Award winner Dick Smith, the recognized father of multipiece overlapping appliances, created the 121-year-old Jack Crabb for Arthur Penn's *Little Big Man* (1970), starring Dustin Hoffman as Jack Crabb.

FIGURE 1.1
Lon Chaney, *The Phantom of the Opera.*
Historical image reproduced by permission of William Forsche.

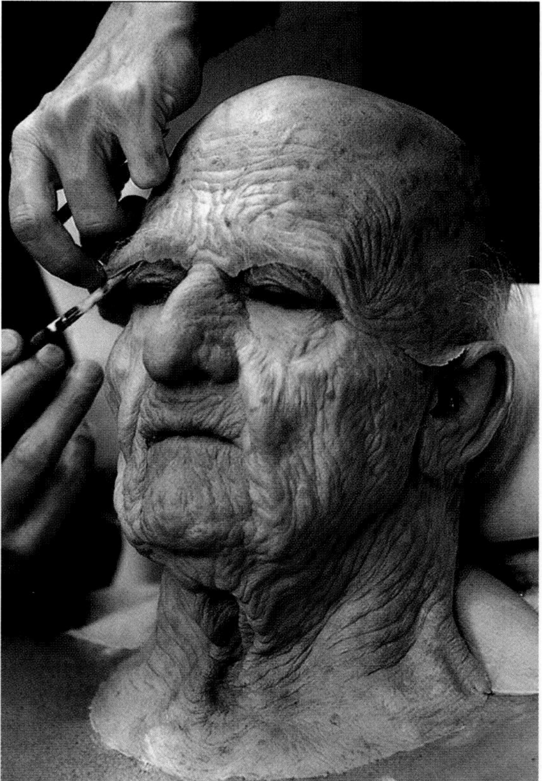

FIGURE 1.2
Dick Smith's multipiece makeup; *Little Big Man.*
Historical image reproduced by permission of William Forsche.

The makeup was created out of foam latex and comprised 14 separate pieces, including hands and eyelids. Four decades later, Smith's process of multiple overlapping appliance pieces is still the industry standard for applying complex makeup, whether in foam latex, gelatin, or silicone. It has since been adopted and improved on by the likes of Joel Harlow, Neill Gorton, Stan Winston, David Elsey, Barney Burman, Rick Baker, Ve Neill, Greg Cannom, Mindy Hall, Matthew Mungle, Vittorio Sodano, Bill Corso, and literally hundreds of other truly amazing makeup artists.

Neill Gorton

Neill Gorton owns and operates Neill Gorton Prosthetics Studio and Millennium FX Ltd. in the United Kingdom, providing special makeup effects, prosthetics, animatronics, and visual effects for films, TV, and commercials worldwide. He is also the man responsible for creating the amazing creatures seen in the BBC's *Doctor Who* since its distinctive 2005 rebirth. Neill's impressive credits include *The Wolfman, Torchwood, Being Human, Saving Private Ryan, Gladiator*, and *Children of Men*. Neill has been an enormous help and encouragement to me and has influenced how I approach almost everything I do in this field.

In Neill's words, "Not many 12-year-olds know what it is they want to do with their lives and eventually succeed at it. Frankly, I'm a bit of an oddity, and at the age of 12 I was already planning my career." This was in a suburb of Liverpool long before anyone had even heard of the Internet. Neill scoured magazines and books for any snippet of information that would help him achieve his goal. At the age of 15, Neill was already working with a mask maker in London; by 17, he was working on his first motion picture.

Like many, Neill was influenced by the stop-motion animation of legendary special effects pioneer Ray Harryhausen. Ray created animated model monsters and dinosaurs for films such as *Jason and the Argonauts*, *Sinbad and the Eye of the Tiger*, and *Clash of the Titans*. At about the same time when Neill was learning about Harryhausen's groundbreaking work, films such as *Star Wars* and *ET* were bringing more lifelike monsters and aliens to the screen through animatronics and prosthetic techniques.

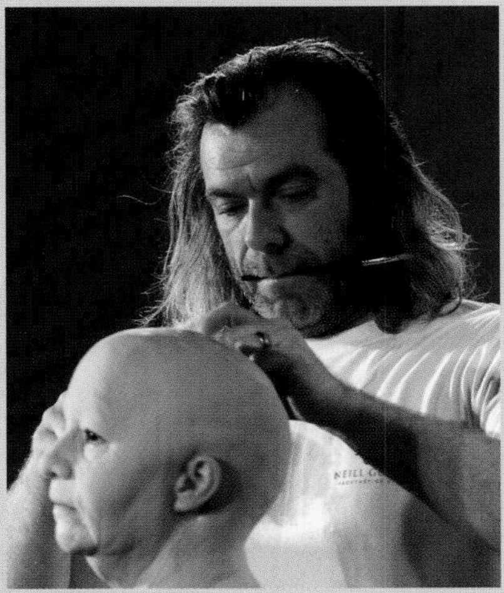

FIGURE 1.3
Neill applying one-piece silicone makeup to Karen Spencer.
Photo by the author.

FIGURE 1.4
Neill and animatronic werewolf he built at the age of 15.
Images reproduced by permission of Neill Gorton.

Neill's attention turned from creating miniature monsters in clay to full-size mechanical beasts and prosthetic makeup. His parents realized how passionate he was and encouraged his new "hobby." By this time, he'd been communicating with a number of makeup and special effects artists by post and received varying advice. Neill says, "Ultimately it watered down to 'Do practical subjects,' so amongst others I chose art, photography, and craft design and technology, which was an amalgam of metalwork, woodwork, and technical drawing."

"Looking back, craft design and technology was one of the better choices I made, because it taught the process of breaking down a product using a basic brief to determine design and function, following through to construction using a variety of skills and materials. All these things are very much a part of the work I do today, and this class gave me the fundamental skills to 'deconstruct' a project into its salient parts and follow it through from beginning to end."

In addition, Neill also studied drama because it gave him more time to experiment with makeup and his artistic skills to see how that role could affect the "other side of the curtain"—how the final performance is perceived by an audience.

"The last piece of the puzzle was chemistry," says Neill. "A special effects man working at the BBC, whose name, sadly, I forget, had kindly written a reply to my young enquiry telling me that chemistry was an important science in this area of work, and I'm grateful to him because he was right. I work in a world dominated by monomers, polymers, and polyesters, endothermic reactions and exothermic reactions, alkalines and solvents. My chemistry skills aren't first rate, but I learnt enough not be totally bamboozled when a rep from a chemical supply company starts waffling on about polymeric chains."

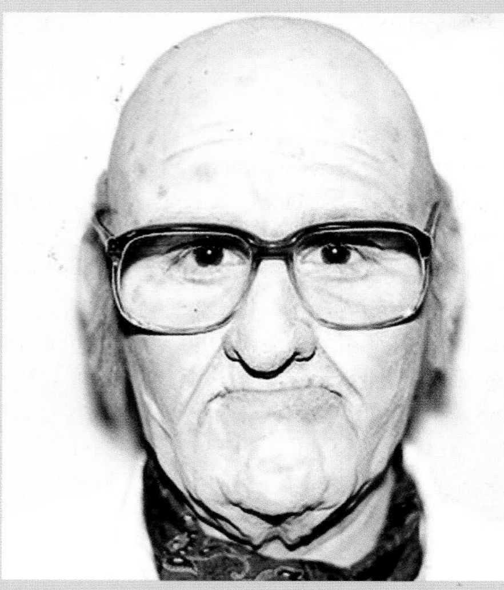

FIGURE 1.5
Neill's first age makeup.
Image reproduced by permission of Neill Gorton.

As a consequence of Neill's persistence, he was offered a couple of weeks' work with a makeup artist by the name of Christopher Tucker. The offer was to assist for a couple of weeks on another theatrical production and helping cast prosthetic appliances for the West End theatrical production of *Phantom of the Opera*.

FIGURE 1.6
Kurt Carley; makeup by Neill Gorton.
Photos by the author.

Neill's expertise in the field has taken him all over the world, and his travels are far from over. Neill says he wouldn't change his career path for anything, but adds, "Were I to be starting out all over again today, finding a proper vocational course in screen prosthetics which fully prepares you for a career as a workshop technician or enhances your skills as a prosthetic makeup artist for on-set work would be like manna from heaven and make the path into the industry so much easier to navigate. Hence the reason for having set up my own training studio for others who want to follow in my footsteps, but with a little less time wasted in wondering which way to turn next and bickering with well-intentioned but curriculum-bound college tutors along the way!"

FIGURE 1.7
Neill and Karen Spencer; finished makeup, IMATS London, 2008.
Photo by the author.

The very first Academy Award for makeup was given to MGM Makeup Department Head William Tuttle in 1964 for his landmark work of transforming Tony Randall in *The Seven Faces of Dr. Lao*, although Tuttle's work was hardly the first notably brilliant makeup since Lon Chaney's self-applied creations some 40 years earlier. The list of remarkable, memorable makeup work continues to grow with each passing year, but some have become indelibly etched in our collective consciousness (in no particular order): Jack Pierce's work on Boris Karloff as Frankenstein's Monster in Universal Pictures' *Frankenstein* (1931); John Chambers' extraordinary work in 20th Century-Fox's *The Planet of the Apes* (1967); and Jack Dawn's Tin Man, Scarecrow, and Cowardly Lion for MGM's *The Wizard of Oz* (1939). A list of cool and favorite makeup could be as long as this book, and if you asked 30 different makeup effects artists for lists of their top 10 favorite makeups, you'd probably get 30 different lists.

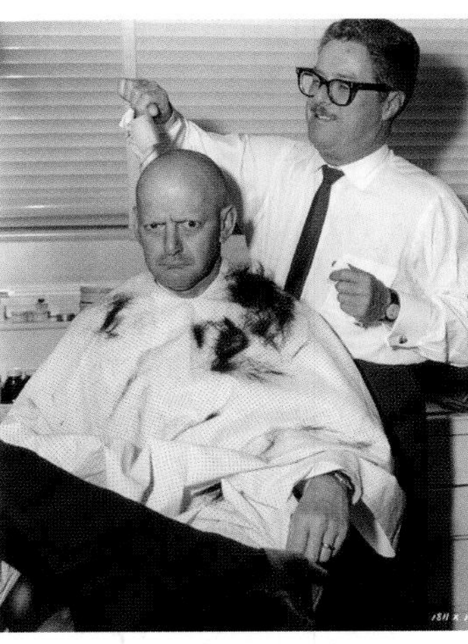

FIGURE 1.8
William Tuttle and Tony Randall; seven faces of Dr. Lao.
Historical images reproduced by permission of William Forsche.

FIGURE 1.9
Lon Chaney and makeup kit; *The Phantom of the Opera.*
Historical image reproduced by permission of William Forsche.

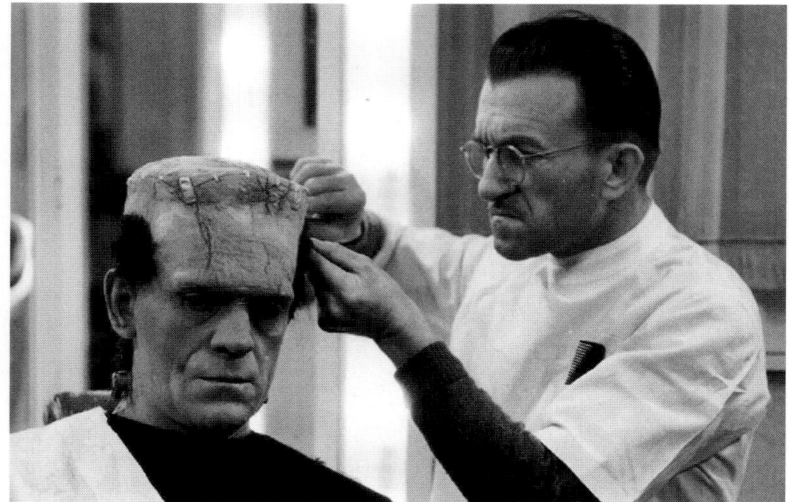

FIGURE 1.10
Jack Pierce and Boris Karloff; *Frankenstein.*
Historical image reproduced by permission of William Forsche.

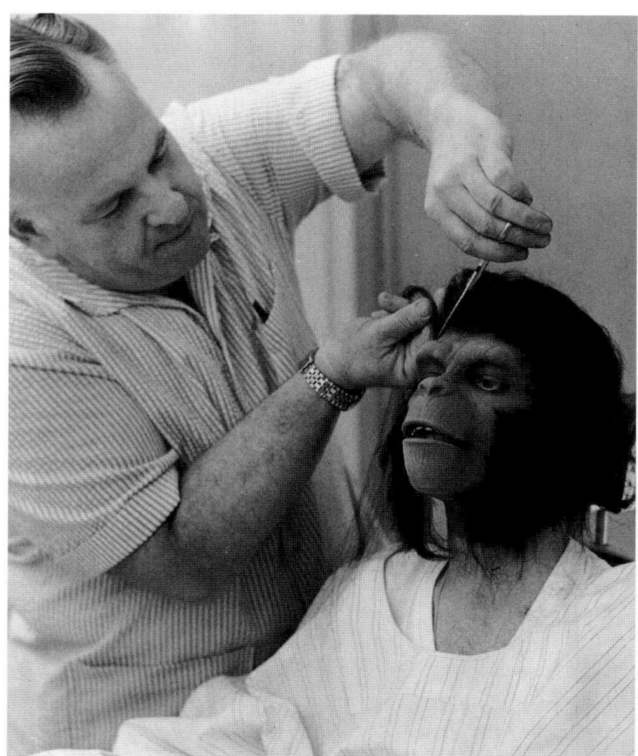

FIGURE 1.11
John Chambers and Roddy McDowell; *The Planet of the Apes.*
Historical image reproduced by permission of William Forsche.

Jamie Salmon

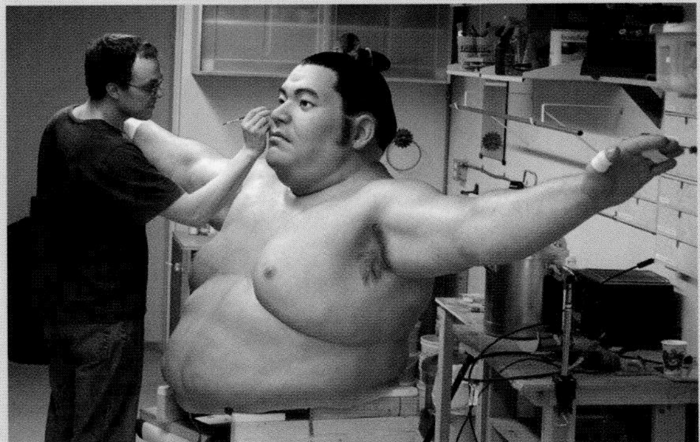

FIGURE 1.12
Jamie detailing Sumo, 2009.
Image reproduced by permission of Jamie Salmon.

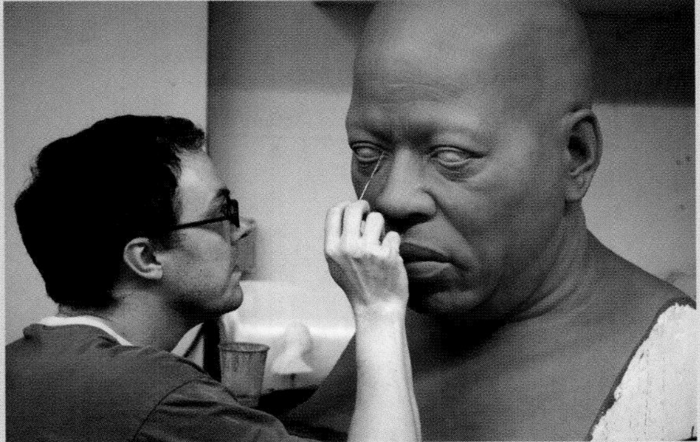

FIGURE 1.13
Jamie sculpting Wreckage head sculpture.
Images reproduced by permission of Jamie Salmon.

Jamie Salmon is a British-born contemporary sculptor living in Vancouver, British Columbia. He specializes in photorealistic sculpture, utilizing materials such as silicone, rubber, fiberglass, acrylic, and human hair. Jamie's wife, Jackie K. Seo is also a remarkable artist; whereas Jamie works frequently in larger-than-life works, Jackie works smaller.

The themes of Jamie's works are varied. He says, "I like to use the human form as a way of exploring the nature of what we consider to be 'real' and how we react when our visual perceptions of this reality are challenged. In our modern society we have become obsessed with our outward appearance, and now with modern technology we are able to alter this in almost any way we desire. How does this outward change affect us and how we are perceived by others?"

Every piece of work that is created in the studio is the result of a painstaking, multistage process that is both artistic and technical. It can take anywhere from several weeks to, sometimes, months to create a piece, depending on its complexity and scale.

Both Jamie's and Jackie's work can be seen on permanent display in the MEFIC collection, which opened in Spain in 2009. MEFIC is a contemporary sculpture museum

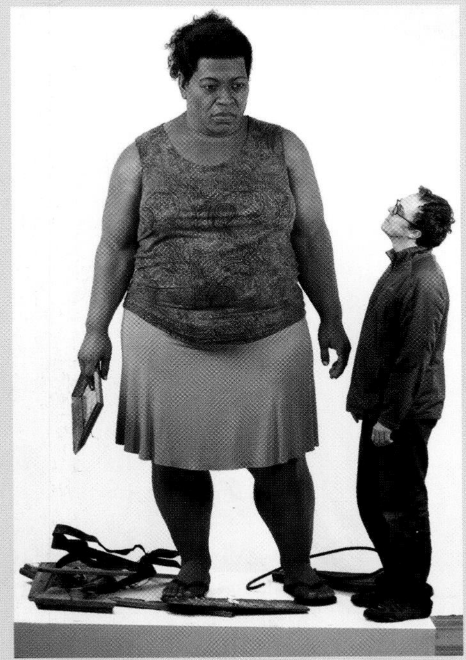

FIGURE 1.14
Wreckage installation.
Images reproduced by permission of Jamie Salmon.

showcasing work from some of the world's most influential modern contemporary artists.

However, Jamie is more than just an incredible sculptor of larger-than-life realism. He is also an accomplished makeup effects artist, whose film work includes *Freddy vs. Jason, Final Destination 2* and *3, Scary Movie 4, The Fog, X-Men: The Last Stand, Snakes on a Plane, Fido*, and *The Wicker Man*.

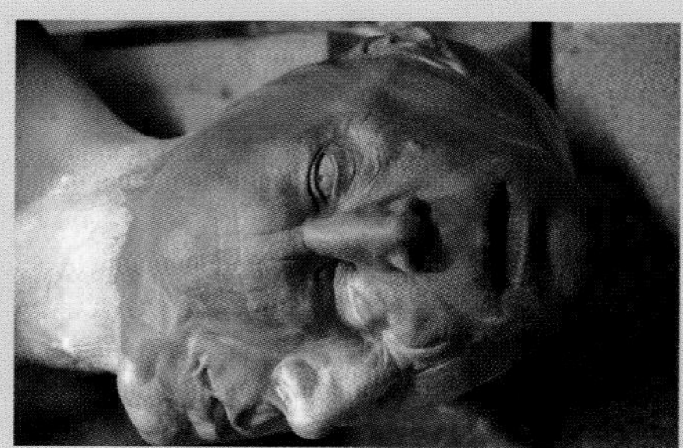

FIGURE 1.15
Fused sculpt.
Image reproduced by permission of Jamie Salmon.

Within the industry, there is some confusion about boundaries; when do special makeup effects stop being makeup, per se, and become special effects (which includes puppetry and animatronics) or the domain of prop designers? Is a severed head made from a lifecast of the lead actor's head and whose eyes blink and neck bleeds a makeup effect, special effect, or a prop? It depends on whom you ask, I guess. Legendary makeup effects pioneer Vincent J-R Kehoe said that although special makeup effects are character work in makeup, they belong to a specialized niche within the industry because creating makeup effects requires skill in painting, sculpting, mold making, and casting as well as in fabricating electronic controllers and articulated figure armatures used in animatronics. Therefore, he said, the work is not just makeup, but also special effects manufacturing.[1]

The field draws graduates not only from art schools but also from the fields of engineering, industrial design, chemistry, and medicine. In fact, a crossover between the worlds of makeup effects and the medical fields is involved in the creation of facial and somato (body) prosthetics.

STAGE VS. SCREEN

Strictly in terms of the end result, there is no discernable difference in the way makeup effects are created for use on the stage or screen. An important point to remember when creating makeup effects is you can *add to* but cannot *take away* when creating the makeup effect. That is, sunken cheeks, for example, would need to be the result of building up around the areas that need to appear sunken, and then taking away so the cheeks *are* sunken.

Although traditional stage makeup (not prosthetic makeup) is meant to be viewed from a distance, many of today's live theater venues put actors and audience within proximity of one another, so makeup of any kind, whether it is aging with highlight and shadow or by creating old age prosthetics, the makeup must read realistically from anywhere in the theater. Where the differences really begin to manifest themselves is in a particular show's makeup budget.

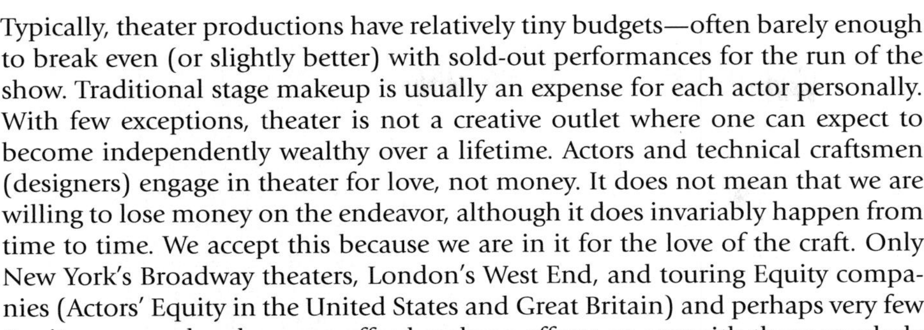

Typically, theater productions have relatively tiny budgets—often barely enough to break even (or slightly better) with sold-out performances for the run of the show. Traditional stage makeup is usually an expense for each actor personally. With few exceptions, theater is not a creative outlet where one can expect to become independently wealthy over a lifetime. Actors and technical craftsmen (designers) engage in theater for love, not money. It does not mean that we are willing to lose money on the endeavor, although it does invariably happen from time to time. We accept this because we are in it for the love of the craft. Only New York's Broadway theaters, London's West End, and touring Equity companies (Actors' Equity in the United States and Great Britain) and perhaps very few Equity venues elsewhere can afford makeup effects on par with those regularly seen on screen.

In film and television, makeup effects are a measure of scale; in theater, they're a measure of volume. Equity shows usually run eight performances a week for several weeks, sometimes longer. Film projects often need many days' worth of appliances for various characters, but other factors can quickly come into play. When an actor is made up with prosthetics for the screen, it often happens early in the morning, and the actor remains made up throughout the day, touched up by the makeup artist between takes, after meals, and so on. If an appliance starts to come loose, as it tend to do at high-movement areas such as the corners of the mouth, the camera can be cut, the appliance touched up, and then the camera rolls again.

When an actor is made up with prosthetics for the stage, it will happen as close to curtain time as possible, and if an appliance starts to come loose during a performance, there is likely to be hell to pay when the actor comes off stage! The same level of professionalism is required whether a performance is taking place before a camera or a live audience; the stakes are immediately higher for stage productions for the following reasons:

- There is no possibility of halting a stage performance to repair or reapply a mischievous appliance.
- Many theaters are quite intimate, with audience members seated mere feet from the stage; if the makeup effects are not applied to perfection, it will be clearly evident to those in the front rows.
- Film and television can employ additional dialogue replacement—rerecording dialogue by lip syncing to video playback—but theater cannot; an actor must be audibly clear and succinct throughout the theater in 3D makeup, and the visible effect of the makeup must also be as effective to people seated in the last row as it is in the first row.

Other things to take into account in creating 3D makeup effects for stage are as follows: Is there going to be a quick change for this character, either in makeup or costume? Does the actor have to put on or take off an appliance, and if so, how long will it take? Must the actor do it alone and in the dark? If clothing must come on or off past a makeup appliance, care must be taken not to damage the makeup, or time must be factored into the change to fix any damage. If it is

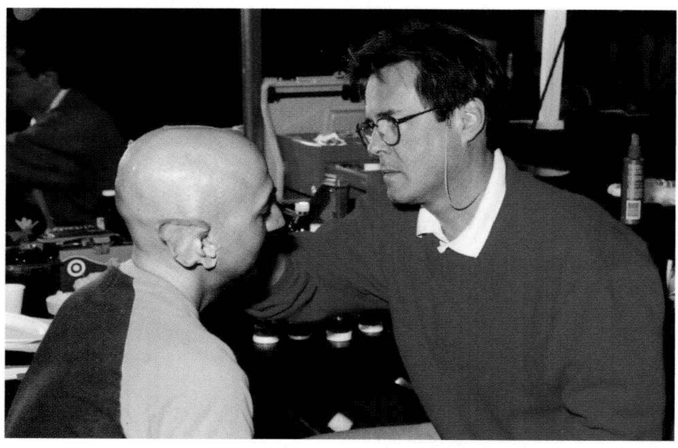

FIGURE 1.16
Author applying prosthetic ears to Nick Sugar for *Bat Boy: The Musical*.
Image reproduced by permission of the author. Photo by Kelly Rooney Pearsall.

a two-performance day, will there be time for the actor to get out of makeup and then back into it before the second show, or will the actor remain made up during the break between shows?

Probably the biggest hurdle to overcome in creating special makeup effects for theater is cost. If you're working on a major Actors' Equity production, it is somewhat less a concern, but not all Equity theaters have enormous subscriber bases to allow producers to create productions from an ideal financial situation. It becomes even more of a concern with small theater companies. For example, special makeup effects for a Denver, Colorado, production of *Bat Boy: The Musical* can become a cost concern because not only must prosthetics be applied, they are not ones that can be easily self-applied, so a makeup artist must be taken into account for each performance.

Many times an appliance application can be simple enough that the actors themselves can be shown how to put them on and take them off without trouble. The "trouble" shows up in the form of having to have a fresh appliance for each performance. I have been working for years to perfect a method of fabricating appliances that are soft enough for an actor to emote through, yet be strong enough to be thoroughly cleaned after each performance and used many times, thereby becoming more affordable. Several years ago, I created actor-applied character appliances that lasted 40 performances for children's productions of *The Garden of Rikki Tikki Tavi* and *Lilly's Purple Purse*.

If I can do that, I'm certain I will also be able to overcome many actors' seeming inability to keep their dressing areas neat and organized and their makeup supplies clean and uncontaminated. Yeah, right ...

There's another way I can think of that hair and makeup for theater differs from hair and makeup for film and television; in theater, hair and makeup fall (to me, inexplicably) under the direction of costumes, whereas for film and television, they are their own departments... as I believe they should be. I've heard the rationale from a few theater costumers that "everything should be tied together thematically." Well, *duh*! That goes for film and television as well, but hair and makeup have always been their own entities. This has long been a soapbox topic for me, so I'll leave this for debate another time, another place. Suffice it to say that I don't know a costumer working in theater who knows a lot (if anything) about hair and makeup—let alone special makeup effects—and certainly has enough, usually, on their plates just dealing with costumes and would prefer to leave hair and makeup to hair and makeup people!

Lighting considerations are often different for makeup effects applications for the stage versus for the screen. Whether you're creating prosthetic makeup for still photography, live theater, video, or film, lighting is always crucial to the way the makeup will be perceived. The biggest makeup concern from a lighting standpoint is the use of color, which is a frequent addition to theatrical stage lighting. Colored gels have a decidedly different effect on your makeup coloring—much different than under the lighting conditions in which the makeup was applied. One way to develop makeup coloration for a stage production is to equip the dressing room with the same colored gels that will be present on stage with the makeup. Another is to do a makeup test on stage under actual stage lighting conditions. If the effect is negative, there should still be time to suggest makeup options. I'd try this route before suggesting that the lighting designer change her lighting plot.

FIGURE 1.17 Leonard Barrett Jr. in *Man of La Mancha*; PHAMALy, 2009. *Makeup and photos by author.*

Amber gels tend to flatter makeup by adding life to flesh tones. Rosco, for example, offers several shades of an amber called Bastard Amber that are quite popular; the Roscolux color range includes four useful Bastard Amber shades, #01, #02, #03, and #04, and two Rose shades, #05 and #305. Another popular Roscolux color for flesh tones is Pale Apricot #304. Surprise Pink is another color that has proved very useful for flattering makeup. There are several Roscolux shades in the Surprise Pink or Special Lavender category: #51, #52, #53, and #54. The Flesh Pink filters, such as Roscolux #33, #34, and #35, enhance the effect of most makeup by reinforcing the pink tones. But be careful of some of the other "pinks." Roscolux #37, for example, leans toward lavender and tends to warm up colors in the makeup base. It may even turn cool makeup gray or blue.

Blue filters transmit little red, so red and pink makeup appears gray and "dead" under blue light. This is an important factor as makeup is normally pink or "rosy" in tone. Blue filters are important in lighting many scenes (moonlight, for example); but care should be exercised when blue light falls on the actor, because it tends to give makeup a cold look. Even greater care is necessary when the darker Rosco blues are used, because they tend to create "holes" in the facial structure, such as hollows in the cheeks. Performers should be cautioned to use rouge sparingly. You should definitely pretest makeup when blues will dominate the stage lighting.[2]

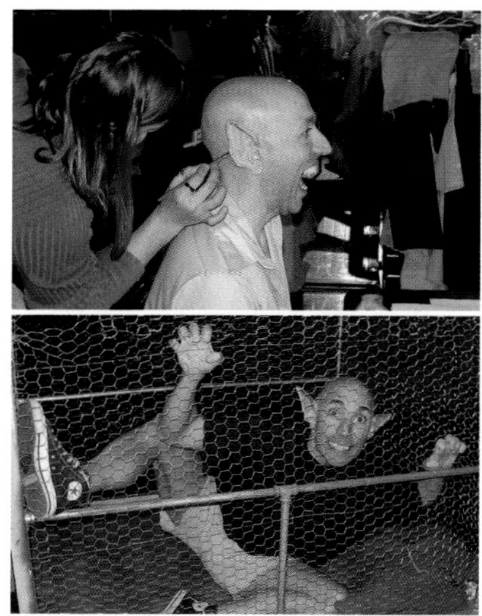

FIGURE 1.18
Makeup artist Kelly Rooney Pearsall applying finishing touches to Nick Sugar in *Bat Boy: The Musical* (top), onstage (bottom).
Photos by author.

Even rather "normal" lighting can appear to change the way makeup is seen differently by the audience than when being applied under similar lighting in the dressing room. The same production of *Bat Boy: The Musical* is a good example. Once the stage lighting was set, we did a makeup test under the lights, and coloring that was a perfect skin tone match under makeup lighting backstage made Bat Boy's enormous ears appear to be several shades lighter under the stage lights. We adjusted the ear color, and the results were outstanding, although under normal lighting backstage, they were too dark. On stage, it was impossible to tell that the actor hadn't been born with those ears!

Suzanne Patterson has offered this simple, yet great way to determine an actor's foundation color. This is particularly true in the age of high-definition work:

Makeup should begin with lighting that is no less than from a 5600 K tungsten lamp with daylight correction. It's at that temperature that all eyes can see the full spectrum of colors, and it will compensate for any skewed color perception deficiencies you may have in reading warm, neutral, and cool skin tones. Neutral is the hardest skin tone for many artists to read because they haven't been properly shown how to read temperature transitions through warm, neutral, and cool.

Neutral is equal amount of warm and cool on the skin and is the second most prevalent skin undertone, next to warm tones. The majority of the population—about 70%—has warm undertones.

FIGURE 1.19
Ve Neill touchups Keira Knightly in *Pirates of the Caribbean 3.*
Image reproduced by permission of Ve Neill.

The easiest way to look for temperature patterning is to look at the inside of the arm for some telltale signs: The veins in a warm undertone will appear green, and a cool undertone will show bluish veins. A neutral tone generally has a blue/green tin to the veins. Be sure you're looking at this under the lighting conditions mentioned above or go outside into actual midday sunlight and examine the arms.

If you think your subject reads warm, then you'll need to match the value. Take a couple of colors in warm that come close to the top tonal value in the skin. Swipe a stripe of each from the side of the jaw down a bit into the neck and let it dry. If it's a match in temperature, then it should look like either a light or dark area on the skin. If it's a match in both temperature and value, then it will disappear into the background of the skin and look like a smooth spot on the complexion. If it isn't a match in either temperature or value, then it will sit on top of the skin as an orange-looking hue. With neutral it will look gray, and with cool it will look peach.

Ve Neill

FIGURE 1.20
Ve Neill.
Image reproduced by permission of Ve Neill.

One of the most well-known, well-regarded, and sought-after makeup artists working in the world today, three-time Oscar winner Ve Neill remains one of the nicest people you are ever likely to meet. Ve knew from a very young age what she wanted to do, and there has never been any doubt since. One of the first makeups she remembers doing was an alien on herself; she wore it to a convention and it was the first time she met Rick Baker. "I had this crazy looking pointed head and there were no ears so I had limited hearing," she said. "My ears were covered, naturally. I especially remember this because Rick likes to bring it up occasionally. I guess he thought it was pretty funny. I thought I looked great of course."

"The toughest part of this industry is trying to do more than just be in it," she said. "For some reason, it is much more difficult for women because you are also the one who takes care of the home and the family. I always tell young women getting into this field to make the decision between having a family and a career. This is a full time gig that requires most of your time. If you want a family they will not see you very much and that's not good. For me, there is nothing tough about it. I guess I just know the ropes now and if something doesn't go right you just simply fix the problem and move on. There is very little that cannot be dealt with as long as you have common sense and knowledge of your craft."

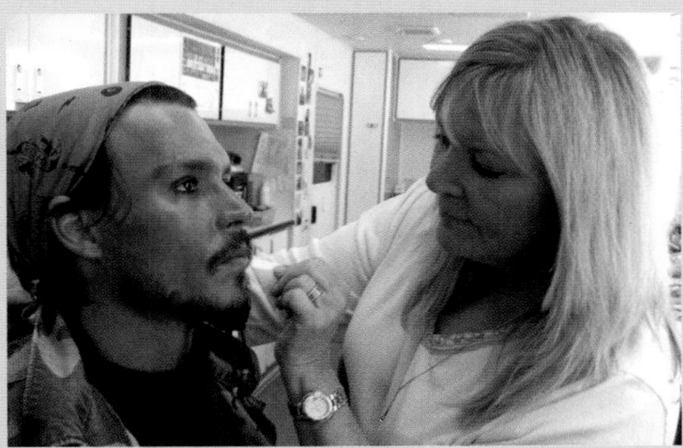

FIGURE 1.21
Ve Neill and Johnny Depp for *Pirates of the Caribbean 3.*
Image reproduced by permission of Ve Neill.

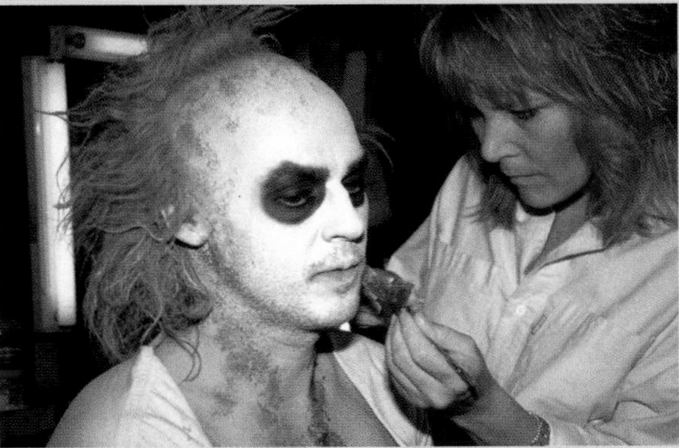

FIGURE 1.22
Ve Neill and Michael Keaton; *Beetlejuice*, 1988.
Image reproduced by permission of Ve Neill.

"All I ever wanted to do was make monsters and aliens and change people in to something or someone else," she said. "Let's face it, you get put in a box in this industry and it's hard to get out. I was an anomaly when I started. First of all, there were like two woman makeup artists and I didn't even think there were any (other women makeup effects artists) at that time. One of these days I'm going to find out who they were; they must have been hidden away at some studio lot in a back room."

FIGURE 1.23
Elizabeth Banks, *The Hunger Games*, 2012.
Image reproduced by permission of Ve Neill.

"I remember when I first got into the union some of the guys would hire me just to see what I was all about. They would have me cut sponges and sharpen pencils and the like. God forbid they should let me do any makeup! The late Fred Phillips was an old friend of mine at the time, and Fred would try to give me jobs now and again. I'll never forget the day he called me up and asked me to come and do *Star Trek: The Motion Picture* with him. I just about fell down! I was so excited and completely blown away. That was my first big union job. Wow!" Ve goes on, saying, "Your career is what you make it. There are plenty of very well established and famous women (makeup) artists that get hired all the time. They're just not known in my circles because they specialize in beauty makeup. By the way, they probably make three times the money I do, so as I like to say, 'Pick your poison wisely ...'"

Among Ms. Neill's stellar credits are some of my favorite movies of all time, including *Galaxy Quest*, *The Lost Boys*, *Mrs. Doubtfire* (for which she won an Oscar), *Beetlejuice* (for which she won another Oscar), and *Edward Scissorhands*.

FIGURE 1.24
Ve Neill and Johnny Depp; *Edward Scissorhands*, 1990.
Images reproduced by permission of Ve Neill.

CONTRIBUTIONS FROM MEDICINE

Many developments regarding the materials used in the fabrication and coloring of makeup effects appliances as well as the adhesives used to hold them in place have come from the field of anaplastology: the art and science of restoring human anatomy by artificial means.

Generally speaking, various kinds of prostheses made by anaplastologists include facial, somato (body), and ocular (eye) prostheses.

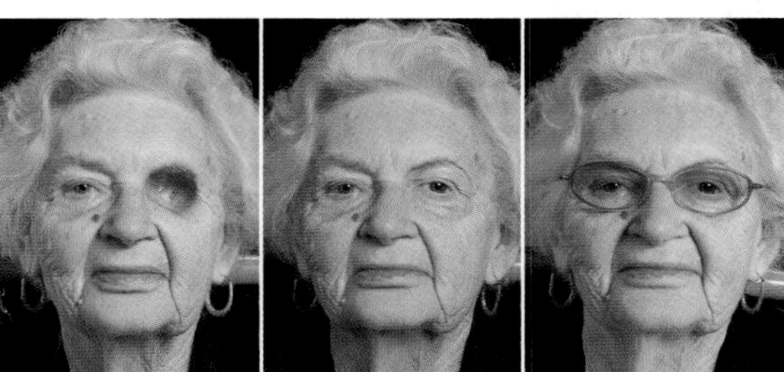
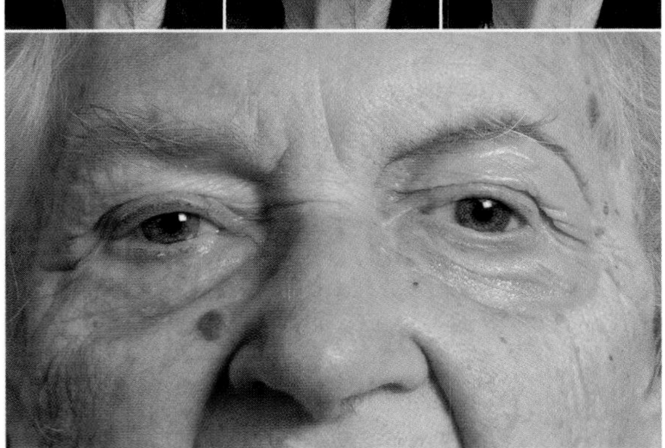

FIGURE 1.25
Silicone prosthesis relies on undercuts in orbital socket for retention; back of prosthesis gel filled to allow insertion into undercuts. Loss of orbital contents due to malignancy.
Images reproduced by permission of Medical Illustration Department, UHL NHS Trust.

This is exactly what makeup effects artists do. It is the job of a special makeup effects artist to create prosthetic appliances to be worn by actors that will transform their physical appearance by replicating anatomy as closely as possible, resulting in a natural and lifelike appearance although interfering with the actor's performance as little as possible.

Just as with prosthetic appliances made for use on stage or screen, even a well-made anaplastic prosthesis may be detectable under close observation. Because prostheses are not living tissue, there are some obvious limitations: An anaplastic prosthesis might not restore normal movement, it will not blush or tan, and it must be removed for cleaning.

The process of making prostheses is the blending of art and science. There is very little difference between the methods of designing and fabricating a prosthetic device for everyday use and one created for a stage or screen character, with the possible exception of some of the materials used for the finished appliance. As a result of development from silicone breast implant technology, silicone gel–filled appliances incorporate a tough elastomeric encapsulator—usually another silicone used as an outer skin, or envelope—over soft silicone gel that approximates the qualities of human skin over soft fleshy or fatty tissue.

Although special effects artists employ the use of foam latex and gelatin as well as silicone as prosthetic appliance materials,

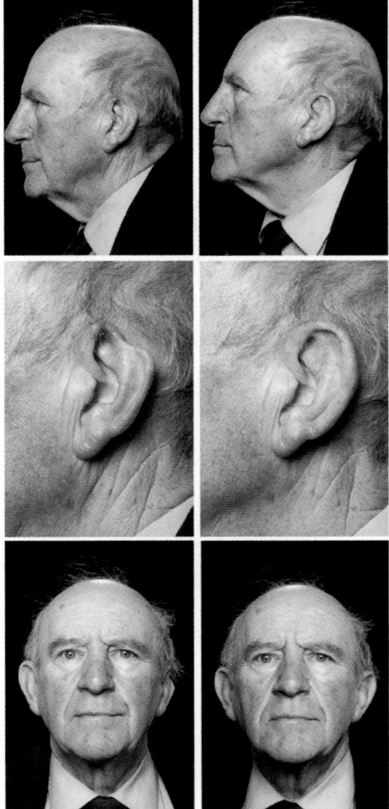

FIGURE 1.26
Partial auricular prosthesis following trauma to pinna; retained by natural undercuts within natural ear.
Images reproduced by permission of Medical Illustration Department, UHL NHS Trust.

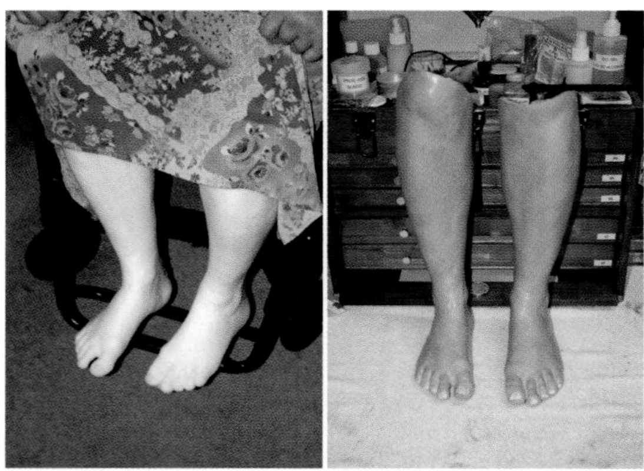

FIGURE 1.27
Cosmetic legs made by author. Unpainted legs during early fitting (left) and finished gams (right). Polyfoam and acrylic polymer skin.
Photos by author.

anaplastologists do not work with gelatin or foam latex. This is where the major differences stop. The results are dependent on the artistic, clinical, and technical skills of an individual professional. A well-made medical prosthesis serves to restore form whenever possible. Anatomical landmarks; facial proportion; symmetry; the direction of skin folds, skin, and tissue textures; and the coloration of the skin are taken into account for creating a convincing, lifelike appearance. This is no different from what a special makeup effects artist does. The steps in the creation of appliances are virtually identical, too.

Materials used in the creation of anaplastic prostheses include ultralightweight silicone and polyurethane. Furthermore, although special makeup effects are attached with a variety of medical-grade adhesives, craniofacial implants made of titanium have greatly simplified the daily management of facial prostheses for everyday applications. However, these titanium anchors do require surgical implantation. Some people become anxious about the possibility of a prosthetic appliance coming loose, which causes them to avoid many social activities. Craniofacial implants can give those people the confidence to participate in more activities, which, together with an improved esthetic appearance, improves their quality of life. The use of these implants has also allowed for the development of new techniques and advanced applications of softer, more flesh-like silicones.

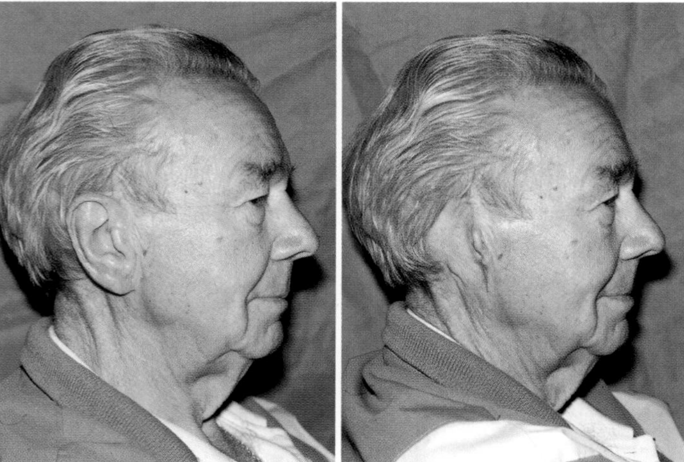

FIGURE 1.28
Adhesive-retained auricular prosthesis in medical-grade silicone. Appliances must be removed and replaced each day. Loss of ear due to malignancy.
Images reproduced by permission of Medical Illustration Department, UHL NHS Trust.

High-consistency silicones with greater tear resistance can be used where edge strength is a priority. The manipulation and mold packing characteristics of these silicones also produce deeper and longer-lasting intrinsic coloration. Nuances in pigmentation and vascularity—that is, the condition of having prominent, visible veins—can literally be captured with a prosthesis by layering color into the mold before polymerization, but this, like any painting technique, relies heavily on the artistic skills of the artist. Achieving the ideal pigment-to-polymer ratio results in a prosthesis that reflects and absorbs light similarly to the adjacent skin. Human skin is not completely opaque, and this balance between opacity and translucence produces a more natural appearance over varied lighting conditions.

FIGURE 1.29
Silicone eye made by prosthetic artist/ technician Matt Singer.
Image reproduced by permission of Matt Singer.

The American Anaplastology Association is an organization that serves to bring together those specialties involved in anatomical restorations and to encourage acceptance and understanding of facial and somato prosthetics among healthcare specialties and providers worldwide. Experts from the fields of anaplastology, maxillofacial prosthetics, medical illustration, ocularistry, prosthetics and orthotics, dental lab technology, prosthetic dentistry (prosthodontics), materials research, clinical cosmetology, biomechanical engineering, medicine, psychology, and other allied fields all participate in the task of improving patient outcomes through research and information exchange. It is through much of this activity that advancements in makeup effects technology occur. Anaplastology is an emerging global profession from which special makeup effects artists can benefit. Their annual conferences and publications offer timely topics on all aspects of restorative prosthetics, as well as conduct workshops on new and innovative developments in biomaterials, technologies, procedures, and approaches.

Greg Nicotero

FIGURE 1.30
Greg signing Walking Dead posters, KNB.
Image reproduced by permission of KNB.

Greg began his film career under the watchful eyes of director George Romero and special effects master Tom Savini in Pittsburgh, PA, but quickly relocated to Hollywood. His skills as an effects coordinator helped him to easily anticipate the needs of the film industry. His personality and sense of loyalty has won over directors such as Frank Darabont, M. Night Shamalyan, and Quentin Tarantino.

His overall effects knowledge has also made him an ideal choice to supervise effects photography. Greg has also directed sequences for George Romero's *Land of the Dead*, the R. L. Stine inspired series *The Haunting Hour*, the Stephen King/Frank Darabont collaboration *The Mist*, and is

FIGURE 1.31
Greg Nicotero, Howard Berger, makeup team for *The Walking Dead*: (Left to right) Andy Shoneberg, Jake Garber, Greg Nicotero, Howard Berger, Kevin Wasner, Garrett Immel, and Jaremy Aiello.
Image reproduced by permission of KNB.

a co-executive producer and the makeup effects supervisor for the AMC hit show of Robert Kirkman's comic book zombie apocalypse series *The Walking Dead* and has directed that show as well.

Greg formed KNB EFX Group Inc. with his close friend and business partner Howard Berger in 1988. Since then, Howard and Greg's talents have been highlighted in feature films including *Dances with Wolves*, *The Green Mile*, *Sin City*, *Transformers*, *Pulp Fiction*, *Boogie Nights*, and *Army of Darkness*.

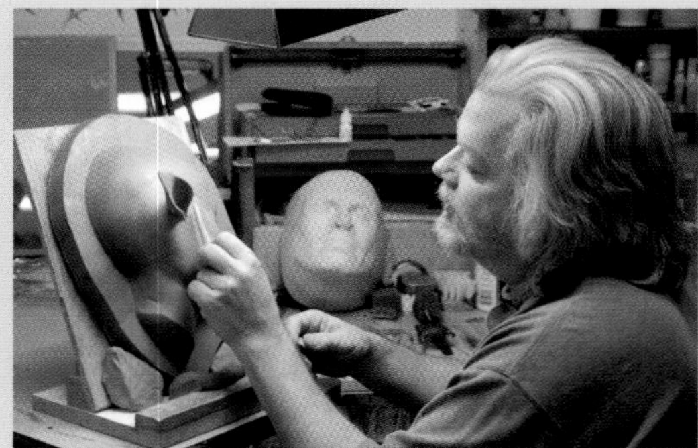

FIGURE 1.32
Andy Shoneberg sculpting centaur ear.
Image reproduced by permission of KNB.

Although it would seem to be a logical place for it in this chapter, it is Chapter 10 that has a step-by-step tutorial by Matt Singer for making your own nonmedical prosthetic-grade silicone eyes.

The Chronicles of Narnia: The Lion, the Witch and the Wardrobe won Howard, Greg, and KNB a BAFTA Award and an Oscar.

FIGURE 1.33
Author's workshop (then and now).
Photos by the author.

THE WORKSPACE

Before you can begin creating makeup appliances from your ingenious designs, you need somewhere to do it. My little indie studio workshop is called BaPo F/X (short for Back Porch) because that's literally where it started way back when: on my back porch.

Actual square footage isn't important as long as you have sufficient room to work on whatever projects you work on and can afford. It will probably never be big enough! I have a way of filling up space rather quickly. However, whether you take up residence in your basement, garage, barn, or back porch or whether you rent or buy a studio, workshop, or warehouse somewhere convenient, make sure you have adequate storage room for your materials, molds, and tools, ample electrical service to run them, and proper ventilation. *And* mellow neighbors who don't freak at the sight of various body parts being shuttled to and fro. My present office and workshop space is total roughly 800 square feet, which is quite cozy; I occasionally work with my friend and fellow sculptor Dave Parvin at his studio in Denver, which is significantly larger than mine. Dave regularly conducts large workshops in his space, so there is ample room to move about freely. I have access to space when I conduct workshops and classes that have too many bodies for me to use my own space.

Workspace that can be dedicated to the tasks necessary for creating special makeup effects is vastly preferable to space that must be shared and used for other purposes. The very nature of the work and the materials and tools involved often all but preclude any other use. The amount of dust and potentially toxic fumes generated by a variety of fabrication processes should be reason enough to allocate a dedicated space.

Makeup rooms in many theaters or film and video studios are usually custom built with the necessary power, lighting, work surfaces, and storage areas to provide a comfortable working environment. This is often not the case when working on location. Our makeup room on location in the jungle of Belize in 2007 for a film called *The Enemy God* was a thatch-roofed, mud-walled, dirt-floored hut, which we shared with geckos, scorpions, doctor flies, and the occasional tarantula. Frequently when we arrived early in the morning, there would be fresh jaguar paw prints in the mud by the door. We had bare bulbs overhead for our lighting.

We may not have had air conditioning or glass in our windows, but at least we had electricity and a roof over our heads. The wardrobe hut flooded every time it rained, which was daily. The point is to make the space you have functional, hygienic, and as comfortable as possible for your cast and fellow makeup artists.

FIGURE 1.34 Author's jungle makeup hut. *Photo by the author.*

Ideally, your working space will be well ventilated, including a mirror and counter space with lights for each working artist. There should also be plumbing with running water, both hot and cold. These conditions will be present in most situations, but when they're not or can't be, you must be ready to adapt to the situation at hand and make it work. You are a professional, after all, right? Or you want to be. The Boy Scouts were onto something when they came up with the motto *Be prepared*.

SAFETY AND HEALTH

In the application of makeup and makeup effects, it is critical for you, the makeup artist, to be aware of the potential for cross-contamination of makeup and accessories. Infections such as cold sores, sties, and any number of other potentially more harmful bacterial or viral infections can be transmitted via makeup sponges, powder puffs, foundations, creams, lipstick, eyeliner, and so on. These can also be passed on via brushes and other tools that have not been cleaned or sterilized properly. Portable autoclaves for sterilizing brushes, scissors, sponges, and other tools of the trade can be purchased for less than $300. Because of this potential for contamination and because the acids in your skin could also be contaminants, you should never touch makeup products with your bare hands. Use brushes, sponges, or spatulas instead. Bulk applicator items can be purchased relatively inexpensively for just such purposes. The same goes for disposable paper palettes that can be purchased at art supply stores.

In the United States, you can obtain health and safety regulations from the Occupational Safety and Health Administration (OSHA) (www.osha.gov); in the United Kingdom and Europe, Health and Safety Executive, publishes the Control of Substances Hazardous to Health Regulations 2002 (www.hse.gov.uk/coshh). In particular, you should be familiar with the correct storage and use of cleaning agents, solvents, polymers, and the like and make certain that the storage areas are clearly marked and in compliance with your local health and safety regulations.

The tools and materials we work with are not toys. Fatalities have been known to result from improper use and storage of numerous tools and chemicals common to the creation of special makeup effects. Thankfully, that number is small. Virtually every product used in the course of fabricating makeup effects has a product material safety data sheet (MSDS) with a product overview and recommended safety precautions. In fact, MSDS information should be gathered and stored on all materials (if available) that a makeup artist uses. These sheets are required when an OSHA representative requests them. Keeping them handy and in your kit, particularly when you are traveling, may actually minimize potential hassles with TSA or other security folks regarding what is in your kit and whether it may still be in your kit when you reach your destination. Try not to think of it as being intrusive, but as doing your part to ensure that your makeup subjects are being well taken care of.

There are enough harmful agents wafting through our daily environments already without adding to our potential health risks. Work only in areas with adequate ventilation. Buy particle masks and a respirator capable of filtering not only dust particles (even mist from airbrushed makeup foundation is not good to breathe) but also toxic fumes such as acetone and naphtha. Purchase boxes of disposable gloves in powder-free latex, vinyl, and nitrile. Get in the habit of wearing safety glasses. I keep inexpensive synthetic paper suits handy for messy days in the shop—which can be most days—because I'm tired of not having any decent clothes to wear. Many of the substances we come into contact with might not be immediately harmful, but harmful levels can build up cumulatively in your system over time. Take sensible precautions and keep both your workshop and makeup room safe and clean and yourself healthy.

The products in your kit should be properly labeled to avoid mistaking acetone for astringent or 99% IPA for distilled water. Hazardous materials should be kept securely in lockable metal cabinets or cases. It is really easy to work safely and hygienically if you simply use *common sense*.

WHAT ARE PHTHALATES?

Phthalates (pronounced *thal-ates*) are a group of chemicals used in hundreds of products, such as toys, vinyl flooring and wall covering, detergents, lubricating oils, food packaging, pharmaceuticals, blood bags and tubing, and personal care products such as nail polish, hair sprays, soaps, and shampoos. What phthalates are used in makeup?

The principal phthalates used in makeup products are dibutylphthalate, dimethylphthalate, and diethylphthalate. They are used primarily at concentrations of less than 10% as plasticizers in products such as nail polishes (to reduce cracking by making them less brittle) and hair sprays (to help avoid stiffness by allowing them to form a flexible film on the hair) and as solvents and perfume fixatives in various other products. Of late, these chemicals have been used as a softening additive into bondo for making 3D Pros-Aide transfers.

It's not really clear what effect, if any, phthalates have on health. An expert panel convened from 1998 to 2000 by the National Toxicology Program, part of the National Institutes of Health, concluded that reproductive risks from exposure to phthalate esters were minimal to negligible in most cases. I do know chemists in the United Kingdom who think that any use of phthalates is a bad idea, at least in terms of being used as a plasticizer or softening agent for making TPAs or bondo transfers. Here's my thinking: When in doubt, punt. My meaning is, if you have any doubts about using a particular chemical or ingredient, find an alternative or do without.

Currently, the Food and Drug Administration (FDA) does not have any compelling evidence that phthalates, as used in cosmetics, pose any safety or health risk. If the FDA eventually determines that a health risk exists, they will advise the industry and the public and will consider its legal options under the authority of the Federal Food, Drug and Cosmetic Act in protecting the health and welfare of consumers.

Matthew W. Mungle

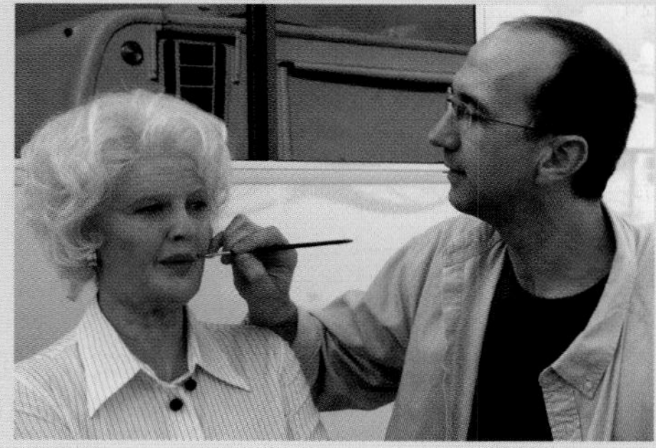

FIGURE 1.35
Matthew finals, Drew Barrymore; *Charlie's Angels: Full Throttle.* *Image reproduced by permission of Matthew Mungle.*

Academy Award winner Matthew W. Mungle is regarded as one of the Hollywood's premier makeup special effects artists. He has over 100 film and television projects to his credit, including *The Bucket List, Schindler's List, Ghosts of Mississippi, Bram Stoker's Dracula, Edward Scissorhands, Six Feet Under, N.C.I.S., House, The X Files, CSI*, and *Women's Murder Club*. Matthew has earned accolades and recognition as one of the industry's top masters of special makeup effects. Along with Neill Gorton, Matthew has had an enormous influence on my career and mentored me through my first feature as a makeup department head and makeup effects supervisor. I credit much of what I know to what I learned from Matthew.

As a boy Matthew recalls seeing *Frankenstein, Dracula*, and *The Mummy*. As he got older, he sent away for theatrical makeup from New York and Dallas specialty stores and experimented with face casts and prosthetics on willing family members and friends. Although his parents thought it was a phase he would soon outgrow, Matthew knew differently. He credits the 1964 release of *The Seven Faces of Dr. Lao*, with makeup effects on Tony Randall by the late William Tuttle as having been his greatest influence and deciding factor in becoming a special effects makeup artist.

Matthew came to Hollywood in 1977 and in 1978 applied to and was accepted into Joe Blasco's Make-up Center, one of Hollywood's top makeup academies that is responsible for training many of the film and television industry's best makeup artists. He credits Joe with his professional start in the industry. "I was a sponge, absorbing every ounce of knowledge I could," he said. "Whether learning the techniques of beauty makeup or casting molds and working with prosthetics, I wanted to be as versatile as I could." Today Matthew is a veteran voice listened to by up-and-coming artists hoping to find their own niche in the industry. Matthew says, "If you want to be a working makeup artist, you need to learn and perfect all areas of the craft."

Matthew's professional career began on low-budget projects that taught him to think quickly on his feet. His first major success was on *Edward Scissorhands* in 1990 with Ve Neill. Years later, Matthew has accumulated an impressive list of credits and an equally impressive genre of box office successes, an Academy Award and multiple nominations, and several Emmys and continued international recognition.

Age makeup has become one of Matthew's strongest calling cards and an area of makeup effects that's definitely challenging. His fascination with artificially making someone young look old prompted him to research more viable methods, such as gelatin, which was first used in the 1930s but later abandoned when the hot lights caused it to melt. With today's less-intense lighting and faster film, Matthew has resurrected the nearly translucent substance, which, when applied, looks and moves like real skin. "I've made it a part of my craft to see how skin moves," says Matthew. "I'm intrigued with how women and men age differently. Both get jowls and tend to get that fold of skin over the top lid of the eyes and bags under the eyes. However, men's ear lobes get longer and women's skin gets creepy and translucent."

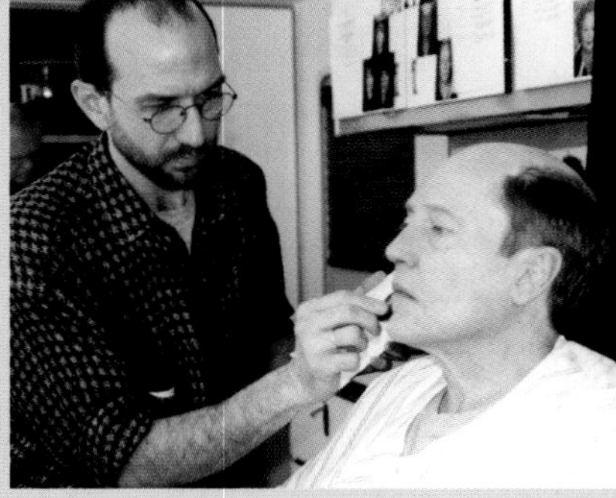
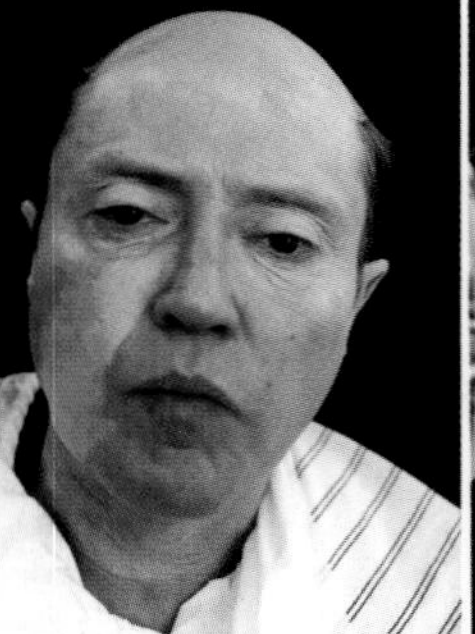

FIGURE 1.36
Age makeup, Christopher Walken; *Blast from the Past. Images reproduced by permission of Matthew Mungle.*

One of Matthew's greatest challenges has been with the Broadway hit, *Wicked*, creating the prosthetic face masks for the production's various characters—the flying monkeys and the talking animals. Balancing his film and TV projects, Matthew continues his work for the show's many productions.

"In my thirty three years working in this business, I've always taken pride in creating subtle 'I didn't know the actor had prosthetics on' type makeups, so it brought me great pleasure to work on Albert Nobbs with Glenn Close," said Matthew. "Glenn had a photo of a manly woman from the 30s that she wanted to base her character on, and I instantly knew the direction we should go which would be a slightly larger nose, earlobes, dental plumpers, no makeup look, and a little eyebrow work. Working with photos I had taken of Glenn at a meeting, I rendered a Photoshop composite of the look we were going for."

FIGURE 1.37
Photoshop render, Glenn Close; *Albert Nobbs*.
Image reproduced by permission of Matthew Mungle.

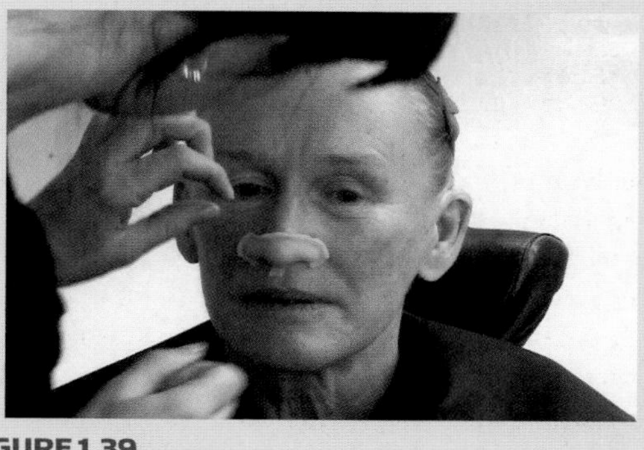

FIGURE 1.39
Albert Nobbs' nose application.
Photo reproduced by permission of Glenn Close, Matthew Mungle.

FIGURE 1.40
Matching skin tones.
Photo reproduced by permission of Glenn Close, Matthew Mungle.

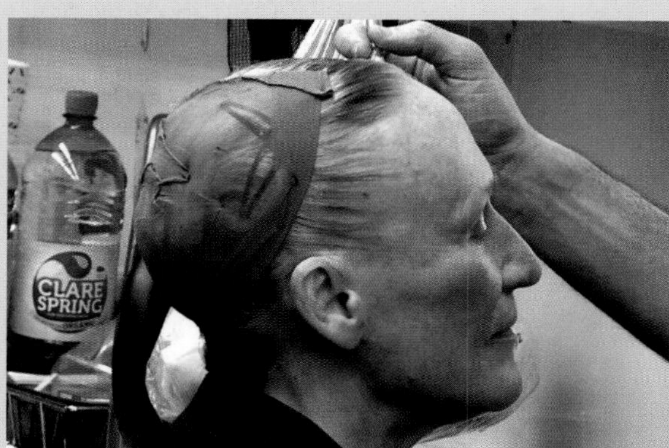

FIGURE 1.38
Preparing Glenn Close Albert Nobbs makeup.
Photo reproduced by permission of Glenn Close, Matthew Mungle.

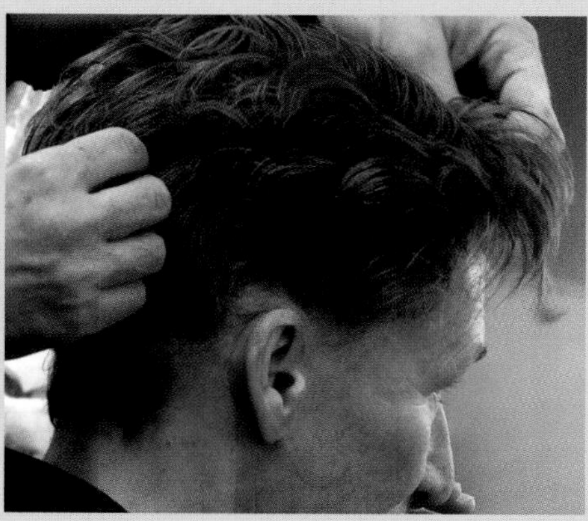

FIGURE 1.41
Wig placement.
Photo reproduced by permission of Glenn Close, Matthew Mungle.

FIGURE 1.42
Final makeup.
Photo reproduced by permission of Glenn Close, Matthew Mungle.

Matthew's process of fabricating bondo appliances—a combination of Pros-Aide® adhesive, Cab-O-Sil filler, and added coloring—has taken off in a big way since Christien Tinsley's success in creating 3D wound appliance transfers for *The Passion of the Christ*. The extremely soft bondo encapsulated in Matthew's alcohol-based "Soft Sealer" skinned prosthetics makes them ideal for use as a small- to medium-sized prosthetic; he created eye bruises for Sly Stallone in *Rocky 6*, casualty wounds for *Poseidon*, and even an upper lip appliance supplied for Guy Pearce as Andy Warhol in *Factory Girl*. These appliances are great for actors who perspire a lot or have to be wet all day and are extremely easy to apply with the lightest touch of 99% alcohol.

"There has been a lot of use of Baldiez; plastic-skinned Plat-Sil gel-filled silicone appliances in the last couple of years," says Matthew. "Thanks to Ryan McDowell, we've had great success making silicone appliances with the Baldiez skin and filled with Plat-Sil Gel 10 platinum-based silicone, which has a very low leach property when highly plasticized. However, I feel in the right circumstance that gelatin, foam latex, and even bondo appliances still have their place in our great world of creative makeup effects."

Matthew is big on not limiting himself to one particular material for casting appliances.

"I use all materials because they each have their own different properties. I try not to limit myself to a certain material because of the outcome of the creation."

PROFESSIONALISM

Working in the entertainment industry is supposed to be fun. We play make believe for a living and sometimes get paid quite well for it, too. However, it is still a business, and a certain sense of decorum can and should be maintained while still having a good time. Being well prepared and well organized is a good start.

Specialty makeup cases abound in a broad price range to keep your supplies organized; there are also inexpensive cases for tools or fishing tackle that are compartmented and will work well. Rather than putting all your supplies together into one kit or even several kits through which you have to search to find things, consider organizing your kits separately: one for straight makeup; one for injury and wound effects; and one for hair. I have, at present count, 15 dedicated makeup cases of various sizes ranging from small to very large, as well as numerous other bags and boxes that can be used to carry anything from tools and towels to hair clippers and silicone paints. I have a case for my electrostatic flocking wand and its accessories. I strongly suggest investing in leak-proof plastic containers for your liquids, gels, and powders. Be able to store your materials so that they won't spill, break, leak, or be damaged. Keep potentially messy substances such as adhesives, artificial blood, glycerin, and dirt powders such as Fuller's Earth (Pascalite) separate from other items in your kits. Before storing liquids such as acetone in plastic bottles, be certain that these materials can be safely stored in plastic. Otherwise, stick to leak-proof glass or metal containers.

I can't say this too many times: *There's no such thing as being too prepared.* Ask my students! I really do say this all the time. Be certain you have enough of everything in your kit to handle unforeseen circumstances, because they will arise. Do you have sufficient adhesive for your appliances? Remover? The *right* remover for the *right* adhesive you're using? Do you have sufficient cleaning materials? Sponges? Cotton pads? Q-tips? Create a checklist you can use for each production and each day. Are all your materials clearly and correctly labeled? I believe it is better to have more than you need and not need it, than it is to need something and not have it.

When purchasing new or replacement stock, be sure it's what you need for the production. Do you know of any special skin care needs of any of your cast? If you will be working out of town or abroad, make advance arrangements to ship-sensitive or hazardous materials—well packed—by air or ground. Traveling by air with many items, even ones in checked baggage that nothing could possibly happen to, can create major headaches, even if you believe you are prepared for them. Trust me. I'll give you an example; I pass along this information because it is a lesson I learned and a mistake that will not be repeated if I can help it. Once, when flying to a remote location out of the country, baggage inspectors painstakingly inspected every individual crème foundation in both of my large studio kits; there must've been close to 100 of them in all. Someone unscrewed each lid and stuck a gloved finger (I'm being presumptuous) into the center of each crème disk and then replaced them in the drawer where they were stored, many of them upside down and all of them without the lids secured. This happened both when I left the United States *and* when I came back through different airports; I don't know if it happened in the United States or at my foreign destination. Nobody claimed it as their handiwork, and there were no witnesses.

Regardless of the culprit, be forewarned. Before leaving on a trip, ensure that the materials you cannot take with you are available at your destination. If they're not, advance ship them. I could do neither and was forced to use them, but I tossed them all (what was left of them) when I returned home. It was an expensive lesson. Ship your kit by ground or by one of the express companies, if possible, for early arrival. This would be the most convenient choice, although not inexpensive. And it's not always possible. Since September 11, 2001, sweeping rules have been put into play governing what can or cannot be brought on board a commercial flight, even in a carry-on bag.

Your makeup area and workshop should be sanctuaries from the anxiety and stress that often pervade a set. Models and actors need a peaceful environment. Although your workshop environment might not be exactly a model of calm, Grand Central Station during the evening rush is not what you want to emulate for your working environment. When people rush, mistakes are made, and then everything goes downhill quickly.

Without some sort of protocol in place, a large set would be utter chaos. On smaller shoots, departmental lines are often blurred, but certain rules of etiquette *always* apply. Every craft has its own protocol for on-set behavior, but there are some universal standards:

- Show up early for your crew call.
- Be polite. Manners you learned in kindergarten still apply when you're an adult.
- Learn and use people's names.
- Ask questions if you're in doubt about what to do.
- Pay attention to what is going on in your department.
- Make your supervisor and everyone on your team look good.
- Stay near the action. Don't leave the set or wherever you're meant to be, unless you tell one of the assistant directors first and have permission to do so. If you can't be found when something goes wrong in your department and someone has to go looking for you, you might well have cost the production significant money while everyone waits for you. If this happens more than once, don't expect to be asked back.
- Remain composed. Occasionally, crew members, even experienced department heads, behave irrationally or even unfairly. If someone bites your head off about something, don't bite back; rise above it. Remain calm and courteous and ask them how they'd like you to proceed. If it's your boss or supervisor doing the yelling, do what they ask quickly and without getting angry or upset. If the angry one is not part of your chain of command, check with your boss before doing anything. If you can weather the storm, it will pass. By maintaining your composure in a confrontational situation, you've made yourself look good.
- Don't embarrass anyone, least of all your supervisor or anyone else you directly work with.
- Unless you are just making conversation or have been given the authority to do so, don't talk to other departments. It might be frustrating, but if you have a problem or suggestion, talk to your supervisor about it. An obvious exception to this rule is when safety is involved.
- Don't brag or be boastful. Ditto for arrogance. Doing good work and being confident in your abilities are not the same as showing off. Let people find out for themselves how good you are and how valuable you are to the department and the production. In other words, Be humble. It isn't that hard.

On-set etiquette is mostly common sense. The following list is by no means complete nor is it new. There are probably as many variations as there are rules. For a makeup artist, it is generally acknowledged that you are expected to be on the set at all times. Ideally, you will be near the camera but far enough out of the way so as not be a distraction or blocking anyone's view of the action. When in doubt about where to be, ask an AD.

- Dress comfortably but professionally on set. Be subtle. Remember: You *are not the star*.
- *Bathe!* We work in very close proximity to actors. Although working with grips who have dirt under their fingernails and don't wear deodorant might be tolerated, it is completely unacceptable for a makeup artist to have dirty hands and body odor.
- Brush your teeth. This is no different from not wearing deodorant. When your face is inches away from your subject, your breath shouldn't make them gag. At least keep gum or mints handy. As a service provider, you should want your subjects to be comfortable and at ease as much possible while you do your job.
- Talk to your actors; when you're applying or removing prosthetic appliances, let them know what you're doing at every stage so there won't be any surprises via sudden movements on your part. But, don't be overly chatty—learn how to read your actor and take cues for when to be quiet.
- Know your script, shooting schedule, and daily call sheets. Knowing how many scenes your actor will be in will give you an idea of your application needs. If your actor is in every shot, your application process will be different than if your actor is being shot for a small insert or short scene, and you can adjust accordingly. The same is true of knowing what the camera setups are going to be; there is no need to do a 30-minute touchup on an actor who is partially obscured in a wide shot.
- Be able to adapt and react. Thinking outside the box is very important, from actors' allergies to certain materials or a director getting a new idea for a makeup that should take an hour to apply and you only have 15 minutes.
- You are providing a service. Your makeup is for the purpose of enhancing and supporting a performance. It's never about the makeup; it is always about the performance. Don't forget that.
- Take your time. Don't dawdle, but don't let a zealous AD or impatient actor fluster you and make you hurry. When you rush, you make mistakes, and that ultimately leads to more delays, frustration, short tempers, and unemployment. Don't let yourself get sucked into a situation that you can't control.
- Resist the temptation to insert yourself into the middle of a discussion or rehearsal to do touchups. A director's last-minute instructions to an actor always take precedence over makeup. Wait patiently until they're done; go in for touchups only if you're certain it's okay. If it appears that you're not going to get the time you need for your finals, inform the first AD. It's the AD's job to coordinate these things; keep the AD or ADs informed of potential problems before they occur.
- If you're not sure how your makeup will read on camera or you need to double check a detail, ask the camera operator if you can look through the camera before doing it.

- To assure makeup continuity, take notes, draw pictures, and take photographs. Old school Polaroid photographs or digital photos of your makeup will most likely be a necessity, and you can refer to them as you work. Keep a detailed file on each actor and each change in his or her makeup. Every artist has his or her own way of keeping track of makeup for each actor. There is now digital continuity software called SavingFace for theater, film, and television. There are even apps for smart phones to keep track of your makeups.
- Sometimes we must be mind readers or, at the very least, intuitive; learn when and when *not* to talk to your actor. Actors might not be in a talkative mood and be getting into character when you are applying their makeup.

In a theater environment (unless you're working on Broadway or with a big touring Equity show), things will usually be a little bit different, frequently more casual, often chaotic, and cramped, but the basic tenets remain unchanged.

YOUR PORTFOLIO

It is generally agreed that your makeup portfolio should contain certain things. How many of these things is not agreed upon, although I think it is safe to say that quality tops quantity. If you ask 10 makeup artists what makes up a good portfolio, you will likely get close to 10 differing opinions. However, you might want to think twice about having only one makeup to show, even if it's a really, really good makeup. You need to show evidence that it wasn't a fluke. Oscar winner Matthew Mungle believes you should have examples of beauty makeup, small and large prosthetic applications, character and age makeup with and without prosthetics, and creature prosthetic makeups.

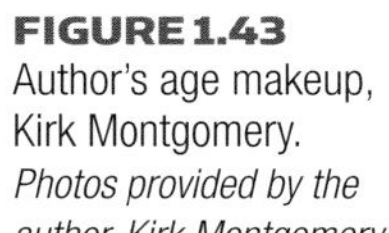

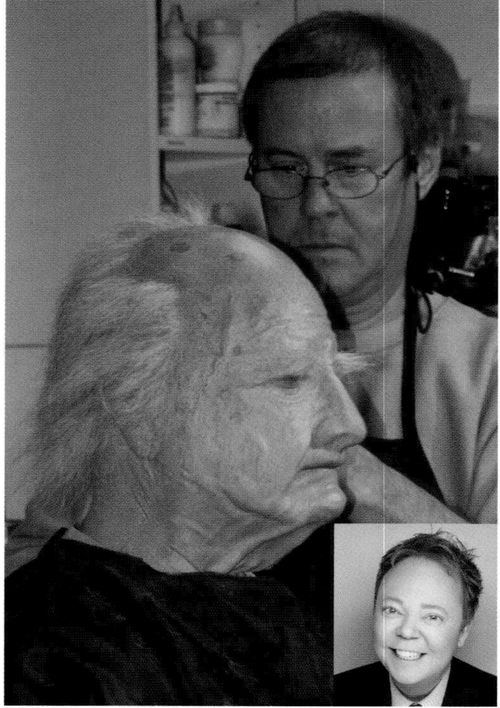

FIGURE 1.43 Author's age makeup, Kirk Montgomery. *Photos provided by the author, Kirk Montgomery.*

Kevin Kirkpatrick echoes my point: "A makeup effects portfolio should only consist of your best work. Honestly, it's not about quantity, it's all about quality." I've watched and listened to my friend Neill Gorton offer constructive criticism when asked to critique a student's portfolio. Neill is a marvelous teacher and an amazing artist, and he is graciously tactful. His advice, in a nutshell, is to *show the makeup clearly;* don't just show a before and after, with the "after" being a screen shot. Frequently, the screen shots are dark with the makeup somewhat obscured. Although that may fit the mood of the scene and the makeup looks great in the storytelling context, how well the makeup was painted and applied can't really be seen clearly. The person looking at your portfolio wants to see the paint job and how good your appliance edges are, not merely how the makeup looked in the actual scene. Whenever possible, have photos taken in good light that show how good your painting and application skills are.

Don't make someone work to see your work. Have a print version of your portfolio, an electronic/digital version, and even an online version where you can direct someone. Be able to show a client your portfolio in the way that they want to see it.

YOUR KIT

There's an adage that goes something like this: "It's not the tools that are used but the artist who uses them." Legendary photographer Ansel Adams said something similar: "The single most important component of a camera is the 12 inches behind it."[3]

The materials in your makeup kit will not make you a better artist; the right materials just make it easier, faster, and more convenient for you to achieve the results you want.

If you were to ask every working makeup artist what he or she has in their kit and what they consider absolutely essential tools to have in everyone's kit, you will likely find a great many different answers (this should no longer surprise you), the same as trying to get a fix on what type of case or cases these tools should be carried around in. Some artists swear by Ben Nye crème foundations; others can't live without Graftobian, Mehron, Krylon, or RCMA products. Still others may say it's MAC or Sephora for them, or nothing. Very few, if any, artists use only one product brand for the simple reason that no one single manufacturer makes everything an artist could possibly use. The Boy Scout motto, "Be prepared," certainly applies in this instance because we makeup artists are frequently called on to come up with a makeup seemingly out of thin air—something unplanned—and if we've got a little bit of everything at our disposal, it becomes much easier to improvise on the spot and (one hopes) look like a hero. Ironically, to be good at improvising requires practice and a very broad knowledge base. Some suggested kit essentials as well as a fairly comprehensive listing of suppliers are included in the Appendix C.

FIGURE 1.44
Kevin Kirkpatrick age makeup "before and after," Dustin Heald. *Images reproduced by permission of Kevin Kirkpatrick.*

CHAPTER SUMMARY

Chapter 1 shared a brief makeup effects history and introduced you to the makeup effects artists Neill Gorton, Ve Neill, Jamie Salmon, Greg Nicotero, and Matthew Mungle. You also should now be aware of differences and similarities between makeup effects for the stage and those for the screen.

We discussed how advances in medicine and medical prosthetics have aided the makeup industry. We also discussed workspace and working conditions, safety and health concerns, professionalism, what should be in your portfolio, and what should be in your makeup kit.

Endnotes

1 Vincent J-R Kehoe, *Special Make-Up Effects* (Focal Press, 1991).

2 www.rosco.com/us/technotes/filters/technote_1.asp#MAKEUP.

3 Ken Rockwell, *Why Your Camera Does Not Matter*, 2006.

CHAPTER 2 

Anatomy and Design

Key Points

- Using computer as a makeup design tool
- Elements of design
- Human body
- Surface anatomy
- Symmetry and proportion
- Geometric analysis
- Distinctions of gender, age, and ancestry

INTRODUCTION

After writing a story (script), perhaps the next most important task is designing and creating the story's physical characters. Of course, this will most likely only apply to a story that needs physical alteration of actors who will be playing characters in the story. But this is where the fun begins (at least for me), and having a solid understanding of human anatomy will make your job that much simpler and that much more enjoyable. Human physiology—the way the body works—is good knowledge to have as well, though it's not as critical as knowing human and animal anatomy is to the success or failure of a special makeup effects artist.

The way we move and the way we look is wholly dependent on our anatomy—our bone structure, how and where muscles attach, how big or small they are, what our skin looks and feels like, and how and where hair grows; everything about us right down to the dirt under our fingernails should be studied and understood. Without this knowledge, our designs, sculptures, and ultimately finished makeups would lack the sense of genuine depth and believability that a truly outstanding, memorable character must have if we are to succeed as makeup artists.

FIGURE 2.1
Werewolf; human/canine anatomy combined.
Image reproduced by permission of Peter Tindall.

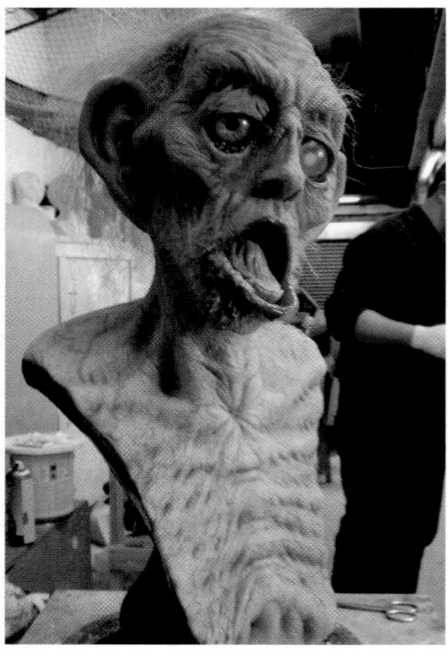

FIGURE 2.2
Zombie; exaggerated human anatomy is still human anatomy.
Image reproduced by permission of Peter Tindall.

As artists, we will never be completely satisfied with our work. Accept that as a given. Nor should we be satisfied. That is the nature of artists. No matter how good we get, there will always be something we could do to be better. We might not always know what that something is; it's simply the way we are. I don't think our work should ever be "good enough" for us. That's not to say that we shouldn't recognize when something is "finished" and move on to the next project, it's just that there will always be room for improvement. In fact, I think that is a good gauge for us as artists: The moment we start thinking that there is nothing we can do to improve, that is the moment for us to reevaluate what it is we're doing and why. Pushing ourselves beyond our "comfort zone" into increasingly more difficult areas is the only way for our skills to improve. And when we get comfortable at the new level, it's time to push beyond it again.

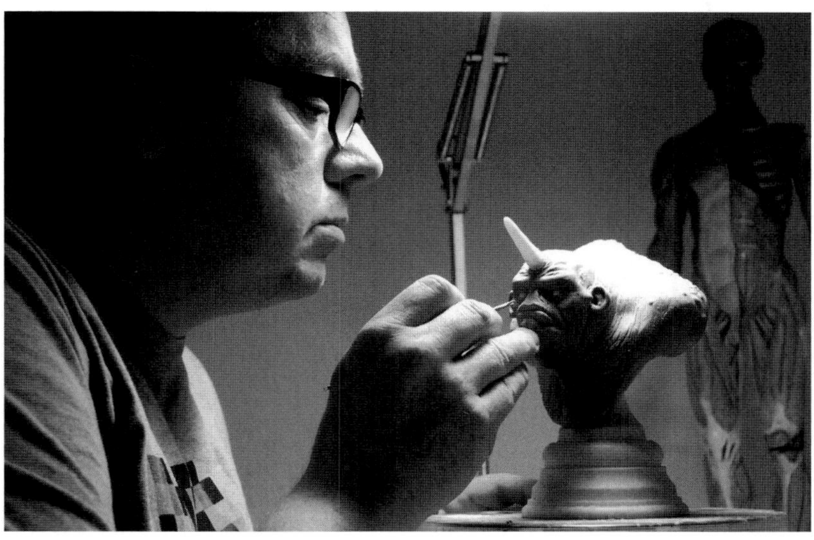

FIGURE 2.3
Pete Tindall sculpting creature in very small scale.
Image reproduced by permission of Peter Tindall.

Our work can always improve, and no matter how skilled we become, there will always be someone who can teach us something new. Iconic dancer/choreographer Martha Graham once wrote to her dear friend and contemporary, legendary dancer/choreographer Agnes De Mille:

> There is a vitality, a life force, a quickening, that is translated through you into action, and because there is only one of you in all time, this expression is unique. If you block it, it will never exist through any other medium and [will] be lost. The world will not have it. It is not your business to determine how good it is; nor how valuable it is; not how it compares with other expression. It is your business to keep it yours, clearly and directly, to keep the channel open. You do not even have to believe in yourself or your work. You have to keep open and aware directly to the urges that motivate you. Keep the channel open. No artist is ever pleased. There is no satisfaction whatever at any time. There is only a queer, divine dissatisfaction; a blessed unrest that keeps us marching and makes us more alive than the others.

USING COMPUTER AS A MAKEUP DESIGN TOOL

The tools we have at our disposal today to aid us in designing characters have vastly improved over the years. But human anatomy is still human anatomy. Whether you draw every aspect of a design by hand, go straight to clay and sculpt what is in your head, or enlist the aid of 2D and 3D software to model and mock up your designs, computers have become as essential a tool as PlatSil Gel 10, WED clay, Ultracal 30, and fiberglass. Today's 3D packages such as LightWave 3D, Softimage XSI, Maya, 3D Studio Max, and Cinema

4D are not merely high-end animation software but staple among character designers as modeling tools, as are the virtual sculpting tools ZBrush and MudBox. Software seems to change more frequently and significantly with each passing year. Adobe Photoshop now has 3D capabilities and is a very powerful previsualization design tool used by many artists, including myself.

A makeup design can be rendered quite believably in Photoshop for approval before tool ever touches clay.

I don't know a working artist today who doesn't have at least a passing relationship with Adobe Photoshop. I can't imagine working without it.

With the aid of software, the design process can be sped up considerably, though the computer is no substitute for a solid foundation in life-drawing skills and knowledge of anatomy. When asked about the skills required to be a sought-after character designer, Miles Teves (*King Kong, Interview with the Vampire, Legend*) is quoted as saying, "A good foundation in life drawing is key. You need to be able to imbue your designs with a sense of realism and nuance that you can only get from studying nature directly."[1]

FIGURE 2.4
Dave Elsey Photoshop previz.
Image reproduced by permission of David Elsey.

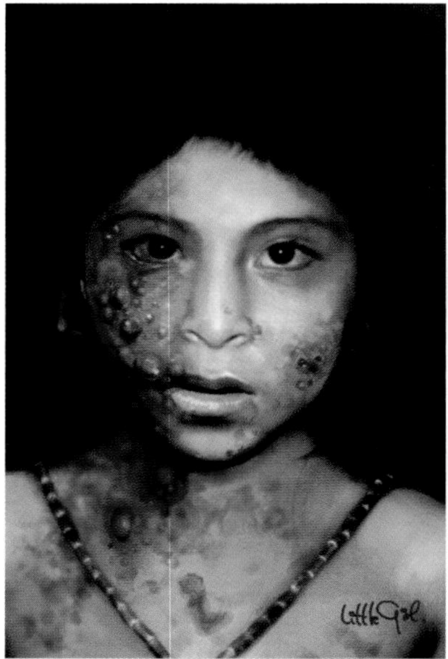

FIGURE 2.5
Plague girl from *Apocalypto*.
Image reproduced by permission of Vittorio Sodano.

FIGURE 2.6
ZBrush Design and sculpture.
Image reproduced by permission of Kris Martins Costa.

FIGURE 2.7
Photoshop image manipulation by the author.
Image reproduced by permission of Drew Soicher, 9NEWS, and the author.

FIGURE 2.8
Al Pacino as Lestat by Miles Teves; *Interview with the Vampire.*
Image reproduced by permission of Miles Teves.

Brian Wade

FIGURE 2.9
Brian Wade character designs.
Image reproduced by permission of Brian Wade.

Brian started his career in special makeup effects when he was still in high school in Studio City, California, helping makeup effects master Kenny Meyers. Continuing to work with Meyers after finishing high school, Brian got a call one day from Kenny's assistant, Erik Jensen, to work on John Carpenter's 1982 effects masterpiece *The Thing* for Rob Bottin.

"That was an amazing time in my life; working with Rob Bottin, having lunch during the week with Rick Baker and his guys who were doing *Videodrome* at the time … Man, life was perfect."

Like many artists in the field of makeup effects, Brian worked for a number of makeup effects shops, each working on different projects. It was, as he calls it, the hey-day for makeup effects; it was pre-CGI, so everything was live action and in camera. During those years, Brian met and worked with many of the industry's best, on projects including *The Terminator*, *Harry and the Hendersons*, *Star Trek IV: The Voyage Home*, *Buffy the Vampire Slayer*, *Blade*, *Bicentennial Man*, *Stuart Little*, *Van Helsing*, *Hellboy*, and *Chronicles of Narnia 2: Prince Caspian*.

In addition to his makeup effects skills, Brian is also exceptionally adept at Pixologic's 3D sculpting software ZBrush, as you can see from these images of his 3D work. In 2002, pal Miles Teves lured Brian to Prague, Czech Republic, for a gig, where he remained for several years. Brian moved back to California in late 2010 and continues to work steadily.

Character designer Patrick Tatopoulos (*Stargate*, *Independence Day*, *I-Robot*, *Face-Off* judge) agrees. "To be a good designer I think you need to have a wealth of knowledge about artistic and cultural styles, about biology, anatomy, and different types of animals. You are constantly observing these things. Then when you draw, you don't need to think about these things; they will inform your work almost instinctively."[2]

A computer as a design aid is just that—an aid. Once a design has been sculpted or modeled in 3D, it can be rotated, lighting can be added or changed, textures can be applied, and images can be printed so that when a physical sculpture must be made, there are views from every angle.

FIGURE 2.10
Brian working on Firefall display for Steve Wang and Biomorphs, Inc.
Photo by the author.

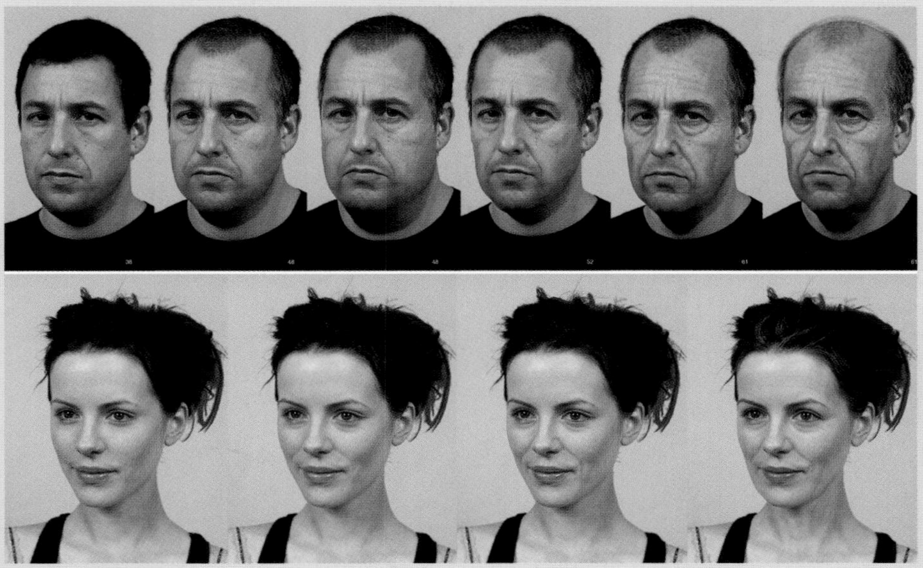

FIGURE 2.11 Previs computer age progression, Adam Sandler, Kate Beckensale; *Click.* *Images reproduced by permission of Kazuhiro Tsuji.*

Miles Teves

Character designer par excellence Miles Teves grew up in a suburban town near the Pacific coast of central California. An avid fan of the usual sci-fi and horror flicks shown on late-night TV as well as a huge fan of *Batman*, *Godzilla*, and *Star Trek*, Miles was a keen artist from an early age, drawing and sculpting and using the family's 8-millimeter movie camera to make his own stop-motion monster movies.

The release of *Star Wars* when he was in junior high school coincided with an increasing interest in art and cinema; at a science-fiction convention a few years later, Miles met special effects genius Rob Bottin, who had just completed the special makeup effects for John Carpenter's superb remake of *The Thing*. Miles showed his portfolio to Bottin and was asked to "keep in touch."

After high school, Miles moved to Los Angeles and studied illustration at Pasadena's Art Center College of Design, which is considered one of the best art schools there is.

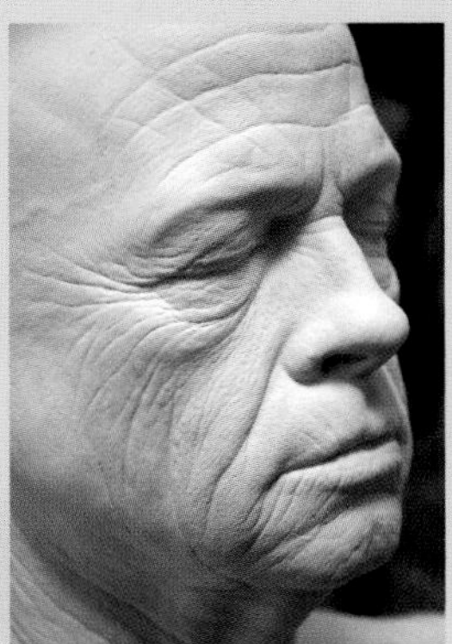

FIGURE 2.12 Old age sculpt, Brad Pitt; *The Curious Case of Benjamin Button.* *Image reproduced by permission of Miles Teves.*

However, after a year he was out of funds and decided to try to get in touch with effects legend Rob Bottin, who

FIGURE 2.13
Meg Muckelbones sketch.
Images reproduced by permission of Miles Teves.

was just beginning work on, ironically, *Legend*. Bottin hired Teves as an illustrator, and soon he was heavily involved in helping to develop the character of Darkness based on a sculpted design by Bottin's key sculptor Henry Alvarez. Miles's success on *Legend* led to more work with Bottin, first on *Explorers* (1985) and then on *Robocop* (1987).

Designing an amazing character must take into account the actor or actress who will portray that character. It all comes back to anatomy and design. Among the key characters Miles had a hand in designing are Darkness and Meg Mucklebones (*Legend*), Robocop (*Robocop*), Lestat (*Interview with the Vampire*), Robin (*Batman and Robin*), dragons (*Reign of Fire*), Jesus (*The Passion of the Christ*), Hell Hound (*Chronicles of Riddick*), Kong (*King Kong*), and Blackbeard (*Pirates of the Caribbean: On Stranger Tides*). Other movie credits include *Explorers*, *Hollow Man*, *Spiderman*, *Terminator 3: Rise of the Machines*, *Van Helsing*, *Pirates of the Caribbean: The Curse of the Black Pearl*, *Ironman*, *Watchmen*, *The Good Girl*, *The Curious Case of Benjamin Button*, *Terminator Salvation*, and *Jack the Giant Killer*. Miles designs with traditional illustration techniques as well as sculpting in clay and using Adobe Photoshop.

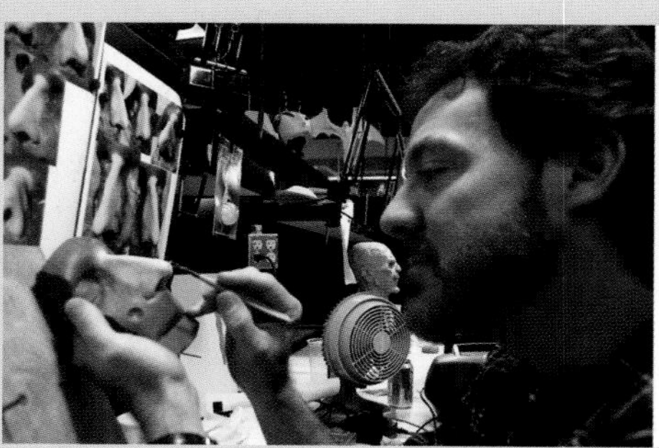

FIGURE 2.14
Miles sculpting noses; *The Passion of the Christ.*
Images reproduced by permission of Miles Teves.

I think that most character designers—that is, designers creating makeups that actors will ultimately wear versus CGI creatures or animatronics—will agree that sculpting in a 3D software package isn't the most efficient use of time and resources when designing, say, an age makeup for a specific actor. Why? Because, first, a cyberscan of an actor's head needs to be taken—you can't work from a 2D photograph in either ZBrush or MudBox—and more often than not the scan will be so dense and need so much cleanup work that it would make more sense to use a package such as Photoshop to create a design right from the start. Photoshop has become an indispensable tool in the artist/designer's arsenal.

I mentioned earlier that more often than not a cyberscan of an actor's head or body will likely be so dense and need so much cleanup work that it isn't really an economical design option. Well, that's changing even as I sit at my computer writing this. Although it is still expensive, it can be done because the software and hardware have advanced greatly. There are now 3D scanners and 3D printers capable of reproducing an actor's entire body in material strong enough to sculpt on. Steve Wang has been printing very large pieces in 3D from digital files, assembling them, cleaning them up, and then remolding and casting them for large installations.

FIGURE 2.15
Fiberglass casting from 3D print. Steve Wang, Tony Grow.
Images reproduced by permission of Steve Wang.

Both MudBox and ZBrush take a little getting used to if you are unfamiliar with sculpting digitally. They work with (but don't demand) the use of a tablet and stylus pen for optimal efficiency. However, once you begin to understand the interface of each program and what the tools are capable of doing, it soon becomes no different from sculpting with actual clay, but with the benefit of not getting bits of clay all over everything in your work area.

FIGURE 2.16
Photo manipulation of Sharon Stone by Miles Teves.
Images reproduced by permission of Miles Teves.

ELEMENTS OF DESIGN

Creating an effective, memorable character makeup is dependent on several things. What is the medium in which the character will be viewed? Is this a character makeup for stage or screen?

FIGURE 2.17
Tim Roth as General Thade; *Planet of the Apes* (2001).
Image reproduced by permission of Kazuhiro Tsuji.

Since essentially everything in a stage production will be viewed by the audience in a "wide shot," the makeup must reflect the reality of the medium. Even makeups designed for the screen must often be bigger than life. Steve Wang has said that when you sculpt a character, you tend to make the detail more exaggerated than in real life because you want those details to show up. "Although we are very often inspired by nature, our aim is not always to reproduce nature—our work is very theatrical and is there to serve the movie," he says.[3]

It also has to be a design that, when fabricated and applied, will allow the actor to wear it and perform in it. For film and television, it becomes important for makeup artists to be in sync with the director of photography so that the makeup—and so the performer—will be photographed in the best possible way to achieve the storytelling objectives. In theater, lighting is the critical element with which to be in sync. How a makeup appears under certain lighting conditions can help or hurt a performance. Story and performance should always take precedence over makeup.

Crucial physical information you need to know about your character before you begin to design should include (but certainly should not be limited to) the following:

- What is the character's general physiology and body shape?
- Is the character nonhuman or animal-like? What does it resemble—a mammal, a bird, a reptile, an amphibian, or an insect?
- Does the character have wings or a tail?

FIGURE 2.18
Street Language sculpt and mid-stage makeup by the author, 2011.
Photos by the author.

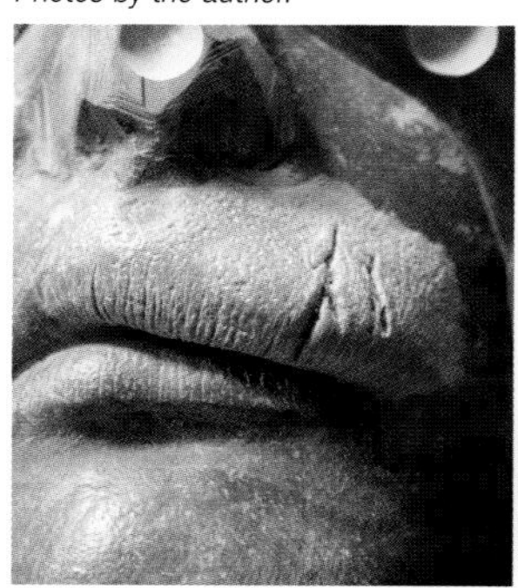

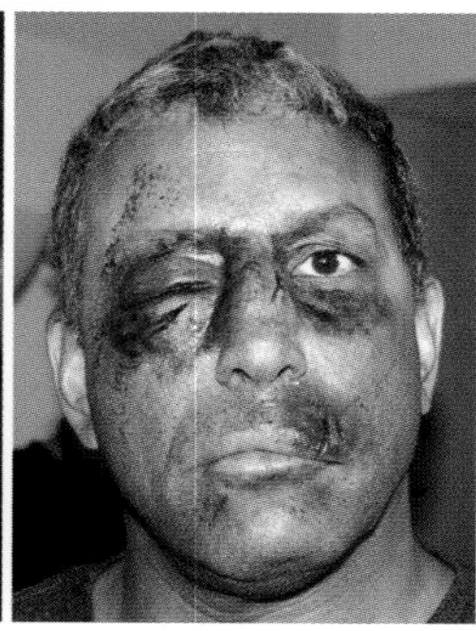

FIGURE 2.19
Zombie bite makeup by the author; Mary Kay Riley; Starz Entertainment, 2011.
Image reproduced by permission of the author. Photo by Cryssie Bender.

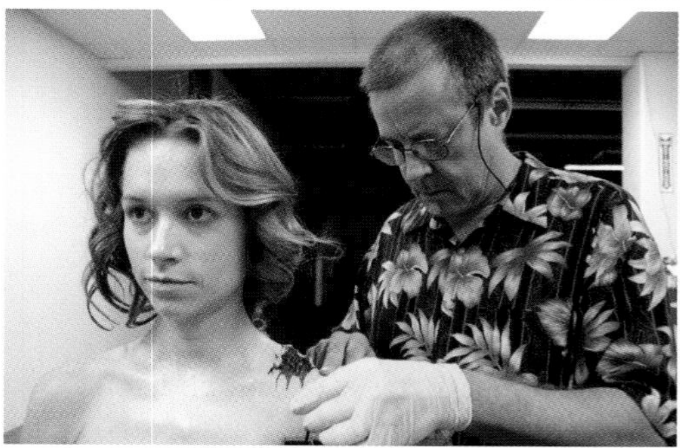

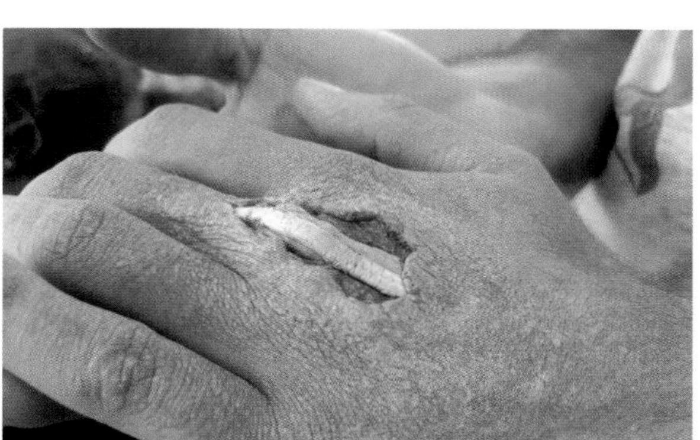

FIGURE 2.20
Student project, Michael Vambenschoten, 2011.
Photo by the author.

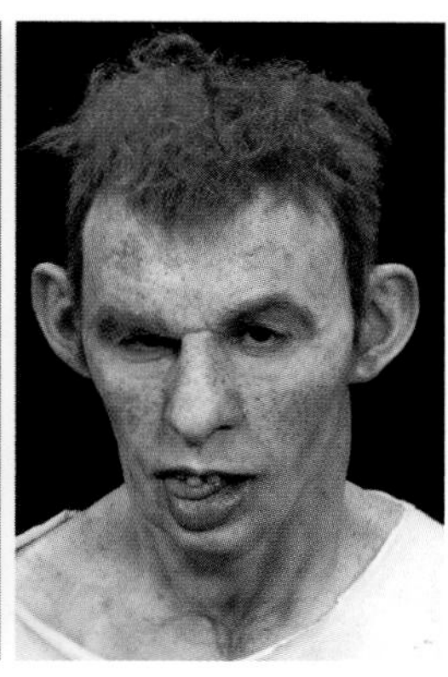

FIGURE 2.21
Character "before and after" by Mark Alfrey.
Images reproduced by permission of Mark Alfrey.

Body Types

There are three *somatotypes*, or body types, associated with men and women: ectomorphic, mesomorphic, and endomorphic. These body types were described by American psychologist William Sheldon, who began his research with 4,000 photographs of college-age men, which showed front, back, and side views. From the study of these images, Sheldon saw that there are three fundamental elements that, when combined, made up these three physical body types.[4]

No one is wholly one of the three without having at least some of the other two at the same time in varying degrees.[5]

The *ectomorphic* body type is characterized by long arms and legs and a short upper body with narrow shoulders.

In addition, ectomorphs are characterized by the following:

- Thin physique
- Small bones
- Flat chest
- Youthful in appearance
- Lightly muscled
- Very little body fat
- High metabolism
- Tall

The literary character of Ichabod Crane (*The Legend of Sleepy Hollow*) is an example of a classic ectomorph.

The *mesomorphic* body type is characterized by a high rate of muscle growth and a higher proportion of muscle tissue. Mesomorphs have large bones and a solid

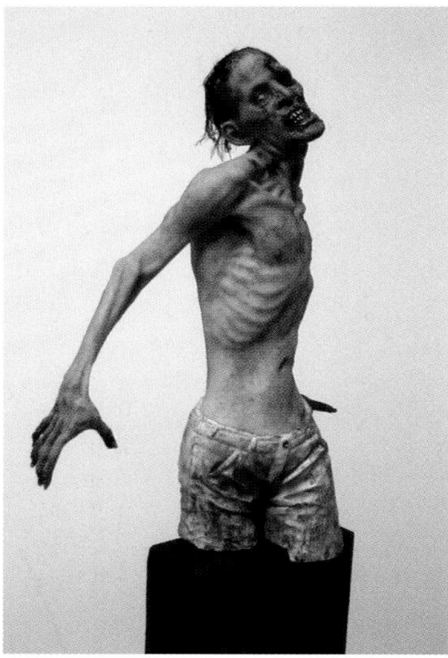

FIGURE 2.22
Maquette by Jordu Schell—ectomorphic zombie.
Image reproduced by permission of Jordu Schell.

torso combined with low body fat levels. They are characterized by the following:

- Broad shoulders
- Narrow waist
- Overly mature appearance
- Physical strength
- Large chest
- Long torso
- Thick skin

The character Tarzan is a classic mesomorph.

The *endomorphic* body type is characterized by an increased amount of body fat. Endomorphs have wide waists and hips and a large bone structure. They are also characterized by the following:

- Soft body
- Slow metabolism
- Round-shaped body
- Round face
- Short neck
- Low muscle mass

FIGURE 2.23
Jerry Kernion, foam latex body suit; Grey's Anatomy.
Image reproduced by permission of Vincent Van Dyke.

Santa Claus is our society's ideal endomorph.

Obviously, you'll need to consider variations within each of these somatotypes when designing your character as well. Sheldon evaluated the degree to which a characteristic was present on a scale ranging from one to seven, with one being the minimum and seven the maximum of a particular somatotype.[6]

In assessing a character's body type, the following variables may need to be considered:

- Is the character from classic fiction or popular culture, or previously unknown?
- Is the genre of the character horror, science fiction, fantasy, or reality?
- Is the character animal, vegetable, or mineral?
- What is the character's gender?
- Does the character have skin? If so, what are its color, texture, and hairiness? Are there variations of these characteristics over the body?
- Does the character have fur? Feathers? Scales? A shell or bony armor?
- How will the character's coloring affect audience perception?

What about stereotypes? Stereotypes are based in reality but tend to be a gross oversimplification of an observed or a perceived trait of behavior or appearance. If you can add familiarity to your character and makeup design without becoming inappropriate or offensive, then do so. However, remain sensitive when dealing with cultural and symbolic elements that may affect your design.

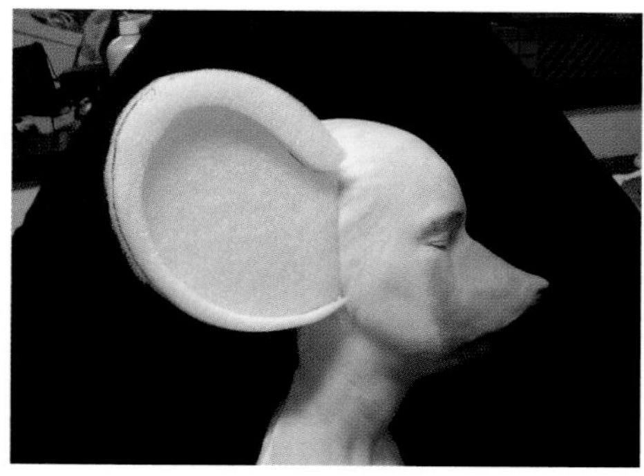

FIGURE 2.24
The author's design for children's theater; Lilly's Purple Plastic Purse.
Photo by the author.

In designing special makeup effects, you must remember that you can add to, but not take away from, a makeup if an actor is going to be wearing prosthetics. There must also be a basis in the reality of biology and physiology; a character with an enormous head, neck, and chest but a lower torso and waist barely large enough for the spine and little else is not likely to have survived long enough as a species to evolve, let alone grow to adulthood with such a physique. The sheer weight of the head, neck, and upper body would topple, splintering the spine like a toothpick, not to mention the question of where the abdominal organs and digestive tract are supposed to be. In creating even a fantasy character, there must be a basis in reality, in human anatomy, *especially* if a human actor has to wear it, even if it is a nonhuman character makeup!

FIGURE 2.25
Ghost of a young girl; *The Enemy God.* Author's design.
Image reproduced by permission of the author. Photo by Paul Cuthbert.

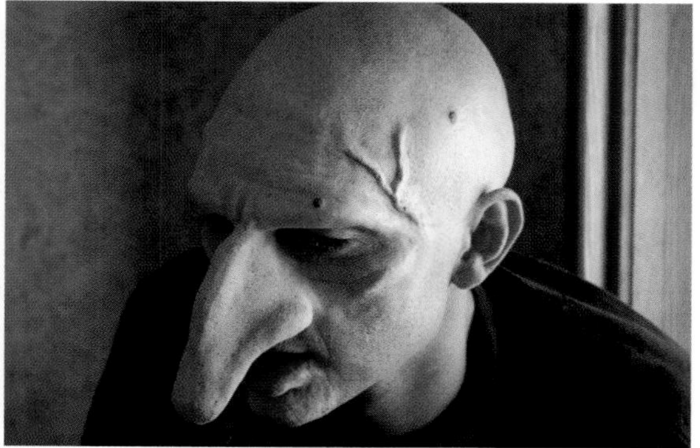

FIGURE 2.26
Foam latex, Chris Kelly; *Ink.*
Makeup and photo by the author.

HUMAN BODY

There are 11 systems that combine to make up the human body: *skeletal* (bone, cartilage, and ligaments); *skeletomuscular* (muscles and tendons of the skeleton); *integumentary*, or the external covering of the body (skin, hair, nails, sweat glands, mammary glands, and their products); *nervous* (brain, spinal cord, and peripheral nerves); *endocrine* (glands and hormones); *cardiovascular* (arteries, veins, and blood supply); *lymphatic* (fluid drainage and immunity); *respiratory*; *digestive*;

urinary; and *reproductive* systems. Our skeletal system—our bones, cartilage, and ligaments—creates a rigid framework that supports and protects our body. But it is the study of principally three systems—the *skeletal, skeletomuscular,* and *integumentary* systems—on which we focus for designing and creating special makeup effects in this book.

Skeletal System

Our bones hold our body in its shape and are the anchor points for most of our muscles. It is the way these bones are put together as our skeleton that gives us the framework around which all other tissues form and characterize our species: erect posture and bipedal locomotion. Our skeleton is divided into two parts, each with clearly different functions:

- The *axial* skeleton (skeleton of the trunk or central skeleton) includes the *cranium, spinal column,* and *thorax*. The primary function of the axial skeleton is to support and protect the internal organs.
- The *appendicular* skeleton includes the upper and lower limbs and the girdle (pelvis). The primary function of the appendicular skeleton is to enable movement and to provide support.

Of the 206 bones in our body, 29 make up the cranium, 26 the spinal column, 25 the thorax, 64 both upper limbs (including the hands), and 62 both lower limbs (including the feet). Our bones are quite strong and very elastic. Depending on their shape, bones are categorized as long, short, or flat. Their sizes vary considerably as well. By understanding and knowing the size, shape, and purpose of each bone group, we can start to envision the way our character makeup will take shape.

Jordu Schell

Jordu Schell is widely regarded as one of the most influential creature designers in the world. Working mainly from his studio in the San Fernando Valley of suburban Los Angeles, he has been designing film and television monsters for nearly 20 years. Jordu has worked on and designed characters and creatures for numerous projects, including *Arabian Nights*, *R.I.P.D.*, *Men in Black III*, *The Thing*, *Cowboys and Aliens*, *Avatar*, *Cloverfield*, *Men in Black*, *Edward Scissorhands*, *The X-Files*, *Predator II*, *Galaxy Quest*, *Evolution*, *My Favorite Martian*, *Alien: Resurrection*, *Babylon 5: The Series*, *The Guyver*, *Bedazzled*, *Scary Movie 3*, and many more.

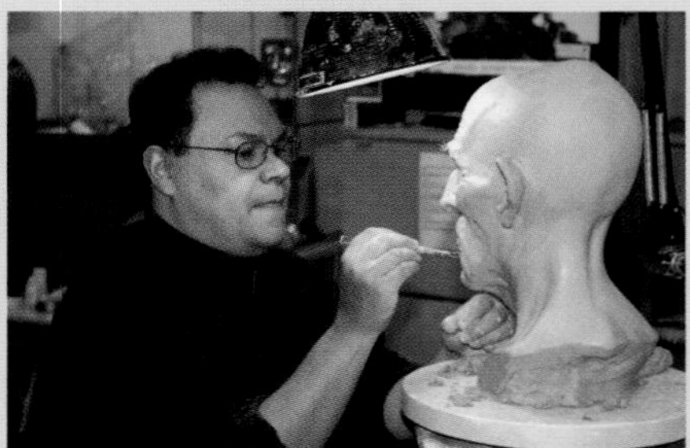

FIGURE 2.27
Jordu Schell.
Photo by the author.

As well as teaching at his own busy facility, Schell Sculpture Studio in the San Fernando Valley, Jordu teaches internationally at a number of well-known shops, including Tippett Studio, Industrial Light and Magic, Blizzard Entertainment, The Monster Makers, Creature Effects, Specter Studios, Vancouver Design, Joe Blasco, Empire Academy of Makeup, and Neill Gorton's prosthetics studio in England.

Jordu's work carries an innate understanding of real-world anatomy that translates into the characters and creatures he designs, rendering his creations wholly believable when you see them in person or on screen; it's as if these beings could ... *do* ... exist. Jordu's talent and skill, plus the fact that he is a remarkably good teacher and that he's simply a really good guy, keep him in very high demand for television and motion pictures. I am thrilled to be able to include Jordu and examples of his work in this book for you.

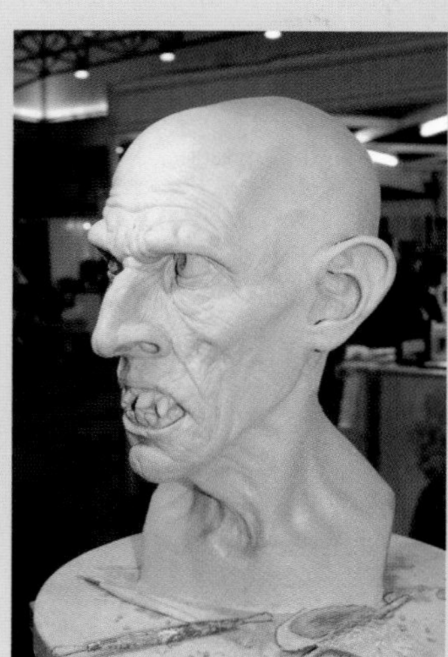

FIGURE 2.28
Finished IMATS London sculpt.
Photo by the author.

FIGURE 2.29
Jordu's Peter Cushing as Grand Moff Tarkin.
Photo by the author.

FIGURE 2.30
Ectomorphic body type, Preeple.
Image reproduced by permission of Jordu Schell.

Some basic orientation terms will help make sense of anatomical terminology and the relationship of one part of the body to another in the descriptions that follow:

Median. The midline of the head and body
Medial. Toward the midline and away from the side of the body
Lateral. Away from the midline and toward the side of the body
Anterior. Toward the front of the body
Posterior. Toward the back of the body
Superior. Toward the top; above; ascending
Inferior. Toward the bottom; below; descending

Howard Berger

FIGURE 2.31
Howard Berger.
Image reproduced by permission of Howard Berger.

FIGURE 2.32
Chris Cera clay pour; KNB.
Image reproduced by permission of KNB.

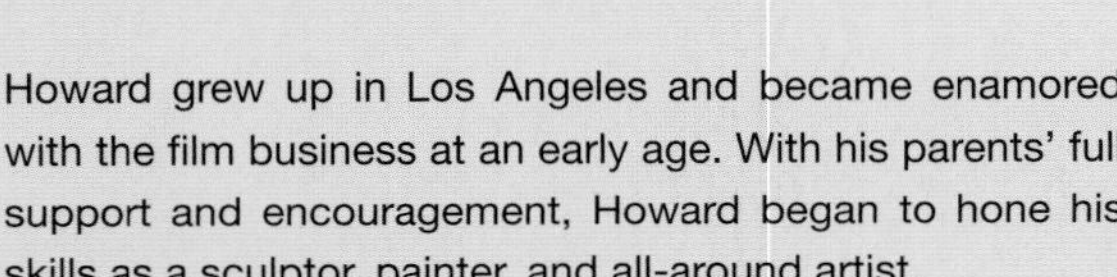

Howard grew up in Los Angeles and became enamored with the film business at an early age. With his parents' full support and encouragement, Howard began to hone his skills as a sculptor, painter, and all-around artist.

When he was 13, Howard met one of his heroes, legendary effects artist Stan Winston. Stan took Howard under his wing and gave him added encouragement, stressing the importance of education. Stan promised to hire Howard after he completed high school with the understanding that he must maintain high grades, prove his attention to detail, and take responsibility for completing his schoolwork. True to his word, Stan hired Howard when he graduated and put him to work on *Predator* and *Aliens*, the first of many dreams to come true for Howard.

He was already making a name for himself in the industry when he met another of his idols, Rick Baker, on *Harry and the Hendersons*, for which Baker won an Oscar for Best Makeup. Over the years, Howard worked for a number of studios and quickly moved up the ladder. In 1988, Howard and Greg Nicotero took a risk and opened their own shop, KNB EFX Group, Inc.

FIGURE 2.33
Sculpting room at KNB.
Image reproduced by permission of KNB.

FIGURE 2.34
Howard and Oscar; *The Chronicles of Narnia: The Lion, the Witch and the Wardrobe.*
Image reproduced by permission of Howard Berger.

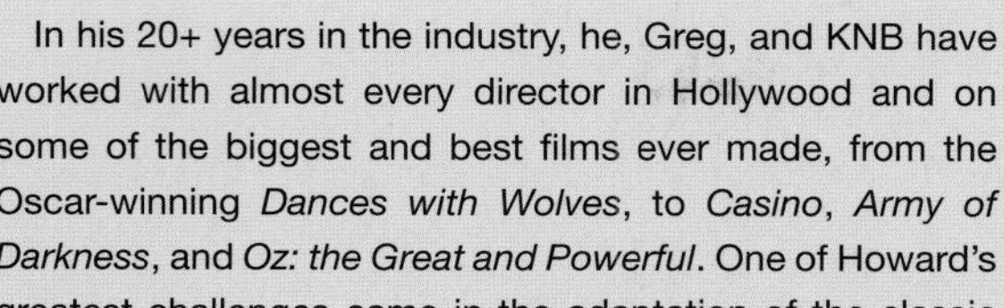

In his 20+ years in the industry, he, Greg, and KNB have worked with almost every director in Hollywood and on some of the biggest and best films ever made, from the Oscar-winning *Dances with Wolves*, to *Casino*, *Army of Darkness*, and *Oz: the Great and Powerful*. One of Howard's greatest challenges came in the adaptation of the classic CS Lewis novel, *The Chronicles of Narnia: The Lion, the Witch and the Wardrobe*. Howard led his team of more than 120 artists at KNB in Los Angeles and 42 artists on location in New Zealand to create the inhabitants of Narnia. For their efforts, Howard was awarded the British Academy Award—the BAFTA—for Best Makeup, as well as his first Oscar.

Skeletomuscular System

There are three types of muscle tissue: striated, smooth, and cardiac. Of the three, striated is the one that will be influential in our makeup design. Viewed through a microscope, striated muscle appears to be striped. Striated muscle is also called *voluntary* muscle since it is under our conscious control. More than 640 voluntary muscles make up 40%–50% of our body weight.[7]

Voluntary muscles are grouped and arranged in two or more layers and give the human form its characteristic shape beneath layers of fat and skin.[8]

HEAD AND NECK

With a few exceptions, cranial muscles comprise two groups: One is located inside the head; the other connects the head to the torso. *Extrinsic* muscles originate at different points of the axial skeleton—at the shoulders, neck, and chest. *Intrinsic* muscles—the ones inside the head itself—originate and insert into the head.[9]

These are the muscles that are needed for chewing, swallowing, and nonverbal communication—our ability to create various emotive facial expressions such as smiling, frowning, and grimacing.

FIGURE 2.35
Head and neck muscles with the shoulder and chest.
Photo by the author. Model by Andrew Cawrse.

FIGURE 2.36
Posterior lateral view of head and neck muscles.
Photo by the author. Model by Andrew Cawrse.

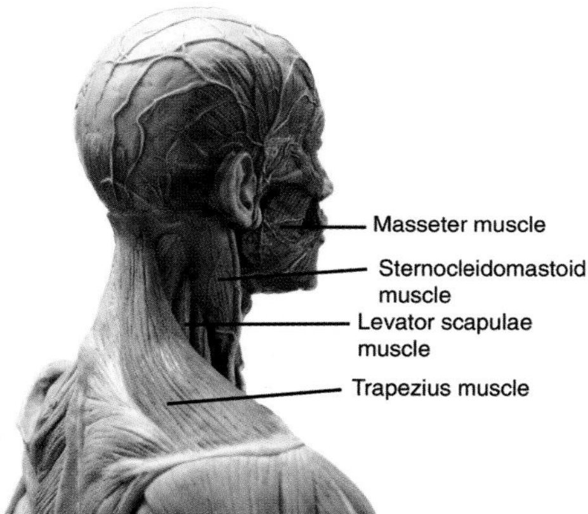

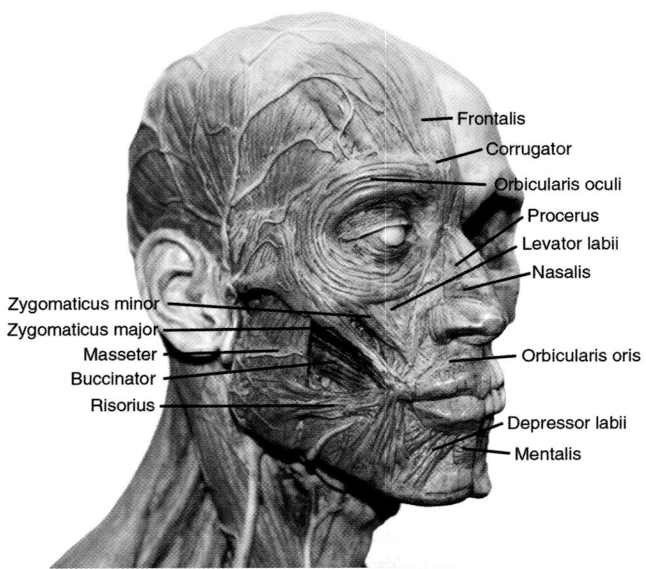

FIGURE 2.37
Facial muscles.
Photo by the author. Model by Andrew Cawrse.

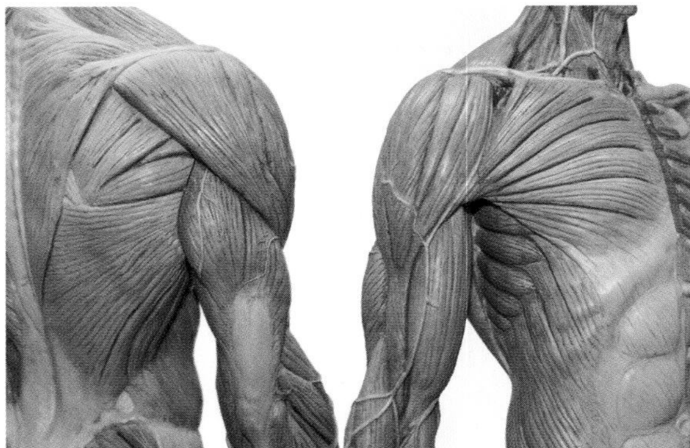

FIGURE 2.38
Anterior and posterior torso and upper limbs.
Photo by the author. Model by Andrew Cawrse.

Muscles of the face, head, and neck that could dramatically affect the physical appearance of a character makeup, the surface anatomy, are the *trapezius* muscle (neck), *sternocleidomastoid* muscle (neck), *levator scapulae* muscle (neck), and *masseter* muscle (jaw).

FACE

It's not so much the muscles of the face themselves that affect the way a character looks, though there are a few that can alter the face's shape; it is how the muscles affect the overlying skin as the skin ages that will create alterations. (We will look at aging later in this chapter.) The muscles of the face include the following:

- *Frontalis (epicranius)* muscle
- *Corrugator* muscle
- *Orbicularis oculi* muscle
- *Levator labii* muscle
- *Zygomaticus minor* muscle
- *Zygomaticus major* muscle
- *Risorius* muscle
- *Depressor anguli oris* muscle
- *Depressor labii* muscle
- *Buccinator* muscle
- *Masseter* muscle
- *Mentalis* muscle
- *Orbicular oris* muscle
- *Procerus* muscle
- *Nasalis* muscle

TORSO AND UPPER LIMBS

Muscles of the torso are divided into muscles of the *thorax* (upper torso or chest) and muscles of the *abdomen* (lower torso). Anterior (front) muscles of the chest and abdomen that are likely to affect the appearance of surface anatomy include the following:

- *Sternocleidomastoid* muscle
- Greater pectoral muscle (*pectoralis major* and *pectoralis minor*) *Clavicular* part
- *Sternocostal* part
- *Abdominal* part
- *Deltoid* muscle (anterior and medial)
- *Rectus abdominis* muscle
- *External oblique* muscle

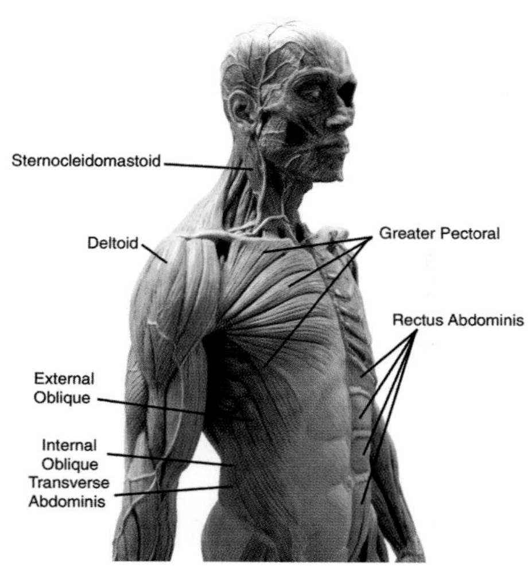

FIGURE 2.39
Anterior torso muscles.
Photo by the author. Model by Andrew Cawrse.

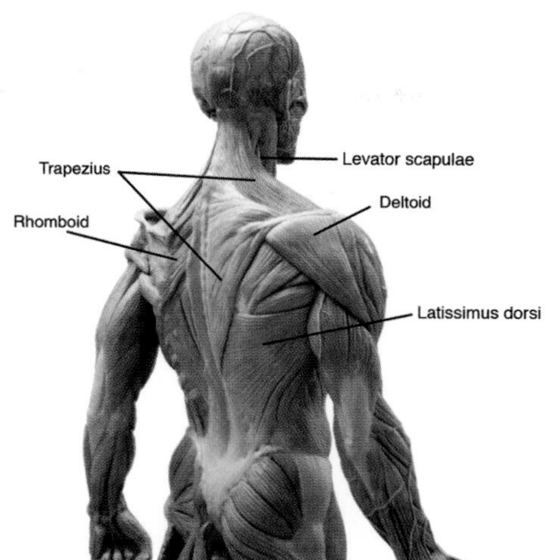

FIGURE 2.40
Posterior torso muscles.
Photo by the author. Model by Andrew Cawrse.

- *Internal oblique* muscle
- *Transverse abdominis* muscle

Posterior (rear) muscles of the back and lower back that are likely to affect the appearance of surface anatomy include:

- *Deltoid* muscle (medial and posterior)
- Upper, middle, and lower *trapezius* muscle
- *Levator scapulae* muscle
- *Latissimus dorsi* muscle
- *Erector spinae* muscle
- *Rhomboid major* and *Rhomboid minor* muscles

The *biceps brachii* is the muscle that shapes the front of the upper arm and bends the arm. The biceps is actually made up of two parts—*biceps* means "two heads"—that attach at separate points above the shoulder joint and converge and attach at a single point below the elbow joint.

The *triceps brachii*—"three heads"—shapes the back of the upper arm and extends it. The three heads attach separately to the humerus bone near the shoulder joint and to the scapula and then converge into a single tendon that attaches at the back of the ulna of the lower arm.

The muscles of the lower arm or forearm—more than 30 of them—consist of long extensor (extending), abductor

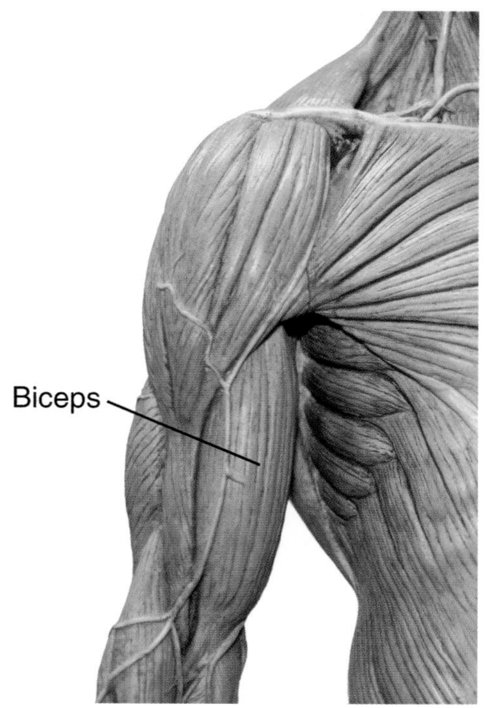

FIGURE 2.41
Anterior view showing the biceps brachii muscle.
Photo by the author. Model by Andrew Cawrse.

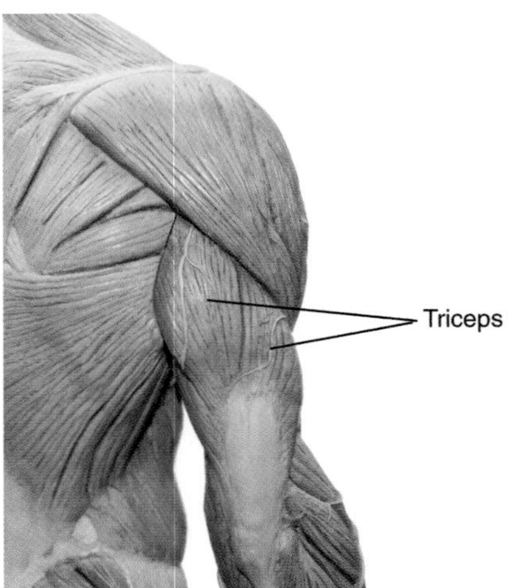

FIGURE 2.42
Posterior view showing the triceps brachii muscle.
Photo by the author. Model by Andrew Cawrse.

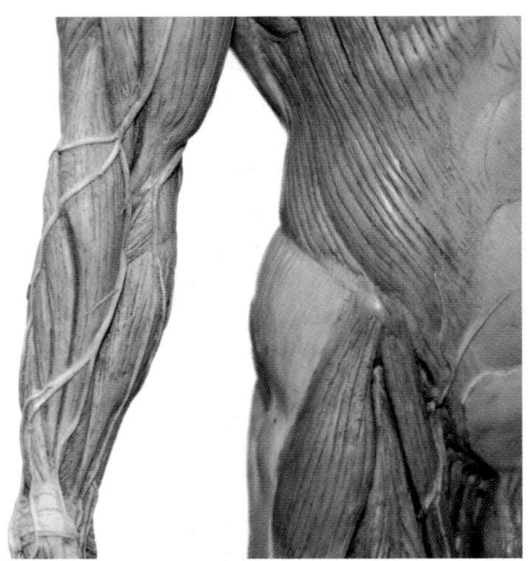

FIGURE 2.43
Anterior view of forearm muscles.
Photo by the author. Model by Andrew Cawrse.

(opposing), and flexor (flexing) muscles that shape the front and back of the forearm and pass into the hand.

There are no muscles in the fingers, only tendons on either side of the finger bones wrapped by lubricated fibrous sheaths. The meaty part of the fingers is fatty tissue carrying blood vessels and nerves and providing a cushion for the flexor tendons when the hand grips objects. The dorsal or back side of the hand is bony, and the tendons are readily visible against the skin; the palm of the hand is more muscular. These palm muscles are enclosed by a sheet of thick connective tissue called *palmar aponeurosis*. This tissue is bonded to the skin above and bones below so that the skin does not slip when the hand grasps a surface.[10]

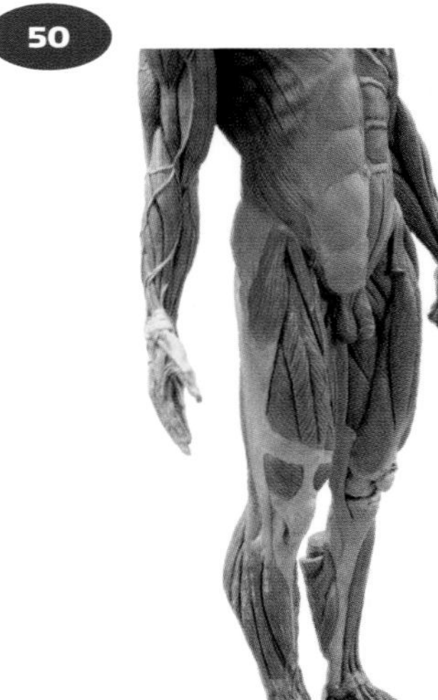

FIGURE 2.44
Anterior lateral view of abdomen and lower limbs.
Photo by the author. Model by Andrew Cawrse.

ABDOMEN AND LOWER LIMBS

Of the anterior torso muscles, *rectus abdominis* and *external oblique* are probably the most recognizable muscles, next to *pectoralis major*. Well-defined rectus abdominis is the classic washboard "six-pack" abdomen we've all seen on bodybuilders.

The hip and thigh bones of the lower extremities are surrounded by some 27 muscles, comprising extensor, adductor, rotator, and flexor muscles. These large, powerful muscles are the ones that enable us to stand from a seated position, supporting almost our entire body weight. Surface definition of these muscles is frequently greater in men than in women.

Quadriceps femoris muscles flex the hip joint and extend the knee. As the name implies, it is a four-part muscle, made up on *vastus lateralis*, *vastus medialis*, *vastus intermedius*, and *rectus femoris*, that begins at the front and side of the femur

near the hip joint and at the base of the spine; these components converge into a single tendon that covers the knee (*patella*) and attaches at the head of the *tibia* bone, at the top of the shin. The *quadriceps* (*vastus lateralis*) and body fat beneath the skin's surface shape the outside of the thigh, whereas *rectus femoris* shapes the front of the thigh. *Sartorius*, the longest muscle of the human body, is both a flexor and an adductor and separates the quadriceps from the thigh's adductor muscles; it bends the knee and pulls and rotates the thigh.

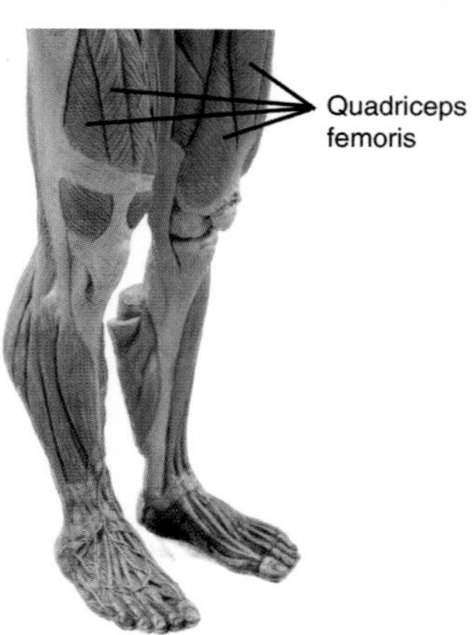

FIGURE 2.45
Quadriceps femoris muscles.
Photo by the author. Model by Andrew Cawrse.

The back of the thigh is shaped by the *semitendinosus* and *biceps femoris* muscles.

Both muscles attach near the head of the *femur* and insert, or end, at the head of the *fibula* in order to be able to flex the knee joint and extend the hip. *Gluteus maximus* is the large muscle of the buttocks; it extends and rotates the hip laterally. The buttocks are shaped by the gluteus maximus and by fatty tissue that covers it beneath the skin.

The bones of the lower leg and foot are accompanied by more than 30 muscles; the muscles of the lower leg are arranged in two sections: one anterior on the outside of the shin and the other posterior, giving shape to the calf.[11]

These muscles are separated by the lower leg bones, the tibia and fibula. These muscles are responsible for our ability to draw our foot back, point it down, and turn it inward or outward. *Tibialis anterior* is a strong, tapered muscle that shapes the front of the leg to the outside of the shin (there is a ridge that runs along the anterior shaft of the tibia).

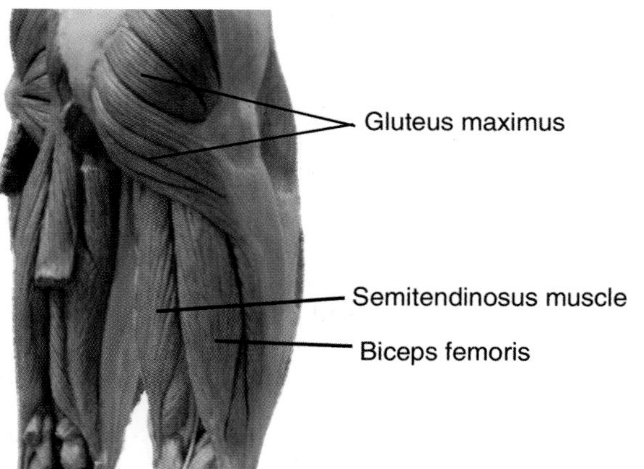

FIGURE 2.46
Semitendinosus and biceps femoris.
Photo by the author. Model by Andrew Cawrse.

The tibialis anterior narrows into a tendon that passes over and under the instep of the foot, allowing us to flex it tightly, pull the foot back, and/or turn it inward. The superficial muscles of the posterior of the lower leg—*soleus*, *plantaris*, and *gastrocnemius*—shape the back of the calf; these muscles share a common tendon, the *calcaneal tendon*, better known as the Achilles tendon, which is a short, thick tendon that is clearly visible at the back of the foot as it attaches onto the upper back of the heel bone (*calcaneus*).[12]

Similarly to the muscles of the hand, the muscles of the foot are mostly beneath, on, or inside the sole. They act on toes to collectively spread them, draw them together, pull them back, or curl them under. The sole is covered with a *plantar aponeurosis* in tandem with the deep fascia pad of the foot. Just like the hand's palmar aponeurosis, it protects the foot, gives attachment to the foot muscles, and holds the skin of the foot firmly in place so that it does not slip as we stand or walk.[13]

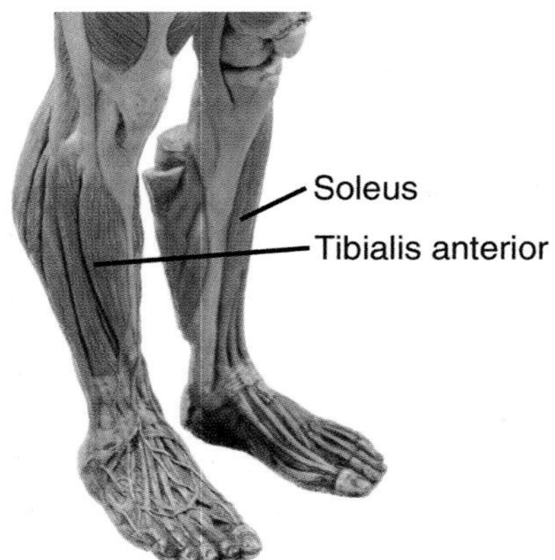

FIGURE 2.47
Tibialis anterior.
Photo by the author. Model by Andrew Cawrse.

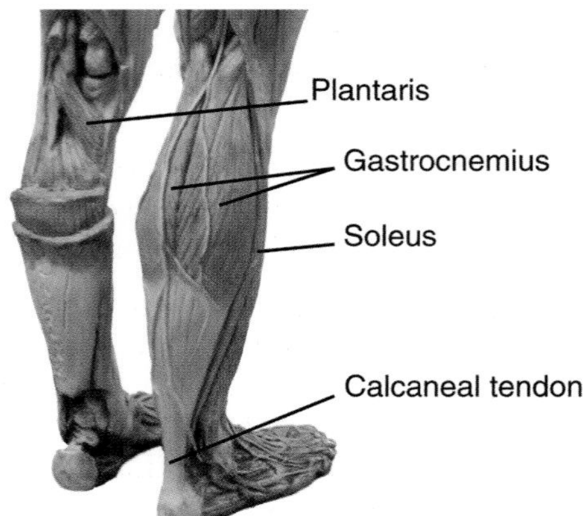

FIGURE 2.48
Soleus, plantaris, and gastrocnemius.
Photo by the author. Model by Andrew Cawrse.

SURFACE ANATOMY

Surface anatomy is the study of the configuration of the surface of the body, especially in relation to its internal parts. The way we are put together beneath the skin manifests itself to a great extent outwardly and is visible. Our skeletons and musculature give us our basic shape, and our skin is the covering that gives those internal structures one overall form that is each of us. From birth, as we grow and develop, our surface anatomy changes because our internal anatomy is changing as well.

The reason that understanding anatomy is so important for us as makeup effects artists is that much of what we do is based on surface anatomy being

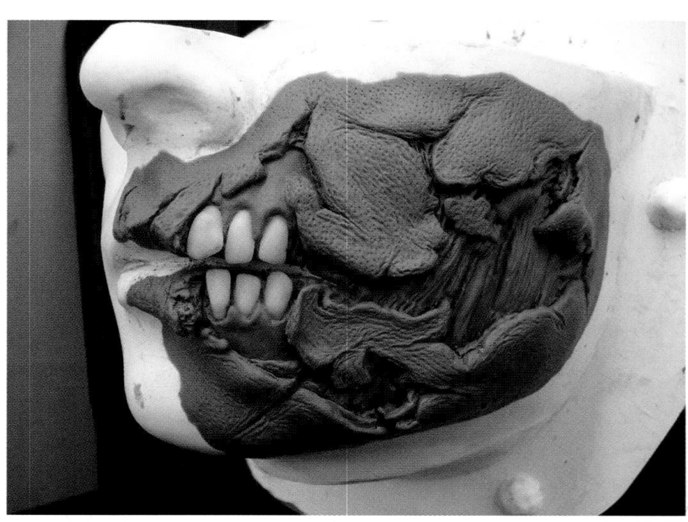

FIGURE 2.49
Ripped face sculpt by Nimba Creations' Tom Lauten shows knowledge of human anatomy beneath skin that helps define surface anatomy.
Image reproduced by permission of Tom and Siobhan Lauten; Nimba Creations.

dictated by underlying anatomy. It is by understanding internal anatomy that we are able to know why there are bumps and hollows on the external surface of the body.[14]

To create prosthetic appliances that will be believable, even if the design is somewhat stylized, we must know what people of every color, gender, size, age, and shape look like and how they move as a result of these attributes.

Also remember that when it comes to designing prosthetic makeup effects, you can add to the anatomy of the actor to create the new character but you cannot take away. For example, if you are given the task of creating the makeup effects for a production with emaciated, starved, and abused concentration camp prisoners, the direction in which you can go is limited. Creating a character of skin and bones requires one of the following:

- Extremely skinny actors
- CGI characters
- Shadow and highlight foundation makeup that may give a stylized impression of a gaunt appearance but will not in actuality make the actors thin

For individuals with no body fat and very little muscle mass, their surface anatomy will show much of the body's skeleton clearly defined just beneath the skin. For example, for the film *The Machinist*, actor Christian Bale was willing to lose one-third of his body weight to play a character in a perilous downward spiral emotionally, physically, and mentally. And he did it.

That couldn't have been achieved any other way than physically, and had the character been physically heavier his character's impact would have been negatively compromised. Was what he chose to do wise and healthy? I don't know, but Christian Bale is physically fine as far as I know. He is just a supremely dedicated and focused actor.

Another outstanding example is Bicycle Girl from Season 1 of AMC's *The Walking Dead*. Actress Melissa Cowan was cast to play the decomposing zombie, and her full-body prosthetic makeup worked—sculpted by KNB's Jaremy Aiello—because she was very thin to begin with.

FIGURE 2.50
Full scleral contact lenses by Cristina Patterson. Sculpt by KNB's Jaremy Aiello; applied by KNB's Andy Schoneberg, Jake Garber, Garrett Immel, Greg Nicotero on Melissa Cowan; AMC's *The Walking Dead*.
Image reproduced by permission of Cristina Patterson.

Eyes, Ears, and Nose

If you are already relatively familiar with human anatomy and its terminology, you might notice some slight variations, perhaps even some conflicting labels, in the terminology used here compared to how you were taught. I have attempted to use the most common anatomical names from numerous anatomy reference books.

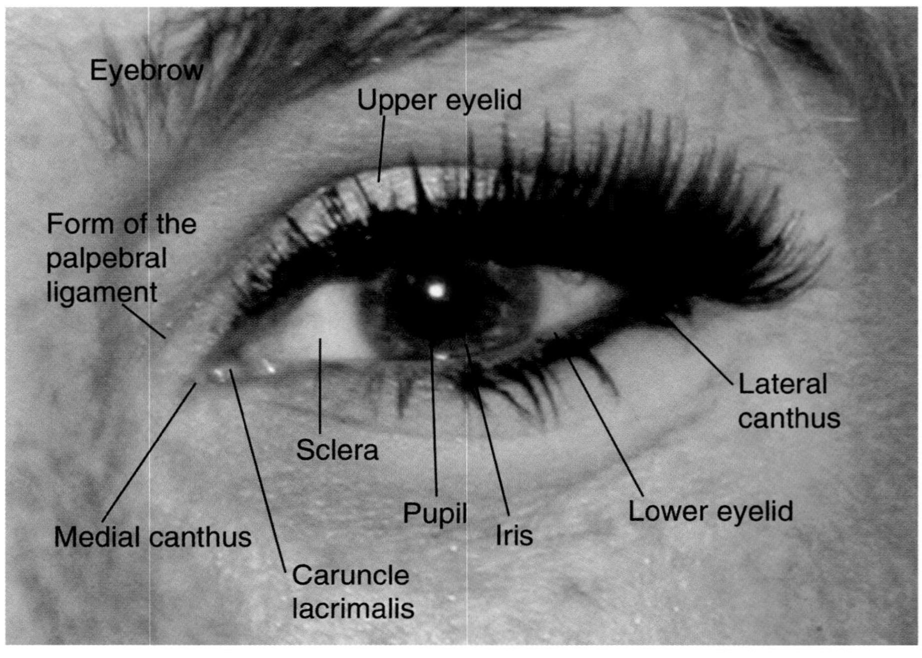

FIGURE 2.51
The eye.
Photo by the author.

To be consistent throughout this book, we also use the labels shown here for individual facial features (eyes, nose, ears, and mouth) as well as other anatomical names discussed in this chapter in the chapter on sculpting the makeup. The nose, ears, and mouth are potential problem areas for undercuts during the mold-making process.

CONTACT LENSES

While we're in the chapter discussing the anatomy of eyes, ears, and nose, let's talk about altering the eyes with specialty contact lenses.

Surprisingly, contact lenses have been around since the late 1800s when German ophthalmologist Adolf Fick fabricated and fitted the first successful contact lens made of blown glass in Zurich, Switzerland, in 1888.

Blown-glass scleral lenses remained the only form of contact lens until the 1930s when polymethyl methacrylate (PMMA or Perspex/Plexiglas) was developed, allowing plastic scleral lenses to be manufactured for the first time. In 1936, optometrist William Feinbloom introduced plastic lenses, which were lighter and more convenient. These lenses were a combination of glass and plastic.[15]

In 1949, the first corneal contacts were developed that were much smaller than the original scleral lenses; they covered only the cornea instead of the entire visible surface of the eye. PMMA corneal lenses became the first contact lenses to have mass appeal through the 1960s, as lens designs became more sophisticated with improved manufacturing technology.

This is a pretty big topic, and I wanted to include just a very small bit of history surrounding contact lenses before coming up to date and how they're used in entertainment. The eyes can play a *huge* role in the overall look of a character/creature's particular design and thus its on-screen or on-stage appearance. Although it can be a major factor in the "reality" of a character, contact lenses represent a relatively small and highly specialized niche within the industry. Contact lenses rightly live within the realm of the licensed eye care professional.

There is a story I've heard that Lon Chaney used the thin milky membrane from an eggshell to create his blind eye effect for *The Hunchback of Notre Dame*. ***It is a myth.*** It is a rather dangerous myth too, one that if you try yourself will result in a nasty eye infection *at the very least*. Chaney wore a blown-glass scleral lens—which was all that existed in the 1920s—and as a result he paid the price of some vision loss. Lesson: Do not mess around with your eyes! Leave your eyes alone. If you want or need specialty lenses for a character or creature makeup, let a licensed eye care professional handle it.

Can you buy special effects contact lenses from anyone other than a licensed professional, say, on the Internet? Yes, you can. Is it a good idea? It's a bad idea. Although it's possible to purchase some really cool-looking lenses online or directly through some retail outlets, flea markets, and touristy beach shops, is it really worth saving a few bucks to risk corneal ulcers, infection, blindness, or total eye loss? That's why the US Food and Drug Administration (FDA) is getting tough on Internet sales of specialty contact lenses and contacts being imported into the States from outside the country. Let me make this perfectly clear, in case what I've already said still hasn't registered: In the United States, only a licensed eye care professional can fit a contact lens.

The FDA defines contacts as prescription devices and requires that they should only be sold and supplied by an eye care professional licensed to do so. That professional is responsible for the lens quality and any adverse effect they may have on the person wearing the prescribed lenses. In fact, *no one* other than a sanctioned technician (which means a licensed optometrist or licensed contact lens technician) can legally take that responsibility. In California, it's a criminal offense for anyone other than a licensed eye care professional to sell and/or handle the insertion/removal and care of contact lenses for production companies.[16]

Why so strict? Because contact lenses are not a one-size-fits-all device. Just as no two fingerprints are alike, everyone has a slightly different eye curvature and eyelid tension. Because of that, anyone who wears contact lenses must go through a thorough eye examination and contact lens fitting to ensure the proper fit of each lens.

In order to have a set of specialty, noncorrective (they can be corrective too) theatrical contact lenses prescribed by a reputable eye specialist, you will need to provide specific information that will be obtained during the eye exam:

1. Current lens refraction
2. Keratometric readings (corneal measurements)
3. Visible iris diameter (in millimeters)
4. Pupil size (in millimeters)
5. Normal eye color
6. An exact color rendering of the effect to be created[17]

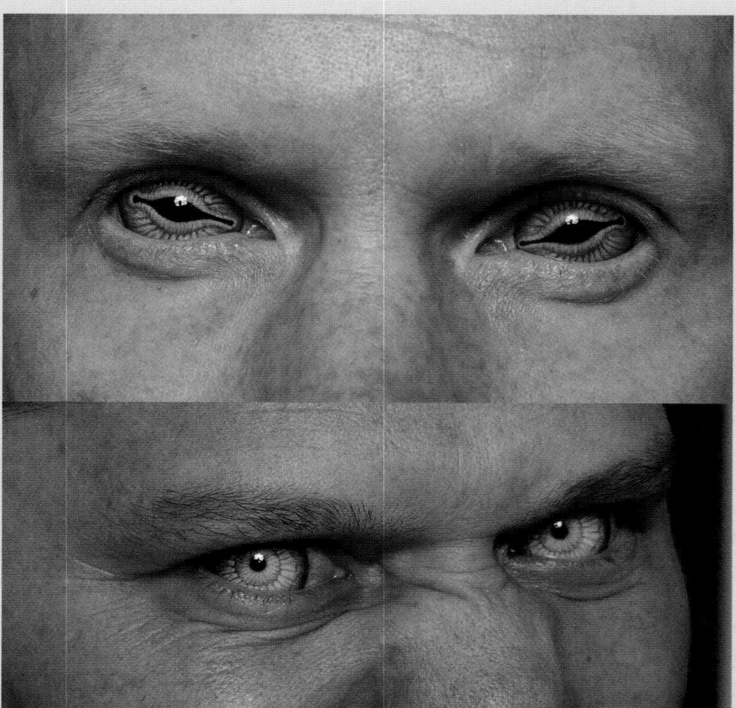

FIGURE 2.52
Hand-painted scleral contact lenses.
Images reproduced by permission of Kazuhiro Tsuji.

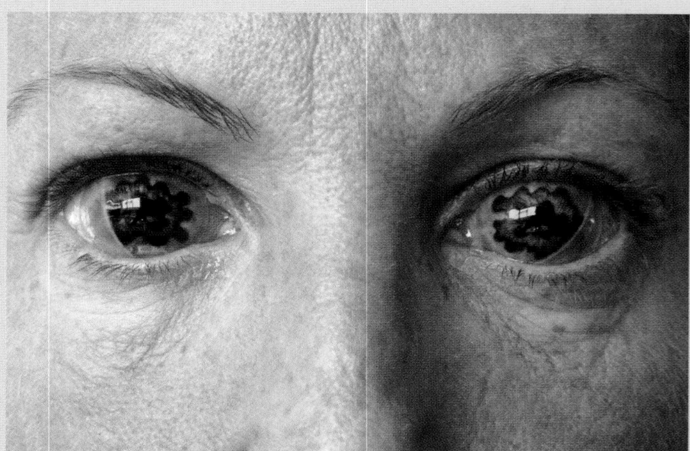

FIGURE 2.53
Scleral lenses by Cristina Patterson; *I Am Number Four.*
Image reproduced by permission of Cristina Patterson.

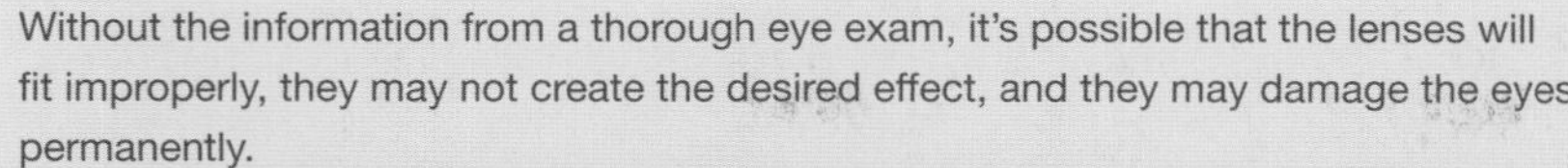

Without the information from a thorough eye exam, it's possible that the lenses will fit improperly, they may not create the desired effect, and they may damage the eyes permanently.

FIGURE 2.54
Lens by Cristina Patterson for *Pirates of the Caribbean 2 & 3*, Stellan Skarsgård; makeup by Ve Neill. *Image reproduced by permission of Cristina Patterson.*

There are basically two types of contact lenses: hard lenses and soft lenses. But there is also a choice between traditional corneal lenses and scleral lenses. Because scleral lenses cover the entire visible white (sclera) of the eye, they are soft lenses today (which is why Lon Chaney developed vision problems—the scleral lenses he wore were rigid, and he wore them too long); traditional corneal lenses can be either rigid or soft. Most theatrical lenses used today are soft, though the only contact lenses available prior to the 1970s were rigid lenses. The drawback to wearing rigid lenses is the reduced wearing time. Because of this, anyone unfamiliar with wearing rigid lenses can only wear them for a few hours at a time until eyelid sensitivity decreases, which can take weeks. So, this may not be the best option for film and television, though it may be fine for theater.

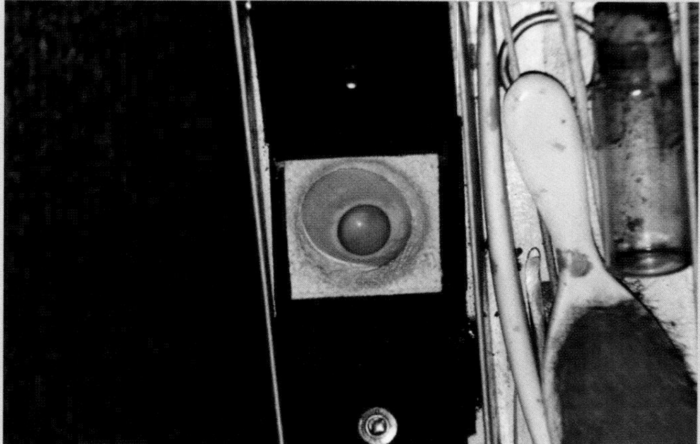

FIGURE 2.55 Lon Chaney blown-glass eye shield; *The Hunchback of Notre Dame.*
Image reproduced by permission of William Forsche.

Full scleral contacts are larger than traditional corneal lenses—18–24 millimeters in diameter; traditional lenses are usually 14–15 millimeters in diameter. Scleral lenses are ideal for effects that call for damaged or diseased eyes—bloodshot, cataracts, hemorrhaged, jaundice, etc.—or full black demon or other monster/creature effects where the full surface of the eye must be covered and to avoid seeing the edge of the lens. Scleral lenses must be physically fit to the eye. Poorly fit lenses will be very uncomfortable to the actor wearing them, may cause unwanted cosmetic appearance problems and, worse, can cause painful corneal abrasions. They are not merely uncomfortable but *painful*.

Specialty lenses can be expensive, though the cost is relative, I suppose. If you are looking for cool eyes to round out your Halloween costume, full scleral lenses may significantly blow your budget. But if you're working on character designs for a major studio release, the cost may not be much of a factor at all. To give you an idea of cost, specialty lenses can run anywhere from $150 per pair to $600 per pair. Perhaps even more for custom, hand-painted lenses.

CRISTINA PATTERSON

FIGURE 2.56
Cristina Patterson.
Image reproduced by permission of Cristina Patterson.

Born in Madrid, Spain, Cristina came to Los Angeles, California, with her family before she could walk. At the age of four, she was introduced to the film industry by her makeup artist mother, Raffaelle Butler, whose work includes *Doctor Zhivago* and *To Kill a Mockingbird*, as well as various TV sitcoms shot on the lot at Paramount Studios. Cristina got her start in the industry as a background and atmosphere performer and did some light acting. Often accompanying her mother on set, Cristina became more intrigued with makeup application than with acting. By the 1980s, she was following in her mother's footsteps, diving into makeup in the motion picture industry, with her skills including straight makeup, special makeup effects, tattoo application/design, and also hair technician work. In 1995, she joined Professional Vision Care Associates as a contact lens technician and in 2002 was promoted to special effects coordinator. Cristina was soon designing and painting contact lenses for film and television and prosthetic lenses for medical patients. She also became responsible for coordinating shows, for special effects lens fittings and exams, and for training and supervising all on-set lens technicians. Cristina is an accomplished self-taught fine art painter, with a particular interest in surrealism. Her work is ongoing to discover new and inventive ways to paint contact lenses. She is well known for her abilities to work closely with makeup effects artists and for her attention to detail. Cristina is highly sought after for her expertise and now works independently as a contact lens designer and technician. Cristina's outstanding work can be seen in many, many high-profile productions, including *Thor*, *Sucker Punch*, *Pirates of the Caribbean: On Stranger Tides*, *Tron: Legacy*, *Star Trek*, and *District 9*.

Some people have attached earlobes, but most people's lobes are free. In fact, free earlobes are twice as common as attached lobes. As I'm sure you've already noticed, in special makeup effects ears are nothing but undercuts—severe undercuts. For the uninitiated, an undercut is any part of a sculpture that creates an overhang that when molded will be grabbed by the other part of the mold and won't let go (primarily when both mold and model are rigid), making it either impossible to get the mold parts separated or breaking off part of the sculpture or mold, or both. None of these outcomes is particularly good.

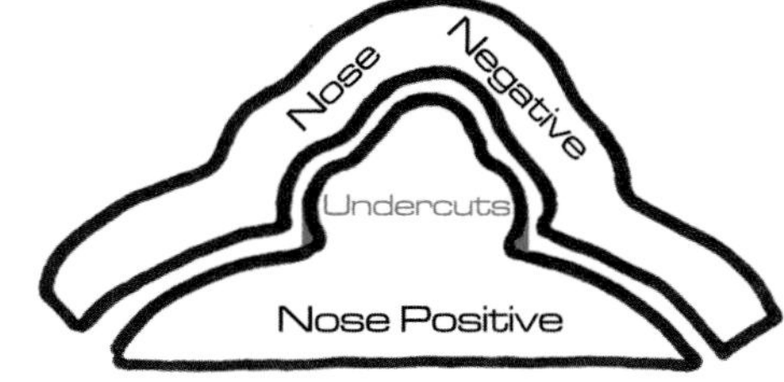

FIGURE 2.57
Undercuts created by nostrils.
Image by the author.

Mouth

The mouth becomes a potential for undercut problems, particularly if the mouth is cast partially open, which is what I recommend.

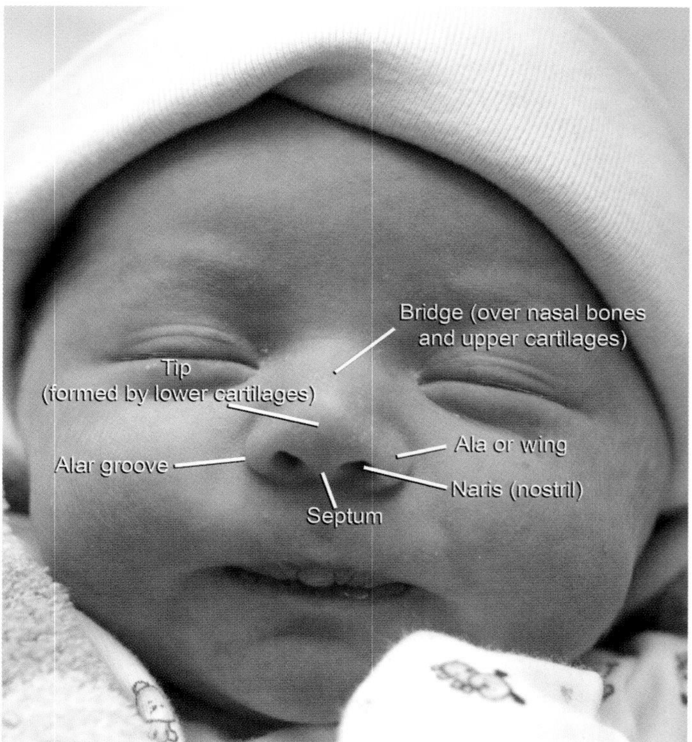

FIGURE 2.58
The nose.
Image reproduced by permission of istockphoto.com.

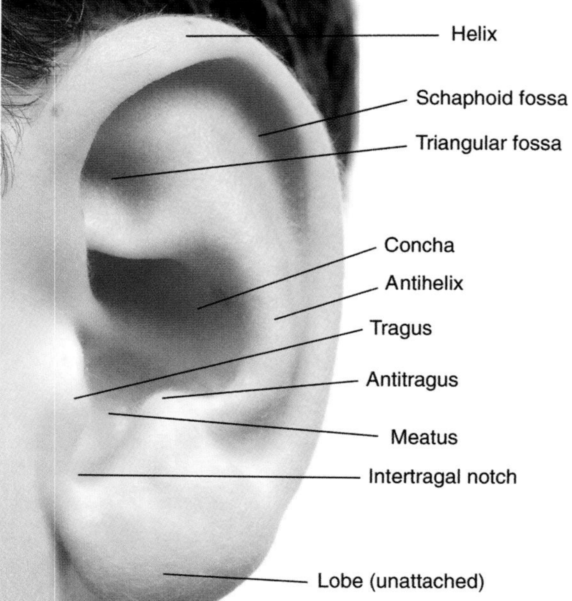

FIGURE 2.59
The ear.
Image reproduced by permission of istockphoto.com.

Skin

The surface anatomy of skin varies on different parts of the body. For example, the skin covering the shoulder and arm is smooth and very movable over the underlying muscle and bone. Over the inside and front of the forearm, the skin is thin and smooth and has very few hairs. The skin on the outside and back of the arm and forearm is thicker and denser and contains more hairs. Around the elbow, the skin is thick and rough and is very loosely connected to the underlying tissue so that it falls into transverse wrinkles when the forearm is extended.[18]

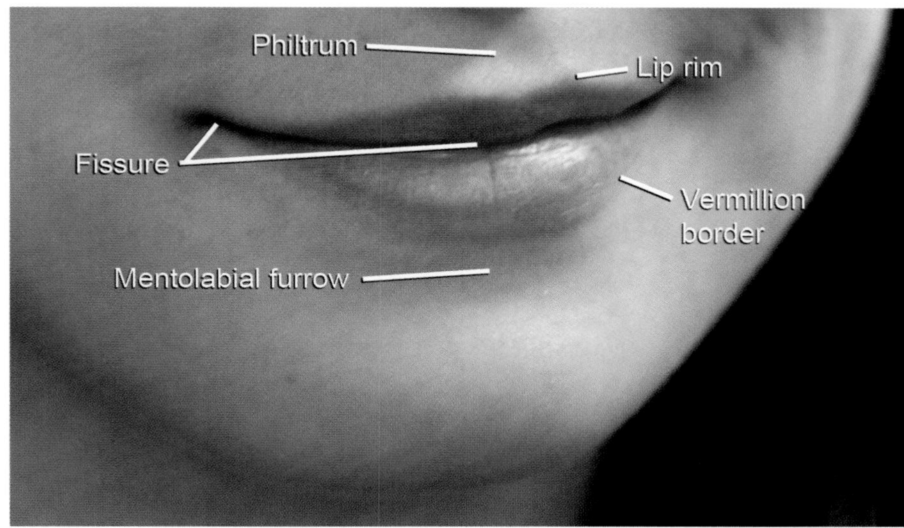

FIGURE 2.60
The mouth.
Photo by the author.

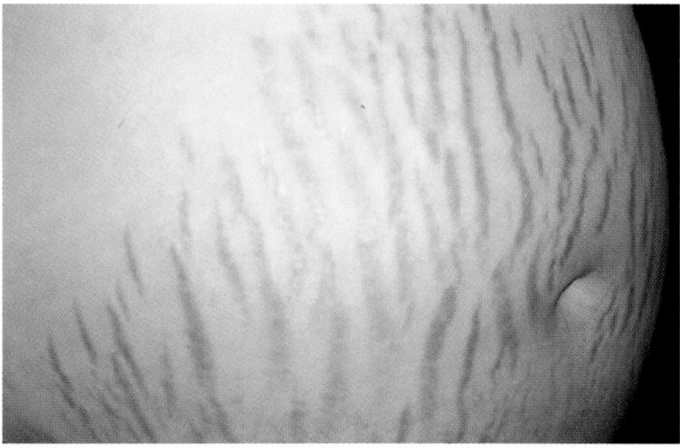

FIGURE 2.61
Abdominal stretch marks.
Photo by the author

SKIN: STRETCH MARKS

Muscles and bone structure define outward appearances, so do veins and the skin itself. Stretch marks are *striae*—furrows, stripes, or streaks in a parallel arrangement—caused when the skin is pulled by rapid growth or stretching.

When skin is overstretched, the normal production of *collagen*, a protein that makes up the connective tissue of skin, is disrupted and results in scarring. But stretching alone is not the cause. It is often seen in pregnant women, children who experience rapid growth spurts, obese people, and bodybuilders. These stretch marks appear first as reddish or purplish lines that may appear indented and feel different from the surrounding skin. They often feel "empty" and soft to the touch.[19]

They generally lighten and fade to a silvery-white hue, almost disappearing over time.[20]

Stretch marks most commonly appear on the abdomen, breasts, upper arms, underarms, both inner and outer thighs, hips, and buttocks.[21]

SKIN: AGE SPOTS

Age spots or liver spots are usually found on skin that is exposed to the sun; despite their name, they have no relation to liver function. They're also known as *solar lentigo*. These spots represent changes in skin color associated with older age and are the result of increased pigmentation in combination with growing older as well as exposure to sun light or other UV light. They commonly begin to appear after the age of 40 and mostly occur on the backs of the hands, forearms, shoulder, face, and forehead—the places most apt to be exposed to sunlight. Age spots are often accompanied by other signs of sun damage, including deep wrinkles; dry, rough skin; fine red veins on cheeks, nose, and ears; and thinner, more translucent-looking skin.[22]

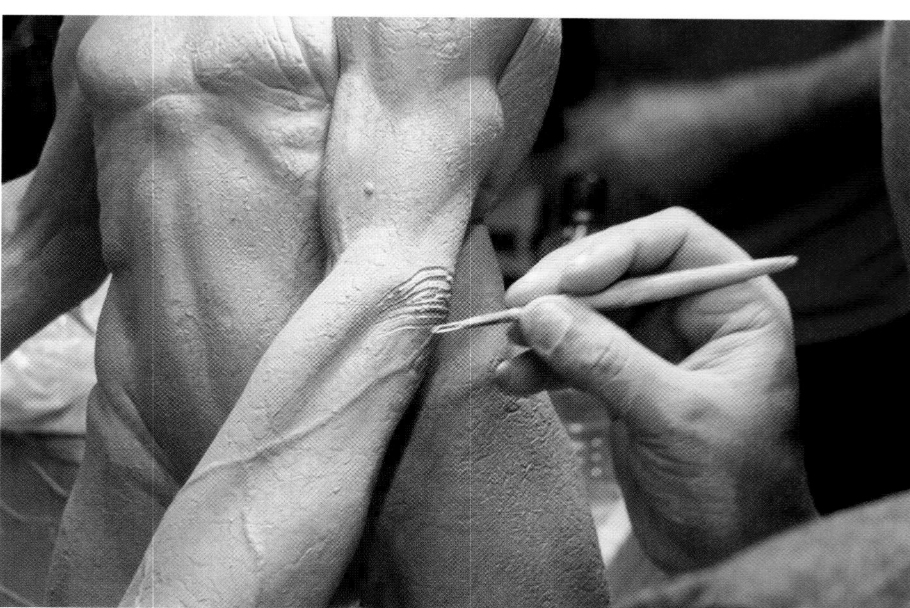

FIGURE 2.62
Elbow wrinkles being sculpted by Jordu Schell at IMATS 2008 in London.
Photo by the author.

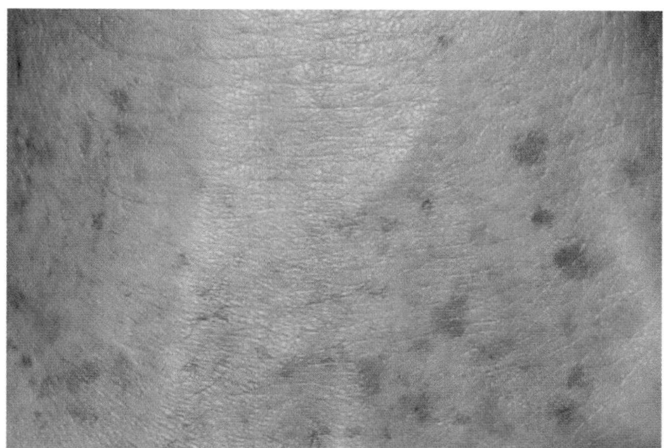

FIGURE 2.63
Age spots.
Photo by the author.

SKIN: FRECKLES AND MOLES

FIGURE 2.64
Freckles.
Photo by the author.

Freckles are spots of melanin pigment in the skin. They are usually tan or light brown, flat, and very small and are usually found in people who are light skinned or have fair complexions. Freckles are often genetically associated with fair hair—blonde and more commonly red—and with light-colored eyes. Freckles are found predominantly on the face but also can appear on any skin that is exposed to sunlight. Freckles are rarely seen on infants and most commonly begin to appear on children before they reach puberty. In adults, most freckles fade with age; people with the fairest skin often don't produce enough melanin, so freckles are always present.[23]

Moles, sometimes called *beauty marks* when found on a woman's face, are similar to freckles and are brought about by a high concentration of body pigment, or melanin, which is responsible for their dark color. Moles can be either subdermal (below the skin) or appear as a pigmented growth on the skin.[24]

SKIN: VARICOSE VEINS AND SPIDER VEINS

Both varicose veins and spider veins can appear almost anywhere on the body; varicose veins are most commonly found on the legs, whereas spider veins most commonly occur on the face around the nose, cheeks, and chin. Varicose veins are veins that have become twisted, bulging, and enlarged and are hereditary. Varicose veins are typically 3 millimeters or more in diameter and are more common in women than in men. On the other hand, spider veins are small, dilated blood vessels that are near the surface of the skin and are rarely larger than a few millimeters.

SKIN: BIRTHMARKS

Birthmarks are pigment lesions on the skin—abnormal tissue usually caused by disease or trauma—that forms before birth. Some types of birthmarks even seem to run in families. There are several types of birthmarks, including the following:

- STORK BITE or ANGEL'S KISS. Pink
  - Irregular and flat
  - Less than 3 inches in diameter
  - Located usually on the neck, head, or top lip
  - Most fade or disappear by 12 months
- MONGOLIAN BLUE SPOT. Bluish, bruise like
  - Irregular and flat
  - About 4 inches in diameter
  - Located on the lower back and buttocks
  - Most common in dark-skinned people; most noticeable in East Asians
  - Might not appear until after birth and gradually fade and have been mistaken for abuse bruises
- STRAWBERRY MARK. Red
  - Raised and lumpy
  - Can appear anywhere on the body
  - Usually appears between 1 and 4 weeks of age; can grow rapidly before stopping and fading; 60% gone by the age of 5, 90% gone by the age of 10
- CAFÉ AU LAIT SPOT. Light brown, like coffee with milk
  - Oval shaped
  - Can appear anywhere on the body
  - One or two spots are common
  - Do not fade with age
- CONGENITAL MELANOCYTIC NEVUS. Light brown in fair-skinned people to almost black in people with darker skin
  - Irregular shapes; usually flat, though large ones can be raised and bumpy
  - Ranges in size from less than ½ inch (11 millimeters) to about 11 inches (30 centimeters)
  - Can appear anywhere on the body
- PORT WINE STAIN. Pale pink at birth; becoming darker with age and changing to a deep wine red
  - Irregular shapes
  - Usually larger than 4 inches in diameter
  - Often occur on the face
  - Occurs in 3 out of 1,000 births
  - Do not fade[25]

SKIN: HAIR

When designing a makeup that will need *postiche* in addition to the other physical characteristics and landmarks we've already discussed, it is important to have at least some understanding of the external structure of hair. Postiche is a French word meaning a covering or bunch of human or artificial hair used for disguise or adornment.[26]

The term has come to describe any article of hair work, from false eyelashes to a full wig. I mention it because it is part of the language and vocabulary of special makeup effects.

Three types of hair are common to all humans:

- *Lanugo*, which is very fine fair that covers nearly the entire body of a fetus
- *Vellus hair*, which is the short, fine "peach fuzz" body hair that grows in most places on the body of both males and females
- *Terminal hair*, which is fully developed hair and generally grows longer, thicker, coarser, and darker than vellus hair[27]

Different parts of the body exhibit different types of hair. From early childhood onward, vellus hair covers the entire body regardless of gender, except for the lips, soles of the feet, palms of the hands, scar tissue, the navel, and certain external genital areas.[28]

At the onset of puberty, hormonal transformations cause some vellus hair on the body to transmute into terminal hair; because the hair is responding to hormonal influence, this hair is known as *androgenic hair*.[29]

SKIN: SCARS

After an injury and a wound heal, scars form, which are areas of fibrous tissue that replace normal skin. With the exception of very small cuts or abrasions, every wound results in scarring to some degree. Scar tissue is quite different from the skin tissue it replaces. For example, hair follicles do not grow back in scar tissue, so this information is necessary in creating a scar effect as part of a makeup design. Scars are part of the natural healing process and as such need to be understood to create authentic scar makeup. Obviously, the greater the damage to the skin, the greater the scar. Most scars are flat and pale and leave a mark of the original injury.

As wounds heal, they go through changes. The initial redness that follows a skin injury is not a scar; it may take days or weeks for the redness to go away and to go from wound to scar, and if you are doing a progressive makeup the stages of a wound are important to know. Wound makeups as well as burns and skin diseases are discussed in Chapter 9.

Two types of abnormal scars result from the body's overproduction of collagen. This causes a raised scar above the surrounding skin.[30]

Hypertrophic scars take the shape of a raised red lump on the skin but don't grow beyond the boundaries of the original wound. They often improve in appearance over time, usually a few years.

Keloid scars are a more serious form of scarring. Keloids are capable of continuing to grow indefinitely. Both hypertrophic and keloid scars are more common

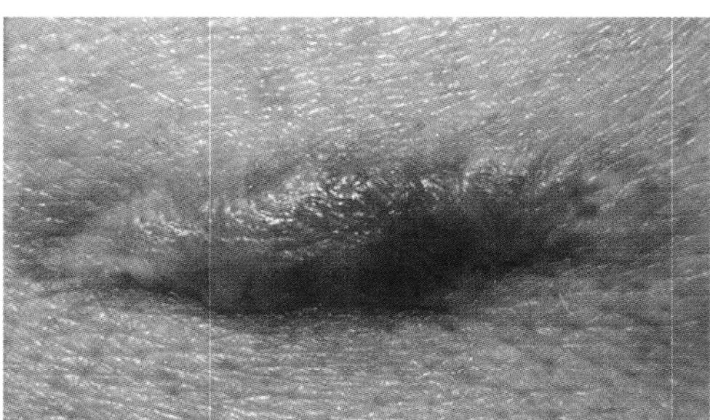

FIGURE 2.65
Hypertrophic scar.
Photo by the author.

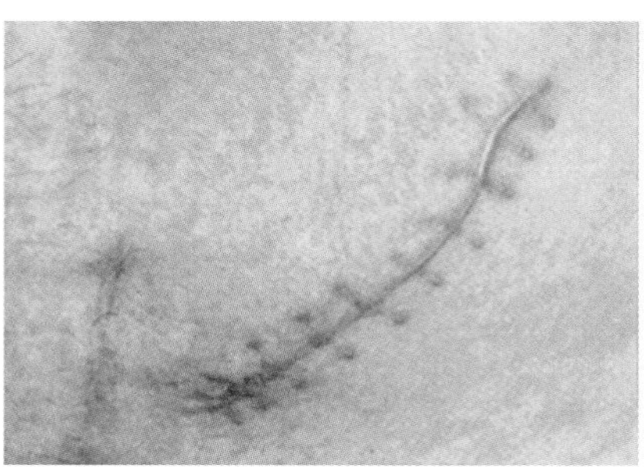

FIGURE 2.66
Hypertrophic scar, surgery.
Photo by the author.

on younger and darker-skinned people. Keloid scars are most commonly seen on the shoulder, chest, and abdomen and are most common among people of Asian or African descent.

Alternately, a scar can take the form of a sunken recess in the skin that has a pitted appearance. These are caused when the underlying structures supporting the skin, such as fat tissue or muscle, are lost. This type of scarring is most typical of acne scars but can also be caused by diseases such as chickenpox. Stretch marks, mentioned earlier in this chapter, are a form of scarring as well.[31]

SYMMETRY AND PROPORTION

Nature is filled with examples of balance and symmetry. The human body is one such example of proportion in nature. Phi (Φ), also known as the *Golden Ratio*, is a proportion that is found often in the natural world as well as in the structure of the human body. Perhaps our appreciation of the classical art and architecture of the Greeks and Romans is due partly to an appreciation, albeit unconscious, of dynamic symmetry.

Anatomical Planes

Before we can discuss dynamic symmetry of the human body, we need to establish a visual frame of reference when proportions are mentioned. Anatomical planes are crucial to describing human anatomy in a way that makes it readily understandable to others. Based on a vertical figure facing the observer, let's compare planes based on a figure whose central axis is horizontal. This is like working in 3D, modeling in the *X*, *Y*, and *Z* axes where *X* is side to side, *Y* is up and down, and *Z* is front to back.

Dynamic symmetry can be expressed in the *Fibonacci series* and in the Golden Rectangle. The Fibonacci series is a series of numbers in which any number of the series is the sum of the two previous numbers, such as $a + b = c$; $b + c = d$. It starts with 1; 1 + 1 = 2; 1 + 2 = 3; 2 + 3 = 5; 3 + 5 = 8; 5 + 8 = 13; 8 + 13 = 21; and so on. The ratio of sum divided by the preceding number approximates 1.62…; 21 ÷ 13 = 1.615; 13 ÷ 8 = 1.625; and so on. This number is called Phi, or Φ.[32]

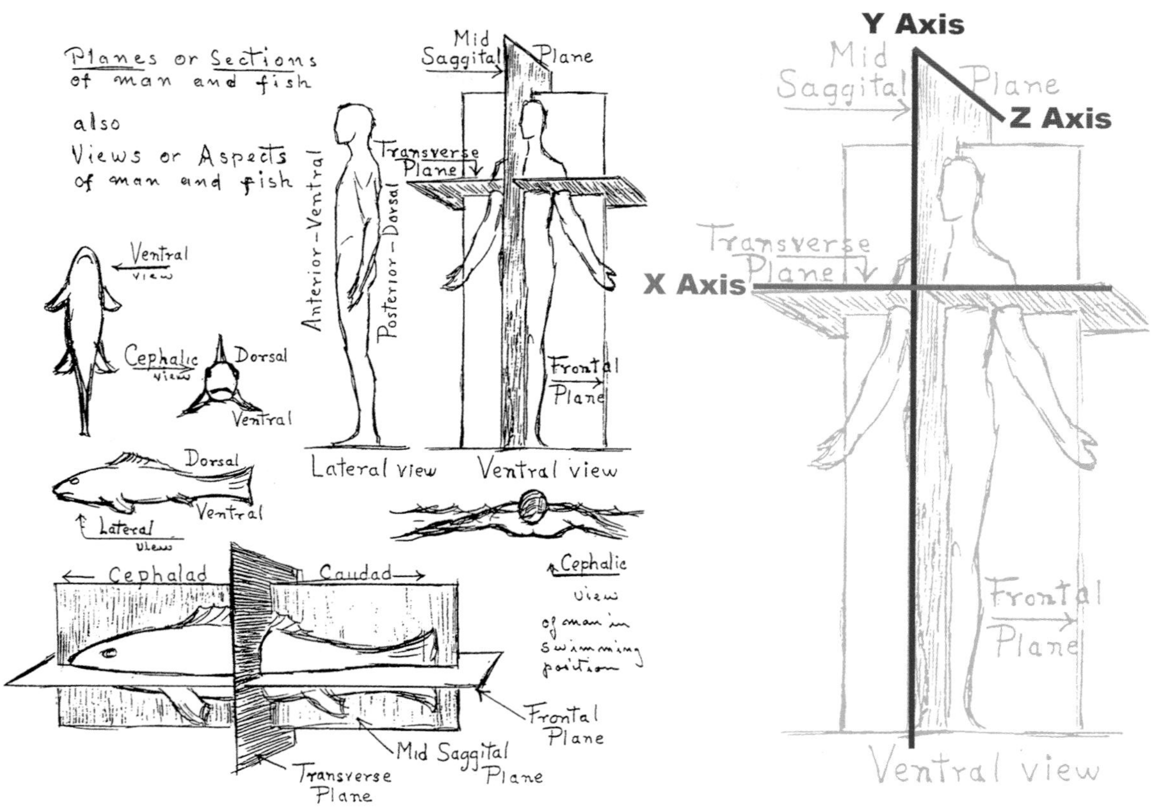

FIGURE 2.67
Anatomical planes of the human figure.
Images reproduced by permission of Eugene F. Fairbanks.

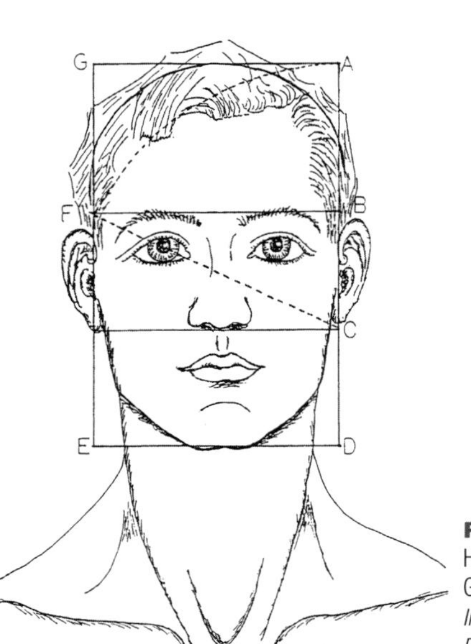

FIGURE 2.68
Head proportions conform to Golden Mean, AD/AC = 1.6 = Φ.
Image reproduced by permission of Eugene F. Fairbanks.

For example, the ratio of the height of a human male head to its width is approximately (on average) 9 inches to 5¼ inches; 9 ÷ 5.25 = 1.61. Many proportions of the human body share this ratio.[33]

Facial Ratios and Phi

As already mentioned, representative proportions and average measurements will not be found in any one person; in creating a figure for a makeup effect or perhaps as a prop, it might be best to work with a live model for truly accurate representation. Nonetheless, Phi ratios are valid and can be used to create accurate and pleasing results.[34]

FIGURE 2.69
Some vertical face ratios approximate Φ, or 1.62. *Images reproduced by permission of Eugene F. Fairbanks.*

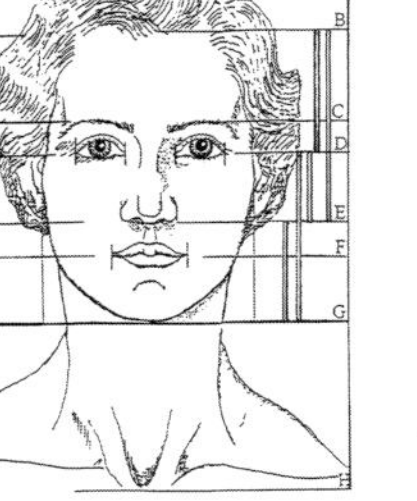
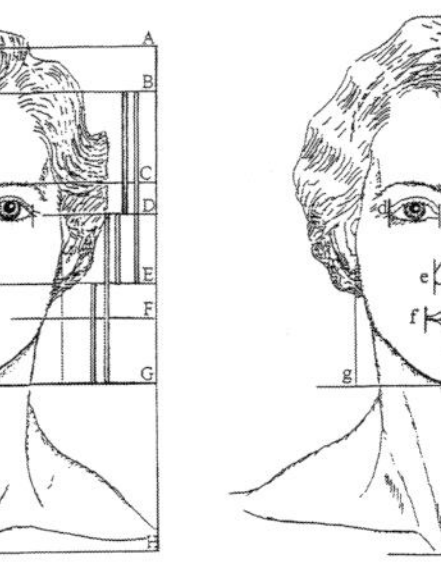
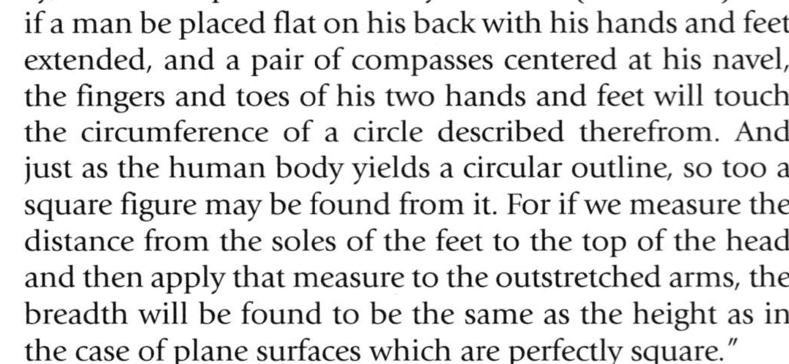

Few people are aware of the significance of Leonardo da Vinci's the *Vitruvian Man* drawing and its relationship to human proportion. Quoting Vitruvius, a celebrated Roman architect under both Julius Caesar and Augustus Caesar, "Then again, in the human body, the central point is naturally the navel (umbilicus). For if a man be placed flat on his back with his hands and feet extended, and a pair of compasses centered at his navel, the fingers and toes of his two hands and feet will touch the circumference of a circle described therefrom. And just as the human body yields a circular outline, so too a square figure may be found from it. For if we measure the distance from the soles of the feet to the top of the head and then apply that measure to the outstretched arms, the breadth will be found to be the same as the height as in the case of plane surfaces which are perfectly square."

Table 2.1 Comparative Male/Female Ratios

Vertical (*Y*):		**Female**	**Male**
Head height ÷ Head width		= 1.45	= 1.51
Vertex to eyes ÷ Hairline to eyes	AD ÷ BD	= 1.32	= 1.29
Eyes to chin ÷ Nostrils to chin	DF ÷ DE	= 1.59	= 1.54
Hairline to eyes ÷ Eyes to nostrils	DB ÷ DE	= 1.60	= 1.67
Eyes to mouth ÷ Eyes to nostrils	DF ÷ DE	= 1.50	= 1.56
Nostrils to chin ÷ Mouth to chin	FG ÷ FG	= 1.45	= 1.46
Transverse (*X*):		**Female**	**Male**
Head width ÷ Lateral eye corners	gg'÷ dd'	= 1.56	= 1.49
Mouth width ÷ Nose width at ala	ff'÷ ee'	= 1.42	= 1.34
Lateral eye corners ÷ Mouth width	dd'÷ ff'	= 1.59	= 1.54
Hairline to eyes ÷ Eyes to nostrils	DB ÷ DE	= 1.60	= 1.67
Eyes to mouth ÷ Eyes to nostrils	DF ÷ DE	= 2.05	= 2.00

Whatever motivates your makeup design, there is a natural law of symmetry you can follow and adapt to the universe where your character exists, but its design must still adhere to a set of symmetrical rules; it is also imperative that the design follow the criteria set for the production, whether theater or film. Nature must give the base from which to build on a design; but since the makeup is to be theatrical and will be worn, it becomes the paramount design parameter to keep in sharp focus.

Through *anthropometry*, the study of the measurement of humans, ratios of other body proportions have been determined, all of which can be extremely beneficial in creating special makeup effects.

Ratios and Body Proportions

The male and female figures in the following two drawings illustrate standing, sitting, and kneeling relationships. Both are standing at eight head heights (eight males and eight females, respectively), with kneeling height at ¾ of standing height and sitting height slightly more than ½ of standing height. You'll notice that the female is a bit more than the male sitting height, since women mature physically earlier than men. The long bones of female legs (the femur) usually don't grow as long as those in males.[35]

The shoulder width of a grown man is equal to ¼ of his height (stature) and also equals two head heights. The span of the same man's arms outstretched from third fingertip to third fingertip is equal to his height and also equal to eight head heights.

By dividing a design in half or into thirds, it could seem to lose some of its subtlety. Not so. Halves and thirds appear to be quite prevalent in studies of the human figure and the face. The head is 1/8 of the total figure; the hair above the forehead is 1/8 of the whole of the (vertical) head. The figure minus the head is divided into thirds to reach the leg length. This process establishes three main lengths: the lower leg, sole of foot to knee; the knee to the ilium crest (pelvis); and the body from the crest of the ilium to the chin.[36]

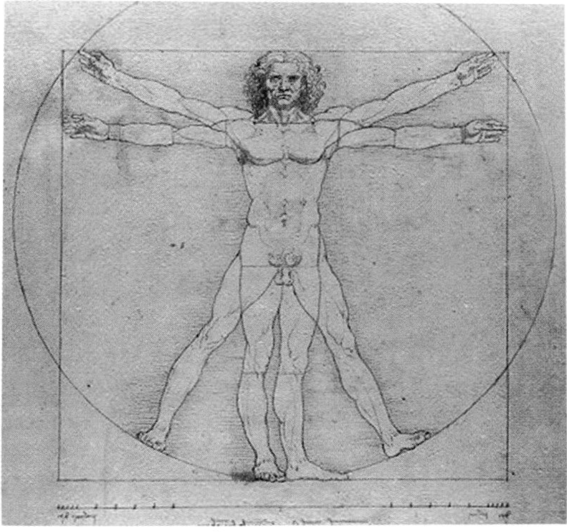

FIGURE 2.70 Leonardo da Vinci's *Vitruvian Man*, illustrating human proportion. *Image reproduced by permission of Luc Viatour.*

The head from chin to vertex is equal to the length of the foot from heel to tip of foremost toe. The face is equal to the length of the hand; the distance from wrist to tip of middle finger equals that from chin to hairline. The neck, from chin to sternal notch, is equal to half the head height.

There are also differences between the male figure and the female figure; to establish vertical measurements for a typical figure, the only measurement needed to begin modeling is the overall anticipated height of the figure. You can then determine what the body proportions will be. However, when measuring people, you'll quickly see that there are loads of individual variations. Not everyone's body will conform to a measurement norm; some people have long necks, some short. Some people have long legs and a short torso, or the like. The drawing and descriptions of human proportions shown and described in this chapter are to be considered as guidelines for assistance only and should not be considered for precise measurements.

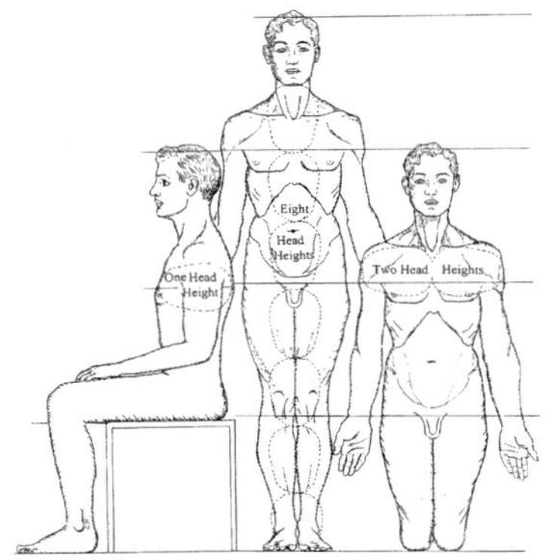

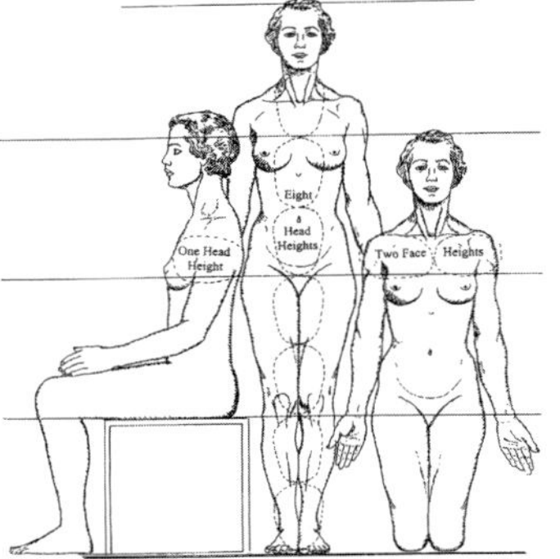

FIGURE 2.71
Male figure of eight heads is illustrated with kneeling height at ¾ and sitting height a little more than half the standing height. In the male figure, shoulders are two head heights wide. Female figure is illustrated with stature at eight head heights. Kneeling height is also ¾ standing height, but sitting height is slightly greater than half the standing height since maturation is earlier in females. The long bones of legs usually don't grow as long as in males. Shoulder width in females is two face heights.
Images reproduced by permission of Eugene F. Fairbanks.

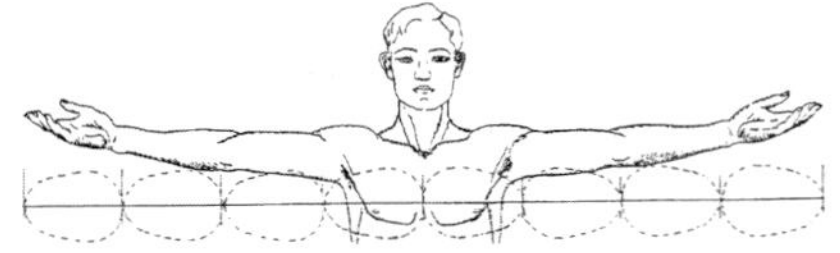

FIGURE 2.72
A man's height equals eight heads.
Image reproduced by permission of Eugene F. Fairbanks in.

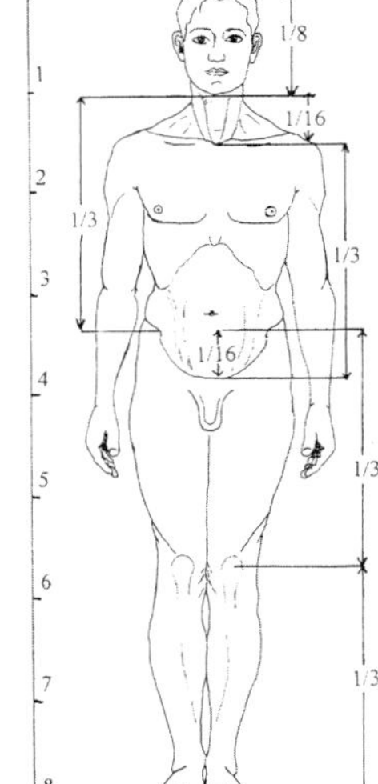

FIGURE 2.73
Body divided into thirds.
Images reproduced by permission of Eugene F. Fairbanks.

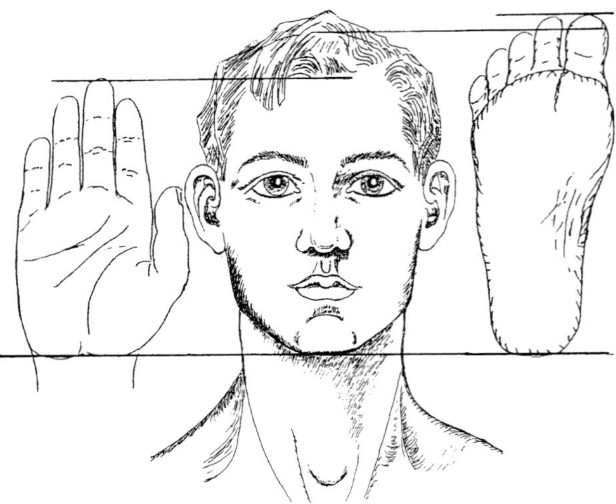

FIGURE 2.74
The male head compared to hand and foot.
Image reproduced by permission of Eugene F. Fairbanks.

GEOMETRIC ANALYSIS

It should be clear that these descriptions are a gross oversimplification of human anatomy and the proportional relationships between different segments and groupings of the body and that I am merely highlighting some areas of interest that I feel should be considered when you're designing and creating for our craft.

Some very interesting geometric relationships come to light when we analyze proportions of the human form. In most geometric analysis, there's a dominance of straight-line shapes and measurements, but there are relatively few such lines when looking at the human body's lines. Instead we see a preponderance of curves and arcs. For example, the *scalenus* muscles on each side of the neck give support to the vertebra laterally, much like the wires that support a utility pole. The *sternocleidomastoid* muscles, responsible for turning the head, cross the scalenus muscles, creating a triangle; the triangle shape is also visible via the *trapezius* muscles (posterior), the *sternocleidomastoid* muscles (anterior), and the *clavicle* (collar bone).[37]

In the torso, an isosceles triangle (at least two equal sides) is formed from the points of the shoulders to the navel. As you can see, there are also a number of proportions that correspond to squares and rectangles in addition to triangles.[38]

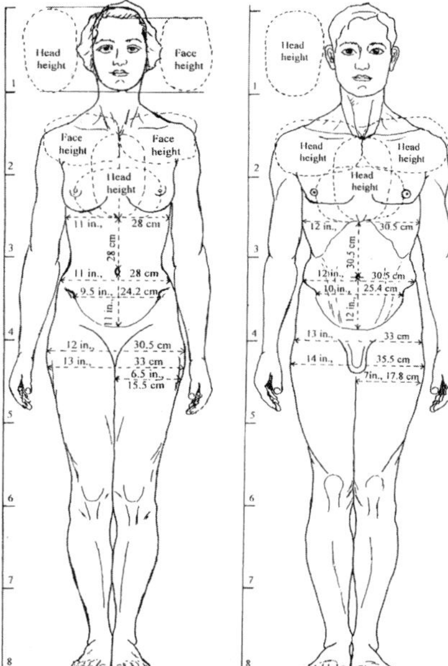

FIGURE 2.75
Male/female proportions.
Image reproduced by permission of Eugene F. Fairbanks.

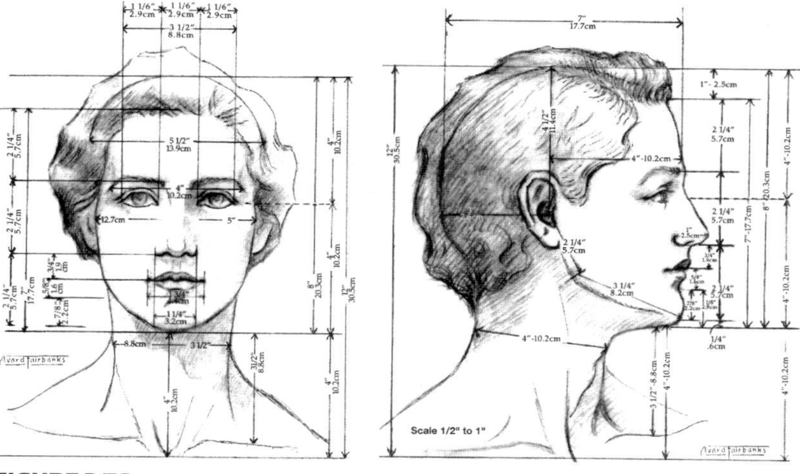

FIGURE 2.76
The female head, detailed proportions, and anterior and lateral views. In the anterior (front) view, the head is divided into two at the level of eyes. Half the face height equals distance between lateral corners of eyes. Mouth width equals ½ distance between lateral corners of eyes. In the lateral (side) view, head and neck are divided into three equal proportions: sternal notch to chin, to corner of eye, and to top of head. Face is also divided into three equal proportions, commonly referred to as nose lengths.
Images reproduced by permission of Eugene F. Fairbanks.

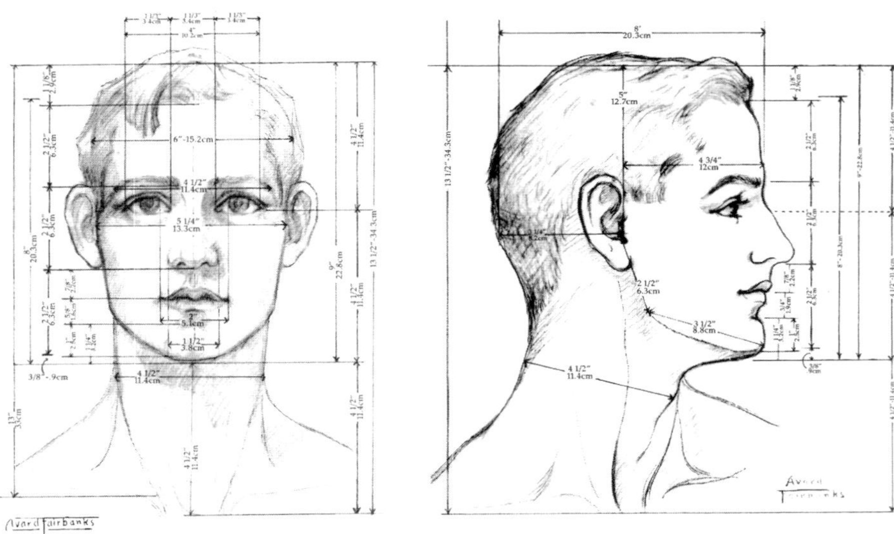

FIGURE 2.77
The male head, detailed proportions, and anterior and lateral views. In the anterior view, the head is divided into two at the level of eyes. As with the female head, half the face height equals distance between lateral corners of eyes. Mouth width equals half the distance between lateral corners of eyes. In the lateral view, head and neck are also divided into three equal proportions: sternal notch to chin, to corner of eye, and to top of head. Eye is half the distance from top of head to chin.
Images reproduced by permission of Eugene F. Fairbanks.

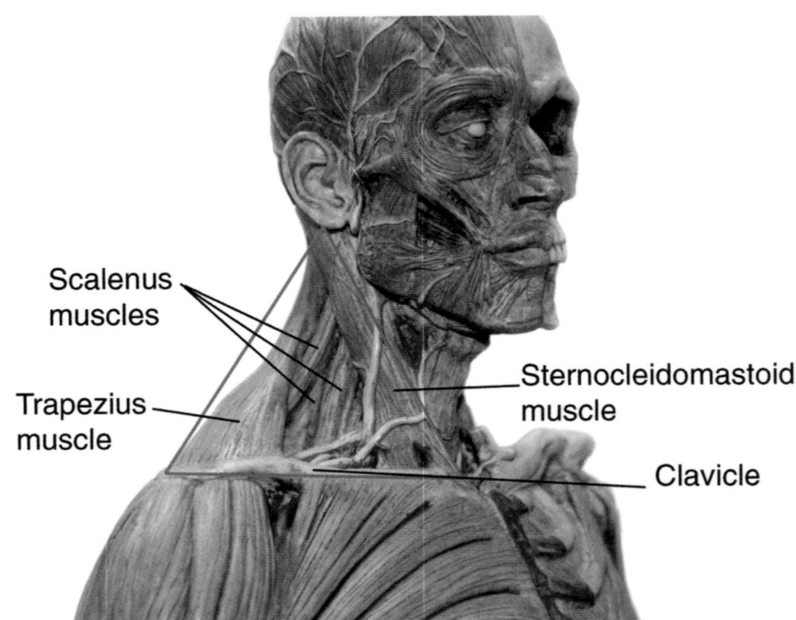

FIGURE 2.78
Clavicle, sternocleidomastoid, and trapezius form a triangle.
Photo by the author. Model by Andrew Cawrse.

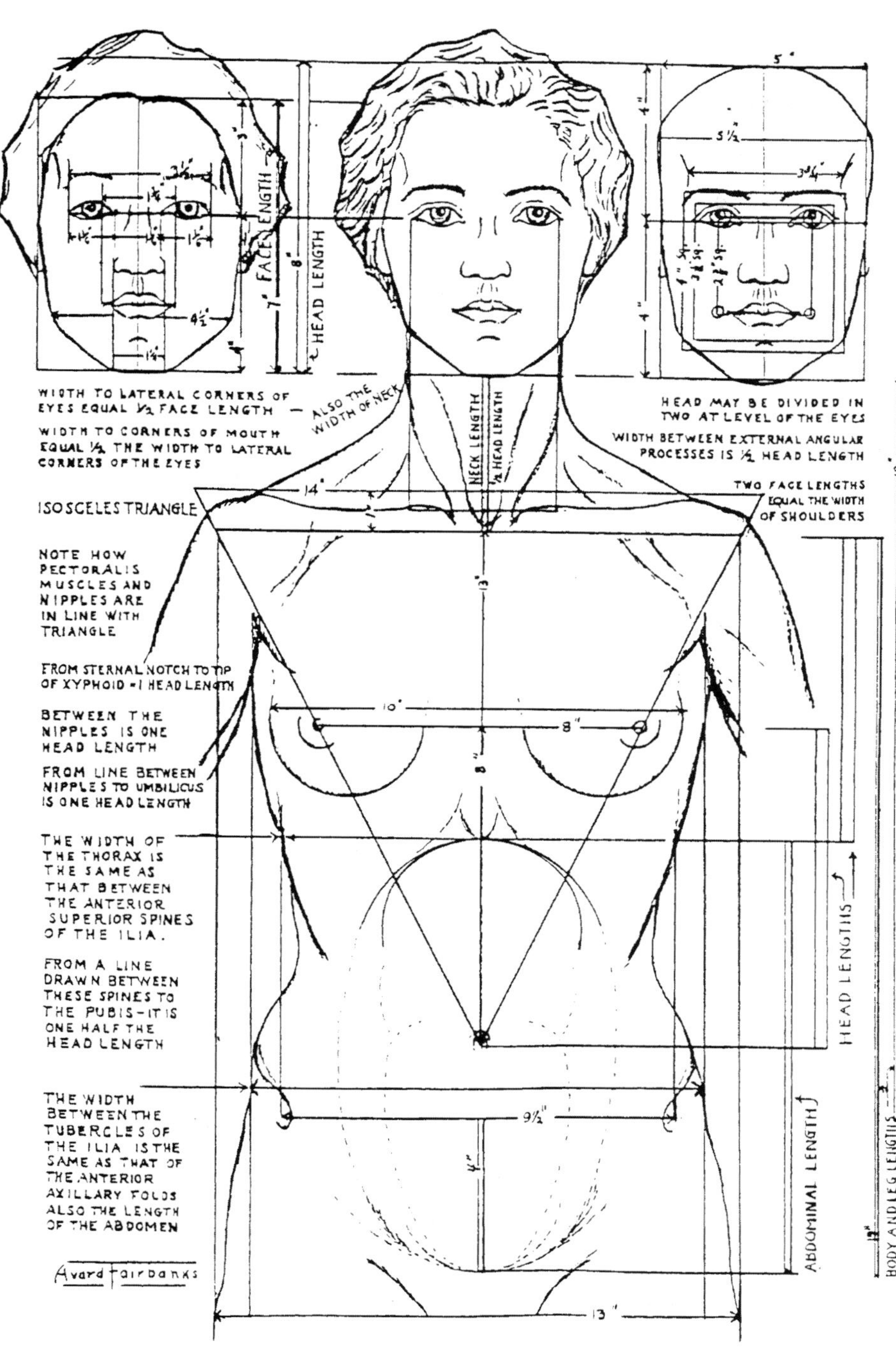

FIGURE 2.79
Geometric analysis.
Image reproduced by permission of Eugene F. Fairbanks.

FIGURE 2.80
Men and women are noticeably different ….
Image reproduced by permission of istockphoto.com.

DISTINCTIONS OF GENDER, AGE, AND ANCESTRY

In the field of forensic art and illustration, there has been a great deal of research into the distinctions of age, gender, and ancestry for the creation—or *re*-creation—of individuals from a variety of information sources. A forensic artist could be given the task of helping to identify an individual from composite drawings, whereas forensic anthropologists can actually reconstruct an individual for identification from skeletal and semiskeletal remains through sculpture. How does this apply to us as makeup effects artists? It should be fairly clear: Much of what we've just discussed regarding human proportion and surface anatomy will come into play when you create age makeups, gender change makeups, and ancestral alterations.

Distinctions of Gender

Physically, there is obvious and readily apparent *sexual dimorphism* between men and women, that is, differences in shape and size between individuals of differing gender in the same species. In many species, including most mammals, the male is larger than the female. For the most part, this is true of humans as well; on average, men are taller than women and have greater body mass and weight. The male face is more angular overall and is usually larger than the female face, and the lower half of the male face is proportionally larger than the female simply because the lower jaw, or the mandible, of the male is bigger and stronger. The jaw angle is usually more severely defined in the male and the chin squarer and more prominent. The forehead is also often more sloping in males than in females, with a hint of a projecting brow ridge.[39]

FIGURE 2.81
The lateral view of growth pattern from 1 month to 6 years and then to 18 years. Proportional comparison of fetal skull (left) and adult skull (right).
Image reproduced by permission of Wes Price, © 2008.

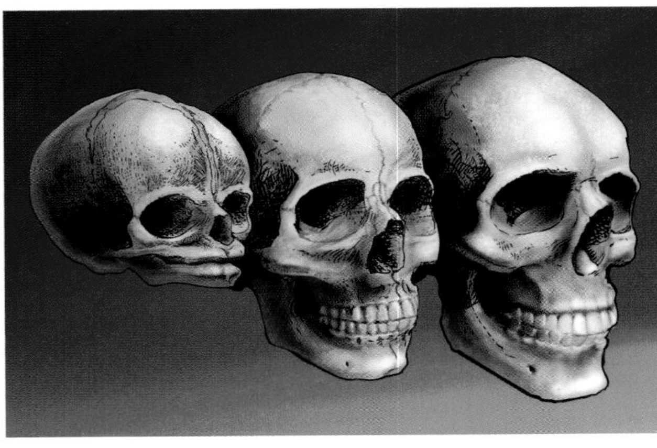

The following are some additional outward physical differences between men and women:

- Men generally have more body hair than women.
- Men's skin is thicker and oilier than women's skin; women's skin tends to be smoother.
- Women generally have smaller waists in relation to their hips; that is, their waist-to-hip ratio is smaller than that of men.

- A man's index finger (second digit) tends to be shorter than the ring finger (fourth digit), whereas women's index finger tends to be longer than the ring finger.
- Women tend to have lighter skin coloration than men, on average, by as much as 3% or 4%.
- Women generally have a lower center of gravity than men—that is, shorter legs and longer torsos relative to their height—as well as a larger hip section.
- Women generally have a higher percentage of body fat than men.
- Women tend to have higher voices than men.
- Men tend to have a more prominent *laryngeal prominence*, or *Adam's apple*, than women.
- Women have enlarged, functional breasts.
- Men generally have greater muscle mass and physical strength.
- Men tend to have shoulders that are wider than their hips.
- Men's skeletal structure is generally heavier than women's.
- Men tend to collect fat deposits around the abdomen and waist (apple shape), whereas women tend to have greater fat deposits around the buttocks, thighs, and hips (pear shape).[40]

Distinctions of Age

As we grow, our bodies go through a series of remarkable physical changes of which we, as designers, must be acutely aware. The proportional change in the amount of lower face is perhaps the most fundamental aspect of facial growth. For example, as a child grows, the face grows downward and forward; the forehead becomes more upright and flat, and the lower part of the head (face) elongates downward and out.[41]

There are other outward manifestations as we grow through childhood into adolescence and puberty and then into adulthood. In fact, ossification—the hardening or calcification of soft tissue into bone—doesn't usually occur fully until around the age of 25.

With the exception of primary sexual characteristics—that is, having either a penis or a vagina—male and female bodies are very similar during childhood. It isn't until adolescence, when boys and girls begin to go through puberty, that noticeable differences between the sexes begin to manifest themselves. During puberty (often between the ages of 9 and 13), both boys and girls quickly begin to gain weight and grow taller. In boys, the body becomes more muscular and the shoulders become wider than the hips; girls develop breasts, and their hips become wider than their shoulders. As they reach adulthood, the secondary sex characteristics noted previously are fully developed.

You may well be asking yourself, "What does childhood and adolescent growth have to do with creating special makeup effects? I can't turn a grown man into a kid." Of course you can't. But you might be asked at some point in your career to turn a middle-aged man into a 20-something version of himself, something Rick Baker and his team were asked to do for several characters in the 2006

Adam Sandler movie *Click*. You may also find yourself in the position to fabricate props—children's bodies, perhaps—for a crime show or horror movie. This information may be useful. I hope it is now and will be later.

Our faces go through a tremendous amount of growth and change from youth to old age. But at the same time, barring physically altering trauma, there is also

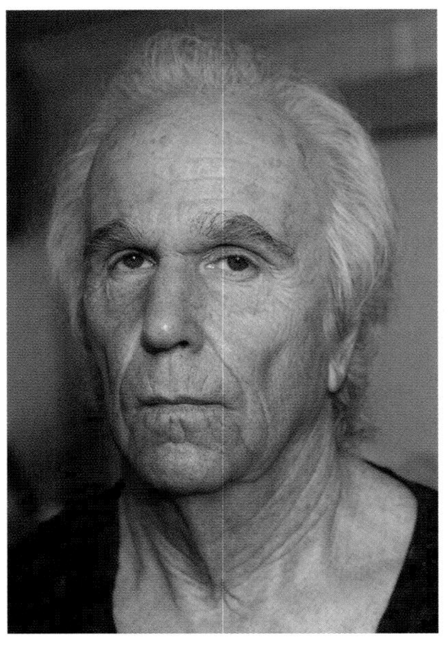

FIGURE 2.82
Age makeup, Henry Winkler; *Click.*
Image reproduced by permission of Kazuhiro Tsuji.

FIGURE 2.83
The author at 3, 7, 11, 13, 15, 18, 32, and 53 years, illustrating gnomatic growth.
Images reproduced by permission of the author's wife and mother.

a significant constancy of appearance. The face of a man or woman looks almost the same throughout his or her life, no matter the age. This phenomenon is known as *gnomatic growth*.

Gnomatic growth is a process that leaves facial features in later years similar to those found in youth.[42] It's due (in part) to the phenomenon of gnomatic growth that missing children can be found alive and be identified years later.

An individual's looks cannot be undermined by age. The first 20 years are constructive and growth oriented; the years after that are degenerative and destructive.[43]

FIGURE 2.84 Karl Langer's skin tension lines look like this.
Image reproduced by permission of istockphoto.com.

Nothing will be more beneficial to your makeup designs than reference images, gobs and gobs of reference images … but a firm understanding of how the human body ages and the physical changes we go through will also aid you immensely in getting your details right. Depending on where it is on the body, aged skin wrinkles and folds in specific directions. These lines were mapped out in detail by the Austrian anatomist Karl Langer in 1861.

Everyone ages differently, and factors beyond genetics also contribute significantly to the aging process. Smoking, alcohol, drug abuse, stress, fitness (or the lack there of), lifestyle, the environment (sun exposure, pollution)—these can all contribute to visible aging, either premature aging or a prolonged youthful appearance. All these things, as well as the medium in which the makeup will be seen, must be taken into account when we design an age makeup. If there will be close-ups, the makeup can be more subtle than if it must be seen on the stage, for example. Furthermore, though you may be presented with the challenge of creating a full-body makeup at some time—perhaps a body to be used as a prop—usually at the most you will be working with the face, neck, and hands and possibly part of the arms, leaving the rest of the body covered.

FACIAL AGING

Creating a realistic and convincing age makeup for any individual requires understanding the physical mechanics of the facial aging process, to project how a particular face will change with age. Every individual ages at a variable rate, but a fairly predictable series of changes seems to occur in a similar order in most people.[44]

For example, wrinkles will first appear in certain locations and then in others, such as first on the forehead and around the eyes and then around the nose and mouth. Steve

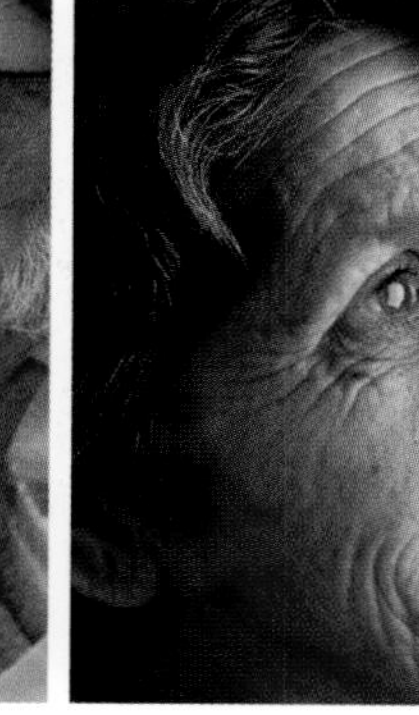

FIGURE 2.85 Wrinkles occur perpendicular to the stretch and pull of underlying muscles.
Images reproduced by permission of istockphoto.com.

Wang once told me about a student who asked him how to get good at something. Using an example of facial wrinkles, Steve said, "Find a good image of a face that has interesting wrinkles you'd like to recreate. Take a piece of tracing paper and trace *just* the wrinkles, and then toss that piece of paper. Take another piece of tracing paper and trace just the wrinkles again." Steve said to keep repeating the process until you can draw the wrinkles perfectly from memory. Effects artist Anthony Grow agrees, saying it takes repeating something at least 11 times for it to become ingrained in memory.

Terminology for the lines and grooves of the face has been published by the American Society of Plastic and Reconstructive Surgeons that is related to the degree of facial line depth, such as transverse frontal lines and nasolabial folds. A progression of wrinkles begins as *lines*, then *grooves*, and matures into deeper *furrows* and *folds*.[45]

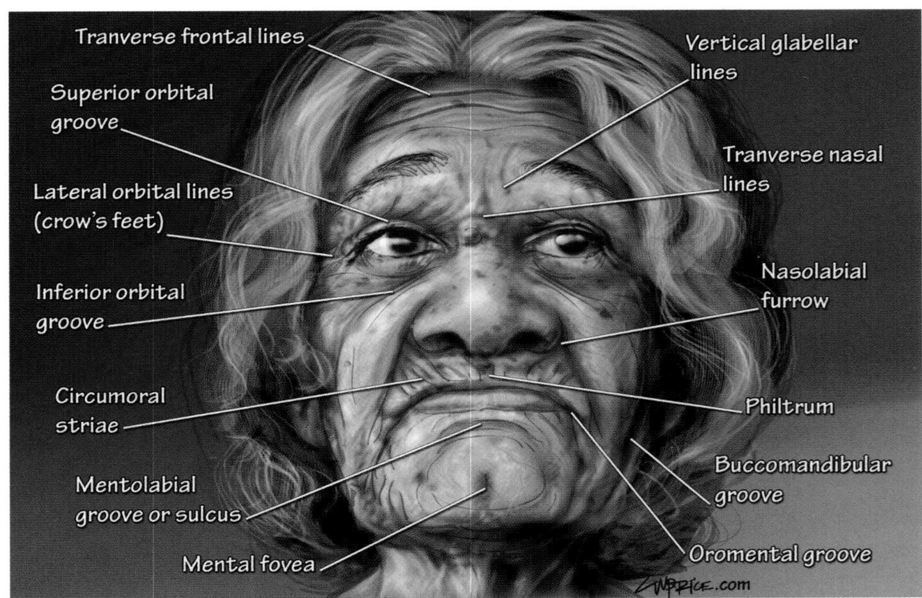

FIGURE 2.86
Facial anatomy.
Image reproduced by permission of Wes Price, © 2008.

Here is a guideline: Wrinkles appear perpendicular to the stretch of underlying muscles. For example, the horizontal (transverse) lines across a forehead are perpendicular to the vertical pull of the *frontalis* muscle of the face. If you understand facial muscles, it will be easier to determine where to place age lines and wrinkles that look natural. The following breakdown by decade was created by a renowned forensic illustrator, Karen Taylor, from research presented in *The Journal of Otolaryngology*, Craniofacial Identification in Forensic Medicine, the Combined Graphic Method (CGM) of Craniofacial Reconstruction, and the Scottsdale Artists' School.[46]

THE 20S

- Fine transverse frontal lines may appear across the forehead.
- Fine vertical glabellar lines may appear in people who frown frequently.
- Fine lateral orbital lines, or "crow's feet," may appear in people who smile often or spend a lot of time in the sun.

THE 30S

- Transverse frontal lines deepen.
- Vertical glabellar lines deepen.
- Lateral orbital lines increase in number and deepen.
- Transverse nasal lines may form across the top of the nose.
- Nasolabial lines or furrows become noticeable.

THE 40S

- The inferior orbital groove may become apparent.
- The eyebrows may descend slightly.
- An excess of upper eyelid may develop and a portion of the superior orbital groove may be obscured at the lateral side.
- The jawline becomes less firm.
- Circumoral striae become noticeable, especially in smokers.
- The lips may begin to thin.
- The oromental groove may begin, depending on facial structure.
- The mentolabial groove becomes more apparent, depending on facial structure.
- Fine lines in the neck become noticeable.

THE 50S

- The inferior orbital groove may define a developing pouch under the eyes.
- Excess upper eyelid tissue may worsen, obscuring more of the superior orbital groove at the lateral side and creating more lateral orbital lines.
- The nasolabial furrow is more noticeable.
- The oromental groove deepens.
- The lips continue to thin, especially in people who had thin lips in youth.
- Dental changes may become apparent, increasing lines accordingly.
- A buccomandibular groove may appear.
- The jawline becomes much less firm.
- Jowls and a double chin may appear.
- Lines in the neck are more noticeable.
- Arcus senilis may begin to appear in the eyes.

THE 60S

- All the aforementioned lines become exaggerated.

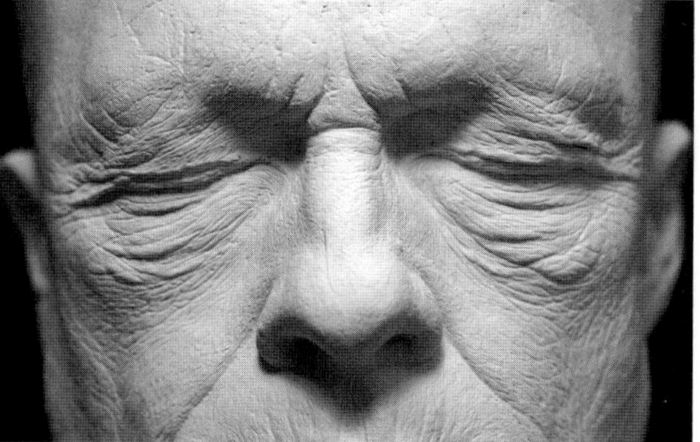

FIGURE 2.87 Age sculpt, Brad Pitt; *The Curious Case of Benjamin Button.* *Image reproduced by permission of Miles Teves.*

- The circumoral striae may cross over the vermillion border of the lips.
- Ears appear to get larger, and wrinkles appear in front of the tragus.
- The jawline is very soft, and tissues under the neck sag.

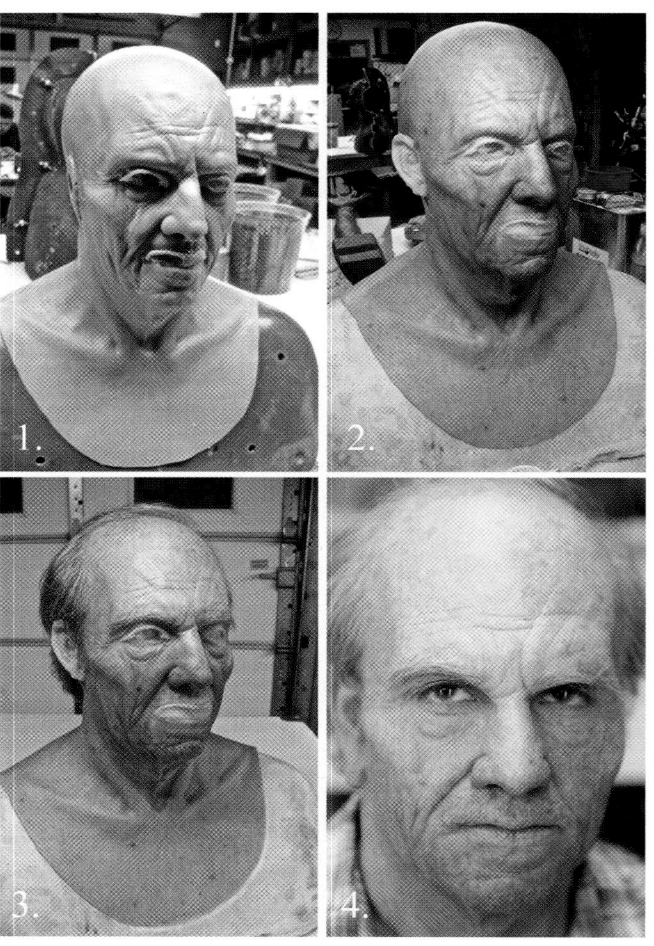

FIGURE 2.88 Vincent Van Dyke age makeup applied by Thom Floutz. 1. Silicone fresh out of mold. 2. Painted. 3. Hair work done. 4. Applied.
Image reproduced by permission of Vincent Van Dyke.

THE 70S AND OLDER

- All the aforementioned lines become more pronounced and defined, accompanied by a marked loss of elasticity of the skin and sagging tissue.

Arcus senilis is a cloudy grayish or whitish arc or circle around the periphery of the cornea of older adults; it's caused by fatty acid deposits in the deep layer of the peripheral cornea. It most commonly occurs after the age of 50 and is most common in men.

Other factors can create an appearance of having aged without much passage of actual time. Hair loss and a slight weight gain can affect the appearance of aging beyond normal chronology. Keep in mind that when you're creating transverse

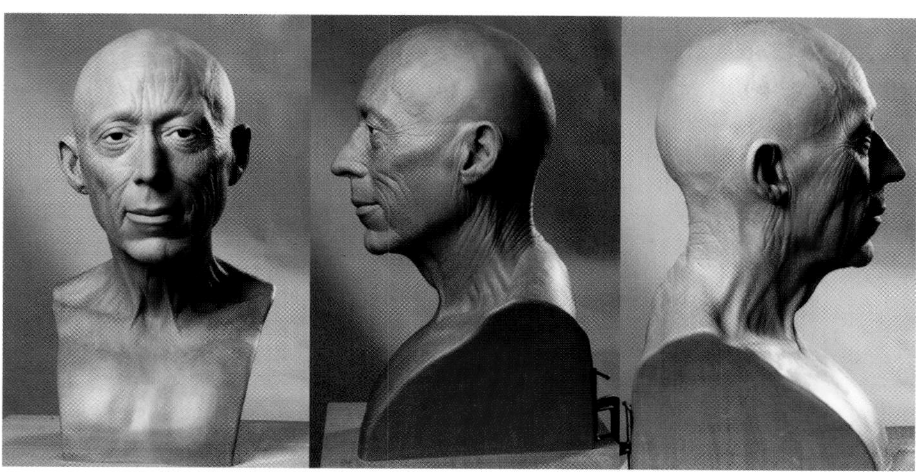

FIGURE 2.89
Sculpture of Dick Smith by Kazuhiro Tsuji.
Image reproduced by permission of Kazuhiro Tsuji.

frontal lines, they can't exist beyond the natural hairline, because they correspond to the perpendicular vertical pull of the frontalis muscle, which stops very near the hairline in most people.

Distinctions of Ancestry

As our society becomes more and more culturally and ethnically diverse, the impact of "race" is becoming more and more diluted as peoples begin to blend with one another and clearly defined descriptions blur. *Race* is a traditionally used term that describes major zoological subdivisions of humankind, which are regarded as having a common beginning and sharing a relatively constant group of physical traits, such as pigmentation and facial and body proportions.[47]

FIGURE 2.90
"Before and after" age makeup, Ben Browder; Farscape.
Images reproduced by permission of David Elsey.

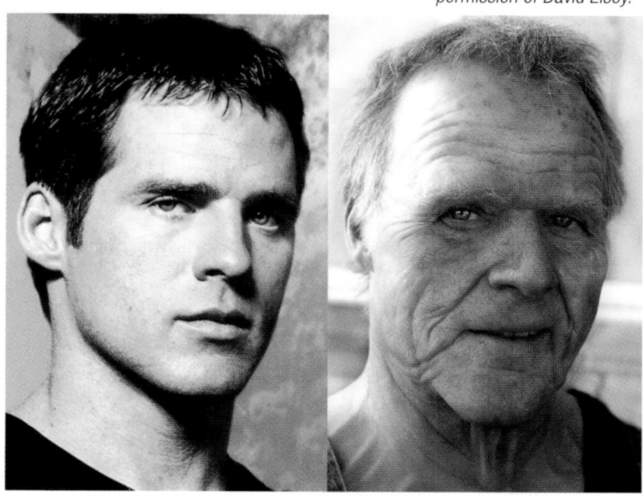

For the makeup of today's population, *ancestry* seems to be a more accurate term. However, as makeup artists and makeup designers we must examine the more traditional overview of the three major racial/ancestral groups to arrive at a distinct physical appearance: Caucasoid, Negroid, and Mongoloid, or the preferred *European derived*, *African derived*, and *Asian derived*.

Of course, there is a multiplicity of physical appearances that exist with each of these groups.[48]

Dr. Henry Field in his 1946 book, *The Races of Mankind*, first described the three

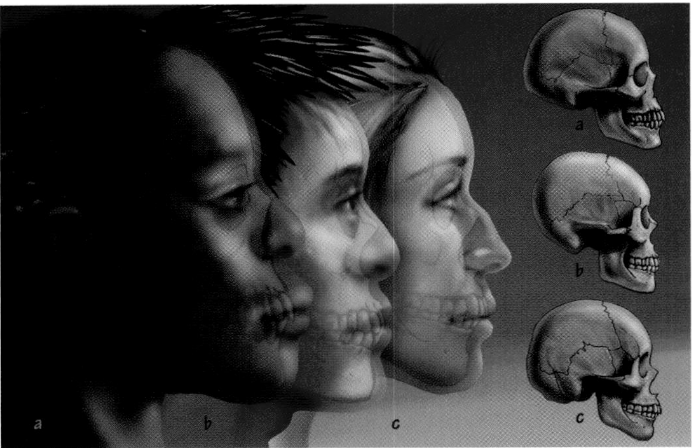

FIGURE 2.91
Lateral view showing the relationship of face to skull, three ancestral groups—African derived (a, left); Asian derived (b, middle); European derived (c, right).
Image reproduced by permission of Wes Price, © 2008.

major racial groups—Caucasoid, Negroid, and Mongoloid—which by today's standards seem quite antiquated,[49] but regardless of how appropriate they are or not there is no denying that physical differences in ancestry do still very much exist. I present them here as a context only for creating a particular ethnic character makeup design.

Structurally, there are immediately obvious skeletal differences (though generalized) between the European-derived, African-derived, and Asian-derived ancestral groups, which are visible in this illustration of facial relationships to the skull shape.

Caucasian people are generally referred to as *white*, though hardly all light-skinned people are Caucasian nor are all Caucasians light skinned. Many Caucasian skulls present a seemingly flat face in profile, with retreating or back-slanting zygomatic bones. The anterior skull shows longer and narrower nasal openings than its African- or Asian-derived counterparts.[50]

In his book, Dr. Field placed European-derived people into three additional groups:

- *Mediterranean*. Iberian peninsula, western Mediterranean islands, southern France and Italy, western Wales, and western Ireland:
  - Short and stocky
  - Olive complexion
  - Dark hair and eyes
  - Long head; narrow, oval face
  - Small mouth
- *Alpine*. Central plateau of France, Switzerland, and what is now the Czech Republic; south into the Balkans and east into Russia and the former Soviet Union:
  - Round head; broad face
  - Dark complexion
  - Dark (brown) wavy hair
  - Thick eyebrows over brown eyes
  - Heavy body hair
  - Sometimes a thick neck; medium to heavy build
- *Nordic*. Scandinavia, northern Germany, part of Holland and Belgium, Great Britain[51]:
  - Tall
  - Light complexion

- Fair hair and blue eyes
- Long head and face
- Prominent nose and chin

Field also wrote about Caucasian people of Africa:

> *The Hamites who inhabit north and northeast Africa … possess dark brown or black hair, which is either curly or wavy in form, and the skin varies in color from reddish brown to dark brown. Their average stature varies from very tall to medium and their build is slender. The typical Hamite possesses a long head, an oval, elongated face with no forward protrusion, thin lips, pointed chin, and a prominent, well-shaped nose.*
>
> *Semites … in a measure the physical traits of Hamites resemble those of Semites. Members of the Semitic group now live chiefly in the extreme north of Africa migrated from Arabia at early dates. The Arabs, who are typical Semites in both physique and language, are usually medium in stature, are dark-haired, and generally have oval faces, with long, narrow, straight noses. There are two typical head forms among the Arabs—one is long and the other broad.*[52]

The African-derived peoples who make up the majority of the group originating in Africa are most frequently referred to as *black*, even though their pigmentation varies broadly from light brown to a very dark brown, sometimes bordering on black. Often the skull exhibits alveolar prognathism, which is a protrusion of the lower face by both the maxilla and the mandible. The anterior nasal openings tend to be wider and shorter than in Caucasians and Asians (Mongoloids), with a broader and flatter bridge. The mouth tends to be broader as well, with fuller, inverted lips. Many African-derived people also have wider set eyes than the other groups.[53]

Field identified four African-derived groups of people:

- *West African*. Coastal West Africa:
  - Long headed
  - Medium stature
  - Well developed, with a heavy torso and massive limbs
  - Long arms and short legs in comparison with the length of the trunk
  - Sometimes a projecting chin
  - Nose is broad, lips are thick; dark eyes and wooly hair
- *Nilotic*. Upper Nile:
  - Taller, greater stature
  - Slender build
  - Longer head in relation to width
- *Pygmies*. Ituri forest, northern Congo:
  - Short, dark brown hair
  - Pigmentation ranging from light brown with yellow tinge to very dark chocolate brown
  - The average stature is short: 4 feet, 6 inches; both body and legs are short

- Round head with some facial protrusion
- Full lips; flat, broad nose
- *Bushmen*. Kalahari Desert[54]:
  - Short, frizzy hair in tufts
  - Little or no facial or body hair
  - Pigmentation ranging from yellow to olive
  - Markedly wrinkled skin at early age
  - Small head, low in the crown; somewhere between long and round head
  - Slightly protruding forehead
  - Very flat and broad nose
  - Dark, narrow, and slightly oblique eyes
  - The average height of males: below 5 feet

We ordinarily think of the Mongoloid group of people—those we think of as Asian derived—as being Chinese, Japanese, Korean, or one of several other varied Asian groups. In actuality, this group of individuals also includes Native Americans and American Eskimos. As such, the group also exhibits a wide variety of physical features and skin colors. When we examine the facial bone structure of the group members, the skull often exhibits a flattened face with a short cranial cavity—that is, a short distance from front to back. The anterior cheeks are wide, with projecting zygomatic bones. The nasal opening is somewhere between that of European-derived and African-derived features. The size of the mouth is also often somewhere in between.[55]

FIGURE 2.92
Eddie Murphy, Wong; *Norbit*.
Image reproduced by permission of Kazuhiro Tsuji.

Field described the following Asian groups:

- *Chinese*. China, Mongolia:
  - Represent a single racial unit, medium in stature
  - Head intermediate, between long and round
  - Pigmentation yellowish brown
  - Oblique eyes, with a Mongolian (epicanthic) fold
  - Hair black and straight
- *Japanese*. Emigrated from southeast Asia; two distinct types:
  1. Fine features: Taller and more slender
     - Elongated face
     - Prominent, narrow, arched nose
     - Straight or oblique eyes; epicanthic fold may be present

2. Coarse features:
    - Short and stocky
    - Broad face; short, concave nose
    - Rounded nostrils
    - Oblique eyes; usually with epicanthic fold
    - Darker complexion

- *American Indians*:
    - Brown skin with reddish or yellowish tinge
    - Dark eyes
    - Straight, coarse black hair
    - Minimal facial and body hair
    - Broad face with high, prominent cheekbones
    - Round head; occasionally long in certain groups
    - Varied stature
    - Nose varying from flat to aquiline (curved or hooked)

- *American Eskimos:*
    - Clearly of Asiatic origin; the most Mongoloid of all American groups
    - Short, stocky build
    - Long head with very broad face
    - Massive jaw and moderately narrow nose
    - Flat sides of head and a ridge along the dome of the skull
    - Eyes with epicanthic fold

FIGURE 2.93
"After" (left) and "Before" (right); Neill Gorton Asian makeup, IMATS London, 2008.
Photos by the author.

I've mentioned the term *epicanthic fold* several times in the previous descriptions of ancestral traits, but you might not know what it means. You should, because it is an immediate ancestral identifier as well as a trait of several disorders, including fetal alcohol syndrome and Down syndrome. An epicanthic fold, also known as an *epicanthal fold* or an *epicanthus*, is a skin fold of the upper eyelid, from the nose to the inner side of the eyebrow, covering the *medial canthus* (inner corner) of the eye.

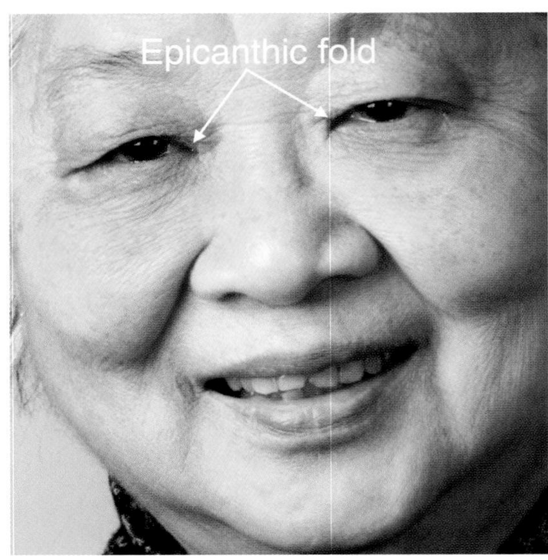

FIGURE 2.94
Asian woman exhibiting epicanthal fold.
Image reproduced by permission of istockphoto.com.

An epicanthic fold is present in all humans in the womb; some children lose them at birth, but many children of any ethnicity may exhibit an epicanthic fold before the bridge of the nose begins to elevate.[56]

CHAPTER SUMMARY

From reading this chapter you should have gained a clearer understanding of how the computer can be put to work as a makeup design tool and how to determine what the elements of your design should be. The importance and relationship of human anatomy to character and creature design should make better sense, as should the subtlety and nuance of surface anatomy, symmetry and proportion, and ways to create believable distinctions of gender, age, and ancestry in your character or creature makeup design.

Endnotes

1 Rickitt, R. (2006). *Designing movie creatures and characters*. Focal Press.

2 Ibid.

3 Ibid.

4 Tyra, & Arraj, J. (1988). *Tracking the elusive human* Vol. 1. Inner Growth Books.

5 Ibid.

6 Ibid.

7 Simblet, S. (2001). *Anatomy for the artist*. DK Publishing.

8 Ibid.

9 (2002). *Atlas of anatomy*. Taj Books.

10 See note 7 above.
11 Ibid.
12 Ibid.
13 Ibid.
14 Fairbanks, A. T., & Fairbanks, E. F. (2005). *Human proportions for artists*. Fairbanks Art and Books.
15 Mandell, R. B. (1988). *Contact lens practice* (4 ed.). Springfield, IL: Charles C. Thomas.
16 Professional Vision Care Associates, Sherman Oaks, CA. Retrieved from http://web.mac.com/eyegirl/PVA/INFO.html.
17 Ibid.
18 Gray, H. (1918). *Anatomy of the human body*. Philadelphia: Lea & Febiger. Retrieved from Bartleby.com, www.bartleby.com/107/
19 Wikipedia. *Stretch marks*. Retrieved from http://en.wikipedia.org/w/index.php?title=Stretch_marks&oldid=165987535.
20 Ibid.
21 Ibid
22 Mayo Clinic Staff. *Age spots (liver spots)*. Retrieved from www.mayoclinic.com/health/age-spots/DS00912/DSECTION=2
23 Wikipedia. *Freckle*. Retrieved from http://en.wikipedia.org/w/index.php?title=Freckle&oldid=166224174
24 Wikipedia. *Melanocytic nevus*. Retrieved from http://en.wikipedia.org/w/index.php?title=Melanocytic_nevus&oldid=166037601
25 Wikipedia. *Birthmark*. Retrieved from http://en.wikipedia.org/w/index.php?title=Birthmark&oldid=164696060
26 Postiche; Dictionary.com, *WordNet® 3.0*, Princeton University. Retrieved from http://dictionary.reference.com/browse/postiche.
27 Wikipedia. *Hair*. Retrieved from http://en.wikipedia.org/w/index.php?title=Hair&oldid=166373232
28 Ibid.
29 Ibid.
30 Wikipedia. *Scar*. Retrieved from http://en.wikipedia.org/w/index.php?title=Scar&oldid=165002945
31 Ibid.
32 See note 14 above.
33 Ibid.
34 Ibid.
35 Ibid.
36 Ibid.
37 Ibid.
38 Ibid.
39 Taylor, K. T. (2001). *Forensic art and illustration*. Boca Raton, FL: CRC Press.
40 Wikipedia. *Secondary sex characteristic*. Retrieved from http://en.wikipedia.org/w/index.php?title=Secondary_sex_characteristic&oldid=166755262
41 See note 39 above.
42 Ibid.
43 Ibid.

44 Ibid.

45 Ibid.

46 Ibid.

47 Landau, S. I., Brantley, S. C. et al. (1968). *Funk and Wagnall's standard encyclopedic dictionary*. J. G. Ferguson Publishing Co.

48 See note 39 above.

49 Ibid.

50 Ibid.

51 Field, H. (1946). *The races of mankind*. C. S. Hammond and Co.

52 Ibid.

53 See note 39 above.

54 See note 51 above

55 See note 39 above.

56 Wikipedia. *Epicanthal fold*. Retrieved from http://en.wikipedia.org/w/index.php?title=Epicanthal_fold&oldid=166374872

CHAPTER 3

Lifecasting

Key Points

- Safety
- Materials
- The process
- Lifecasting teeth
- Lifecasting face and neck
- Lifecasting full head and shoulders (bust)
- Lifecasting hands, arms, legs, and feet
- Lifecasting full body, prone

INTRODUCTION

Without intending to cause alarm, I begin this chapter with a disclaimer: *Lifecasting has the potential to be quite dangerous if done incorrectly*. Some of the materials used in lifecasting may encapsulate body hair, enclose or block orifices, cause serious allergic reactions, and create substantial heat that can cause serious burns. That being said, lifecasting is a skill that's not difficult to learn and, once learned, can be used to create myriad lifecasts of body parts, including full-body lifecasts.

Since this book is intended as both a makeup effects primer and one that also provides more advanced information, it is strongly suggested that if you've never done a lifecast before, you should take a physical class or a workshop before attempting to do it alone. Although the information in this chapter is more than sufficient for you to make a lifecast on your own, first get some training with a professional, before venturing into this domain. If you insist on being a self-starter, I suggest you to begin by making a cast of someone's hand or foot rather than their head.

Dave Parvin

A former Marine aviator, Dave Parvin, is essentially a self-taught sculptor who began carving in wood before he was 3 years. His primary subjects are people, and he strives to bring life to his sculptures by carefully defining the underlying muscles and bones of the human form. Unlike most of the artists who have contributed to this book, Dave didn't come to the decision to become a full-time artist until later in life, after the jet he was flying lost power to both engines while in flight, making him realize that there's no time like to present to follow your dreams.

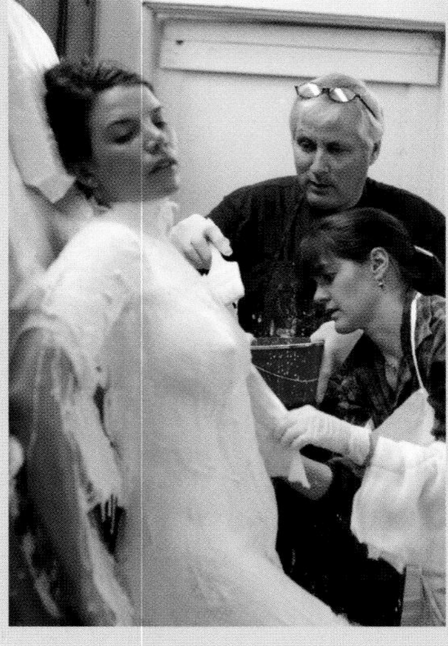

FIGURE 3.1 Dave Parvin's lifecasting workshop, Denver. *Image reproduced by permission of Dave Parvin.*

Known mainly for his bronzes of the human figure, Dave also works in other media. He became interested in lifecasting as an anatomical reference, but it occurred to him that it was very much like three-dimensional photography. Since then, Dave has become one of the best lifecasters in the world and is widely recognized as one of the innovators of the form, continuing to develop new and better ways to approach the craft.

Dave regularly presents workshops and seminars on lifecasting techniques at his studio in Denver, Colorado, and has presented internationally as well, including seminars at IMATS in California and England. *Art Review* magazine has called Dave "the premier lifecasting expert in Colorado, maybe in all the West." Dave is also a founding member of the Association of Lifecasters International (ALI) organization.

SAFETY RISKS

Compared with making molds of inanimate objects, lifecasting can pose some potential safety hazards. Since the mold is made directly on an actor's body, the materials must be safe and approved for use directly on the skin. There is also the potential for injury if the subject is being lifecast in a standing position and faints from holding a stationary pose for too long. Feelings of claustrophobia and anxiety can also be a reaction for some actors enclosed in a mold, and it can seem to gain weight the longer it is on the subject.

When lifecasting the face, you must take great care so that the actor can continue to breathe when a mold covers her mouth and nose; the nostrils must be kept clear but *not with straws*. There are two reasons not to use straws in a subject's

nose when making a lifecast: the straws significantly change the shape of the subject's nose and even the very slightest of bumps will cause a rather impressive nosebleed. Don't ask me how I know that. It's always a good idea to ask your subject beforehand if she generally has trouble breathing out of both nostrils; if your subject is congested and stuffed up, she will need to take measures in advance of the lifecasting session that will allow her to breathe comfortably while the alginate is covering her face. It is also possible to do a lifecast with the mouth open just slightly. This can even help if you need to sculpt onto the lips of the lifecast.

NOTE

When lifecasting someone's face and neck, there are a few Dos and DON'Ts to keep in mind:

DO release the eyebrows and eyelashes with a very light coating of Nivea skin cream, petroleum jelly, or cholesterol cream.

DON'T put plaster directly on the skin. It gets hot when it cures, will absorb the skin's moisture, and may fuse with the skin if not released properly. Just don't do it.

DO have your subject sitting upright. Unless the prosthetics you create will go on someone who is lying down, gravity has a way of pulling on our bodies, which will affect how an appliance fits when applied.

DON'T put straws in the nostrils; just be careful to keep them clear. Straws will deform the shape of the nostrils and can cause nosebleeds.

DO make sure you cast enough of your subject's face and neck to be able to sculpt a usable prosthetic appliance with good blending edges.

While most alginates used for lifecasting are considered hypoallergenic—meaning that few people (if any) are allergic—in rare instances, models can have allergic reactions to a material. But far from lifecasting being a negative experience, every model finds it interesting, and most models actually find the experience to be somewhat enjoyable, not unlike getting an extended—albeit unusual—facial. Some even fall asleep!

As a professional makeup effects artist, you're responsible for the appropriateness for any material you use in a given circumstance, much like hairstylists. Hairstylists are responsible for the materials they use on their clients and many of the materials may be outright hazardous, for example, some hair color and perm chemicals. Performing small tests for allergic reactions is a good idea.

Whether it is silicone, adhesives, alginates, or other, most of these materials are considered cosmetic items since they come in contact with the skin, and although many contain FDA-certified ingredients, most have no FDA certification requirements. Although many may have the art and craft "NON TOXIC" status, they are not FDA or medical grade. You may use already many of these materials without being aware of it; many of them are widely used in our industry and other industries—Cab-O-Sil, for example, fumed silica. The need of certificate or license to use them depends on the use and where you're doing the work. *It's up to you to find out.*

Confidence in a particular product's safety is one of the biggest concerns when considering the numerous professional products available to us as artists. You also have a responsibility to educate the novices in our industry until they're competent enough to perform services as a professional.

As an artist, you should know intimately the consequences of any material you're using on your client. Products are *For Professional Use Only* because they're intended for use only by professionals. Most of these materials are required to have an MSDS since they are not FDA-certified. You should have technical data sheets and MSDS for everything you use if they are available. Find out.

I've lost count of how many lifecasts I've done personally or supervised—quite a few—but I've never experienced an allergic reaction or had someone faint (I've had subjects get a little wobbly). I consider myself fortunate. Most fainting spells are mild and brief, but they can still be frightening. If your subject is standing, don't let them lock their knees; that will lead to fainting. Be ever vigilant!

Other safety concerns to be aware of constitute the lifecasting materials themselves—alginate, silicone, and plaster. The alginates used for lifecasting come as a very fine powder, and even when mixed very carefully with water they may create a substantial amount of dust. Many alginates also contain crystalline silica, which can cause silicosis—a disabling, nonreversible, and sometimes fatal lung disease caused by overexposure to respirable crystalline silica—so it is advisable to guard against breathing the dust while mixing your alginate. Most manufacturers of alginate make a version that is silica-free. Smooth-On makes one called Alja-Safe; EnvironMolds makes it with the SILFREE tag.

Silicone that is safe for application directly to the skin, such as Smooth-On's Body Double, EnvironMolds' LifeRite, Accu-Cast's Accu-Sil 35, and Mould Life's Life Form, should only be used in a well-ventilated room; you should also do a small test on the back of your subject's hand a day or so before to ensure that there is no allergic reaction. If you notice any type of skin reaction, do not use the product. When working with platinum silicone such as Body Double, LifeRite, Accu-Sil 35, and Life Form, if you wear gloves you will want to wear vinyl or nitrile gloves, not latex gloves, as the sulfur in latex will inhibit if not completely prevent the cure of the silicone rubber. I'll discuss about silicones in more detail later.

There are reasons you might want to use skin-safe platinum silicone for your lifecast instead of alginate, but there is a significant cost difference. Just to give an example of cost difference between the two materials, the amount of alginate needed to cast someone's face and neck from the ears forward, across the top of the head, and down to the clavicles could cost $5.00–6.00 (£2.5–3.0); the same amount of skin-safe platinum-cure silicone can cost 10 times as much. Platinum is not cheap, and the more platinum in the silicone, the faster it will cure. Silicone won't dry out and shrink like alginate. You don't need to cast a positive immediately and you don't need to make a secondary mold from the positive, because the silicone will last a very long time and can be used many times before the silicone begins to degrade. You must weigh various factors to determine whether the cost of lifecasting with silicone is worth the benefits.

TIP

Consider doing a very thin coat of platinum lifecasting silicone—just enough to cover the body parts you need to cover—and then apply a thicker coat of fast-curing tin silicone on top of that after the platinum silicone has cured. Tin silicone is less expensive than platinum, and it will bond well to the platinum silicone. Be sure to use a thixotropic, fast-cure tin silicone.

There are artists who do lifecasting by applying plaster directly onto the skin of their subjects. I'm talking about faces. No offense intended to those who do, but I avoid it, and so should you, and I'll tell you why. Reason 1: Plaster heats up as it sets; the thicker the plaster, the hotter it gets—hot enough to cause real burns. Reason 2: Plaster absorbs moisture and can seriously dry out your skin. In addition, if someone is foolish enough to apply plaster directly to the skin and has failed to release the skin properly beforehand so the plaster can be removed, there is very distinct possibility that the plaster will fuse to the subject's skin and hair, making the removal of the plaster very difficult and painful. The reality of the danger of direct application of plaster to skin was illustrated in January 2007, when a 16-year-old girl in Lincolnshire, England, suffered third-degree burns after encasing her hands in plaster as part of a school art project. Why she thought she'd be able to pull her hands out escapes me, but she subsequently had both thumbs and all but two of her fingers amputated. Be forewarned! We are well into the 21st century as I am writing this, *and I know for a fact* that there are *still* people lifecasting other people using plaster. All I can do is shake my head.

John Schoonraad

John Schoonraad has been lifecasting for film, television, and the arts for over 20 years. Accompanied by his sons Tristan and Robin, John and his U.K. team are masters of the lifecast, having done over 1,000 of them, from hands, feet, and heads to full bodies.

Among John's many prominent models are actors Laurence Fishburne, Gary Oldman, Joaquin Phoenix, Kate Winslet, Patrick Stewart, Russell Crowe, and Tom Hanks. He has successfully brought his skills and innovative ideas to the areas of special makeup effects, prosthetics, and

FIGURE 3.2
John and Sly Stallone on location; *Rambo 4*.
Image reproduced by permission of John Schoonraad.

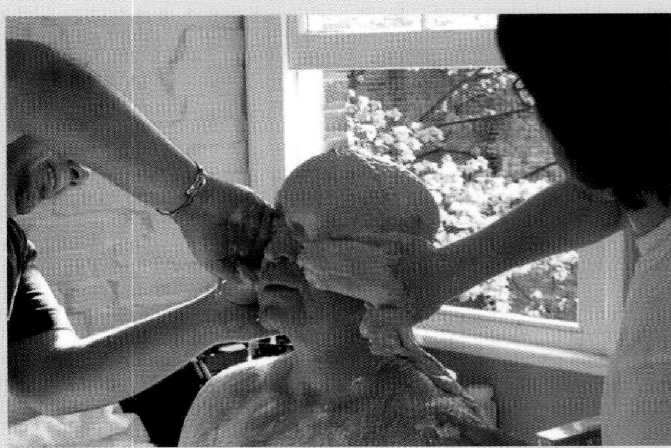

FIGURE 3.3
John and assistant lifecasting Bob Hoskins.
Image reproduced by permission of John Schoonraad.

special effects, and he has applied them to films such as the 2008's *Rambo*, the award-winning Gladiator, and the *Saving Private Ryan*. He also worked with pop celebrities David Bowie, Robbie Williams, and Bjork.

Rightly considered among the best lifecasters in the world along with Dave Parvin, John and his sons Robin and Tristan continue to make an impact on the entertainment industry as talented effects sculptors, craftsmen, and mold makers.

FIGURE 3.4
A rare "eyes open" lifecast by John Schoonraad.
Image reproduced by permission of John Schoonraad.

THE MATERIALS

There are almost as many variations in the list of materials used for making a lifecast as there are artists who do them. That's a bit of an exaggeration, but there is no one set list of materials used. Most artists continue to use the materials with which they were taught the process, working from the adage: If it ain't broke, don't fix it. Other artists continue to experiment with materials to become more efficient and achieve higher quality. Dave Parvin continues to experiment and develop fresh methods for streamlining the lifecasting process for both himself and his models.

Dave is arguably one of the finest lifecasters in the world and uses procedures and materials that might not be appropriate for beginners. For example,

Dave eschews the use of plaster bandages for making mother (support shell) molds and prefers instead to brush impression dental plaster directly onto the alginate mold, laying small pieces of cheesecloth onto it, and then painting plaster into the cheesecloth for reinforcement. Dave does this less for economic reasons (plaster bandages can be expensive; impression dental plaster is far less expensive) but because he's exceptionally good at it. Dave also says this is the best, most efficient method as well for ensuring that the resulting cast comes out flawlessly. I've tried it several times and usually wind up wasting more plaster than I care to think about. It is also less-expensive Dave's way; one box of a dozen 6-inch plaster bandage rolls costs more than a 100-pound bag of impression dental plaster. However, for me, the ease of using plaster bandages outweighs the savings; just be careful not to cause indentation in your mold by pressing too hard!

A number of commercially available alginates are of sufficient quality for prosthetics work, including FiberGel and MoldGel from EnvironMolds in Summit, New Jersey; Accu-Cast Imperial Body Gel and Accu-Cast 390, 680, and 880 by Accu-Cast of Bend, Oregon; Prosthetic Grade Cream (PGC) by Teledyn-Getz, and Algiform from Pink House Studios in St. Albans, Vermont. New ones continue to be introduced to market. A more extensive list of suppliers can be found in the supplier's appendix.

Following is a list of materials and tools you may need/want to create a lifecast from start to end in a stone (gypsum) positive made from the alginate lifecast. As I mentioned, there is no one prescribed list of tools and materials, and the following list is in no particular order of importance nor necessarily comprehensive, but lifecasting is relatively standardized throughout the industry, so for the most part consider this list complete. After you've become proficient at lifecasting, I'm sure you'll decide to modify the list to suit your needs. This list also includes materials you may use to sculpt your character makeup appliance in clay once the lifecast has been made.

- Non-sulfur oil clay
- Kitchen timer or darkroom timer
- Plaster bandages (4- and 6-inch rolls)
- Polygrip or other dental adhesive
- Eyebrow pencil (water soluble)
- Painter's rags or paper towels
- Plastic wrap
- Jiffy-Mixer
- Large screwdriver (flat)
- Hair dryer
- Misc. plastic buckets
- WED clay
- Scrub brushes/pads
- Wood blocks (misc. 2- × 4-inch pieces)
- Misc. plastic cups
- Rubber spatula
- Petroleum jelly
- Masking tape
- Loose-weave burlap, hemp or fiberglass mat
- Ruler
- Wire cutters
- Drill
- Alginate

- Acetone
- Cholesterol cream (hair conditioner)
- Plastic drop cloths
- Pros-Aide adhesive
- Q-tips
- Mineral spirits or Naphtha
- Algislo or baking soda/water solution
- Spirit gum and spirit gum remover
- Handle (½″ electrical conduit)
- Salt and/or terra alba
- Hair clips
- Large and small craft sticks
- 99% Isopropyl alcohol (IPA)
- Sculpting tools
- 1-inch chip brushes
- Hot-glue gun
- Ultracal 30
- Utility towels
- Tincture of Green Soap
- Sharp knife
- Hammer
- Krylon Crystal Clear
- Water
- Duct tape
- Pencil and notepad
- Chisel
- Pliers
- 1-, ¾-, and ½-inch router bits and a ¼-inch drill bit
- Large plastic bowls
- Scissors
- Bald cap(s)
- Sharpie marker
- Cotton batting or cheesecloth
- Superglue
- Misc. plastic containers
- Acrylic fortifier, bonder, or Acryl 60

You might not even come close to using all the materials listed above, but these are all common to most lifecasting procedures, and you may find that you prefer some over the others. They are listed only as a convenience for you to decide what fits best your style. Somewhere in my shop is a container of plastic surgical towel clips that are great for holding thin alginate edges to the plaster mother mold, and so on… This is just one example of things that can be used for purposes other than their original intended use.

THE PROCESS

Creating makeup effects requires a number of skill sets, including lifecasting, sculpture, mold making, and appliance casting, painting, and application techniques.

Overview

In most professional settings, the skill sets needed for creating a character makeup are most often practiced individually because each requires a good deal of concentrated expertise; however, it is not uncommon to find individuals who are adept at wearing the many hats necessary to take a project from concept to completion by themselves.

Once a negative mold/lifecast has been created in alginate, it must be immediately filled with a gypsum stone material called Ultracal 30 to make a positive from the alginate negative.

It is important that this could be done very soon after the alginate mold is completed, because it will begin to dry out almost immediately. If your positive is not a precise copy of your subject, the finished appliance will not fit properly when it is applied to your subject later; when water evaporates out of the alginate, it shrinks as well as dries.

Ultracal 30 is *much* harder than plaster when cured. I sometimes refer to it as *Plaster-zilla*. The form of the prosthetic appliance is sculpted in oil/wax clay on top of the newly cast positive after the positive has been cleaned up.

FIGURE 3.5
Ultracal 30 detail coat brushed into alginate negative.
Photo by the author.

Vittorio Sodano

FIGURE 3.6
Vittorio and friends with David di Donatello Award for *Noi credevamo.*
Image reproduced by permission of Vittorio Sodano.

FIGURE 3.7
Vittorio at work.
Image reproduced by permission of Vittorio Sodano.

Italian makeup effects artist and designer Vittorio Sodano was born in Naples, but began his rise to the top in London at the age of 16, sculpting and working as a prosthodontist in a British effects laboratory.

Vittorio's major cinema debut came with the 1999 film *Prima che il Tramonto* (*Before the Sunset*) directed by Stefano Incerti, for which he was recognized for Makeup and Special Effects at the Locarno Film Festival. His expertise led him to become the personal makeup artist for several of Italy's leading actresses, including Margherita Buy, Laura Morante, Mariangela Melato, and Valeria Golino.

Vittorio is considered by many to be among the best when it comes to age makeup and was nominated for an Academy Award and won a coveted David di Donatello Award (the Italian Oscar) for his outstanding work in *Il Divo* (2008).

FIGURE 3.8
Vittorio's aging Toni Servillo; *Il Divo*.
Image reproduced by permission of Vittorio Sodano.

FIGURE 3.9
Vittorio's makeup; *Apocalypto*.
Images reproduced by permission of Vittorio Sodano.

FIGURE 3.10
Vittorio's makeup; *Apocalypto*.
Images reproduced by permission of Vittorio Sodano.

FIGURE 3.11
Vittorio's makeup; *Apocalypto*.
Images reproduced by permission of Vittorio Sodano.

He also received an Academy Award nomination for his work on Mel Gibson's *Apocalypto* (2006) and won a David di Donatello Award for his work on the 2010 film *Noi credevamo*. A few of Vittorio's lengthy film credits include *Casanova*, *The Black Dahlia*, *Fade to Black*, and *Safe House*.

CORRECTED POSITIVE

Many times, it will be necessary to create what is known as a *corrected positive* before beginning to sculpt what will become your prosthetic appliance or appliances. When this becomes the case, I do not use Ultracal 30 to make my initial positive, but will use Impression Dental Plaster or Lab Dental Plaster (just two of several varieties of plaster that are available) or sometimes good ol' Plaster of Paris. Plaster of Paris is too soft and fragile to use for a positive that you will eventually sculpt on, but if you know you will be making a corrected positive, it's fine. It only has to last long enough to clean up and make another mold.

In this instance, I needed a corrected positive of my friend, actor Brian Landis Folkins, for some generic appliances I was going to make for several different projects. So, I took a much-used Ultracal positive I had lying around of Brian and added a WED clay flange, or rim, around the existing lifecast, and then cleaned up a few dings and blemishes with a bit of Chavant Le Beau Touche oil clay.

The next step was to spray the WED clay with a thin coat of Krylon Crystal Clear, and when it dried, brush up silicone over the flange and lifecast, and then add a plaster mother mold. Silicone mold making will be discussed later at much great length, so don't be alarmed that I'm glossing over it here.

The process of creating a corrected positive for sculpting will be looked at in depth in the chapter about mold making and breaking down the sculpture.

FIGURE 3.12
Clay up on positive for corrected cast. Mold by Carl Lyon.
Image reproduced by permission of Vincent Van Dyke.

FIGURE 3.13
Finished silicone negative of corrected cast. Mold by Carl Lyon.
Image reproduced by permission of Vincent Van Dyke.

FIGURE 3.14
Finished epoxy positive of corrected cast. Mold by Carl Lyon.
Image reproduced by permission of Vincent Van Dyke.

When you sculpt, it is very important that the edges of the clay could be made as thin as possible to create an invisible edge; the clay is a stand-in for what will eventually be the foam latex (or silicone, foamed gelatin, etc.) appliance, and only extremely thin edges will allow it to blend seamlessly when it is applied to the subject's face.

If the prosthetic will be cast in silicone, the clay must be sulfur-free or the silicone may not cure and you will be left with a mold filled with a gooey mess that will be a royal pain to clean up. This is especially true of platinum-cure silicone; tin-cure silicone is more forgiving, but why tempts fate? We'll discuss silicone in greater detail later in this book; get into the habit of using sulfur-free clay for all your work, no matter what material your appliances will be made of.

Once the sculpture is complete, a new negative must be made. Along the edges of the positive mold or on the clay dividing wall, mold keys or mold points must be sculpted or drilled/routed to make sure that the parts of the mold will fit together correctly.

When the second sculpt is completed, a second mold must be made. This will result—in the simplest form—in two pieces of a mold: a positive of the original lifecast and a negative of the lifecast with the character design sculpted in.

FIGURE 3.15
Front and back halves of fiberglass mold.
Image reproduced by permission of Neill Gorton.

After the sculpted clay is completely removed and the two halves of the mold are thoroughly cleaned, the prosthetic material, whatever it may be—foam latex, gelatin, or silicone—is added (poured, brushed, or injected) into the two-part mold, and the mold is clamped or bolted tightly closed and the material cures, creating the beginning of a special makeup effect.

When the appliance is removed from the mold, trimmed, gently washed, and dried, it is ready to be seamed, pre-painted, and applied. Airbrush has become the preferred method (for many artists, but certainly not all) for painting appliances in the 21st century, allowing even opaque material such as foam latex to be painted with numerous layers of transparent pigment to give the impression of the translucency of human skin.

TEETH

Altering the appearance of the teeth can add a significant dimension to a character makeup, and there are several ways to change the appearance of teeth to varying degrees. The easiest way is with tooth wax; a prosthetic device that fits over existing teeth is the most difficult. Fangs, decayed, rotting teeth, and the like can be achieved commercially from kits such as Billy Bob Teeth, Dr. Bukk, Scarecrow, and Toothfairy Teeth relatively inexpensively. There are also paints designed to be applied directly onto the subject's teeth for different looks. These colors are for temporary use only. Sets of acrylic and porcelain teeth can also be purchased from dental supply companies.

However, if you want to have a set of truly unique and original teeth for your transformational character makeup, it will be necessary to create the teeth from scratch by first taking a cast of your subject's teeth. This is especially important for theater or film work that requires your character to speak. The results can be quite amazing, but this is a complicated process that borders on professional dental work. I don't really need to tell you this, but it is illegal to practice dentistry without a license. Common sense should also tell you that custom dental prosthetics for theater, film, and television work should never be worn for any extended period of time. Also, they should not be worn while eating.

Taking dental impressions is easy enough that you can do it to yourself. It is actually not a bad idea to practice on yourself and become familiar with the procedure before trying it on someone else. However, I would refrain from taking impressions of teeth with braces, caps, crowns, or bridges without consent and approval of the subject's dentist.

The materials for dental prosthetics are very specialized and can be purchased from dental supply companies as well as numerous makeup effects suppliers. A comprehensive list of suppliers is included in Appendix C.

- Upper and lower impression dental trays—small, medium, and large
- Dental die stone or Ultracal 30
- Misc. cups
- Acrylic activator (monomer)
- Dental acrylic powder: tooth shade, gum shade
- Petroleum jelly
- Sandpaper
- Water
- Dental acrylic monomer
- Dental alginate
- Craft sticks or small metal spatula
- Silicone mold rubber
- George Taub's Minute Stain kit
- Small brushes
- Dremel
- Rubber base tray mold
- Sulfur-free oil or wax clay

FIGURE 3.16
Dental impression trays.
Photo by the author.

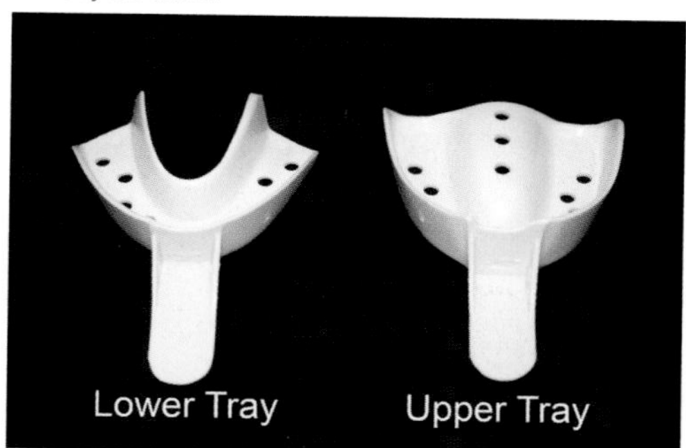

We placed our discussion of casting teeth before casting the face, because if dental prosthetics are required as part of the character makeup, they must be completed before a face lifecast can be made, so that your subject can be wearing them during the lifecasting. If they are not worn during the lifecast, the appliance will not fit correctly when the teeth are in place and the prosthetic is applied.

Before you begin, determine the size of the dental trays you will need to use for the impressions. Dental trays come in different sizes: small, medium, and large. Try each to find the correct one for your subject. Then, place a cape or some sort of covering around your subject to avoid getting your subject's clothing messy.

The dental alginate that I use is Algitec dustless alginate impression material by Patterson Dental Company of St. Paul, Minnesota. There are a number of dental alginates you can use. Follow these steps:

1. Wear gloves when casting an actor's teeth; it's a good idea hygienically, and it's simply better for your subject's confidence in you.
2. Brush a very light layer of petroleum jelly over the front of your model's teeth.
3. Begin by mixing a small amount of alginate with water. The alginate comes with specific instructions; as you use the alginate and become comfortable with it, you'll be able to mix it by eye and feel.
4. Mix for about 45 seconds or until the alginate becomes a thick paste. Refer to the manufacturer's instructions for specific mixing instructions. Then use a craft stick or small spatula to spread it into the upper plate tray. Mix the alginate thick so that it won't run down your subject's throat; this will also help obtain a better gum impression.

Fill the tray completely; if it overflows, scoop the alginate back into the tray. You will have only about 2 minutes total working time before the alginate sets fully. Your water temperature should be about 72°F (22°C). Cold water retards the set and warm water accelerates it.

It may also be advisable to invest in an infrared digital thermometer. It will come in handy for many tasks. Radio Shack sells one for about $75 (£40) that I have found invaluable. It is a very handy little gadget I learned about from Dave Parvin—just one of many tips I have received from a truly amazing artist and a good friend. I'm sure you can find something similar elsewhere for less money. I just happen to be a Radio Shack junkie.

Next, do the following:

5. Once the (thick) alginate is in the tray, run the tray under water for a moment if it is handy and form the alginate into a tray-like shape.
6. Open your subject's mouth wide and press the tray gently into position; then close the subject's mouth. Carefully pull the upper lip over the tray if possible.
7. You may want to ask your subject to lean slightly forward in case the alginate isn't quite thick enough; this will help prevent alginate slipping toward the back of the throat.

FIGURE 3.17
Dental tray in subject's mouth. Very attractive. *Photo by Brandon McMenamin. Image reproduced by permission of author.*

This process can be somewhat messy, so it's a good idea to have your subject's head tilted slightly down. This will prevent runny alginate from running down the throat, and many people tend to collect a lot of saliva in their mouth during this process, creating rather excessive drool! Did I mention how much fun this is? *Don't hurry*. Keep the

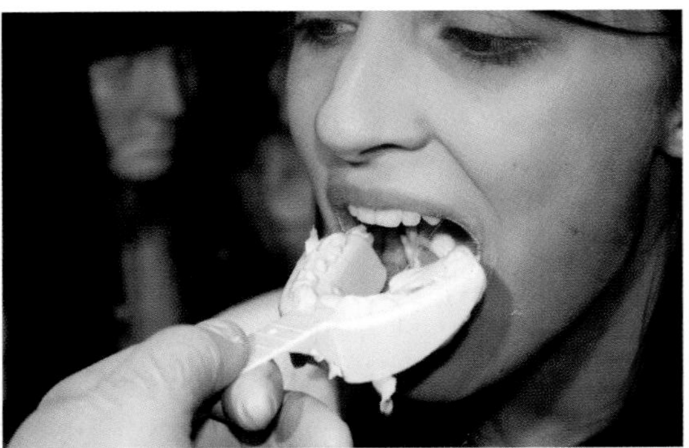

FIGURE 3.18
Removing impression. Watch out for drool!
Photo by the author.

subject's mouth closed, and don't move the tray. Hold it steady until the alginate is fully set.

Now, do the following:

8. When the alginate has set, have your subject flex her lips. Ask the subject to close her lips around the tray and blow. This will introduce air between the set alginate and the teeth, making removal much easier. Have a paper towel or napkin ready for your subject to remove any residual alginate that may still be in her mouth or to wipe away saliva. Because the solidified alginate is mostly water, it is soft and rubbery and will begin to dry out quickly. You can wrap it in wet paper towels or submerge it in water to prevent shrinkage while you mix the dental stone or while you prepare to cast the lower teeth. This step is necessary only if you are going to take an impression of the lower teeth before casting the upper teeth and the alginate will be setting for a while.
9. Casting the lower teeth follows the same procedure as the upper teeth, but you must be sure to mix the alginate properly and thick because the lower tray must be upside down when it goes into the subject's mouth; you do not want the alginate to run out of the tray after you've filled it.
10. Once you've got both upper and lower impressions made, it's time to make positives. You can use either dental stone or Ultracal 30. There are numerous types of dental stone available from different manufacturers. Whip Mix Corporation, one of the manufacturers whose products I use, has 22 different gypsum dental stone materials available at this writing.

FIGURE 3.19
Tray with alginate impression of lower teeth.
Photo by the author.

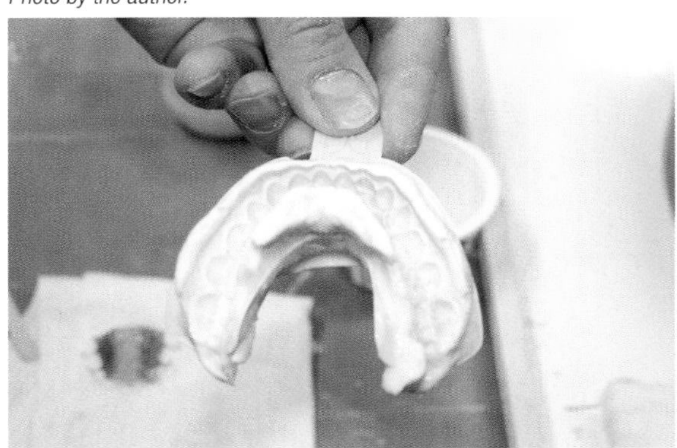

FIGURE 3.20
Whip mix dental stone and rubber base molds.
Photo by the author.

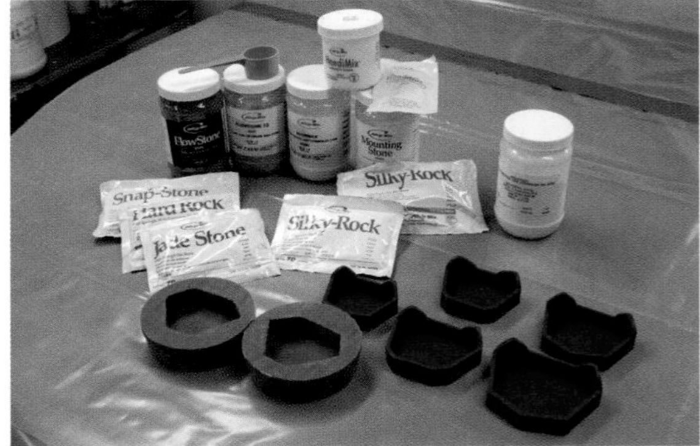

11. Dental supply companies sell rubber base molds you can use to cast a nice, professional-looking stone base for your teeth to sit on, or you can make one yourself by shaping some oil clay and make a silicone mold of it. You will need this after the next step.
12. Mix enough dental stone to fill your tooth tray; with a small brush, begin to apply the stone to the alginate negative. Shake it a bit to get any small bubbles to rise. You will notice that the stone liquefies as it is shaken. This gentle shaking also helps ensure that the Ultracal 30 (let's just call it Ultracal from here on) makes its way completely into each tooth cavity. When all the tooth spaces are filled, build up the Ultracal slightly higher than the edge of the dental plate and let it sit for about an hour before demolding it.

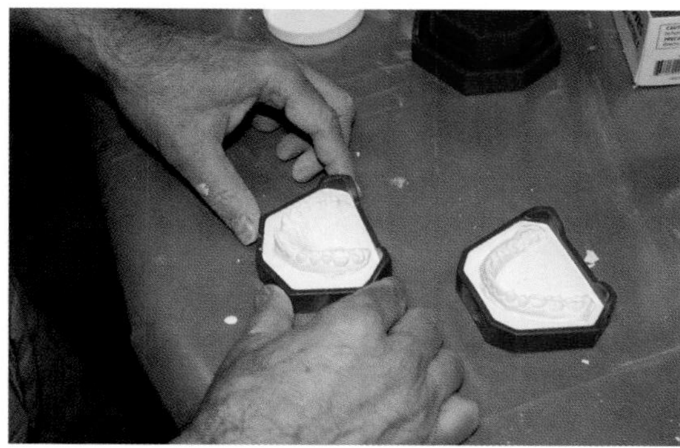

FIGURE 3.21 Stone impressions laid into base molds.
Photo by the author.

If you want to make the Ultracal stronger than it already will be, mix 50% acrylic fortifier (or Acryl 60) and 50% water when you mix the Ultracal. You can buy cement acrylic fortifier at just any hardware store, especially the Big Box stores like Lowe's or The Home Depot. Acryl 60 can also be purchased at most Ace Hardware, True Value, or Home Depot locations. In addition, if you cover your Ultracal cast with plastic before it sets, the plastic will help the Ultracal retain moisture as the heat builds up when it cures, making the stone stronger still. At least that's what I've been told; I have no way of proving or disproving it.

Next:

13. Remove the stone cast from the alginate and dental tray. Clean up any rough edges around your cast and remove or patch any blemishes that are present. Mix another small batch of Ultracal, enough to fill the rubber base mold. Make it thick so that the teeth will not sink.
14. Gently tap the mold to get rid of any air bubbles or air pockets trapped inside the mold. As the Ultracal begins to set, carefully place the teeth into the wet Ultracal (with the teeth facing up, of course), being careful to leave the gum and frenum membrane visible. The frenum membrane is the thin flap of tissue that connects the upper gum to the upper lip. You can feel yours with your tongue. It important to keep this flap visible on your cast so you have a gauge of how far you can sculpt your teeth appliance later.
15. After you have done this for both the upper and lower teeth, make a silicone mold of them so that you can make duplicate positives of the upper and lower teeth. This is

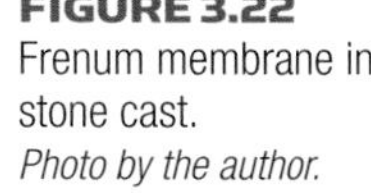

FIGURE 3.22 Frenum membrane in stone cast.
Photo by the author.

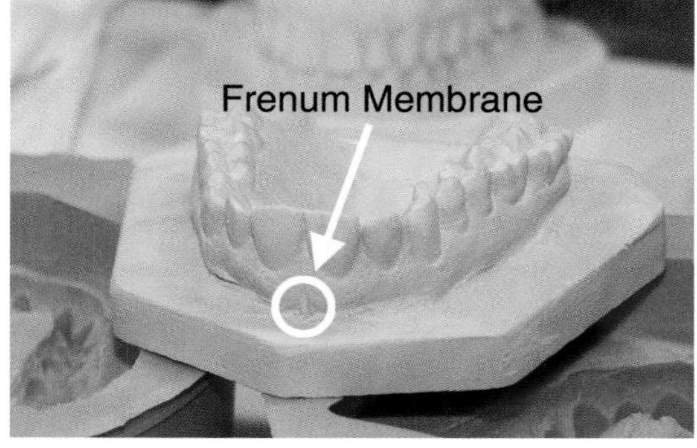

not essential to do, but it can be very useful for at least two reasons: You will have a clean reference model to refer to when sculpting your appliance, and if you somehow manage to break one of your positives, you won't have to start from scratch again by taking new impressions; you will already have a mold and can simply mix more stone and fill it.

16. There are a variety of silicones that you can use for this step. The procedure is the same regardless of the silicone you choose. I like to use Smooth-On's Mold Max 30, a tin-cure (also called a *condensation-cure*) silicone because I won't need these molds to last a long time and therefore don't need the expense of platinum silicone. Since the first edition of this book, Smooth-On has introduced a platinum mold rubber series called Mold Star; Mold Star has become my primary silicone rubber (when I can afford it).

We will get into a much more detailed discussion of silicone in later chapters, but for now there are two basic cure types of silicone used in makeup effects: *condensation cure* and *addition cure*. They are very different and are not intermixable.

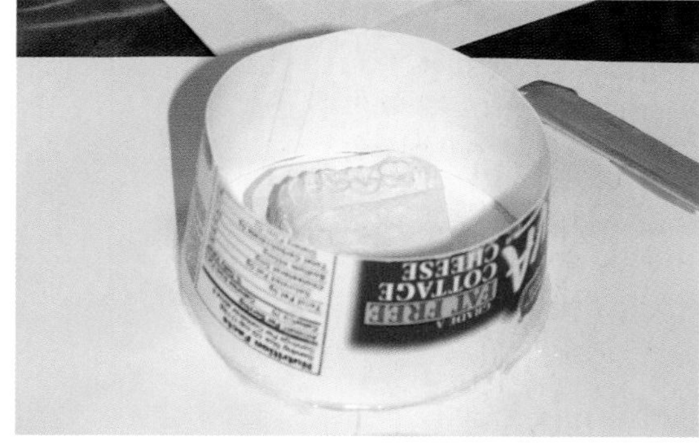

FIGURE 3.23
Teeth ready for silicone molding.
Photo by the author.

17. Next, cut two large plastic containers apart and hot-glue them to a piece of Formica board or something similar, such as Masonite. I also use pieces of smooth-coated board shelving cut into 10 × 10- or 12 × 12-inch squares. The containers must be large enough for the teeth cast to fit inside each one and still have at least half an inch (about 12½ millimeters) of space between the cast and the edge of the container.

18. Mix silicone to pour over the teeth. Do you still remember your geometry from high school? To find the volume of a cylinder, which is essentially what we're using here, $V = \pi r^2 h$. Translated, that's *Volume* = 3.142 × *radius*^{2} × *height*, where the radius of a circle is half the diameter (width of a circle), which is the distance from the one outer edge to the other outer edge through the center of the circle. The volume of silicone you'll need to mix is that number minus the displacement of the teeth cast. If that seems like too much work, it's actually pretty easy to eyeball it. The thing to keep in mind here is not to be wasteful of silicone. It's your money or your client's money.

19. Using either a triple-beam scale or an accurate digital scale, measure your silicone according to the manufacturer's recommendations and mix the components thoroughly. It's better to mix too little than too much if you're eyeballing it. Silicone sticks to silicone, so if you make your batch too small, mix up a bit more and pour it onto what you've already poured once it is firm; it doesn't have to be fully cured. If you use Smooth-On Mold Max 30, you can decrease the kick time by using FastCat 30 instead of its regular catalyst. By increasing the amount you use in proportion to the rubber base, you can decrease the kick time to minutes and can usually demold in less than an hour.

However, accelerating the silicone like this significantly weakens it to the point that it may become brittle and crumble within days. You can use a fast-setting platinum silicone and demold in a very short time. Adding heat will also accelerate platinum silicone curing; it will also affect tin-cure silicone, but not as much. However, more air bubbles are more likely to escape and not cause problems if you let the silicone cure overnight.

20. Lastly, pour the thoroughly mixed silicone over the teeth, making sure that the silicone rises above the uppermost teeth by at least ¼ of an inch (about 6 millimeters). When the silicone is completely cured, it will feel like hard rubber. Demold the teeth and lightly brush a very thin layer of petroleum jelly inside the molds as a release agent. You shouldn't really need it, but this will ensure that your next stone cast will pop out easily.
21. Mix another batch of Ultracal or dental stone and fill the molds. When they're filled, tap the molds to release any trapped air bubbles and make them rise to the surface. You can demold the teeth in about an hour. Remember that you can use a 50/50 mix of water and acrylic fortifier and cover the molds with plastic to get a stronger stone cast when using Ultracal. Once the teeth are demolded, you're ready to begin sculpting the teeth and gums that your character will need for the makeup effect.

FIGURE 3.24
Silicone poured over cast of teeth.
Photo by the author.

FACE AND NECK

Face and neck lifecasts are probably the most common for creating makeup effects, since most makeups can be achieved with small appliances rather than full head and shoulder appliances. I'm sure there are artists who would disagree, but face and neck lifecasts are certainly what I do more of. Here's how to do it; use the materials list from above.

As mentioned in the beginning of this chapter, you might not come close to using all the materials listed above, but these are pretty common to lifecasting, and you may find that you prefer some materials over others. They are listed only as a convenience for you to decide what fits best your style and budget.

It will be advantageous for you to arrange everything you will need ahead of time so that you will be able to reach it easily and work in an efficient and a timely manner once you begin. It is worth noting again that there is no single way to approach lifecasting a face and neck. If you were to poll 50 artists about the way they do a lifecast, you are likely to get 25 different methods or more. I learned one way but have altered my methods several times over the years. I will probably continue to do so as materials change and advance. The description that follows is a process that works well for me, but once you've become comfortable with the process, you are likely to come up with your own way to approach it.

FIGURE 3.25
Plaster bandages cut for mother mold.
Photo by the author.

1. Cut the plaster bandages into lengths of about 8 inches (about 20.5 centimeters), 10 inches (about 25.5 centimeters), and 12 inches (about 30.5 centimeters). Make several of each. Also cut several thin strips that will be used to reinforce the nose along the bridge and septum.
2. Premeasure the alginate you will be using into a plastic container. Also premeasure the amount of water you will need into one of your larger plastic containers. You might want to use the 1-gallon bucket even though we're not mixing a large batch of alginate, because the Jiffy-Mixer® is likely to cause some splatter. To minimize it even further, set the 1-gallon bucket in the 5-gallon bucket before firing up the Jiffy Mixer. The water temperature should be about 80°F (about 27°C).

You can certainly use cooler water or warmer water. The 80°F (about 27°C) water temperature is comfortable for most people. Cooler water will cause the alginate to set more slowly; warmer water will accelerate the set time. Refer to the recommendations of the particular alginate you are using, because they could differ somewhat as to the ratio of alginate to water. With most alginates, a ratio of 5 ounces of alginate per 1 pound of water will give you a nonrunny, workable mixture that spreads easily and stays where you put it. I strongly suggest a bit of self-experimentation before you begin putting alginate on your subject's face.

You might also want to do a pH test on your water supply. Most tap water will be just fine for mixing alginate, but some city water supplies contain chemicals that will interfere with the way alginate sets, causing partial or complete cure inhibition. It's rare, but it does happen. If you are in any doubt, use distilled water from your local grocer; it's inexpensive relative to other materials you'll be using. Alginate also has a lifespan, and old alginate or alginate that has not been stored properly will also lose its ability to set up. It never hurts to do a test if it's been a while since you've used your materials.

TIP

Alginate has a definite lifespan, and old alginate or alginate that has not been stored properly will lose its ability to set up. Always do a test if it's been a while since you've used your materials.

Here we will be using EnvironMolds' FiberGel. FiberGel has a set time of 4–5 minutes (which means we will need to work quickly) and contains a matrix of tiny synthetic fibers. The fibers not only add tear resistance and strength to the alginate, but they also help prevent running and dripping. The fiber matrix also allows the alginate to retain moisture, thereby reducing the shrink rate and keeping your mold soft and flexible far beyond the usable time of most other alginates once they've set. This allows for more delayed

TIP

Here's a tip to save having to turn to Appendix D: If you want to mix a certain number of pounds of alginate, you can use the accompanying graphic in reverse to determine how many quarts of water you'll need to use (instead of measuring the water by weight). A typical face cast requires about 1/4 pound (4 ounces) of alginate mixed with 1 pint of water. Remember that there are 2 pints to a quart and 4 quarts to a gallon. A gallon of water weighs just over 8 pounds, so a pint of water weighs approximately 1 pound. An entire head needs about 1 1/4 pound and up to 2 pounds for a front or rear torso, depending on how thick or thin you want the mixture.

I think it's a good idea to begin by using the manufacturer's suggested mix ratio, then do a test of your own to find the right ratio for your application; Dave Parvin calls this the Goldilocks Method—find the mixture that's not too runny, not too thick, but just right...

casting times without the loss of detail if necessary. This was one of Dave Parvin's many innovations.

We will be casting our subject seated in an upright position. I've heard that some artists like to cast a face with the subject lying flat. I've never met anyone who does it that way unless the final result requires a character to be lying flat. Lying down could be quite comfortable for the subject, but when the subject is lying flat, gravity will pull the skin and muscles of the face downward in a way that can distort the lifecast as well as prevent the resulting appliance from fitting properly when the subject is standing or sitting upright.

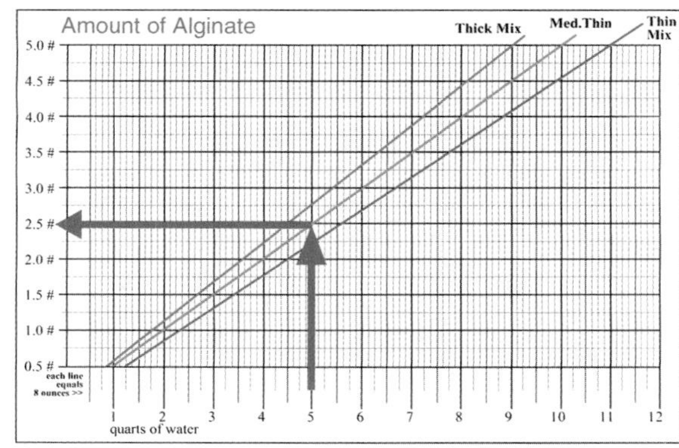

FIGURE 3.26
How much alginate to use.
Illustration by the author.

3. Place your subject in a comfortable chair, preferably one that can be raised and lowered. Cover your subject's body and clothing with plastic, carefully attaching it with tape at least an inch below the level of your cast. Make it easy on your back and your assistant too by having your subject seated high enough that you're not bent over uncomfortably to do the cast.
4. Apply a bald cap to your subject. Applying bald caps properly is a necessary skill, and we'll talk about a full bald cap application elsewhere in this

book. But for lifecasting, we need only apply the cap well enough to provide us with a good cast, keeping the subject's hair out of the way. Begin by flattening your subject's hair using water and a non-oily gel or hairspray. Aqua Net hairspray works very well. Dampen the hair with water, then spray with Aqua Net, and comb flat. Gently blow-dry.

You don't need to use an expensive bald cap—a regular theatrical cap will do, just make sure that it is large enough to cover your subject's head. In a pinch, you can use plastic wrap tightly around your subject's head, held in place with Scotch tape. However, I am a firm believer that anything worth doing is worth doing well, so we'll use a bald cap made from scratch using slush latex built up in several layers on a plastic head block. These can be purchased at a nominal cost and will definitely come in handy in your work. Carefully and comfortably place the bald cap snugly on your subject's head, pulling it down to cover the ears.

FIGURE 3.27
Fitting bald cap onto subject's head.
Photo by Chase Heilman. Image reproduced by permission of author.

5. Using the eyebrow pencil, lightly mark the cap around the subject's ears and draw a line across the top of the head from the middle of one ear to the other. If the ears do not need to be included as part of the lifecast, you won't need to cut the cap to go around the ears. This will also prevent concerns of undercuts later in the process of creating your appliance.

6. Before gluing the cap down, you might want to trim the front closer to your subject's hairline; otherwise, you can carefully pull back the front edge of the cap and apply adhesive to your subject's forehead, then press the bald cap down onto the forehead. If you're using Pros-Aide®, the glue dries sticky and transparently. Press the cap down until it holds. If you're using spirit gum, wait until it is quite gummy before pressing the cap down.
7. Carefully start to secure the sides and back of the bald cap, making sure the cap is going to hold before moving on to the next section.
8. There should be no wrinkles on the head forward of the line drawn between the ears. If there are, carefully lift the cap at the edges and reposition it until the surface is smooth. Lastly, mark your subject's hairline with the eyebrow pencil. This line will transfer to the alginate and then to the Ultracal. This line is important because it shows exactly how far we can sculpt on the forehead and sides of the face without going into the hair.
9. Apply a small amount of cholesterol cream or petroleum jelly to your subject's eyebrows, eyelashes, and any other facial hair. Use K-Y Jelly or petroleum jelly to lightly cover the bald cap one inch beyond the line drawn across the top of your subject's head. This will ensure that the alginate will not stick to the bald cap.

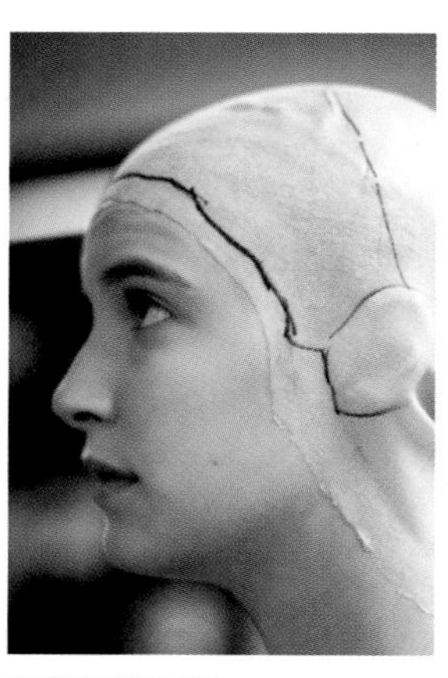

FIGURE 3.28
Lines drawn across top of head, around ears, and along hairline.
Photo by Chase Heilman. Image reproduced by permission of author.

10. Before applying the alginate, explain the procedure to your subject so that there will be no surprises during the lifecasting. It is very important that your subject has no trouble breathing through both nostrils, because the mouth will be completely covered with alginate. Now would also be a good time to find out if your subject is claustrophobic. If that is the case, your approach to making the lifecast must be altered to do the cast in sections. Ideally you would know this kind of information well beforehand so other arrangements could be made. Last-minute changes do happen, but the less you can leave until the last moment, the better.

Make any last-minute adjustments to your subject before you mix the alginate; make sure her head is aligned straight and not tilted, turned, or cocked at an angle and that she is sitting up straight. A misalignment can result in a lifecast that might look fine overall but that will be inadequate for sculpting a makeup appliance, because it will be distorted or turned.

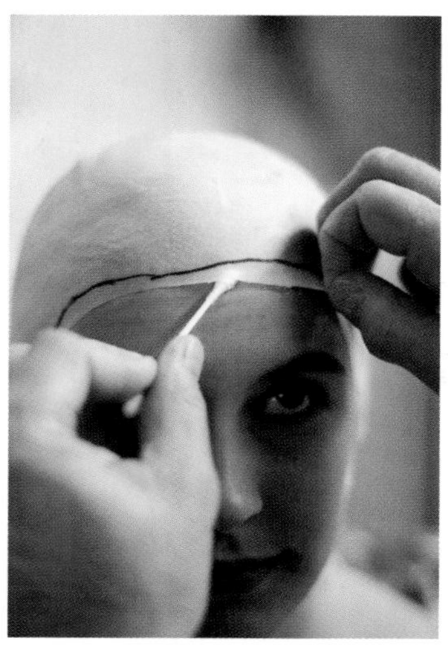

FIGURE 3.29
Final adjustment to bald cap.
Photo by Chase Heilman. Image reproduced by permission of author.

If your character will have dentures, now is the time for your subject to put them in so that the lifecast can be taken with false teeth in place. This will prevent the makeup from fitting incorrectly when it is applied later.

11. Now, it's time to mix the alginate. For the alginate, we'll be using—EnvironMolds' FiberGel—the manufacturer recommends using between 4.75 and 5 ounces of alginate powder per 16 ounces (1 pound) of water by weight. Look at the clock or start your timer when you begin to mix the water and the alginate powder so that you'll know how much time you have before the alginate begins to set. To do a face and neck cast, we'll mix 10 ounces of FiberGel alginate with 2 pounds (32 ounces) of warm (80°F/27°C) water. Always add the alginate powder to the water and not vice versa. The alginate can be mixed with your hand, but I don't recommend it; mixing with an electric drill and a Jiffy-Mixer bit is much faster and mixes the alginate and water more smoothly and thoroughly. Be careful not to start the drill too rapidly because you will likely put a cloud of alginate dust into the air! This is not good, particularly if the alginate you use has silica in it, as some do. If you are working with another person, divide the labor so that one person is spreading the alginate and the other is keeping an eye on the subject's nostrils, making sure that they remain clear and unblocked. Properly mixed alginate should not run, but never take anything for granted in such instances. It is also possible that you'll need to add a very small amount of water to your alginate if it is too thick. Remember to keep talking to your subject as you spread the alginate, telling her what you're doing and just letting her know that you're still there and are paying attention. It is reassuring. Lifecasting requires trust.

Every artist works a bit differently with alginate. You might want to wear gloves—latex, vinyl, or nitrile—or you might prefer to work barehanded. I suggest gloves. The reason is that you can quickly remove them to put on a fresh pair and

FIGURE 3.30
Spreading alginate.
Photo by Chase Heilman. Image reproduced by permission of author.

instantly have clean hands! Keep in mind that room temperature, water temperature, your subject's body temperature, as well as how quickly or slowly you work will all affect the lifecasting. Ideal working conditions (for me) are a room temperature of 69–72°F (20.5–22°C), 45–45% humidity, 80°F (about 27°C) water temperature, and normal subject body temperature (98.6°F/37°C).

12. Next, begin to spread the alginate with your hand, starting at the top of the head where the line is drawn between the ears and move downward on the face, leaving the nostrils for last. When I say spread the alginate, I mean s-p-r-e-a-d the alginate; you will get fewer surface bubbles when you spread rather than just blobbing it on. But be careful not to spread the alginate too thin. It should be at least ½ inch thick and no more than 1 inch or its own weight will begin pull it down.
13. When you get to the subject's eyes (which should be closed already), be certain—and careful—to gently press the alginate into the inner corners of the eye and under the eyelashes with your fingertips. Make sure to do the same with the eyebrows, getting alginate thoroughly into them. If you've released them properly, the alginate will come off beautifully, and when you make your stone positive, there should be no eyebrows on it at all. As you apply the alginate, make sure no air is trapped between it and your subject. Use your fingers to follow the contours of your subject's face with the alginate.

NOTE

A note about release for your subject's eyes: Cholesterol cream may cause stinging for some people; I have never experienced it, but if you have any concerns, it is always best to err on the side of caution. Use petroleum jelly instead. Lightly.

FIGURE 3.31
Preparing to apply alginate to mouth.
Photo by Chase Heilman. Image reproduced by permission of author.

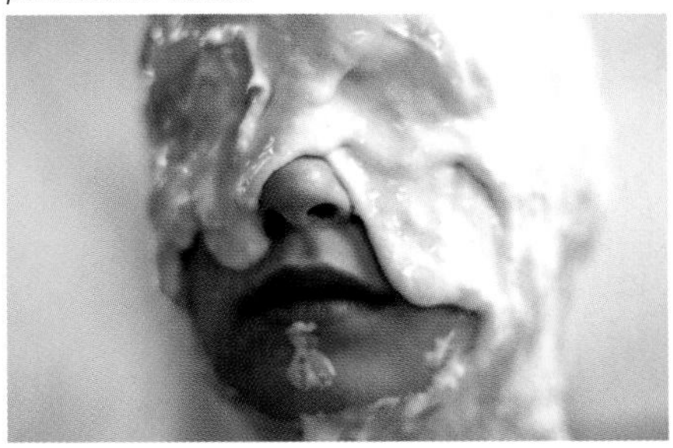

14. Do the same with the sides of the face, stopping just in front of the ears, making sure to get good alginate coverage into all the lines and creases in the face. When you cover the mouth, use your fingers to work alginate into the corners of the mouth and in the mouth crease between the upper and lower lips. If your subject's mouth is slightly open, that's fine. The goal is to have the subject's mouth in a normal, relaxed position. In fact, if your makeup design includes upper and/or lower lip pieces, having more lip exposed during the lifecast will be beneficial during the sculpture phase of your project.
15. Next cover as much of the subject's neck as needed for your makeup design. Make your coverage as even and symmetrical as possible. Lastly, cover the nose, being careful to keep the nostrils clear. You might want to use a small craft stick to spread the alginate

evenly and as closely to the edges of the nostril as possible without creating a blockage.

16. If the alginate does run, carefully lift it back up over the face, always in a spreading motion. Another method of getting good coverage around the nose—and the nose is a critical part to do well—is to tell your subject to take a deep breath and hold it. Then cover her nose completely with alginate, making sure to get around the nostrils, and then have your subject blow out sharply through the nose to clear the nostril openings of alginate.
17. Quickly use a craft stick to remove any dangling alginate before your subject takes another breath and inhales a bit of alginate. Your subject can then resume breathing normally, and you can further refine the alginate around the nose with your finger or craft stick. I have gotten flawless results this way, with no problems. If you choose to try this method, you might want to do the subject's nose first, while her mouth is still clear and it is possible for her to breathe through her mouth while you clear the nostrils. Then proceed with the rest of the face, taking care to keep a watchful eye on the nostrils as you work, to make sure they remain unobstructed.

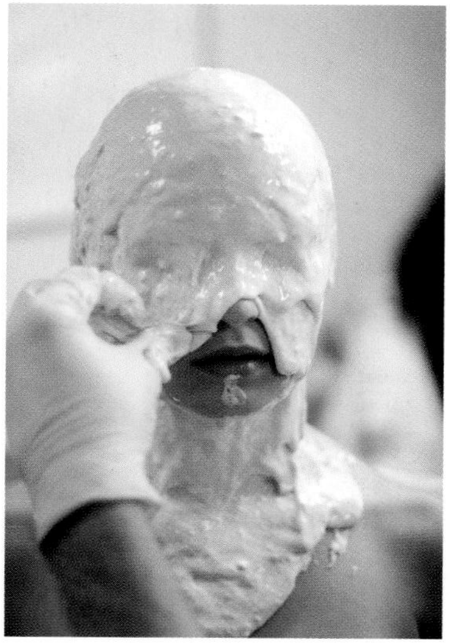

FIGURE 3.32
Save nostrils for last.
Photo by Chase Heilman. Image reproduced by permission of author.

Don't force alginate between the lower lip and teeth, because the lower lip will protrude and give you a result with which you will probably be unhappy. Talk to your subject as you apply the alginate to remind her not to relax her mouth too much, which could result in a droopy lower lip. A bit of tension should remain around the mouth so that the weight of the alginate won't pull it down unduly.

FIGURE 3.33
Keep nostrils clear.
Photo by Chase Heilman. Image reproduced by permission of author.

If you work quickly, you should have no trouble covering the entire face and neck with one batch of alginate. Try to have an even layer of coverage on the face, with no thin spots. It is especially important to try to get the alginate as thick as possible around the edges, eyes, and nose. If you find you need more alginate, it is important to know that alginate will not stick to itself once it has set up, meaning that you cannot apply freshly mixed alginate to set alginate and get the two to bond. However, there is a way to make it happen.

A product called Algislo, available from EnvironMolds, can be used as an alginate retarder, bonder, or softener. This is another Dave Parvin innovation. Algislo is a base that reacts with alginic acid in the alginate to soften it enough on the surface to create a bond between it and fresh alginate. Or if you simply need a bit more working time, you can use it per its directions when mixing the alginate to get a longer working time. You can also create a similar result by making a

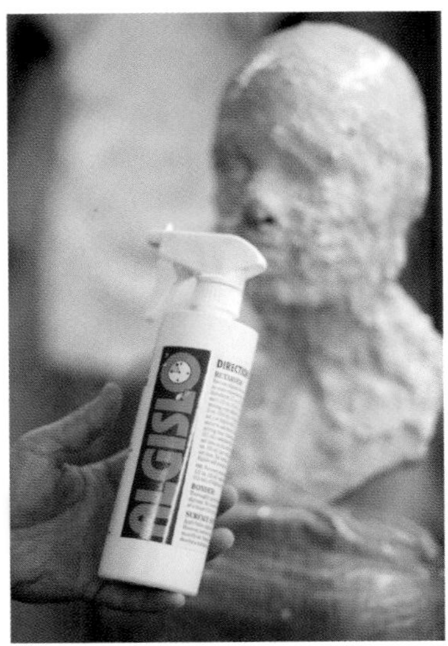

FIGURE 3.34
Algislo slows cure of alginate and helps alginate stick to alginate.
Photo by Chase Heilman. Image reproduced by permission of author.

solution of baking soda and water. Experiment beforehand to find the right solution for your needs.

Back to work:

18. Before the alginate sets, add some fuzz—cotton from a roll—while the alginate is still sticky. The cotton fuzz will stick to the alginate, and the plaster bandages will stick to the cotton as well, making sure that your mother mold (the support mold) conforms precisely to the alginate mold. You don't need much. Press gently so you don't push all the way to bare skin.

You may opt to use cheesecloth cut into small, single-thickness pieces in lieu of the cotton for the same purpose. Make sure you get cotton fuzz or cheesecloth all the way to the outside edges of the alginate so that the mother mold will adhere tightly at the outer edges. Otherwise, there is a possibility of the alginate folding in on itself when you are making the positive, particularly if the alginate is thin.

19. Now that the alginate has set, it is time to apply the plaster bandages as a shell—a mother mold—to support the alginate. If you were to remove the alginate now, before the mother mold is applied, you would wind up with a floppy impression of your subject's face that will not hold its shape. To make the mother mold, you will need to dip the precut strips of plaster bandage into slightly warm water with a pinch of salt. You will definitely want to wear gloves for this process. Warm water will accelerate the cure of plaster, as will a pinch of salt. Terra alba—dried powdered plaster—will also accelerate the cure of plaster to a fraction of its normal set. If the water is too warm, however, you can actually inhibit the cure of the plaster. Fold the plaster strip in half, with the plaster side out. Dip it into the water, then carefully squeeze out some (but not all) of the water before applying it to the alginate. You want the cotton to become soaked so the plaster will stick to it. When you're finished, there should be a buildup of about four layers of plaster. Begin by creating an outside edge and work your way in toward the center of the face.
20. Make sure that your plaster strips overlap one another, with the thickest layers on the outside edges. Press gently but firmly to make sure that there's no airspace between the alginate and the plaster. If you press too firmly, you risk creating a distortion in the alginate and the resulting stone positive. Also, if your mother mold is not thick enough, the weight of the stone when you make your positive may distort the shape of the mold, also ruining your cast.

FIGURE 3.35
Cotton fuzz helps plaster and alginate stay together.
Photo by Chase Heilman. Image reproduced by permission of author.

Here is a good place to discuss in more detail the argument for brushing on plaster with a brush and laying strips of cheesecloth into it for strength instead of

TIP
Terra alba will accelerate the cure of plaster; so will a bit of salt; so will warm water. However, hot water will actually inhibit or prevent the cure of plaster, so be careful with the temperature; test beforehand. White vinegar added to the water in small amounts will retard, or slow, the cure of plaster.

FIGURE 3.36
Detail showing plaster attached to bandage.
Photo by Chase Heilman. Image reproduced by permission of author.

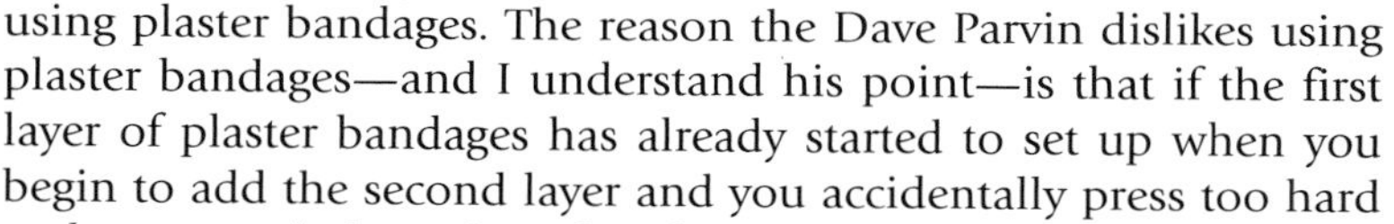

using plaster bandages. The reason the Dave Parvin dislikes using plaster bandages—and I understand his point—is that if the first layer of plaster bandages has already started to set up when you begin to add the second layer and you accidentally press too hard and create an indentation, the plaster will not spring back. That will also cause an indentation in the alginate and will result in an indentation in the stone positive when it is cast.

It is important to note that not all plaster bandages are created equally; some contain more plaster than others. Gypsona plaster bandages seem to be quite popular; I use them frequently. They are similar to Specialist bandages (made by Johnson & Johnson and BSN). I also use Cliniset bandages from EBI; they can be purchased from FX Warehouse in Florida. You'll find a comprehensive appendix of suppliers in the back of this book. There are several brands available; it is important to find one that has a lot of plaster impregnated into the fabric of the bandages. Woodland Scenics sells a plaster bandage used for model railroad scenic construction; it has the most plaster of any bandage I have ever used, and it is also by far the most expensive.

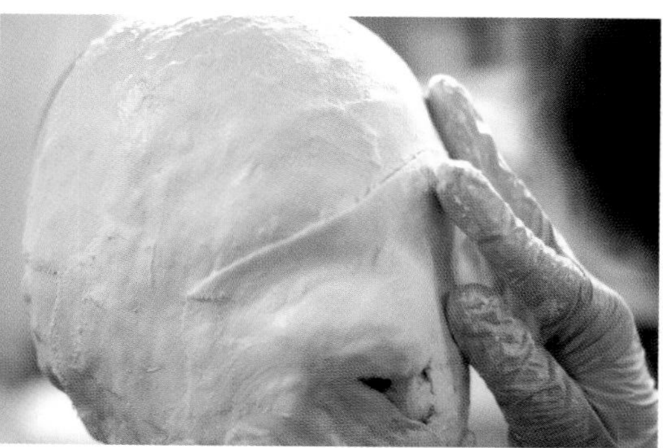

FIGURE 3.37
Applying plaster bandages as mother mold.
Photo by Chase Heilman. Image reproduced by permission of author.

Brushing on plaster as a substitute for plaster bandages can be done in the following way. Note that the logistics of this process dictate that it should be attempted only when two people are creating the lifecast, not one:

- After the cotton fuzz or cheesecloth has been pressed into the uncured alginate (the alginate should now be fully set), mix up a shallow bucket of impression dental plaster (set time 2–3 minutes) and use a 2- or 3-inch chip brush to brush on a layer of plaster over the fuzz-covered or cheesecloth-covered alginate, making sure to continue keeping the subject's nostrils open. Use a 2-inch brush on the face; a 3-inch brush is a bit too big.

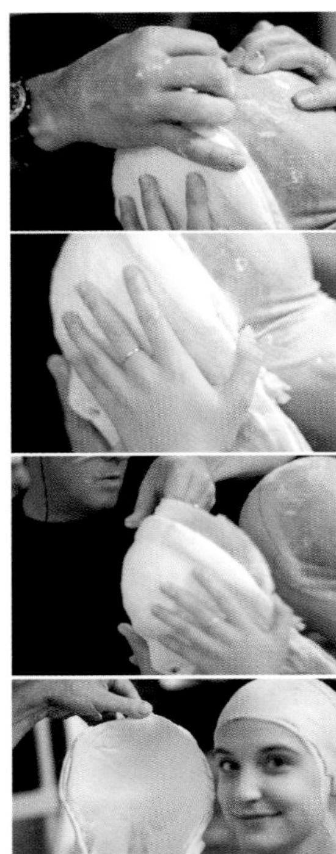

FIGURE 3.38
Removing alginate and plaster mold.
Photo by Chase Heilman. Image reproduced by permission of author.

Rinse your chip brushes in a bucket of water before the plaster sets, to keep them viable for more than one application.

- As soon as this layer has been brushed on, the second person will begin gently applying a layer of cheesecloth to the wet plaster, matching the contours of the alginate and plaster. Repeat this step. Your plaster shell should be about 3/16 to ¼ inch (5–6.5 millimeters) thick. You can also add cut fiberglass fibers to the remaining plaster and spread it onto the mold by hand for added strength.
- After the plaster has heated and then begun to cool, it is cured and you can remove the mold from your subject.

Now let's resume the step-by-step application of plaster bandages for the support shell:

21. Use some of the smaller cut pieces of plaster bandage across the bridge of the nose horizontally and the thin strips along the ridge of the nose and over the septum between the nostrils and the upper lip. Be careful to keep the nostrils unobstructed. It would be a shame to risk starting over when we're almost ready to make our positive!
22. When the plaster shell has set up–remember, plaster heats up when it is curing—that is, it is beginning to cool (time may vary, but it may be about 15 minutes), it's time to remove the mold from your subject's face. I assure you, she is ready, too. Total time to this point—*including* the bald cap application—should be somewhere between 30 and 45 minutes, on average. Variables will be the alginate you use, water temperature, and so on. The actual application of plaster, whether with bandages or brushing on with cheesecloth, may take about 12–15 minutes.
23. To remove the mold, ask your subject to begin puffing out her cheeks and wiggling her face. This will help begin to break any suction between the alginate and skin, and the mold will begin to separate. Have your subject lean forward slightly and help by cupping their face in their hands while you begin to separate the mold from the bald cap at the top of their head.

TIP
The first layer of plaster bandages will begin to set before you are finished applying all of the bandages so be careful not to press too hard, creating an indentation in the plaster that won't bounce back, and will deform the alginate, and the subsequent positive gypsum casting.

It is possible that your subject might feel some resistance on the eyelashes and eyebrows and on any facial hair that was exposed, such as sideburns or moustache. Not to worry, unless you forgot to release them with cholesterol cream or petroleum jelly! The alginate will let go, though you could find a stray hair or two left in the alginate.

24. Ask the subject to keep her eyes closed because the sudden change in lighting could be uncomfortable after this much time. The lifecast should now easily pop off into your hands.

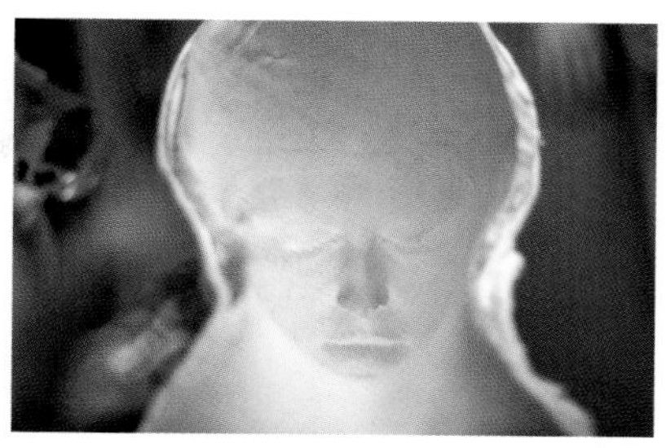

FIGURE 3.39
Sometimes lighting can make negative appear to be positive.
Photo by Chase Heilman. Image reproduced by permission of author.

You now have a negative mold of your subject's face. Take a close look to examine it. A few minor air bubbles are nothing to be concerned about. Those can easily be cleaned up once the positive has been made. More serious imperfections may require that the entire process be repeated. If all is well, we need to make our positive before the alginate begins to dry. If the alginate is thin at the edges, it could already be changing color and drying. It doesn't take long. When the alginate dries, it shrinks; it is mostly water, after all. If you are working with another person, you might want to have him or her help get your subject cleaned up while you prepare to make the stone positive. If you are working alone and your subject needs your help to remove the bald cap, put some wet shop towels inside the alginate mold and around the edges to keep it moist until you are ready to make the positive.

TIP
Add glycerin to the water in a 1:1 ratio, and you will have a longer working window with your cured alginate for getting a gypsum positive cast. The addition of glycerin will retard the drying-out process, making the likelihood of multiple pulls possible from the alginate mold.

Before you begin to mix the Ultracal for the positive, you need to plug the nostril holes in the lifecast mold, or the Ultracal will run right out of the mold. You can either use a small piece of WED clay or oil clay into the holes or mix up a small amount of dental alginate to fill the holes. Be very careful not to push whatever you use too far into the cavity or you risk deforming the nose and ruining the positive. If you don't know what WED clay is yet, it is a water-based clay that contains glycerin so it will stay moist longer. WED stands for Walter Elias Disney; it was developed for Disney sculptors to create maquettes for Disneyland attractions. Other water clay may be substituted for WED, such as CT3, but I prefer WED clay.

Now do the following:

1. Place the lifecast upside down (face down) supported in a shallow box.
2. Wearing gloves, pour about a cup of water in a small plastic bucket, then sprinkle Ultracal into the water. Let the water soak into the Ultracal before beginning to mix; that will help prevent lumps. Continue to add Ultracal powder until it is about the consistency of a Goldilocks milkshake—not too thick and not too runny.

FIGURE 3.40
Water soaking into Ultracal; acrylic fortifier added to water.
Photo by the author

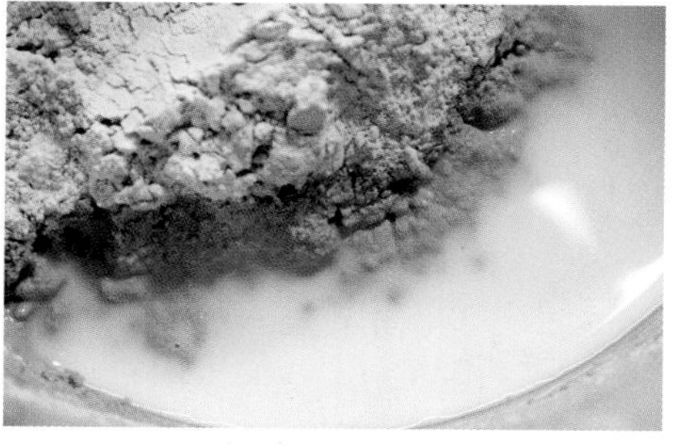

NOTE

If you allow water to soak into plaster just as with the Ultracal, but do not stir, the plaster will not begin its cure reaction until it is agitated. When you begin to stir, the reaction begins; this way you can have multiple batches of plaster ready to go. It is important that the containers be clean and free of any residual plaster or this will not work.

TIP

If you're interested, the official mix ratio for Ultracal 30 is 38 parts water to 100 parts Ultracal by weight. Using 1 cup of water for our example: One cup of water weighs about ½ pound, or 8 ounces, so, how much Ultracal 30 will you need to add to the water? If 8 ounces = 38 parts water, then 1 part water = 8/38 or 0.21 ounce = 1 part. Therefore, 100 parts Ultracal 30 = 0.21 · 100 or 21 ounces of Ultracal 30.

You are going to create a detail layer in the mold and brush it into every nook and cranny of the negative with a 1-inch chip brush. Brush the Ultracal into the negative and bring it up the sides of the mold. You can take your time with the Ultracal since it won't begin to set up for 15 or 20 minutes. Jostle and tap the mold to release any trapped air bubbles from its surface. You will notice that the Ultracal liquefies even more when it is jostled and shaken, so you will need to brush up the walls of the mold again.

FIGURE 3.41
Brushing Ultracal into alginate mold.
Photo by Chase Heilman. Image reproduced by permission of author.

The goal of this step is to create a pure Ultracal detail layer about ¼ inch (6.5 millimeters) thick over the entire surface of the alginate negative. It is up to you whether or not to use Acryl® 60 or another acrylic fortifier when you mix the Ultracal. It will add strength to your stone positive, and that will be an advantage if you will be making your appliances with foam latex. (Adding acrylic fortifier will also make repairs easier when mixed 50/50 with water.)

If you need more Ultracal than you initially mixed, add a little more water and then more Ultracal and continue with the detail layer. When you're done with the detail layer, you might want to rinse out your chip brush in a cup of water so that you can use it again. *Whatever you do,* don't *rinse it in the sink or pour any uncured Ultracal down the drain!* Ultracal will set up even under water, and if it sets in your pipes, you will help your plumber buy a lovely vacation home in Europe or the Caribbean. Any excess Ultracal you still have in a small mixing bucket can come in handy later as a mold base. Once the Ultracal has gone through its curing process, you can just pop it out of the bucket and set it aside somewhere handy.

3. Now, after your detail layer has cured, in about an hour … actually, there are a couple of schools of thought on this: One says it's better to let the

Ultracal cure completely before applying a new layer to it (Ultracal will stick to itself); I find it's better to add more Ultracal before the first layer completely cures. Just make sure it's set up enough to hold its shape and not be affected by the next step. (When in doubt, and most certainly when you are getting accustomed to working with a new material, it is best to err on the side of caution until you really know the properties of the materials you're working with.) Mix another batch of Ultracal, more this time than for the detail layer; the consistency of this batch should be that of a thin milkshake. We are going to be adding the burlap pieces in this step to add strength to our Ultracal. The burlap will act like rebar in concrete, as a strengthening support. Dip a piece of burlap into the Ultracal, then press it onto the Ultracal in the negative mold, making sure to eliminate any air pockets. Do this over the entire mold, overlapping the pieces of burlap. You can even use pieces of cheesecloth or chopped fiberglass fibers. We want to build up two or three layers of Ultracal and reinforcing material and then a final layer of only Ultracal for a beauty layer. The final thickness of the positive should be about an inch (2.6) centimeters, no less.

TIP

Never pour uncured Ultracal, plaster, or any gypsum stone material into a sink and down the drain, because it will set under water and could ruin or permanently block the pipe anywhere from the drain to the main sewer line. You may consider installing a plaster trap under the sink where you're working to help ensure your drain pipe and sewer line doesn't jam up with unwanted gunk. You can purchase them from numerous sources online in a variety of sizes and configurations.

FIGURE 3.42
Brushing detail layer into negative.
Photo by Chase Heilman. Image reproduced by permission of author.

FIGURE 3.43
Building up thickness of Ultracal and burlap.
Photo by Chase Heilman. Image reproduced by permission of author.

> **NOTE**
> I prefer using cut or torn pieces of fiberglass mat instead of burlap or cheesecloth; cheesecloth is really too wimpy, and both cheesecloth and burlap have a North/South-East/West weave that is not as structurally strong as the random intertwining of fibers in fiberglass mat.

FIGURE 3.44
Adding handle to positive.
Photo by Chase Heilman. Image reproduced by permission of author.

4. As the beauty layer is beginning to set, use the rubber kidney tool to smooth the Ultracal. Again, anything worth doing is worth doing well. Even though few, if any, other people will see the finished stone positive, you should want it to look good. Another reason is that if the surface is too rough, you could easily cut or scrape your hands when handling it during the other stages in your makeup creation. Try not to bleed on your mold.
5. You need to make a handle for the positive. The handle can be added as the beauty layer is applied. There is a reason we don't just make a solid stone positive—two reasons, actually: a solid positive would be heavier than necessary, and having no handle would make it awkward to manipulate and very difficult and virtually impossible to lift from the negative mold we will make later of the sculpted prosthetic. Take the piece of metal conduit you precut and have standing by and place it inside and across the back of the positive; it might need to lie at an angle. Dip two of the long strips of burlap into the remaining Ultracal and wrap one around each end of the metal handle, securing it to the positive.
6. When you have finished smoothing the beauty layer and the handle, cover the mold with plastic. Remember that the plastic will help retain moisture as the Ultracal heats during its cure, adding additional strength.
7. After your positive has cooled, you can remove it from the alginate and plaster mold. Will it look good? Will there be huge air bubbles? Is the nose deformed? Will you have to start over?! It's time to find out. With your fingers, begin to gently pry the plaster and alginate shell away from your Ultracal positive around the edges. As the mold begins to pull away from your positive, it should begin to loosen more and more, to the point where you can grab the handle and pull it out of the mold.

FIGURE 3.45
Covering with plastic during cure.
Photo by the author.

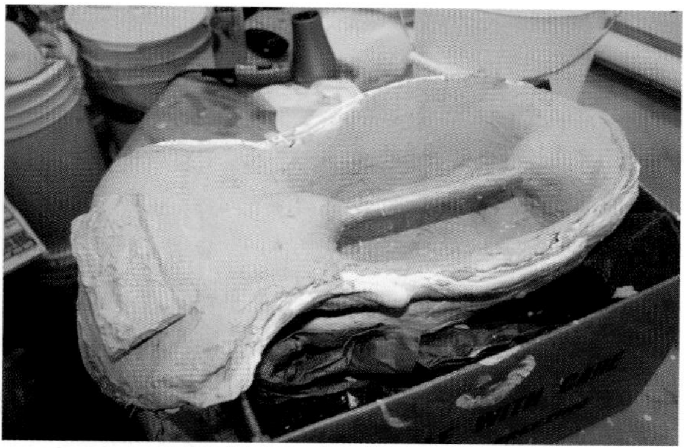

FIGURE 3.46
Stone positive almost ready to be pulled from mold.
Photo by the author.

There may well be some small bubbles or blemishes on the surface, but those are easy to chip away, and if there are any holes, unless they are enormous, they should be easy to patch and fill by mixing a bit of Ultracal with Acryl 60/acrylic fortifier and/or concrete bonding adhesive, and water (1:1 ratio). There is always a bit of cleanup to do on a positive, especially at the nostrils because they were left open and then had to be plugged.

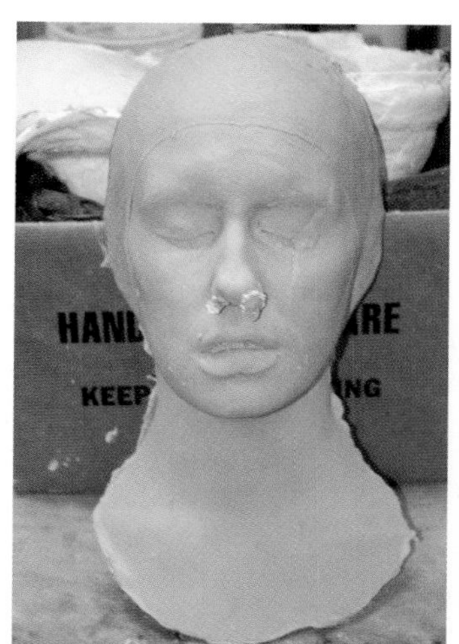

FIGURE 3.47
Stone positive ready for cleanup.
Photo by the author.

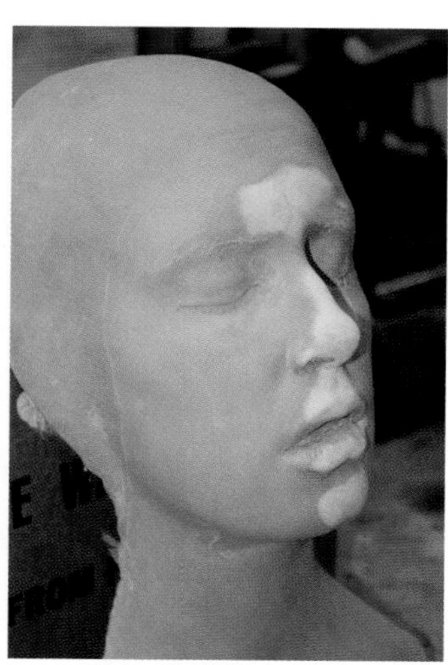

FIGURE 3.48
Cleaned-up positive.
Photo by the author.

With a small chisel and hammer, you can carefully pop the Ultracal "booger" off each nostril and then clean up further with a little sandpaper or a Dremel. If there is any edge work to clean up, you can use sandpaper or a rasp. Once the cleanup is done, you are ready to begin sculpting your makeup design.

BUST: HEAD AND SHOULDERS

Our lifecasting is going to get progressively more difficult. From here on out we will be working "in the round." We will follow many of the same steps for making a lifecast of a face and neck, but we'll include the back of the head as well as the shoulders. We'll need more plaster bandages for a full-bust lifecast—about four times as many. This may be a good project to use brushed impression plaster and cheesecloth. If you want more working time for your plaster, you may try impression dental plaster or regular Plaster of Paris. This will be a lengthier process for your subject as well, so if you choose to use the brush method, perhaps it would be a good idea to first practice on something—or someone—other than your subject. We will begin by duplicating the first several steps for creating a face and neck lifecast. We will also need essentially the same materials listed above.

TIP

You should always mix a test batch of alginate when working with new material; mix characteristics may vary slightly from batch to batch. It is better to simply *stop* if something isn't working to your expectations rather than continuing and trying to fix it on the fly. This will also prevent you from wasting more money and material. The list is essentially the same.

EnvironMolds' MoldGel alginate mixes best with a ratio of 3.5–4 ounces of alginate per 1 pound (16 ounces) of water. We'll go with 4 ounces per pound of H_2O; so, for a head and shoulders lifecast, front and back, we will need approximately 40 ounces of alginate, which means we'll need 10 pounds of water (160 ounces). (In case you didn't know, a gallon of water weighs 8.3 pounds. It's math time again for those of you who need help: there are 16 ounces in 1 pound. If we need 4 ounces of alginate per 16 ounces of water, we need 40 ounces of alginate, simply divide 40 by 4 to get the number of pounds of water we'll need.)

TIP

Suppose you want to use less than a pound of water or less than 4 ounces of alginate (MoldGel). How do you determine how much you need of each material? What is the ratio of alginate to water? It is 4 to 16 ounces, or 4 divided by 16, which is 0.25, or 1⁄4; so a 1:4 ratio. Therefore, if you want to use 2.75 ounces of water, you multiply 2.75 by 0.25 to get the amount of alginate or 0.68 ounce. (There are 28.3495231 grams to 1 ounce; 0.68 ounce is 19.27 grams, and 28.3495231 multiplied by 0.68 gives the total in grams.)

Since we are doing a full head and shoulders lifecast, you need to make sure the bald cap is glued down fully around the head. If your subject has long hair, take the time to flatten it well enough against your subject's head or down the neck so that it won't create a bulge that will be a problem to clean up. If hair sticks out below the

TIP

It's prudent to wear a dust mask when mixing alginate, because some alginate contains silica. Breathing silica can lead to serious respiratory problems.

bottom of the bald cap, be sure to thoroughly release it with cholesterol cream, or cover it with plastic wrap. Lastly, mark your subject's hairline with the eyebrow pencil. This line will transfer to the alginate and then to the Ultracal.

We will begin with the back of the head, neck, and shoulders. Look at the clock or start your timer when you begin to mix the water and the alginate powder so you'll know how much time you have before the alginate begins to set. For this step, we'll need to mix half the alginate and half the water: 20 ounces of MoldGel alginate and 5 pounds (80 ounces) of warm (80°F/27°C) water. Always add the alginate powder to the water and not vice versa. Remember, properly mixed alginate should not be runny.

TIP
Always start with the back of the subject's head and body so that you have face contact with your subject for the longest period of time possible to keep them engaged, involved, and aware of what is going on.

I prefer to wear gloves; I can change quickly and have clean hands immediately to continue working. Keep in mind that room temperature, water temperature, and your subject's own body temperature as well as how quickly or slowly you work will all affect the lifecasting. The alginate is also bound to stick to your hands, whether you're wearing gloves or not. I also like to have an extra small bucket of water handy to dip my hands into, which helps keep the alginate from blobbing too much on my hands, which makes it easier to spread.

- Before spreading any alginate, dip your hands into the water, which will allow you to spread the alginate more easily without it sticking as much to your gloves or your skin. Then, take a handful of alginate and begin to *spread* it with your hand, starting at the top of the head where the line is drawn between the ears and move downward on the back of the head toward the shoulders.
- Spread alginate behind and into the ears (if the ears are not covered by the bald cap). *Try not to push alginate into the ear canal.*
- Before the alginate sets, add some fuzz while the alginate is still sticky.
- Once the alginate has set, it is time to apply the plaster bandages to support the alginate. To make the mother mold, you will need to dip the precut strips of plaster into slightly warm water with a pinch of salt. You will definitely want to wear gloves for this task. Fold the plaster strip in half with the plaster side out, giving a double thickness of plaster bandage. Dip it into the water and carefully squeeze out most (but not all!) of the water before applying it to the alginate. You want it wet, but not sloppy.

TIP
If too much water has been squeezed from the plaster bandage, the cotton fuzz or cheesecloth won't be soaked and the plaster might not adhere to it, causing the mother mold to separate from the alginate mold, potentially resulting in a bad cast.

> **NOTE**
> When doing a full head and shoulders in-the-round lifecast, some people will do the back of the head entirely with plaster bandages and use no alginate at all—there is little detail on the back of the head and neck, usually—and others may create a plaster bandage outer frame before applying alginate inside the frame. I've already stated my opinion about disliking using plaster directly against the skin; I am merely presenting other commonly known methods.

- When you're finished creating the mother mold, there should be a buildup of about four layers of plaster bandage. Make sure that your plaster strips overlap one another, with the thickest layers on the outside edges. Make your edges as clean as you can make them. Press gently but firmly to make sure that there is no airspace between the alginate and the plaster. If you press too firmly, you risk creating a distortion in the alginate and the resulting stone positive. In addition, if your mother mold is not thick enough, the weight of the stone when you make your positive could distort the shape of the mold, also ruining your cast. It is better to use too much than too little. Plan accordingly.
- Once the plaster shell has begun to cool, we can prepare to do the front. First clean off any plaster that got onto your subject's face, neck, and shoulders that could interfere with the alginate. Furthermore, if the line of alginate across the head, neck, and shoulders is not straight and neat, you can neaten it by carefully cutting away the offending alginate with a dull palette knife.
- Next, brush a line of petroleum jelly over the edge of the plaster mother mold, about 2 inches (5 centimeters) in width. It might help to add a bit of food coloring to tint the petroleum jelly so that it can be easily seen. Since most alginate will not stick to itself once it has set, we only need to make sure that the plaster will not stick to itself and encase your subject in a plaster and alginate case. Tincture of Green Soap is also a good release you can use, as is Murphy's Oil Soap.
- Now it is time to mix the rest of the alginate. Look at the clock or start your timer when you begin to mix the water and the alginate powder so that you'll know how much time you have before the alginate begins to set.
- Spread the alginate with your hand; starting at the top of the head, spread the alginate up to and just beyond the alginate on the back half of your subject. Make sure that you get good contact along the edge so that there will be little or no seam between the two halves of alginate. Do this all the way around the edges and then spread alginate everywhere else, moving downward on the face and leaving the nostrils for last.
- When you get to the subject's eyes, gently press the alginate into the inner corners of the eye and under the eyelashes with your fingertips. Do the same with the eyebrows, getting alginate thoroughly into them. As you apply the alginate, make sure no air is trapped between it and your subject.

Use your fingers to follow the contours of your subject's face with the alginate.

- Do the same with the sides of the face, stopping at the back edge of the ears (getting inside the ears, *but not into the ear canal*), making sure to get good alginate coverage into all the lines and creases in the face. When you cover the mouth, use your fingers to work alginate into the corners of the mouth and between the upper and lower lips. If your subject's mouth is slightly open, that's fine. The goal is to have the subject's mouth in a normal, relaxed position. In fact, if your makeup design includes upper and/or lower lip pieces, having a bit more of the lip exposed during the lifecast will be beneficial during the sculpting phase of your project.

TIP

Another method that is used when lifecasting the face is to do the nose first, using a small batch or alginate; this can be done to make the rest of the process go much faster because you aren't as concerned with the nostrils becoming covered, and full attention can be paid to the nose, making certain that alginate gets good coverage. A baking soda solution can be applied to the nose alginate, retarding the cure, and making it sticky so that the new alginate will stick when applied to the rest of the face.

- Cover as much of the subject's neck as needed for your makeup design. In fact, you need to come down as far in front as you did in back; come straight across the chest in front. Make your coverage as even and symmetrical as possible. Lastly, cover the nose, being careful to keep the nostrils clear. You might want to use a small craft stick to spread the alginate evenly and as closely to the edges of the nostril as possible without creating a blockage. If the alginate does run, carefully lift it back up over the face.
- If you work quickly, you should have no trouble covering the entire face and neck with one batch of alginate. Try to have an even layer of coverage, with no thin spots. It is especially important to try to get the alginate as thick as possible around the edges, eyes, and nose. In this case, we don't want the edges too thick, because we still have to build the plaster shell for the front half of the mold.

TIP

Try having your subject take a deep breath and hold it on your command; cover her nostrils with alginate and tell her to blow out sharply through her nose to reopen the nostrils. Clear any obstructing alginate and then she can breathe normally again. This will result in a very good impression of the nose and nostrils.

- Before the alginate sets, add the cotton fuzz or cheesecloth.
- Apply plaster bandages just as you did for the back, but overlap the back with the front just up to the edge of the petroleum jelly, not beyond. We need to be able to get the two halves apart. As with the back, when you're

finished, there should be a buildup of about four layers of plaster. Because we are making a larger mold, you might want to add reinforcing strips of plaster in front and back and along the bottom.

TIP

You might want to create a flange and keys made of plaster for the front and back halves of the mold instead of overlapping the front and back; the two halves can then be held together with drywall screws afterward. Or, the front and back can simply butt up together and the two parts be taped and/or clamped together prior to filling the mold with gypsum.

- When the plaster has begun to cool, draw marks with a Sharpie or other marker to help line up the two halves again when you pour the stone positive. Just as with the face and neck lifecast, ask your subject to begin puffing out her cheeks and wiggling their face to help demold. This will help begin to break any suction between the alginate and the skin, and the mold will begin to separate. It may be a bit difficult for her, but have your subject lean forward slightly cup her face in her hands while you begin to separate the mold from the back half of the mold and her body. Your subject could feel some resistance on the eyelashes and eyebrows and on any facial hair that was exposed. Not to worry, unless you forgot to release them with cholesterol cream or petroleum jelly! The alginate will let go, though you may find a stray hair or two left in it. Ask your subject to keep her eyes closed because the sudden change in lighting may be uncomfortable after this much time. When you've removed the front half of the mold, set it down somewhere safe and carefully remove the back half.
- While your subject is getting cleaned up, mix a bit of dental alginate or grab a small chunk of WED clay and carefully plug the mold's nostril holes without deforming the shape of the nose. Then, put the mold halves back together

FIGURE 3.49
Have subject help with removal of lifecast.
Photo by the author.

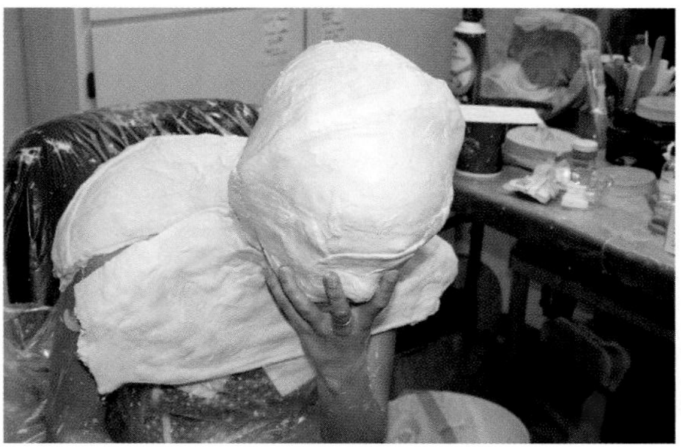

FIGURE 3.50
When mold halves are put back together, seam should almost be invisible.
Photo by the author.

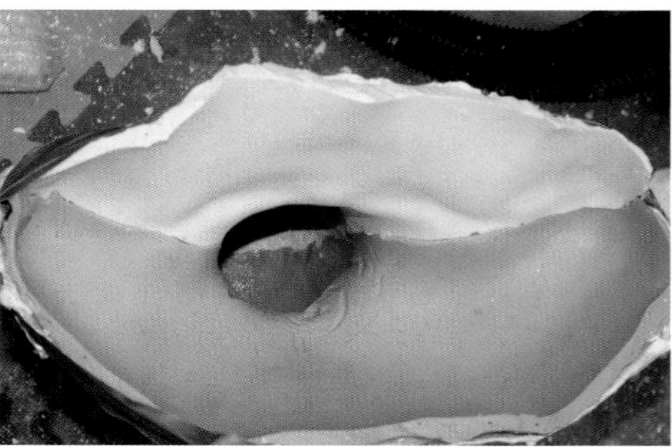

carefully and secure the halves with duct tape, or you can take the time to wet some more strips of plaster bandage and wrap them around the mold to hold the pieces together. Examine the seam to make sure it is tight. If you've lined up the two halves properly, the seam should be almost invisible.

- Use a large bucket or sturdy box with foam or newspaper (or both) padding in the bottom to support the mold while the stone is poured.
- Mix a large batch of Ultracal, enough to fill the head cavity up to the neck. It should not be too thick or too runny—about the consistency of a milkshake. There is a formula for mixing Ultracal: The mix ratio is 38 parts water to 100 parts Ultracal by weight, but I've found—and anyone who works with Ultracal will tell you the same thing—that it is easy to judge your mixture by eye and by feel. (How much you affect the structural integrity of the stone by not following the mix ratio is arguable.) Ultracal is easy to mix by hand; you should definitely wear gloves when working with it. Although the powder is fine, it is still abrasive, and like plaster, it will draw moisture from your skin, so over time, your skin will dry and crack. I didn't use gloves the first several times I worked with it, and then while I was mixing a batch—for about the eighth or ninth lifecast of the day—I noticed that it was turning pink … Anyway, when you're mixing the stone, add the Ultracal powder to the water a little at a time so that there will be fewer lumps to break up as you mix with your hand. You can use a mixer if you want to, but since Ultracal has such a long working time, speed won't actually gain you anything except quicker lump-free Ultracal and lots of air bubbles.

FIGURE 3.51
Support mold so that it can be easily filled.
Photo by author.

FIGURE 3.52
Finished positive (smooth base added).
Photos by the author.

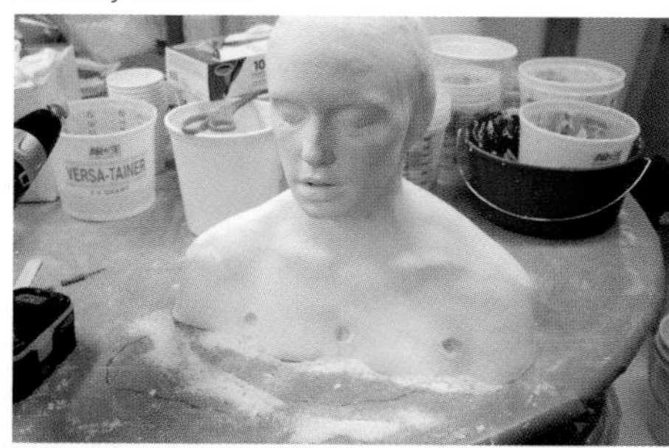

- Pour the Ultracal into the mold. With a gloved hand, reach inside and work your hand around the surface of the mold to dislodge air pockets. You can also gently bounce the bucket or box supporting the mold to dislodge air bubbles. Then, with your hand, bring some of the liquid Ultracal up the sides of the mold. We want to create a detail layer in this mold also, before adding layers of Ultracal with burlap or fiberglass mat. It should be about 1/8 to ¼ inch (3–6.5 millimeters) thick.
- Once the detail layer has begun to cool, you can begin to add Ultracal with burlap in three or four layers. We want our cast to be hollow because if we were to make it solid, it would be very heavy, unwieldy, and extremely difficult to work with. Your finished stone cast should be no more than an inch thick.
- Cover the mold with a plastic bag so that it will strengthen during its cure. I've heard that retaining moisture while it heats will make the stone stronger. Whether this is actually true or not, I have not been told by a gypsum expert. As long as it does not purportedly make the stone weaker, there's no reason not to give it a try. Because this is a larger stone cast than the face and neck cast, it will take longer to fully go through its cure process. In about 2 hours, you can demold the bust.
- With a bit of luck, when you carefully pry apart the plaster and alginate mold halves, your stone bust cast should look just like your subject, only in Ultracal.
- A bit of cleanup with some sandpaper and a rasp is all that's left; then we'll create a smooth aesthetic base for the bust using a piece of Formica board or Masonite or even a piece of sheet plastic.

FIGURE 3.53
Bust is placed into fresh stone to create smooth base.
Photo by the author.

- Place the bust on the nonstick surface and trace around the base with a marker. This line will be the guide for the batch of Ultracal that will be mixed and applied to square off the bottom of the bust, making it smooth and better looking.
- Mix some Ultracal and apply it around the inside of the bust at the bottom. Then place Ultracal along the inside of the traced line on the nonstick surface and put the bust down onto it. As the Ultracal begins to set, take a rubber kidney tool and scrape away the excess, and with a damp paper towel make the edge nice and clean. Once the Ultracal has completely cured, you can easily loosen the bust from the nonstick surface and remove it. A little more cleanup may be needed, and you'll be ready to begin sculpting.
- To save time later, go ahead and drill keys near the base of the bust for lining up the mold. You can use a ¾-inch (19 millimeters) round router bit in an electric drill to create the keys. Make three in front and three in back.

NOTE

An alternative to casting a hollow Ultracal positive is to simply cast a solid Plaster of Paris positive (yes it'll be heavy) and then make a silicone matrix mold of the plaster positive; you will then have a mold you can cast hollow in fiberglass or epoxy that will be much lighter than a gypsum positive. How to do this will be discussed in Chapter 5. This involves more steps, but is a better way in the long run, I think.

HANDS, ARMS, LEGS, FEET, AND EARS

The intended end use of hands, arms, legs, and feet will determine how these body parts will be lifecast. If you need the body part in the round, you'll need to cast it one way; if you need only one side, you will cast it another way.

For as small as they are, it's a challenge to lifecast ears. Because of the many severe undercuts, getting a good impression of a model's ears can be difficult, but it's not impossible, obviously. Care must be taken to get the alginate into every nook and cranny of the ear to avoid thin areas and trapped air bubbles.

Hands and Arms

More often than not, when it comes to makeup effects for hands and arms, you will find yourself working with hands more often than arms unless the makeup involves much more of the body, such as with a creature suit, a muscle suit, or a fat suit, in which case the entire body will likely be cast. With hands, too, unless close-ups will be involved, you might be able to create the necessary effect with nothing more than applying makeup, not prosthetics.

TIP

A few drops of dish soap in a spray bottle filled with water creates "wet" water; a very small amount of soap will reduce surface tension and allow better surface contact between alginate and skin.

Legs and Feet

Much of the time, you will want to cast your subject with the leg straight, in a standing position; even if you want a leg bent at the knee, the process will be the same. Your subject's comfort is very important for this process because she will need to hold the same position for an extended period of time, so you need to come up with a system in your workspace that will let you make your subject comfortable

TIP

Remember the Goldilocks Principle when mixing alginate: if the alginate is too thin and runny, you'll get air bubbles; if the alginate is too thick you'll get air bubbles. You want the alginate to be *just right*. Alginate should be thin enough to spread easily but thick enough to stay where you put it, with very little or no downward movement.

and still provide you with the room you need to make the lifecast. Even if you encase the leg in one batch of alginate and make a cut to separate the leg and alginate, you will make (at least) a two-part mother mold. Creating some sort of keys will help hold the soft mold and rigid mold together in registration.

Ears

Ears are interesting bits of anatomy, and you need to take great care to create a convincing appliance—whether it is an earlobe extension to simulate gauged piercings, ear tips for a fantasy character or alien, or a full ear prosthetic that needs to sell an audience up close.

If you cast a head and shoulders bust, casting ears separately from the head and shoulders lifecast can provide you with ears to complete the head or with base ears from which to create character ears. Let's begin by cutting the bottom off a large deli container about 4½ inches (11.5 centimeters) in diameter and 3 inches (7.5 centimeters) deep. Be careful cutting off the bottom of the container!

1. Cut a slit in a piece of clear plastic sheet (such as from a large lawn bag) about 10 × 10 inches (25 × 25 centimeters) and fit it over your subject's ear. You will need a piece for each ear. Use spirit gum (which I do not like) or Pros-Aide to glue the plastic at the edges around the ear for a clean casting. You might need to trim the plastic a bit first so there won't be any wrinkles. Use tape if you need to keep the outside edges of the plastic lying flat.
2. Make a thin line of nose and scar wax or use tape and place it along the larger edge of the plastic container to help prevent alginate from running out.

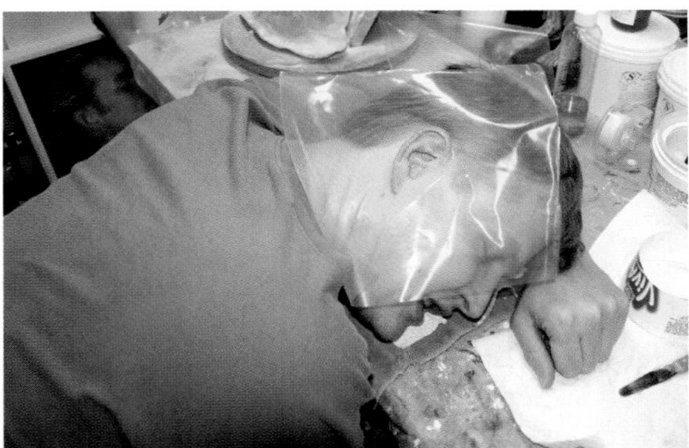

FIGURE 3.54
Plastic covering subject's head to prevent alginate sticking to hair.
Photo by the author.

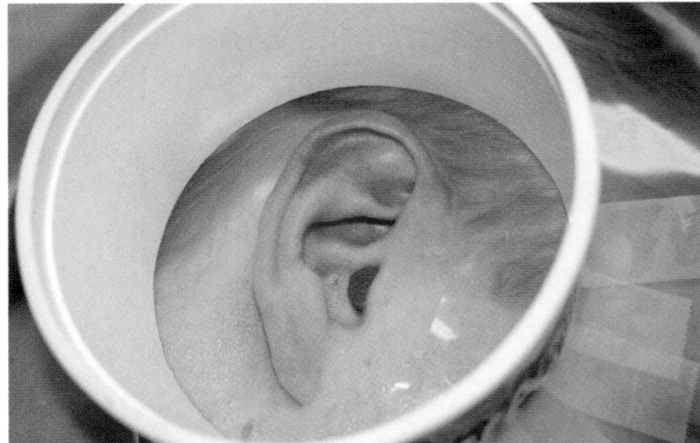

FIGURE 3.55
Ready to fill with alginate.
Photo by the author.

3. Have your model's head rested on a table or against his hand so that his head and ear are horizontal, where it must remain until the alginate mold is removed. Although it is not necessary, for your model's added comfort place a piece of cotton or piece of foam earplug into his ear canal to close it.

4. Place the plastic container over your subject's ear and make sure it is centered. Press it and the nose wax down so that it sticks to the plastic. Check for gaps and seal them with extra wax if necessary.
5. You might decide to use dental alginate because it sets quickly. EnvironMolds has a dental alginate called Hollywood Impressions, and there are others that are listed in Appendix C. Accu-Cast 390 alginate—which is not a dental alginate but it's just quick setting—has a working time of 3 minutes and is also a choice you might consider. Working with warm water, the MoldGel will set pretty quickly. Mix a small batch of alginate by eye—don't worry about the formula here—to a consistency that you can easily pour but not too runny. When it's mixed, pour it into the plastic ring of the container until it is about ½ inch (12 millimeters) past the top of the ear. Use your finger to make sure the alginate gets behind, under, around, and into every bend and fold of the ear. *Try not to get alginate deep into the ear canal.* Let the alginate set.
6. Next, gently separate the container from the plastic covering your model's face, starting from the front of the ear so that you don't damage the alginate negative. The alginate is fairly thick, so it will not dry and shrink rapidly, but if you want to cast the other ear before making a stone positive, wrap the alginate in wet cloth or paper towels. Then repeat steps 1 through 6 on your model's other ear.
7. When you're ready to cast positives of both ears, cut strips of craft foam about 1½ inch wider than your alginate container is thick. Wrap the foam around the plastic container to form a wall and secure it with masking tape, gaffers tape, or duct tape. There should be no gaps between the foam wall and the edge of the container for the Ultracal to seep through.

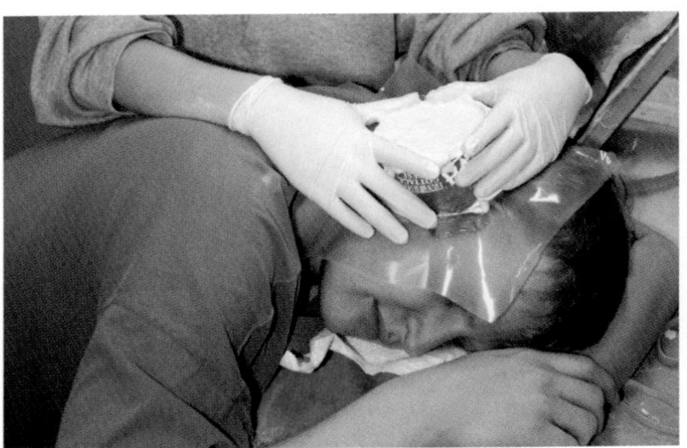

FIGURE 3.56
Alginate ear mold ready to remove.
Photo by the author.

FIGURE 3.57
Thin foam wall supporting Ultracal in alginate.
Photo by the author.

8. Mix a batch of Ultracal large enough to cast both ears and a base. Don't mix the Ultracal too runny, but you should be able to pour it. Pour the Ultracal slowly into the mold and let it fill up the ear cavity. Before it is

completely filled, tilt, tap, and rotate the mold to get the Ultracal into all the spaces. You can also gently squeeze the entire mold to get rid of trapped air pockets. Then continue to fill the mold until the Ultracal is about an inch thick above the alginate. Tap it gently until the air bubbles all disappear and then let the stone cure.

9. When the Ultracal has cooled, remove the foam wall and the plastic container, which should come off easily. With a dull knife or spatula or a slightly sharpened wooden craft stick (you don't want to scratch or otherwise damage the positive), you can begin to cut away the thickest part of the alginate.
10. When you're certain the Ultracal is fully cured, remove the rest of the alginate a little at a time from front to back so that you don't risk breaking off the Helix and Scaphoid fossa.
11. With a rasp or sandpaper, smooth out any defects or rough areas, and your ear positives are ready for sculpting.

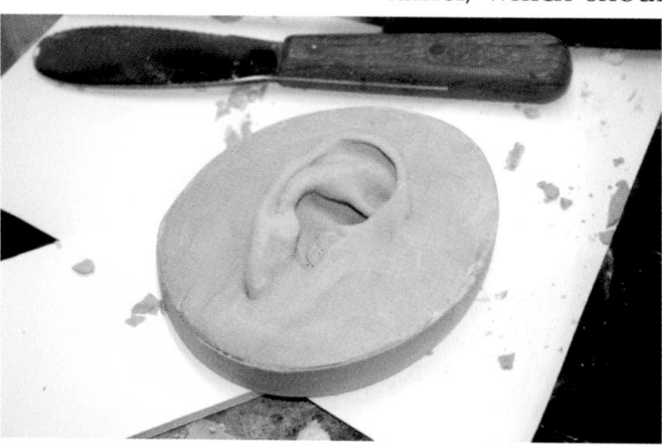

FIGURE 3.58
Ultracal ear cast.
Photo by the author

FULL BODY

Why would you want to do a full-body lifecast? I can think of only two reasons that apply to makeup effects work for stage or screen. The first is for the purpose of creating a body or corpse, in which case the task is somewhat easier because the lifecast will most likely be done with the subject in a prone position. The second would be for the purpose of creating a body form that will be used to create a sculpted costume or body suit.

To do a full body, front and back, will require about 15 pounds of alginate (about \$120 or £61.5); to do the same job with a skin-safe silicone will require about 3 gallons of (platinum) silicone. The cost difference between alginate and silicone for a project of this size is enormous. You must know before starting what your time allotment will be to perform the task and whether or not you will need more than one "pull," or copy, from the mold. The advantage to using silicone is that you do not have to make a stone or foam positive from the mold immediately because once silicone has set, it will not dry out and any shrinkage will be negligible. With alginate, a positive must be made fairly soon after the alginate mold is removed, because it will begin to dry out quickly due to the water it is made with. However, if you need to make multiple copies, you can make a silicone mold from your positive using a much less-expensive tin silicone.

Before we go any further, let's also discuss the materials we could use for casting our positives: oil or wax clay, Ultracal 30, plaster, Hydrocal, or urethane. Here are the characteristics of each:

- Sulfur-free oil-based clay or wax-based clay is ideal for melting and brushing into molds where additional takeaway sculpture and texturing may be needed. Often, rigid urethane foam is cast as a reinforcing element to the positive after the clay has been brushed in and allowed to cool. Rigid urethane foam is lightweight and can be quite strong.

- Ultracal 30 has the lowest expansion of any rapid-setting gypsum cement available. Ultracal was designed to give the patternmaking industry the ultimate in a gypsum cement tooling medium. It is also ideal in the makeup effects industry for its ability to withstand repeated heating and cooling, which is necessary when fabricating foam latex appliances. Since prosthetic appliances must fit precisely to sell the illusion of reality and believability, Ultracal is outstanding mold making due to its exceptional hardness and accuracy of detail.
- Impression dental plaster and Lab dental plaster are harder than regular Plaster of Paris; they set faster and have a negligible amount of expansion compared with Plaster of Paris. However, I would not recommend any plaster as a casting medium for prosthetic appliances; in fact, I would not use plaster of any kind for prosthetic fabrication except as a mother mold/shell material or as a core model that will be reworked (as a corrected mold) and molded again.
- Hydrocal from U.S. Gypsum offers higher strengths than typical plaster products (such as #1 Potter's Plaster, Impression dental plaster), though it is not as strong as Ultracal. It can be used in a variety of arts and crafts applications in addition to makeup effects work. Hydrocal is especially designed for thin sections, which require high green (early) strength to minimize breakage during removal from intricate molds.

Full Body: Prone

To create a dead body lying prone, we first need a live body lying prone. Since we will only be casting one side of a subject, we need less alginate than for a full body front and back. For this task, we need about 8 pounds of alginate.

Since this is a learning exercise, let's make it an exercise that won't frustrate you to the point of looking for another line of work. How about a corpse laid out on an autopsy table? Seems simple enough. You need a model who won't mind lying absolutely still for a while. You also need a surface large enough for your subject to be posed on as well as a space large enough to work in comfortably without everyone running into each other like the Keystone Cops! My studio is too small, so we enlisted Dave Parvin's studio, which is quite roomy. There were six of us working, including our model.

If we mix all our alginate at once, it will solidify way before we're done applying it to our model, Nicole. Since we don't want that to happen, we will mix up a smaller amount and add to the alginate we've already applied. Remember that alginate will not stick to itself once it has set up, *unless* we do—what? We need to retard the set. We can do that in one of the two ways: (1) we can use colder water, which is usually less comfortable for subjects than warm water (since this particular subject will be modeling for a corpse, we want her skin to be relaxed, not all hard and goosebumpy) or (2) we can spray our alginate with Algislo or a solution of baking soda and water to react with the surface of the alginate and make it sticky and able to receive new alginate and stick. We will use this method to also get cotton fuzz and cheesecloth to stick to the alginate for the plaster mother mold.

The positive from this lifecasting session will be different from the ones created up to this point. Instead of making an Ultracal positive, this positive will be only another step toward a finished camera-ready piece. We will make an oil clay skin and urethane foam-core positive. We need to do substantial sculpture work on this positive if we are to have a convincing autopsy subject.

We'll do this lifecast in two stages. Stage one will be a cast of the body minus the head; stage two will be the cast of the head. When both lifecasts are completed, we will put the two molds together and reinforce the seam with plaster before we fill the mold and make our one-piece positive. When the two casts are put together, a layer of melted clay will be brushed into the alginate mold—at least ½ inch in most places, thicker in others, depending on what your ultimate autopsy corpse design entails.

After putting water in the bottom of the roaster oven, you need to put as much of the clay as you can safely put into the top of the roaster and turn the thermostat to just under 200°F (93°C); somewhere between 175°F and 200°F should be fine. It will take a while for the clay to liquefy—probably several hours, depending on which clay you actually use, so plan ahead.

1. Divide the alginate into separate containers with about 1 pound (16 ounces) of alginate in each; set one of the containers aside for the head. We are using EnvironMolds' FiberGel. That's eight batches. If we mix the alginate to the ratio of 5 ounces of alginate per pound of water, we will need 3 pounds or 3.2 ounces (51.2 ounces) of 80°F (about 27°C) water for each batch; for the math challenged, that's 3.2 ounces of water per 1 ounce of alginate. It would be ideal to have the water premeasured before starting. (Interestingly, a fluid ounce of water weighs 1 ounce, so 1 pound (16 ounces) of water is 16 ounces by volume as well.)
2. You shouldn't need to release your subject's skin with anything—petroleum jelly or cholesterol—unless there is hair present that could get caught in the alginate. If that is the case, work cholesterol or petroleum jelly thoroughly through the hair so that it will release easily when the alginate is removed. Our model Nicole wore an old bikini bottom that she didn't care about; we thoroughly released the fabric with vegetable oil so that the alginate would not impregnate itself into the fabric and would separate easily.
3. With your subject being comfortable in position, mix one of the batches of alginate and begin to apply it at the neck and work your way down the body, making sure to spread the alginate, not just glob it on. Even though we will be doing sculpture work on the positive, we still want

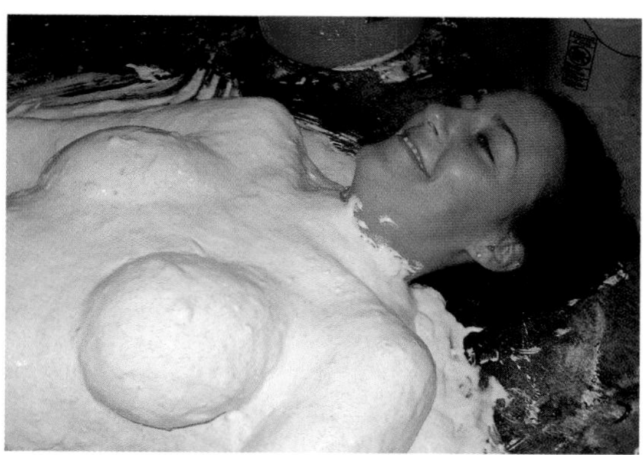

FIGURE 3.59
Nicole covered with EnvironMolds FiberGel. Fibers are clearly visible in alginate.
Photo by the author.

to avoid air bubbles and make our cast as good as possible. Be careful to not spread the alginate too thinly. We can add more alginate if necessary, but try to do it evenly to begin with. The alginate should be between ¼ and ½ inch (about 6–12 millimeters) thick.

4. While the first batch of alginate is being applied, a second batch should be getting mixed so that it can be applied immediately after the first one, before it has started to set up. While the alginate is being mixed and applied, someone also should be making sure the cotton and cheesecloth will be ready to apply once the alginate has been fully applied.
5. Spray the alginate with Algislo. For best results, the surface of the alginate should be sprayed before it sets. This will act as a surface set retarder, giving you time to apply cotton or cheesecloth on the surface. If that's not possible, the surface should be recently set. Spray the surface rather than using a paintbrush; the results will be more even, and you want to avoid pulling on a tacky area. Rub the Algislo on the alginate with a gloved hand to determine whether it is sticky enough for cotton fuzz and cheesecloth to stick. When it is, dab the cotton onto the alginate and pull back, leaving some of the fuzz, which will be enough for plaster to adhere to. Lightly press cheesecloth onto the alginate, especially near the edges of the alginate.
6. For the plaster mother mold, you will want to use Impression dental plaster or 1 Potter's Plaster (with terra alba to shorten the set time) as the primary shell and plaster bandages for adhering wood supports after the shell has set. Mix a small bucket of plaster; mix only as much as you can use working fairly quickly, because you don't want the plaster to kick while most of it is still in the bucket. Brush the plaster into the cheesecloth and smooth it as you go. As you brush a layer of plaster onto cheesecloth, have another of your team add more cheesecloth on top of the fresh plaster. While this is taking place, more plaster should be mixed in a new bucket. Remember, if you mix new plaster in a container that has setup plaster in it, the hard plaster will cause the new plaster to kick much more quickly than if it had been mixed in a clean bucket.

FIGURE 3.60
Cheesecloth imbedded in alginate, ready for plaster application.
Photo by the author.

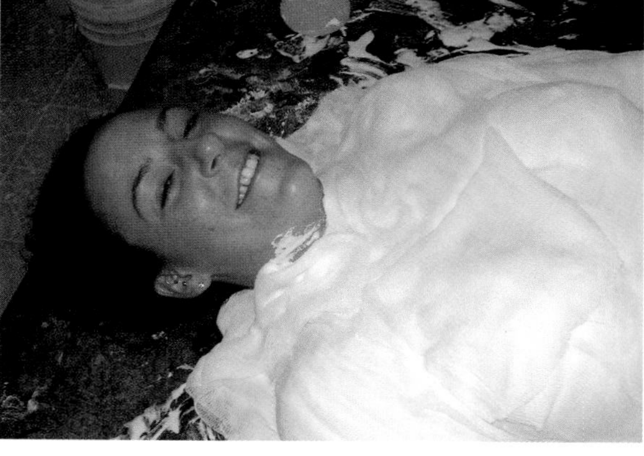

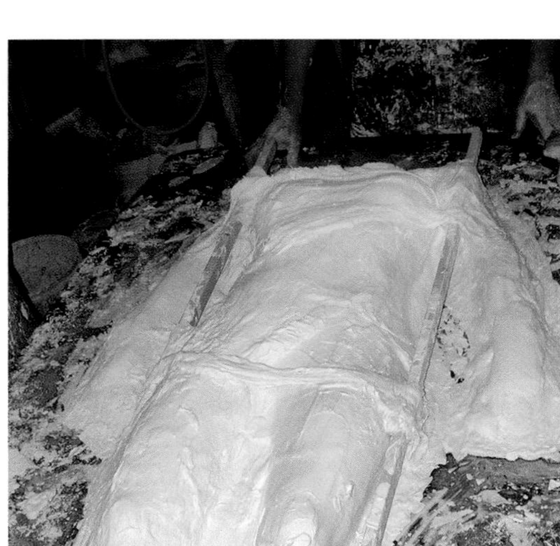

FIGURE 3.61
Wooden supports attached to plaster shell with plaster bandages.
Photo by the author.

7. When the plaster mother mold has set, the mold can be *carefully* removed. We have not built the supports yet. While the model is getting cleaned up and ready for the next step (casting the head), the supports can be attached using the wood strips of 1 × 2 inches long. The purpose of these supports is to prevent the mold from buckling or cracking from the weight of the clay, plaster, and alginate when it is repositioned for attaching the head and then for removing the positive once the mold has been filled. One long piece should be positioned along the torso and leg on each side of the mold. The shorter pieces are to be laid across the log pieces and screwed together. Once the four pieces of wood are attached to each other, they need to be attached to the plaster mother mold. Plaster bandages wet in 50/50 mixture of water and acrylic bonding agent can be wrapped around the wood joints and pressed onto the plaster shell to form a strong bond.
8. Mix up a batch of plaster using the same 50/50 mixture of water and acrylic bonding agent and spread it over the wood joints and plaster bandages to give the mold a really strong connection between the wood and the plaster shell.
9. Now it's time to cast our subject's head so that we can attach it to the body. Since we used Dave Parvin's studio space for this project, we'll also use one of his techniques for casting a head: no bald cap. Dave's lifecasting is almost used exclusively for the cast to become artwork, so incorporating the subject's hair into the cast is usually critical when the head is involved. Since we are going to do extensive resculpting once our positive is made, it is really irrelevant whether the hair is there or not. Cholesterol is thoroughly worked through the subject's hair so that there will be no problem removing the alginate cast. Then, casting the face proceeds normally. Notice the fibers in the FiberGel that give it remarkable tear strength.

FIGURE 3.62
Nicole's face covered with alginate.
Photo by the author.

10. We leave the nose for last, making sure to keep the nostrils clear before pressing cotton fuzz into the alginate and then letting it set up.
11. Plaster is applied to the alginate and cotton fuzz, just as with the body. Plaster is brushed onto the fuzz; cheesecloth is laid into it and layers built up until we have three or four

layers of plaster and cheesecloth. Our mother mold is about ½ inch (about 12 millimeters) thick.

12. When the plaster has cured, it's time to wake up our model and remove the cast from her head. It should come right off, with marginal pull, if any, against the hair. Nicole's job is done; while she showers off and gets ready to leave, the head and body can be assembled.
13. Some minor trimming might be necessary to line up the neck seams on both molds and then some fresh plaster can be mixed—either 1 Potter's Plaster and cheesecloth or plaster bandages—and the seams bonded.
14. After the plaster seam has cured, carefully flip the mold and support it underneath with foam, rags, crumpled newspaper, or anything you have handy to keep it level and wobble free.
15. Open the roaster oven (someone should have been checking periodically to see how melted the clay is) and begin to brush the clay into the alginate mold with the large chip brushes. Be careful to make good contact against the alginate with the clay when it is brushed in so as to not leave gaps and air pockets. Toes and fingertips might be especially tricky to get clay fully into it. Build up the clay thickness to ½ inch through most of the mold, thicker where you will do takeaway sculpting—for a traumatic wound, perhaps. We used about 50 pounds of clay in the mold. The next step is to fill the remaining cavity with rigid urethane foam. We used Smooth-On's Foam-It!® 5 urethane foam that is a 1:1 mix ratio by volume and expands to seven or eight times its original volume; a little goes a long way.

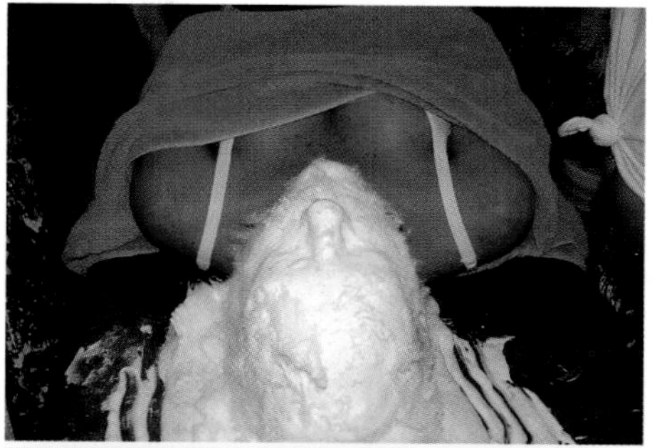

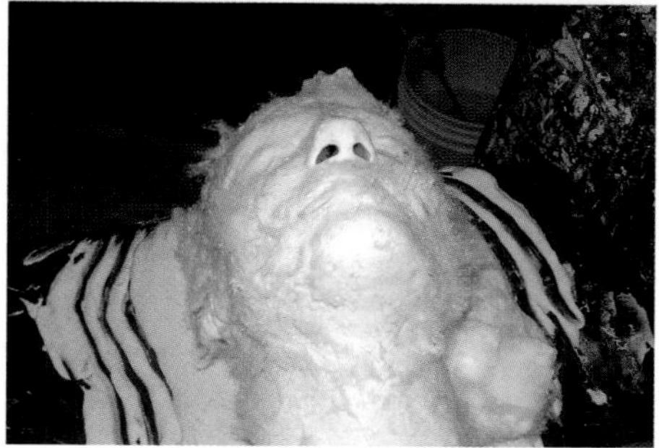

FIGURE 3.63
Cotton fuzz attached while alginate still sticky.
Photos by the author.

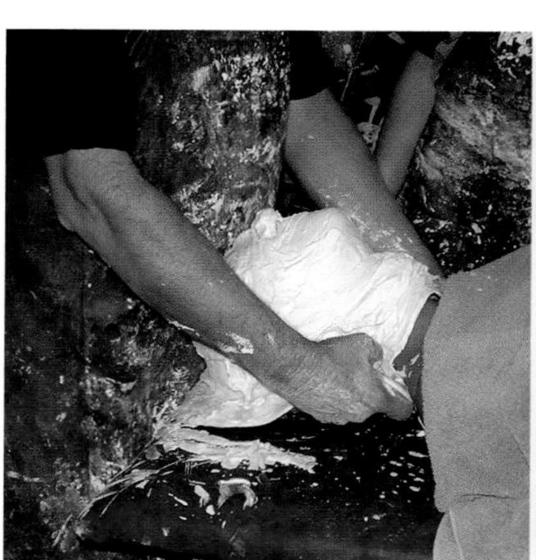

FIGURE 3.64
Properly released, alginate mold comes off easily.
Photos by the author.

16. Mix small batches at a time and pour it into the mold, brushing it into the mold until you see it begin to rise. It becomes tack free in several minutes and develops handling strength in about 20 minutes. Full cure is 2 hours; the foam goes through a heat reaction during its cure also. If you pour freshly mixed foam liquid onto risen foam that has not begun to solidify, it could collapse, so be aware of that as you work.
17. Since quite a bit of melted clay was put into the mold and the foam also generated heat during its cure, it would be a good idea to let the mold cool overnight and demold the positive the next day. At the very least, you should wait several hours before attempting to demold the clay and foam positive. If the clay is not completely cooled and back to its restive state of hardness, you could damage the positive when you begin to peel away the plaster shell and alginate.
18. You might need to do some sanding or cutting to flatten the foam backing so that your positive cast will lie flat when it is turned over to remove the mold.
19. Take your time removing the plaster and alginate. The plaster is quite hard and will require effort to cut and pull it away without damaging the positive.

FIGURE 3.65 Alginate mold ready for melted clay to be brushed inside; Dave Parvin, Kelly Rooney, and Elliot Summons. *Photo by the author.*

Now you have a full body cast of a prone body. There is still much work to be done, but now the real fun can begin!

Full Body: Standing

Creating a front and back standing body form is not as difficult as it sounds. It can be achieved with the subject clothed or unclothed, with little difference in the end result. Much will depend on your model's level of modesty and what is required for the final product. Any clothing the model wears must be thin and form fitting, such as a spandex bathing suit.

Lifecasting is a critical part of creating prosthetic makeup effects for theater, television, and film as well as props and animatronics. The steps outlined previously are certainly not the be-all and end-all of lifecasting techniques. As I've mentioned, there are many ways to accomplish the same task. After completing your own application of these processes, you are certain to discover a way that will suit you well.

Here are a few lifecasting tips and suggestions to keep in mind:

- Spread the alginate when applying it; you'll get fewer bubbles when spreading than when just laying it on.
- Add fuzz—cotton from a roll—before the alginate sets, while it is still sticky; cotton fuzz sticks to the alginate and gives the plaster something to adhere to.

- Try cheesecloth instead of cotton.
- To repair alginate tears or to add two coats, use Algislo or a baking soda/water solution to soften the alginate enough for new alginate to stick to it.

Try using Impression dental plaster or Lab dental plaster with cheesecloth instead of plaster bandages.

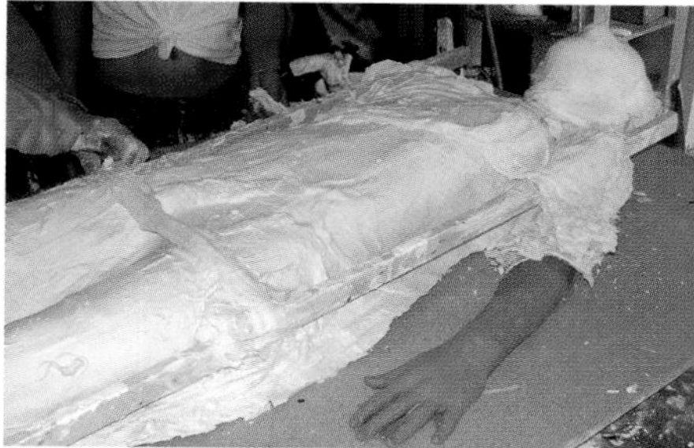
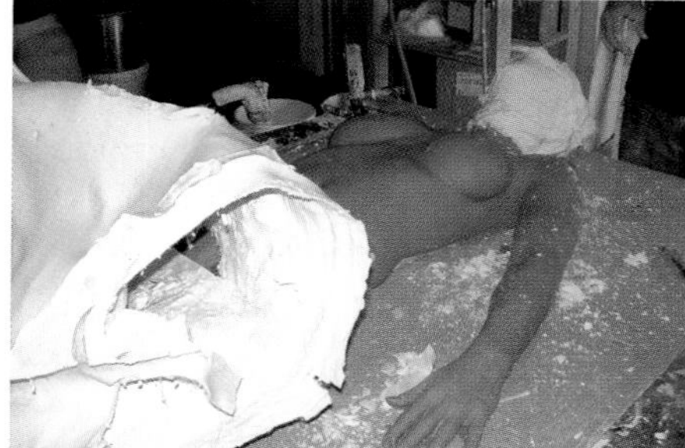

FIGURE 3.66
Plaster and alginate carefully peeled away revealing finished figure.
Photos by the author.

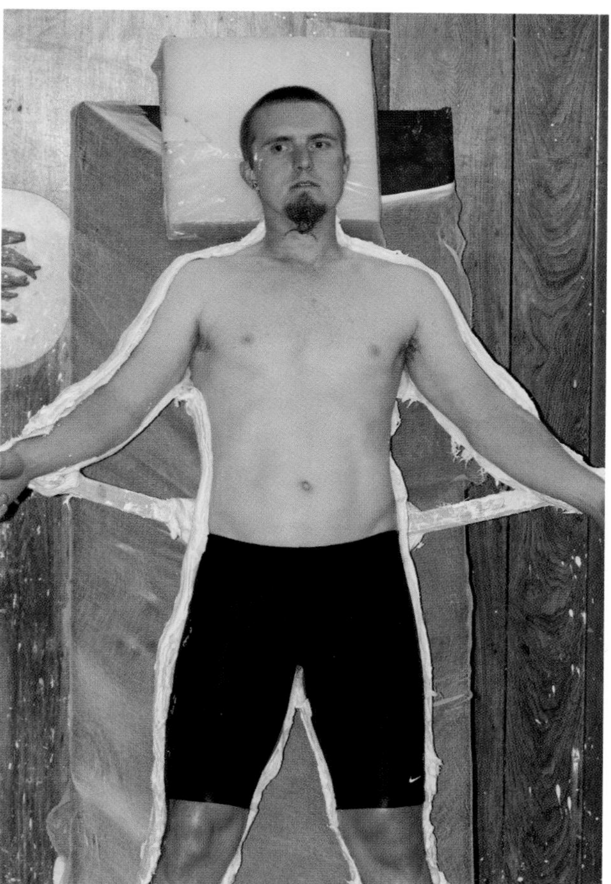

FIGURE 3.67
Full body standing lifecast. Model, Will Chilen.
Photo by the author.

- Use terra alba to get your plaster to set faster. A pinch of salt in the water will also help plaster set faster; slightly warm water will make plaster set faster, but *hot* water will actually inhibit the set of plaster.
- A small amount of white vinegar will slow the set of plaster.
- Use plaster-coated rolled cheesecloth along the outer edges of a mother mold to add strength.

- Mix 50% acrylic fortifier with 50% water to mix plaster for a stronger plaster or Ultracal.
- The warmer the water used to mix alginate, the faster it will set up; cooler or cold water will give you longer working time.
- Rule of thumb with most alginates (some of EnvironMolds' alginates need only 3–3.5 ounces of alginate per 1 pound of water): 5 ounces of alginate to 1 pound of water will prevent the alginate from running. A full torso (front) will use 40 ounces of alginate and 8 pounds of water (1 gallon of water weighs roughly 8 pounds).
- If you're casting with clothing, use vegetable oil as a fabric release.

CHAPTER SUMMARY

This has been a lengthy chapter with lots of information to retain; you should now be familiar with:

- How to make good dental impressions
- Lifecasting using alginate versus skin-safe platinum silicone
- The safety risks
- The materials needed
- Making gypsum positives
- Mixing ratios and determining material amounts
- The various methods and the overall process of creating a lifecast for special makeup effects

CHAPTER 4

Sculpting the Makeup

Key Points

- Materials
- Preparation
- Sculpting tools: Making your own
- Types of clay
- Sculpting: Blocking, refining, and finishing

INTRODUCTION

By now you should be more than ready to get some clay under your fingernails. However, before any sculpting for a prosthetic appliance can begin, the positive that you'll be sculpting on must be properly cleaned up and prepared, and you will need to have your tools and other materials ready so that you can work without interruption and not continually be looking for something you need. Having a prepared workspace with everything you need in plain sight and within reach will maximize your efficiency. I can't do anything without music playing in the background, so there's that to consider too.

MATERIALS

You might not need everything listed here—you may want more, but these are all commonly used in this chapter's procedures:

Chavant Le Beau Touché, NSP or Monster Clay

Rotating sculpture stand

Ultracal or resin positive

- Misc. sculpting tools: wood and metal
- Freeman sheet wax
- Misc chip brushes
- Misc. small brushes
- Plastic wire brush
- Cat or dog hair brush
- Plastic toothpicks
- Lighter fluid, mineral spirits, Naphtha, 99% IPA or WD-40™
- Toothbrush
- Baby powder
- Reference photos
- Serrated scraper
- Heavy plastic sheet

Thomas Floutz

Thom's passion for makeup effects started when he was young. It was the images of an American GI in a Japanese bathhouse who had an eye that opened in the middle of his back and then grew into a second head. Thom was never the same after seeing that. "I knew this was what I wanted to do with my life. I wanted to grow extra body parts on myself," reflects this Oscar-nominated makeup effects wizard.

FIGURE 4.1
Thom working on actor Doug Jones.

"And I knew that the way to do this was to mix the right chemical potions and drink them. Part of the reason that this made sense to me at the time was that my dad was a chemist. But more than that, it was just my impressionable kid brain seeing the obvious solution as it started to be shaped." Years later Thom found out that the film that pushed him over the edge was called *The Manster*. "I watched it again recently and it doesn't hold up… but no matter, it did what it was supposed to do. It helped guide me to this path that I've been on professionally for the last 25 years, and also to find an easier way to make the transformations."

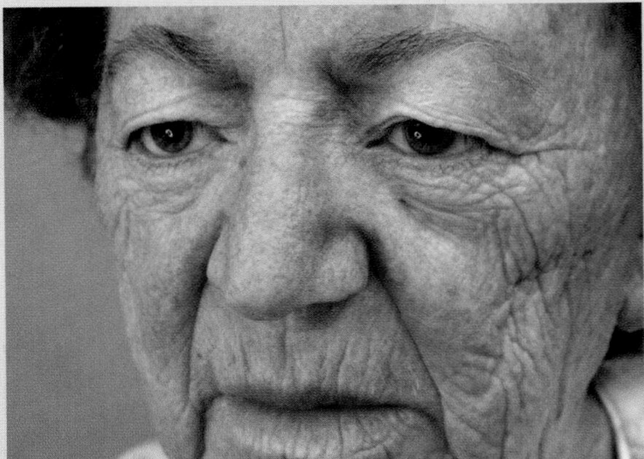

FIGURE 4.2
Marre Sculpt and paint by Thom Floutz; Hair by Nicole Michaud; Seaming by Chris Walker; Eyes by Michael S. Pack.
Image reproduced by permission of Thom Floutz.

Thom's credits include *Hellboy II: The Golden Army*, *Breaking Bad*, *X-Men: First Class*, *Nip/Tuck*, *Grey's Anatomy*, *Private Practice*, and *Sucker Punch*.

FIGURE 4.3
Sculpt by Brian Wade for Firefall game display by Steve Wang's Biomorphs, Inc.; paint by Thom Floutz.
Photo by the author.

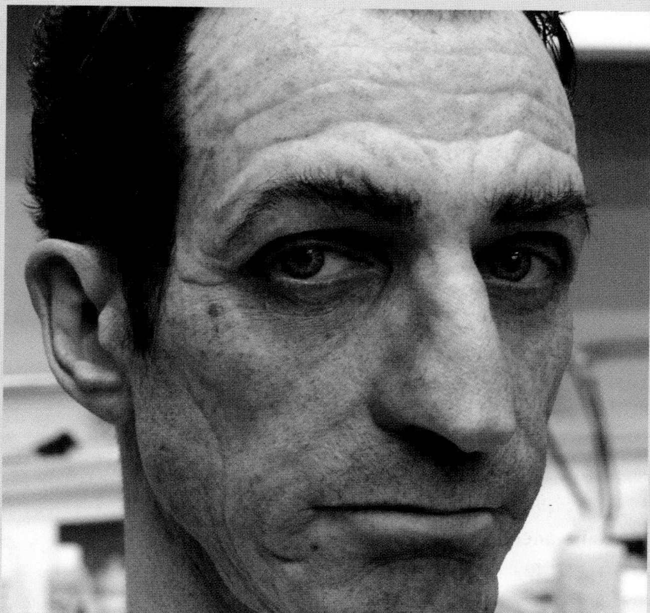

FIGURE 4.4
Butcher makeup applied by Thom Floutz on Doug Jones.
Image reproduced by permission of Thom Floutz.

PREPARING THE POSITIVE

Putting that first piece of clay onto a gypsum lifecast to create something new is a great feeling. But first, there is a bit of cast preparation to do. I will presume that your lifecast positive has been cleaned up—minor imperfections repaired and edges smoothed and rid of any roughness. Often it is necessary to brush a very light layer of petroleum jelly over the surface of your stone positive, then rub it into the surface; this will help the oil clay adhere to it. Make sure that there is no dust left over from your cleanup of the positive before you apply the petroleum jelly. If there is, wipe the cast with a damp cloth or paper towel to remove dust or tiny pieces of Ultracal that might mix with the petroleum jelly and make a gritty or otherwise yucky surface.

TOOLS

There is no set number or type of tools to use for sculpting your makeup. That, I imagine, is pretty obvious. What might not be obvious are the tools themselves. They could be expensive store-bought tools; they might be homemade

FIGURE 4.5
Creature designer Jordu Schell working on Stonehenge Demon; IMATS London, 2008.
Photo by the author.

jobs or even found objects. I'm sure Jordu Schell and Thom Flouts have sculpted entire heads with nothing more than a Popsicle stick. In fact, I've watched Jordu create a creature sculpture from start to finish in less than a full day, and it was amazing! But Jordu is Jordu.

If you're interested in some DIY sculpting tools, they're very easy to make and inexpensive. Go to your favorite hobby store and pick up some 1/8-inch (3 millimeters) or 3/16-inch (4 millimeters) brass tubing (or steel or aluminum) and some 1/32-inch (1 millimeters) wire; then swing by Guitar Center or Musician's Friend and buy an inexpensive set of heavy guitar strings—they can be acoustic or electric, but they must be steel strings. One last stop at Ace, True Value, Lowe's, or The Home Depot for scroll-saw or small band-saw replacement blades.

You will also need a few tools to help you make your new sculpting tools:

Soldering torch
Solder
Pliers
Wire snips
Dremel with a cutting wheel
Bending pliers
Crimping pliers

1. Cut the tubing into 4½- or 5-inch (11.5–12.5 centimeters) lengths with the Dremel®.
2. For a rough loop, cut a length of the low E string (the fattest wound string) about 2½ inch (6.35 centimeters) long and bend it into a triangular shape. Cut another of the same length and bend it into a U shape.
3. Fit both ends of one piece of the bent wire into one end of the 3/16-inch (5 millimeters) tube and make sure it is in as far as you want it; you do not want it to be so far out that you will risk bending and breaking it off at the tubing when working with it later. Crimp the tubing shut around the guitar string with your pliers and solder it in place. This will also add strength at the join point. Repeat for the other end with the other piece of E string.
4. For other loop tools, use the 1/8-inch (3 millimeters) tubing and the other guitar strings, repeat the process in Steps 1–3. Create whatever shapes you need for carving, blending, and shaping.
5. To create a rake tool using the saw blade, you will need to heat the blade with your soldering torch so that the blade will not snap as you bend it. Bend the blade *slowly* (so that it won't snap) into the curve you want. Then, cut it with the wire snips or the Dremel. I shouldn't have to remind you to wear safety glasses when you're using the Dremel, but I will anyway. Wear safety glasses!

6. Stick the ends of the bent blade into the tubing, crimp, and solder. You might need to file down some of the blade's teeth to fit into the tube end if the blade is too big. You can do that with your Dremel.
7. Another tool that could come in handy is what I call a wrinkle rake. It consists of several pieces of guitar string stuck into the ends of a 1/8-inch (3 millimeters) piece of tubing, crimped, and soldered. This is a terrific tool for creating lip wrinkles, eye wrinkles, and a number of various creases and wrinkles on the skin.

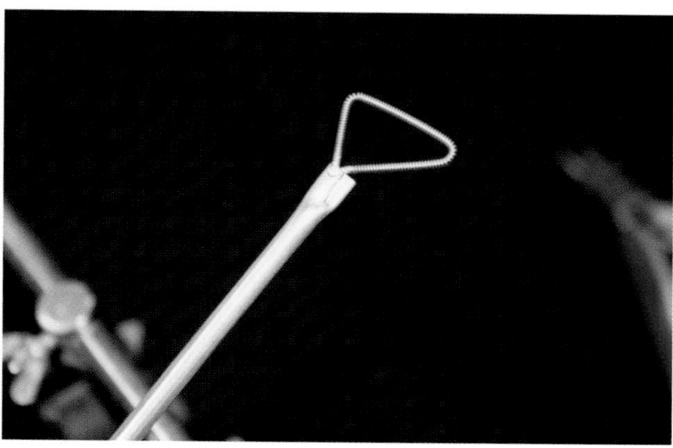

FIGURE 4.6
Homemade sculpting tools: brass tubing and guitar string.
Photo by the author.

If you are less inclined to make your own tools or want to supplement your own handiwork with other tools, Ken Banks sells a variety of terrific loops, rakes, and so on, which will last you a lifetime, at http//www.kenstools.com/. They are outstanding.

The most common tools you will use for your sculpture are rakes, wires (loops), steels (scrapers), and hoggers. Rakes are serrated tools used for removing clay efficiently. Wires or loops are useful for intricate detail work and they don't need much pressure to remove clay from the sculpture. Steels or scrapers are used to smooth out the sketched-in clay that has been raked. Some steels also have serrated edges and can be used as rakes to blend bits of clay, removing unwanted highs and lows on the clay surface. Hoggers are essentially large wire tools—more blade than wire—used for removing large hunks of clay. I use them mainly for scraping chunks of clay off the supply block to add to the sculpture.

Clay

I've already mentioned that I think it's a good idea to get into the habit of never using clay with sulfur in it, whether you're using silicone for your appliances or not, for the simple fact that sulfur will inhibit the cure of just about every type of silicone.

SULFUR CLAY: FORGET IT

If you are intending to cast silicone appliances for your makeup… well, anything that has come into contact with the sulfur-infused clay may prevent your silicone from curing. I've heard rumors that it's not even a good idea to say the word *sulfur* around uncured silicone! I hope I haven't upset the sulfur clay aficionados out there, but facts are facts, and sulfur and (uncured) silicone just do not play well together. There are new products available that make inhibition problems less common (I'll talk about them later), but for now let's continue to follow the guideline that removes any clay with sulfur in it from your inventory.

So why do manufacturers put sulfur in clay at all if it is so bad for curing silicone? According to Chavant, maker of Professional Plastiline, NSP, Le Beau Touché, and Da Vinci Italian Plastilina, sulfur is used in some of its clays because it is an inexpensive nontoxic filler that enhances the surface texture of the clay, giving it a unique, silky feel. Arnold Goldman of Monster Makers in Ohio (USA) has a sulfur-free wax clay that is outstanding; it has a low melt temperature and a very low tack feel that won't stick to your tools or fingers when sculpting. It is also less dense than most other oil clays, delivering about 25% more clay per pound, and is called Monster Clay.

WED CLAY

Perhaps you're a water clay lover and want to use WED (which stands for Walter Elias Disney) clay or other water-based clay for your sculpting. Admittedly, it is easier to work with if you are just starting out. Just beware of the pros and cons before starting so that you don't wind up screaming bloody murder when your clay dries out and cracks into chunks or is so wet it resembles a California mudslide. Lightly spritzing your clay with a bit of water from a small spray bottle or using a mixture of water and glycerin will keep your clay nice and workable.

An advantage of water clay over oil clay is its ability to take texture stamps more easily with less pressure. You do need to be careful not to press so hard that you alter the shape of your sculpture when you press the stamp into the clay. If the clay is too wet, the stamp will simply make a smear; just when your clay starts to begin to feel leathery is a great time for carving and shaping your design and for using texture stamps. Water clay is also very easy to work with quickly because it is so soft. A design can be roughed out in a relatively short amount of time. If you are relatively new to sculpting, I suggest you practice with WED clay or other water clay because it is easy to work with. Try roughing up some anatomy studies in WED before moving on to the harder, more difficult to work with oil clay.

OIL CLAY

Chavant Le Beau Touché is the oil clay I prefer to use; it is a popular clay among many makeup effects artists, including Mark Alfrey and Neill Gorton, although I also like Chavant NSP Medium. It's a firm clay, but it is easily warmed for malleability and takes texture stamps fairly easily without damaging the sculpt by pressing firmly into the clay surface. Oil clay can also be melted and poured or brushed, but I'll talk more about that later. Artists use other clays; a list of materials is included in Appendix A. Le Beau Touché is not the firmest clay to work with; NSP may be the firmest you will want to work with unless you are also involved in sculpting prototypes and models for props: armor, weapons, and so on. For that kind of work, I suggest a material called Casteline, a wax-based clay that is very hard (some also say that it is very difficult to work with); it is available at The Compleat Sculptor (see Appendix C for contact information). Ralph Cordero's TMS Studio Wax is used extensively by sculptors in the collectibles market. There are also numerous industrial design clays that are very hard and are ideal for carving, shaping, and styling extremely detailed models; some are even de-aired; entrapped air is removed, making the clay more dense, smoother, and great for achieving fine extrusions. Like the oil clays used by makeup effects designers, some of these clays can also be melted and poured or brushed into molds. Chavant makes very lightweight, hard sulfur-free clay called Y2-Klay that is outstanding for sculpting extremely fine detail. I have begun using Monster Makers' Monster Clay almost exclusively since its introduction. There are a number of prominent artists who are also using it.

Reference Photos

Trying to sculpt from memory alone is difficult at best, and practically impossible if your skill level is below "expert." Maybe your ego won't let you "cheat" by looking at photos that represent portions of what you are going to create, but I don't know an artist worth his or her salt who doesn't maintain a "morgue" filled to overflowing with images of all sorts—eyes, ears, noses, lips, hands, teeth, wrinkles, scars, scabs, pimples, cleft chins, turkey necks, age spots, pores, moles, and so on. You name it. In the digital age, I suppose those magazine pages are supplemented with Googled pictures downloaded from the Internet. "Ask and ye shall receive!" It all depends on what you need to augment your memory and make your design interesting and appropriate for the character.

If you have a digital camera, you might even want to go out on your own in search of interesting faces and bodies to add to your reference library, if you aren't already doing just that. Be sure to be polite when asking if you can take someone's photograph; don't approach someone with a wonderfully weathered face full of character and say, "Ma'am, I've never seen wrinkles like that except on an elephant!" and expect to get a favorable response. But to be on the safe side, have a supply of photo releases at the ready, or snap unobtrusively and discretely from afar with a telephoto lens if your people skills need work. But as a makeup effects artist, I certainly hope that isn't the case!

TEETH

If teeth are going to be a part of your character makeup, they need to be completed first, before a lifecast is done of your actor's face. If the teeth are not done before the lifecast is taken and if they aren't worn when the lifecast is made, the makeup will not fit correctly when the teeth are put in, because the face will then deform and cause the makeup to buckle or wrinkle improperly. Completing the teeth first is a priority.

Materials

Dental articulator	Petroleum jelly
Small sculpting tools	Mineral spirits
Small fine brush	Al-Cote dental separator
Dental wax	Dental waxer/Wax pen

NOTE

You may want to invest in a wax pen, an electric wax carver with precise temperature control settings and interchangeable tips for delicate work or for fast wax removal or carving harder waxes.

Take the upper and lower teeth positives you made in Chapter 3 and rub on or lightly brush a little petroleum jelly to help the clay stick to the stone. For this, I'll use Chavant Le Beau Touché sulfur-free oil-based clay.

1. Place bits of tooth-shaped clay over each tooth on the positive; keep the thickness close to the thickness and shape you want the finished teeth to be. Keep in mind that your actor probably won't want to have to take speech lessons to learn to speak all over again when wearing these new choppers!
2. Anchor the clay to the positive with a sculpting tool and remember to anchor the underside too.
3. Start creating the gum line with small sausages of clay and smooth the clay with one of your tools. We're still roughing everything in at this point.
4. Next, start defining the tooth root structure. You can even begin to do some preliminary smoothing with a small brush dipped in a very small amount of mineral spirits, WD-40, or lighter fluid to soften the clay.
5. To maintain strength in the new teeth, you might want to mark a piece of wire to show a depth of 1 millimeter; if your tooth sculpt is less than that, you risk breakage of the finished piece anywhere the thickness is less than 1 millimeter.
6. Periodically check the bite with the uppers and lowers to ensure that your actor's mouth will close correctly. The proper dental term for this is *occlusion*.
7. If you're doing lower teeth as well as uppers, your job will be doubly difficult because you want to create dentures that will be strong, will allow your actor to speak or sing, *and* will maintain normal occlusion.
8. When you've finished sculpting the new dentures, you are ready to mold and cast them, which will be covered in Chapters 5 and 6.

NOTE

To ensure correct occlusion, mount upper and lower casts to dental articulator using dental stone or plaster.

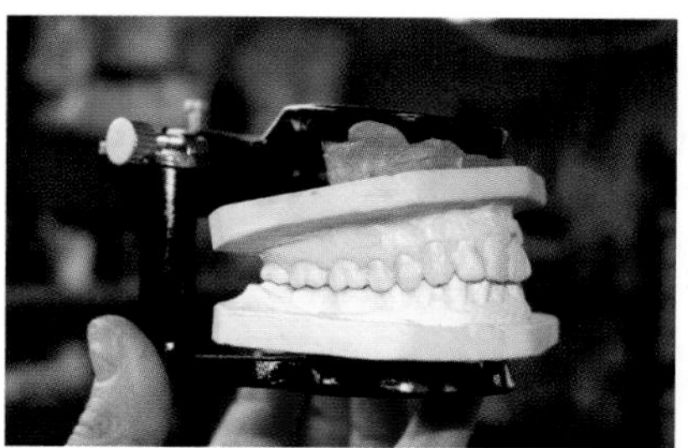

FIGURE 4.7
Teeth impressions mounted to dental articulator.
Photo by the author.

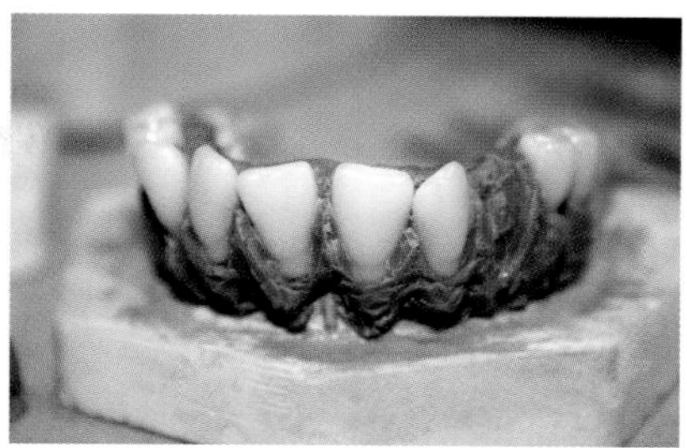

FIGURE 4.8
New dentures being sculpted with acrylic teeth and Monster Clay.
Photo by the author.

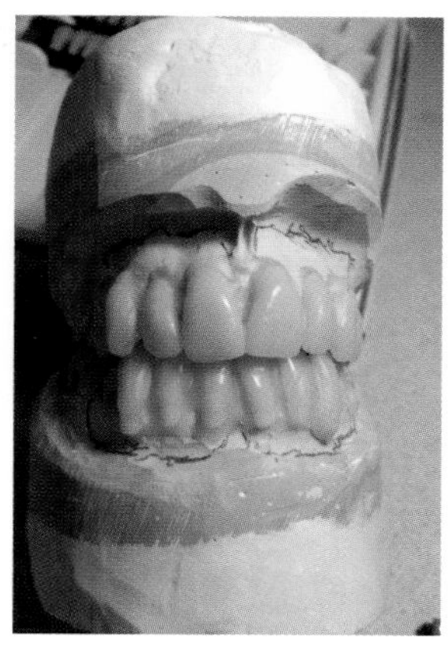

FIGURE 4.9
Beginning new denture sculpt on stone impression with wax and acrylic teeth.
Image reproduced by permission of Darren Grassby.

SCULPTING THE FACE

I don't draw nearly as much as I ought to and as a consequence my skills aren't nearly as good as I would like them to be—or as good as I think they *should* be. That's partly to do with being an artist; I don't think I ever believe my work is as good as it could be, but it's also partly because I'm not very good at saying no and there's always a lot on my plate. Anyway, the point I'm trying to make is that rather than work from sketches of a particular makeup design, as many artists do, I prefer to take what I see in my head and begin directly with sculpture. Whether you work from sketches, photos, 3D renderings from ZBrush or images printed from your mind's eye, the process is essentially the same. There's no right or wrong way to sculpt a character makeup, but there are some steps and tips I will share that I have learned over the years, some from artists who have contributed a great deal to this book. I will add this, however: I do not know anyone who works without reference of some kind, without at least one very good image as they work.

Kazuhiro Tsuji

FIGURE 4.10
Kazu and portrait of Dick Smith.
Image reproduced by permission of Kazuhiro Tsuji.

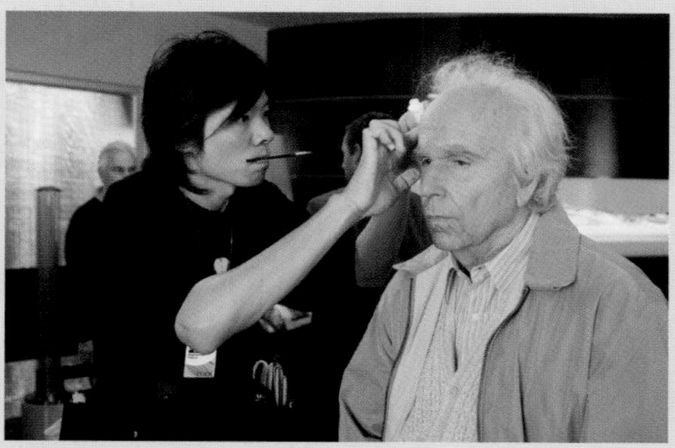

FIGURE 4.11
Kazu and Henry Winkler for *Click*.
Image reproduced by permission of Kazuhiro Tsuji.

FIGURE 4.12
Kazu's Abraham Lincoln on Chris Walker; wig by Sylvia Nava; beard by Justin Stafford.
Image reproduced by permission of Kazuhiro Tsuji.

Kazu, as he is known to friends and acquaintances, is an artist's artist. Born in Kyoto, Japan, Kazu has been interested in art, movies, science, and technology since his childhood. During high school, he focused his career aspirations on special makeup and became a student of Dick Smith's Advanced Makeup Course. Dick saw in Kazu what all of us working in the industry have come to know: This man has a gift.

In 1996, Kazu was sponsored by Rick Baker to work on *Men in Black*. This began the longstanding relationship between Kazu (as project supervisor and makeup artist) and Rick that has lasted ever since. Projects include *Batman & Robin*, *The Devil's Advocate*, *Mighty Joe Young*, *Life*, *Wild Wild West*, *Nutty Professor II*, *How the Grinch Stole Christmas*, *Planet of the Apes*, *Men in Black II*, *The Ring*, *The Haunted Mansion*, *Hellboy*, *The Ring Two*, *Click*, and *Norbit*. Baker won the Oscar for *Men in Black* and *How the Grinch Stole Christmas*, and Kazu was a key in helping create those makeups. Kazu also won a BAFTA award for *How the Grinch Stole Christmas* and was nominated for *Planet of the Apes*. He won the Hollywood makeup artist and hair stylist Guild Awards for *Planet of the Apes* and *How the Grinch Stole Christmas*. He received Oscar nominations for *Click* and *Norbit*.

If you are going to be creating a multipiece, overlapping makeup, you need to coat your stone positive with two or three thin layers of Al-Cote® dental separator (and let it dry) before you begin to sculpt. Why? Because once you've decided how the sculpture will be broken up, you need to be able to get those pieces separated from the positive and from each other without destroying them. To do that, your finished sculpt will need to be soaked in water to float off the clay pieces so that they can be resculpted. Don't fret; this task will be covered in Chapter 5. This design is a one-piece face and neck, with a separate lip piece and ears.

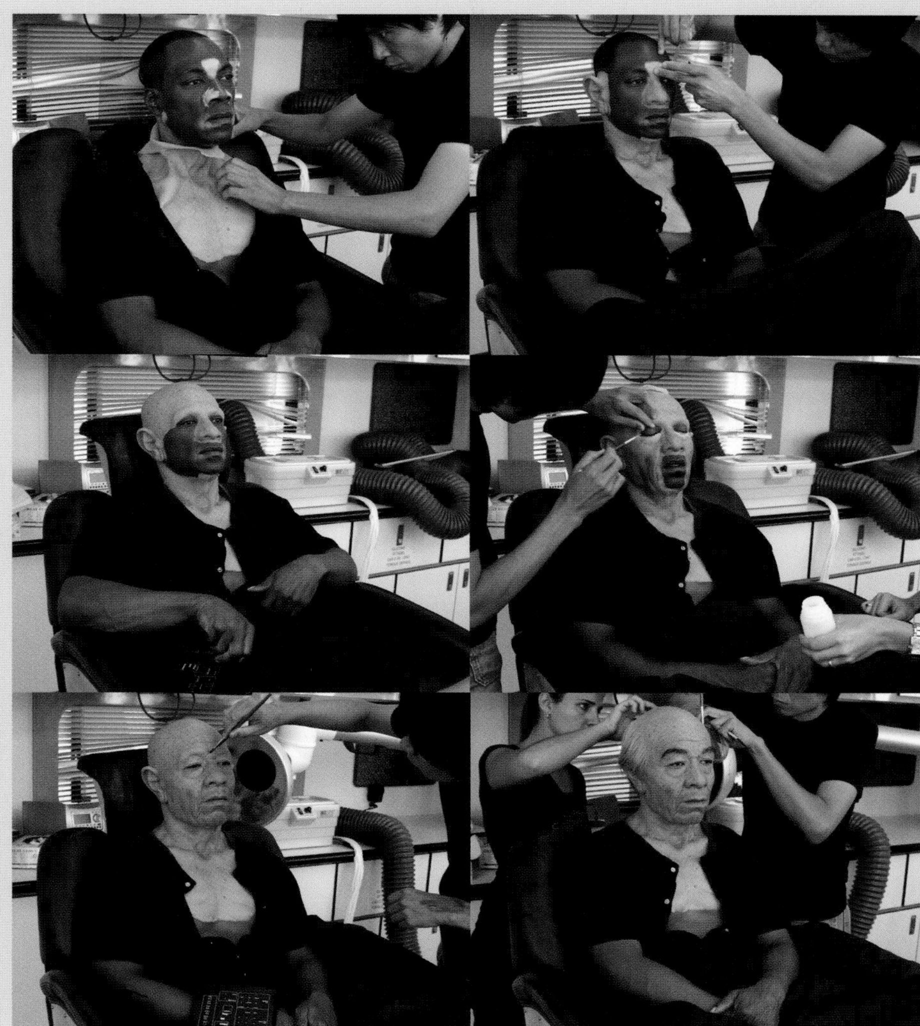

FIGURE 4.13
Makeup progression, Eddie Murphy; *Norbit*
Image reproduced by permission of Kazuhiro Tsuji.

Blocking the Sculpture

Follow these steps:

1. Place the positive of your actor's face, also known as a *buck*, upright on the sculpture stand so that it will be easy for you to work with. Take a good look at the cast and become familiar with the face.

This is the blocking stage, the roughing stage. Neill Gorton suggests simply picking out features and details that you want to translate from the lifecast

FIGURE 4.14
Lifecast ready for sculpting.
Photo by the author.

FIGURE 4.15
Rough Joker sculpt showing how six pieces (plus wig) will work together.
Image reproduced by permission of Frank Iippolito.

to the sculpture. Take a pencil and lightly, loosely draw lines on the face that correspond to lines on the cast to make them more obvious for when you begin to place clay on the cast. If you sculpt lines that are counter to where the face will actually move and bend, creases in the face will not move and deform correctly and it will look wrong. It will *be* wrong.

This is an ideal time for your knowledge of facial anatomy to kick in. Remember that skin develops creases and wrinkles that are perpendicular to the direction that the underlying muscle pulls. I think it's a good idea to have a small makeup mirror nearby when you're working, so you can use your own face for additional reference. Take a moment now and look in the mirror; make an exaggerated, forced smile and notice the way wrinkles and creases appear on your face against the pull of your facial muscles. If the makeup you've decided to sculpt is of an older character, you can incorporate the way the skin will begin to sag and hold wrinkles and creases because there is less elasticity in the skin.

2. Begin to place bits of clay on the cast where you've drawn lines. This is the roughing-in stage of the sculpture and can be done with just clay and your fingers. You might find it useful, if not absolutely necessary, to have at least one reference photo visible near your sculpture, with features similar to what you are trying to recreate on your actor's cast. You might even have several reference images to work from. Try not to have so many that you stop using your instinct, your own vision, for the sculpture. There are so many different ways skin can bend and simply be that your inspiration can become blurred and unfocused. Find one representative inspirational image if you can and look at others only when you get stuck for a particular shape, wrinkle, crease, or fold.
3. You might want to use a small tool or two to help press the bits of clay together, but continue to place bits and pieces of clay—Neill rolls out small pieces, "sausages" of clay, he aptly calls them—along the natural lines and folds of the face where the pencil lines have been drawn, along the forehead, the cheekbone, and so on. This is a very early stage of sculpting, you're blocking it, and it will begin to take a coherent shape bit by bit, piece by piece. At this stage, you can work fairly quickly because you are merely blocking out the shape, creating an overall impression of what it will eventually become.

4. At this point, there should be clay over most of the face, and you can use one of your wooden shaping tools to begin sketching lines in the clay where eventually you will place details in the skin: finer lines and wrinkles. Here is where, once you've built up clay on the face to create new features—the nose, cheeks, brow, and eyelids—you can begin to blend the pieces of clay together into more of a whole. You've placed the face cast on a stand that you can rotate. It is important to be able to rotate your sculpture easily so that it can be seen from different angles quickly (even upside down) to ensure relative symmetry on both sides of the face.
5. Take one of your wooden tools and begin a light crosshatch over the chunks of clay that you placed with your hands; you will "rake" the surface with the wooden tool and start to smooth and blend rough areas into more of a whole. You don't necessarily want to redefine what you've already done, but to refine the rough spots, to unify your sculpt. Sculpture is about working from the outside in—creating rough shapes, then making them more and more detailed in stages until you ultimately have a finished sculpt that is ready to be molded and cast in an appliance material.
6. Continue adding clay and blending it until your entire sculpture is blocked, until all the main features and shapes have been created and clay is everywhere that it needs to be. When the sculpture is roughed in completely, you can begin to refine it further.

Refining the Sculpture

It can't be emphasized enough that the process of sculpting prosthetics demands that the sculpture be defined by the face underneath. Someone, an actor, must wear it and emote through it.

A certain amount of the work—the *art* of sculpting prosthetics—is a *feel* when something is or isn't right and that can only come about through practice—through the act of sculpting. A *lot* of sculpting. It should not be forced.

1. Since we are beginning to refine the sculpture, you need to refine your tool selection, choosing tools that will allow you to create finer nuances in the sculpt. You might want to try a medium rake tool or loop tool to go over the surface, creating areas of slightly more definition.
2. After you've gone over the sculpture to some degree, take the plastic wire brush (plastic bristles) and lightly brush over the surface where you've been working with the rake and loop tools. Essentially what you are doing is removing tool marks left by the loop and rake. Repeat Steps 7 and 8; carve in some detail, then brush over it to remove tool marks. Create lines, but remove bumps and lumps and unwanted tool marks. The plastic bristle brush will likely leave bits of clay on the surface of the sculpt as you brush; you can get rid of these by lightly whisking them away with a chip brush.

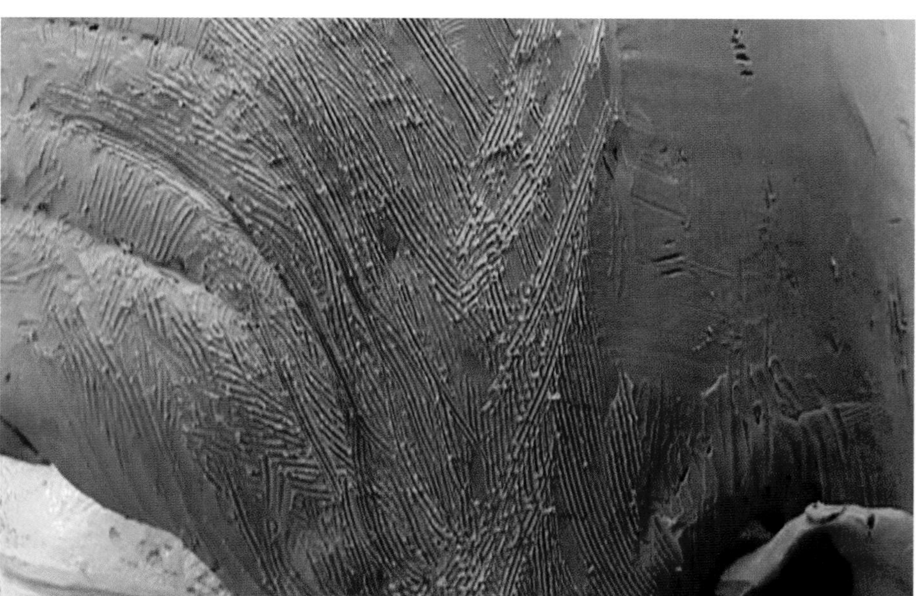

FIGURE 4.16
Refining the sculpture with a medium rake tool.
Image reproduced by permission of Neill Gorton.

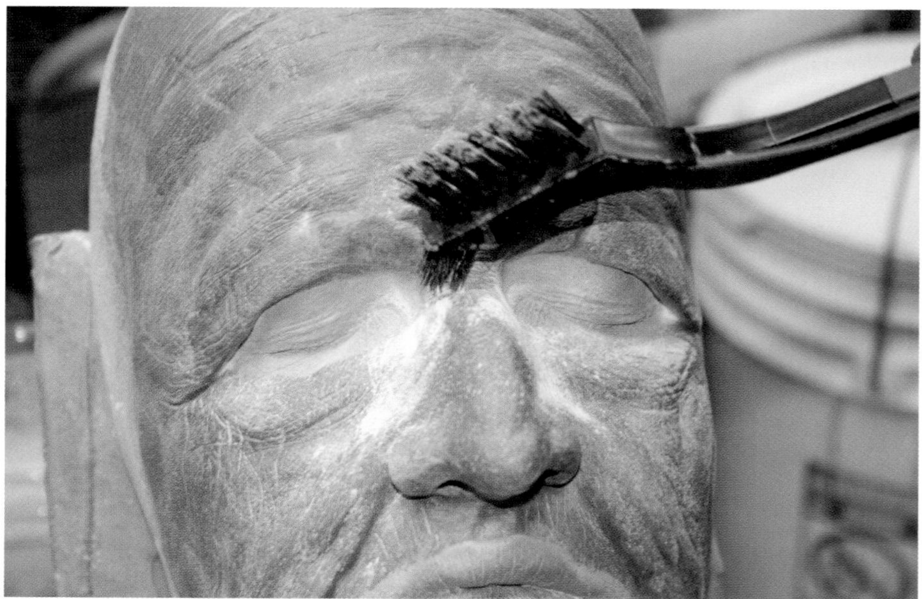

FIGURE 4.17
A plastic bristle brush can be used to soften harsh lines created by a pet brush raked across the clay.
Photo by the author.

Skin texture is like skin coloration; it is multifaceted and multilayered. There is texture within texture. There is depth to the wrinkles. Some are sharp, some are soft, some are deep, and some are shallow. Skin wrinkles and creases are varied. Don't fall into a trap of making all the wrinkles and folds at the same depth or length. The more varied and nonuniform the wrinkles, the better they appear. At this stage of the sculpture, you're still using the equivalent of medium-grit sandpaper.

3. Pour some of the solvent into a cup and, with a chip brush, brush over the surface of your sculpture. The liquid will soften the clay; break down the surface to smooth out any blemishes. You will probably want to use a smaller-detail brush to get into tighter areas of detail on the sculpture because the partially dissolved clay becomes slurry and the chip brush could be too large to effectively get into the tighter spots and brush it out.
4. Some of the detail you created will likely soften too much with this step, so you will need to go in with one of your small loop tools and recarve that detail, then brush over it with a soft brush to take some of the hardness of the crease away.
5. Brushing lighter fluid or other softening liquid onto your clay will keep the clay soft for several hours, most likely, until all the solvent has evaporated. It might be advisable to let the sculpture sit overnight to ensure that the surface will be hard enough to work with again and not be too soft and sticky.
6. When you come back to it, brush talcum powder or baby powder over the entire sculpture where you had brushed the solvent to soften the clay. Why? Because now you're going to use the pet brush on the clay. Notice as you run the brush across the clay that it creates and leaves behind lots of tiny beads of clay that the wires of the brush have scraped up.

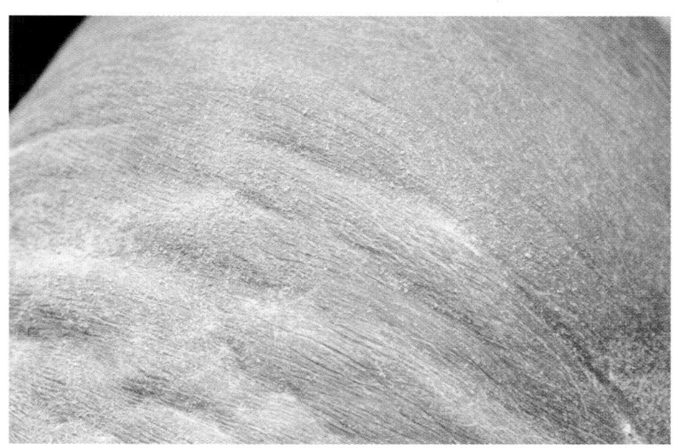

FIGURE 4.18
Powder causes clay to bead up when raked with a stiff brush instead of being smeared across the sculpture.
Photo by the author.

If the surface doesn't have powder on it, all the tiny lumps of clay will stick to the sculpture and be nearly impossible to remove. When the clay has been powdered first, you can take one of your chip brushes and whisk them away. I've even used pieces of stipple sponge to knock away these bits of clay. The powder also acts as a very mild abrasive that will allow you to take a chip brush that's been cut down, making it a bit stiffer, and brush back over the lines created by the pet brush to soften them.

7. Some of the lines created by the pet brush might be a little too harsh, so you can go over those with the plastic bristle brush or a toothbrush and continue to refine and increase your detail in the sculpture, underlying texture. You should really be able to see the texture upon texture I mentioned after Step 2. You'll be adding pore texture shortly.

The texture of human skin varies across the face. The skin of your forehead is different, thinner, than the skin on your cheeks, which is different from the skin on your nose or your neck. This is why studying surface anatomy is very important to us as artists; we must work from a foundation of reality to create a realistic, albeit often stylized believability, in our makeup design and sculpture.

8. You can repeat Steps 6 and 7 over and over again, even using a very small amount of solvent on the clay to brush out some detail and then create even more detail by carving with a tiny loop tool, powdering, and repeating the process again until the sculpture has the look and feel you are going for. Create fine lines, coarse lines, sharp lines, and soft lines and brush them each back in succession so that you have a skin texture with layers and layers of lines and wrinkles.

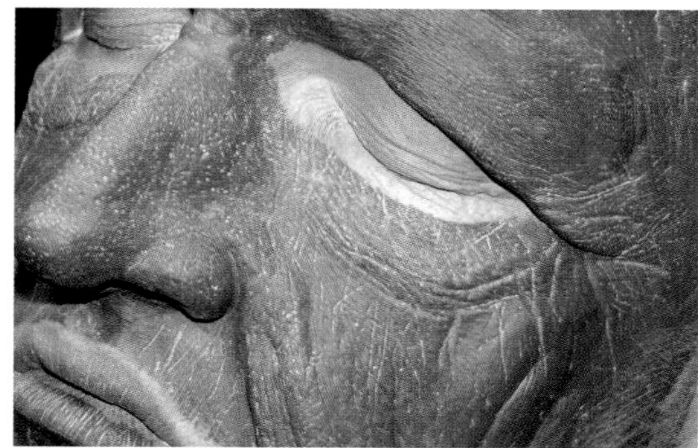

FIGURE 4.19
Layered wrinkle texture.
Photo by the author.

I can't tell you when your sculpture is complete; only you can know that. However, you should be getting pretty close, which would be time to add some pore texture. One way to add pores is with a texture stamp. Brushing several layers of latex over an orange peel until you have a fairly thick piece of rubber with bumps on it is frequently used as a texture stamp; its pattern is somewhat random, but in actuality, for skin pores, I think it's too uniform, and you need to do it by hand, without using texture stamps. By all means, experiment and make your own choice. There is no prescribed way to do this work; you must find methods that work for you and give you the results that you want, not what I or anyone else wants. Here I am merely presenting options and ways that I know work well.

Pores are not always uniformly round; some are deep and some are almost invisible. Pores on the face are often an oval shape. They are elliptical and elongated. They also follow the direction of the skin. The same goes for facial hair or whisker follicles. These pores will all be sculpted by hand, and there's no quick and easy way to do it except as carefully and as randomly as you can.

9. Pick one of your small tools, perhaps a small loop or a small burnishing tool, and begin making small indentations across the nose with the tip. Brush them back, softening them, then make some more. You can use a sharper tool, such as a toothpick, and poke it into your thick plastic that you've laid over the clay. Create varying depths of these pores. Then brush those pores back, making them softer. Repeat this process until you're satisfied, then move on to another part of the face, such as the cheeks.
10. Because the pores need to follow the direction in which the skin is hanging, the elongated pores need to be vertical and not horizontal. Try it if you like and I think you'll see that it just feels wrong. You might want to use a narrow tool such as a dental spatula poked into the plastic that

can give you a very thin pore. When you brush them with powder and a chip brush, brush in the direction of the skin and the pores, not across. If you need to add more lines, do it. At this point, you are creating almost the last bits of detail. Continue to add pores until you don't need to add any more. Gently brush away any imperfections with powder and a chip brush.

11. Make a small container of clay slip or slurry by mixing some thin clay scrapings and some of whatever solvent you've been using. With this very loose clay, you are going to create tiny bumps on the skin. In addition to lines and pores, there are small raised bits of skin. This step is not absolutely essential, but it adds to the overall texture of the sculpture and, under varying lighting conditions, if the skin only has recesses instead of ridges and bumps, it won't have the same effect or impact as if you take the time to add some tiny raised bumps on the skin, particularly around the chin and at the base of the neck.

The bumps will shrink as the solvent evaporates, and you might need to add more. The effect is well worth the time it takes to add this additional detail to your sculpture. Of course, how much of this you'll be able to do will be completely dependent on how far you are able to sculpt on the neck.

12. The last step before molding your sculpture will be to make certain all your edges are as fine as you can make them. Perhaps I should have mentioned this earlier, but I think it's a good idea to turn the sculpture upside down and look at it from underneath. This is a good way to see if there is anything wrong with your sculpture that hasn't been readily evident from looking at it normally, from above. Everything is probably fine, but better safe than sorry, right?

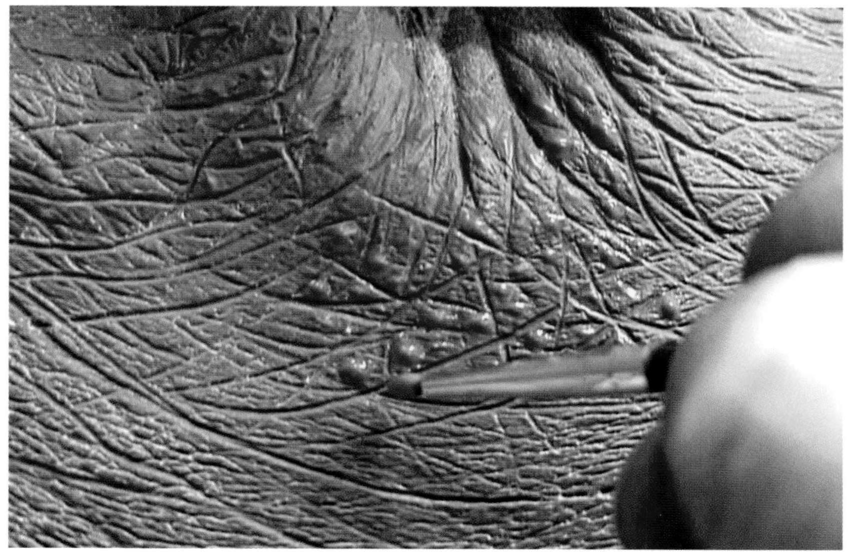

FIGURE 4.20
Bumps added with clay slurry—clay dissolved in mineral spirit or naphtha. *Image reproduced by permission of Neill Gorton.*

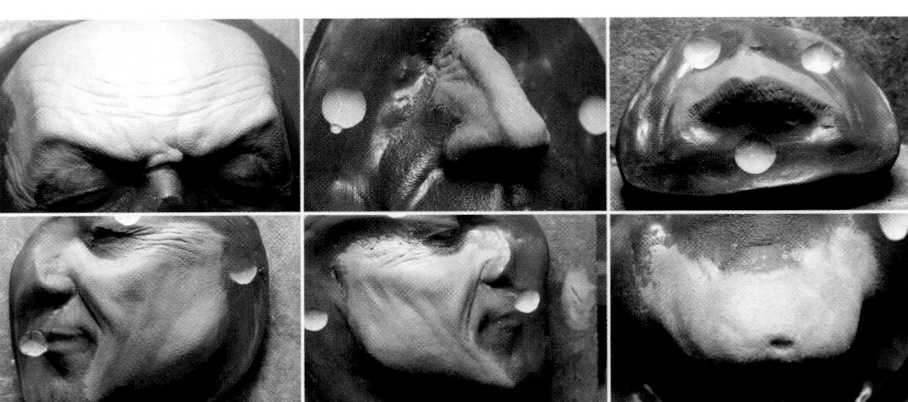

FIGURE 4.21
The Joker's upper lip, chin, left cheek, right cheek, nose, and forehead beginning to get texture.
Images reproduced by permission of Frank Ippolito.

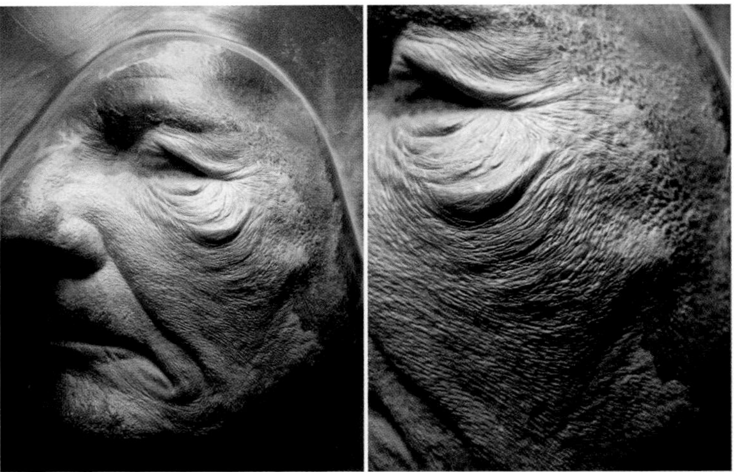

FIGURE 4.22
Super skin texture detail on appliance by Vincent Van Dyke.
Image reproduced by permission of Vincent Van Dyke.

Barring any unforeseen need to do any additional sculpting, you should be ready to make a mold of your face. That will be covered in Chapter 5.

SCULPTING THE FACE, HEAD, AND NECK

The process of sculpting a full head and neck differs from sculpting the face exactly the way you think it would differ: there's more to sculpt. However, there is a little bit of preparation of the lifecast prior to beginning the sculpture. It needs to be placed securely onto a disc that will allow the sculpture to be easily rotated and looked at from different angles.

Since this sculpture will involve the entire head and neck, not just the face, clay will need to be built up around the entire cast, with care taken to leave room for the ears and surrounding tissue of the head.

Steve Wang

One of the most respected makeup effects designers in the world, Steve's talents as a designer, sculptor, painter, and supervisor have been highly sought after for years. Steve is as popular with effects fans—if not more so—as his on-screen contemporaries are in today's hottest blockbusters.

Although Steve is mostly retired these days from working as a makeup effects artist, he is hardly resting on his laurels, and barely has a moment free. He is in constant demand. Perhaps best known for his work on the predator in *Predator*, Abe Sapien from *Hellboy*, Gill Man from *The Monster Squad*, and Marcus from *Underworld: Evolution*, Steve's skill as an artist is only getting better.

Born in Taiwan, Steve and his family moved to the United States when he was 9 years. He'd always been fascinated by masks, and shortly after arriving with his family, he discovered a passion for mask collecting and then mask making fueled by Halloween, which does not exist in Taiwan.

As a veteran makeup artist and creature designer, Steve has worked with fellow veterans before him including Stan Winston, Rick Baker, and Dick Smith.

He's received high praise for his two film adaptations of the manga superhero, Guyver (*The Guyver* and *Guyver: Dark Hero*). Steve and his brother write, produce, and direct as the "The Wang Brothers."

FIGURE 4.23
The author with Steve Wang.
Photo by Destiny McKeever. Photo reproduced by permission of the author and Steve Wang.

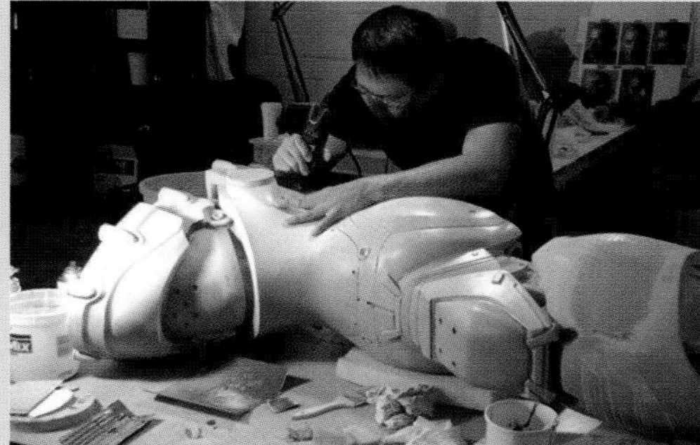

FIGURE 4.24
Steve cleaning up Jim Raynor; *Star Craft 2*
Image reproduced by permission of Steve Wang.

FIGURE 4.25
Steve working, Jim Raynor sculpt.
Image reproduced by permission of Steve Wang.

FIGURE 4.26
Yellow Firefall suit for *Red 5 Studios.*
Image reproduced by permission of Steve Wang.

BLOCKING THE SCULPTURE

Just as with the face and neck sculpture, you will rough in shapes and refine them in stages, bringing out detail a little at a time until the design has been completed.

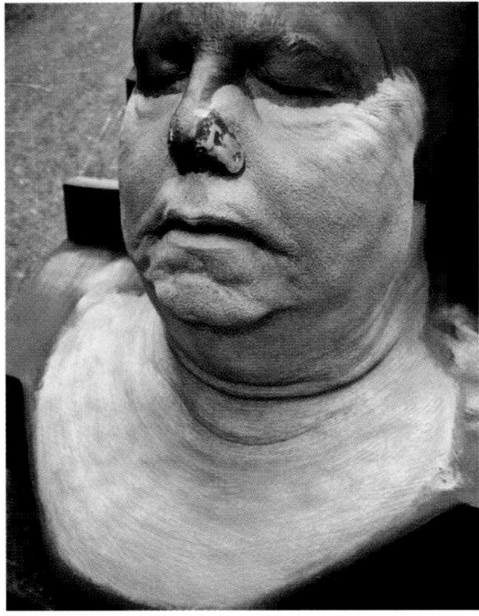

FIGURE 4.27
Grey's Anatomy sculpt by Vincent Van Dyke.
Image reproduced by permission of Vincent Van Dyke.

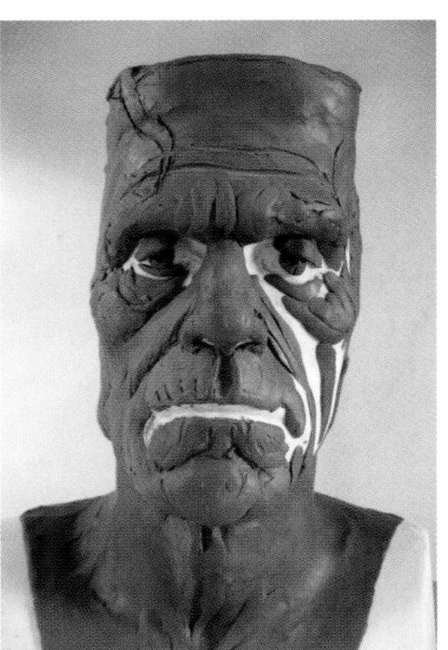

FIGURE 4.28
Roughing in Frankenstein's Monster sculpt.
Image reproduced by permission of Neill Gorton.

1. Loosely draw lines on the face with a pencil that correspond to facial lines on the cast to make them more obvious for when you begin to place clay on the cast, as you can see Neill Gorton doing in the accompanying photos.
2. Begin to place bits of clay on the cast where you've drawn enhancing lines. This is the roughing-in stage of the sculpture and can be done with just clay and your fingers.

Some of the areas of the face and head will be sculpted very thinly by necessity, meaning that there will be very little appliance material in some places. This is critical for the actor's performance because the thicker the appliance, the harder it will be for nuances of facial expression to translate through it and be perceptible to the audience. Never lose sight of the fact that everything we do is in support of the performance. It is never about the makeup; it is always about the performance.

Since this makeup will eventually cover the entire head, you want to make certain that there is a minimum thickness around the head to prevent overstretching of the appliance or buckling during application, which will create serious headaches. You might find it useful to create a depth gauge by marking a piece of heavy-gauge wire, the type used in some of your loop tools, at ⅛ inch, or about 3 millimeters. This uniform thickness around the entire head will also give the whole head a sense of uniformity.

3. Slice off some thin slabs of clay as close to ⅛ inch as you can and begin covering the cast all the way around, except for the face and ears.
4. Create some rough ear shapes that you can put on and take off simply as a point of reference and to make the head look a little more familiar.
5. Once you've covered the head with a uniform thickness, use a serrated scraper to blend the surface and then smooth it all out, tying all the pieces into one whole.
6. You might want to use a small tool or two to help press the bits of clay together, but continue to place bits and pieces of clay—those little "sausages" of clay—along the natural lines and folds of the face where you drew those pencil lines.

This is a still very early stage of sculpting, and it will start to take on the shape of your character. At this stage, you can work fairly quickly because you are still just blocking out the overall impression of what it will eventually look like.

FIGURE 4.29
Continuing to rough in facial shape.
Image reproduced by permission of Neill Gorton.

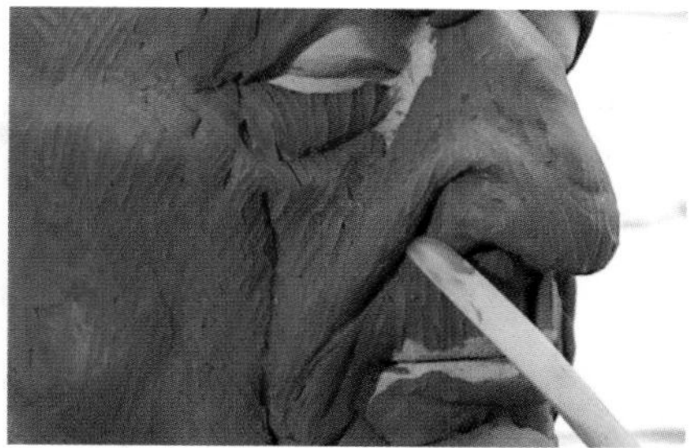

FIGURE 4.30
Refining the clay little by little.
Image reproduced by permission of Neill Gorton.

7. You can begin to use one of your wooden shaping tools to sketch lines in the clay where you will place details.
8. Take a tool and start a light crosshatch over the clay that you placed with your hands, rake the surface with the tool, and start to smooth and blend rough areas into more of a whole. You don't want to redefine what you've already done, just refine the rough spots.
9. Every so often, put the rough ears on if you need a different perspective. A head without ears looks a little odd.
10. Continue adding clay and blending it until all the main features and shapes have been created and clay is everywhere that it needs to be. When the sculpture is roughed in completely, you can begin to create the detail.
11. Since we are beginning to add minor detail to the sculpture, you need to refine your tool selection, picking tools that will allow you to create increasingly finer nuances in the sculpture. Try a medium rake tool or loop tool to go over the surface, creating areas of more definition.
12. After you've gone over the sculpture to some degree, take the plastic bristle brush and go over the surface where you've been working with the rake and loop tools. Essentially what you are doing is removing tool marks left by the loop and rake. Repeat Steps 11 and 12, carve in some detail, and then brush over it to remove tool marks. Create lines, but remove bumps and lumps and unwanted tool marks. The plastic bristle brush will likely leave bits of clay on the surface of the sculpture as you brush; you can get rid of these by lightly whisking them away with a chip brush and a little baby powder.
13. Lightly brush solvent over the surface of your sculpture so that you can smooth out any blemishes.
14. Some of the detail you created could likely soften too much or fill in with this step, so you might need to go in with one of your small loop tools and recarve some detail and then brush over it with a soft brush to take away some of the hardness of the crease.
15. You might want to let the sculpture sit overnight or have something else you can work on while you wait to ensure that the surface will be hard enough to work with again and not be too soft and sticky from the solvent.

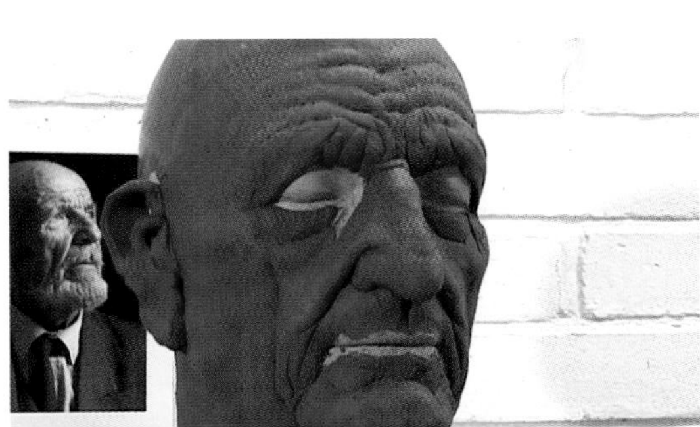

FIGURE 4.31
By placing ears roughly on the sculpture, you get a better overall feel for the sculpture.
Image reproduced by permission of Neill Gorton.

16. Make sure the clay is firm again when you come back to it and then brush talcum powder (baby powder) over the entire sculpture where you had brushed the solvent. Now you're going to use the pet brush on the clay. If the surface doesn't have powder on it, all the tiny bits of clay will stick to the sculpture.
17. Make a small container of clay slip or slurry by mixing some bits of clay scrapings and some of whatever solvent you've been using. With this very loose slip, you are going to create tiny bumps on the skin, just as you did on your face sculpture.

The effect is well worth the time it takes to add this additional detail to your sculpture. Anything worth doing is worth doing well, and it's the little things that will help your work stand out from others who won't make the extra effort.

FIGURE 4.32
Detail is added on top of detail for a sense of skin depth.
Image reproduced by permission of Neill Gorton.

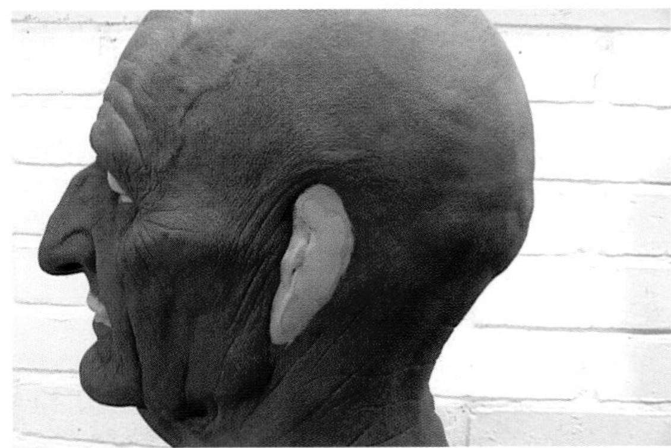

FIGURE 4.33
Neill's sculpture ready to be molded; cast in silicone.
Image reproduced by permission of Neill Gorton.

Make sure the edges of your sculpture are as thin as you can make them and clean off any excess clay from the sculpture. You should now be ready to make a mold of the sculpture so that you can cast your appliance.

SCULPTING HANDS

Up to this point, we've been sculpting for age prosthetics; everything that has been done in the previous sections can be adapted to suit any type of character sculpture. That is true of this section as well.

Blocking the Sculpture

Pull out some reference photos you have of old hands so that you won't be working from memory. You could find it necessary to only sculpt up clay on the backs of the hands and part way out onto the proximal phalanx, or first bone of each finger, including the thumb. What you don't create in clay to become an appliance you might be able to create with a wrinkle stipple technique I'll discuss in Chapter 10.

1. As with all sculpture, begin by placing small bits of clay onto the positive. You can work on both hands at the same time or one at a time; it's up to you. If the clay doesn't seem to want to stick to the Ultracal, you can try brushing a thin layer of petroleum jelly into the stone first (if your positives are stone); then, the clay should have a grab hold. This particular sculpt is on hands cast in fiberglass.
2. Loosely draw lines on the hand with a pencil that correspond to tendons and veins on the hand casts to make them more obvious for when you begin to place clay onto them.
3. Begin to place bits of clay on the cast where you've drawn enhancing lines. This is the roughing-in stage of the sculpture and can be done with just clay and your fingers.
4. You might want to use a small tool or two to help press the bits of clay together, but continue to place bits and pieces of clay—those little "sausages"—on the hands where you drew those pencil lines.
5. Continue adding clay and blending it until all the main features and shapes have been created and clay is everywhere that it needs to be. When the sculpture is roughed-in completely, you can begin to create the detail.
6. Refine your tool selection, picking tools that will allow you to create finer nuances in the sculpture. Try a medium rake tool or loop tool to go over the surface, creating areas of more definition.
7. Take the plastic bristle brush and go over the surface where you've been working with the rake and loop tools.
8. Create lines, but remove bumps and lumps and unwanted tool marks. The plastic bristle brush will likely leave bits of clay on the surface of the sculpture as you brush; you can get rid of these by lightly whisking them away with a cut-down chip brush and a little baby powder.
9. After you've applied solvent to soften the clay, use a smaller-detail brush to get into tighter areas of detail on the sculpture where clay slurry may have filled it in.
10. The clay will be soft for several hours until all the solvent has evaporated.
11. When the clay is firm again, brush powder over the entire sculpture where you had brushed solvent. Just as on the face and head, you're going to use the pet brush on the clay now. If the surface doesn't have powder on it, all the tiny bits of clay will stick to the sculpture and might be difficult to remove.

Make sure the edges of your sculpture are as thin as you can make them and clean up any excess clay on the sculpture. You should now be ready to make molds of your sculpture so that you can cast your hand appliances.

FIGURE 4.34
Clay is added gradually and continually refined until the correct shape has been reached.
Photo by the author.

FIGURE 4.35
Hand sculpts finished with flashing added; ready to make negative molds.
Photo by the author.

SCULPTING EARS

Ear appliances can be tricky, too, mainly because parts of them can often be quite thin. As we age, our ears get longer; a study by Dr. James Heathcote,[2] a general practitioner in the United Kingdom, concluded that our ears get bigger on average by 0.22 millimeters annually.

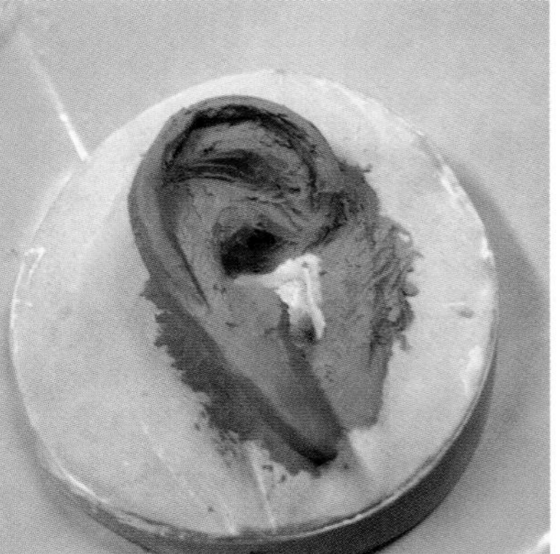

FIGURE 4.36
Ear appliances being roughed in. Natural undercuts have been minimized.
Photos by the author.

BLOCKING THE SCULPTURE

1. Take the ears you cast in Chapter 3 and begin placing small bits of clay onto them. Have your reference images handy so that you can sculpt from them. Remember that if the clay doesn't seem to want to stick to the Ultracal, you can try brushing a thin layer of petroleum jelly into the stone first; then the clay should want to grab hold.

2. Ear skin is very thin and is textured differently than skin elsewhere on the head, at least above the earlobes. For the most part, the skin covering the ears is smooth, including the earlobes. Begin by filling in the areas around the *triangular fossa, schaphoid fossa,* and *meatus* with clay to eliminate the undercuts and sculpt a new tip onto the helix.

You might find it easier to work on both ears simultaneously than one at a time; that way you can compare as you go.

3. Decide whether you're going to create ears with attached lobes or free lobes; in Chapter 2, I mentioned that most people have free lobes by a margin of nearly 2 to 1. Will your character have gauged lobes, that is, a large hole that objects can be stuck through? That could be interesting; so would the mold. Remember that every cool design has to be moldable, and I mean moldable in a time and cost-efficient way; otherwise, the design may not work.

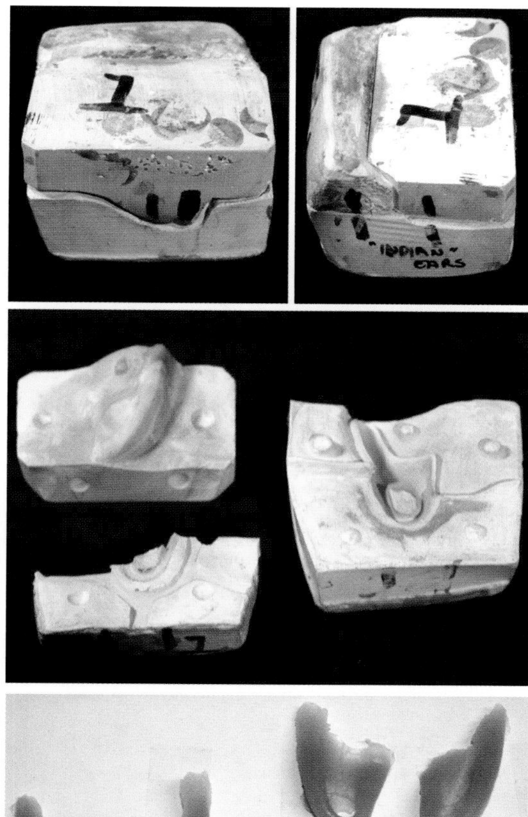

FIGURE 4.37
Multipiece molds by Matthew Mungle for *The Indian in the Cupboard* and gauged earlobe extensions cast in flocked silicone.
Photos by the author.

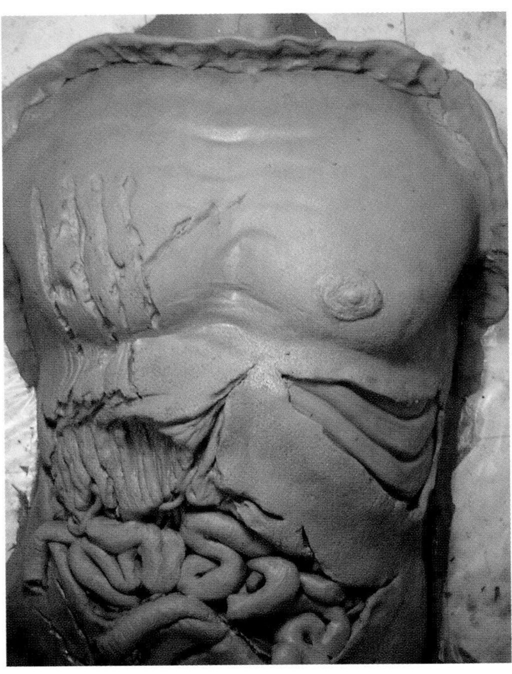

4. Once you have your new ear shape roughed in, you can begin to smooth the clay and blend the edges off to nothing. Use solvent to soften the clay, then smooth the clay with a soft brush. After the solvent has evaporated and the clay has hardened again, you will be able to carefully create the molds for the ears.

Don't forget that sculpting is sculpting, whether it's gauged earlobes for a period piece about the Mayan culture, a disemboweled torso for a zombie film, or an overlapping facial piece that will fit onto a companion cowl for a sci-fi epic. Take time to plan out what you need to do, what you're going to use for reference, how you're going to accomplish it all in the time you have, and so on.

FIGURE 4.38
FX torso in WED clay.
Image reproduced by permission of Darren Grassby and Ian Jowett.

FIGURE 4.39
Lizard face sculpt to overlap companion cowl piece.
Image reproduced by permission of Neill Gorton.

CHAPTER SUMMARY

Chapter 4 introduced you to methods for sculpting prosthetic appliances in sulfur free, oil-based clay, the purpose of WED clay, and useful sculpting tools, even how to make your own tools. You also learned how to prepare your finished prosthetic sculpture for molding, which will be covered in Chapter 5.

Endnotes

1 Can inhibit silicone.

2 Dr. James Heathcote, *British Medical Journal* (December 1995).

CHAPTER 5

Breakdown of the Sculpture

Key Points

- Tools and materials
- Releases and sealers
- Making the negative mold
- Keys, flashing, and cutting edge
- Types of molds

INTRODUCTION

Breaking down the sculpture is the process of determining the way a complex makeup must be separated for mold making and preparing it properly for the mold-making process. Not all makeup sculpture will need to be broken down, but molds will always have to be made, and this chapter is all about preparing the sculpture for mold making and then making the molds. There are different types of molds, each with its own design concerns. I forget who told me this, and I apologize for not attributing the quote, but "Good molds aren't *made*, they're *designed*."

Kevin Kirkpatrick

In 2004, Kevin enrolled in Tom Savini's Special Makeup Effects program at the Douglas Education Center near Pittsburgh, PA. It turned out to be a good decision. Upon graduation in 2006, Kevin got a call from Savini asking if he'd be interested in working on a project for 4 months in Cairo, Egypt. Kevin readily said yes and was soon on a plane bound for North Africa. Four months turned into 9, and Kevin returned to the States as a seasoned veteran of makeup effects.

"I learn a lot when I experiment with materials I have no idea how to use," said Kevin. "Of course it doesn't always work out, but a lot of times I stumble upon happy accidents. I believe that there is more than one way to make things work, and I enjoy trying to find that way." It's the thinking outside the box that keeps Kevin's wheels spinning.

In his relatively short time in Los Angeles, Kevin has joined SAG as a puppeteer and Local 706, the Union for Makeup Artists and Hairstylists. He's already worked alongside many of his heroes and has been able to travel to exciting places. Most important to Kevin has been being able to provide a better quality of life for his daughter who is his greatest inspiration. "I love what I do and I just want to keep making my dreams a reality each and every day."

Kevin's credits include *Sucker Punch, True Blood, The Wolfman, Pirates of the Caribbean: On Stranger Tides, Wonder Woman, The Lone Ranger*, and *Abraham Lincoln: Vampire Hunter*.

FIGURE 5.1
Kevin applying makeup to a character in Sucker Punch.
Image reproduced by permission of Kevin Kirkpatrick.

FIGURE 5.2
Kevin Kirkpatrick.
Photo by the author.

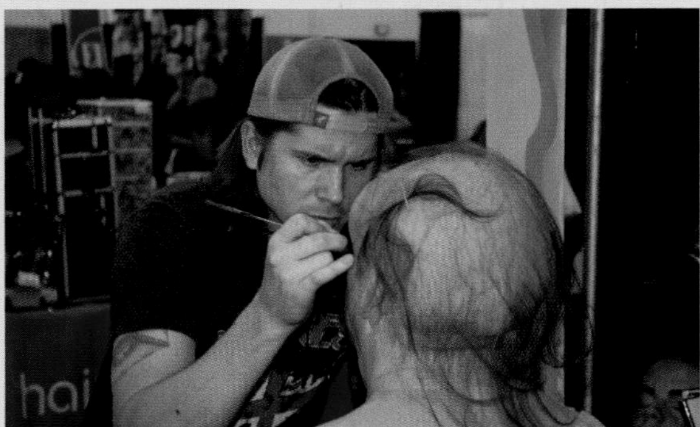

FIGURE 5.3
Kevin and Brian Hillard.
Photos by author.

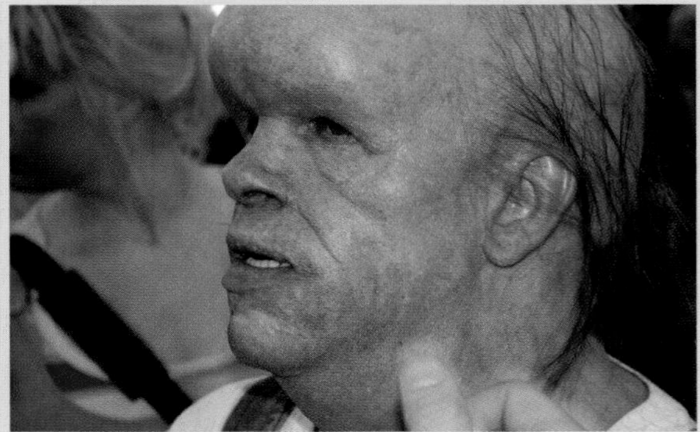

FIGURE 5.4
Kevin and Brian Hillard.
Photos by author.

TOOLS AND MATERIALS

> **NOTE**
> You may not need or want all these materials—they are listed simply as an aid.

- Ultracal
- 1- and 2-inch chip brushes
- Sculpting tools
- Hemp fiber
- Drill and ½- or ¾-inch (12 or 19 millimeters) round router bit
- Sharpie or other marker
- Chavant NSP Medium or Monster Makers Monster Clay
- Solvent—naphtha, mineral spirit, and 99% IPA
- Alginate
- ⅜ inch (1 centimeter) foam core
- Misc. containers
- Formica board or Masonite (× 2)
- Clay cutter
- Coarse sandpaper
- Petroleum jelly
- Plaster bandages
- Soft brushes
- Scissors
- Misc. mold keys
- Safety glasses
- Palette knife
- Polyethylene sheet (drop cloth)
- Burlap fabric (loose weave)
- Fiberglass mat, cloth, and tissue
- WED clay or other water clay
- Chavant Le Beau Touche non-sulfur oil clay
- Hot glue gun
- Misc. wood pieces of 2 × 4 and 1 × 2 (about 6–10 inches)
- Plastic wrap
- Paint stir sticks
- Rasp or sandpaper
- Two large flathead screwdrivers
- Superglue activator/accelerator
- National Institute for Occupational Safety and Health (NIOSH) respirator
- Latex, nitrile, and vinyl gloves
- Utility knife
- Green soap tincture

I strongly suggest you to read this chapter all the way through at least once before attempting what follows. That way there shouldn't be any surprises. As I've said before, the Boy Scout motto is a good one for makeup effects artists, too: Be prepared!

RELEASE AGENTS AND SEALERS

Release agents are materials that allow you to separate cast objects from molds. There are two categories for most release agents: barrier and reactive (or chemically active) types. *Barrier* release agents work by forming a barrier between the form (the cast) and the mold. Paraffin wax is an example of a barrier release, as is Al-Cote, which I explain in the next section. *Chemically active* release agents are releases that have an active ingredient that is usually some type of fatty acid, such as soap, that is dissolved in some sort of a carrier, such as alcohol (e.g., tincture of green soap). Palmolive dish soap dissolved in 99% IPA works very well.

Sealers are liquids or sprays that are absorbed into porous surfaces to seal against moisture, making the surface essentially no longer porous; they can act as both a seal and a release for some materials. Not all materials need to be sealed and/or released, although for some applying a mold release will make demolding easier and will most likely prolong the life of the mold. A pretty comprehensive listing of suppliers for releases and sealers is included in the appendix at the back of this book.

MAKING THE NEGATIVE MOLD

For a makeup that may cover an entire bust—the entire head and neck, for example—it is probable that the makeup will need to be broken down so that there will likely be several overlapping prosthetic pieces, each with its own mold of two or more pieces. One very important bit of information you need to know of this chapter is this: *If you are creating a makeup that will ultimately be cast in several pieces that will overlap, the initial lifecast must first be coated with a separating agent*, such as Dentsply's Al-Cote (liquid foil). If you don't use a separating agent between your stone positive and the clay sculpture, you will have a devil of a time getting the clay off in intact sections to create overlapping pieces—if you can get the clay off at all without destroying your sculpture.

So, let's assume that you applied two or three coats of separator to your positive before you began sculpting with your clay. You need to decide how you are going to break the sculpture apart; in doing this, you will also be determining how the pieces will fit back together, overlapping, so that there will be no semblance of a seam anywhere on the makeup.

1. With a thin wood tool, create a separating line on the clay where you want it to part. Make the line somewhat random so that the dividing lines and subsequent edges will be less obvious. Make sure to press hard enough to reach the positive under the clay.
2. Fill a large basin or tub with water, enough to completely submerge your sculpture, and carefully place the sculpture into it.
3. Let it soak for about 24 hours to be certain the water has had time to reach the Al-Cote and liquefy it. By doing this, you will be able to "float" the clay off your sculpture.

> **NOTE**
> Soak the sculpture in cold water, not warm or hot—you don't want to soften the clay so that it becomes too soft and becomes damaged when you remove it. Monster Clay is great for sculpting appliance that will need to be floated. Because of the high wax content, Monster Clay will literally float off a gypsum buck (lifecast), whereas other clays often need some assistance.

4. There will likely be Al-Cote residue left on the clay; you should carefully wash it off with water and a chip brush. You want the clay to be clean to ensure that it will adhere to the new cast you will be placing it on.

5. You will need to make additional positives that will be used to resculpt individual pieces that will overlap. Carefully set aside the clay you have removed from the original sculpture.
6. Blend the rough edges of the sculpture where you have removed clay and smooth it.
7. Now mix a batch of alginate large enough to just make a cast of the area you need to recreate plus an inch or so beyond it.
8. You might or might not need to create a plaster mother mold of the alginate, depending on the size of the piece. When the alginate has set, carefully remove it, place it level on a support, and mix enough Ultracal to fill the alginate mold.
9. If the new piece you are making is small, such as a lower lip, you will need to create a base for it.
10. You will need to create an alginate or silicone mold and Ultracal positive for each separate overlapping piece of your makeup, so repeat steps 8 and 9 as many times as necessary.
11. Place the clay you removed from the original onto the new positives and seat it well; blend and smooth the edges and finish adding skin texture detail if you haven't already done that.

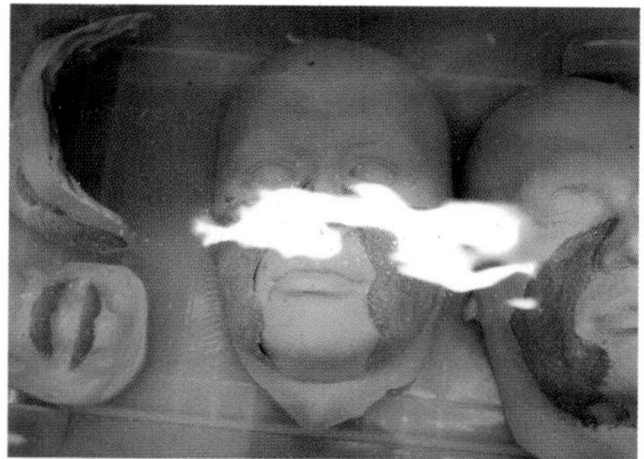

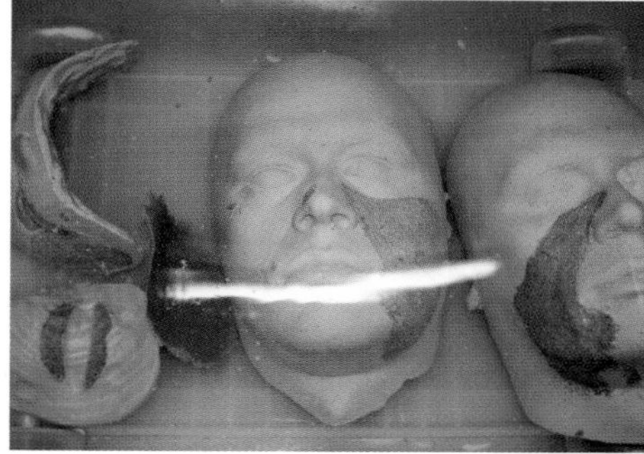

FIGURE 5.5
Floating a sculpt off a stone positive.
Photos by the author.

NOTE
For smaller pieces—such as a cheek appliance—you will be able to float the clay off of the gypsum positive in a shorter period of time than overnight; then it is really important to use cold water to soak the sculpt before floating off the appliance sculpt. You may also want to use a much firmer clay—a wax-based clay—that will help retain fine edges.

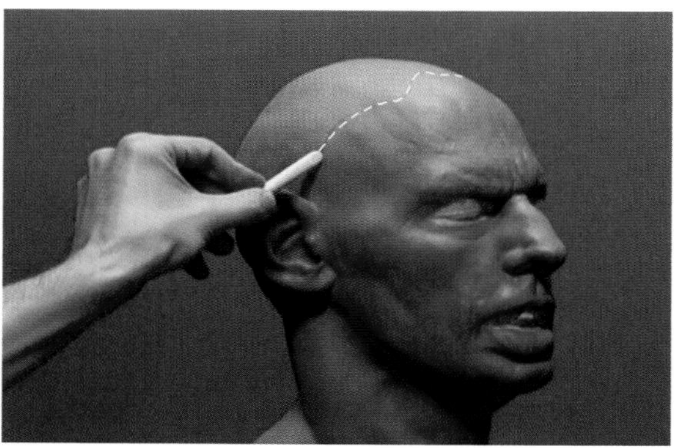

FIGURE 5.6
Dotted lines show where cut is made in clay to separate sculpture.
Image reproduced by permission of Mark Alfrey.

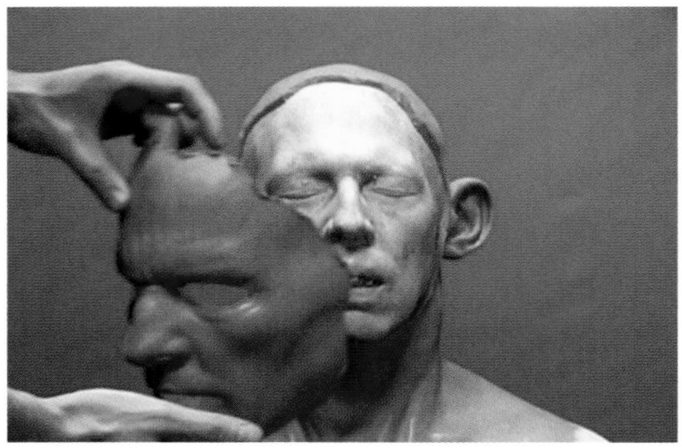

FIGURE 5.7
Lifting off the face portion after soaking it in water overnight.
Image reproduced by permission of Mark Alfrey.

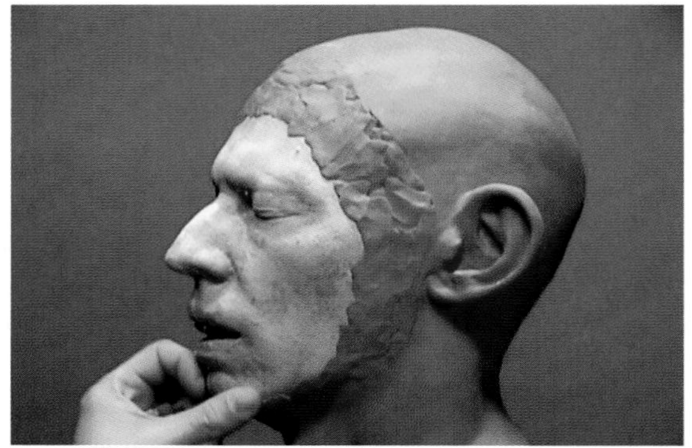

FIGURE 5.8
Clay must be extended and smoothly blended where parts will overlap.
Image reproduced by permission of Mark Alfrey.

KEYS, FLASHING, AND CUTTING EDGES

Now you will drill keys and flashing around the new pieces you've created. *Keys* are for precise registration of two or more mold parts so that they will fit together perfectly. Keys can be created by drilling rounded shapes into the positive (no undercuts!) or by placing clay or rubber shapes at even distances around the mold wall you will create.

Flashing is thinly placed (about 1/8 to 1/4 inch) over all the exposed areas of the mold and trimmed to within 1/8 to 1/4 inch from the edge of the sculpture for your appliance.

The flashing needs to be cut away from any drilled keys. The purpose of flashing is to create space for excess appliance material to escape when the mold parts are clamped together to cast the appliance pieces in gelatin, foam latex, or silicone.

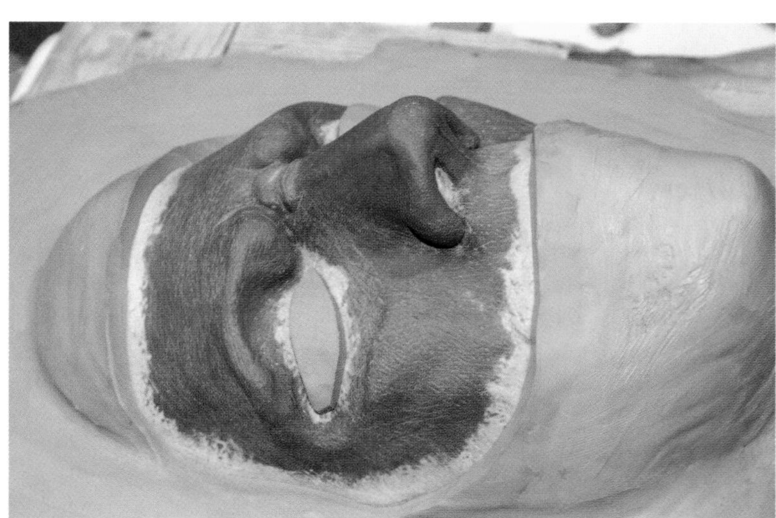

FIGURE 5.9
Flashing placed on the face sculpture.
Photo by the author.

There is a very good reason that the flashing stops just shy of the edge of your appliance sculpture. Do you know the reason? It's to create a *cutting edge* for the appliance you will cast later in the mold you're about to make. A cutting edge is the point where the negative part of the mold comes into physical contact with the positive, creating a separation of excess material that will escape into the space created by the flashing and the material that is pressed into the space created by your sculpture to make the appliance. When done properly, it will leave you with ultrafine edges that will be very easy to blend off onto your actor's skin or overlapping pieces when you apply the makeup.

Building the Clay Wall

After the keys and flashing have been made, you'll divide the sculpture by creating a dividing wall along a predetermined line that will prevent creating undercuts. Traditionally in sculpture, this dividing wall is created using metal shims (thin wedges) pressed into the sculpture to create a separating line between two mold halves. You can use shims, but for this, we'll use water clay instead of shims because shims may damage the sculpture more.

1. Before cutting and placing clay, take a Sharpie or similar marker and mark small dots along the line you intend to follow with the clay wall—a line that will prevent formation of undercuts that will possibly damage the mold.
2. Using a clay cutting tool, either a wire cutter and a piece of Masonite with paint sticks glued to each side (the width of the clay block) or an adjustable clay cutter, cut slabs of clay about 1/2 inch thick; lay them flat and cut strips about 2 inches wide and 4 or 5 inches long.

FIGURE 5.10
John Cox making the dividing wall perpendicular to the sculpture and the edge clean and smooth; make the wall as close to 90° as you can make it.
Photo by the author.

3. Begin to place these strips of clay along the dotted line you made along the ridge line of the sculpture, pressing down hard enough to get a good connection between the clay and the sculpture but not so hard as to cause a bulge at the contact point. You want the clay wall to be perpendicular to the sculpture and the edge to be clean and smooth; make the wall as close to 90° as you can.

A perfect wall will have no gaps where the water clay meets the oil clay. The clay in these pictures is Laguna WED clay.

4. Build the wall all the way around the sculpture. It is critical that the meeting point be closed and neat. You can use a small dental tool and a fine, soft brush dipped in water to smooth the clay in critical areas. You don't need to use much water. Alternate between smoothing and brushing until the seam where the wall meets the sculpture is perfectly smooth.
5. When the wall is finished, spray the sculpture (the side you're going to cover with Ultracal first) with a light coat of Krylon Crystal Clear. When it is dry, spray another coat and then spray a coat of Dulling Spray over the Crystal Clear. The reason for the Dulling Spray is to prevent the Ultracal from beading up and rolling off the sculpture when you brush on your thin detail coat.

> **NOTE**
> A method used in traditional fine art sculpture that is also used in effects work—particularly with very large sculptures—is the practice of laying up shims, or dividers, which can be made of thin metal or plastic. I've even seen coated playing cards used as shims to create a wall around a sculpture.

FIGURE 5.11
Playing cards make a very good retaining wall. *Image reproduced by permission of Rich Krusell.*

Building a Different Clay Wall

There is another way to do a wall for your sculpture: It can be done with your sculpture laid flat instead of standing upright.

1. Cut enough clay (about ½ inch to 12 millimeters thick) to lay your sculpture on face up. Cover the clay with plastic wrap to keep the clay from sticking to your sculpture. The clay is to prevent the sculpture from denting by being laid on a hard surface.
2. Place your sculpture on the plastic-covered clay. If you are working with just a face sculpture, you might not need or want to try this method; it works well for a full head (360°) sculpture. On the other hand, if you have only a face sculpture, it must be laid flat, facing up, because it would be awkward at best to try to mold it in an upright position.
3. So that you don't wind up using more WED or other water clay than you need to, you can first build up around the perimeter of your sculpture with precut lengths of 2 × 4-inch and 1 × 2-inch wood, or you can build platforms using pieces of ⅜-inch (1 centimeter) foam core and a hot glue gun.
4. Once you've built a perimeter using either wood or foam core, proceed with your clay just as described in steps 1–5 in the preceding section, following a line around the sculpture that will prevent undercuts that would keep the front and back halves of the mold from separating.

NOTE

Another way of preparing your sculpt for molding is a method I have tried and learned from Gray Taxidermy, the largest marine taxidermy company in the world. The process involves placing the model (sculpture) in a sandbox (covered with plastic to contain the sand and away from contaminating the sculpture with sand grit), with the sand simulating the edge of the mold; the sand can easily be contoured and shaped to create a smooth bed for the clay that will be added next to create the actual dividing wall. Once one side is molded, the sculpture is turned over and the process repeated. This is being presented merely as another option for prepping a sculpture for molding. It may not always, or ever, be practical for your applications, but it works well for Gray, having molded a 1,400 lb Blue Marlin in Kona, Hawaii, using this method.

Once you have made it through spraying Krylon Crystal Clear and Dulling Spray, you are ready to begin applying a thin coat of Ultracal for your detail layer. You should have all your supplies laid out and ready to begin, even before you start to build the clay wall around your sculpture. If you wait until you've already done the dividing wall before getting everything you need to make the Ultracal mold, the clay could already be drying out to the extent that you can see separation at the contact point on the sculpture due to shrinkage that occurs

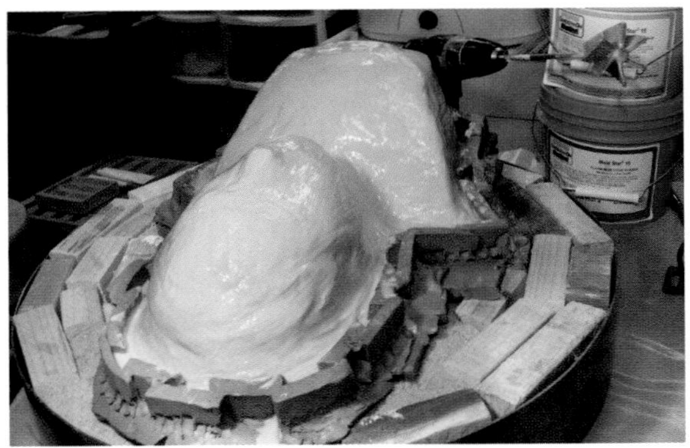

FIGURE 5.12
Brush up mold using bed of sand to brace model (sculpt) for molding.
Photo by author.

FIGURE 5.13
Build up a perimeter with wood and/or foam core before creating the clay wall.
Photo by the author.

when the clay dries. You don't need to work fast, but if you have all your tools and materials handy and ready to go at each stage, you won't need to rush and hence won't forget important steps.

STONE (GYPSUM) MOLDS

Stone molds, also called *gypsum molds,* are organic molds made with a base material of hydrated calcium sulfate, used for making Plaster of Paris, cement, Hydrocal, and Ultracal, among others. Gypsum has quite a few varied uses, from making drywall and fertilizer to being a major source of dietary calcium and also an ingredient in Hostess Twinkies! White Sands National Monument in New Mexico is a 275-square-mile expanse of white gypsum sand. Well, enough history; it's time to make your mold.

This process is exactly the same as when you made your Ultracal positive in Chapter 3 after taking your subject's lifecast; only this time we're making a negative, not a positive.

1. Spray the sculpture with a layer of Crystal Clear and let it dry. Then spray a layer of Dulling Spray to give the Ultracal a surface to adhere to.
2. Mix enough Ultracal to create a ¼-inch thickness that is the consistency of a thin milk shake—loose enough to brush easily with a 1- or 2-inch chip brush.
3. Begin brushing the Ultracal onto the sculpture, making sure to get Ultracal into all curves and creases such as the nose and the ears. Brush in all directions. This will help eliminate any trapped air bubbles.
4. As the Ultracal begins to thicken, dribble and brush more onto the sculpture until you have built up a thickness of about ¼ inch.
5. When your detail layer has gone through the heating phase of its cure, mix up some new Ultracal. You will add pieces of burlap fabric as you

apply the next batch of Ultracal, building up a thickness of three or four layers of burlap. Thoroughly press each piece down to remove trapped air and then overlap each piece of burlap by at least 1 inch.

6. After the burlap layers have cured, add a final beauty layer of just Ultracal that will give your mold an overall thickness of about 1 inch.

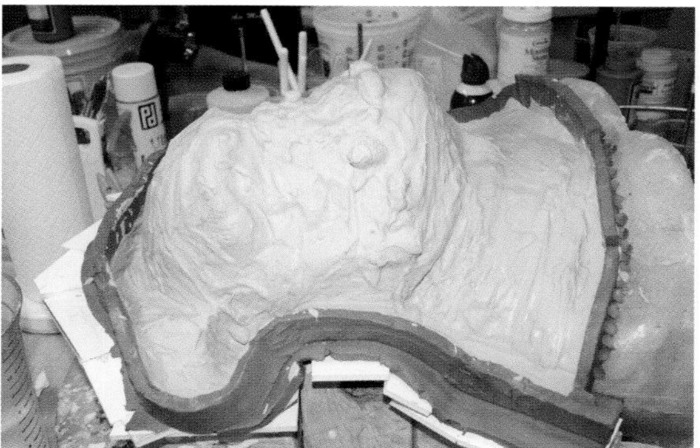

FIGURE 5.14
Brush on a detail layer of Ultracal, being careful to prevent trapping air bubbles.
Photo by the author.

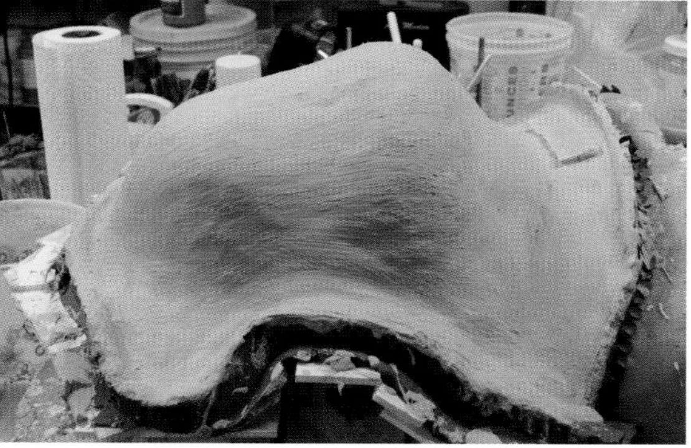

FIGURE 5.15
Build up three or four layers of burlap for reinforcement, overlapping each piece by about an inch. Give the mold a slightly rough texture on the outer layer for a good grip when handling the mold.
Photo by the author.

Some folks prefer to use hemp fibers or fiberglass mat fibers instead of burlap fabric as the reinforcing material they put in the Ultracal. It is nothing more than a personal preference and whether the materials are available in your area. For me, burlap and fiberglass mat are a 3-minute ride to Home Depot, but I have to order hemp online. You'll find a list of suppliers in the appendix at the back of this book, so let's continue.

7. When this half of the mold has fully cured and is cooling down, you might begin to remove the clay wall from around the sculpture.
8. Next, carefully remove the 2 × 4s and 1 × 2s or the foam core; if you've used foam core and hot glue, spray the glue with cyanoacrylate (Superglue) activator/accelerator. It will soften the glue so that it's easier to remove. Next remove the clay base that was being supported. If your sculpture has delicate parts such as ears, be very careful when removing the clay so that you don't damage it.
9. Once the clay is removed, you can use coarse sandpaper or a rasp to remove sharp edges and smooth the edges of the mold, removing excess Ultracal.

TIP

If you've used hot glue in any stage of your mold making, spray the cooled, dry hot glue with cyanoacrylate (Superglue) activator/accelerator. It will soften the glue so that it's easier to remove!

10. When you've done this and cleaned away the clay you've already used, carefully turn the mold over, supporting it under the edges of the mold flange (the part sticking out perpendicular to the sculpture) with the wood and some of the clay you used on the other side.
11. Spray this side of the mold with Crystal Clear and Dulling Spray and then lightly brush any exposed Ultracal with a thin layer of petroleum jelly. Brush about 1 or 2 inch down the side just to be safe.
12. Add small pieces of clay about 12 inches apart all the way around the mold; line them up opposite one another if you can. These will be used as pry holes to aid you in getting the two mold halves apart. You might also want to draw a mark with a Sharpie below the pry mark on the mold in case any Ultracal accidentally covers it. It will be easier to find later.
13. Now cut a slab of clay about 1 inch thick and trim the edges smooth. Use a paint stick to measure a width of about 1½ inches and cut the slab into strips. Begin placing the clay strips around the perimeter of the mold and press it down onto the Ultracal so that it will hold.
14. When you've finished, spray another coat of Crystal Clear so that the clay gets coated and spray a layer of Dulling Spray.
15. Now repeat steps 1–4 for the back side of your mold. You will eventually begin to know how much Ultracal to use for certain projects, but it's easy enough to mix up a little more if you find you haven't mixed enough. Unlike plaster, Ultracal has a substantial working time—hence its name, *Ultracal 30*.
16. Just as with the positive you made in Chapter 3, you might choose to cover the Ultracal with a plastic bag to hold in moisture as the stone heats. It is supposed to make the stone stronger; I don't know if anyone's actually run tests, but I tend to see the glass as half full. It won't weaken your mold, and it doesn't add to the cure time. However, it will mean that there is moisture in your mold, and if you're planning to run foam latex in it soon, you'll need to get rid of all that water or risk ruining your latex appliances. We discuss more about that in the next chapter.

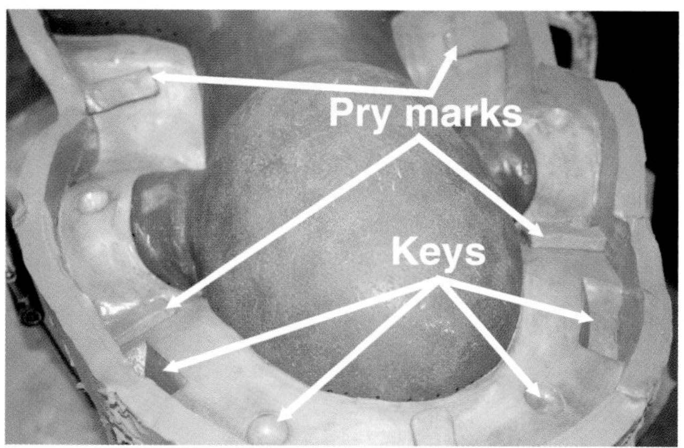

FIGURE 5.16
Add small pieces of clay about 12 inches apart all the way around the mold; these will be used as pry holes to aid you in getting the two mold halves apart. Also build a 1-inch retaining wall around the flange of the stone mold. (Yes, this is a different sculpt and a different mold!)
Photo by the author.

OTHER TYPES OF MOLDS

Gypsum molds are not the only kinds of molds you can make that are used for special makeup effects. In fact, the entire procedure just described can, in most cases, be substituted with a positive cast in fiberglass or epoxy (and then sculpted on), and the negative be made by brushing on a detail layer using a gelcoat in either epoxy or fiberglass and then adding laminating layers with reinforcing material like chopped glass or cut pieces of fiberglass cloth of mat for strength. These molds are much lighter than gypsum, although fiberglass requires a respirator and proper ventilation. We'll cover epoxy and fiberglass molds later in the chapter.

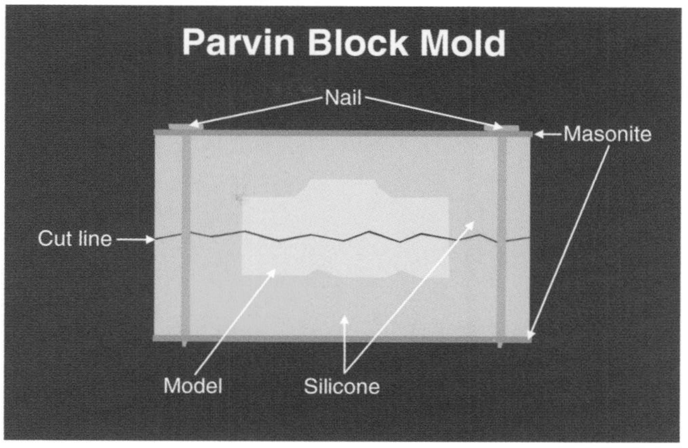

FIGURE 5.17
Side view cross-section diagram of Parvin block mold.
Illustration by author.

We'll look at the other types of molds one by one and talk about their uses and how to make them. Other materials used for mold making include silicone rubber, fiberglass, urethane rubber, and urethane plastic resin. The two-piece front and back mold you just made is called a *case mold*, but there are case molds that are made in numerous pieces that must be bolted together. There are matrix molds, flood molds, box molds, block molds, plate molds, brush up molds, injection molds, pour molds, pressure molds, and vacuum molds.

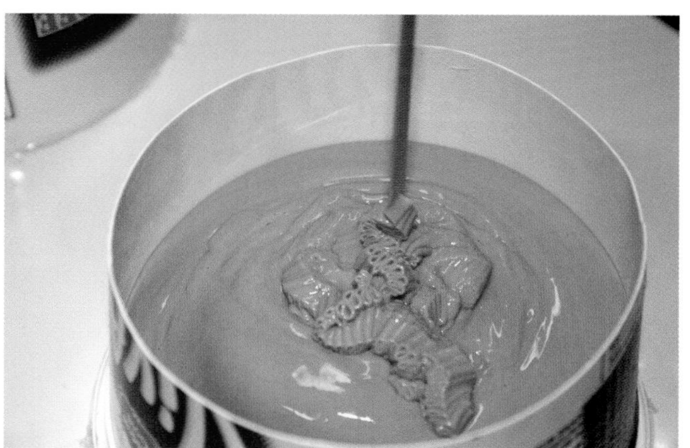

FIGURE 5.18
Flood or pour mold is exactly what name implies.
Photo by author.

Some of these names might be confusing, so let me do a bit of clarification. A *box mold* is just what the name implies—it is made by creating a box shape around the sculpture that is to be molded.

However, sometimes the shape that needs to be molded will not conform to a basic four-sided box shape without causing an inexcusable and unnecessary waste of mold-making material. Box molds are also known as *block molds* for the same reason: their block shape. These box/block molds can be, and most often are, made with silicone rubber or urethane rubber, but they can also be made out of plaster, Ultracal, or urethane plastic resin. That material can be poured, or flooded, in and hence the names *flood mold* and *pour mold*. They're really all just different names for similar molds.

If you really want to get technical, I suppose you could call the Ultracal case mold you've made a *brushed case mold* as you essentially brushed on the Ultracal to create the mold. What matters is that there should be no confusion about terminology among people working together on any given project.

Like the other molds I've described, a *plate mold* describes what it is: a flat, one-piece mold resembling a flat plate or a slab. Plate molds are essentially box

FIGURE 5.19
Various silicone plate molds.
Photo by author.

molds. I use plate molds for making small, thin appliances such as Pros-Aide transfers, which will be discussed in another chapter.

These types of molds are frequently used for creating generic prosthetic appliance pieces such as cuts, scars, bullet holes, and the like, by sculpting the particular injury or feature on a flat surface and then creating a box mold around the sculpture and casting it in stone or plastic. Don't forget to release the surface on which you are making the mold or you could fuse them together and never get them apart. The way these molds are used is usually as follows: Gelatin or silicone is cast into the negative of the sculpted feature and excess material is scraped away with a flat scraper of some sort, leaving a piece that is flat on the back with very fine edges. I'll show you how in Chapter 6.

SILICONE (PART 1)

By Naomi Lynch

Silicone is a synthetic polymer, which cures, or vulcanizes, at room temperature into a rubbery material. This is known as Room temperature vulcanization (RTV) silicone. It comes in very firm and soft forms, and it is inert once cured, heat resistant, and flexible. RTV silicone rubber is used in the movie, entertainment, and special effects industry and in theme parks. Soft "skin" silicone rubbers, used by makeup and FX artists, were developed specifically for SFX makeup artists, and certain kinds are also used in the medical prosthetics industry. It is also used, in an uncured form, as a lubricant, which will be apparent to anyone who has ever spilled uncured silicone on the floor.

RTV silicone comes in varieties, but the first thing to realize is that there are two main types. These are classified based on the catalyst used to turn the uncured, liquid, silicone polymer into a solid product. One is known as *tin silicone*, because its catalyst is a tin-based chemical, and the other is known as *platinum silicone*. To further complicate this, often you will hear them described not by the type of catalyst but by the manner of combination and vulcanization (curing process). That is, *tin-based silicones* are also known as *condensation-cured silicones*, whereas *platinum silicones* are *addition-cured*.

Tin-based systems come in two different types:

One-part materials contain all the ingredients needed to produce a cured material. They use external factors—such as moisture in the air, heat, or the presence of ultraviolet light—to initiate, speed, or complete the curing process.

- Typical uses—Building sealants, high-consistency rubber compounds, coatings for electronics, and medical bonding adhesives.

- Advantages—Easy to use; low- or room-temperature cure (although, in some cases, cure can be accelerated by heat).
- Disadvantages—Moisture-curing materials may take 24 hours or more to fully cure; precautions must be taken to protect the material from the cure initiator before application.

Examples include window and bathroom caulking. These silicones are not suitable for mold making or prosthetics; they do have an unexpected application in painting silicone models.

Two-part systems segregate the reactive ingredients to prevent premature initiation of curing. They often use the addition of heat to facilitate or speed cure.

- Typical uses—High-speed, high-volume operations, such as the application of silicone release coatings or pressure-sensitive adhesives, injection molding of liquid silicone rubber, and soft skin adhesives for healthcare applications
- Advantages—longer shelf life, high-speed cure (some materials cure within seconds), and the ability to carefully control bath life and cure time by manipulating the formulation.
- Disadvantages—mixing required; often requires more sophisticated processes and formulating/application expertise.

Platinum silicones only come in the two-part system. We will be looking at two-part systems here.

Platinum or Tin?

Both types have unique properties that make them suited to certain applications. For instance, if high temperatures are anticipated, then addition cure silicones (platinum catalyzed) are typically a better choice. But for economy, general mold making, and prototype applications, condensation cure (tin catalyzed) would be preferable.

Condensation cure (Tin)—Two-component silicone rubbers are less expensive and better for most general mold making and prototype applications than platinum silicones. They use tin salts and titanium alkoxide for catalysts. Most (but not all) condensation cured silicones are mixed at a ratio of 1 part catalyst to 10, 20, or even up to 100 parts of silicone base! They are usually (but not always) measured by weight, not volume, and accurate scales are essential. You can add things to them like fillers, colors, and so forth without appreciably affecting the cure.

Tin silicones are not particularly sensitive to inhibition, meaning they will cure at room temperature over virtually any surface. They're easy to mix and de-air, because they have a relatively long curing time, which allows bubbles to rise to the surface. The cure time can be reduced either by increasing the amount of catalyst used or by adding special activators. *Warning: Over-accelerating your silicone will dramatically reduce its usable life, by causing brittleness and deterioration, in direct proportion to the amount used*. Tin silicone molds are excellent for casting polyester, epoxy, polyurethane, masonry, gypsum, and candle wax. Tin silicones have a relatively long working time and a long period after gelling before they can be demolded. When mixing, if you miss a little bit, don't stress, it will usually cure anyway.

Advantages

- Cost
- Resistant to catalyst poisoning or substrate inhibition—they set over almost anything
- Adhesion
- Versatility

Disadvantages

- Tin silicone appliance and molds leach silicone oil over time and become brittle, as the catalyst is unstable. Because of this they cannot be used for any purpose requiring a long shelf-life or in contact with skin (or food).
- Tin silicone molds cannot be used for casting platinum silicone in (see note at end of article[1]).
- Need air and moisture to cure, not good for confined spaces.

Addition cure (platinum)—Two-component silicone rubbers offer superior heat resistance and cure with virtually no shrinkage. Their catalysts are platinum and rhodium.

Most (but not all) platinum silicones are mixed at a ratio of 1:1. Platinum silicones are usually (but not always) measured by weight; however, some can be measured by volume.

Platinum rubbers can be inhibited by tin, sulfur, or amines, in fact a whole heap of things you probably never thought about. Latex is a no-no, so you can't use latex gloves while mixing them; nitrile is the best choice. You can't use them on a wet surface like water-based clay without sealing it or on plastiline sculpting products with sulfur in them; you need a nonsulfur clay. You can't use them in the same room where foam latex is being made or baked in, and other airborne contaminants can also inhibit. Fresh fiberglass must have the styrene baked out or be left to cure for a week or so or it will inhibit. Adding too much or the wrong kind of pigment, accelerator or retarder, can also inhibit. However, despite their fussiness, they can be cured in total confinement, and the cure rate can be dramatically accelerated with heat. Finished molds are ideal for casting epoxies, low-melting-point metals, and polyurethanes. They can be accelerated by adding an accelerating agent, but as they have a very short gel time in comparison with tin-based systems, you are more likely to want to slow them down. This can be done with a retarder or simply by chilling the components before use. They also have a much shorter working time and a considerably shorter cure time, which can be both an advantage and a disadvantage, according to purpose. Mixing must be done thoroughly and evenly or you will be left with uncured parts, and if you are too vigorous, air bubbles can be a problem, unless you have a vacuum degassing chamber.

Advantages

- Cure without by-products and can be accelerated by heat with no loss of "library" life.
- Clear, deep-section cure, no shrinkage.
- Cures in a vacuum, so good for multipart molds.
- Texture can be altered with additives to make a "fleshier" more flexible product for SFX, prosthetics, and animatronics.
- Good adhesion.

- Certain formulations are safe to use directly on the skin, either for molding or for building up realistic skin effects.
- Certain formulations are used as medical adhesives or to attach other silicone pieces, and some are self-adhesive in their uncured state.

Disadvantages

- Potential for catalyst poisoning and substrate inhibition.
- Catalyst cost can be prohibitive in large amounts.

Both types have a limited shelf life in their uncured state. It is not advisable to buy larger quantities than you are likely to use in that time period (usually specified on the manufacturers information). The "library" life, that is, the life of the cured silicone varies by product and you should check with the manufacturer if it is important. As a guideline, tin products may last as little a matter of months (if over-catalyzed or accelerated) or as many as 10 years, while platinum can last indefinitely under optimum conditions.

Kato DeStephan

Kato grew up as a "Monster Kid," watching the classic Universal and Hammer monster films *Star Trek* on TV and reading copies of *Famous Monsters of Filmland* magazine. "My interest in makeup goes back as far as I can remember," says Kato. "I carried Richard Corson's *Stage Makeup* and Al Taylor's *Making a Monster* with me through part of Junior High and all through High School." In 1986, Kato met Dick Smith, a fellow New Yorker, and started visiting him at his home in Larchmont almost weekly. "It was so inspiring to be in Dick's workshop with the dummy of Linda Blair from *The Exorcist*. I learned to sculpt at his work bench!"

In 1990, Kato moved to Los Angeles and landed a job at Steve Johnson's XFX and considers his time working and learning from Steve some of the best years of his life. During that time, he worked with and learned from Bill Corso, Dave Dupuis, Joel Harlow, and Mike Smithson. "I learned so much from these incredibly talented guys!" Among the projects Kato worked on at XFX were the films *Pet Sematary II*, *Batman Returns*, *Innocent Blood*, *Freaked*, and *Zoolander*.

"I was really ambitious and wanted to learn as much as possible about not only prosthetics but also beauty makeup. It was necessary to learn not only how skin moved but also about all of the subtle colorations to it. I

FIGURE 5.20
Kato DeStephan.
Image reproduced by permission of Kato DeStephan.

realized that my friends who could do prosthetic and straight makeups—their work really stood out. That was the look that I wanted to emulate."

Kato has also worked on *Fantastic Four: Rise of the Silver Surfer*, *Boogeyman 2*, *Watchmen*, *Cabin Fever 2: Spring Fever*, *Underworld: Rise of the Lycans*, *G.I. Joe: Rise of Cobra*, and J.J. Abrams' *Star Trek*. "If there is a movie that is the second in a series or has the word "Rise" in the title, I work on it!"

Of working in the biz, Kato considers himself to be very fortunate. "The days may be long, sometimes the pay is low, and the conditions may not be ideal, but… I feel so lucky to be a makeup artist!"

FIGURE 5.21
Kato with actor Bo Hopkins for Of God and Kings.
Image reproduced by permission of Kato DeStephan.

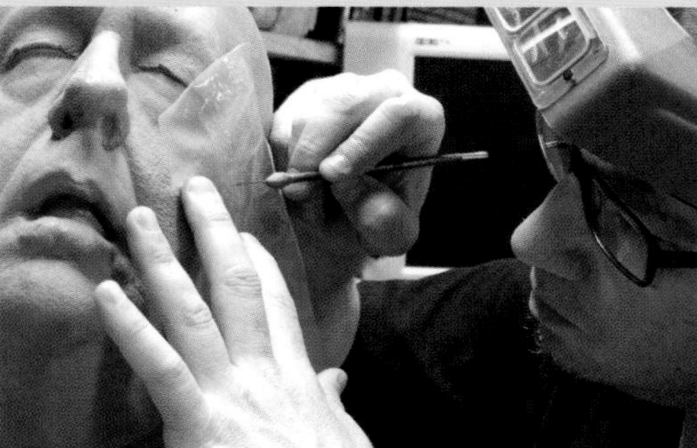

FIGURE 5.22
Adding texture to a clay pour for a segment of A, B, C's of death.
Image reproduced by permission of Kato DeStehpan.

SILICONE RUBBER MOLDS

Rubber molds made with silicone can be quite versatile and, when made thick enough, don't necessarily require the support of a rigid support shell or mother mold. Working with silicone doesn't require a degree in chemistry either, but it sure wouldn't hurt! What I mean is, silicone is an interesting creature, and I think it is worthwhile for me to go into some of its quirks and idiosyncrasies so that you won't literally get yourself into a mess that is difficult to clean up. I will go into more detail about silicones in Chapter 6, but here are some basics. Take a look at the sidebars in this chapter and Chapter 6 for a much more comprehensive look at silicone.

This information was just covered in Naomi's wonderful silicone sidebar (part 1), but is important enough to bear repeating. Of the two types of silicones, condensation cure (tin) and addition cure (platinum), condensation cure silicone is the most tolerant of outside influence. Of the two main types, condensation cure silicone is most widely used in mold making due to its resistance to cure inhibition (not setting up because of contamination by an outside agent).

The second type of silicone, addition cure, cures by a self-contained chemical reaction. Addition cure silicones will cure in a vacuum, and there is virtually no

shrinkage, although the shrinkage with condensation silicones is also nominal. However, being able to cure in a vacuum is one of addition cure silicone's benefits. I guess that's true if you work in outer space. Addition cure silicones are also mixed in two parts, and when they're mixed, air bubbles get trapped in the thick liquid silicone, which is bad. The silicone must be degassed, which requires a vacuum chamber. Right now you're probably thinking, "Oh, man! Where the heck am I gonna get one of those?!" Not to worry. If you feel compelled to buy one, Harbor Freight sells a 2-gallon pressure/vacuum pot for less than $100. They're really not that hard to find. If you know what you're doing, and you will because you're reading this book (depending on which silicone you use), you don't have to have a vacuum chamber to get rid of the air bubbles, but it could help. However, you would still need a vacuum pump, and they're a bit more costly. The one I have is a two-stage vacuum pump—a Robinair 15500 1/3 Hp 5CFM (cubic feet per minute) pump that cost me about $250 a couple of years ago. It'll suck the chrome off a trailer hitch. Not really, but it does the job quite well.

FIGURE 5.23
A 2-gallon pressure/vacuum chamber from Harbor Freight.
Photo by the author.

NOTE

Although condensation cure silicone (tin cure) may be the most common mold making silicone, addition cure silicones (platinum cure)—while often more expensive—are fast catching up with the condensation cure silicones because of their longer library life and lower viscosity, making them less necessary to be degassed.

NOTE

Guy Louis XVI and his company, FuseFX, have a product called BondFX, which, when used for surface preparation, will enable you to use a platinum silicone in a tin silicone mold or even allow the two silicones to bond together. I use BondFX and now have no trouble casting platinum silicone into a tin silicone mold.

NOTE

Smooth-On Inc. owned company Mann Formulated Products has a product called *Inhibit X*, which is essentially a platinum solution that stops cure inhibition when using platinum silicone rubber. I can tell you from personal experience that it works very well. As a test, I sprayed two thin coats onto a sheet of latex and then spread a small amount of platinum silicone onto the latex, and the silicone cured! I've also sprayed small patches of slightly uncured (tacky) platinum silicone with it, and the sticky patches of silicone fully cured within minutes. But just because I'm telling you it works doesn't mean it always will. The planets may just have been aligned correctly at the moment I tried it.

Knowing how sensitive platinum silicones are to cure inhibition is very important because of the materials you choose for your prosthetic appliances. If you make foam latex prosthetics in a mold and later decide you'd rather make a silicone version, you may well be out of luck. Likewise, you can't cast platinum silicone prosthetics in a mold with tin silicone parts, because it won't cure either. Ah, chemistry! Gotta love it. I'll save more about silicone for the next chapter.

CONTOURED OR CONFORMING MOLDS

Contoured or conforming molds are becoming more commonly used in prosthetic application because of the ease and precision of the application process; however, there is quite a bit of set up on the front end to facilitate such ease, speed, and precision of application, so they may not be well suited for all types of appliances.

Conforming molds came into the spot light with 2008's *The Dark Night* and Conor O'Sullivan's marvelous Joker makeup on the late Heath Ledger, for which Conor was nominated for an Academy Award along with fellow mufx artist John Caglione Jr.

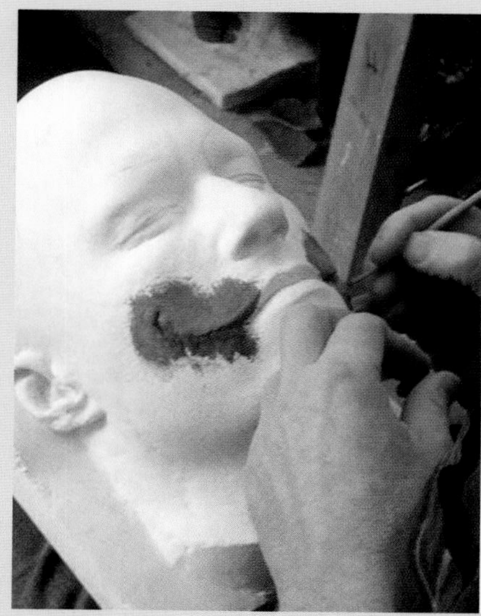

FIGURE 5.24
Joker appliance sculpt (left) Joker appliance, Heath Ledger (right).
Images reproduced by permission of Conor O'Sullivan.

Conforming molds are best suited for smaller pieces, such as the Joker's facial scars, or for subtle old age cheeks—pieces that will be no thicker than 5 or 6 millimeters (about ¼"). Appliances of this thickness can often be a bit tricky to apply because they are delicate and, therefore, a bit floppy; keeping the pieces in the mold for direct application makes them much easier to apply.

FIGURE 5.25
Finished conforming mold.
Image reproduced by permission of Neill Gorton.

This will be more of an overview of making conforming molds; Neill Gorton has a very excellent DVD that describes the process step by step in greater detail, and he has been generous enough (as always) to allow me to share it with you. There are lots of steps to create this type of mold; so, for the full, unabridged training, I suggest you pick up a copy of Neill's DVD. Conor O'Sullivan also has online training to make conforming silicone molds called *The Silicone Solution* (www.siliconeprosthetics.com).

In a nutshell, you'll need a clean positive cast in a very hard plaster on which you will sculpt and float off your prosthetic sculpt—I suggest Hydrocal or Ultracal in the United States; the point is, regular plaster of Paris is too soft—to begin this lengthy process.

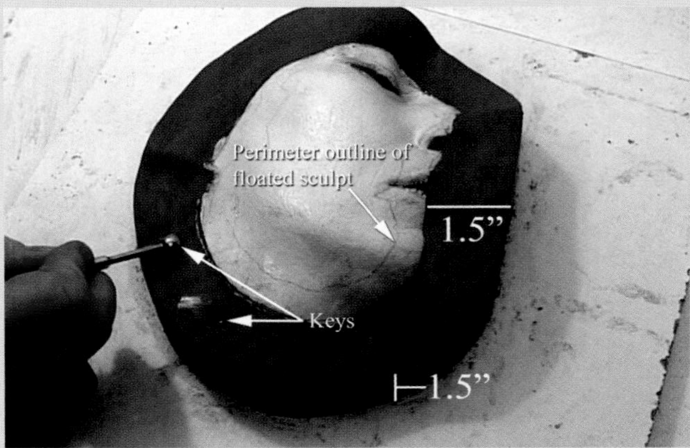

FIGURE 5.26 Stone positive with flange. *Image reproduced by permission of Neill Gorton.*

1. Raise the cast so that its lowest point is about 1.5 inches high and create a clay flange around the cast about 1.5 inches wide with its inner edge about 1 inches (25 millimeters) from the edge of where the appliance will sit. That inch beyond the edge of the appliance will define the area of the conforming mold. Make sure that it lies level because silicone for the appliance will need to pool in the center. Add both raised and recessed keys.

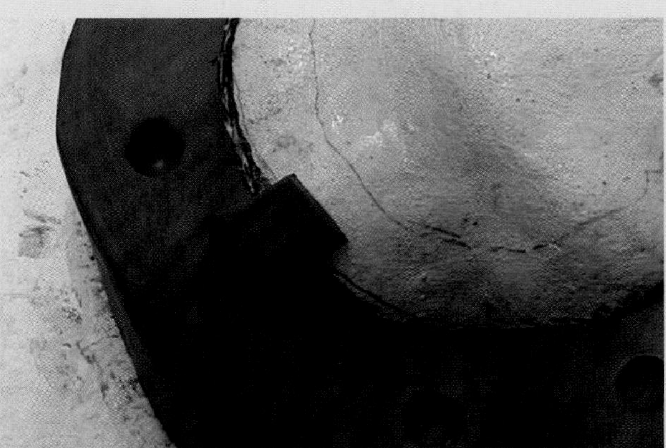

FIGURE 5.27 Raised key. *Image reproduced by permission of Neill Gorton.*

2. Make a silicone block mold of this piece using a firm 30 or 40 shore tin silicones, making sure that the wall of the block mold is thick enough to work as a support wall without further reinforcement for the steps to follow. The silicone should be poured to about ½ inch above the highest point of the sculpt.

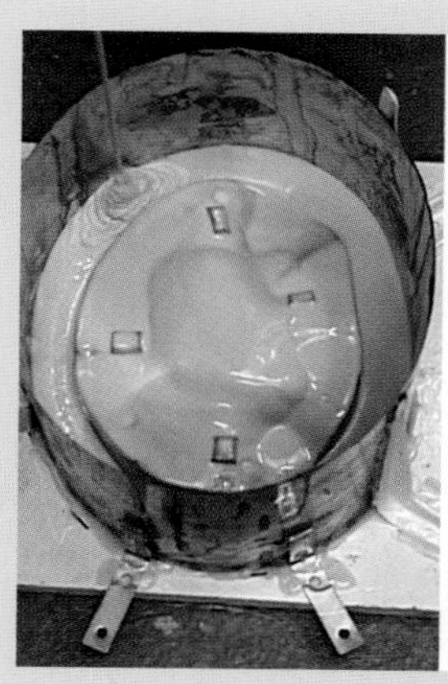
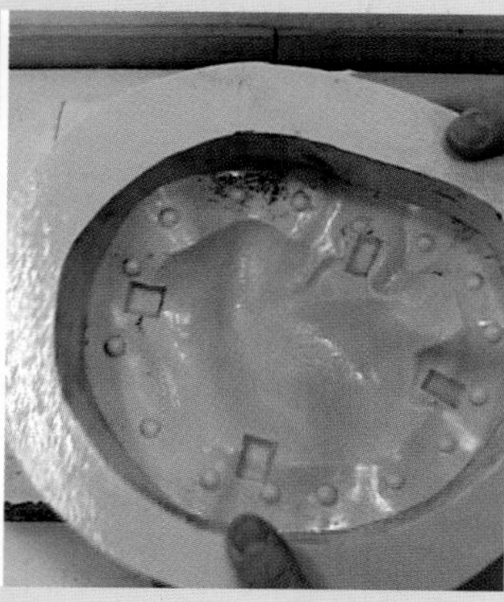

FIGURE 5.28
Silicone block mold.
Images reproduced by permission of Neill Gorton.

3. When the silicone is cured, trim the raised edge on the bottom caused by surface tension. This is necessary so the mold will sit perfectly flat when turned over to fill. We will need to pour a new positive in this mold in two parts—in two pieces. Add the clay from the flange back into the silicone mold to section off the flange area in the mold, and fill the void (the face area) with the same gypsum you've been using—Hydrocal, Ultracal, etc.

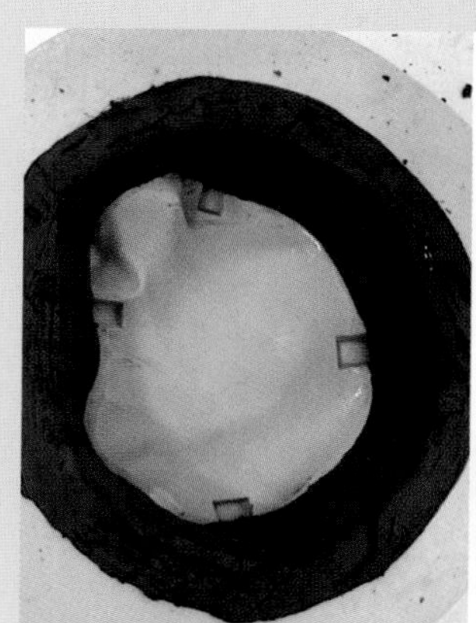
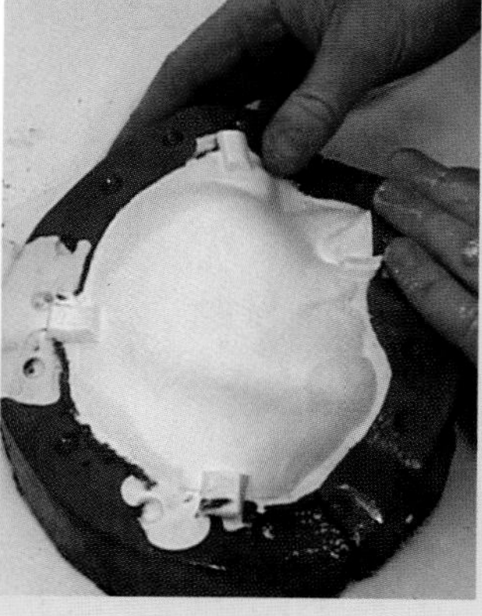

FIGURE 5.29
Clay filling flange area; new positive minus flange.
Images reproduced by permission of Neill Gorton.

4. When the stone is cured, remove the new positive core and clean it up well. This will be our new Master Positive. This piece will go back into the silicone mold and we will add a stone flange. This is where it may start to get a little confusing; we need the flange, but it is a "waste mold" meaning we won't need it in the final stage, but it is important to help us get there. Drill three keys into the sides of the positive to register the flange to the positive and add a release such as Al-Cote or other dental separator. When the separator is dry, place the positive into the mold; it should fit perfectly in place. Add some weight to it to help ensure that it doesn't move when we add new gypsum to the mold.

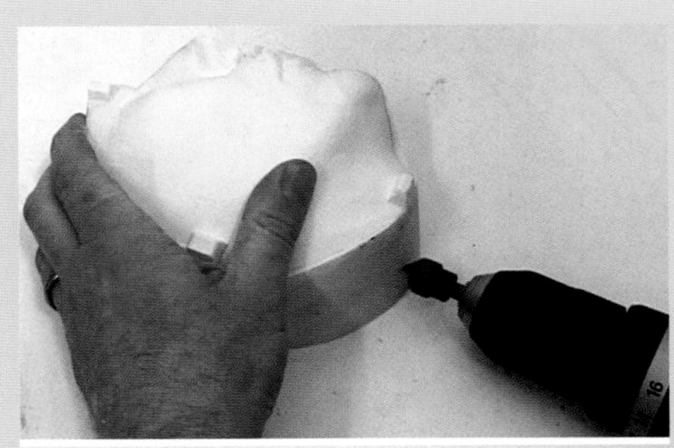

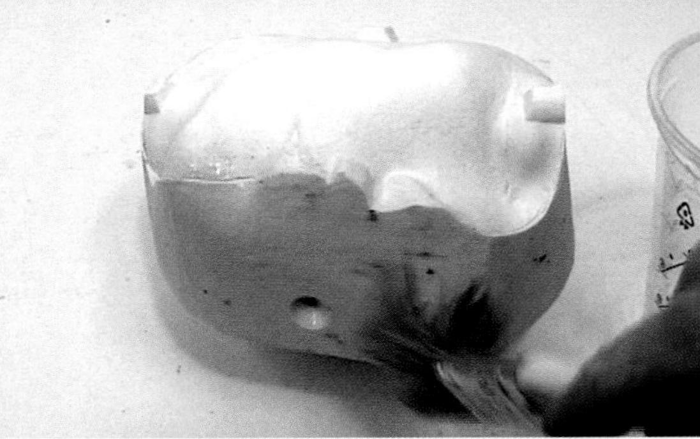

FIGURE 5.30
Drilling new keys; brushing separator; adding gypsum for new "waste" flange.
Images reproduced by permission of Neill Gorton.

5. Now we're ready to put the floated sculpt back onto the new positive with the disposable flange.
6. It will probably be necessary to use a silicone adhesive (Telesis 5, Telesis 7, Snappy G, etc.) to get the clay to adhere sufficiently to the stone positive so the sculpt can be detailed and completed.
7. When the sculpt is finished and ready to mold, use a Sharpie marker to mark the line between the inner core and the waste flange. We're ready now to make a two-part jacket or matrix mold.

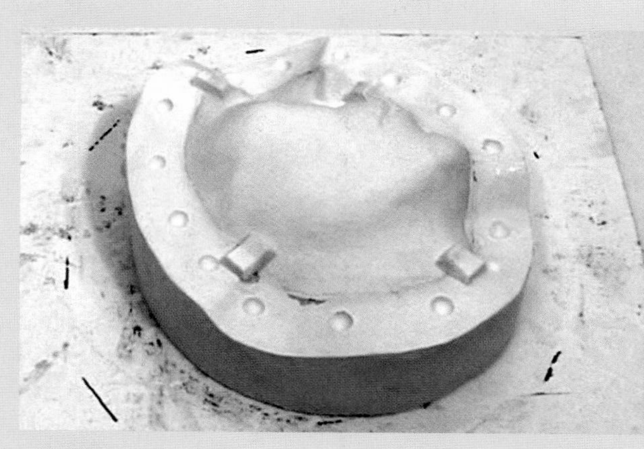

FIGURE 5.31
New positive with "throw away" flange.
Image reproduced by permission of Neill Gorton.

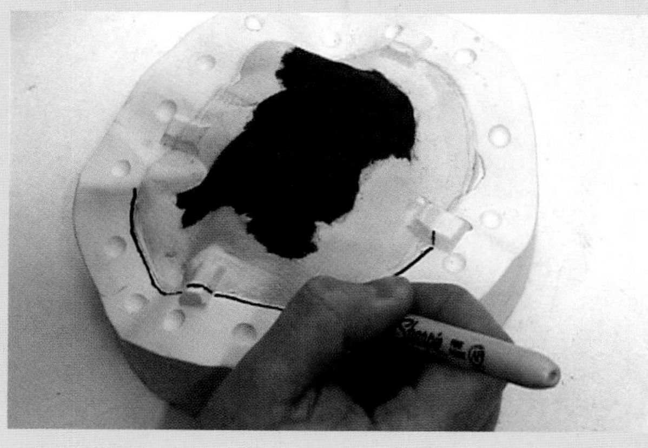

FIGURE 5.32
Line showing separation between inner core and waste flange.
Image reproduced by permission of Neill Gorton.

8. Carefully cover the sculpt with a piece of wet paper towel and lay a uniform thickness of WED clay over the sculpt (8 millimeters or ⅜ inches) all the way to the edge of the core/flange separation line, just overlapping. Use clay to fill in any imperfections that may be on the flange. Smooth the clay as much as possible; the silicone that will replace the clay is going to be relatively clear, and the smoother the clay is, the clearer the silicone will be.
9. When the clay is as smooth as you can get it, add pour tubes/keys; pack the tubes with clay to make them more solid and help them stick in the clay. I use the plastic tubes that come in the center of Gypsona plaster bandages. Add several as in this photo.
10. Build a clay wall around the piece; don't forget to add pry marks! Give the wall good height; it doesn't matter if some of the tubes get covered. We'll drill them out later. Spray with two or three light coats of Krylon Crystal Clear, then a good dose of Epoxy Parfilm, and then fill with gypsum. To make sure the gypsum has cured sufficiently, let it sit overnight before demolding.

FIGURE 5.33
Wet paper towel and clay covering the finished sculpt.
Images reproduced by permission of Neill Gorton.

FIGURE 5.34
Plastic tubes as pour tubes/keys.
Image reproduced by permission of Neill Gorton.

FIGURE 5.35
Ready to demold.
Image reproduced by permission of Neill Gorton.

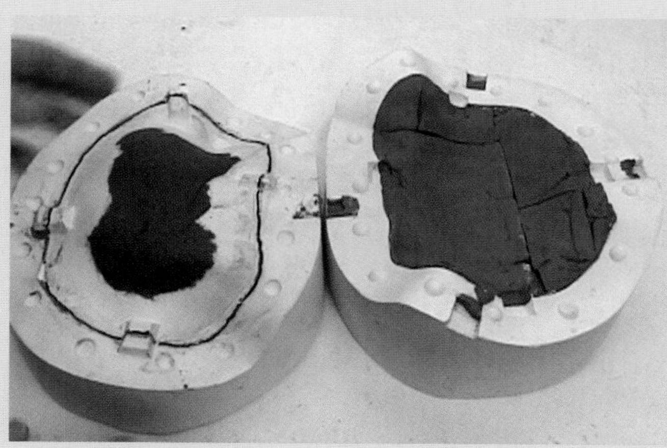

FIGURE 5.36
Demolded, ready to clean up.
Image reproduced by permission of Neill Gorton.

11. Demold carefully so as not to damage the sculpture. The WED clay should come out cleanly. Keep the clay handy because you will need its volume to know how much silicone to mix for the next step.
12. Pull out the plastic tubes (carefully); drill out the blockages and then counter sink the holes making them funnel shaped for pour holes. These holes must be very clean; you do not want any clay bits or gypsum to get trapped in the silicone when you pour it. Use Crystal Clear to seal the holes.
13. Add flashing to the sculpt on the core. Create your cutting edge about 7 or 8 millimeters, about ¼ inches; if your cutting edge is too wide, you'll get a thick edge because not enough silicone will be pushed out of the way. If our cutting edge is too thin, the edge of the appliance becomes too difficult to distinguish. *The flashing must stop before the dividing line between the core and the waste flange or the mold will not close properly.*

FIGURE 5.37 Counter-sinking pour holes/keys. *Image reproduced by permission of Neill Gorton.*

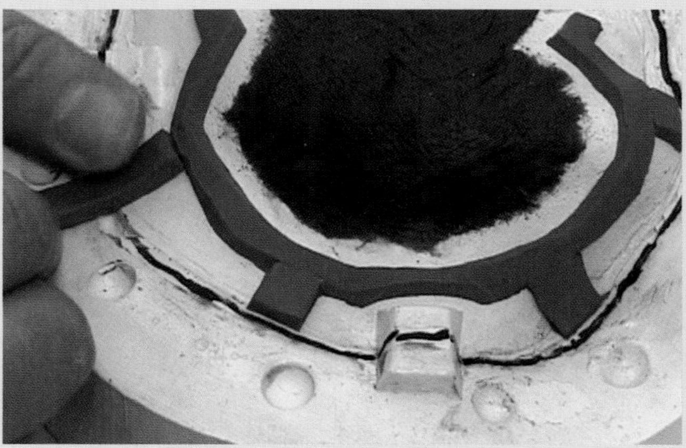

FIGURE 5.38 Adding flashing and cutting edge. *Image reproduced by permission of Neill Gorton.*

14. Spray the inside of both halves of the mold with Epoxy Parfilm and then carefully close the mold; spray the outside of the mold with epoxy Parfilm also and wrap with plaster bandage to join (temporarily) the mold halves.
15. Mix slightly more silicone than the volume of the clay to compensate for filling the pour hole keys; Degas if possible. Fill the mold through the pour holes, tilting the mold slightly to ensure that there are no trapped air pockets in the mold. When the mold is filled, cover the holes with Saran Wrap (plastic wrap and cling wrap) to make sure no foreign objects accidentally make it into the silicone. We don't want any schmutz or bugs committing suicide.
16. When the silicone is fully cured, carefully demold and remove the plastiline from the mold with a wooden tool so you don't damage the silicone. Then carefully trim away the excess silicone.

FIGURE 5.39
Wrap mold with plaster bandage to join halves.
Image reproduced by permission of Neill Gorton.

FIGURE 5.40
Filling mold.
Image reproduced by permission of Neill Gorton.

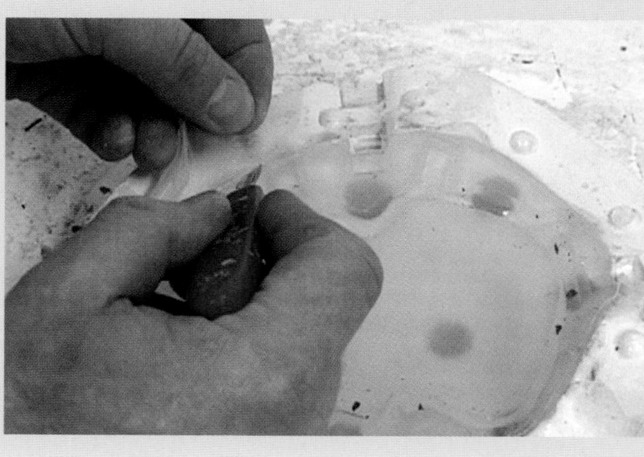

FIGURE 5.41
Trimming excess silicone.
Image reproduced by permission of Neill Gorton.

You want to make a duplicate mold so that you will be able to cast multiple appliances. (You didn't think you'd go to all this trouble just for a one-off, did you?!) Brush a thin layer of petroleum jelly over just the gypsum not on the silicone. Fill the pry marks with clay and build a new WED clay wall. You'll no longer need the waste flange; it can be carefully separated from the core positive.

17. Mix up a good mold resin (e.g., BJB TC1630) and then clean up the new Master positive once it's demolded.

FIGURE 5.42 Prepping to make duplicate mold. *Image reproduced by permission of Neill Gorton.*

18. Trim the pour sprues/keys (cut them off about halfway); use petroleum jelly (just a little) or dish soap to help re-seat the sprues back into their holes.

FIGURE 5.43 Making BJB TC1630 Master. *Image reproduced by permission of Neill Gorton.*

19. When you place the positive core back into the silicone negative, there should be a couple of millimeters of space where the gypsum of the positive and the gypsum of the negative do not touch. They should not touch anywhere. When you cast an appliance piece, place a weight on top of the mold, which will push down and create a gasket seal for a perfect appliance edge.

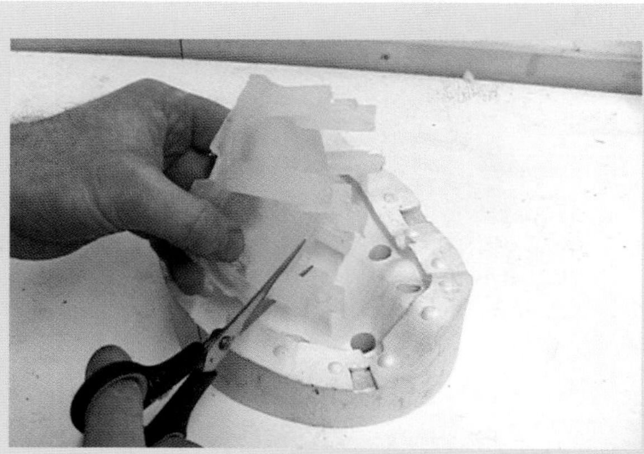

FIGURE 5.44
Trimming silicone sprues/keys.
Image reproduced by permission of Neill Gorton.

FIGURE 5.45
Positive and negative do not touch.
Image reproduced by permission of Neill Gorton.

20. You can now make a duplicate silicone mold for the appliance. Place the gypsum jacket over the new resin Master positive; spray the outside with Epoxy Parfilm and join the two halves with plaster bandage like before and fill the mold with silicone, just as before.

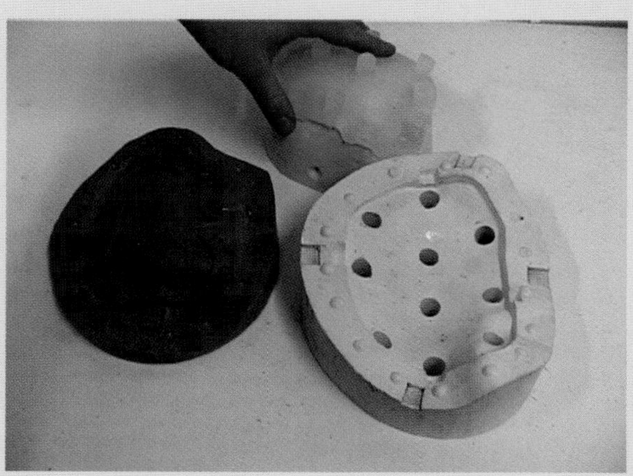

FIGURE 5.46
Finished pieces.
Image reproduced by permission of Neill Gorton.

MATRIX MOLDS

Matrix molds are arguably the best, most accurate molds you can make, but they could be overkill for some applications due to the amount of work that can go into making them. (In the United Kingdom, matrix molds are simply called jacket molds.) This particular type of mold is called a *matrix* mold because it consists of two parts—it is a composite mold consisting of a soft core and a rigid outer shell—that are melded into one cohesive unit. The rigid outer shell is created first and then the softer and more fluid molding material (silicone) between the shell and the sculpt is introduced. This process is best used for complex shapes.

There are also two ways to approach a matrix mold: as a brush-up mold or as a pour-up mold (it's the pour-up method that gives the matrix mold its name). One is more accurate than the other and also takes more time. The process begins similarly to the way you make a two-piece case mold for a sculpture, with the sculpture lying horizontally on a bed of clay covered with plastic wrap. I mentioned this at the beginning of the chapter, but in case you've already forgotten, read through the following steps and then make sure you have all the tools and materials necessary before proceeding.

This particular mold has a one-piece silicone core that will be cut to remove the model. Here is a drawing of the mold my friend Stuart Bray helped me make. The support jacket is epoxy and urethane, but it could be fiberglass, urethane, or even gypsum.

FIGURE 5.47
Stuart Bray's drawing of our matrix mold.
Photo by author.

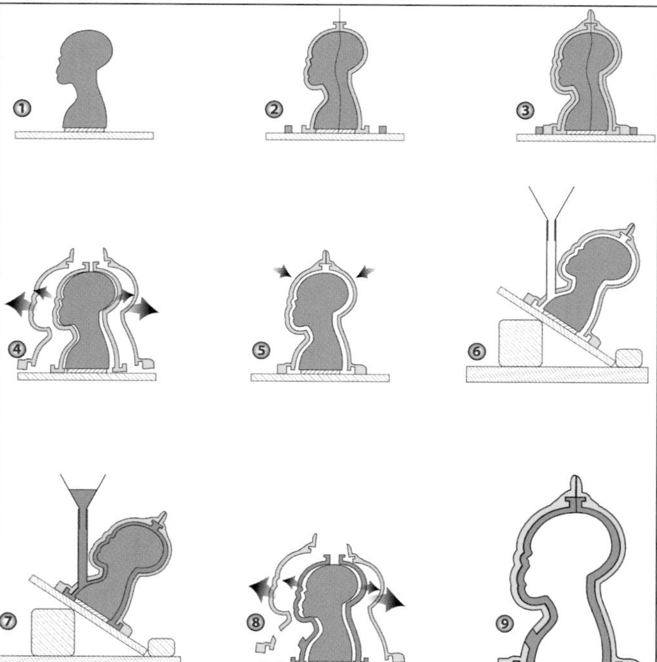

Many people opt to do a two-piece (and sometimes three) silicone core and jacket. Doing it this way all but eliminates a seam, particularly on a sculpt that has intricate details all over the place as this zombie sculpt does.

FIGURE 5.48
Zombie bust ready to mold.
Photos by author.

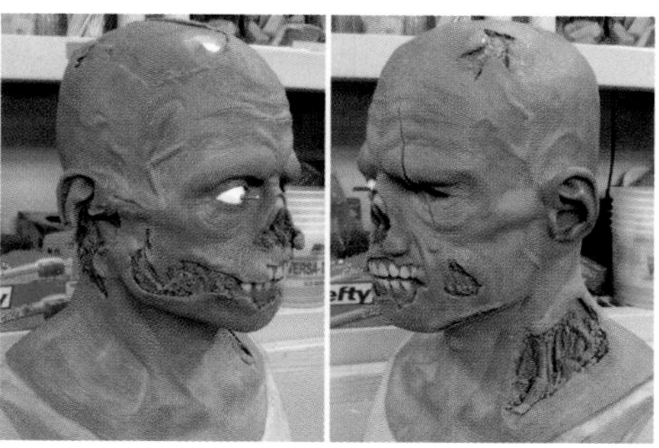

1. Wet sheets of paper towel and carefully cover the sculpt. Cover as much of the sculpture as you can with wet paper towel, gently and carefully pressing it into the contours of the sculpture.
2. Cut thin strips of clay about ½ inch thick and place them around the sculpture, then cut thin slabs to cover the rest of the sculpture.
3. Blend the clay together and smooth it. Be very mindful of undercuts with this clay covering and avoid making them. You should always be aware of the potential for undercuts at every stage of your projects. Remember, an undercut is any curve or indentation you can't see when looking straight down at your sculpture.
4. Once the clay is smooth, cut additional strips and place them down the middle of the sculpture and across, perpendicular to the strip on the midline. These will become registration keys for the silicone and support shell.

   In case you haven't yet figured it out, the clay with which you have covered the sculpture and built keys will eventually be replaced entirely by silicone. Every artist has his or her own way of doing it—how they place keys and so on. The effectiveness of the resulting mold made by different artists remains the same despite slight differences in methodology.
5. For this mold, we use thin metal shims to create the dividing wall that will separate the front and back halves of the support shell, the rigid jacket part of the mold. A good deck of playing cards also works exceptionally

FIGURE 5.49
Stuart Bray adding wet paper towels to sculpt to protect it from WED clay.
Photo by author

FIGURE 5.50
Stuart Bray slicing thin slabs of WED clay to cover sculpt (left); covering sculpt with WED clay (right).
Photos by author.

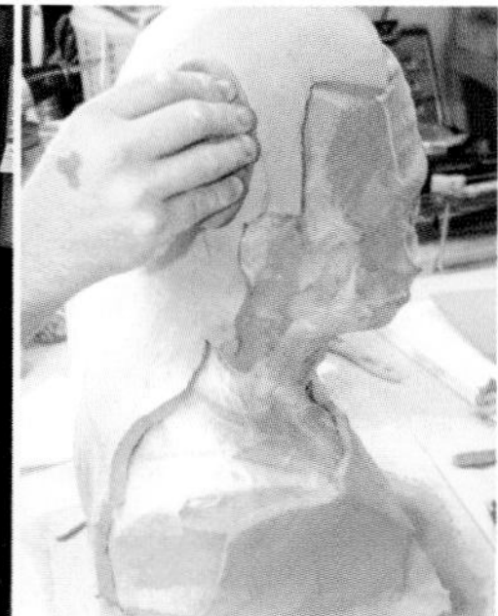

FIGURE 5.51
Author and Stuart adding keys.
Photos by Cryssie Bender.

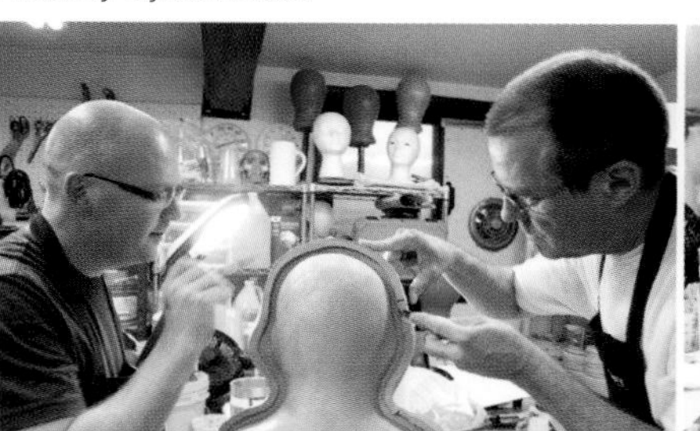

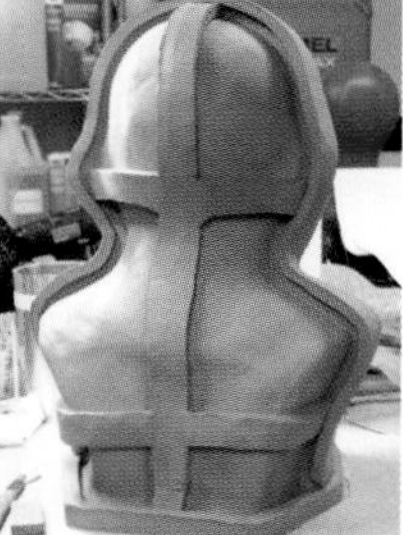

FIGURE 5.52
Metal shims as dividing wall between jacket mold halves.
Photo by author.

well and are actually quite a bit easier to manipulate than metal shims, and you're much less likely to draw blood using them, too.

6. Once the dividing wall has been constructed, spray the WED clay with two or three coats Krylon Crystal Clear, then a coat of Dulling Spray. The dulling spray may help prevent the epoxy resin for the support shell from simply rolling off the Crystal Clear when you brush on the first layer.

Because this doesn't really need to be a detail layer, you don't need to use an epoxy gelcoat (although I did). You can mix chopped glass or layup small pieces of fiberglass mat for reinforcing strength into the resin; you can also use a urethane or microballoon filler. We did a final layer of a urethane paste with fibers.

The finished mold is very strong, but much heavier than necessary. If I was going to do this again (and I did), I'd use epoxy dough sandwiched between two reinforced layers of laminating resin for exceptional strength and ultralight weight.

FIGURE 5.53
Plasti-Paste II outer layer.
Photo by author.

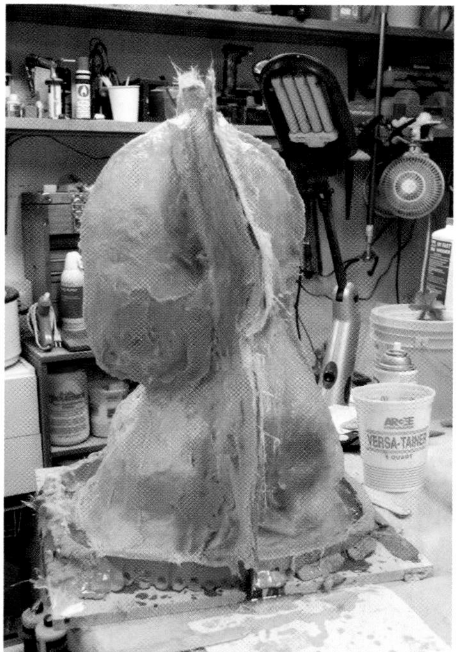

7. Once the jacket of the mold is fully cured, carefully open the mold a little at a time, using a pair of large screwdrivers or some similar tools; the mold will begin to release itself from the gradual torque being applied by adding craft sticks. Open from opposite sides simultaneously to avoid too much pressure in one area.

FIGURE 5.54
Finished mold (untrimmed); author and Stuart.
Photo by author.

FIGURE 5.55
Carefully opening mold.
Photo by author.

FIGURE 5.56
Save WED clay for weighing.
Photo by author.

8. Once the mold is opened, carefully remove the paper towels and any clay from the sculpture. Toss the paper towels, but keep the clay handy; you'll need to weigh it or determine its volume. Using a soft brush and water, clean any remaining WED clay from the surface of the sculpture.
9. Use a smooth detail tool to repair the clay around the edges of the sculpture, smoothing it and filling any gaps.
10. Remove all the clay from the inside of the mold halves and, along with the clay you already removed, weigh it or determine the volume.
11. Clean the inside of the support case mold and scrape down any sharp edges on the keys that might have been formed by resin leaking over the edges.
12. Take a Sharpie or some permanent marker and make several dots at low points (which will become high points) all around the mold where you'll drill bleeder holes; these holes will allow air to escape when silicone is poured into the mold as well as provide an escape for some excess silicone. Make sure to brush away any resin dust so that the bleeder holes will remain clear.
13. Next, drill a 1- to 2-inch hole in the jacket of the mold at a high point of the mold; it is not critical that it be at the highest point on the mold itself as long as the top of the pour spout (which will fit into the hole you just drilled) is higher than the highest point of the mold. This is the point at which you will fill the mold with silicone. You will be using a long cardboard tube or PVC pipe fitted with part of a plastic soda bottle as a funnel that you will hot-glue into the 1-inch hole you drilled. You might

FIGURE 5.57
Pouring from high minimizes bubbles.
Photo by Cryssie Bender.

find that you will have to tweak the size of the hole a bit to get your funnel to fit before gluing it in place.

It isn't actually important how big the hole you drill is, although it should be big enough in diameter so that there's plenty of room for the silicone to pour at a decent rate. What's important is that the hole you make allows your funnel to fit.

14. This mold had bolt holes drilled before opening the newly cured halves for the first time. Before you do your silicone pour, make sure that the mold is securely bolted, closed, and hot glued around the seams to prevent possible leakage. This includes the base to which the sculpt is attached.
15. If you haven't weighed the clay yet, do it now using an accurate scale. You need to know how much silicone to mix without being wasteful. You may decide to use a tin RTV silicone instead a platinum RTV silicone for cost, but platinum silicones will last longer.

You can also determine the amount of silicone by volume; whatever the volume of the clay, divide by two to get the amount each of A and B (platinum silicones are almost always a 1A:1B mix ratio).

16. Now it's time to mix the silicone. Which silicone you use is up to you. The silicone that I used as my "go to" mold rubber was a condensation-cure or tin RTV silicone, but there are addition-cure or platinum RTV silicones that I now prefer to tin-cure silicones; many of them are now of such low viscosity and fast cure times that you can use them with confidence that there will be no air bubbles trapped at the detail surface of your mold—without degassing.

I now prefer Smooth-On's Mold Star series platinum silicones (both shades of blue) over their Mold Max series, although Silicones Inc., Polytek, and others also offer a variety of exceptionally good mold-making silicones. Things you will want to consider are shore hardness (how soft or hard the material is when fully cured), shrinkage when cured, pot life (how long you have to work with it before it begins to set up), and demold time (how long you have to wait before you can safely remove the mold when it is fully cured). You will find a listing of manufacturers in the appendix at the back of this book.

NOTE

The higher the shore strength number, for example, shore 30, the harder the rubber; the lower the number, the softer the rubber.

When the silicone is mixed, air bubbles are created that you do not want to negatively affect your mold. Ordinarily you would de-air or degas the silicone in a vacuum chamber, but that will not work here because of the volume of silicone to be used, although it could be mixed in smaller batches. However, there is another way that will work just fine for our purposes.

TIP

100% clay = 70% silicone by weight

Whatever your clay weighs, multiply that number by 0.7 to get the weight of the silicone you will need. For example, if your clay weighs 1,200 grams, you'd multiply that by 0.7 and see that you will need 840 grams of silicone: 1200 · 0.7 = 840. Of course, this is only a guesstimate. If you are mixing your silicone by volume—most platinum silicones are a 1:1 mix ratio by volume—keep track of the volume of clay that you use and you will know the volume of silicone to use. You will want to mix a bit more than you need to compensate for the pour tube volume, and so forth.

17. Pour the silicone slowly in a thin stream into the mold funnel from a height above it; this will stretch and break up most of the air bubbles.

NOTE

This could require some practice, so you don't end up pouring silicone all over the place. If you're uncertain about your ability to hit a target from above, *practice first!*

You also want to be using a silicone rubber with a long cure time; that will allow any remaining air bubbles to rise in the mold, away from the surface of the sculpture, where you absolutely do not want them.

18. As the silicone fills the mold cavity, it will begin to seep out the bleeder holes. As each hole begins to leak, plug the hole with a dry wall screw or a piece of WED clay.
19. The silicone cure time should be anywhere from 4 to 24 hours, depending on which silicone you used. When the silicone is fully cured, remove your funnel and cut away the excess rubber.

FIGURE 5.58 Silicone being poured into mold.
Photo by Cryssie Bender.

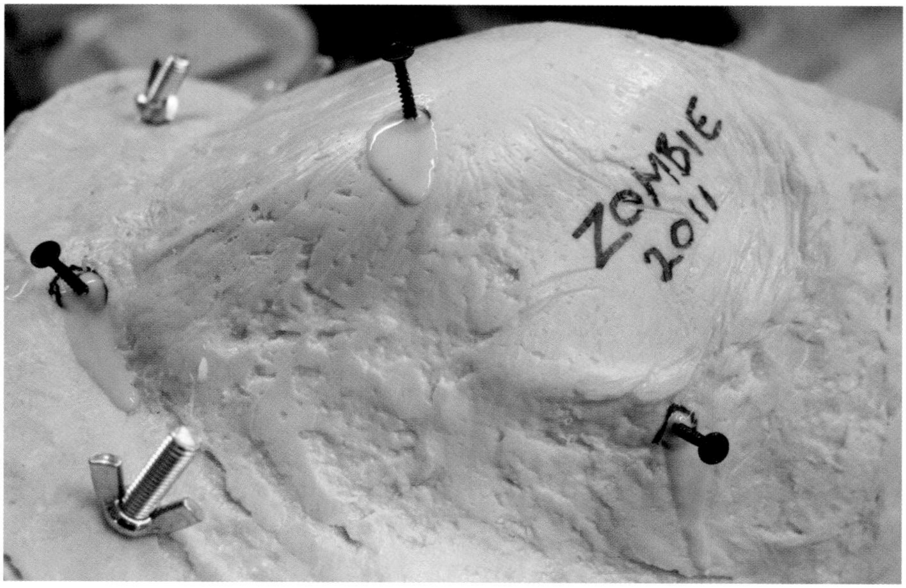

FIGURE 5.59
Bleeder holes filled and plugged.
Photo by author.

NOTE
Many newer, lower viscosity silicones have shorter cure times, which means fewer bubbles without degassing and faster demolding times.

Removing the hot glue may be a little trouble, but if you spray it with Superglue activator, it will soften and be easier to peel away. Then carefully open the mold with the proper tools inserted into the pry holes, just as you did before.

20. If this was a two-part silicone core mold, the next step would be to remove the clay from the other half of the mold and weigh it, as you did for the other half. Then repeat the steps to fill the cavity. Since this is a one-piece core and a two-piece jacket, repeating those steps is unnecessary.
21. When this silicone has cured, you can open the mold and begin removing the clay sculpture. Be careful not to damage the silicone as you're digging out the clay. You should use dull wooden tools as you get close to the silicone.
22. After you've removed all the clay, separate the inner silicone core of the mold from the outer

TIP
Superglue activator sprayed on hot glue will soften it so that it's easier to remove.

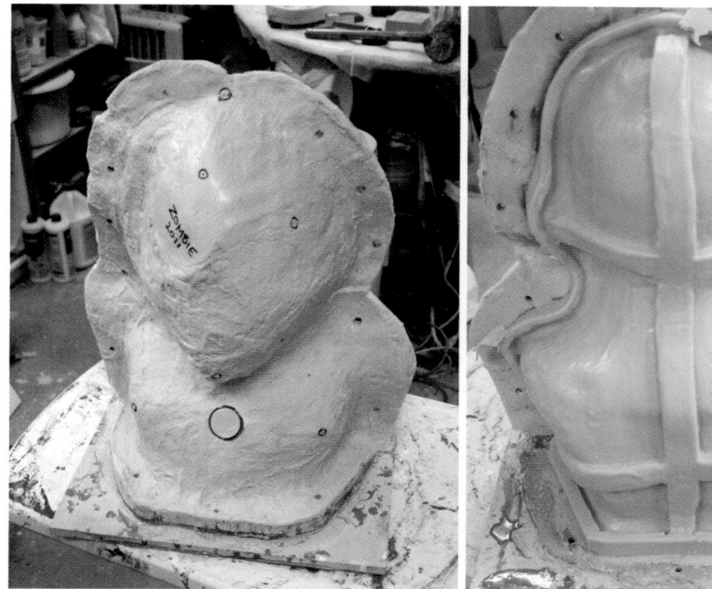

FIGURE 5.60
Matrix mold with pour spout and back jacket removed.
Photo by author.

rigid jacket of the mold. Cut off the little rubber protrusions (called *sprues*) from the bleeder holes so that it will be easier to reseat the silicone into the case mold. Cut them off flat by pulling on them slightly so they stretch, and then cut them off flush with the surface of the silicone.

23. Any clay still stuck to the silicone can be softened from removal with 99% IPA, mineral spirit, or naphtha—something that you can use as a solvent for the clay that will not damage the silicone—into the silicone and then brush out the remaining clay with a chip brush that has the bristles cut down.
24. Seat the silicone core back into the corresponding jacket halves. Feel around the silicone to make sure that there are no spaces between the silicone and the stone. When you're certain the silicone and the stone are seated together perfectly, put the mold halves together and strap the mold closed. When you look into the mold, you should not be able to see a noticeable seam line where the silicone was cut to remove the sculpt.

Your matrix mold is finished and ready for production!

The alternative to making your matrix mold using the steps just described is to do a brush up mold using thickened silicone instead of doing a cavity pour.

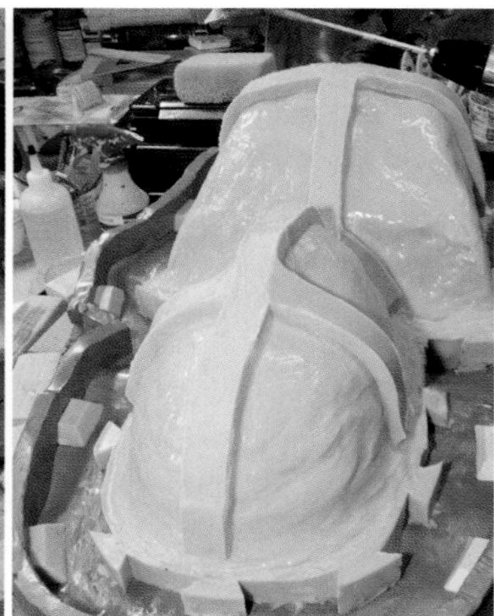

FIGURE 5.61
Brush up core without and with keys.
Photo by author.

One of the disadvantages of doing a mold this way is the silicone may be thinner and thicker in some places than in others, which can cause the silicone to pull away from the shell of the mold if not keyed sufficiently well or be a little difficult to separate from the jacket. Or it can tear. One way to help avoid thin spots is to do multiple layers of silicone and tint each batch a different color so it is easy to see where you've already brushed. Another disadvantage can be the creation of air pockets if the silicone you're brushing is too thick.

You may want to consider brushing on a thin detail layer of unthickened silicone before adding thickened silicone to ensure no air pockets against the surface of the sculpt.

Once you've achieved the thickness you want, brush a thin wash of naphtha over the outer layer of silicone before it cures to smooth it out. Because you're doing this only on the last, outer layer, you don't need to be concerned about shrinkage when the solvent evaporates. A few other tips for smoothing the outer layer of silicone are to use a wet (with water) cloth or paper towel to smooth the silicone, water with a bit of dish soap, or even a slice of fresh potato. That's not a typo.

FIGURE 5.62
Jacket mold applied to brush up core.
Photo by author

The advantage in making a brush up mold is that the shell mold is made once the silicone has been applied, so there are fewer steps and it may take less time to achieve. Then again, it may not.

The keys on the sculpt and around the perimeter of the clay flange and wall are precast and laid in place. The long strips are placed and then pinned and "glued" with silicone.

Once the silicone is cured, you're ready to make your jacket one side at a time just as described above.

FIBERGLASS MOLDS

Working with fiberglass requires safety precautions. You must wear a respirator, and there must be adequate ventilation where you work with this material. I do not say this lightly. Fiberglass gel coat and laminating resin contain proprietary polyester resin and styrene monomer, the vapor of which is quite harmful and flammable. Without adequate ventilation and a fitted NIOSH–approved respirator, you could quickly find yourself up to your chin in floor.

As a casting material and mold material, fiberglass is outstanding. You can even use it as a mold material for baking foam latex in an oven in less time than it takes using a stone mold. It is extremely lightweight and very tough. I was really leery of ever working with fiberglass until Neill Gorton convinced me that it is really easy to use. He was absolutely right, and if *I* can make it turn out well, *anybody* can!

The process is somewhat similar to making a stone mold, in that a detail layer is brushed onto the sculpture first and allowed to set before adding laminate reinforced layers. However, that's pretty much where the similarities end. Compared with Ultracal, fiberglass weighs nothing. This will make for far easier handling and much quicker curing times when you're making foam latex appliances, and time is money in this business.

Unlike silicone, latex, or urethane rubber molds, fiberglass is relatively inflexible. That is, it will not "give" in the way those other materials will. At least, it probably won't give as much or at the points where you want it to. In fact, compared to those materials, fiberglass is downright immobile. If you make a fiberglass mold of a hard or rigid object that has undercuts of any kind, you will find yourself with a mold that you cannot remove without breaking the mold, the sculpture, or both (if you can get the parts separated at all). Seriously, even a seemingly insignificant undercut may wreak havoc. Be very, very careful before building a fiberglass mold or any rigid case mold.

In addition, and I cannot stress this point enough so I'm saying it again: Fiberglass resin is very toxic in its liquid state. You need to work in a room with good ventilation and wear a NIOSH-approved respirator. Serious respiratory problems or death is considered to be unattractive life choices, so I suggest you try to avoid them whenever possible.

Because you will be creating a flange wide enough for you to bolt the two (or more) sections of the mold together, the clay wall will need to be wide as well.

Why do the mold pieces need to be bolted together? Although the fiberglass mold you make will be very strong and stiff, it will be thin, and because it is thin and also fairly large, there will be inevitable flexibility. By bolting the pieces together around the mold flange, the flexibility is taken out of the equation, making the mold very firm and holding its shape for casting inside it.

WED clay or other water clay
Misc. containers
Fiberglass mat, etc.
Gel coat
Laminating resin
Rubber gloves
Water spray bottle
Paper towels
Clay tools
Soft brush
1-inch chip brushes
NIOSH-approved respirator
Utility knife
Plaster bandages
Petroleum jelly
PVA release
Epoxy Parfilm or Synlube 531 Crystal Clear, varnish, or shellac
Safety glasses
Wood base
Polyethylene sheet

To build a fiberglass matrix mold of a bust, you'll need the following tools as well as materials listed at the beginning of this chapter:

Fiberglass gel coat is thicker than the laminating resin (polyester) used to apply fiberglass mat and fiberglass cloth, although some fiberglass resin is considered all purpose or general purpose. If you decide to use an all-purpose resin, you might find it helpful to thicken it with a filler such as Cab-O-Sil (fumed silica). It will need to be mixed thoroughly and left for a while to ensure that all the fumed silica particles dissolve and disperse throughout the polyester resin. Finding the right gel coat and laminating resin should not be too difficult, but the listing of suppliers in the appendix might be helpful if you cannot easily find what you are looking for locally. Most suppliers have online ordering capabilities and shipping.

Gel coat is available in different colors, so don't let color selection confuse you. Although there are differences in polyester formulation for laminating resin, mostly in terms of stiffness or surface finish after cure, those properties will not conflict with whatever gel coat is used.

FIGURE 5.63
Fiberglass mold pieces should be bolted together for strength. *Image reproduced by permission of Neill Gorton.*

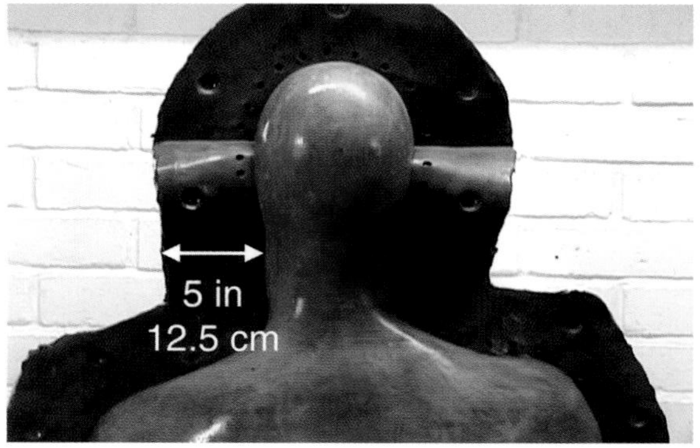

A note about using fiberglass cloth versus fiberglass mat: Fiberglass cloth is strong and is often used where it could be visible and where aesthetics are important. One of the downsides of fiberglass cloth is that because the strands are neatly woven, the layers do not intermesh as they do with the loose, disorganized strands on the fiberglass mat. Therefore, the layers of cloth sit on top of one another rather than meshing together the way they do on the fiberglass mat. This might or might not be a concern for the type of mold being made, but I'm putting the information out there for you to weigh. Fiberglass tissue is very thin, very fine fiberglass mat and is sometimes referred to as *veil*. It is outstanding for reinforcing and laminating fine detail areas.

Fiberglass resin contains *styrene*, which reacts with the glass fibers in the fiberglass mat, cloth, and tissue, softening it (essentially dissolving it) so that it is easy to shape and mold around forms. Styrene is the primary reason for using proper ventilation and wearing eye protection, rubber gloves, NIOSH-approved respirator, and even coveralls.

The principal health effects due to styrene exposure involve the central nervous system. These effects include subjective complaints of headache, fatigue, dizziness, confusion, drowsiness, malaise, difficulty in concentrating, and a feeling of intoxication. The International Agency for Research on Cancer classifies styrene as a potential human carcinogen. Acute health effects of styrene are generally irritation of the skin, eyes, and the upper respiratory tract. Acute exposure also results in gastrointestinal effects. Chronic exposure affects the central nervous system, showing symptoms such as depression, headache, fatigue, and weakness, and may cause minor effects on kidney function. Additional information about recognizing occupational hazards and health effects associated with styrene can be found at www.osha.gov/SLTC/styrene/recognition.html.

I know these warnings make working with fiberglass sound rather frightening. It really isn't. However, I would be remiss if I did not identify potential problem areas so that you can easily avoid them by working smart and being safe.

For outstanding step-by-step instructions for creating a fiberglass core (positive) and fiberglass matrix mold, I strongly recommend purchasing Neill Gorton's four-DVD series, *Creating Character Prosthetics in Silicone*.

FILLERS

In casting core positives or even when making molds, it is often desirable to add some kind of filler to the polyester resin to give it added strength and longevity. Depending on the need, there are different fillers that will give different properties to the materials they're added to. For example, adding fumed silica (Cab-O-Sil) as filler to a material such as polyester laminating resin will cause the silica to act as a thixotropic agent, making the laminating resin thicker. It also enhances tensile strength, abrasion resistance, and stiffness. Adding chopped fibers to that same laminating resin will make it stronger as well. Metallic powders can also be added as fillers. These will make a material stronger as well as heavier; heavier metal powder will add weight proportionally by volume as well as tint the material to the metallic color. Other fillers, such as certain types of microspheres, not only can add strength to a material but can make it lighter, depending on what material the spheres are made of. Aluminum powder added to polyester resin for fiberglass mold fabrication, for example, will increase the hardness and abrasion resistance of the surface.

RESIN MOLDS

Forton MG (FMG), although technically a gypsum product (Hydrocal is the main ingredient), is considered a resin casting material because it incorporates plastics and fiberglass. FMG consists of a modified gypsum (hence the name modified gypsum [MG]), FGR-95, dry melamine resin powder, a hardener, a liquid polymer called Forton VF-812, and chopped fiberglass. The advantages of FMG over fiberglass are that it is odorless and nontoxic and it cures much faster. Another advantage is that it can be cast directly into an alginate mold, unlike polyester and epoxy resins. The disadvantages are that there are more components to measure and measurement must be precise, so an accurate gram scale is essential; in addition, it is heavier than polyester or epoxy resin molds. By my math, advantages outweigh disadvantages for Forton MG

You can also substitute Densite HS for the FGR-95. FGR-95 is Alpha gypsum from US Gypsum, whereas Densite HS is from Georgia Pacific but is also Alpha gypsum. What *is* Alpha gypsum? Alpha gypsum is made by processing batches of gypsum under high pressure; it has a lower water-carrying capability and is used where strength is required, as in mold making. *Ahhhh...* So what's Beta gypsum? When the hemi-hydrate of gypsum (two gypsum molecules for every one molecule of water) is formed by calcining (heating to the point of burning to ash) in kettles at atmospheric pressure, it's called Beta gypsum. *Ohhhhhh...* now don't you wish you'd paid attention in chemistry class? Sources where you can get Forton MG are listed in the appendix. A similar gypsum-based resin product is called duoMatrix, from Smooth-On.

Forton MG really doesn't need fillers for strength because it already has them as part of the system. However, you can add metallic powders or marble powders to it to simulate the look and feel of foundry castings or natural stone sculpture. The surfaces can then be patinaed using foundry etching acids or be polished to a high shine.

EPOXY MOLDS

Epoxy molds can be constructed the same way fiberglass molds are made; the major advantage to making epoxy molds is that wearing a respirator is not mandatory so long as you have good ventilation. Wearing gloves is still essential, however.

First, a detail gelcoat layer is laid down, followed by up to three laminating layers of epoxy with chopped glass, fiberglass cloth, or fiberglass mat. Unlike polyester resin, however, epoxy does not contain styrene, so the fiberglass material will not actually dissolve in it, but it will provide sufficient reinforcement as to make your laminating layers of epoxy quite strong, while the mold wall remains thin and lightweight.

SYNTACTIC DOUGH

A relatively new addition to the makeup effects artist's arsenal of mold making materials is syntactic dough, a two-part epoxy dough that is an extremely lightweight and extremely strong material used in industrial die making. It can be drilled and tapped, and for makeup effects mold making, it is becoming quite popular because of its weight, strength, and heat resistance. It takes longer to reach its full cure hardness than other epoxies, polyester resin, urethanes, or gypsum, but its light weight and high strength is undeniable. The best way to use it is in conjunction with a laminating resin—another epoxy, polyester, or urethane. First, apply a detail surface gel coat of epoxy, polyester, or urethane and then add one or two layers of laminating resin with fiberglass mat or fiberglass cloth. Although the laminating layer is still tacky, mix the dough according to the manufacturer's instructions (they will vary by manufacturer, and there are a few—Adtech, Smooth-On, Factor II, United Resin) and press the compound out in all directions until you have the desired thickness; ½ inch (13 millimeters) should be plenty thick, maybe thinner, depending on what you're molding. Thicker won't hurt either; the dough is so light weight that a mold an inch thick (2.5 centimeters) overall will still be substantially lighter than a gypsum mold. It will bond to the laminated layers. Finally, add a couple more layers of laminating resin with fiberglass mat or cloth.

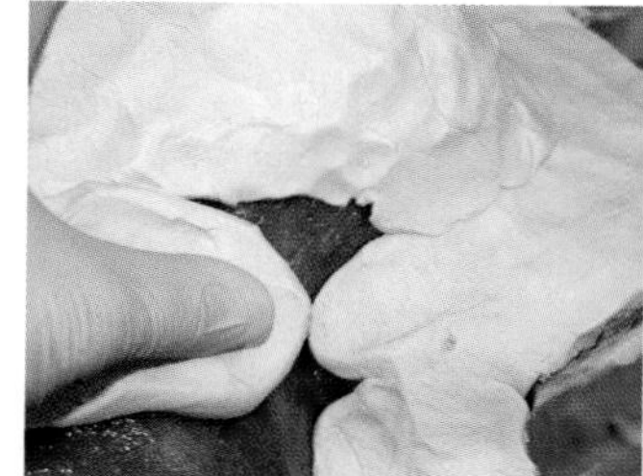
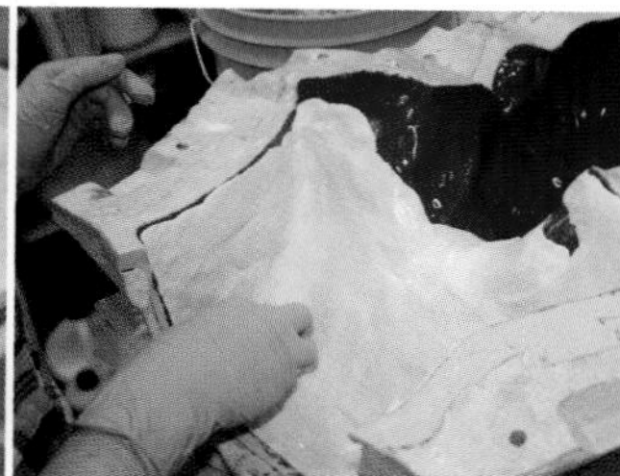

FIGURE 5.64
Epoxy mold using epoxy dough.
Photos by author.

I've been asked if these light epoxy molds can be used to bake foam latex. Absolutely, yes.

URETHANE MOLDS

Urethane is just one more way to go in the world of mold making for special makeup effects. Actually, when we use the term *urethane* as it pertains to the work that we do and the uses we have for it, the name has been shortened from *polyurethane*. There is a specific substance called urethane, also known as *ethyl carbamate*, and the two should not be confused. For our purposes, when you see the word *urethane* in the context of special makeup effects, it means *poly*urethane.

Urethane formulas cover an extremely wide range of stiffness, hardness, and densities. These materials include low- and high-density flexible foam used in upholstery and bedding as well as in makeup effects prosthetics (known as *cold foam*), which will be discussed fully in Chapter 6; low- and high-density rigid foam used for thermal insulation; soft-solid elastomers used for gel pads, print rollers, and mold making as a substitute for some tin-cure RTV silicones; and hard-solid plastics used as electronic instrument bezels, structural parts, and mold making as well, as a substitute for epoxy and polyester resin molds. Urethanes are widely used in high-resiliency flexible foam seating, rigid foam insulation panels, microcellular foam seals and gaskets, durable elastomeric wheels and tires, electrical potting compounds, high-performance adhesives, and sealants, Spandex fibers, seals, gaskets, carpet underlay, and hard plastic parts.[2]

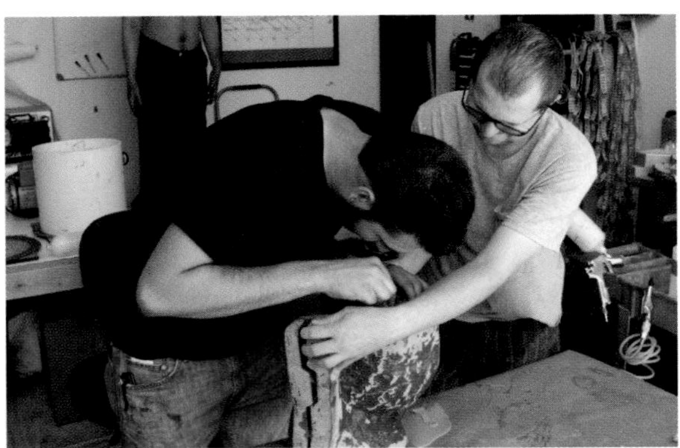

FIGURE 5.65
Photo by author.

One particular urethane that I like to use for making small block case molds is BJB Enterprises' TC-1630 urethane resin. It is a two-part urethane with filler added. BJB cautions that platinum silicones will not set up against the TC-1630, but I have not found that to be the case.

Smooth-On also makes a urethane paste with embedded fibers called PlastiPaste II, which is quite nice for creating mother molds. It holds a vertical surface without sagging and cures to a strong, durable, and relatively lightweight plastic.

For the most part, the use of these materials is the same as their counterparts, with a few notable exceptions. One of the reasons we use silicones extensively for mold making is that silicones are essentially *self-releasing;* that is, almost nothing will stick to silicone except other silicone. Urethane rubbers, on the other hand, are not self-releasing. In fact, they are the opposite: Urethane rubbers are adhesive. To prevent adhesion between urethane rubber and the porous surface of a cast (made of Hydrocal, plaster, Ultracal, or the like), it must be sealed and then released. Casts made of thermoplastic, which includes urethane plastic, epoxy, and polyester resin (fiberglass), must be sealed with shellac or PVA and then released. When in doubt about what to use, manufacturers recommend a small test application to determine the proper release agent. That is a good idea, considering how much work goes into a project before reaching this point. It'd sure be a shame to have to start over.

All liquid urethanes are moisture sensitive and will absorb atmospheric moisture. Using water-based clays is not recommended. Mixing tools and containers should be clean and made of metal or plastic; mixing urethane with a wooden stir stick can cause problems merely via atmospheric moisture retained in the wood, even if you're working in a humidity-controlled environment. If you choose to make your mold using urethane rubber instead of silicone and you plan on building the dividing wall with WED or other water clay, it is absolutely imperative that the clay be well sealed with Crystal Clear, and dry, before applying the urethane! *I strongly suggest a test with sealed clay and a bit of urethane before trying this on a project.*

This is quite true also of urethane plastic used for a hard outer shell of a matrix mold, for example. If you are using WED clay or other water-based clay to form barriers and walls, it must definitely be well sealed to prevent moisture contact with the urethane. It will bubble and foam if there is any contact with any moisture from water. Use another material to form your walls.

Working with silicone does not require that you wear a respirator or work in a well-ventilated environment (although it's not a bad idea to have good ventilation anyway), but it is strongly recommended that you wear safety glasses and gloves to minimize the risk of contamination and irritation. However, working with urethane shares essentially the same hazardous risks of working with fiberglass resins: epoxy and polyester. Mixing should be done only in a well-ventilated environment while wearing a respirator. Rubber gloves and safety glasses are also strongly advised. Before working with any of these materials, you should read and be familiar with each product's material safety data sheet.

With these exceptions, working with urethane follows the same procedural steps as working with gypsum, silicone, fiberglass, and epoxy. We won't repeat the step-by-step process in this book. You can easily go back and figure that out on your own.

COLLAPSIBLE CORE MOLDS AND 'PUZZLE' MOLDS

All images reproduced by permission of Brian Best

This category of mold making can give even the most seasoned effects artist a moment of pause. And if you think general mold making is time consuming and difficult, creating collapsible core molds will turn your hair gray. But if you're not one to back away from a challenge, and you actually like to solve puzzles, then by golly this is for you!

Both "collapsible core" and "puzzle" refer to the same type of mold: a mold with an inner core that is designed to come apart as part of the demolding process to allow easy removal of the cast appliance as well as producing a piece with no outward seams or connecting lines. Some are more complex and complicated than others, but what this type of mold allows you to do is create a single prosthetic appliance when you would have to create it with multiple pieces using a more traditional mold making technique; otherwise, you'd be creating the risk of damaging the prosthetic, or the mold, or both when trying to remove the finished cast.

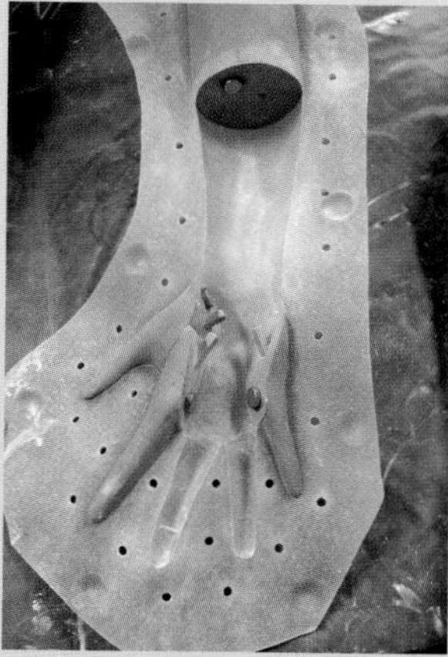

FIGURE 5.66

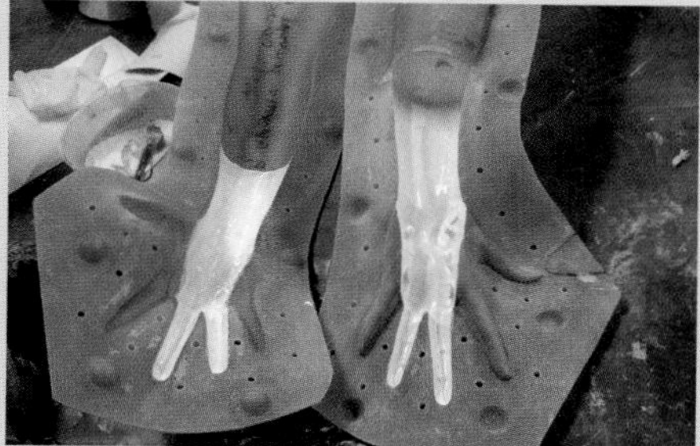

FIGURE 5.67

FIGURE 5.68

FIGURE 5.69
Vincent Van Dyke and Carl Lyon demolding encapsulated silicone appliance.

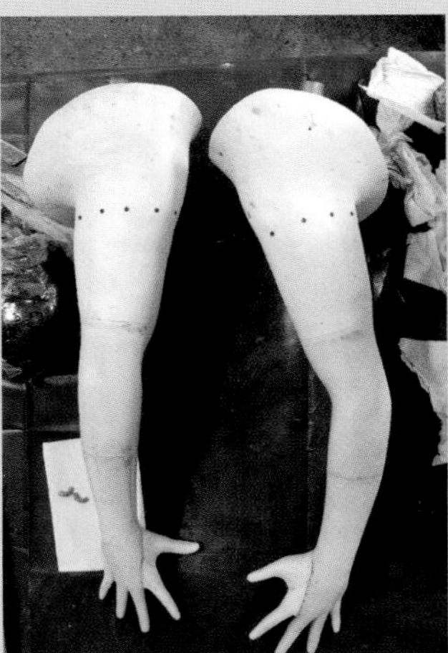

FIGURE 5.70

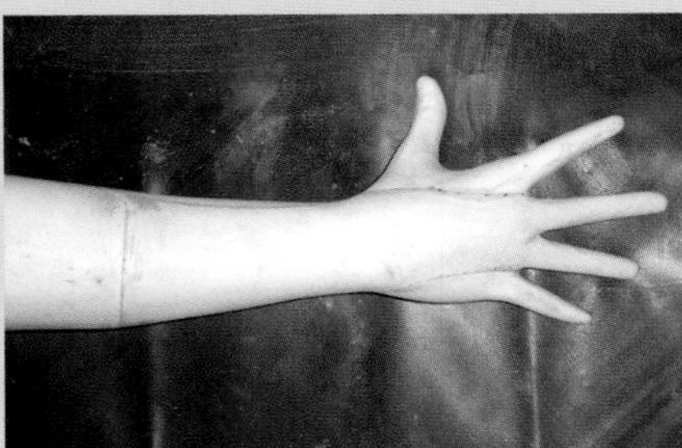

FIGURE 5.71

Figures 5.66 through 5.69 show the prototype sections (gray glass reinforced plastic [GRP] and auto filler composite with magnets) being converted into the master core (white GRP with magnets). Figures 5.70 and 5.71 show the final GRP core. Figures 5.72 through 5.76 show the final exterior jacket molds (flexible interior with a GRP jacket). Figure 5.77 shows the final hands cast in silicone. These were cut down from the full arm size to allow for certain suits to be lighter when the full costume was in use. Brian initially used a flexible polyurethane rubber for the interior one-piece wrap-around mold. However, he decided the next epoxy arm core/jacket mold will be made with a platinum silicone interior. Both can be used successfully to cast the final platinum silicone skin (the appliance); Brian prefers using silicone as a molding material because it is safer and cleaner to use than urethanes.

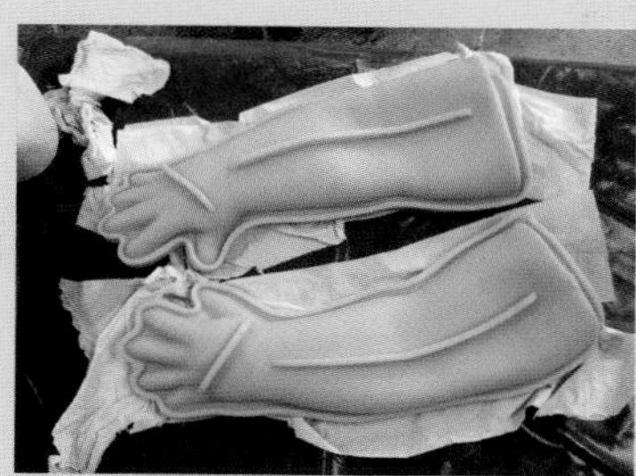

FIGURE 5.72

FIGURE 5.73

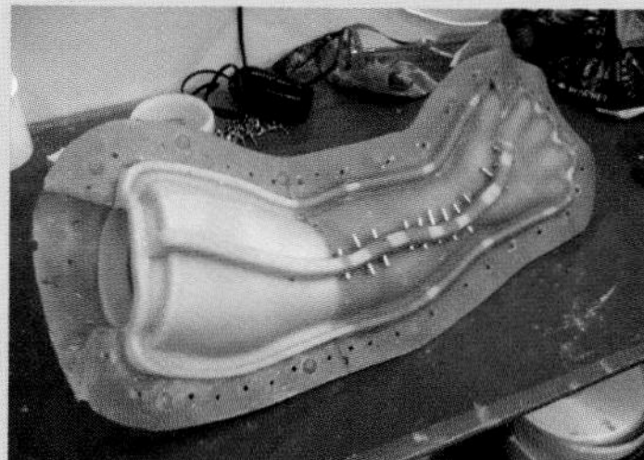

FIGURE 5.74

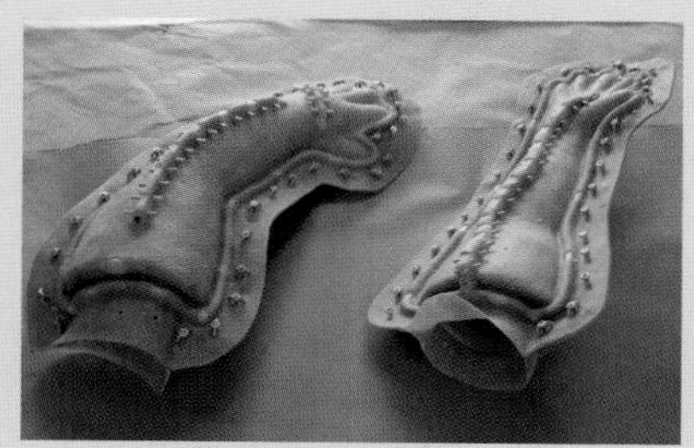

FIGURE 5.75

FIGURE 5.76
Image reproduced by permission of Brian Best.

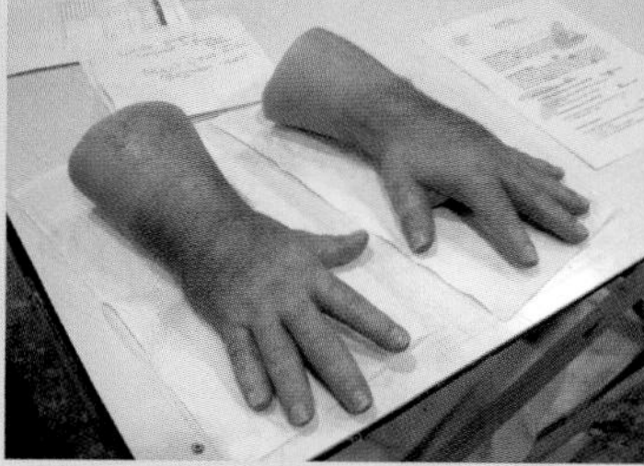

FIGURE 5.77
Image reproduced by permission of Brian Best.

A collapsible core is used when you want to produce to prosthetic appliance, such as a sleeve, with no seams. The best solution is to place all your seams inside the core of the mold. With all the seams inside the actual mold itself (built up on the final sculpture/core), the appliance can then be processed in one piece rather than multiple pieces.

This hand/arm core is designed to be used in conjunction with a one-piece silicone/two-piece epoxy jacket mold. These figures show how a collapsible core can be converted into any given casting material.

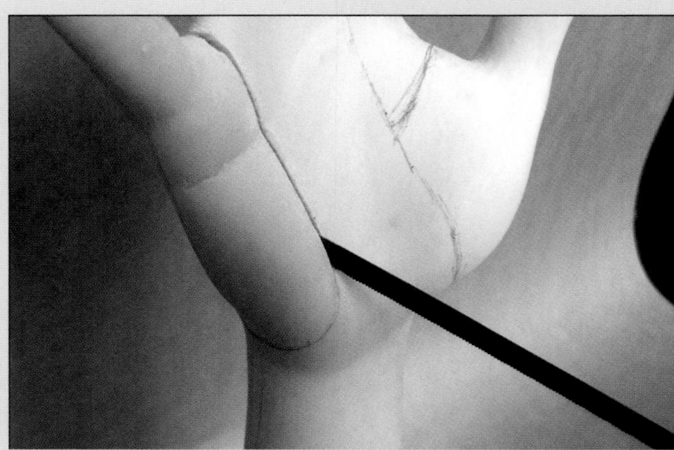

FIGURE 5.78
Image reproduced by permission of Brian Best.

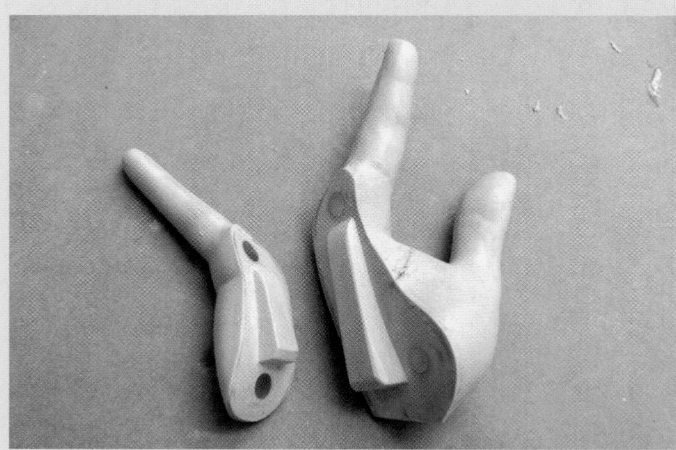

FIGURE 5.79
Image reproduced by permission of Brian Best.

Figure 5.78 shows the GRP hand/arm cast being cut up into the desired sections. Figure 5.75 shows the GRP sections cast in polyester filler and with magnets in place.

Figure 5.80 shows the GRP cut sections in polyester filler. Figure 5.81 shows the sections placed in the core mold to produce the main section.

Figure 5.82 and Figure 5.83 show how you can cast the collapsible core sections; this example shows injecting with polyurethane casting resin.

Figure 5.84 through Figure 5.87 show the hand/arm sections being cast in epoxy and the final collapsible hand/arm core as an epoxy/carbon composite.

These cores can be simple to produce, but they need to be thought out before sculpting commences. The sculpture design usually determines how the core is collapsed. A thick sculpture will need a minimal breakdown. If the sculpture is very thin, the core may require more pieces to successfully remove it from inside.

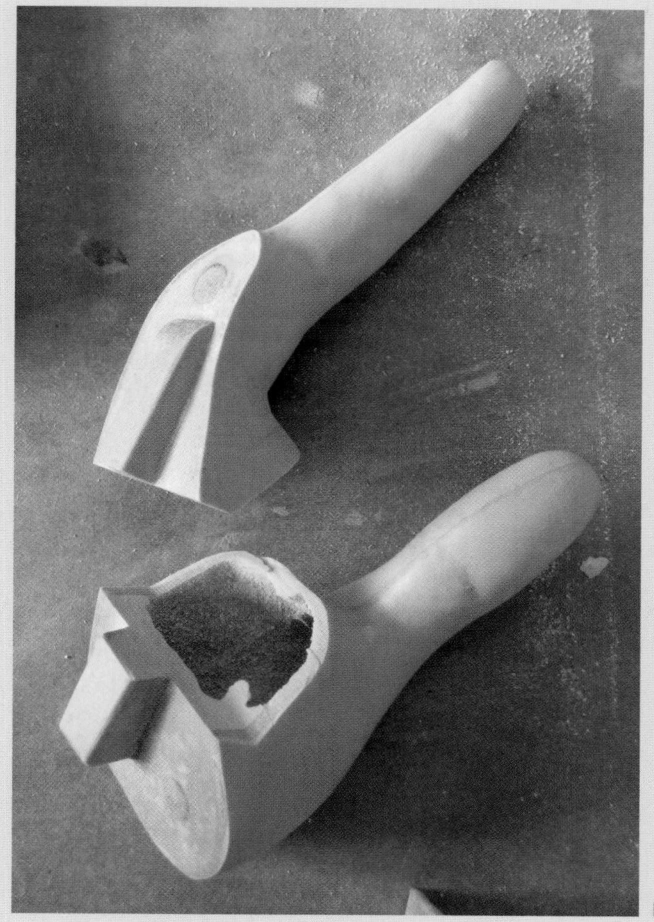

FIGURE 5.80

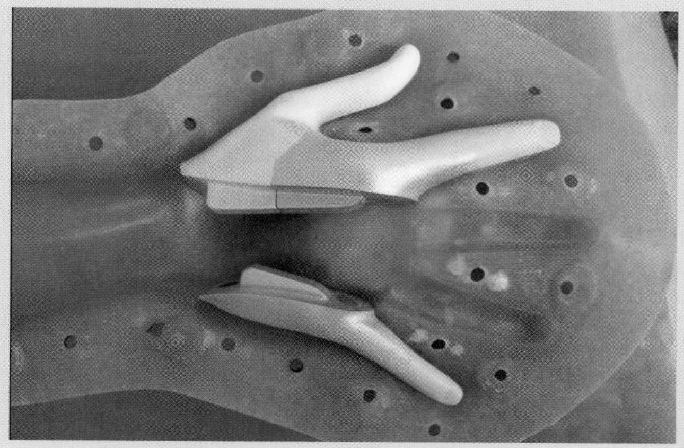

FIGURE 5.81

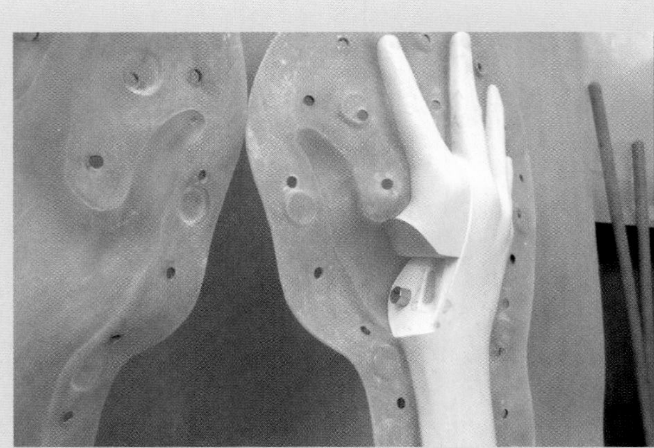

FIGURE 5.82
Image reproduced by permission of Brian Best.

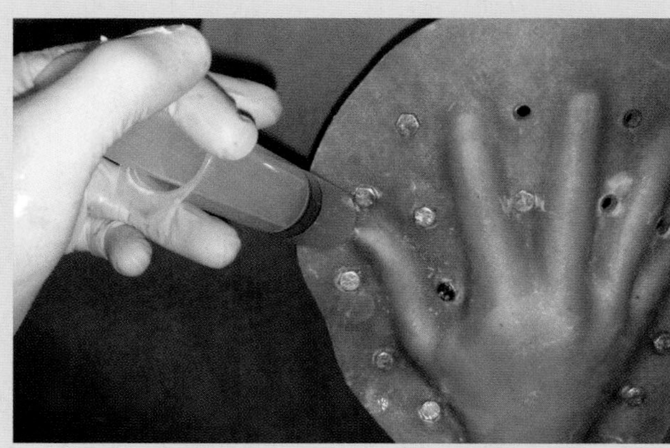

FIGURE 5.83
Image reproduced by permission of Brian Best.

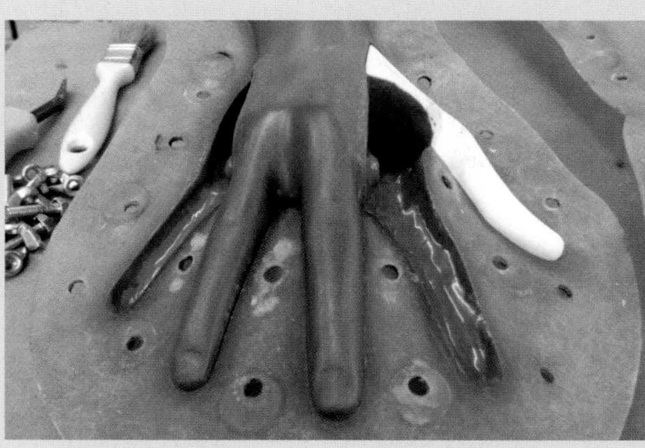

FIGURE 5.84
Image reproduced by permission of Brian Best.

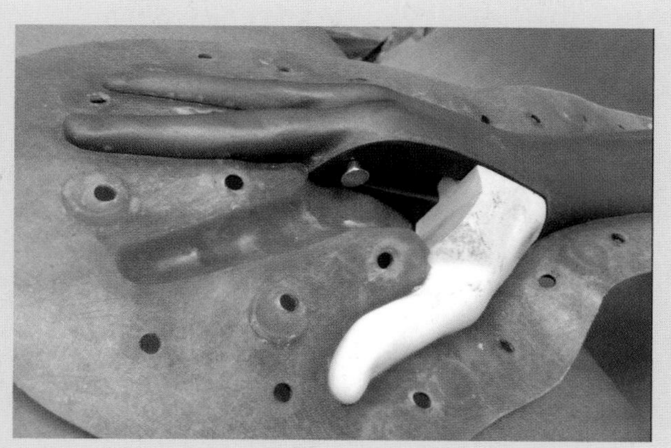

FIGURE 5.85
Image reproduced by permission of Brian Best.

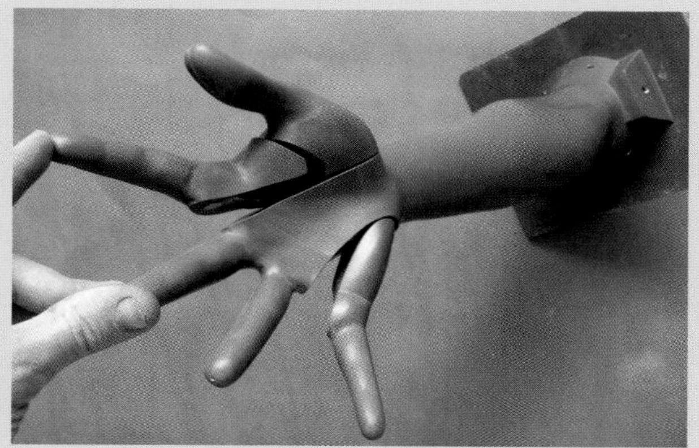

FIGURE 5.86

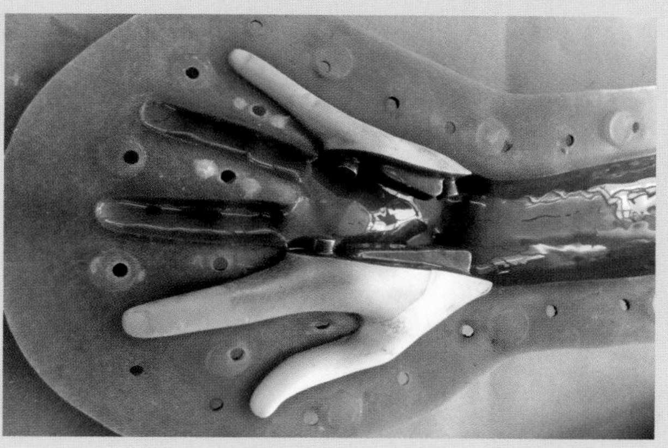

FIGURE 5.87
Image reproduced by permission of Brian Best.

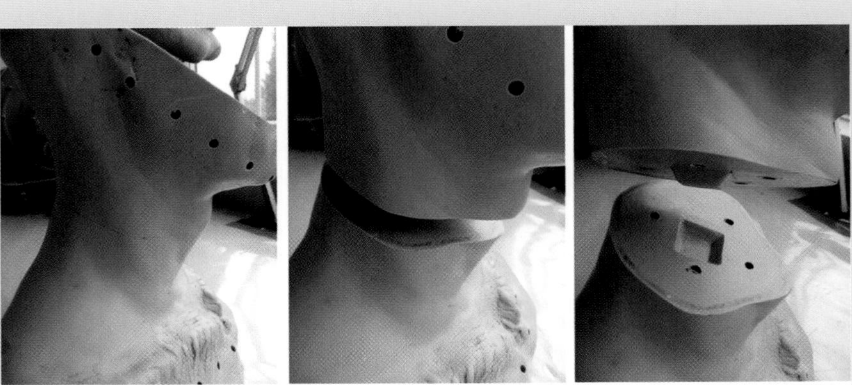

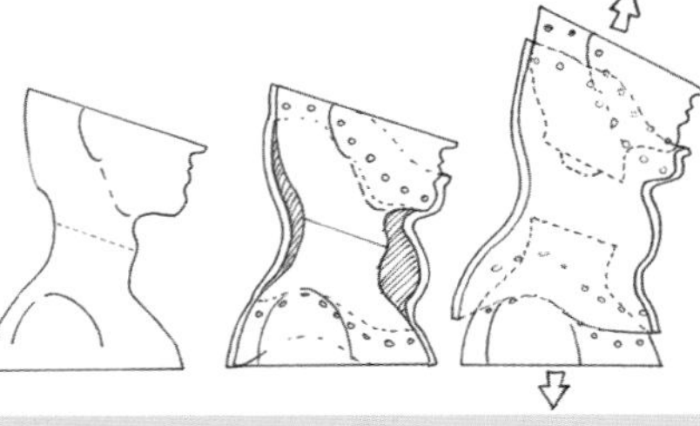

FIGURE 5.88
Two-part neck mold.
Images reproduced by permission of Brian Best.

This neck mold is a simple GRP example; the same process could easily be produced as a gypsum mold. It is broken down into two sections. A line was initially drawn across the neck to define the area where both sections can be removed without any undercuts. A saw was used to cut the neck into halves. One section of the neck was place onto a thin sheet of plastic (about 0.5 millimeter or 3⁄16 inch), drawn around with a marker and then trimmed to produce a plastic disc. A sculpted location key was added to the center of the disc, and the disc was then taped onto one of the neck sections (either section is okay). A gel coat was then applied, followed by GRP.

Once cured, cleaned up, and waxed/released, the other section was added, again simply by securing with tape. Again, a gel coat was applied followed by GRP. Before demolding the two sections, a drill was used to add four bolt location points, which will accurately keep the two sections aligned properly. A core mold is quite useful during this process; by laminating each section within this core mold, you will keep the accuracy of the original form.

CHAPTER SUMMARY

- This chapter describes the steps needed to break down a sculpture into the parts needed for mold making.
- You received a crash course in silicone.

- You learned to make conforming molds.
- You learned about the types and importance of release agents and sealers.
- Re-sculpting for multipiece makeup was illustrated.
- The purpose and placement of keys, flashing, and cutting edges was described.
- You learned how to construct a sturdy clay retaining wall around your sculpture.
- You learned about different types of molds and mold materials and were given descriptions of them.
- You learned about fillers.
- You were given a glimpse of collapsible core molds.

Endnotes

1 Just when you thought it was safe, a crucial point to remember when making silicone molds is to think ahead to your finished piece. If you need a final result made out of platinum, then your mold will need to be platinum, because yep, you guessed it, tin silicone is one of the many things that inhibit the cure of platinum silicone. Conversely, tin silicones will set over platinum without any problems. There have recently been a couple of products developed by one manufacturer that coat the silicone with a protective substrate (e.g., FuseFX) and are therefore supposed to allow use of a tin silicone mold with a platinum cast, but they are not yet widely available and have not been tested with all manufacturers' products.

2 Wikipedia contributors, "Polyurethane," *Wikipedia, The Free Encyclopedia*, http://en.wikipedia.org/w/index.php?title=Polyurethane&oldid=177688842.

CHAPTER 6

Casting the Appliances

Key Points

- Understanding silicone (continued)
- Coloring silicone intrinsically (internally) for translucence
- Gel-filled appliances, filling the mold, and removing the appliance
- Foam latex and its properties
- Running foam latex
- Casting urethane (cold) foam
- Casting gelatin and foamed gelatin
- Casting dental acrylic
- Painting and seaming (cleaning up) appliances and teeth

INTRODUCTION

This chapter describes the methods for creating prosthetics using silicone, foam latex, foam urethane, gelatin, and foamed gelatin and dental acrylic. Rather than make a laundry list of materials needed to cast prosthetic appliances, I will add the list of materials specific to a particular type of appliance, such as foam latex, gelatin, and silicone, for each section.

David Elsey

FIGURE 6.1
Dave Elsey and Benicio Del Toro; *The Wolfman* (2009).
Image reproduced by permission of David Elsey.

To many, Dave's résumé reads like a cult-film dream list: He created creature effects in *Alien 3*; worked as a special makeup-effects artist on *Hellraiser*, *Mission: Impossible*, and *Indiana Jones and the Last Crusade*; and honed his animatronics skills in the cult classic, *The Little Shop of Horrors*. He is perhaps most well known by genre fans for his role as the creative supervisor on the sci-fi TV series *Farscape*, for which he designed and maintained up to 600 different creatures.

For his role as the Creature Shop Supervisor for *Star Wars: Episode III, Revenge of the Sith* (for which he was nominated for an Academy Award), Dave and his makeup effects team were responsible for bringing to life all the animatronics, prosthetic creatures, and characters seen in the film. Dave was at the forefront of the Creature Shop team responsible for such Episode III creations as the Wookies, the Utapauns, charred Anakin Skywalker, and the twisted Emperor Palpatine.

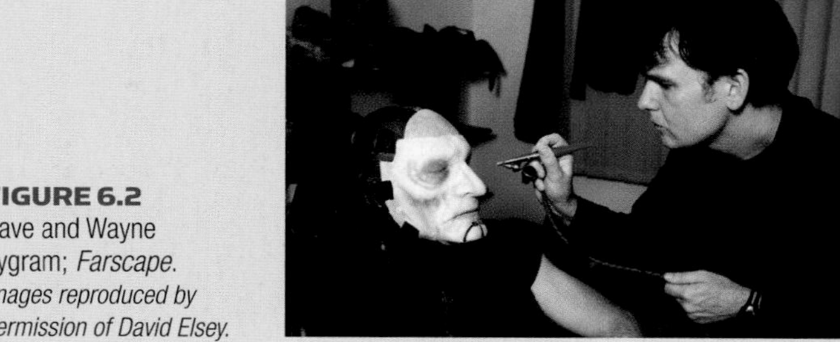

FIGURE 6.2
Dave and Wayne Pygram; *Farscape*.
Images reproduced by permission of David Elsey.

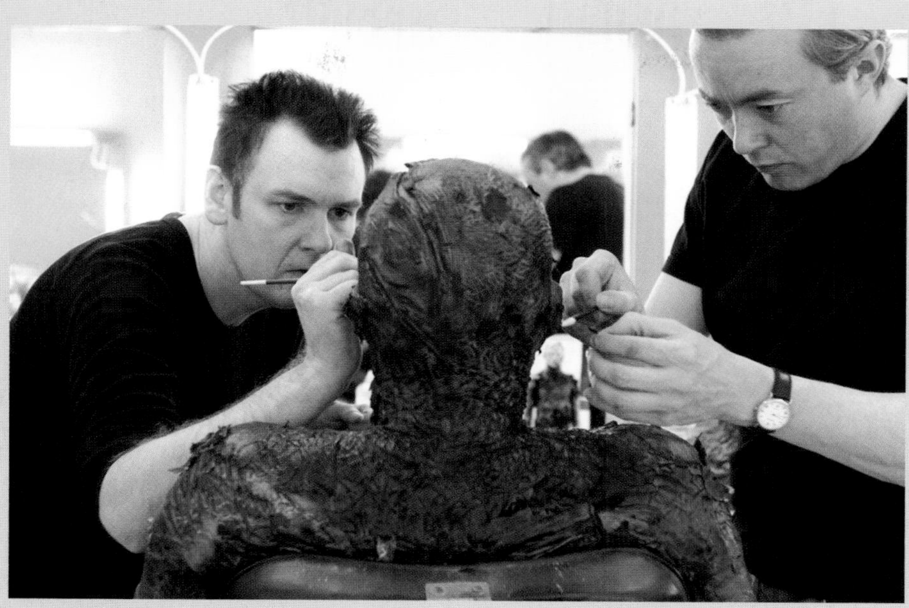

FIGURE 6.3
Dave, Colin Ware, and Hayden Christensen.
Images reproduced by permission of David Elsey.

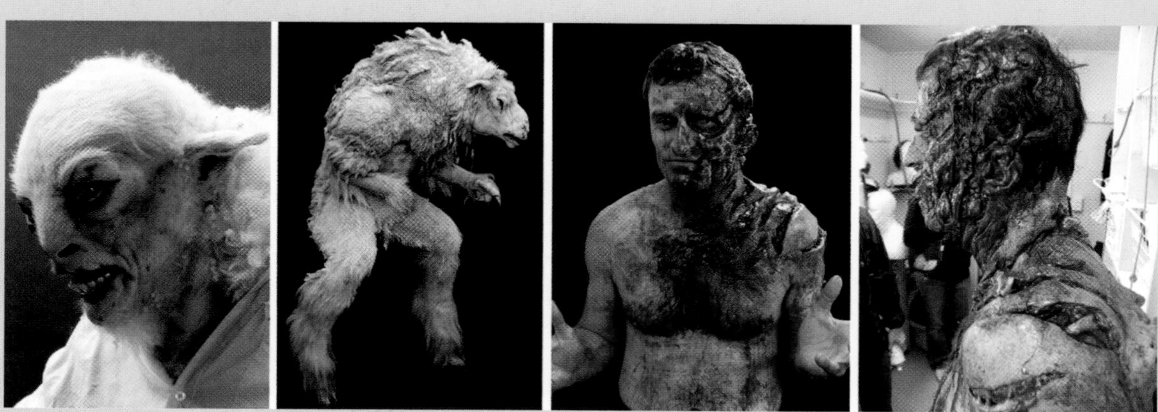

FIGURE 6.4
Black Sheep.
Images reproduced by permission of David Elsey.

More recently, Dave worked on *X-Men: First Class* and was the co-creature supervisor as well as creating the additional creatures for Spike Jonze's *Where the Wild Things Are*. In 2008, Dave worked in London with makeup effects legend Rick Baker and fellow book contributors Neill Gorton and John Schoonraad on makeup effects for a remake of the 1941 Lon Chaney, Jr., horror classic *The Wolf man*, starring Anthony Hopkins and Benicio Del Toro; Dave and Rick were awarded an Oscar.

SILICONE: PLATINUM AND TIN

I've talked at length about one of the materials commonly used for creating prosthetic appliances, but only as it applies to mold making: silicone. As for prosthetics, appliances made of silicone look and feel remarkably like real skin. They certainly can, anyway. And they're made mostly using platinum RTV silicone because platinum silicone is safe for using directly on the skin.

There are also some wonderful tin RTV silicones available for prosthetics, specifically encapsulated tin silicone gels; they can be accelerated, but as you'll recall, a fast catalyst will ultimately weaken the silicone. Perhaps that won't happen quickly enough to be a problem for your application if it's immediate. If you make multiples of a piece with the intention of storing them over time, they may become unusable, even brittle, if the cure is accelerated. This can happen within a matter of days, especially if you use only a fast catalyst and none of the regular catalyst. I've seen it happen with some of my tin RTV mold rubber; I am making a presumption that it will be true for other silicones as well.

Silicone appliances can be cast in a number of types of molds, including Ultracal, Hydrocal, fiberglass, Forton MG, urethane, and even silicone, provided it's supported by a jacket mold. However, remember that platinum silicone cannot be cast into a tin silicone mold; it will not cure. Platinum into tin is not okay. Tin into platinum is okay; tin into tin is okay; and platinum into platinum is okay. But the molds *must* be released well to prevent the new silicone from permanently bonding to the silicone of the mold.

COLORATION

One of the great things about silicone is its similarity in look and feel to human skin when it is colored intrinsically with pigment. Human skin is actually translucent. When silicone is colored internally with any number and type of pigments, most notably colored rayon flocking, the silicone color has actual depth, just like skin.

FIGURE 6.5
Adding pigment.
Photo by author.

Silicone can also be colored intrinsically with opaque pigments that significantly lessen the sense of depth and translucence; however, if the amount is very small, translucency can be maintained. This is something that will require experimentation on your part; there is no formula for coloring silicone, although many agree that pigmenting roughly 1% of the total silicone volume is good. You can always add pigment, but you cannot remove it. I believe you want to maintain slight translucency, not go completely opaque with your coloring. I will tell you this, too: Silicone can be very difficult to paint. Silicone is resistant to acids, bases, solvents, chemicals, oils, and water. Virtually *nothing* sticks to silicone except other silicone.

The method I use most often is one I learned from Neill Gorton, and it works well. I will make a mark on my mixing stick with a Sharpie marker and add drops of pigment into the silicone a few drops at a time and stir. When I lift the stick out of the silicone (I do this individually to part A and part B, *not* when they're mixed together), I'll let it drain mostly off the stick, and if I can just barely see the mark on it, then the amount of pigment will give just the right amount or translucence. If I can still see the mark clearly, I need more pigment; if I can't see it at all, I need to add more A/B.

If you choose to forego intrinsic coloring and you color your appliance extrinsically, you will need to use a silicone-based coloring system. You can achieve relatively decent results with a crème foundation that is not silicone based, but the moment your actor rubs his nose or accidentally brushes against something or someone, that makeup is going to wipe right off, no matter how much powder or sealer you applied to set the makeup. Fortunately, there are some terrific silicone-based airbrush paints and makeup foundations designed for use on silicone appliances. Canadian artist Guy Louis XVI's FuseFX platinum silicone paint system has become quite popular and is widely used. You can also color with alcohol-activated pigments, such as Premiere Products' Skin Illustrator palettes, developed by Kenny Myers, and WM Creations' Sta-Color palettes, developed by Matthew Mungle. Just know that this method will rub off.

FIGURE 6.6
Sampling of FuseFX silicone pigments.
Photo by author.

Joshua Turi

Josh has been working as a Special Effects Makeup/Makeup Artist for over 20 years. The Makeup bug bit him at the age of 11 when he saw a makeup artist applying wound makeups on an actor. Immediately knowing that this was what he wanted to do, he immersed himself into learning everything he could about makeup and special effects. After a chance encounter with another artist at the age of 16, Josh's first-ever effect appeared in the feature film *Strong City* (aka *Dark City*).

FIGURE 6.7
Joshua Turi.
Image reproduced by permission of Joshua Turi.

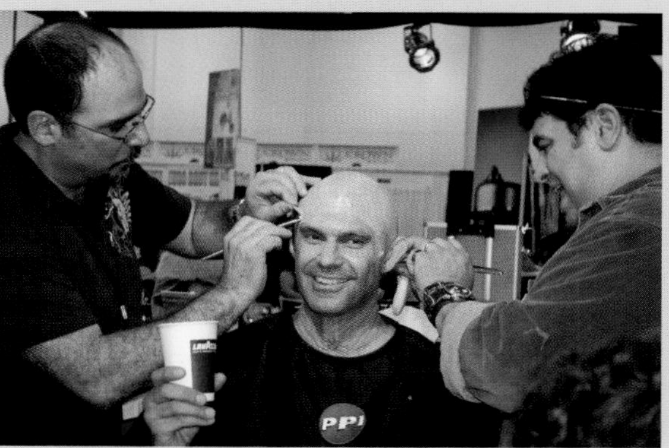

FIGURE 6.8
Josh Turi and Louie Zakarian; SNL makeup; IMATS LA.
Photo by author.

FIGURE 6.9
Josh Turi and Louie Zakarian; Count Chocula makeup.
Photo by author.

FIGURE 6.10
Makeup for TV commercial.
Image reproduced by permission of Joshua Turi.

Since then, Josh and his company *Designs to Deceive* have provided makeup and makeup effects for close to 100 films, dozens of television programs, 6 Broadway shows, and numerous print ads.

Since 2000, Josh has been a Key Makeup Artist/Lab Tech for *Saturday Night Live* working alongside Louie Zakarian, and together have been honored with two Emmy Awards for their work on *SNL*.

Materials

We won't detail a set list of tools and materials that you'll need to cast an appliance in silicone, for the simple reason that although there are certain similarities in the process for casting any silicone appliance, each makeup will be different. Here are the items that you will most likely want/need to have:

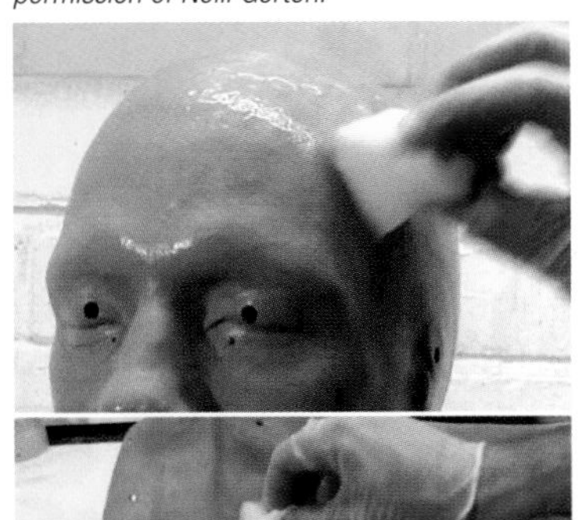

FIGURE 6.11
Stippling thin encapsulating layer of silicone into mold.
Images reproduced by permission of Neill Gorton.

- Two-part silicone
- Nonlatex (nitrile or vinyl) gloves
- Mixing sticks
- Mold
- Mold straps or clamps
- Screwdriver
- Vacuum/pressure chamber
- Mixing containers
- Digital scale
- Mold release
- Powder
- Air compressor
- Syringe (60–100 ml)

Silicone can be cast into a mold in more than one way. It can be poured, brushed, stippled, or injected. Or it can be cast using combination of these methods. The way the silicone gets into the mold is largely dependent on the type of prosthetic being cast. A full-head cowl appliance would be impossible to pour. A thin layer of silicone could be stippled into the mold halves first to ensure that all details have been captured before placing the mold pieces together and then injecting the balance of the silicone into the mold.

De-airing/Degassing Silicone

Because silicone is relatively viscous as a liquid (compared with water), air bubbles easily become suspended in it when the components are mixed together. For that reason, it is often recommended that silicone be de-aired or degassed in a vacuum chamber before it goes into the mold. You can eliminate air bubbles (or at least make them very, very small—almost invisible) by pressurizing the silicone instead of pulling a vacuum. You still need a pressure chamber to do it, but air compressors are far less expensive than vacuum pumps and you probably already have access to an air compressor.

Degassing silicone with a vacuum pump requires that the silicone to be degassed be in a container several sizes larger than the original volume of silicone because when the air begins to leave the silicone, it will froth and bubble madly and expand in volume several times its original volume for 2 or 3 minutes until all the air is exhausted and the silicone collapses back to just under its original volume. It's quite a sight!

FIGURE 6.12 Venturi-type vacuum pump.
Photo by author.

Small vacuum/pressure chambers can be found rather easily online, and if you're dead-set on vacuum de-airing, for about \$18 (£9.66) from Harbor Freight, you can buy a Central Pneumatic air-vac, a Venturi-type vacuum pump that uses air pressure to create enough vacuum to de-air your silicone in a short order!

Your air compressor needs to generate at least 90 pounds of pressure to pull 28.3 (71.9 centimeters) inches of mercury at sea level. From the same vendor, you can also find a 2½-gallon pressure paint tank that is great for pressure or vacuum for under \$100 (£53.59). With a little more effort, you can replace the opaque metal lid with a clear Plexiglas (¾–1 inch thick or 2–2.5 centimeters) cover so that you can see what's going on inside. Often, however, simply allowing the silicone to sit at room temperature until the air bubbles have risen to the surface and disappeared is all you need to do before pouring or injecting the silicone into the mold cavity provided the silicone is slow setting.

GEL-FILLED SILICONE APPLIANCES

If you've ever held a silicone breast implant in your hand (pre-implantation), you know how soft and squishy they are or can be. Squeeze your cheeks (gently) or feel your (or someone's) love handles that's the consistency and softness a gel-filled appliance (GFA) should have. The best GFAs are made with a gel that has a much firmer consistency than you'd find in a silicone breast implant or breast enhancement product.

GFAs are arguably the single most difficult type of prosthetic appliance to make by reason of the steps involved in merely casting the appliance into the mold. The silicone gel must *fill* something; it is a GFA. The gel is one component. The other, an envelope or capsule, must be created for the gel to fill. How is that accomplished? By using an encapsulator, which can be silicone or a liquid-like vinyl cap material that will cure to a solid, flexible skin. Using an encapsulator other than silicone could cause the gel and the encapsulating envelope not to bond well and to separate (because nothing sticks to silicone except other silicone), causing unwanted and largely unfixable problems with the appliance. As long as you don't try to add a platinum gel to a tin encapsulator, the silicones should cure and bond permanently to each other without a problem. However, the "deadened" or softened silicone gel is quite sticky on its own and may provide enough adhesion to bond well to the encapsulator. A spray of 3 M spray cement over the encapsulator before adding the silicone to the mold will also help with adhesion. Baldiez and Super Baldiez—acetone- and alcohol-soluble vinyl cap plastics from Mouldlife—have become Industry Standard materials for encapsulating GFAs. Kryolan's Glatzan L cap plastic can also be used very effectively, as well as Michael Davy's Water Melon. The amount of deadener is something of a personal taste issue, but common ratios of deadener to silicone (A and B together) can be up to 250%.

Filling the Mold

Prepping the mold is the first order of business. Depending on how long it's been since the mold was made, it might need to be cleaned again to ensure that no contaminants such as dust and stray hairs have found their way onto the negative surfaces of the mold interior.

Once the mold pieces are clean and dry (if they're stone molds), they will need to be sealed and released; if the mold is made of fiberglass or other resin, it probably doesn't need to be released, although it's never wrong to release a mold if you have any doubt as to whether the silicone will stick without it.

Injection Filling

To inject silicone into your mold, at least two holes must be drilled in the mold positive: one to inject silicone through and the other to allow air to escape as the mold fills. The syringe for injecting the silicone should be made of polyethylene or polypropylene and should not have a latex rubber end on the plunger that would cause platinum silicone inhibition—it won't cure. Make sure that the mold pieces have been thoroughly released, including the injection hole and the vent hole.

1. Release the mold pieces.
2. For creating a GFA, brush or stipple a thin coat of mixed silicone encapsulator material on both halves of the mold, positive and negative. *Be careful not to stipple silicone over the cutting edge of the appliance mold.*
3. When the encapsulator material begins to set, close the mold and clamp or bolt securely together.
4. Allow the encapsulator material to fully cure inside the mold. You might want to accelerate the cure by applying heat. As a rough guide, the recommended cure schedule for a 1-inch-thick Ultracal mold is 2–3 hours at 200°F (93°C).
5. Allow the mold to cool.
6. Mix the gel components together and add pigment and/or flocking, then de-air them in an evacuator (vacuum chamber); or simply let the air

bubbles rise and disperse on their own (only if you're using a slow-cure gel). Fill the syringe with the gel and slowly inject it through one of the holes until it begins to come out of the second hole.

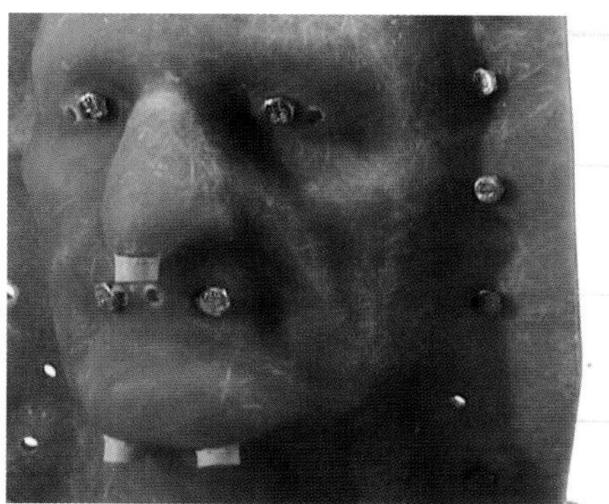

FIGURE 6.13
Hand-tighten bolts, then tighten with wrench.
Image reproduced by permission of Neill Gorton.

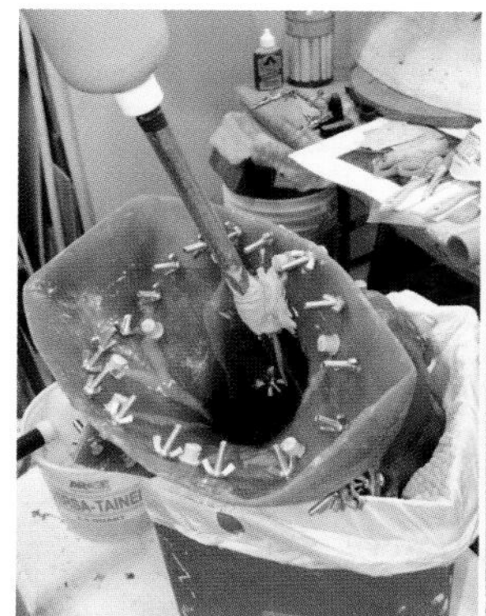

FIGURE 6.14
Hand-tighten bolts, then tighten with wrench.
Photos by the author

NOTE

To know how much silicone gel to mix, you need to use the weight (or volume) of the clay you saved from the appliance sculpture, and then mix a bit more than that so you have room for overflow. It's better to have a bit more than you need than not quite enough and need to start over.

7. Carefully remove the syringe and gently tap the mold, and tilt it to work any remaining air through the holes.
8. Reinsert the syringe and top off the mold with gel if necessary.
9. Allow the gel to cure at room temperature for 24 hours (or as long as the manufacturer recommends) or place it back into the oven for 1–1½ hours at 200°F (93°C) for the gel to cure. Allow the mold to slowly cool enough to handle (90°F–100°F/32°C–37°C)—if the mold is gypsum, it may crack if cooled too quickly—and *carefully* demold the appliance. Wash off any release residue and trim the injection and bleeder sprues.
10. Cover the trimmed sprue points with fresh encapsulator material and allow it to cure. Then, powder the appliance; it is ready for painting and application.

You should store your appliance in an airtight plastic bag if it's not going to be used in the near future. For painting, it would be handy to have a duplicate of the positive for the appliance to lie on or a generic positive so that the prosthetic will have the relative shape it is supposed to have.

You do not have to be making a GFA to inject silicone. Injecting silicone merely ensures that you will have an easier time filling a more complex mold shape. The steps are the same, minus encapsulator.

TIP
Brushing a light dusting of talcum of baby powder into your mold before pouring will help draw your prosthetic material into tight spaces through a physical phenomenon called *capillary action*; the talc releases surface tension, drawing liquid into spaces it would otherwise be prevented from entering due to the physics of surface tension.

Hand Filling

The hand-fill method for making a GFA is similar to the injection method, although the injection hole and vent hole are not necessary.

1. Release the mold sections the same way you would if you were going to inject the silicone. Make sure the release is completely dried before the next step.
2. Brush or stipple a thin coat of mixed silicone encapsulator on both halves of the mold, positive and negative. You might want to experiment with thixotropic agents if you find the encapsulator is too runny, even when stippled on thinly. You shouldn't need to, however.
3. Mix up the silicone gel and allow it to de-air; when the encapsulator has dried (but not cured), pour the gel into the mold negative. If you are going to color the gel intrinsically, now is the time to do it!
4. Fit the positive carefully into the negative and clamp the two halves together securely and then oven cure it at 200°F (93°C). Again, the recommended length of time is 2–3 hours for a 1-inch (2.5-centimeters) Ultracal or other gypsum mold. The remaining three steps are exactly the same.

NOTE
The oven curing is not essential. If you do not have access to an oven or hot box, the silicone will cure at room temperature; it will simply take longer. The results will be identical.

Removing the Appliance

1. Allow the mold to slowly cool enough to handle (90°F–100°F)—if the mold is gypsum, it may crack if cooled too quickly—and carefully demold the appliance.
2. Wash off any release residue and trim the injection and bleeder sprues.
3. Cover the trimmed sprue points with fresh encapsulator material and allow it to cure. Then, powder the appliance; it is ready for painting and application.

The steps for casting a regular silicone appliance are exactly the same—injected or hand-filled, minus the encapsulator; the oven curing is also an option and by no means a necessity. In fact, if you use Polytek's Plat-Sil Gel-10 platinum RTV silicone, it kicks pretty quickly (within 15 minutes at room temperature) and can usually be demolded in less than an hour with no additional heat.

Vincent Van Dyke

"The first thing I can really remember watching and getting really inspired by was the *Hunchback of Notre Dame* with Lon Chaney," says Vince. "I was in awe of it even though it was silent and I was so young, but it was enough to keep my interest. I immediately ran to my makeup kit at the time - I must have been 6 or 7 - and grabbed some silly putty and some of my mom's makeup and went to town ..."

FIGURE 6.15
Vince sculpting in WED clay.
Image reproduced by permission of Vincent Van Dyke.

"Ever since, I have had a true passion for creating characters. Eventually I realized that this was a possible profession and I never thought twice about anything but doing what has now been an amazing career for me."

FIGURE 6.16
Vince opening small urethane block mold.
Photo by author.

Vincent Van Dyke has been creating characters for over 10 years and working professionally in the industry for almost as long for other companies. In a very short time, he has been nominated for three prime-time Emmys for his work on *Grey's Anatomy* and *Nip/Tuck*. Now, with his own company, he hopes to continue to bring creatures and characters to life the Van Dyke way. What way is that? "My goal," says Vince "is to bring a sense of realism into everything I create, even if that means it does not exist in this world. If it's not believable, then you've lost everything, including your audience. In a time where People's expectations for makeup effects are so high the bar must be raised constantly. To stay up on this you must have a fresh outlook on things that may have been done before and bring a new twist to them. I hope that is something that comes across in my work."

FIGURE 6.17
Hanging man sculpture.
Image reproduced by permission of Vincent Van Dyke.

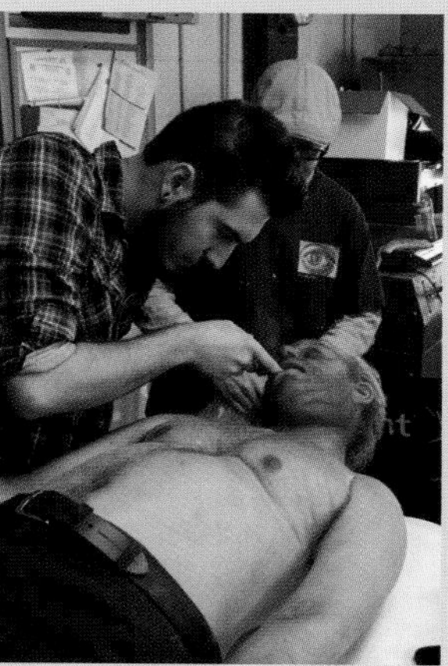

FIGURE 6.18
Vince and Carl Lyon fitting Hanging Man teeth.
Photo by the author.

Vincent's credits include *Nip/Tuck, Grey's Anatomy, Star Trek, Day of the Dead, Tropic Thunder*, and *The Lost Tribe*.

CONFORMING MOLDS

In Chapter 5, there was an overview of making conforming molds; here, we'll cast an appliance into one.

The first step is to prep are both the silicone negative jacket mold and the gypsum positive.

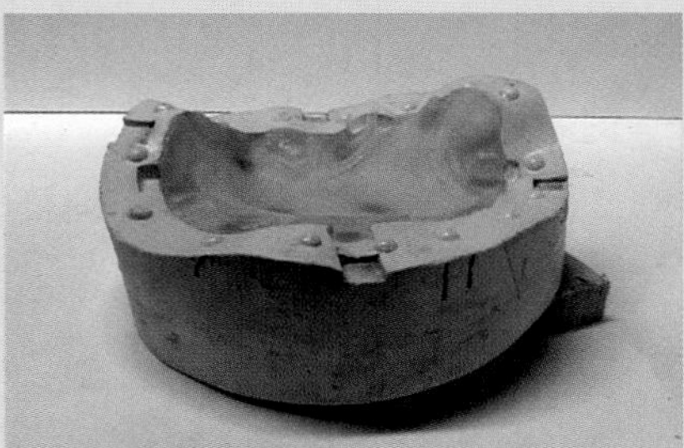

FIGURE 6.19
Negative mold ready for silicone.
Image reproduced by permission of Neill Gorton.

1. Release the positive with Al-Cote dental separator or the equivalent. Let it dry, then spray with Epoxy Parfilm. Release the silicone negative with Epoxy Parfilm also. Brush just a very thin bit of petroleum jelly into the gypsum jacket, so it will be easy to re-seat the silicone into it. Do not get petroleum jelly on the flange; we will be spraying Super Baldiez, and we want the Baldiez to stick to the flange, not release from it.
2. Lightly dust the silicone negative with baby powder or pure talc; blow off the excess to leave a matte surface.
3. Using an airbrush or a sprayer such as one by Preval that can be purchased inexpensively at just about any hardware store in the United States (I'm certain there are equivalents in the UK and elsewhere), spray five or six layers of thinned Super Baldiez (thinned 4:1 99% IPA:Baldiez) into the negative, letting each layer dry before adding the next. If a spray method is unavailable, you can sponge in the Baldiez, stippling each layer carefully.

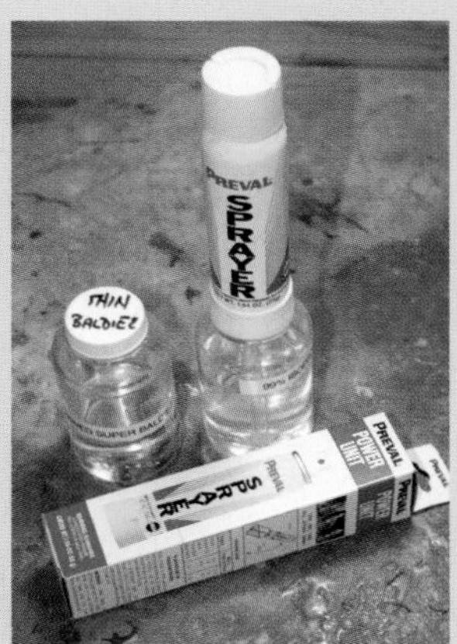

FIGURE 6.20
Preval sprayer.
Photo by author.

Now you're ready for the silicone to go into the mold. The silicone negative mold should sit, so that the silicone will pool evenly like in the bottom of a bowl when it is poured into the mold. Of course, you kept the clay from the prosthetic sculpt and the flashing so you'll know how much silicone (and deadener) to mix.

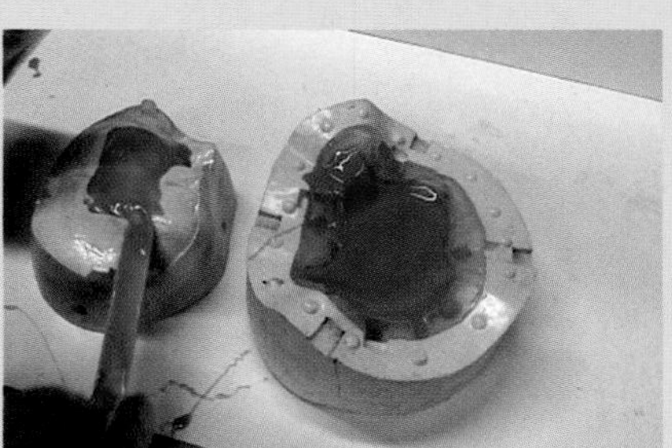

FIGURE 6.21
Silicone into mold.
Image reproduced by permission of Neill Gorton.

4. We want the silicone to be deadened for three reasons: (1) to make the silicone soft and flesh like; (2) to help it adhere to the Super Baldiez; and (3) to help the appliance adhere to the skin when applied (with adhesive). Mix the silicone—de-gas if you can—and

pour the silicone into the mold. Brush a little onto the gypsum positive too, to help prevent air bubbles from forming when you put the two pieces together.

5. Add just enough weight to the top of the mold to ensure a good edge without displacing the silicone negative.

FIGURE 6.22
Closing mold.
Image reproduced by permission of Neill Gorton.

FIGURE 6.23
Place just enough weight on top to ensure good edge.
Image reproduced by permission of Neill Gorton.

6. When the silicone is fully cured, submerge the mold in warm water for about 10 minutes and gently help release the suction.

FIGURE 6.24
Submerge mold to release silicone.
Image reproduced by permission of Neill Gorton.

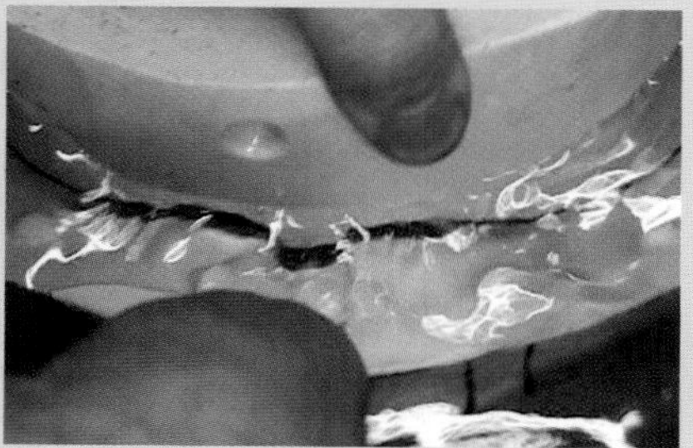

FIGURE 6.25
Release suction gently.
Image reproduced by permission of Neill Gorton.

7. Let the water drain from the negative and let it dry by itself (you can use a hair dryer, but be careful not to blow any dust of foreign debris into the silicone); do not touch the silicone with tissue or paper towel; it is very sticky!

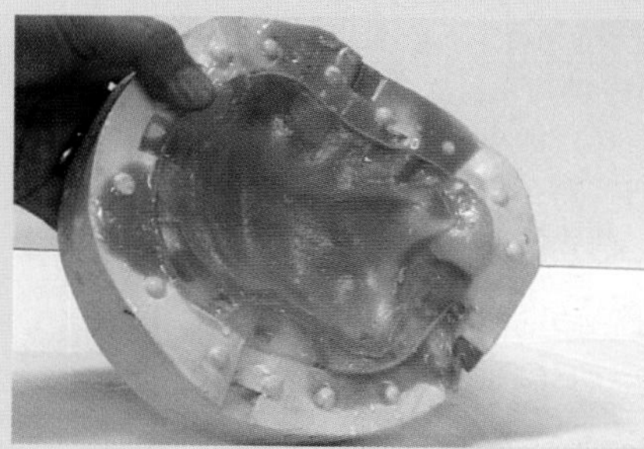

FIGURE 6.26
Drain and let dry.
Image reproduced by permission of Neill Gorton.

8. Clean wet Al-Cote separator off the gypsum positive.
9. Be careful to keep the appliance in the mold, but remove the silicone negative from the gypsum jacket. You may need to use small, sharp scissors to help; trim away overlapping silicone and Baldiez.

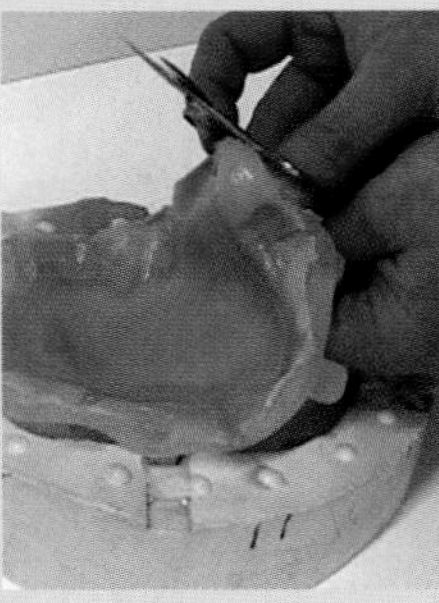
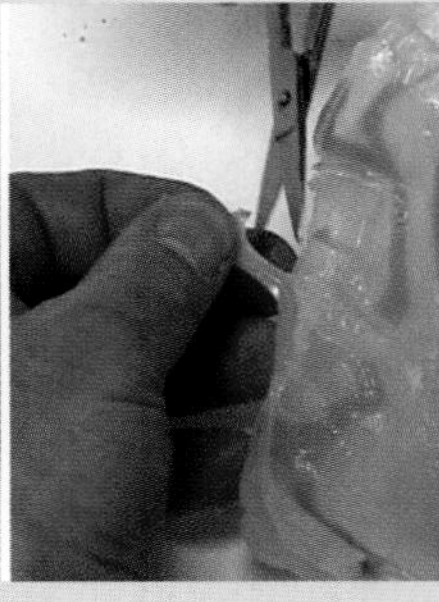

FIGURE 6.27
Carefully remove silicone negative from gypsum jacket (left); trim excess flashing and Baldiez (right).
Images reproduced by permission of Neill Gorton.

10. With a small soft brush, brush a layer of Super Baldiez over the sticky flashing, so it won't be sticky anymore. The appliance is now ready for application. Set the piece aside in a small covered container. You can also brush a light dusting of baby powder talc over the silicone to temporarily remove the stickiness.

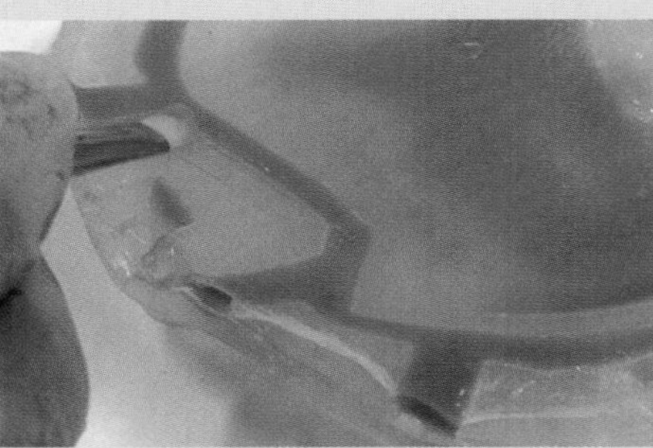

FIGURE 6.28
Brush Super Baldiez over sticky flashing.
Image reproduced by permission of Neill Gorton.

Foam Latex

As a material for making prosthetic appliances for special makeup effects, foam latex is, in my opinion, unrivaled for performer comfort. Materials such as silicone might mimic the appearance and feel of human skin more believably and realistically, but silicone does not breathe, and an active actor wearing silicone appliances will begin to perspire rather profusely beneath the silicone if it is worn for an extended period of time, as many actors must. Gelatin will probably start to melt. Don't get me wrong; the material for a given appliance should not be chosen randomly or by economy, and I have nothing against working with silicone or gelatin as an appliance material.

Appliance materials must be chosen based on numerous factors such as climate, shot framing, performance, and budget. There are a number of foam latex systems on the market, and they are listed in the appendix on the companion Web site.

I particularly love foam latex for its texture and feel. When it's made well, it feels better than velvet, and every subtle expression and nuance of emotion is translated beautifully through the foam from the performer; it *becomes* the performer. A nearly full-face appliance will likely weigh less than an ounce and, when applied, is almost undetectable by the actor wearing it. Foam latex breathes somewhat—certainly more so than silicone or gelatin, so it is comfortable and an actor can wear it all day long, as is frequently the case. Adhesion techniques can also help channel away perspiration from the performer aiding in the actor's comfort level over time.

FIGURE 6.29
GM Foam (top) and Monster Makers foam latex (bottom) components.
Photos by author.

Materials

Foam latex components (latex base, foaming agent, curing agent, gelling agent, and color)

Misc. additives
Timer
Digital scale
Oven mitts
Mold straps mixer and bowl
Appliance mold(s)
Foam latex oven
Foam injector

QUIRKS

However, although foam latex is extremely light, strong, breathable, and expressive, there are some qualities that could be construed as negatives by some. I must confess, to get that extremely light, strong, breathable, and expressive appliance, there are a number of hoops that must be jumped through to get there. Although every material used to make prosthetics has quirks and idiosyncrasies, foam latex is probably the most difficult material to work with overall, from several perspectives.

First, foam latex is opaque. You can't see through it. Unlike silicone and gelatin, which can be colored intrinsically to be semitransparent or translucent, just like real human skin, foam latex is naturally opaque. To create the semblance of translucency, the appliance must be painted with numerous transparent layers of pigment, usually with an airbrush, to achieve the look of real skin.

Second, foam latex requires a heat cure in an oven, and it *cannot* be the same oven you use to bake tollhouse cookies and Thanksgiving turkeys!

FIGURE 6.30
Rescued kitchen appliance terrific for baking small to medium prosthetics.
Photo by author.

Why? Because third, foam latex gives off toxic fumes during the heat cure that will render your oven forever unfit for cooking. There are a few alternatives, one of which is building your own makeshift oven using infrared heat lamps in a well-insulated plywood box. I can show you how, if you're interested. I am now using an old GE consumer oven that I rewired from 220 to 110 volts. It's not very large, but I can fit a two-piece mold for a full-face appliance and two smaller molds in it pretty easily. I might be hard pressed to get a full bust mold for an over-the-head cowl in it, but it has served its purpose well, and I couldn't pass up the price—*free*—when a neighbor remodeled his kitchen and asked me if I had any use for his old oven. (On the plus side, I get terrific results with it.)

Whatever you use as your latex oven, your foam latex should cure in an oven that cannot exceed a controllable/maintainable 200°F. Ideally, foam should cure no hotter than 185°F (85°C). I frequently cook it at 170°F (about 77°C) for a longer time, as I will describe a little further on. Lower temps (150°F-ish) for an even longer time will result in softer foam.

Foam latex is time and temperature sensitive. When I was first learning how to run foam, I remember mixing the foam according to the instructions for using GM Foam and watching the foam solidify in mid pour from the mixing bowl into the mold. D'oh! It was like watching a cartoon.

Foam latex shrinks. The thicker the foam, the more it shrinks. That's not to be confused with the volume of the foam; lower-volume foam (heavier) will shrink more than high-volume foam (lighter) because it has more air and a lesser proportion of foam latex components. It is water loss that causes shrinkage in the foam. Because higher-volume foam stretches more than denser low-volume foam, any shrinkage that does occur can usually be compensated by stretching, with little force exerted on the foam.

What the mold is made of also contributes to the shrinkage of the foam or the lack thereof. A porous mold-like Ultracal will cause the foam to shrink less because it absorbs moisture from the foam. Foam latex, being essentially a foam rubber sponge, will collapse into itself when it moves, such as with a fold of neck skin; silicone appliances displace themselves remarkably like real tissue. These are tradeoffs that you must decide on during the design (and budgeting) phase of your makeup. Foam latex is more delicate than silicone and rarely survives removal in one piece at the end of the day, necessitating fresh appliances for each performance day the actor is in makeup. Silicone, if handled and treated carefully, can be robust enough even for delicate edges to survive multiple applications.

Before I describe the process for running a batch of foam latex, let me give you a little backstory on latex itself. Latex is a natural liquid that comes from the hevea tree grown in Malaysia, Thailand, Indonesia, the Philippines, and other tropical countries. The tree is tapped and a small amount of latex (only a few ounces) is collected from each tree before the cut on the tree congeals and heals itself. Each tree is tapped only once every 2 days. According to GM Foam's technical information, over 95% of all natural latex is concentrated by a method called *centrifuging*. The result is a high-quality product containing 60%–65% solids, used mainly for dipping compounds such as rubber gloves and condoms. The remaining latex, which is less than 5% of the world's production, is concentrated by another method called *creaming*, a process whereby ammonium alginate is added to the raw latex, causing separation. The watery "serum layer" is drained from the vats, leaving a higher concentration of latex.

Ammonia is added as a preservative; this prevents the latex from coagulating, leaving the final concentration at approximately 68% latex solids. Creamed latex separates over time and will continue to separate unless it is shaken on a weekly basis, to keep it mixed and fresh. This type of latex has a greater stretchiness than the centrifuged latex, so it is also considered the best latex for making prosthetic foam.

As latex is a natural product, its composition is dependent on environmental conditions. The hevea trees and the latex are affected by how much rainfall there is in a given season, how many sunny days, how young the trees are, and so on. Thus, the quality of rubber varies from season to season, year to year, and month to month. These fluctuations can wreak havoc for artists running foam for makeup effects, because the latex will behave differently all the time. What GM Foam does when it purchases creamed latex is to calibrate its own latex base. When the company receives the latex, it first adjusts the pH balance, then conditions the latex with additives, and finally makes a special blend with other types of latex. By doing this, GM Foam can carefully control the cell size, foam volume, flow, and gel time. This means that if you follow the instructions provided with GM Foam latex, the foam should perform exactly as predicted, every time. In theory, although there is significant science involved in making foam latex prosthetics, it is every bit as much an art.

Provided that you have already created your appliance sculpture, made the molds, and dried, sealed, and released them properly, you are now ready to run some foam! Basically, the operation goes like this: A batch of latex is mixed together with a foaming agent, a curing agent, and a gelling agent and maybe even a little pigment for color. It is whipped into frothy foam at high speed in a mixer; I use a 5-quart KitchenAid, kinda like beating egg whites into meringue. Then it's poured or injected into the mold, and the mold is placed in the oven and heated at 170°F (76°C) for about 4½ hours. Any temperature above 185°F (85°C) and you will risk overcooking your foam and ruining it.

FIGURE 6.31
Mold ready for oven.
Photo by author.

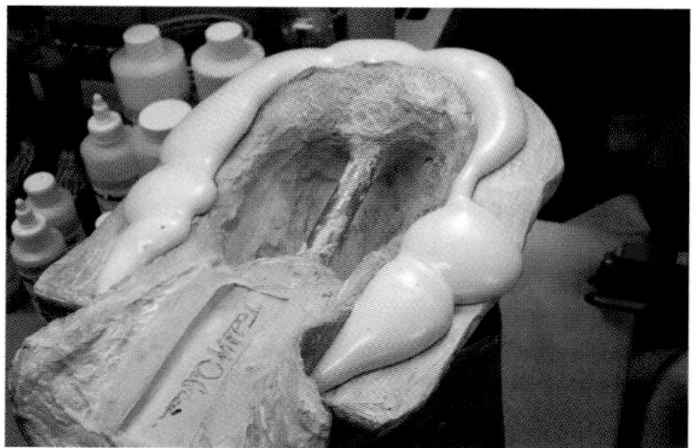

Regardless of your location, some experimentation in mixing the foam might be to find the right blend of mixing for your foam. Gil Mosko, creator of GM Foam, makes a point of telling people, "Don't be a slave to the schedule. All mixers run differently and many conditions can affect how the foam will rise in the mixer." A key point to remember is that *you must be able to pour the foam from the mixing bowl into the mold.* If the foam is too light and fluffy, which happens when you achieve a very high volume of foam, you may get a really, really soft-cured foam, but you are also very likely to have enormous empty cavities where the foam was unable to get into all parts of the mold due to the lightness of the high-volume foam and its nonpourable condition.

Running Foam Latex

A typical batch of foam latex consists of 150 grams of high-grade latex base, 30 grams of foaming agent, 15 grams of curing agent, and 14 grams of gelling agent. There are other ingredients and quantities that can be added for different foam characteristics, but this is a good place to begin. As I mentioned, this operation is time and temperature sensitive as well as humidity sensitive; optimal conditions would be in a room at 69°F–72°F (20.5°C–22°C) and with 45%–55% humidity. I am based in Colorado, so I have humidity (rather, the *lack* of humidity) to contend with as well as a lower high-elevation air pressure that also affects what I do. The above "optimal" conditions are based on mixing at sea level, so I'll stick with that, because most of you will probably be working at lower elevations.

FIGURE 6.32
Accurate scale essential for foam latex.
Photo by author.

Weigh the first three components—the latex base, the foaming agent, and the curing agent—and add them to the mixing bowl. It would be good for you to have an accurate digital gram scale.

Weigh out the gelling agent into a small cup and set it aside. We won't add that until we're almost done mixing. If you're adding pigment, put a few drops of your color into the bowl, too. Then place the mixing bowl into position and you are ready to begin. This will be a 12-minute mix. A timer that will count down is a plus, but if you can tell time and count, a clock or a watch will suffice. (Because you're reading this book, I know you're all very smart.)

1. Your mold must be sealed and released—both the positive and the negative—to prevent the foam latex from sticking and tearing when you attempt to remove it after it cures. If you are using GM Foam, follow the simple instructions for GM's release agent. If you are using different foam, do as you're instructed for that product. Price-Driscoll's Ultra 4 Epoxy Parfilm works pretty well (but only if the stone mold you're using has been sealed and is no longer porous).
2. For the first minute, mix the ingredients on speed 1.

3. For the next 4 minutes, whip the ingredients on speed 10. This will froth the foam and increase the volume in the bowl. As I've already said, Gil Mosko, GM Foam's founder, says to not be a slave to the schedule. Once you understand how foam latex works, you will be able to adapt to any situation.

What the high-speed mixing does in addition to creating high-volume foam is to remove ammonia from the latex. Too much ammonia loss and your foam will gel too quickly; not enough ammonia loss and your foam might not gel at all. It might seem like you need a degree in chemistry to run foam (it certainly wouldn't hurt) but that is why there is a mixing guideline to follow, so you don't have to know specific pH values and other scientific-type stuff. Simply understanding the function of the ingredients and the stages of the process should be enough information to do some experimentation, such as:

- The *foaming agent* bonds as a soap that bonds to the cells of the latex, lowering the surface tension of the latex and allowing it to froth and rise more easily.
- The *curing agent* contains sulfur to help vulcanize (strengthen and add elasticity to) the latex.
- The *gelling agent* creates a reaction that changes the foam from a liquid into a solid.

FIGURE 6.33
Mixing foam with KitchenAid mixer.
Photo by author.

Record notes of what you do when you are just beginning to work with foam latex as well as when you make changes to any part of the process. Things you might want to include in your notes are as follows:

- Air temperature
- Humidity
- Curing agent (amount, brand, date, and batch number)
- Foaming agent (amount, brand, date, and batch number)
- Gelling agent (amount, brand, date, and batch number)
- Latex base (amount, brand, date, and batch number)
- Additives: accelerators, stabilizers, etc.
- Mixing times
- Pigmentation (amount and color)
- Gel time: start and finish
- Baking time: in and out
- Oven temperature
- Mold: Ultracal, fiberglass, old, new, etc.
- Results

Prepping the Mold

Foam can be run in a variety of molds including gypsum, fiberglass, and epoxy. Ultracal is porous, so it needs to be properly sealed and released to prevent the foam latex from adhering to the mold. Every bit as important as sealing and releasing the mold is making certain that there is no moisture left in the mold before baking foam latex in it. This is important for two reasons. Residual moisture in the mold will prevent moisture from the latex being absorbed by the mold, thereby causing the foam to shrink more after curing. Moisture in the mold can also cause steam pockets to form within the mold, which can ruin the foam. Water heated under pressure (as in a clamped, sealed mold) can boil at a lower temperature than normal (212°F—100°C), such as those needed for baking foam latex (under 200°F). To prevent that from happening, your stone molds should be heated for several hours at nearly 200°F (93°C) to remove any residual moisture. This is particularly true of new molds.

The same is true of fiberglass molds—not to remove residual moisture (because there is none) but to vent off styrene remaining in the mold, which can react badly with the sulfur given off during the foam latex-curing process and transfer to the foam.

Okay, back to the process.

1. Turn the speed down to 4 for 1 minute. This stage will begin to refine the foam, breaking up the biggest bubbles.
2. Turn the speed down to 1 for the last 4 minutes to further refine the foam. When there are 2 minutes left, begin adding the gelling agent and continue mixing for 12 minutes. It is critical that the gelling agent be mixed well, and depending on what mixer you use, the methods of assuring that the gelling agent is sufficiently mixed can vary.
3. At 12 minutes, turn off the mixer and remove the bowl and you are ready to carefully fill your molds.

FIGURE 6.34
Testing to see whether foam has gelled.
Photos by author.

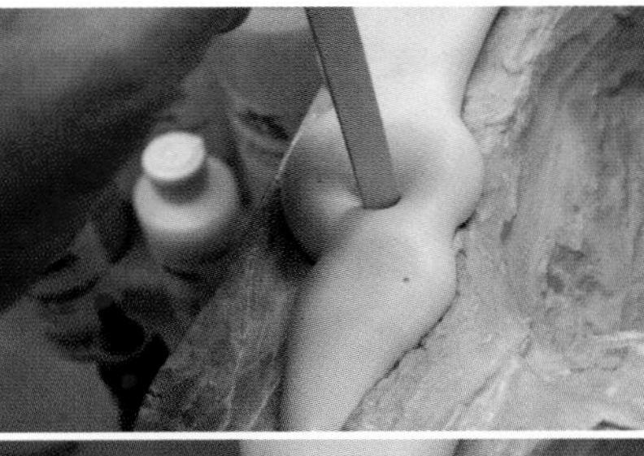

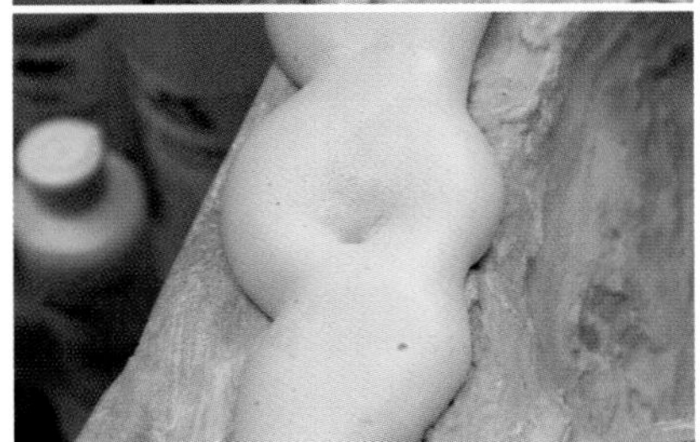

Once the foam has gelled (you can tell by gently pressing on the foam; it should give a little and bounce back), you can place the molds in the oven and heat them until the foam is fully cured.

Filling the Mold

There are really only two ways to get foam latex into the mold: pouring it in or injecting it into the negative mold. For molds that are no larger than a face, pouring works very well.

If there are deep areas in the mold, such as a long nose for the character of Cyrano de Bergerac (think Steve Martin's character in the movie *Roxanne*), you might first want to use a spoon or a spatula to get some foam down into the nose tip to ensure that it fills and doesn't create an air pocket before you pour or spoon in the rest of the foam. You will learn over time how much or how little foam you actually need to place in the mold to fill it; when you press the positive into the negative, the foam will spread out and into other areas of the mold. If there are

deeper portions the foam needs to reach, you will want to use a spatula, craft stick, or even your hand (in a rubber glove!) to spread it into those areas to avoid trapping air.

As the foam is pressed outward by the positive, the excess has to go somewhere; that's why you created flashing when you made the mold. It might even be worthwhile to have drilled small escape holes, called *bleeders*, in the positive to help facilitate the escape of air (and preventing pockets of trapped air) and excess foam latex. Foam latex has a lot of resistance to compression, and for your appliance to have fine, ultra-thin edges, both halves of the mold must be able to close completely and touch at the mold's cutting edge.

It's often necessary to inject the foam latex into a mold—say, for a full-head cowl piece or large three-piece mold (one inner core positive and two front and back negatives) that would be difficult or very messy to hand pour.

Large foam injection syringes are available for sale from several sources listed in the appendix. When foam is injected, it is fundamentally different than when you pour the foam onto an open mold. The mold is tightly closed, making it almost airtight, and the act of injecting foam into the mold will create pressure in the mold; air in the mold will need to escape. Without numerous small bleeder holes drilled or bleeder channels etched into the mold positive, foam will not be able to flow easily into those areas.

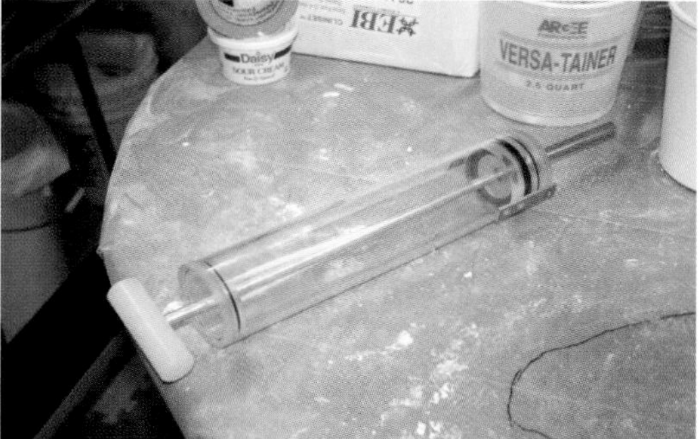

FIGURE 6.35
Foam latex injector.
Photo by author.

Heat-Curing Foam

Once the mold is closed and the foam has gelled, it's time to pop it into the oven. But first, you need to understand the following: (1) higher temperatures make the foam gel faster and (2) higher humidity makes the foam gel faster. To correct these conditions, follow these tips: in hot and/or muggy conditions, use less gelling agent into the mix and pour it sooner. Another way to extend your working time is to add extra foaming agent, which will prevent the latex from gelling too fast. GM Foam offers a product called Foam Stabilizer that is designed for use in high-humidity, high-temperature environments.

The following points are also very important to understand before embarking on a foam run:

- The cure "window" is larger at lower temperatures. At 185°F (85°C), foam can take 3 hours to cure, but at 4 hours, it could be over cured. This over-cured foam loses tear strength and in extreme cases becomes crumbly. The same foam, cured at 165°F (about 78°C), could take 5 hours to cure, but even if cured for 7 hours, it would still be fine. In other words, a low-temperature cure could have a 3-hour window where the cured foam would be usable. A 200°F (93°C) cure may only have a 20-minute window where the foam is usable.

- Steam lakes are areas of foam that have been pushed away from the mold surface by pockets of steam and then cured into that incorrect shape. These areas have all the detail of the sculpture, but they are depressed and too dense. This is a hazard in nonporous molds, such as epoxical and fiberglass, or molds that have not been properly predried. However, it is a problem that can be remedied:
  1. The first step is mold preparation. Nonporous surfaces are to be coated with a thin solution of paste wax (such as Johnson's wax for floors) that has been cut with 99% alcohol. This "alcowax" should be thin and runny. Brush it into the inside of the mold, do not allow to pool, and when it's dry, brush it out with a dry brush. The mold surface will become polished and shiny. More important, the mold surface will be sealed from outgassing, which causes sites for steam leaking to begin.
  2. Cure at a lower temperature (for a longer time). GM Foam recommends curing at 165°F (78°C) for 5–7 hours for this kind of mold.

FIGURE 6.36
Foam piece ready for demolding.
Photo by author.

Removing the Appliance

Once you determine that your foam is fully cured, turn off the oven and let the molds begin to cool. If you try to cool the molds too rapidly, they will crack and break; you do not want to rush the process! When the molds are still warm to the touch, you can carefully demold your appliances; they will come out more easily when warm than if you let the molds cool completely. Carefully pry the mold halves apart and help remove the appliance with the use of a blunt wooden tool (so you don't scratch the mold's surface detail), powdering as you go to keep the thin foam edges from sticking together. I want to stress this point: You probably went to a fair amount of trouble to ensure that your appliance would have thin, beautiful edges; if you are not careful and methodical about powdering the appliance during removal, your thin beautiful edges will fold over on themselves and become thick ugly edges that you can't separate.

After you've removed the appliance, it must be gently washed in warm water containing only a few drops of dishwashing liquid (I use either Ivory or Palmolive dish soap) to remove any residual sulfur from the curing agent. Repeat this procedure until there is no more visible residue in the water, then rinse until all the soap is gone, and gently squeeze out the water; you might want press the appliance between two towels, then allow it to dry completely on the lifecast so that it will maintain its shape.

When the foam pieces have been washed, dried, and powdered, they should be stored resting in their natural curvature in airtight containers, away from light if

possible. It is convenient to use either zip-lock plastic bags or plastic refrigerator containers that have airtight lids. These baggies or plastic containers can then be stored in a cardboard box or any other opaque container that can keep out the light. If stored like this, foam latex pieces can be kept for years without any deterioration. If a foam piece is stored or left to air out with a crease or fold in it, the piece could wind up with a permanent crease line or indentation. Store the appliances in their natural curvature.

FIGURE 6.37
Foam appliances ready for painting and application.
Photo by author.

Now the foam is ready for painting and application.

The appendix at the back of this book includes more detailed information from GM Foam about run schedules.

COLD FOAM (URETHANE)

Cold foam is urethane foam and is called *cold foam* because it is not heat cured like foam latex; urethane foam cures at room temperature. Cold foam (Kryolan makes a urethane foam soft enough for prosthetic work) is an alternative to foam latex and could be a good place to begin working with foam instead of with latex simply because it does not require a lengthy heat cure and can be ready to use quickly. Cold foam is not to be confused with poly foam, which is also flexible urethane foam but has a different use and density associated with it.

That said, urethane foam is *not* a substitute or replacement for foam latex. It is a different material with different properties. It is soft foam suitable for facial and body appliances; however, it's not as soft and pliable as foam latex.

You will probably want to work with good ventilation and might actually want to wear a NIOSH-approved respirator (for the ammonia vapors), but working with foam latex does not mandate that you do so; it is not inherently dangerous to your health. Cold foam, on the other hand, contains isocynates, which are considered quite toxic. It is strongly suggested that latex, nitrile, or vinyl gloves be worn in addition to a respirator. At no time should the components of foam in its liquid state come in contact with the skin or clothing; they will adhere to most surfaces, so it is important to wear proper protection when you handle the liquid components. It's always better to err on the side of caution.

It's been called to my attention that in recent years, more people have been developing allergic reactions to urethane, so I offer this caveat (as I do with the use of ALL materials)—TEST, TEST, TEST! Make certain that your actor is not allergic to anything you are using against their skin, and take all necessary precautions to ensure your subject's health and safety.

Materials

Cold foam is a two-part A and B mixture, mixed in a ratio of 35A:65B, so an accurate gram scale is necessary.

- Digital scale
- Challenge 90 release agent
- High-speed drill
- Wire beater (made from wire hanger)
- Mold clamps or mold straps
- Latex, nitrile, or vinyl gloves
- Appliance mold
- Kryolan two-part Cold Foam System
- Food coloring
- Respirator
- 99% alcohol (for cleaning molds)
- Misc. disposable cups
- ½- or 1-inch chip brushes

FIGURE 6.38
Kryolan Cold Foam.
Photo by author.

Part A should be the color and consistency of a light maple syrup. Part B should be off-white or cream colored and the consistency of cream. The release agent (Challenge 90) should be light beige liquid and should be shaken well before using.

Quirks

The Kryolan cold foam instruction sheet suggests working in a room temperature of at least 80°F (about 27°C). That might be a bit warm, but colder room and mold temperatures can cause the foam to fail occasionally. High humidity can also cause foam to fail; ambient room humidity and even wooden stir sticks with any moisture can cause the foam to collapse. Stone molds or plaster molds must be clean and thoroughly dried before using. New molds can be oven dried for several hours at about 200°F (93°C); air-drying molds can take as long as several days.

Sometimes it is possible to reconstitute a collapsed piece by carefully crushing it; you will hear a popping sound like the noise when you crumple and twist bubble wrap. What you are doing is popping cells in the urethane, allowing the foam to return to its molded shape. Sometimes this will work, sometimes it won't.

The shelf life of cold foam is limited once the product containers have been opened. The chemicals are affected by exposure to air and light; therefore, the components should be stored in a cool, dry, dark area and used fairly soon after purchase. Keep the containers tightly sealed after each use. The manufacturer's recommended shelf life is 6 months after manufacturing, but I've made excellent pieces with foam components much older than that.

Prepping the Mold

If you are using a stone mold that has been thoroughly dried, it must be sealed to make it as nonporous as possible before applying the release agent. New or *green* molds or molds that haven't been used in a while should receive a second coating of release. All coats of release should be thin and dry before proceeding. Care must be taken in demolding the foam to prevent tearing the skin. Stone molds can make removal of urethane foam difficult, so beware. Every surface that the foam touches must be released because of the foam's tendency to stick to anything it comes in contact with when it sets up.

Like foam latex, finding the right amount of material to pour into the mold will take some experimentation before you become adept at just "knowing." It will partly be a factor of calculating the volume of the appliance and partly knowing how much the foam will expand as the mixed liquid components turn to foam. When you mix foam latex, the volume is dependent on whipping speed and time. With urethane foam, it rises of its own accord; under the best of circumstances, the cold foam will expand seven times its original liquid volume. The molds used for urethane foam must have escape holes drilled for excess foam to get out. If too much foam is put into the mold and the mold is then clamped tightly shut, the resulting foam will be dense and less flexible than if just enough is added and expands into all the cavities of the mold.

Although cold foam can be a pain in the neck because of its high sensitivity to any moisture, what I like about it is how tough it is compared to foam latex. It isn't as soft as foam latex, although a softer foam can be achieved by increasing the ratio of part A (I'm talking mere drops for a small mold; too much A could prevent the foam from skinning at all); an appliance made of cold foam can be used repeatedly because it is less susceptible to tearing during removal. I have had pieces made that've lasted for as many as 40 stage performances, without wear noticeable from the audience. In fairness, I must attribute at least some of that success to conscientious actors.

According to Kryolan, the optimum working temperature for the foam is 113°F (45°C). You can achieve this by placing the mold halves, the positive and the negative, in an oven set on warm—about 120°F (about 49°C) in most ovens. Heat the molds until they're warm to the touch. If that's not possible, try using a blow drier on high for a few minutes.

Filling the Mold

Let me reiterate the importance of working in a room with adequate ventilation and a respirator. The release agent alone is reason enough for it. Whew! Just as for foam latex, make notes of what you do for each batch. The more you use cold foam, the better your results will be.

Before beginning, place a cup or other container on the scale and tare it (zero it out):

1. Pour part B into a container; add food coloring to tint if needed. Experiment beforehand for color and amount. Unfortunately, food coloring choices are rather limited compared with pigment selections for other materials.
2. Pour part A into a container (the ratio is 65:35 B:A by weight; multiply the weight of part B by 0.53 to get the weight of Part A; 35 divided by

65 = 0.53). You can pour both parts into the same container if you are able to accurately do so.

3. As soon as the two parts have been added together, mix them quickly. The best results will be achieved by whipping the mixture with an electric drill and wire whisk; bending a long piece of wire (such as a coat hanger) works well. If you mix by hand, stir the mixture as quickly as possible until the foam starts to increase in volume.
4. Immediately pour the foam into your mold and clamp the halves tightly closed. The setting time is usually around 8–10 minutes but can take longer, depending on the temperature of the molds and the room.
5. Cleanup can be done with soap and water but be prepared for the fact that you might not get all the foam off your tools. Definitely wear rubber gloves for this!

There is a heat reaction when the foam begins to rise; the foam might begin to rise very suddenly, so be careful to keep your working area clear of anything you care about. Urethane foam is quite unwilling to give up anything it envelops.

Removing the Appliance

The cold foam will be ready to demold in approximately 30 minutes. Because cold foam is not as soft and stretchy as foam latex, care must be taken when opening the mold so that you don't tear the appliance or separate the outer skin from the inner foam structure.

The formula for Kryolan cold foam is designed to make it safer and easier to use and hold up to repeated washings; it can be applied and worn immediately after demolding, although you might choose to wash it first and let it dry as you do with foam latex pieces. Cold foam takes paint and makeup well and can be used with any of the adhesives used for silicone and foam latex. From a cost standpoint, cold foam is less expensive than foam latex.

Cold foam is just another choice available to you as a makeup effects designer, and the decision to use it instead of another material should be based on a number of factors, not the least of which is skin sensitivity of the performer who will wear it. Kryolan's Research and Development department continues to refine the formula and has stated that "one in a million people" might be sensitive to the foam and develop a rash; so far, there have been no breathing or respiratory side effects. Just as with every substance you work with as a makeup artist, you should be familiar with each product; MSDS product sheets from the manufacturers are available and contain information on just about everything imaginable for their products. All you have to do is ask for them.

GELATIN AND FOAMED GELATIN

The gelatin in Jell-O is what enables you to create all sorts of different shapes. I'm sure you've all heard of gelatin, but what exactly is it? Gelatin is a structural protein called *collagen* that is found in many animals, including humans. In fact,

collagen makes up nearly one third of all protein in the human body. Collagen is a large molecule that our bodies use to make skin, bones, and tendons both strong, flexible, and elastic.

To manufacture gelatin, manufacturers grind up bones, hooves, and connective tissues of cows, pigs, and sometimes horses and treat these parts with either a strong acid or base to break down the cellular structure of the tissue and release the collagen and other proteins. After this treatment, the resulting mixture is boiled; during this process, the collagen protein is broken down, resulting in the creation of gelatin. Yummy!

Because of its versatility, gelatin is a common ingredient in many foods and can be used in many ways; gelatin is used in foods from chewing gum to yogurt. It is even used to make capsules for medications and vitamins to make them easier to swallow.

By now some of you may be wondering, "What the heck does this have to do with special makeup effects, Todd?" Well, in addition to gelatin being used as an ingredient in foods and cosmetics, it is also one of the primary materials used in creating prosthetic appliances, along with foam latex and silicone. Gelatin has been used to create makeup effects since the 1920s.

Materials

You can find a number of formulas for making your own gelatin on the Internet, as well as purchasing pre-made gelatin prosthetic material from various industry suppliers. When describing gelatin, manufacturers refer to *bloom*. The *bloom factor* or *bloom strength* of gelatin is an industrial standard that measures the relative firmness of the gelatin in a cured state. Gelatin used for makeup effects work usually has a bloom factor of 300, whereas gelatin you can purchase from your local grocer (Knox brand gelatin, for example) will have a bloom somewhere between 200 and 250.

This might be just fine for work you will be doing, but just be aware that the tear strength will not be as high as when using a gelatin with a bloom of 300. (The 300 bloom gelatin is also more expensive.) However, there are additives you can put into your gelatin formula that will also increase tear resistance, strength, and durability.

- 300 bloom gelatin (UK gelatine)
- Glycerin (UK glycerol)
- Distilled water
- Appliance mold
- Zinc oxide powder
- Quick rise yeast
- Epoxy Parfilm
- Elmer's Glue (white)
- Ascorbic acid powder (vitamin C)
- Liquid plastic sealer (alcohol based)
- Petroleum jelly (for release)
- Microwave
- Sorbitol (liquid)
- Scale
- Microwave-safe bowl(s)
- Baking soda
- White vinegar

Vegetable oil spray (release)
Tartaric acid (cream of Tartar powder)
Witch hazel (for blending edges)
Misc. plastic cups
Large craft sticks

There are so many formulas for making gelatin suitable for prosthetics that I've listed every ingredient I remember ever seeing in a recipe. Probably not all of them should be used in the same formula if you want to have a product that is soft, light, and strong enough to use. Fortunately, none of the individual elements is expensive; in fact, gelatin is the least expensive of the prosthetic materials used for makeup effects. Gelatin ingredients are inexpensive, and you can buy just about everything you need to create gelatin appliances at your local grocery store and pharmacy. Experiment! Or you can buy premade gelatin, both foaming and nonfoaming, that needs only to be heated and poured into a released mold. Several suppliers are listed in the appendix on the companion site.

Some of the ingredients listed above may seem oddly out of place, so let me describe the purposes of some that might not seem obvious:

- Vinegar: foaming agent
- Ascorbic acid (vitamin C): foaming agent
- Baking soda: foaming agent
- Zinc oxide: strengthener (but will reduce translucency)
- Tartaric acid: foaming agent
- Quick-rise yeast: foaming agent
- Sorbitol: reduces shrinkage, increases strength
- Elmer's Glue: adds strength and stability

Quirks

Gelatin is more translucent and moves better than some materials, has a very realistic texture, and doesn't take much makeup to get good cover. However, gelatin breaks down with heat and perspiration; that is, it melts and dissolves, respectively. There are several effective workarounds for sweat-related problems, but heat, such as working under hot stage lights or on location near the equator, is another matter, and there's not much you can do about that except use something other than gelatin.

Gelatin is considered to be *hypoallergenic*, that is, allergy free for use on most people. That's a good thing. Gelatin is also considered *hygroscopic*, which means that it has a tendency to absorb moisture from the atmosphere. This is both good and not so good: *Good* in that it allows gelatin to be soluble—to liquefy and dissolve. With the addition of water, the gelatin particles swell and expand, actually absorbing up to 10 times their weight in water (which, in turn, can make gelatin appliances somewhat heavy); *not so good* in that gelatin appliances can swell in proportion to humidity changes in the air and shrink over time through evaporation.

One way to help minimize this change due to humidity is to substitute glycerin for almost all the water used in the gelatin appliance formula. This is very good for creating a variety of wounds and injuries—cuts, burns, bullet holes, swelling, and the like. This gelatin can be colored with flocking material, food coloring, or powdered cake makeup and stored in small squeeze bottles to be heated until the gelatin liquefies. This is similar to a number of gelatin effects kits that are available commercially. Just be very careful not to overheat the gelatin; because it is organic material, it can be severely damaged or ruined if heated too much (or too often), and you don't want to burn your actor by applying gelatin that is too warm. *Always test the temperature before application!*

As I mentioned, glycerin is also hygroscopic, so some formulas replace some of the glycerin with sorbitol, which is derived from corn syrup and is less affected by changes in humidity than glycerin. Sorbitol also increases the structural integrity of gelatin formulas, making them more tear resistant, which is critical for prosthetic work. (I've seen formulas that added Elmer's® white glue for the same purpose with good success.) Zinc oxide can also be used in small amounts to add strength and greater tolerance to temperature changes (remember, gelatin tends to melt when heat is applied). You will have to experiment when using zinc oxide because it will affect the translucency of your finished gelatin appliance. Zinc oxide powder is the preferred form, but sometimes it can be tough to find; however, zinc oxide ointment will work. Regardless of the formula you wind up using and calling your own, keep your finished appliances in air-tight plastic bags, away from the light and in a cool place. They will last much longer.

For prosthetic appliance work, the gelatin you use will need to be light and soft—foamy. So, the recipe I'll give you is for a foaming gelatin. The resulting gelatin will not be as light and soft as foam latex, but it will be substantially lighter and spongier than a solid gelatin appliance and definitely lighter than silicone gel.

NOTE

You can double, triple, or quadruple these formulas. Very small batches aren't as easy to mix as a medium batch, which this describes; but once you've mixed a medium batch, you can take smaller amounts from it and use them in small molds.

Filling the Mold

A basic gelatin formula (you will notice that the following recipe does not have sorbitol, white glue, or zinc oxide—do some experimenting—a good makeup effects artist must be part mad chemist):

- 160 grams (¼ cup) glycerin
- 40 grams (⅛ cup) gelatin
- 1 gram (1 teaspoon) quick rise yeast
- 3.5 grams (3.5 teaspoons) distilled water
- Pigment color of your choice (you can also use colored flocking, food coloring, or powdered cake makeup)

1. In a microwave-safe bowl, pour the glycerin. Slowly add the gelatin granules to the glycerin. If you are adding a pigment, mix the pigment into a small amount of glycerin before adding it to the batch. Heat the glycerin and gelatin in the microwave for 1 or 2 minutes, in 5- to 10-second increments, being careful to *prevent bringing the gelatin to a boil*. If the gelatin boils, the collagen in the gelatin will be destroyed and you will need to start over. Gelatin melts at about 70°C or close to 160°F, depending on altitude.

FIGURE 6.39
Foaming gelatin rising.
Photos by author.

2. When the gelatin has completely liquefied, pour the gelatin into a plastic quart cup. Let the gelatin cool completely (you can put it in the freezer or refrigerator; you're essentially making Jell-O), then remelt the gelatin in the microwave three or four times—again in 5- to 10-second intervals, so it won't boil—to ensure that all the water has evaporated from the glycerin, to minimize shrinkage of the finished appliance.
3. Before going on to the next step, apply a very thin layer of petroleum jelly, vegetable oil (PAM), or Epoxy Parfilm on both the positive and the negative of your mold as a release agent so that the gelatin won't stick to the mold surface when you demold your appliance.
4. When you're ready to cast your appliance, mix the yeast with the water and let this mixture sit for at least 2 minutes; melt the gelatin, being careful not to let it boil, then add the yeast and water mixture, stirring it into the melted gelatin. It will immediately begin to foam.
5. Stop stirring and let the gelatin mixture rise until it stops, then stir well with a large craft stick to refine the gelatin—that is, to remove large air bubbles and to make the foam mixture consistent. It should be the consistency of meringue. If the gelatin cools too much, reheat it briefly, so it is pourable. Like foam latex, foamed gelatin can be poured or injected into a mold.

NOTE

Instead of using the water/yeast mixture to make the gelatin foam, you can substitute a small amount of vinegar and/or baking soda to achieve the same result. Ascorbic acid powder (vitamin C) will also cause a foaming action. You do not have to foam the gelatin to achieve an excellent appliance. It is presented as an option, albeit a good one, I believe. Gelatin can have some weight to it (though it's still lighter than silicone), and foaming the gelatin will make it lighter by using less material.

6. It is a good idea to heat the negative half of your mold in a warm oven until it is warm to the touch. This is an optional step, but it could provide a better appliance surface. The positive can be either heated or

chilled before foaming your gelatin. If chilled, it should be cold to the touch but not frozen. The goal is to speed up the gelling time. Pouring warm foam into a frozen mold, or even a cold one, could crack it, which, as you can imagine, would be bad. Experimentation will dictate what is best.

7. When your foam is ready to pour, fill your mold; use a spatula or large craft stick to work the gelatin into the warm negative mold and close it immediately.

Be careful not to trap air bubbles when you're closing the mold. Clamp or press the mold halves together tightly to ensure a thin blending edge of the appliance and then place the closed mold into a freezer or refrigerator to gel. Depending on the size of your mold and the temperature, it could take anywhere from 30 minutes to an hour or more before the appliance is ready to be demolded.

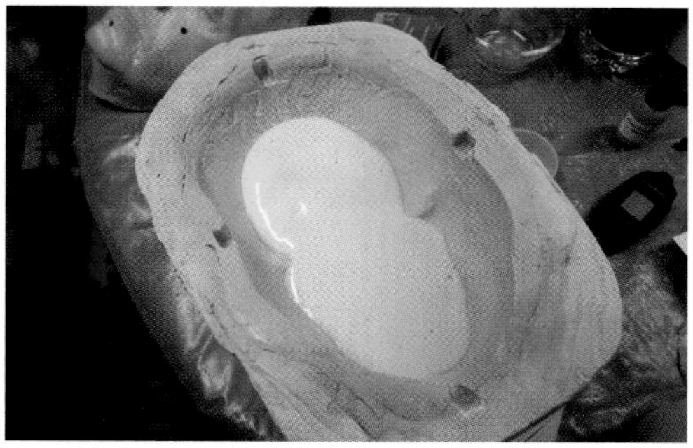

FIGURE 6.40
Foaming gelatin going into mold.
Photo by author.

Removing the Appliance

You can tell when the foamed gelatin has set by touching the overflow or any remainder from the mixing bowl; if it bounces back, it's ready to demold.

1. Carefully open the mold halves and find an edge; begin to remove the piece, powdering the gelatin as you go, to prevent it from sticking to itself. Place it back on the positive and it is ready for painting and/or application.
2. If the appliance piece is going to be applied to the skin, a barrier layer is recommended between the gelatin and the skin to prevent perspiration from prematurely breaking down the piece (dissolving it).
3. Apply a light plastic (such as bald cap plastic), vinyl, or acrylic layer over the areas of the appliance that will come in contact with the skin. Pieces for around the eyes—swollen bruises or eye bags, for example—should be completely sealed; you can even encapsulate gelatin in the same way you encapsulate silicone (but not with silicone as the encapsulator).
4. After sealing, powder the piece again before storing it in an airtight container. Another option is to also cover the back of the piece (but *not* the edges!) with Pros-Aide® adhesive in addition to the sealer, allow it to dry, and then powder it.

Before moving on to casting dental appliances, I'm going to share another recipe with you for gelatin appliances—a nonfoaming one—from Matthew Mungle:

- 100 g Sorbitol (70%) liquid
- 100 g glycerin
- 20–30 g of 300 bloom gelatin
- Coloring: flocking, food coloring, powdered cake makeup, etc.

Here's how to prep are and fill the mold and remove the appliance.

1. Mix the ingredients together and let them sit, preferably overnight, so that the gelatin has time to dissolve in the glycerin and sorbitol.
2. Heat in a microwave (in a microwave-safe container) for approximately 2 minutes (in 10- to 15-second increments), stirring frequently.

Do not let the gelatin boil (bubble or foam) that will burn the gelatin, causing it to change color and leave bubbles in the finished appliance.

3. Gently swirl and jostle the mixing container to get rid of any air bubbles in the gelatin.
4. Carefully pour the gelatin into the warmed mold, holding the container as close to the mold surface as possible.

FIGURE 6.41
Melted gelatin in microwave-safe container.
Photo by author.

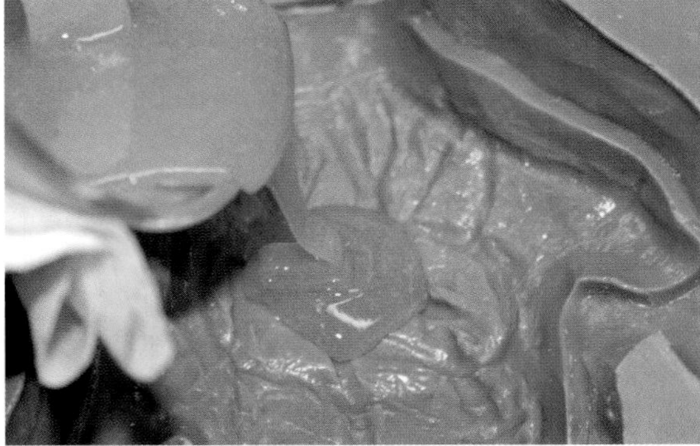

FIGURE 6.42
Slowly pour gelatin from near mold surface.
Photo by author.

Pouring from top (high) may cause the formation of air bubbles becoming trapped (with silicone, pouring from higher up causes air bubbles in the silicone to stretch and break).

5. Tilt the mold from side to side, allowing the gelatin to coat the surface of the mold and allowing air bubbles to escape.
6. Press the positive into the negative and close the mold tightly.
7. Allow the gelatin to cool and set up.
8. Carefully remove the positive, trying to keep the appliance in the negative. If there are bubbles, they will be easier to repair if the gelatin is still in the negative.
9. Trim around the flashing at the cutting edge and powder the inside of the appliance.
10. Carefully begin to peel up an appliance edge and gently remove the piece, powdering as you go. Powder both sides of the appliance.

I've already suggested that you take some time and experiment with gelatin because it is quick, easy, and inexpensive. What's also cool about it is that if your appliance turns out badly in the mold, you can simply clean out the gelatin, remelt it, and pour it again! There is a caveat, however, eventually the collagen in the gelatin will begin to break down from the repeated heating, but in the learning stages, that doesn't really matter, because you probably won't be making an appliance for a major project while you're just learning how to do gelatin well (I hope).

You will notice that the two formulas/recipes for gelatin I gave you are quite different; I can't say that one is better than the other (Matthew Mungle, however, might disagree). Much of how you make the gelatin is dependent on the way it will be used. If it is going to be for a prosthetic appliance, one way could be preferable over another, but if you are making a prop body part, you could decide on a different formula to suit the project.

Michael Davy, veteran makeup artist and the inventor of foaming sponge gelatin (which I think is fantastic), has developed a method of foaming his water-based vinyl cap plastic Water-Melon. The recipe is in Appendix B.

DENTAL ACRYLIC

I'll start this section off with another disclaimer because, next to your eyes, your teeth are the most sensitive and delicate body parts you will be working with. Now you're probably thinking, "Eyes, I can understand, but teeth? Really? They're hard. There are a lot of them. They're designed for tearing through meat and chewing food into itsy bitsy little pieces!" True, we don't always think of our teeth as sensitive and delicate until something is *wrong* with them, and then we find out how tough (or not) we *really* are. Many of us would certainly divulge state secrets if some lunatic went to messing with our sensitive and delicate teeth. Anyone remember Dustin Hoffman and Laurence Olivier in *Marathon Man*?

For this reason alone, I caution you about the risk involved in working in and around anyone's mouth without being a licensed dental technician. *Any dental appliance that is not made by a licensed dental technician is to be considered and treated as cosmetic only, not therapeutic or corrective*. Cosmetic (theatrical) dental appliances are not suitable for chewing food. Never use force when inserting or removing a cosmetic dental appliance. I stated this in Chapter 3 and am reiterating it here in case you missed it there: It is illegal to practice dentistry without a license. (I must've been a lawyer in a past life to feel the need to say something so obvious. Sorry.) Although I'm still on the subject, you should never attempt to take an impression of someone's teeth if they're wearing any kind of braces, real dentures, or removable bridge.

Materials

One of the materials used in making theatrical teeth appliances is a liquid monomer that dissolves the dental acrylic powder; you will need to wear a good NIOSH-approved respirator that is rated for organic vapors whenever you are working with monomers. This stuff is unpleasant! This protection will hopefully help

FIGURE 6.43
Vacuum formed teeth.
Photo by author.

ensure that your brain continues to function properly for years to come. Never use monomers near any open flame or sparking heat source, either. Monomer vapors are heavy and will seek the lowest point; do not use monomers in any room that has floor vents that lead to a heater or furnace or you may get to see your neighborhood from the air through thick smoke and flames.

If you will be casting acrylic in a silicone mold (and you will), you need to know that all silicones will absorb monomer. So, if you cast acrylic in your silicone mold more than twice in a row (in close succession), the silicone will swell, making the dentures you are casting thinner than they are supposed to be. Using a hair dryer (on *low*) on the mold for a few minutes will evaporate much of the monomer that's been absorbed. The mold should be cool before you use it again. A spray release agent such as Frekote, designed for molded polymers in silicone molds, will help prolong your mold life.

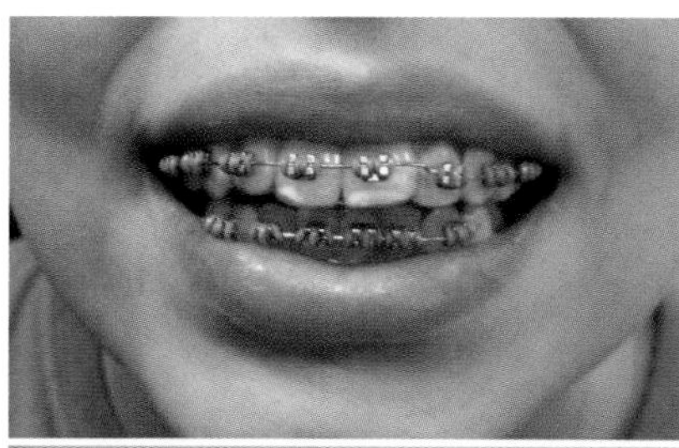

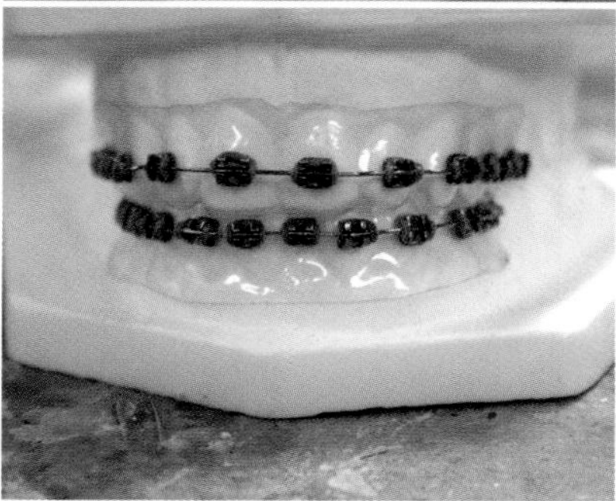

FIGURE 6.44
Vacuum formed teeth with braces hardware.
Photos by author.

Vacuum forming has become another method of creating dental appliances, particularly for thin painted veneers directly over someone's own choppers, or for creating the illusion of wearing a retainer or braces. The wires and supports can be glued directly to the thin clear plastic molded veneer and then slipped right over the actor's own teeth and no one in the audience will be the wiser.

- Flexacryl acrylic powder
- Gum shade acrylic powder
- Round-nosed pliers
- Variable-speed Dremel
- Al-cote dental separator
- 400 and 800 grit wet/dry sandpaper
- Mechanical pencil
- X-acto knife with #11 blades
- Tooth shade acrylic powder
- 0.028 ball clasps
- Acrylic liquid monomer
- Misc. Dremel bits
- Medium bowl with hot water
- Dental wax
- Glycerin

TIP
Curing dental acrylic under water and at 30 psi of air pressure will cause the acrylic to cure faster, denser, and with fewer surface flaws.

Filling the Mold and Removing the Appliance

The process of casting dental appliances can be rather complicated and time consuming, considering how small they can be, but considering how important our mouths and teeth are, it is important to take great care to do this task well. Sculpting and casting dental appliances is fun, but be prepared for disappointment. This job is not easy and takes much practice to become proficient; unless you are called on to do this regularly, dentures might be an aspect of makeup effects that you'll want to leave to a specialist.

1. Place your dental positive in water and then brush it with a coat of Al-Cote dental separator. When the first coat is dry, add a second coat. You might also opt for a thin layer of petroleum jelly instead of or in addition to the Al-Cote.
2. Put some dental wax in the indentations between the teeth. This is fairly easy to do, but the wax must be melted; you can also use wax or oil clay instead of dental wax. This will prevent the dental acrylic from filling that space—which is an undercut—and risk breaking the stone when you remove the acrylic cast from the positive.
3. Mix a 50/50 batch of tooth shade acrylic with Flexacryl with monomer and slowly pour it into the mold when it starts to thicken, tilting it back and forth to make sure the material gets into all the cavities of the mold.
4. Press the positive into the mold, but don't press so hard that suction is created when you remove your hand; you don't want to suck air into the mold with the acrylic.
5. Now you can do one of two things: You can place the mold in a bowl of hot water to cure the acrylic (it must be large enough to submerge the entire mold) or you can submerge the mold in a pressure chamber; Harbor Freight and Northern Tool & Equipment sell a 2½-gallon paint tank that is perfectly suitable for this task. You need to have an air compressor that is capable of delivering 30 psi of pressure, which isn't much. This will cause the acrylic to cure faster, denser, and with fewer surface flaws. You can demold after about 20 minutes.
6. Remove from the appliance any excess acrylic that will prevent extra thickness in the finished appliance, which you don't want.

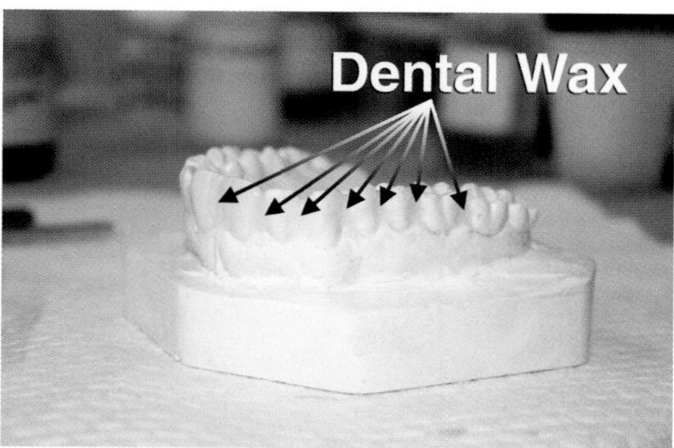

FIGURE 6.45
Dental wax removes potential undercuts that can hinder denture removal.
Photo by author.

Now, here is where I would ordinarily be done with casting dentures. All that remains is to trim away any acrylic that might be causing pressure or discomfort, paint them with Minute Stain, wash them, and wear them. What follows is more advanced, and I strongly suggest that you practice quite a bit before attempting this task for a paid gig. These next steps (steps 7 through 23) border on the realm of a professional dental technician. *I'm providing this information as information only and do not advocate its use.*

7. Draw lines on the teeth and gums with a mechanical pencil to show where the incisal layer is; this is a translucent outer layer on all teeth. Use the Dremel to carefully grind off some of the acrylic, leaving a thin layer

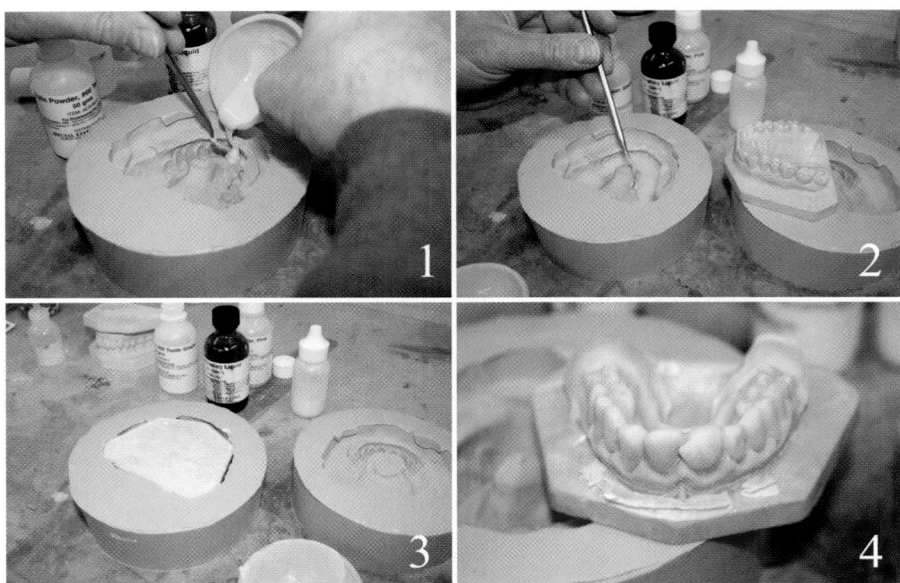

FIGURE 6.46
Dental acrylic poured into mold (1), assuring full coverage (2), positive pressed into negative mold (3), and finished cast (4) ready to trim and paint.
Photos by author.

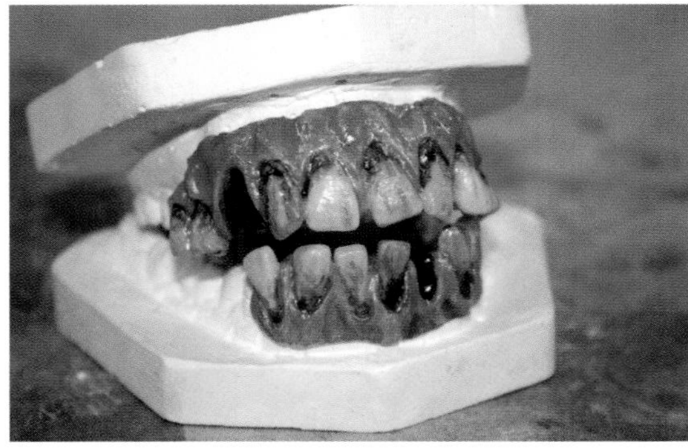

FIGURE 6.47
Simple dental appliances; upper and lower.
Teeth and photo by author.

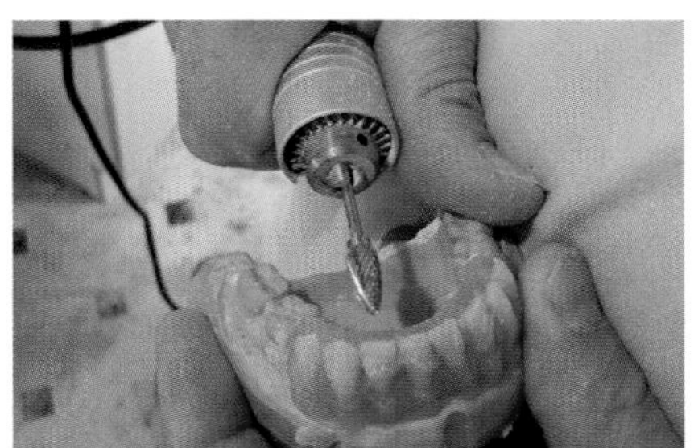

FIGURE 6.48
Using Dremel to trim.
Image reproduced by permission of Darren Grassby.

around the teeth at the gums and at the base of the teeth in a somewhat jagged pattern. You will be recasting the teeth with clear dental acrylic, thereby adding a sense of depth.

8. Remove the pencil markings with a Q-tip dipped in monomer.
9. Brush Al-cote over any exposed stone on the positive before casting the dental acrylic to ensure that it won't bond to it.
10. Mix 1 ounce of clear acrylic with 1 teaspoon of tooth shade acrylic with monomer—enough to liquefy the powder; when it begins to thicken slightly, pour it into the mold and press the positive back into the mold. You can repeat step 5 now. After the teeth have been demolded, they need to be prepped for casting the gums. Take the mechanical pencil again and draw around the teeth at the gum line. Then take the Dremel and remove as much of the existing acrylic covering the gums as you can, leaving a thin layer only. Then remove any remaining pencil markings with another Q-tip® dipped in monomer.

NOTE
Wear a dust mask to avoid inhaling acrylic from grinding.

11. Because more dental acrylic is going to be added (pink gum color), we want to prevent it from bonding to the teeth.
12. Mix 1/4 ounce of Al-Cote separator with 1/4 teaspoon of glycerin. Brush four coats onto any surface you don't want the gum color to adhere to. Make sure that each coat is completely dry before adding the next.
13. Mix the gum color, and when it begins to thicken slightly, pour it into the mold and then press the positive into the mold. When the excess acrylic gets spongy and bounces back when you press into it (return memory), you can demold the positive.
14. Cut around each tooth at the gum line and the vestibule area (small cavity where the midline frenum muscle attaches the upper lip to the gums) with an X-acto knife (#11 blade).
15. Carefully remove the gum acrylic from the teeth, front and back, as well as gum material that is covering the soft palate. *Note*: This might be easier said than done. Then remove the appliance from the positive and do a rough trim with the Dremel, grinding almost to the base of the teeth on the back side. Be careful not to grind through the acrylic and into the stone positive!
16. As an additional anchoring option, you can add a ball clasp to the appliance to help hold it in place, but it is not an essential step. Carefully bend the clasp into a curve that will fit around the back tooth of the appliance. Glue the wire in place with a drop of Superglue.
17. Use the Dremel to remove a section of the gums so that the appliance can be placed back on the stone positive without affecting the placement of the clasp.
18. Release the area of the positive with a bit of petroleum jelly and place the appliance back on the positive. Mix up some new pink gum acrylic and carefully rebuild the gum over the wire clasp. When the acrylic has begun to set, place it in hot water to cure.
19. Use the Dremel to smooth out the new gum acrylic to match the rest of the appliance. Also grind down any high spots or rough areas on the inside. Be careful not to grind a hole in the appliance! Sand any rough edges with high grit wet/dry paper.
20. Use the same 400 and 800 grit paper to sand the front of the teeth and gums; then use a fine grit silicone point bit over the appliance, followed by a bristle brush bit to clean off any silicone residue. Then use a rag wheel bit with some acrylic polish to buff the appliance to a shine.
21. Use an old toothbrush and some dishwashing liquid to remove any remaining polishing compound from the appliance. The last step before painting the teeth will be to reline the inside of the appliance with a soft acrylic.
22. Brush a thin layer of petroleum jelly over the front and back of the positive. Then mix some Flexacryl (2:1) with monomer. The flexible nature

of Flexacryl will make the appliance more comfortable to wear. Work quickly; this could set up rather fast.

23. Rub the inside of the appliance with a Q-tip dipped in monomer and then place the Flexacryl evenly on the inside of the appliance before placing the appliance onto the positive. Clean up any excess with another Q-tip dipped in monomer. Cure the acrylic in hot water and remove it. Then trim the excess, and it's ready to paint and wear!

NOTE

Don't leave the appliance on the positive for several hours or overnight without removing it at least once after the acrylic has cured. If you don't remove the appliance from the positive soon after curing, you may never get it off the positive! You don't need to ask me how I know this, either.

SILICONE (PART 2)

By Naomi Lynch

Not all silicones can be thickened effectively, and some work only with their own specially composed additives. There are different thixotropic agents for platinum and tin silicones. Don't mix them up. Some silicones thicken a lot, others hardly at all. TEST!

You shouldn't mix different types of uncured silicone either. Each is specially formulated to give a specific result and may not work correctly if you mess with that. However, you can add another layer on top of the first once it has passed the gel stage.

The following are the residual solvents or monomers that may inhibit cure:

- Chlorinated hydrocarbons that contain amine stabilizers
- Alcohols—ethanol, methanol
- Esters—ethyl acetate, vinyl acetate
- Compounds with unsaturated bonds

These are "temporary inhibitors," i.e., once they evaporate, they won't affect the cure, as opposed to permanent inhibitors that are permanent. Sometimes if you haven't let the solvents evaporate completely, this may affect the cure, but if you leave the mold for a few days, it may set properly, as the solvents disappear.

Residual solvents that don't inhibit cure include nonchlorinated aromatic and aliphatic solvents—toluene, xylene, Hexane, and mineral spirits.

Therefore, stuff like lighter fluid and naphtha shouldn't cause problems, but isopropyl alcohol can.

I recommend covering your sculpt between working sessions to avoid the chances of airborne contaminants settling on it.

If the room temperature is cool, that can interfere. Low temperature alone won't stop curing, it just slows it down. A rule of thumb I remember from somewhere was that every 10° below 73°F doubles cure time. Which means every 5–6° below 23°C will double cure time; however, you can blast it with a dryer or heater once it has gelled to stop that or even rig up a "hotbox" to give it a warm environment.

SEAMING AND PAINTING SILICONE APPLIANCES

As has already been pointed out, nothing really sticks to silicone except other silicone, which can make silicone somewhat difficult to paint, especially if you want the paint to stay put. This section deals with paint options as much as (if not more so) with painting technique. Each makeup that you create will be different, so how you paint it and what you use to paint it will differ as well.

Let's begin by taking for granted that you have given your silicone appliance (or appliances) a foundation color that is at least in the ballpark of the base color you need for the overall makeup. You would have done this as you mixed the silicone before casting the appliance. But first we have to clean up the appliance by getting rid of seams and other surface blemishes that don't belong and should be corrected.

FIGURE 6.49
Seams before seaming.
Photo by author.

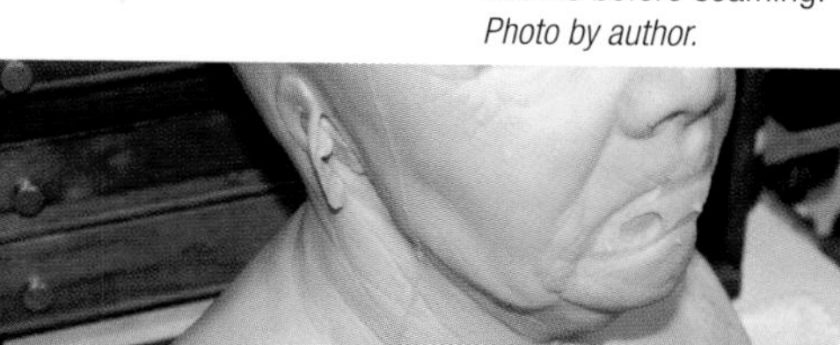

Seaming and Patching

The term for cleaning up seam flashing and surface blemishes is *seaming*. The process actually *de-seams* the prosthetic.

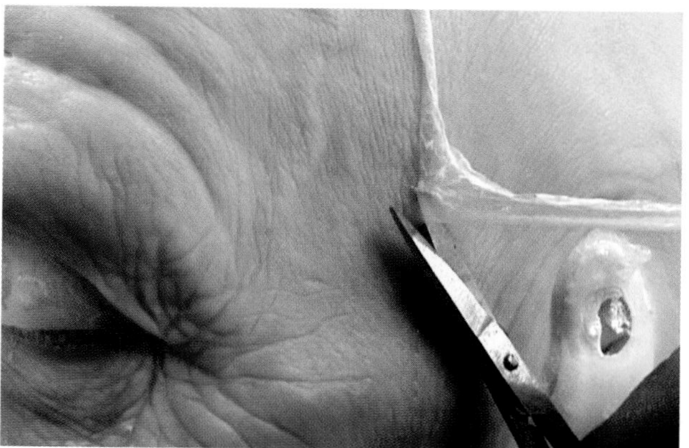

FIGURE 6.50
Start with small sharp scissors; lift seam flashing and trim carefully.
Image reproduced by permission of Neill Gorton.

SILICONE

Starting with a small pair of sharp, fine scissors and your fingers (careful!) or a good set of tweezers, carefully lift the seam flashing and trim as close to the surface as possible.

Neill Gorton suggests that rather than simply trimming the flashing to the surface, which often still leaves a detectible remnant, cut a very slight channel along the seam. It is much easier to fill a small channel than to mask small bumps that could be left behind by simply trimming the seam close. These channels and indentations can be patched invisibly with small amounts of the same mixture of silicone used to cast the appliance initially.

After flashing and other blemishes have been cut away, very carefully clean the surface of the prosthetic with a little isopropyl alcohol or acetone to remove fingerprints, dirt, dust, powder, mold release residue, or whatever. If the piece has been handled, you need to give it a good, gentle cleaning so that the silicone patch will grab and stick properly. Be careful to avoid appliance edges.

Using a small, accurate digital scale, mix a small amount of the silicone in the same proportion used for the appliance. Then, working in only small areas at a time on the seam—no more than 3 inches (about 7.5 centimeters)—it will be easier but somewhat dependent on the silicone you use. Using a platinum-cure silicone such as Polytek's PlatSil Gel-10 will allow you to work quickly. The following steps will work best if your appliance is resting on either a soft foam or a rigid foam form of your model.

1. Apply a thin line of silicone along the channel cut using a small dental spatula to place the silicone.
2. Then place a piece of clear plastic wrap (cling film) over the patch and lay it down carefully to make sure there are no trapped air bubbles. It is best if you can pin it taut in place. If the patch is on the neck, you can use tools to match and follow existing wrinkles and so on. A hair dryer will also accelerate the silicone cure.
3. As the silicone begins to thicken and set up, indentations can be added on top of the plastic wrap. After the silicone is fully cured, the plastic wrap can be carefully peeled away (nothing sticks to silicone, remember?), leaving an invisible patch where there was a noticeable seam before. Voilà! Perfect.

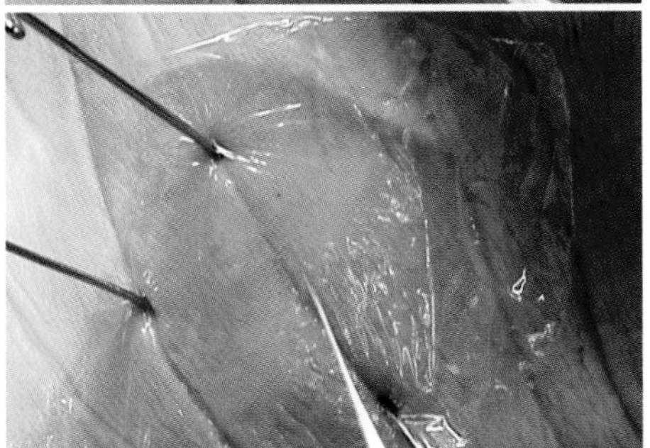

FIGURE 6.51
Apply thin line of silicone along channel cut using small dental spatula to place silicone. If patch is on neck, you can use tools to match and follow existing wrinkles.
Image reproduced by permission of Neill Gorton.

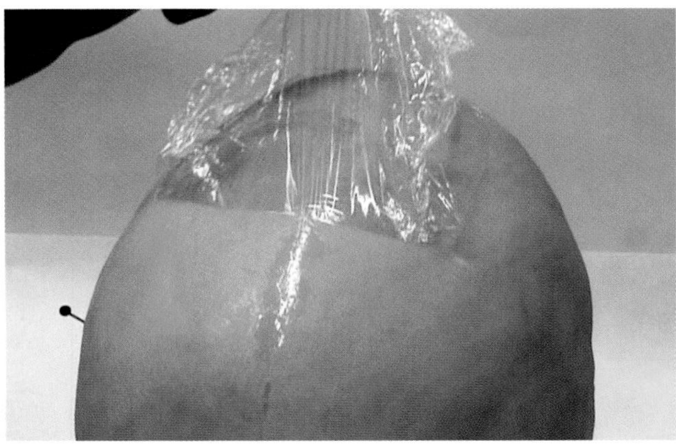

FIGURE 6.52
After silicone cured, peel away plastic wrap, leaving invisible patch where there was noticeable seam.
Image reproduced by permission of Neill Gorton.

FOAM LATEX

Seaming and patching foam latex can be a real pain in the caboose if you actually try to seam and patch with foam latex, because it requires a heat cure again. Unfortunately, foam latex is probably the best material to use because it will be the same as the rest of the appliance. However, in many cases, seams are in areas of the appliance where you may be able to get away with using a different material that doesn't move in the same manner as the foam. It probably won't really be enough for anyone to notice but you.

Pros-Aide makes a terrific patching material, and there are two ways to use it. First, you can pour a small amount into a small cup and let it sit exposed to the air for a while; as the water evaporates from the adhesive, it will thicken up and you can then fill the seam or blemish. As the Pros-Aide begins to dry, you can texture it carefully with a tool or a (damp) stipple sponge. When it is dry (it will be completely clear when dry), powder it, and you're good to go. You can also add a small amount of Cab-O-Sil to fresh Pros-Aide to thicken it into a paste and apply in the same manner. Pros-Aide mixed with Cab-O-Sil is affectionately called *bondo* after the car body filler Bondo. Oddly enough, the Pros-Aide will still dry clear, even though the Cab-O-Sil is white (unless you've added a lot of the filler). A fine brush dipped in 99% IPA (isopropyl alcohol) can be used to feather the edges to nothing while the Pros-Aide is still soft.

You could even try a bit of melted gelatin as a seaming and patching material on foam latex, provided you don't apply it when the gelatin is too liquid and seeps into the foam. A fine brush dipped in hot water can be used to smooth the gelatin. Texture the same way as the Pros-Aide;® freshly set gelatin is very sticky until it is powdered, so a light dusting of powder may facilitate texturing if the appliance needs it.

GELATIN AND COLD FOAM

If your appliance is made of gelatin, I do not recommend using gelatin as the seaming material. The reason should be pretty obvious: You must melt gelatin to apply it to a seam, and melted gelatin is hot—warm, at least—and gelatin melts when it gets too warm or wet; hence, you don't want to remelt the appliance you've just spent considerable time and effort to make. Use Pros-Aide instead. Pros-Aide (bondo) is also the preferred method of seaming cold foam (urethane foam).

Painting the Appliance

Painting prosthetic appliances can be handled in a variety of ways, and your method should be decided based on a combination of personal preference, personal style, the material of the appliance you'll be painting, and whether you'll be painting it before or after application.

PAINTING SILICONE

Toby Sells is one of the most popular and sought after makeup effects artists on the east coast. His company, Toby Sells Creature Make Up FX Shop has been responsible for the makeup effects on such films as *Dance of the Dead* and hit TV shows like *The Vampire Diaries* and AMC's *The Walking Dead* (KNB Efx Group, Inc.) As a freelance makeup effects artist, Toby has been on the makeup effects teams of *Zombieland* (Tony Gardner's Alterian Studios) and *The Crazies* (Robert Hall's Almost Human, Inc.).

FIGURE 6.53
Toby and friend.
Image reproduced by permission of Toby Sells.

Toby: I started out making the zombie bust from Smooth-On's Mold Max 25. Most people come out of the gate bound to lose the race because they won't make their skins opaque enough. Although human skin is slightly translucent, it's about 98% opaque. The magic in making a paint job look great is a very opaque silicone skin with layer upon layer of spatters and flicks of very, very translucent color; otherwise, it will turn out looking like a bad wax museum figure.

Using Shinetsu Silicone Caulk, I make a paint base by dispensing it into a glass jar or a medical specimen cup. I then add an equal amount of mineral spirits. Mix until it's uniform. This will be the "master batch" because to shoot this through an airbrush, it'll have to thin down another 50% when adding pigments.

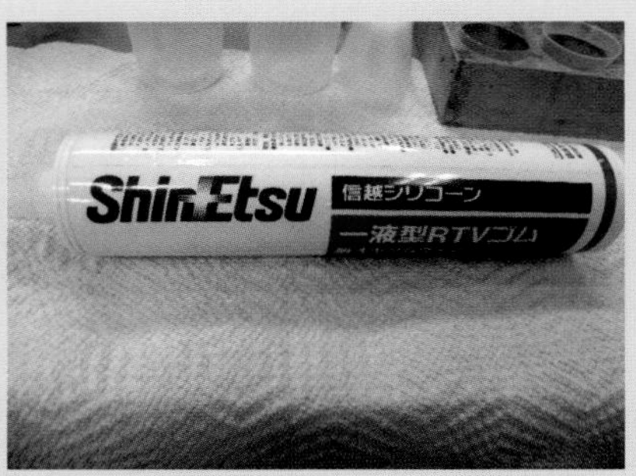

FIGURE 6.54
Shinetsu Silicone Caul.
Image reproduced by permission of Toby Sells.

I mixed 50/50 Raw Umber and Magenta oil paints and then added it to the thinned master batch. Add the oils carefully; you want to make it translucent.

I used a Paasche H with a #5 tip to apply the wash coat. The purpose of the wash coat is to fill in all the fine detail and help it pop just a little through all the other layers of paint that we will be adding. Apply the wash coat moderately, careful not to pool up any paint in the recessed areas. I dry the paint with a hair dryer between coats.

FIGURE 6.55
Thinned raw oil paint.
Image reproduced by permission of Toby Sells.

With my Paasche H, tip #3, I spatter a mixture of paint consisting of Asphalt oil color, again very translucent. I spatter the entire head twice to get the desired look. You can also cut down a 1-inch chip brush and flick the colors on. I prefer the airbrush, but it does come in handy for moles and freckles!

Next, I made a more opaque paint by adding Burnt Umber to our thinned base, spattering the entire head. I then added Ivory Black to the Burnt Umber Paint, still using my Paasche H but with a #1 tip this time. I went in and began to make small noodles and squiggly lines (mottling) around the wounds, the mouth, between the teeth and around the eyes. Then back to the Paasche H with a #5 tip and lightly spattered the entire head, then blow dried; this helped the colors start to pop, so that I have an idea of where to go next.

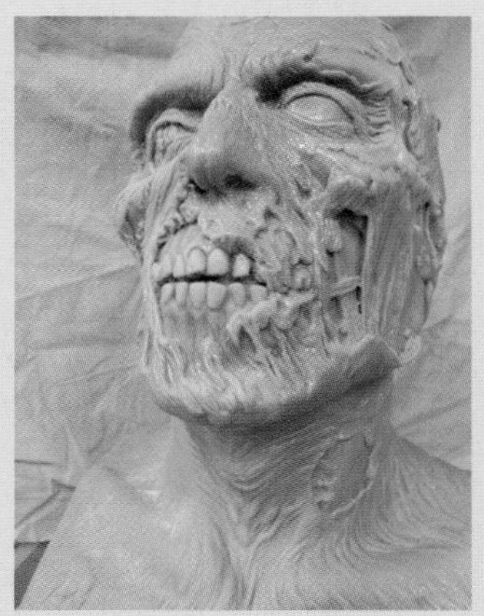

FIGURE 6.56
After thin wash coat applied.
Image reproduced by permission of Toby Sells.

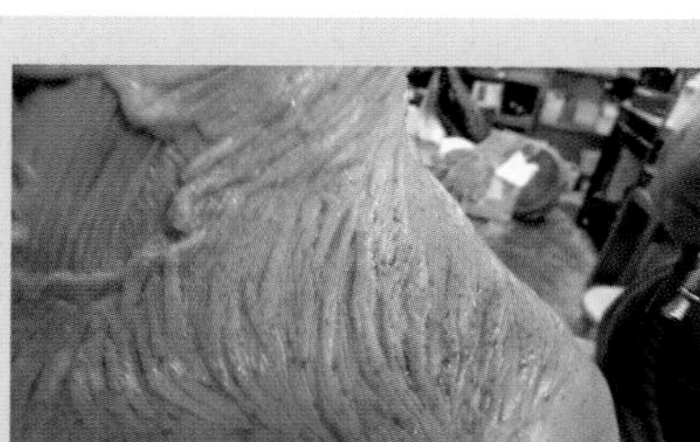

FIGURE 6.57
Spatter burnt umber.
Image reproduced by permission of Toby Sells.

FIGURE 6.58
Reel Creations alcohol activated palette.
Image reproduced by permission of Toby Sells.

I use Reel Creations Palettes and Airbrush Inks a lot when painting silicone with caulk-based paints. I activated the colors on the "Shades from the Crypt" palette with 99% alcohol, and on a wax mixing palette, I pour out some of my thinned silicone paint base. Using a small brush or spatula, I began transferring the alcohol paints to the silicone on the mixing palette. Using "Mocha" in the paint base, I went in with a fine detail brush and punched in some small details around the wounds, teeth, and random areas. Then with "Vein" from the Shades of the Crypt palette, I punched up some detail with a fine brush around the wounds, inside the ears and in other random spots.

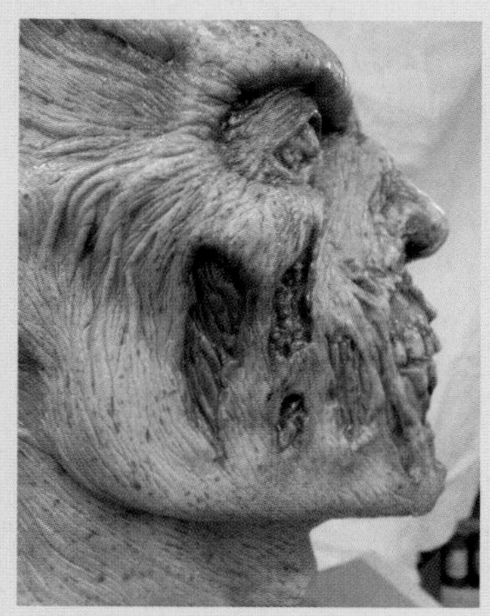

FIGURE 6.59
Punching up detail.
Image reproduced by permission of Toby Sells.

Back to the airbrush for a little while, I mixed up yellow ochre and light blue with my paint base and spattered the whole head and dried it.

Mixing naphtha crimson and light blue (about 50/50) oil paints, I made the paint a bit more opaque. I then went in with an Iwata double action airbrush and did more noodles around the exposed muscle tissues, the gums, wounds, and then randomly all over the head, and blow dry.

Taking the burnt umber, the naphtha crimson and light blue paint from earlier, I made a brownish purple. I used my Iwata to accentuate the more recessed areas and random noodles, highlighting around the edges of the rotting flesh and tissue.

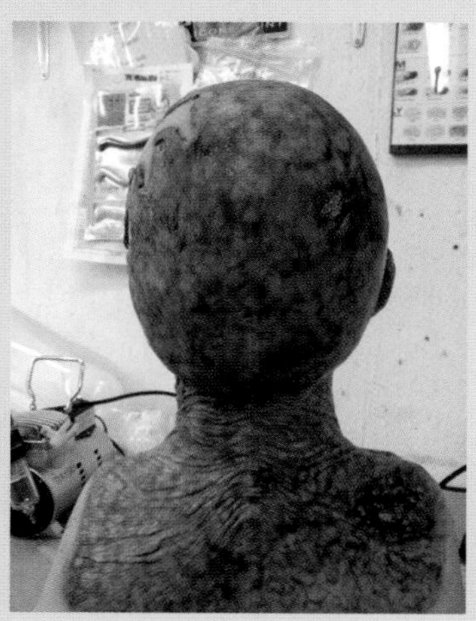

FIGURE 6.60
Airbrush noodles.
Image reproduced by permission of Toby Sells.

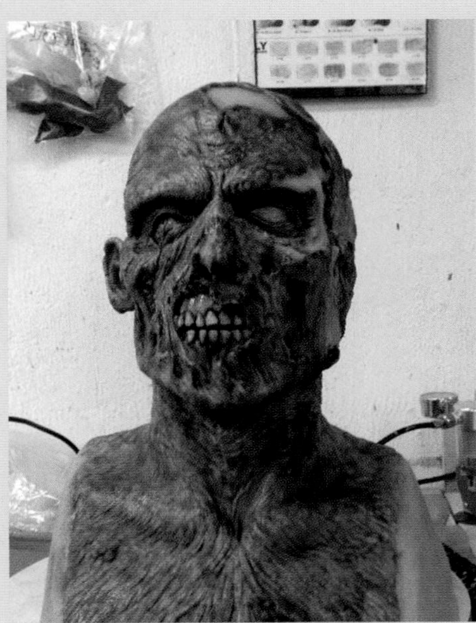

FIGURE 6.61
Mottling of the flesh using an Iwata airbrush.
Image reproduced by permission of Toby Sells.

Adding white oil paint to a drop of burnt umber, making a light earthy tooth shade, I went in with the Iwata and carefully painted the silicone teeth and all exposed skull and bone.

Darkening the tooth shade paint with a bit more burnt umber, I went back with the Iwata and darkened the base and in between the teeth, followed by the same paint with a tiny bit of Yellow oil paint and then punched up random areas of the teeth.

After inserting the acrylic eye and gluing it with Smooth-On's "Sil-Poxy," I added the thinned silicone paint base on to a clean wax palette. Then I activated my "Postmortem Palette" (TOBY SELLS' FX ARTS) with alcohol. I used black, envy (a dead green color), and afterlife (a very earthy brown) and went back in with a fine detail brush and punched up the detail between the teeth, around the gum line, the eyelids, and back over the edges of the

FIGURE 6.62
Carefully airbrushed teeth and exposed skull.
Image reproduced by permission of Toby Sells.

FIGURE 6.63
Detail of teeth and misc. hairs.
Image reproduced by permission of Toby Sells.

rotting flesh. Then I punched in "Liver-Mortis" and a tiny bit of "Primer Greg" in various areas to finally dial it all it.

The final step of the painting process was to seal the entire head with five or six layers of the thinned paint base, to which I add TS-100 or Cab-o-sil to matte the shine down. I let the head dry over night. I then punched Yak Hair in random spots over the head, eyebrows, beard, and mustache area.

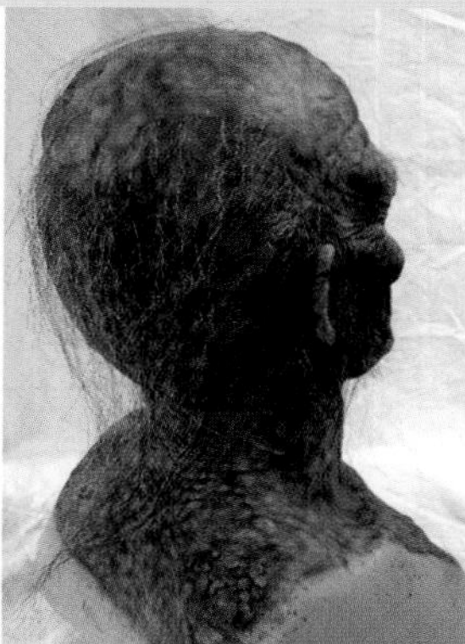
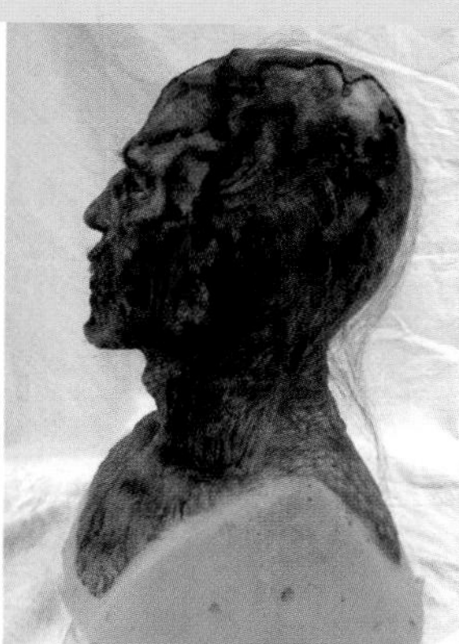

FIGURE 6.64
Finished zombie bust.
Image reproduced by permission of Toby Sells.

SILICONE

To save yourself time and paint, I suggest that your appliances be precolored at the time you cast them. Because the silicone we use for prosthetics is clear or translucent, it is an excellent material for intrinsic (internal) coloring. You can color the silicone with either a pigment that approximates the character's coloring or with rayon fiber flocking material mixed to approximate the character's coloring. Materials you'll need:

- Alcohol palette
- Naphtha or white spirit
- Clear RTV silicone caulk
- Scissors
- Misc. sponges
- Wood craft sticks (for mixing)
- Clear RTV silicone adhesive/sealant
- Fine disposable brushes
- Heptane (Bestine rubber cement thinner)
- One-inch chip brushes
- 99% IPA in a spray bottle
- Mixing cups
- Silicone pigments or artist oil paints
- Hair dryer
- Vinyl or nitrile gloves

NOTE

Nothing sticks to silicone except other silicone. To paint silicone in a way that won't rub off with normal wear, your silicone appliance must be painted with silicone paint; that is, silicone that has been pigmented and thinned for application with an airbrush or fine bristled brushes.

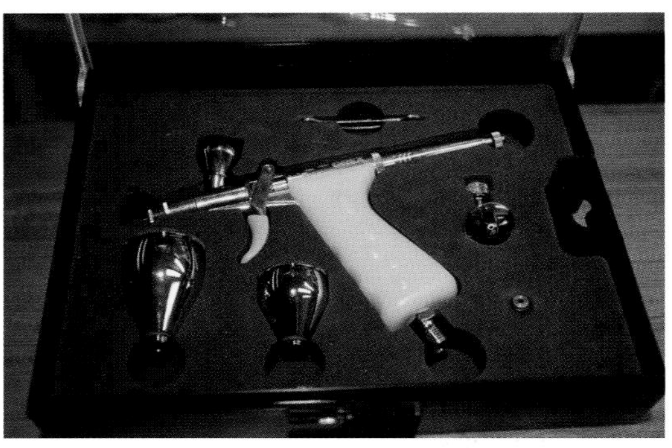

FIGURE 6.65
Grex gravity feed pistol grip airbrush with magnetic quick-change tip. *Photo by author.*

An airbrush might seem to be a more practical and an efficient way to paint an appliance, regardless of what material it is made of. It comes back to personal preference and how you were taught (or are being taught). For painting appliances, I believe you will be better off not using an airbrush and instead using chip brushes and cut-down chip brushes. Don't get me wrong, I love airbrushes; I have six of them ranging in size from very fine detail to big enough to paint a house. But unless you have an assistant whose job is to keep your airbrushes clean and unclogged, you will spend more time cleaning your needles and nozzles every time you change colors, even if you are using several at a time.

Airbrushes clog quite easily, *especially* when you (try to) run thinned silicone through them. I was taught how to get superb results using thinned RTV silicone adhesive and RTV silicone caulk as the medium for applying color to silicone appliances. I think it worth noting that this method of painting is for preapplication of the appliance, not postapplication. RTV silicone caulk is tin silicone, and uncured is not approved by FDA for applying directly on skin.

1. Start off by thinning the silicone adhesive (sealant) in a cup with some heptane, Bestine (rubber cement thinner), or naphtha so that it is a pretty thin wash of about 10 parts solvent to 1 part silicone.
2. Of course, you have a polyfoam (soft or rigid urethane foam) form of your model that the appliance is resting on to hold its shape and facilitate easier painting.
3. Brush this clear wash onto your appliance, but be careful not to paint all the way out to the edges. Because there is a lot of solvent mixed with the silicone, you can ruin the edges; the silicone will absorb the solvent and swell.
4. Because you seamed with silicone gel, this wash will also create a thin layer of silicone over the seam patch. This wash of silicone adhesive will kick very quickly, setting up in less than an hour and resulting in a very strong bonding surface for the color you will add next.
5. You can use either silicone pigments to make your flesh tones or whatever color you need for your appliance, or you can use artist oil paints, which will work just as well. These colors will be used as detail highlight and shadow coloring on various parts of your appliance.
6. Mix another thin wash of silicone, this time mixing naphtha with some of the RTV silicone caulk instead of heptane, Bestine, or naphtha with silicone adhesive. The ratio is about 10:1—10 parts solvent to 1 part silicone.
7. Mix a bit of the color you need and brush it onto the appliance, getting into all the creases and folds. Dab off any excess with a piece of sponge and continue until you achieve the effect you're going for.
8. Next take one of the chip brushes and cut the bristles down about halfway. The next step is to flick or spatter paint onto the prosthetic. This can be done by alternating heavy and light amounts. Mix another batch of

silicone with naphtha in the same ratio and mix colors to complement the complexion you are creating.

9. With your fingers (wear nonlatex gloves), flick the brush bristles so that the paint spatters randomly onto the appliance.
10. Use another chip brush with longer bristles and tap it against the handle of the cut-down brush to apply spatter in a slightly different way, with different spatter amounts.

You could also do this with an airbrush. Be careful with the amount of color; it's very easy to overdo it, particularly with reds.

11. When you've spattered sufficiently, you can move on to adding vein color if it is appropriate to the prosthetic, dabbing with a sponge to remove excess color. Vein coloration should be very subtle.
12. You can continue to add color in the form of moles and age spots, if that is appropriate to the makeup, or you can stop and let the silicone paint cure, which will take several hours.

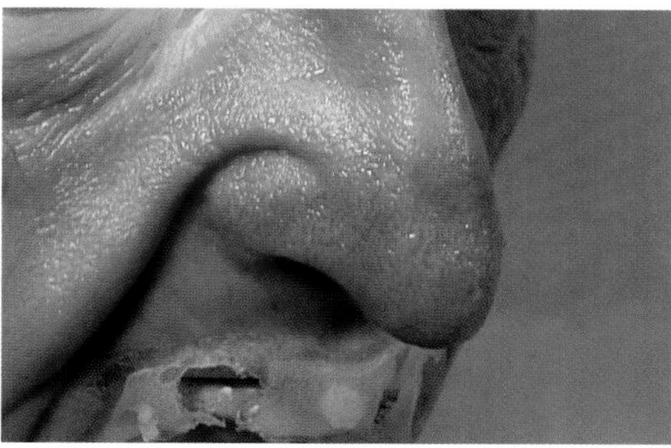

FIGURE 6.66
Use wash of silicone adhesive (caulk) to prime painting surface.
Image reproduced by permission of Neill Gorton.

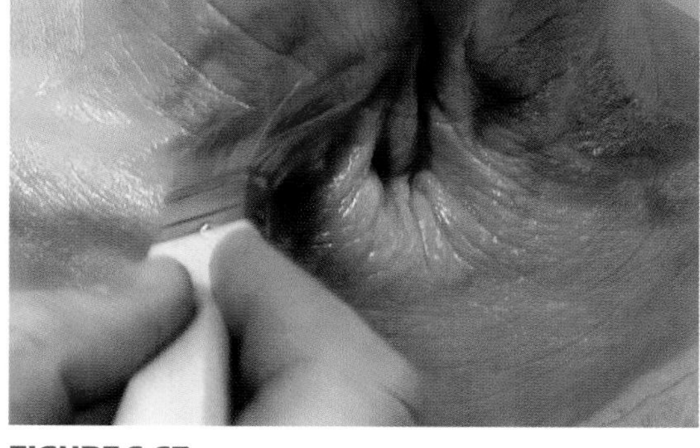

FIGURE 6.67
Mix color and brush onto appliance, getting into creases and folds. Dab excess with sponge; continue until desired result achieved.
Image reproduced by permission of Neill Gorton.

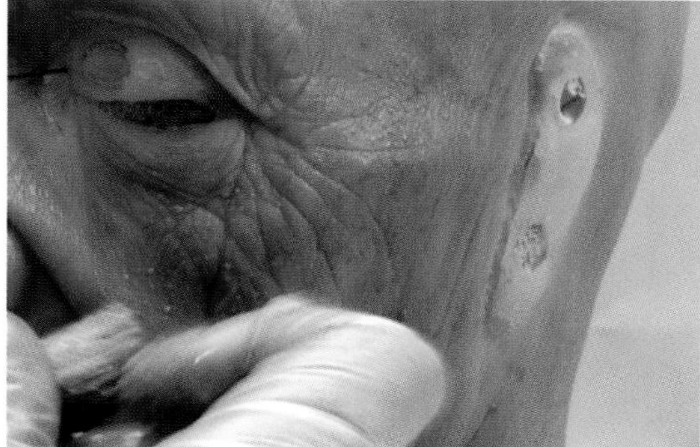

FIGURE 6.68
Flick brush bristles to spatter randomly onto appliance (wear nonlatex gloves).
Image reproduced by permission of Neill Gorton.

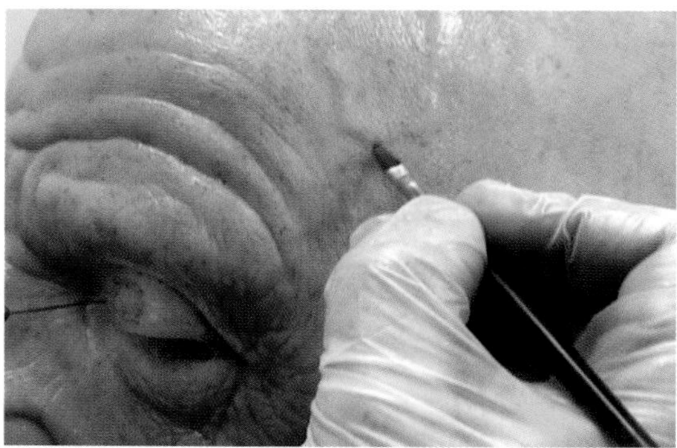

FIGURE 6.69
Vein coloration should be subtle.
Image reproduced by permission of Neill Gorton.

When the silicone has set, the appliance is ready for application. Then you can finish painting the appliance with an alcohol-activated color palette once the prosthetic is glued in place.

Mark Garbarino

Mark has racked up a 20-year-plus career as a creator of sculptures, costumes, puppets, and special makeup effects. After moving to Los Angeles in 1987, Garbarino began specializing in the area of special makeup effects, contributing puppets for films such as *The Abyss*, *Nightmare on Elm Street*, *Hot Shots 2*, *Virus*, *Hellraiser 4*, and *Bicentennial Man*.

FIGURE 6.70
Mark Garbarino (left), Jackie Chan, and David Snyder in China; *Forbidden Kingdom*.
Image reproduced by permission of Mark Garbarino.

As a special makeup effects coordinator, Mark's team won Emmy Awards for the television series *Babylon 5* and *Buffy the Vampire Slayer*. Mark was honored with an individual Emmy nomination in 1997 for *Babylon 5*, for the outstanding makeup for a series, and again in 2003 for prosthetics on *Six Feet Under*.

Mark was also nominated for the Local 706 Hair and Make-Up Awards for Best Prosthetics, transforming John Voight into Howard Cosell for the film *Ali*. Other film makeup highlights include *The Nutty Professor 2, Pearl Harbor, Artificial Intelligence, Pirates of the Caribbean*, and *Constantine*. International film experiences in Hong Kong and China include *Home Sweet Home (Karina Lam), Running on Karma, Kiddult* starring Andy Lau, *Tak-wa, Eyes 10*, Jet Li in *Fearless* and *Ci Ma*, and Jackie Chan in *The Forbidden Kingdom*.

Mark has taught special makeup effects at the Shanghai Theater Academy but continues to maintain his home in Los Angeles. Mark's plans include working more in Asia and expanding the character makeup possibilities for China's film stars.

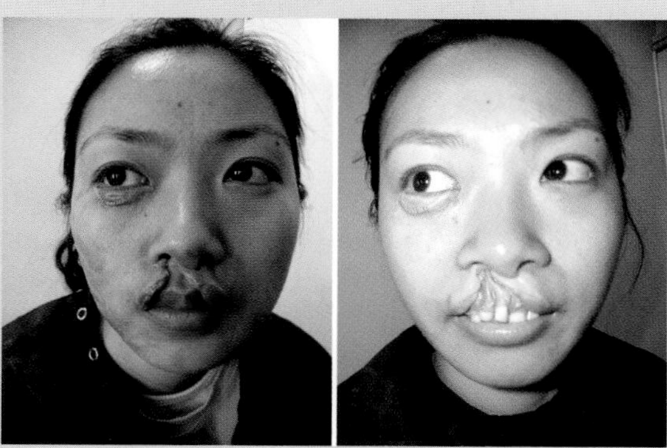

FIGURE 6.71
Yi Ding, silicone lip, eyelid (left); cleft denture appliance (right). Applied and painted by Mark Garbarino; designed by Stan Winston Studios.
Images reproduced by permission of Mark Garbarino.

FIGURE 6.72
Mark Garbarino, Andy Lau, and Jeff Himmell.
Image reproduced by permission of Mark Garbarino.

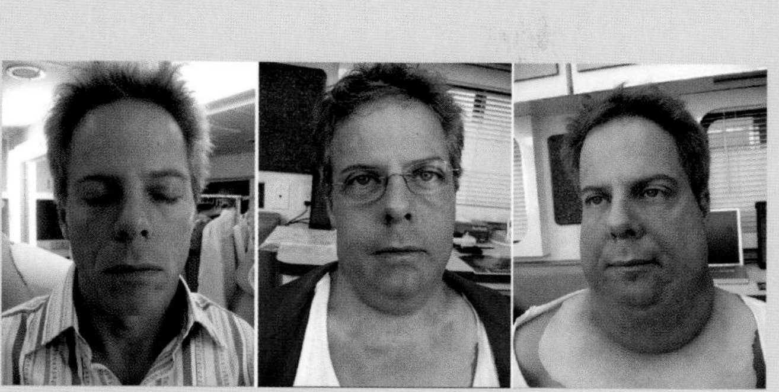

FIGURE 6.73
Greg German, makeup by Mark Garbarino.
Images reproduced by permission of Mark Garbarino.

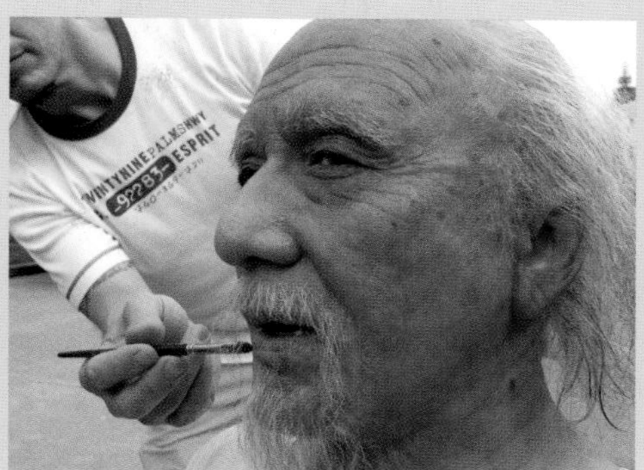

FIGURE 6.74
Mark and Jackie Chan; *Forbidden Kingdom.*
Image reproduced by permission of Mark Garbarino.

FOAM LATEX

Foam latex can be tinted during the batch mixing process to approximate the character's skin tone as closely as possible, and then it can be detailed after the appliance has been washed, seamed, and patched. As you should recall, foam latex is opaque, so any sense of tissue depth will be the result of painting, not the result of intrinsic coloring.

The process for painting a foam latex appliance is essentially the same as for painting a silicone appliance (with the notable exceptions of needing to use silicone paint for a silicone appliance, and *you do not want to paint latex with silicone paint*). One thing to be aware of is that foam latex is essentially a very soft sponge, so application of color should be sparing, applying just a little at a time and letting it dry to avoid saturating the foam with paint. Light airbrush or the previously described spatter technique works well.

Here are the materials you may need:

- Alcohol palettes
- Chip brushes
- 99% IPA in a spray bottle
- Artists' acrylic paint
- Makeup sponges
- Artists' oil paint
- Plastic cups
- Scissors
- Fine brushes
- Pros-Aide
- Airbrush and compressor
- Nylon stocking

1. With your appliance resting on a shaped form, open your color palettes and pick your colors.
2. Spray the color you will use first with alcohol and begin to liquefy the color with a cut-down chip brush. You do not want the color too saturated or concentrated or it will go onto the appliance too rich and vibrant and

will look artificial. The color should be soft and natural; add color gradually to give the appearance of depth.

3. Repeat step 2 for the other colors as well. Human skin, or any skin for that matter, is not one solid, uniform color. There are reds and blues, browns, yellows, and greens in our coloration.
4. Interchange spatter techniques by using the cut-down brush and your fingers as well as tapping the longer bristle brush against the handle of another brush or even against your hand.
5. Try getting some color on your fingers and gently dabbing your fingers onto the appliance to create age spots, if appropriate.

It's very important to have a plan before you begin painting your appliance. You should have lots of reference photos as well as an already formed idea of what you want the finished piece to look like. As artists, part of our unwritten job description is that we have to see all the things that other people, ordinary people, don't notice but that are there nonetheless—things like the way the skin at the tip of your knuckles where the digits begin is a bit pinker than the rest of the skin surrounding it, or that the color of the skin on the back of your hand is a good representation of the coloration of your face, or that the skin on the back of your arm is a different texture than the skin on the bottom of your arm and so on.

6. Repeat steps 2–5 until you get the effect you want and then stop. Learn to know when to stop. That's something you'll have to learn to recognize on your own.

Once the appliance is applied, you can finish up with an alcohol palette or you can stipple and brush other makeup, such as Ben Nye.

Another industry standard for painting foam latex is with PAX paint, a 50/50 mixture of acrylic paint and Pros-Aide adhesive. The Pros-Aide helps keep the acrylic pliant and flexible once it dries; it won't crack, which it would eventually do otherwise. PAX can be applied with a sponge-and-stipple technique or an airbrush, or both. If you have the time to do it, airbrush is a wonderful tool, especially if you have at least two or more so that you can dedicate colors to each airbrush. If you have only one, it can become a real chore because of clogs and having to clean the brush for every color change. There are several brands available, and the choice is personal—whether you choose Grex, Iwata, Paasche, Thayer-Chandler, or Badger—but you should only consider a double-action airbrush, one that allows you to control both air and the amount of pigment. I have three Iwata, a Grex and two Paasche airbrushes, and two Iwata compressors. Two of the airbrushes I've been using since I was in college way back in the 20th century.

Applying PAX with a makeup sponge or sponges is fine and pretty simple. Running PAX through an airbrush, though doable, is asking for trouble, in my humble opinion. Here's what I suggest:

1. Apply your base foundation with PAX by hand.
2. Mix oil paint in the color or colors you want to apply next with the airbrush, and then add 99% alcohol. Stir it well, breaking up as much of the oil medium as you can.

3. Strain the alcohol/oil paint mixture through a piece of nylon hose (stocking) so that only colored alcohol filters through, leaving the oil medium in the nylon.
4. Run this through your airbrush in a stipple pattern; the alcohol evaporates almost instantaneously, leaving behind only the color. This is *much* easier to clean out of your airbrush than PAX. It is also a nice, translucent color to which you can add to achieve your skin coloration.

How do you stipple with an airbrush? Airbrushing for makeup requires very low pressure to begin with and an even lower pressure to get the airbrush to spit and spatter for the stipple effect. All you need to do is lower the air pressure of your compressor (3–4 psi should be all the pressure needed) and remove the needle cap (if your airbrush has one; it ought to). Your airbrush should be set to stipple. Test it first on a piece of waxed palette paper for the pattern you want before trying it on your appliance. Now you're in business.

This brings up a safety point. The very nature of an airbrush puts vapor into the environment where you're working. Even though it's not a lot of vapor and most of the pigments you will work with are nontoxic and not a health hazard, you are still breathing in foreign matter in very tiny particles. If you use an airbrush, please consider wearing a mask or respirator.

You can't very well ask an actor to wear a mask if you are applying airbrush makeup to their face; however, for this reason, it might be a better idea to use a chip brush and hand-spatter technique with alcohol-activated palette colors for this application. The actor can take a deep breath and close his eyes for a moment, you can apply the spatter, and then your subject can open his eyes and breathe.

GELATIN AND COLD FOAM

Both gelatin and cold foam (soft urethane foam) will require a sealer before painting. There are a number of acrylic sealers that can be used and will work just fine. Why do gelatin and urethane foam need to be sealed before coloring? For the same reason, they need to be sealed before application.

1. If you apply adhesive to gelatin without a sealer, the adhesive won't stick very well, and when gelatin gets wet, it begins to lose its shape and becomes weak. If you try to paint unsealed gelatin, the wet paint will seep into the gelatin in ways you can't control as well as weakening the gelatin by dampening it by applying a light coat of acrylic sealer: Kryolan's Fixier spray, Reel Creations' Blue Aqua Sealer, Ben Nye's Final Seal, plastic cap material (which works great), or BJB Enterprises' SC-115. I think this stuff is awesome, especially as a thin coating over polyurethane; it is water based and dries very quickly to form a very soft, stretchy skin.
2. Remember how you've been told that nothing sticks to silicone except silicone? Things we need to use really don't like to stick to the cold foam, either. However, applying a light coat of an acrylic sealer (BJB SC-115 is my preference for using with cold foam) will allow paint, or even makeup, to grab and stay. One word of caution: Apply just a small amount, a very

light coat at a time, to prevent the urethane from wrinkling and collapsing due to moisture. It will return to its proper shape when all the moisture is gone. Because you are creating a watertight seal on the urethane, you want to make sure no moisture is trapped within the foam.

Once the appliances have been sealed, painting can proceed in the same manner described for painting foam latex above. You'll need the same materials.

Painting Teeth

Getting your prosthetic choppers looking right for the makeup you've created might be the easiest part of the whole process, but it's by no means the least important. By *easiest* I mean it represents the least amount of surface area to color. Painting teeth to look natural (for character or creature makeup) is as critical as sculpting them to look real in the first place.

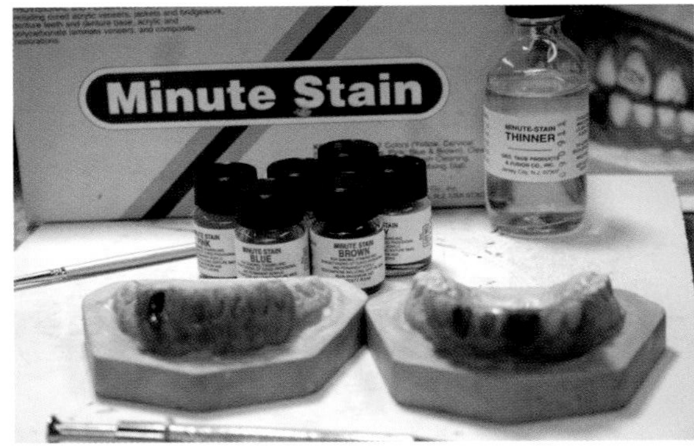

FIGURE 6.75
Painted with George Taub's Minute Stain.
Photo by author.

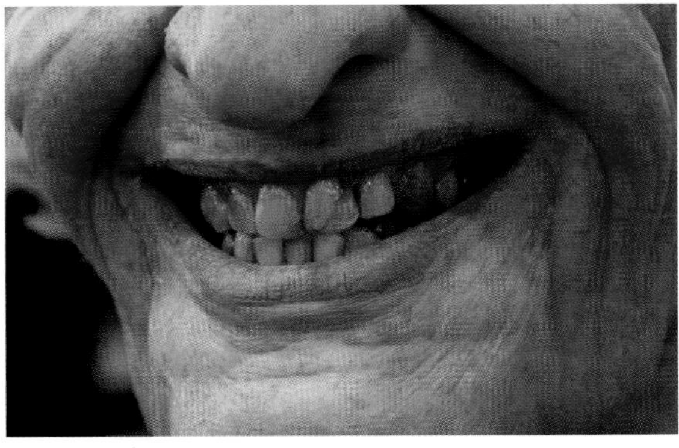

FIGURE 6.76
Clear vacuum formed denture veneers painted with Skin Illustrator; makeup by Neill Gorton.
Photo by author.

Provided you've already done all the prep work to get the dentures ready to be worn, you don't need much else than what's listed below. You might or might not need or want to use the Ben Nye temporary stains on these teeth, but you will definitely want them in your kit, so in this case, I think it's better to have them and not need them than to need them and not have them.

MATERIALS

- George Taub Minute Stain 7 color kit
- Fine sable brushes (¼ inch)
- Minute Stain Black and Violet
- Ben Nye temporary tooth stains
- Alcohol-activated palette

Using Minute Stain is really quite simple; Taub recommends the seven-color kit for effects work due to its colors for looking natural as well as darker stains such as pink and brown. The seven colors in the kit are yellow, cervical blend (kind of a toffee/tan), gray, white, pink, blue, and brown, plus a clear glaze, thinner (for colors) brush cleaner, brush, and a small ceramic mixing slab.

The following instructions for using Minute Stain come directly from George Taub Products and David R. Federick, DMD, ScD:

1. Shake the Minute Stain bottles gently to disperse pigments. Shake bottles vigorously only if intense, concentrated colors are desired.
2. Dip the brush into bottle, wipe the excess off at the bottle neck, and bleed additional excess from the brush onto a ceramic or glass mixing slab. The pigments should be evenly dispersed.
3. Quickly apply the stain to the surface of the restoration using a minimum of straight, even strokes. Let the surface dry. Setting time is 10 seconds.
4. Stains must be applied thin. Clean the brush in the thinner bottle after each application and dry with a paper towel.
5. The translucent colors may be built up in intensity with multiple applications using a slight overlap of coats to create a gradual color shift.
6. Apply two coats of Clear Liquid & Glaze to protect the colors and provide a glaze-like finish. Allow each coat of glaze to completely dry between applications, cleaning the brush in thinner each time.

NOTE

Keep the bottles tightly sealed when not in use. Clean the bottle necks and the insides of caps to maintain a proper seal. Add a few drops of thinner periodically (or as needed) to maintain proper, thin consistency. Once colors have set on the slab, do not try to revive them. Go back to the bottle(s) for a new mix.

SPECIAL EFFECTS

Color suggestions:

- *Yellow*: To deepen shading of 66-67-69-73-77-78.
- *Cervical blend*: To deepen shading of 62-65-68-81-85; interproximal stain.
- *Blue, white*: Incisal blend, decalcified areas.
- *Gray*: To tone down shades and produce tetracycline shading; incisal stain.
- *Brown*: Tea, coffee, and tobacco stains; surface erosions.
- *Pink*: Root surfaces.
- *Color mixes*: Yellow-brown, orange (yellow-pink), purple, or violet (blue-pink).
- *Technique*: Blend the colors on a slab with brush of thinner; mix well. Bleed excess on slab before applying to restoration. For reapplication of the mixed color, add some thinner to the mix on the slab, bleed excess, and reapply to the restoration.
- *Fractures*: To create a hairline fracture illusion, score the facial surface with a fine scalpel and scrape off the flashing. Place brown over the score line

and wipe off the excess immediately. The brown will seep into and remain within the score line. If color does not penetrate, repeat with scalpel to make the line deeper. Do fracture lines before incisal staining.

- *Occlusal*: To highlight grooves, pits, and fissures, bleed brown onto these surfaces with a fine brush or instrument.
- *Decalcification*: Use a fine brush or instrument tip with white to create this effect. The spot should be matted and asymmetrical for best effect.
- *Tobacco and erosion-type effects*: Use brown and/or concentrated cervical blend. Layer color for the most realistic effect.
- *Incisal*: Delicately place blue or gray along incisal edge, perpendicular to the edge, unevenly in three or four strokes, to cover the entire width of the incisal area. It is best to dilute the gray with thinner for best control.
- *Root surfaces*: Use a thin pink or cervical blend to create the effect.
- *Denture base staining*: Use pink as it is or concentrated for intense colors and/or blend with white or blue on a mixing slab. Add thinner to the mix. Apply in quick, even strokes.
- *Lighten shades*: Dilute white on a slab with thinner or glaze to reduce intensity. Apply one or two thin coats.
- *Tone down colors*: Dilute gray with thinner to reduce intensity and place directly over (stained) surface or first blend with stain on initial application.

NOTE

To remove unwanted stains when shading is incorrect, grind it off with a rubber wheel, and repolish the acrylic resin. If Minute Stain bottles solidify, fill bottles with thinner, let stand 5 days, and stir. Should liquid merely thicken (from solvent evaporation), just add thinner to the proper consistency. If the stain becomes too thin, add clear liquid to restore the body. Do not use monomer to dilute colors.

Shake bottles gently to produce light, translucent colors. It is not necessary to disperse all pigments in the bottle. Doing so could create an intense, concentrated, and unnatural stain.

Here are some helpful hints:

- Do not have excess stain on the brush when you apply to the resin surface. This could cause color runoff resulting in too-intense pigment buildup, visible brushstrokes, colors not drying uniformly or rippled, and grainy surfaces. Always bleed excess off onto the slab before applying color.
- In cervical areas, it is best to apply in straight, even strokes in a vertical direction from cervical to gingival or cervical to incisal.
- Apply stains quickly. Use a large (#1) brush (camel hair) for large surface areas to minimize brushstrokes. Use a fine brush for smaller, delicate areas.
- To clean the slab, use a single-edge gem razor blade and scrape the surface clean. Use thinner to clean small, loose scraps from the slab surface.

- Always clean the brush between each application of color and when finished and wipe it dry on a paper towel. If bristles have stiffened after the last use, simply dip into thinner for a few seconds to revive. Do not use inexpensive plastic brushes, because solvent will destroy them.
- Allow surfaces to dry before reapplying additional or new colors. Doing so will help you avoid creating unwanted brush marks.
- To remove excess (dried) color around small areas, such as along a fracture line or occlusal grooves and fissures, dip a clean brush in thinner, bleed the excess onto a slab, and immediately wash the affected area gently, until unwanted colors are brushed away. Wipe clean.
- For concentrated or intense pigment, dip the brush into the bottom of the bottle.
- If pigment streaks, simply blend on the slab until it is uniform.
- If colors are too intense, blend on the slab with thinner of glaze, bleed excess off the brush, and apply.

These instructions provide more information than you will need as a makeup artist, unless you suddenly decide to go to dental school.

CHAPTER SUMMARY

- In this chapter, you were given a further understanding of silicone and coloring silicone intrinsically (internally) for translucence.
- Silicone GFAs, or GFAs, filling molds, and removing appliances were also described in detail.
- Foam latex and its properties were outlined, as was the process for running foam latex.
- Casting urethane (cold) foam described; casting gelatin and foamed gelatin.
- Casting dental acrylic detailed step by step.
- This chapter also detailed the steps involved in painting and seaming appliances and the procedure for painting theatrical dentures.

CHAPTER 7 

Applying the Makeup Appliance

Key Points

- Pre-application skin care
- Adhesives
- Application techniques
- Removers
- Removal techniques
- Post-removal skin care

INTRODUCTION

The process of applying 3D prosthetic appliances has in many ways come full circle. In the days of what is considered the first modern use of foam latex prosthetic appliances, the 1940s and 1950s, the appliances were made as one piece; they were essentially masks. These one-piece foam appliances continued to be the norm until the late 1960s, when it is believed that iconic makeup artist Dick Smith became the first to employ the use of multiple overlapping appliances to create a complete makeup—on Dustin Hoffman as the 121-year-old Jack Crabb in *Little Big Man*.

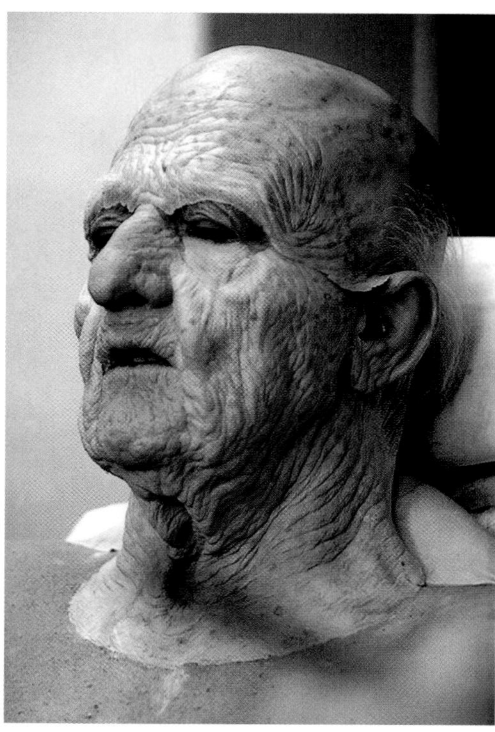

FIGURE 7.1
Dick Smith's *Little Big Man* makeup.
Image reproduced by permission of William Forsche.

This process set a new standard of application of prosthetic appliances, and it continues to be the standard method of application. However, the one-piece appliance never went away and has begun to see a resurgence in popularity, particularly in television, where time for application is in short supply. This chapter examines each method, both one-piece and multipiece; you will most likely have occasion to use both in your career. The one-piece continuous appliance is being used with amazing results by Neill Gorton, whose silicone appliances are astonishingly real, even in tight close-up. The multipiece overlapping approach is also used to great effect by makeup artists. The chief difference between the one-piece approach and the multipiece approach is in the number of pieces and the time it takes to apply them. The results can be equally stunning.

Christopher Tucker

Christopher Tucker is a legend to fans and artists alike; he certainly is to me. He was born in Hertford, England, and studied at London's famed Guildhall School of Drama and Music and became an opera singer. His film career began with no less than a lavish production of *Julius Caesar*, starring Charlton Heston and Sir John Gielgud. He also created all the age makeup for the award-winning BBC series I, Claudius.

His reputation as a brilliant makeup artist led to him designing and creating age, character, fantasy, celebrity look-alikes, animatronic makeup effects, and prosthetics for film, television, commercial, and stage productions in both Great Britain and abroad. Christopher has pioneered numerous techniques and the use of materials such as foam latex, silicone, and gelatin. He also designed the first animatronic eye for a television commercial.

Chris made it possible for an American actor to turn into a werewolf in one take without the use of digital effects for *The Company of Wolves*. His early men in *Quest for Fire* won both an Oscar and a BAFTA for makeup, and his

FIGURE 7.2
Christopher Tucker, author; IMATS London, 2008.
Photo by the author.

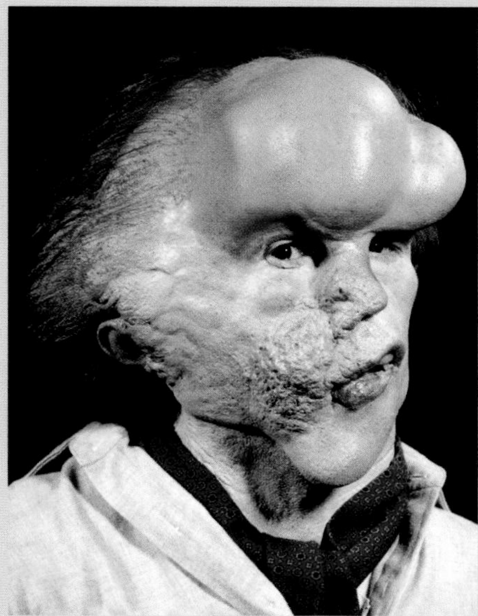

FIGURE 7.3
John Hurt; *The Elephant Man.*
Image reproduced by permission of Christopher Tucker.

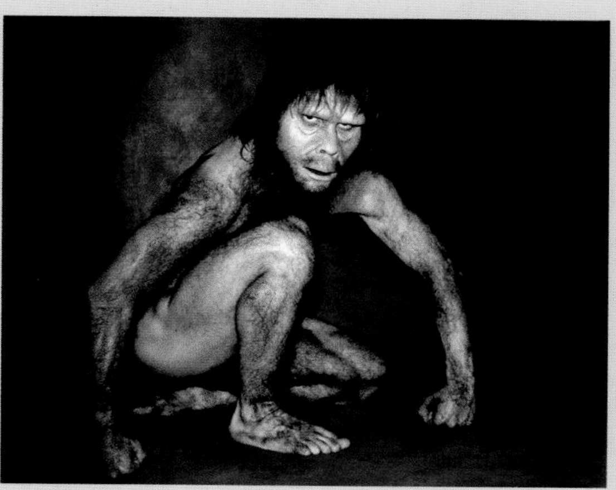

FIGURE 7.4
Neanderthal Man; French Ministry of Culture.
Image reproduced by permission of Christopher Tucker.

FIGURE 7.5
Darryl Hannah; *High Spirits.*
Image reproduced by permission of Christopher Tucker.

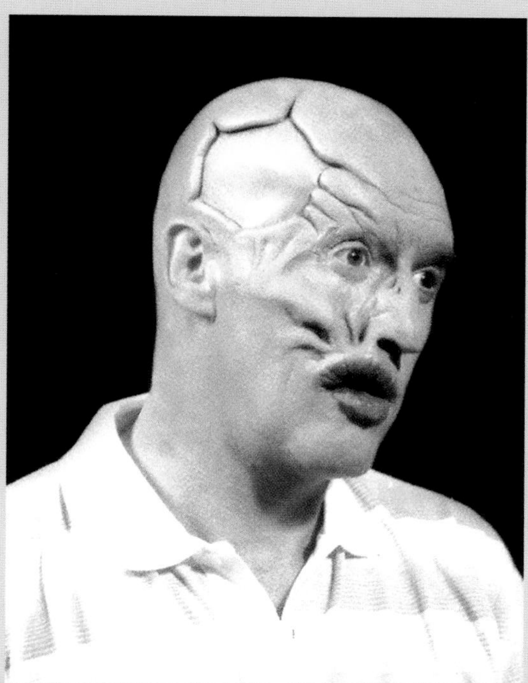

FIGURE 7.6
Michael Crawford; *The Phantom of the Opera.*
Image reproduced by permission of Christopher Tucker.

work on the creature characters in the *Star Wars Episode IV* cantina scene is still a topic of conversation among *Star Wars* devotees. His interests in science, chemistry, engineering, sculpting, and photography have greatly helped in this changing world of special makeup effects; he is also fluent in computer-created image creation and manipulation with programs such as Photoshop.

The Royal Shakespeare Theatre asked Chris to create the hump for Richard III and Cyrano de Bergerac noses for Sir Derek Jacobi. He considers that his career peaked when David Lynch asked him to save his film *The Elephant Man* and design and fabricate the *Elephant Man* makeup for John Hurt. No other previous makeup had been so involved; the head had 15 different foam latex and silicone rubber parts, some of them overlapping (which had never before been attempted). It took 7 hours to apply and was used only on alternative days of shooting and rehearsing.

Chris is also responsible for *The Phantom of the Opera* makeup designed for the original production starring Michael Crawford in London; he continues to be involved with *Phantom*. He has been educating makeup artists at home and abroad and continues to be highly sought as a lecturer by professionals in medicine, education, and entertainment.

SKIN TYPES

There are three basic skin types: dry, oily, and a combination of both dry and oily. Prior to prosthetic application, each of these needs to be addressed in pretty much the same manner, because what we are doing is preparing the skin to accept adhesives so that it will not adversely affect the appliance's ability to stay put.

Usually all that needs to be done is to apply a mild skin cleanser and astringent. Make sure that your model arrives wearing no makeup; any existing makeup must be removed completely and then the skin cleansed, or the adhesives will not work properly. It is also important that your model has no open sores where you will be applying prosthetics or any makeup, for that matter. You would think that this is so obvious that I wouldn't need to mention it. Wrong. I once had an extra show up on set for body paint with an open infection the size of a tennis ball on his shoulder. It was amazing … and disgusting. Needless to say, I immediately grabbed the first AD who sent him straight to the hospital!

In addition to cleansers and astringents to make sure that your model's skin is clean and oil free, there is another skin care concern I want to bring to your attention. It never occurred to me before, but once it did it fundamentally changed the way I approach every application.

I had the opportunity to be the makeup designer for a unique stage production of The Wiz in 2006, and for the Cowardly Lion I designed a full-face makeup in two pieces that was cast with Kryolan Cold Foam. The actor playing the lion had been working in an unpainted version of the appliance for about a week before dress/tech rehearsal. Application and removal had gone without a hitch, as I had hoped and expected, until the first night of dress.

When it was time for us to get our actor out of the appliances, *they wouldn't come off!* We had been using Premiere Products' Telesis 5 silicone adhesive and Telesis Super Solv remover, which is a great combination. All week long, the prosthetic had come off like putting a warm knife to butter. It was a cinch. But no, this time the prosthetic would not budge! The harder we tried, the more difficult it seemed to become. We tried a different bottle of Super Solv—no change. Then a different remover altogether. Nothing! Then another. Aargh! My actor was getting freaked out (did I mention that he is sightless?), not to mention that his skin had become red and irritated…

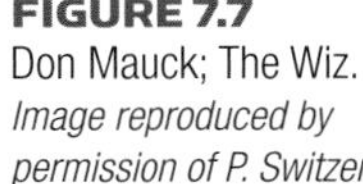

FIGURE 7.7
Don Mauck; The Wiz. *Image reproduced by permission of P. Switzer.*

I started to flop sweat like Albert Brooks in *Broadcast News*. What should have taken us all of 10 or 15 minutes took almost *2 hours*. I felt like a beginner. First thing the next morning I called Premiere Products and explained what happened. The first words out of Scott

Heinly's mouth were, "Does he drink?" Long pause on my end. "Well, yeah," I said, "But it's not like he's a drunk!" Apparently, *any* alcohol in the body will exit with perspiration through the skin. Alcohol is an inhibitor to the adhesive remover. (Light bulb goes on!) My actor was sweating profusely during dress rehearsal because he was wearing a big furry lion suit! D'oh! He hadn't been sweating noticeably in the week before dress/tech because he hadn't been in the full costume, and without the sweating the adhesive and remover worked perfectly. It never would have occurred to me that this would be a problem. I won't make that mistake again.

So what can be done when you have an actor who wants to kick back with a cold one (or two) after a long day's rehearsal? Two words: *barrier layer*. There are a number of products on the market, but the one I used to solve my problem was the one suggested and provided by PPI called Top Guard. It is an acrylic resin-based surface barrier that works just the way it says in the literature: It's a water- and perspiration-resistant surface primer that reduces skin irritation, increases prosthetic adhesion, and allows for easier removal. Just a thin application of Top Guard on the skin prior to the adhesive (let it dry first) and all was in perfect harmony again. Life was good! Top Guard is now part of my regular application regimen, no matter what. Plus it actually makes removal and cleanup easier. That alone is worth the cost of admission to me.

ADHESIVES

There are more adhesives than there are Baldwin brothers. Many of them are fine for just about any type of application. Others are better suited for specialty applications, mostly because of cost than any other reason.

Almost everyone is familiar with the adhesive *spirit gum*. Certainly in the theater community, it's the only adhesive most theater folk seem to be familiar with at all. I don't like spirit gum. Spirit gum is derived from mastic gum, which is harvested from mastic, a small evergreen shrub or tree in the pistachio family. Widely used in theater for applying wigs, beards, and moustaches, spirit gum (also called *mastix*) tends to be a skin irritant for almost everybody, which makes it a less-than-desirable choice as a prosthetic adhesive. Perspiration has a tendency to weaken and dissolve spirit gum; so in situations where an actor will perspire significantly, spirit gum would not be the best choice. On the other hand, spirit gum is relatively inexpensive compared to other adhesives used for applying prosthetics. Spirit gum can be thinned with acetone or hexane (if you want it to dry extremely fast). It is preferred by hair folk to glue lace pieces. I still don't like it.

The adhesives that are the most popular in the makeup effects business are medical-grade adhesives that are either acrylic or silicone based. Some of these (silicone adhesives) can be rather pricey (nearing $100/£54 for 4 ounces), but fortunately a little goes a long way. They can (should) be thinned without weakening the adhesive strength, and the holding power is astounding.

Pros-Aide is a water-based acrylic adhesive from ADM-Tronics that was originally developed as a bumper sticker adhesive. Have you ever tried to remove a bumper sticker? Graftobian and Ben Nye also make their own versions of Pros-Aide, which has—at least in the mufx industry—become a part of the vernacular, much the way Kleenex has come to mean any brand of tissue. Pros-Aide is a great adhesive that goes on white, dries clear, and remains pliant and *very* sticky (though there is a tack-free version available). It works best when applied to both the skin and the appliance as a contact adhesive.

Liquid latex can also be used as an adhesive, but it's not advisable to use it on appliances because it has a tendency to build up and it will come loose if the wearer perspires freely. (Most appliances/adhesives will be affected by perspiration.) If used regularly, a skin prep/astringent called Sweat Stop, available from Michael Davy Film and TV Makeup, will inhibit perspiration somewhat where it is applied. You can also use zinc oxide powder prior to applying the adhesive; zinc is an ingredient in antiperspirants.

Tami Lane

Oscar winner Tami Lane began working with Howard Berger, Greg Nicotero, and Bob Kurtzman at KNB EFX Group shortly after college.

Tami remembers liking monsters when she was a little girl but not liking monsters the way we attribute it to "Ooh, I wanna make monsters when I grow up!" Tami told me about a time when she was a little girl in a store with her mother and saw an interesting magazine on the rack. Leafing through, she saw pictures of amazing creatures. Then a hand reached in from over her head and snatched the magazine out of her hands and placed it high on the rack; it was her mom. "You are never, ever to look at that again!" Tami found out later that it was a magazine called *Fangoria*.

FIGURE 7.8
Tami Lane.
Photo by Howard Berger. Image reproduced by permission of Tami Lane.

FIGURE 7.9
Tami Lane, Peter Dinklage; *The Chronicles of Narnia: Prince Caspian.*
Image reproduced by permission of Tami Lane.

FIGURE 7.10
Tami Lane, Colin Farrel; *Fright Night.*
Image reproduced by permission of Tami Lane.

In the early days of her career, many of the artists working at KNB, like Gino Acevedo, took Tami under their wings and taught her everything from mold making and casting to painting. It was going back to school again. She graduated from cleaning-out molds and painting creatures to finally being asked to go on location by Greg Nicotero for John Carpenter's *Vampires*. She was only supposed to go for a week to help set up but ended up staying for the entire show and was asked to do two lead hero makeups.

Now a permanent resident of New Zealand, Tami is among a very small, elite group of women who are at the top of their game in a very male-dominated industry. She splits her time between the United States and New Zealand, but her work takes her all over the world. The last time I talked to Tami she was still in Wellington, New Zealand, hard at work as prosthetics supervisor on J. R. R. Tolkien's *The Hobbit* (parts 1, *An Unexpected Journey*, and 2, *There and Back Again*). Among Tami's stellar credits are *The Chronicles of Narnia: The Lion, the Witch and the Wardrobe* for which she won an Academy Award; *Surrogates*; *Water for Elephants*; *The Lord of the Rings*; *Spawn*; and *Fright Night*. She and her work blow me away.

FIGURE 7.11
Tami Lane, Steven Rooke as faun; *The Chronicles of Narnia: Voyage of the Dawn Treader.*
Image reproduced by permission of Tami Lane.

APPLICATION TECHNIQUES

To be good at something requires practice. Don't expect to become sought after as an on-set master of applying makeup appliances if you aren't really good at it. You must practice!

Just as with most aspects of creating special makeup effects, there is no one prescribed method for applying a transformational makeup, whether it is one piece or multiple pieces that overlap to create the makeup. An obvious first step in applying a prosthetic appliance is to clean the skin using 99% isopropyl alcohol (IPA), regular 70% rubbing alcohol, or another skin cleanser that is nonoily. It is imperative that the skin be oil and grease free to make for better adhesion when the appliance is applied.

The material your appliance is made from is not as important as being methodical and careful in the application. Nor is the adhesive you use as important. That being said, the appliance material and the adhesive are indeed important, relatively speaking. A few things about the adhesives you will most likely encounter are as follows: Acrylic adhesives, such as Premiere Products' Telesis Beta Bond and ADM Tronics' Pros-Aide, go on white and dry clear; they also dry tacky and work best as a contact cement with the adhesive applied to both the skin and the appliance. Both surfaces should be powdered after the adhesive dries; the glue can then be reactivated with 99% alcohol at the time of application. The silicone adhesives, such as Snappy G or Telesis, go on clear and dry clear and are only slightly tacky when dry, not to the extent of Pros-Aide, for example. Silicone adhesives also work best when applied to both the skin and the appliance, let dry, and then press firmly together.

Attaching the Appliance

MATERIALS

- Silicone adhesive
- Q-tips
- Small cups
- Adhesive remover
- Isopropyl myristate
- Powder and applicators
- Beta Bond
- Adhesive thinner
- Misc. makeup brushes (for adhesive)
- Pros-Aide
- 99% IPA
- Pros-Aide remover
- Beta Solv

If you're doing a makeup comprising several overlapping pieces, there should be a preestablished order in which to apply them:

1. Before applying any adhesive, position the piece (or each piece one at a time) and check it for a proper fit. Ordinarily, any flashing is left on the piece until application. If the piece needs to be trimmed, do it very carefully; trimming is often best achieved by hand-tearing the flashing away, keeping the blending edges thin and slightly irregular. It is easier to disguise an uneven line than a straight one.
2. After the trimming is completed, replace the appliance and check again for fit and anything that might have been missed and still needs to be trimmed.
3. With the piece in its correct position, powder along the edges with a face powder that is either lighter or darker than the natural skin color. This will show the area where the adhesive needs to go.

4. It is usually best to work from the inside out when applying prosthetics; the appliance piece is more manageable that way, especially if it is a large piece, a heavy piece, or both. Sometimes a second pair of hands is advisable so long as the application area doesn't get too crowded with fingers or the like. You will have to find what works best for you; you could decide to begin from the visible powdered edge and work your way across the piece.

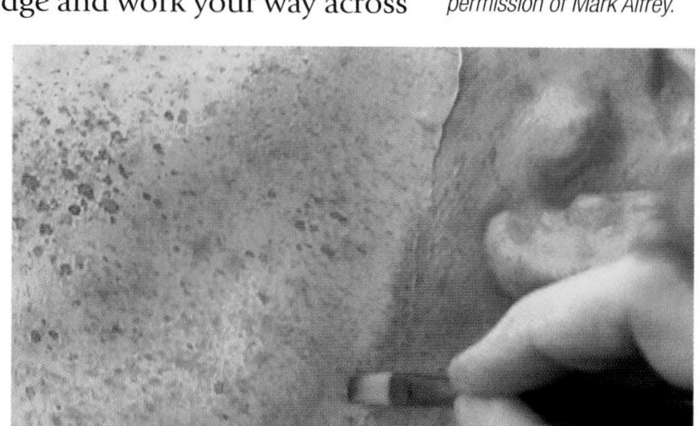

FIGURE 7.12
It's easier to disguise uneven lines than straight lines when blending edges.
Image reproduced by permission of Mark Alfrey.

5. If you're using an acrylic adhesive (e.g., Pros-Aide®), brush on a thin layer of adhesive and allow it to dry before pressing the appliance onto the sticky surface. There is a misconception that more adhesive will make the bond stronger, which is not so. It will only cause a buildup of adhesive, not make it stronger.
6. *Carefully* place the appliance into position, pressing gently; you could find that the foam applicator sticks or the end of a brush might be helpful in getting good surface contact between the skin and the appliance. If you need to reposition it, brush lightly with alcohol, carefully lift the piece, let the alcohol evaporate and the adhesive dry again, and then press the appliance back into place.

Trying to realign a piece after it has been set in adhesive can result in wrinkles and folds that will be difficult to fix or hide.

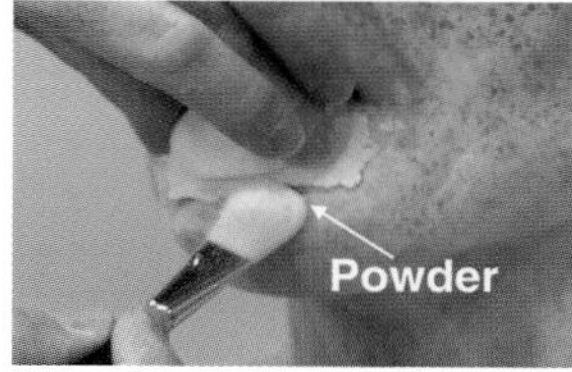

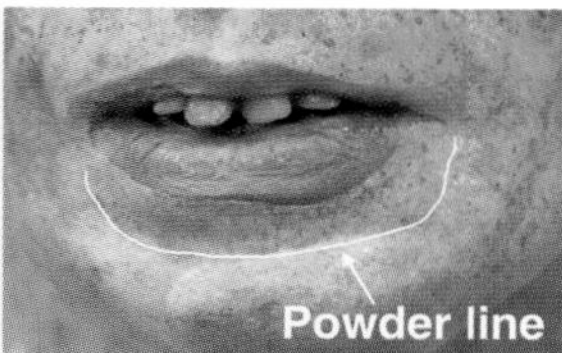

FIGURE 7.13
With piece in position, powder along edges to show the area where adhesive goes.
Images reproduced by permission of Mark Alfrey.

7. If you're working from the inside out, carefully press down and out in all directions until you reach the edges. You could find that helping to keep the thin appliance edges up can be accomplished with a good pair of tweezers and pressing outward from where glued appliance part toward the edges, letting them gently settle into the adhesive, pressing down with a powdered foam applicator.
8. If you are applying a multipiece makeup with overlapping edges, work in the order necessary for the pieces to work and fit correctly. Repeat the appropriate steps.

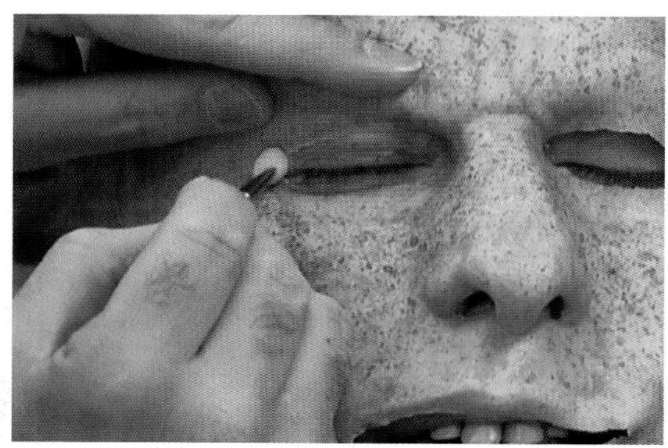

FIGURE 7.14
Foam applicator and brush end are helpful in getting good surface contact between the skin and the appliance.
Image reproduced by permission of Mark Alfrey.

MONSTER MAKEUP

With over 20 years' experience, Conor McCullagh has worked on projects from major studio productions to low-budget indie features. It was during a high school ceramics class that Conor discovered *Fangoria* magazine and realized he could make more than pots and vases out of clay.

He spent 14 years in Los Angeles, working for theme parks and apprenticing under John Caglione Jr., the Oscar-winning makeup artist for *Dick Tracy*. Conor eventually made his way into feature films and television, including *The Mighty Morphin' Power Rangers, Mars Attacks*, *Freddy vs. Jason*, *Seed of Chucky*, *The Vampire Diaries*, and *The Hunger Games*. Conor teaches at the Joe Blasco Makeup School and was the competition winner of the first season of the hit Syfy reality series *Face Off*.

FIGURE 7.15
Conor McCullagh.
Photo by the author.

"For the *Mad Monster Party*, I wanted to create an old ghoul on Addy Miller," Conor told me. Addy has the dubious distinction of being the first walker to be put down on AMC's *The Walking Dead*—she was the little girl at the convenience store in pajamas and a robe, holding a teddy bear. "I thought it would be creepy to have an old, scary, wrinkled face on a petite body."

Conor started with a corrected positive cast in Smooth-On epoxy. He accentuated Addy's cheek bones and brow, along with adding mass to the nasal labial folds, jowls, and a lot of tendons and wrinkles.

Once the sculpture was finished, Conor bonded bolts through the eyes and mouth to ensure a tight cutting edge when casting the prosthetic.

A cutting edge was laid around the entire sculpture, including the eyes, nostrils, and mouth. The clay was

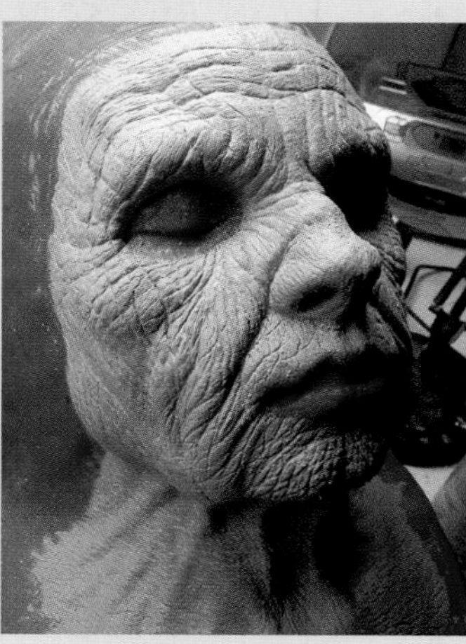

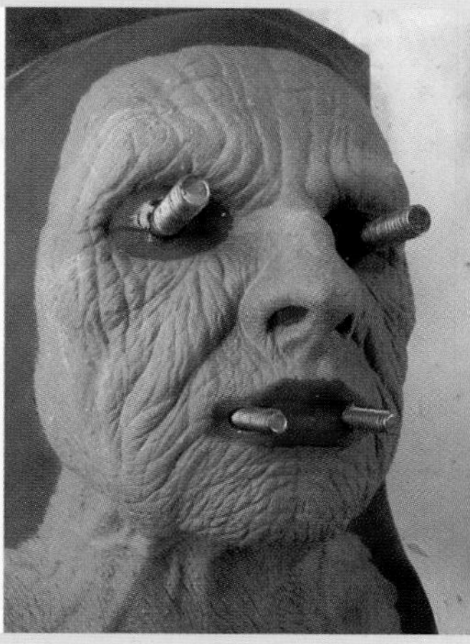

FIGURE 7.16
Sculpt on corrected positive (left); bolts added to positive to ensure tight cutting edges (right).
Images reproduced by permission of Conor McCullagh.

sealed with a clear acrylic spray and then the unwanted acrylic spray, was removed from the cutting edge with lacquer thinner and a small paint brush. One coat of wax spray release was sprayed over the entire surface before molding.

Conor used Smooth-On EpoxAcoat RED for the surface coat, bushing everywhere and then using an air hose to pop any air bubbles trapped in the mix.

Once the surface coat was set, Conor used Free Form epoxy dough to fill in the recessed areas before coating the entire surface in ½ inch of dough. With the dough still soft, he brushed on a layer of EpoxAmite laminating resin and proceeded to laminate five layers of 1-ounce fiberglass cloth over the entire molding surface.

After demolding and cleaning out the clay, he trimmed and sanded the mold to get rid of any sharp fiberglass hairs and then used epoxy putty and some large washers to create a flat area around each bolt.

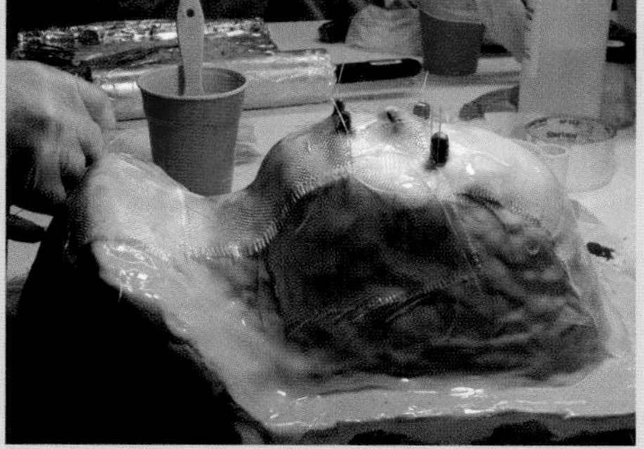

FIGURE 7.17
EpoxAcoat RED applied to positive (top); layers of laminating epoxy and fiberglass cloth (bottom).
Images reproduced by permission of Conor McCullagh.

To cast the silicone prosthetic, Conor prepared the mold by brushing in a layer of dish soap, drying it with a hair dryer, and then spraying in two coats of wax release agent.

For this prosthetic, Conor wanted to use Super Baldiez because it's alcohol soluble. He thinned it out until it easily sprayed through an airbrush (at least 4:1 IPA:Baldiez ratio). Since Super Baldiez is not as strong as regular Baldiez, he skinned the positive and negative with seven layers each. As a binder, Conor then airbrushed one layer of a Telesis 5 (thinned with Telesis thinner) over the encapsulating layer on the positive and the negative. The mold is ready for silicone; Conor mixed Dragon Skin FX Pro with 70% Slacker additive and a little pale skin tone he made with So-Strong pigments. To minimize any trapped air in the silicone, the silicone was degassed before pouring it into the mold.

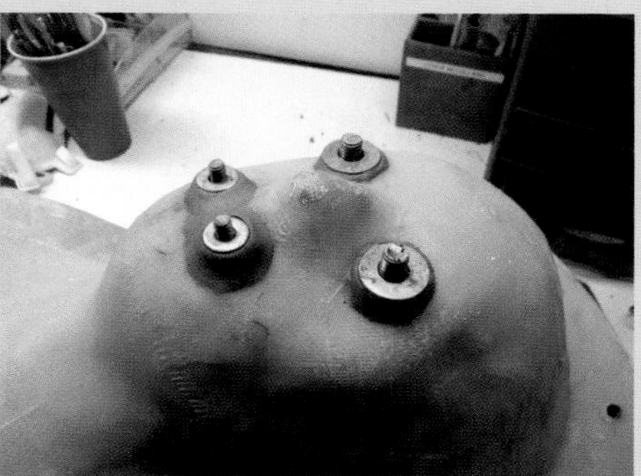

FIGURE 7.18
Adding washers reinforces each bolt hole.
Image reproduced by permission of Conor McCullagh.

FIGURE 7.19
Filling mold.
Image reproduced by permission of Conor McCullagh.

Once everything was ready, Conor plugged the bolt holes with a little clay and then poured it into the negative. By placing the positive back into the negative, the bolts in the eyes and mouth simply pushed the clay plugs out of the way and he was able to bolt the mold shut.

When the silicone cured (about an hour later), the entire mold was placed in a tub of water to let the dish soap reactivate and release the prosthetic from the walls of the mold. The piece turned out beautifully. (Note: In the image, it appears as if there is delamination around the cutting edge. This is just air pockets behind the prosthetic as it was still wet from demolding.)

Conor pre-painted the prosthetic with a combination of hand painting and airbrush spattering. The last thing Conor did before application was hand punch very thin, sparse eyebrow hair.

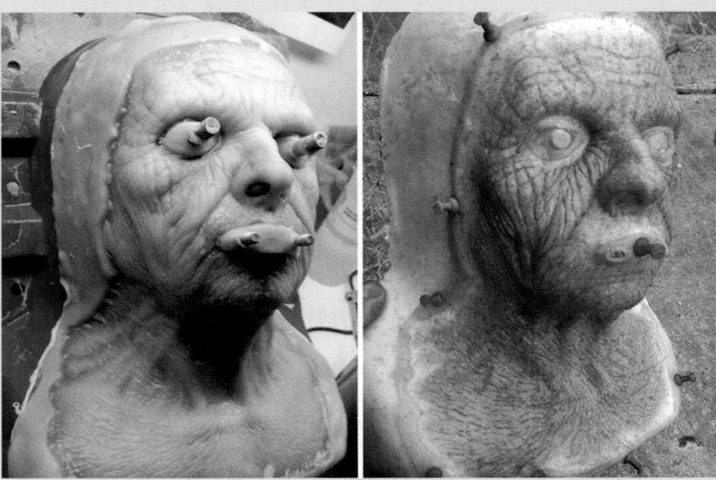

FIGURE 7.20
Demolded appliance, ready for paint (left); painted with airbrush and spatter technique (right).
Images reproduced by permission of Conor McCullagh.

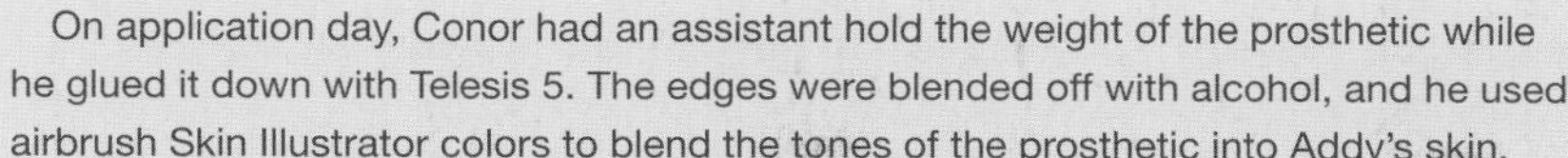
On application day, Conor had an assistant hold the weight of the prosthetic while he glued it down with Telesis 5. The edges were blended off with alcohol, and he used airbrush Skin Illustrator colors to blend the tones of the prosthetic into Addy's skin.

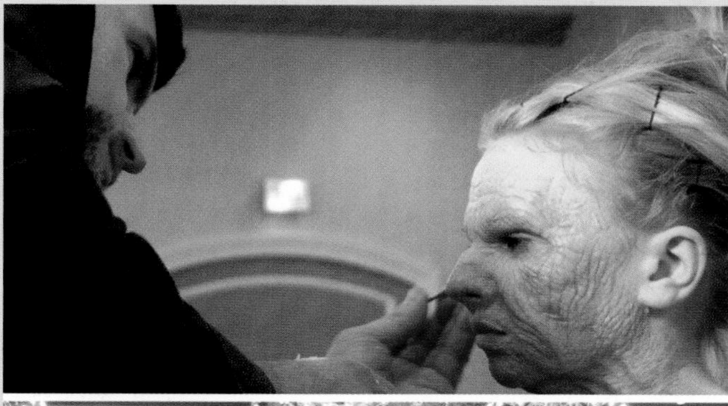

FIGURE 7.21
Conor, Addy.
Images reproduced by permission of Conor McCullagh.

The "Techniques" section mentioned that dry, powdered Pros-Aide can be reactivated with 99% alcohol at the time of application. With the appliance piece positioned in its final location, lift a portion of the appliance and, with a brush that has been dipped in 99% IPA, re-wet the powdered adhesive on the skin and press the appliance into place. Proceed with the application, reactivating the adhesive a little at a time until the entire appliance has been glued into place.

When applying large silicone pieces, you can employ a similar process of gluing the appliances in place. As I mentioned, Telesis 5 dries slightly tacky and should be powdered to prevent its sticking to something it isn't supposed to stick to, such as your finger or a brush, in which case it will try to ruin your life. I credit the following nifty information to Neill Gorton, from whom I learned it, though similar discoveries often happen at the same time worldwide, as has been true of many discoveries throughout history.

Silicone adhesive (chemists, please forgive this oversimplification) is essentially nothing more than a very thin, very soft silicone solution. When the solvent carrying the silicone evaporates, what is left behind is silicone. This makes sense, since nothing sticks to silicone except other silicone, and it sticks to us because it's … sticky.

When the Telesis 5 adhesive begins to get warm due to trapped body heat caused by the large silicone appliance (silicone does not breathe and thereby traps heat and moisture), it gets sticky again. This tackiness, coupled with suction pressure during application, ensures that the appliance stays in place. The following example illustrates reactivating the Telesis 5 silicone adhesive using nothing more than body heat and a large silicone appliance. At the International Makeup Artist Trade Show (IMATS), held on January 26 and 27, 2008, in London, Neill Gorton demonstrated the application of a one-piece silicone appliance that was a full head and face appliance. Neill transformed the lovely, young, blue-eyed blonde Karen Spencer into an elderly Chinese woman, including painting the appliance, in less than 2 hours! (Patching and seaming were done earlier.)

Because Neill does quite a bit of prosthetic work for television, it was important to streamline the makeup process to suit a television timetable. Typically, a makeup of this size could be (and often is) done in several overlapping pieces, for example:

- Bald cap for wig application
- Forehead piece
- Nose piece
- Epicanthic eye-fold piece (× 2)
- Upper lip piece
- Ears (× 2)
- Lower lip piece
- Chin
- Cheeks (× 2)
- Neck piece

Achieving a makeup in that way would require numerous molds, starting with a full head and shoulders bust, from which additional casts would be made for sculpting individual pieces. This becomes a time-consuming logistics puzzle. In

FIGURE 7.22
Karen Spencer, "before and after"; IMATS London, 2008.
Photos by the author.

truth, there could be times when the multipiece overlapping appliance makeup is the better way, but not always.

To begin, Neill Gorton and Stuart Bray applied a bald cap to Karen to keep her hair manageable and out of the way. Had this makeup been for a show and not a demonstration, the piece would most likely have already been painted; in fact, for a show, it is likely that several appliances would have been created and painted to match. Since silicone is more durable than foam latex, a silicone appliance of this size could easily be used more than once if treated well and properly maintained.

1. The first step is to apply the bald cap.

Obviously, everything needed for the makeup application needs to be arranged in advance so that the operation flows smoothly and without delays while the artists look for something:

- Small scissors
- Adhesive brushes
- Chip brushes
- Alcohol palettes
- Silicone adhesive and thinner
- 99% IPA in a spray bottle
- Powder and applicators
- Miscellaneous sponges

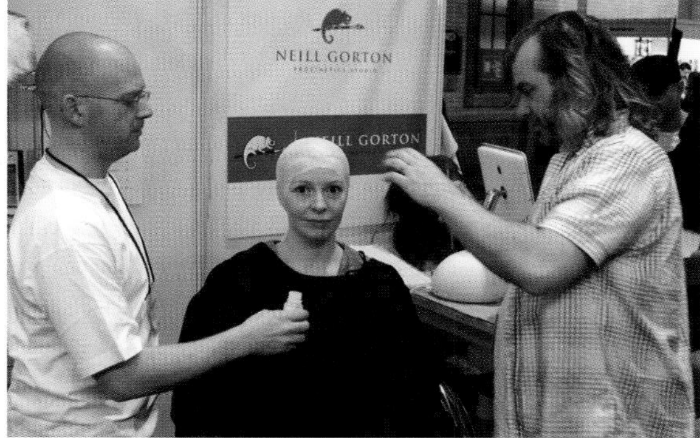

FIGURE 7.23
Neill, Stuart Bray apply bald cap to keep hair out of way.
Photo by the author.

Flashing has already been removed from the eyes and ear but still remains around the mouth. The reason the flashing is left intact is to help hold the piece together and not sag under its own weight. This makeup is actually two silicone pieces: the main appliance and a small lower lip appliance. Having a separate lip piece reduces potential stress for a thin area or a large appliance and leaves a larger opening to facilitate applying adhesive inside the appliance.

2. Next comes the application of adhesive, in this case Telesis 5 silicone adhesive thinned about 1:1 with Telesis thinner. Neill is helped by Rob Mayor of Millennium FX to cover every surface of Karen's head that will come in contact with the appliance using Telesis 5. When the adhesive is dry, it is lightly powdered to remove any tack.
3. The appliance has been resting on a rigid foam copy of Karen's head, and together Neill and Rob carefully roll the appliance up and off the form to prevent damaging the silicone GFA (did I mention that this is a gel-filled appliance?). Then they place the piece on top of Karen's head, roll it back down, and reposition it, carefully nudging the appliance into place.
4. While Neill begins to apply fresh adhesive along the jawline and under the chin (through the mouth and the ear holes), Karen's body heat is already beginning to reactivate the Telesis 5. Gently pressing and smoothing along the neck helps create suction and good surface contact between the appliance and the skin.
5. Neill carefully glues the appliance along the lower eyelid and blends off the edge with Pros-Aide.

FIGURE 7.24
Materials for application and painting.
Photo by the author.

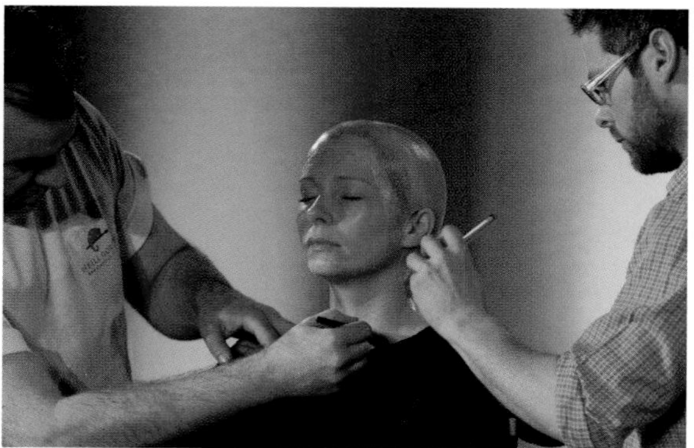

FIGURE 7.25
Neill, Rob Mayor applying adhesive.
Photo by the author.

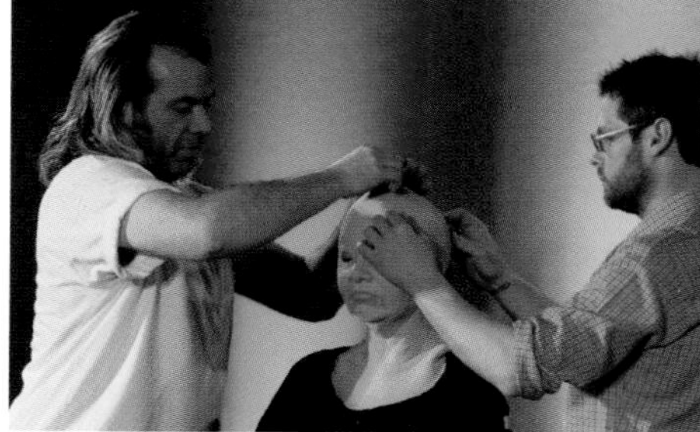

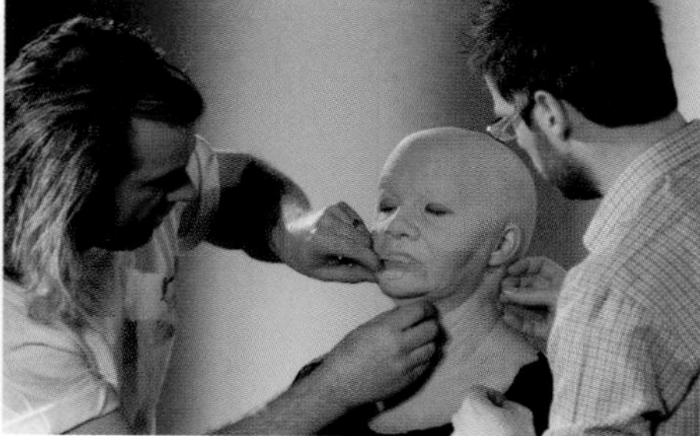

FIGURE 7.26
Nudging into alignment.
Photos by the author.

6. After the adhesive has been applied and the piece is in place, Neill places the lower lip by applying a small dab of Telesis 5 in the middle of the lip appliance. The flashing is left on so that there is more surface area to handle while he makes sure the lip fits properly.

The lip piece is a GFA also, but the envelope is made of plastic cap material, the same blend of polyvinyl acetate that bald caps are made of. The same mixture of silicone gel (Polytek Plat Sil Gel 10 with a high percentage of softener) is encapsulated between thin layers of bald cap material. By encapsulating with the cap material, we can easily blend the edges off to nothing using a small brush and 99% IPA.

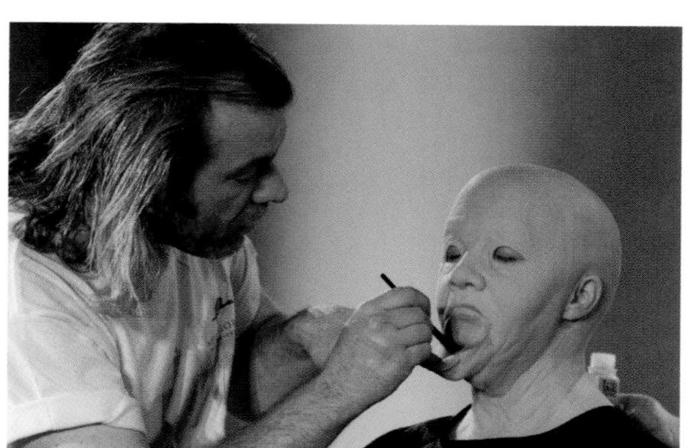

FIGURE 7.27
Body heat reactivating Telesis; Neill applies adhesive along jawline and under chin.
Photo by the author.

7. Working from the middle outward, the rest of the lip is glued in place and the flashing melted away with 99% alcohol. There is no visible seam line whatsoever.
8. While Neill has been gluing under the chin and along the jaw and gluing the lip, Rob has been using Pros-Aide to blend the edges around the ears. (I'll talk more about concealing edges in the next section.)

9. The last thing to do before painting the makeup is to give Karen a way for heat to escape. Because silicone doesn't breathe, it retains everything, especially body heat, and since this makeup includes a lace-front wig (provided by Campbell Young) the vent hole cut in the silicone and slits in the bald cap will never be noticed when the makeup is complete.

It should be noted (here is as good a place as any) that during the casting of the full GFA appliance being applied here, a strip of mesh similar to wig lace but less stretchy—more like tulle—was placed in the mold along the top midline of the head so that there would be very little give to the appliance. On real people, the scalp is attached rather firmly to the skull, and there's not much stretch in any direction; by doing essentially the same to the appliance, the silicone on the top of the head will not over-elongate and allow the appliance to be ill fitting.

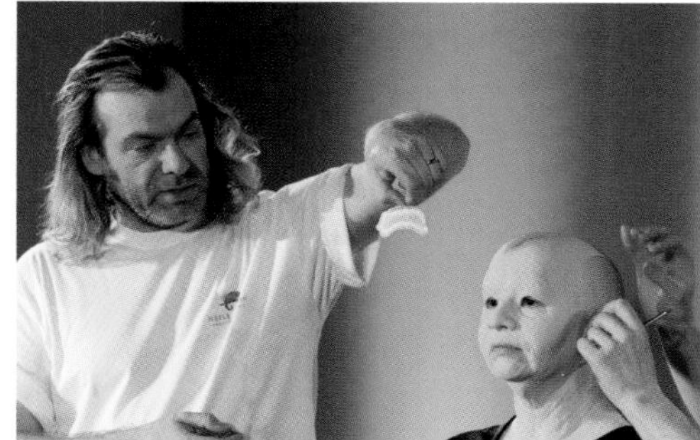

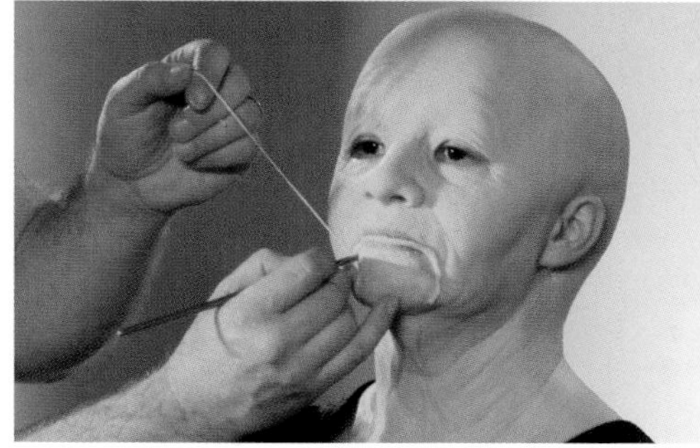

FIGURE 7.28
Lip piece and flashing separated with 99% alcohol.
Photos by the author.

FIGURE 7.29
Neill cuts a hole in silicone appliance covered by wig.
Photos by the author.

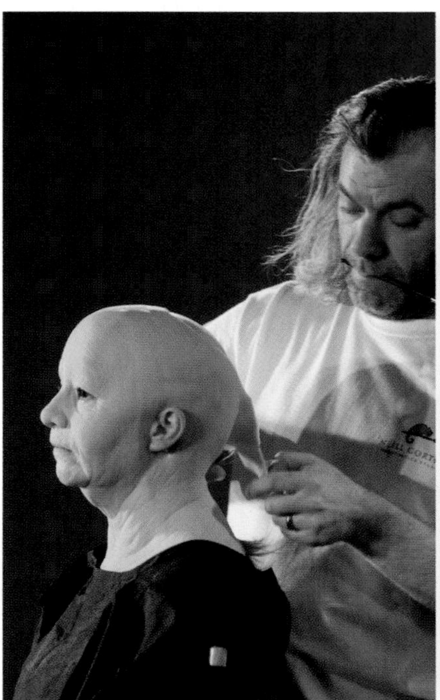

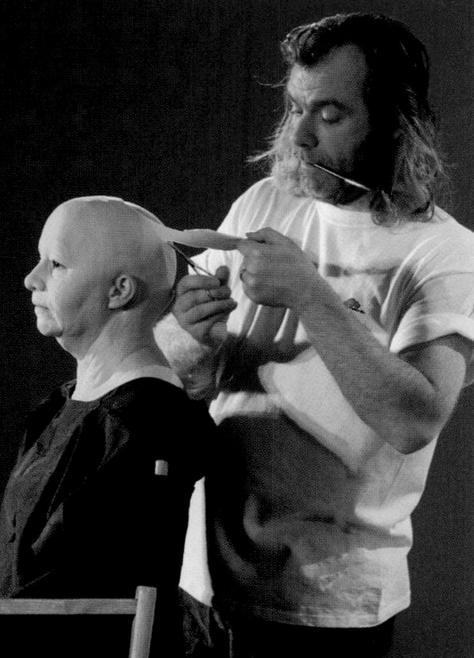

Amy Mills

Among the growing number of standout women in our industry is Amy Mills, whose husband Chris is also a makeup effects artist; together they run a company called Silver Shamrock Lab, Inc. Halloween is almost a religion in their home.

FIGURE 7.30
Amy, Doug Jones.
Image reproduced by permission of Amy Mills.

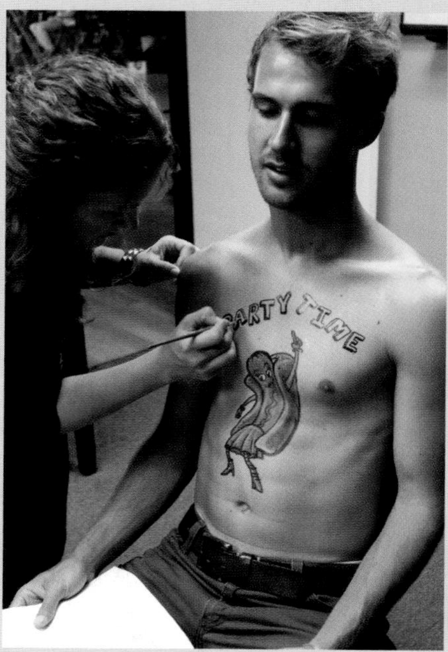

FIGURE 7.31
Hand-drawn tattoo for a TV commercial.
Image reproduced by permission of Amy Mills.

From Ottawa, Canada, Amy has always had an artistic bent. She attended the fine arts program at York University, receiving numerous awards in recognition of her makeup and costuming at the national level at the annual dramatic arts competitions. Amy used any excuse she could muster to slap some makeup on an unwitting friend or family member, and she credits her parents with being instrumental in fueling her love for makeup.

Following graduation from college, Amy moved to Burbank, California, to attend MUD. She graduated in the top percentile of her class and proceeded to dive headlong into the industry. Amy works in all aspects of makeup: photography, commercials, television, live performances, and movies. Her work has been seen on CSI: Crime Scene Investigation and Deadliest Warrior and several Hallmark Channel, History Channel, and Biography Channel programs. She has worked with Cirque du Soleil and on a number of indie films. Amy

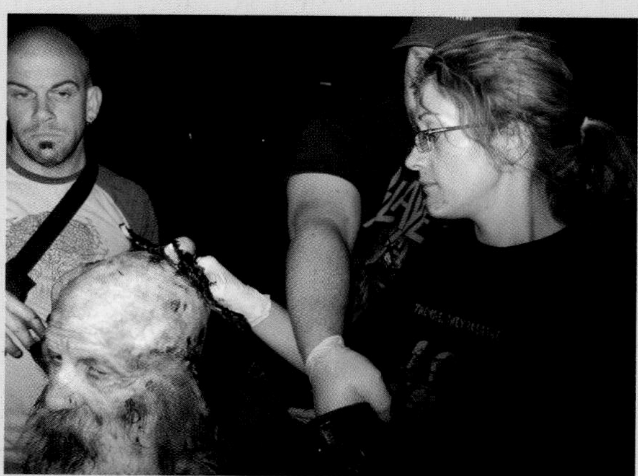

FIGURE 7.32
Amy, Brian Hillard applying gore.
Image reproduced by permission of Amy Mills.

was fortunate to spend 6 months working in Egypt on a medical drama called Critical Moments as the head of the sfx department and joined the Makeup Artists and Hairstylists Union [Local 706] in 2010. From time to time, Amy teaches at her old school MUD in areas of beauty and character makeup.

FIGURE 7.33
Amy with mufx props.
Image reproduced by permission of Amy Mills.

Conforming Molds

To apply a prosthetic appliance made using a conforming mold (as described in Chapter 5), first position the piece on your subject's face using the measuring appliance, and make subtle marks with an eyebrow pencil.

Instead of using Telesis or Snappy G to glue the appliance, for this we're going to use Smooth-On's Skin Tite skin-safe platinum silicone. It was developed for use as a silicone adhesive, a blender, and a means to create direct on-the-skin buildups for wounds, etc. Any skin-safe quick set platinum silicone will work for this.

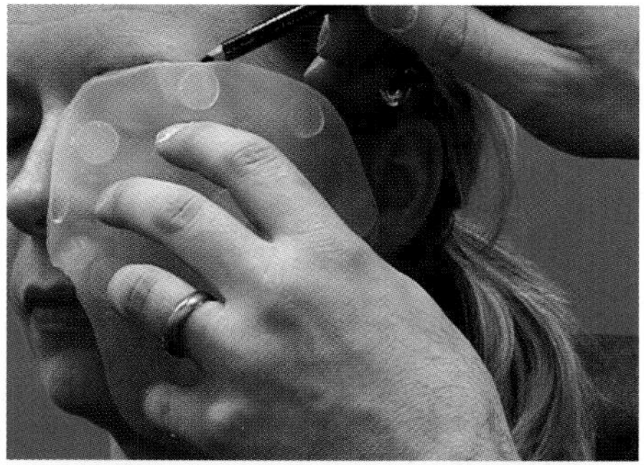

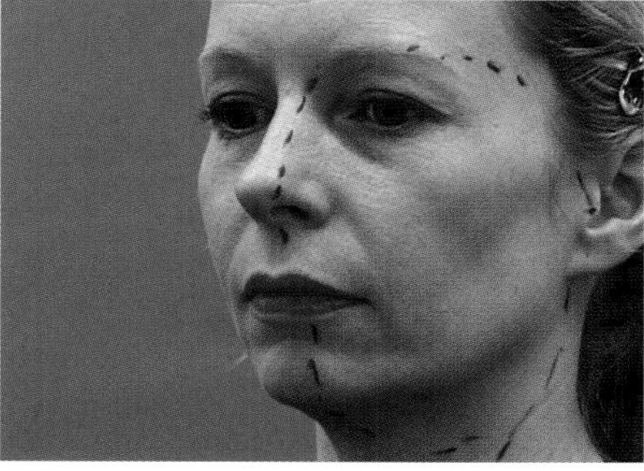

FIGURE 7.34
Positioning marks being made with eyebrow pencil (top); positioning marks (bottom).
Image reproduced by permission of Neill Gorton.

Stipple silicone lightly onto the back of the piece, making sure to go only part way onto the Baldiez skin edge (if you created your piece with a Baldiez

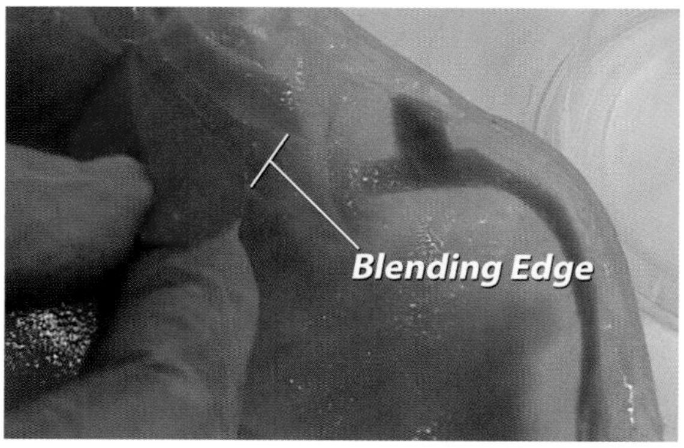

FIGURE 7.35
Stippling Skin Tite partway into Baldiez blending edge.
Image reproduced by permission of Neill Gorton.

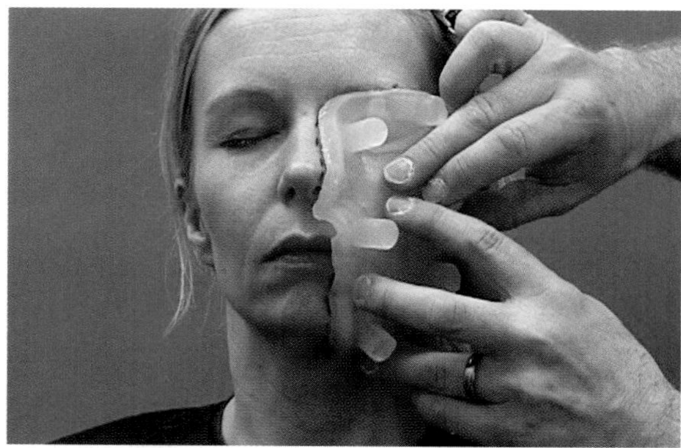

FIGURE 7.36
Hold in place until silicone is cured.
Image reproduced by permission of Neill Gorton.

skin—this method virtually guarantees a seamlessly blended edge); this will ensure a good blending edge that can then be blended off with 99% IPA with no silicone beneath it.

Skin Tite has a working time of about 5 minutes before it begins to kick, which should be ample time to stipple it onto the appliance and then position it on the face.

Once the silicone is fully cured and firmly stuck in place, you can begin to carefully separate the appliance from the mold. Then blend off the edges, separating the flashing with 99% IPA.

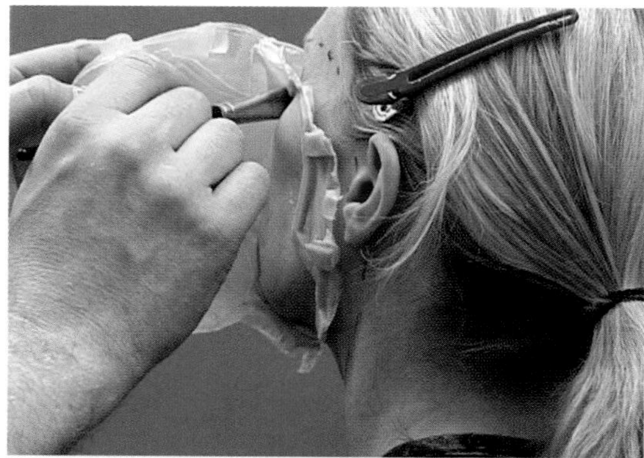

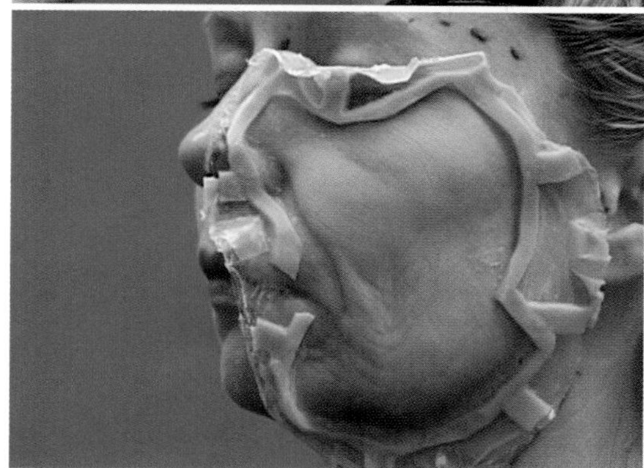

FIGURE 7.37
Carefully separate appliance from mold once silicone has cured (top). Appliance ready for edges to be blended, and flashing removed (bottom).
Image reproduced by permission of Neill Gorton.

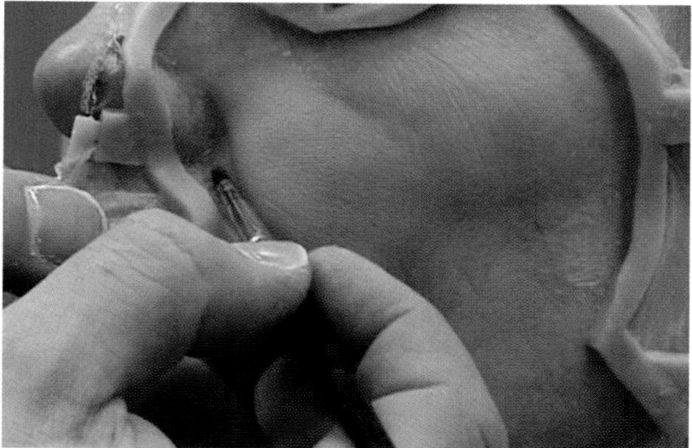

FIGURE 7.38
Blending edges and removing flashing.
Image reproduced by permission of Neill Gorton.

Once the edges are dissolved away the flashing has been removed, and lightly stipple Pros-Aide (*NOT* bondo) over the edges to help with any additional blending and sealing of the appliance before painting.

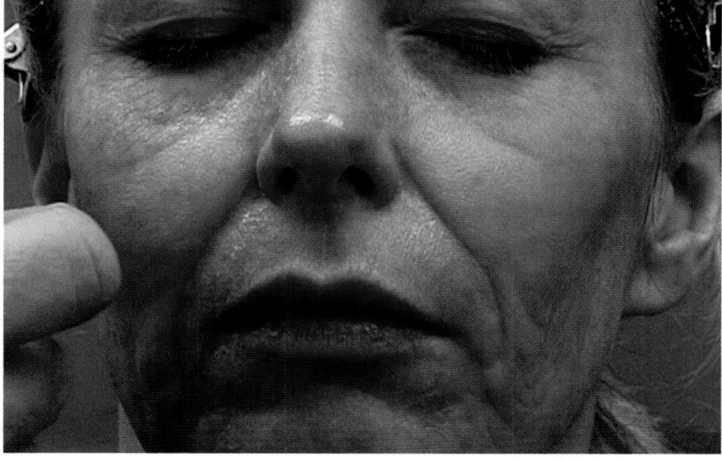

FIGURE 7.39
Cheek appliances complete.
Image reproduced by permission of Neill Gorton.

Blending the Edges

Concealing appliance edges is what helps sell the believability of your makeup. If your appliances have been made well to begin with, blending off the edges is not particularly difficult. You do need to be conscious of very thin edges and not let them fold over on themselves, which can cause them to stick, and then they can be difficult to separate and can even tear. If your edges are thicker than they should be or if they are torn or wrinkled, the following, or many variations, may work to conceal edges and overlaps. I will also caution you at this point that if you are working with an appliance that has previously been applied and had makeup on it, such as a Ben Nye crème foundation or something other than an alcohol-activated palette, concealing edges might be difficult if not impossible because none of the materials commonly used for blending and concealing edges will adhere well to makeup and they will come loose. Any residual makeup must be completely removed and cleaned so that there is no residual oil left from the makeup to inhibit the adhesive used for hiding edges.

So let's assume you are applying a fresh, unused appliance for the first time:

1. Apply the piece as described previously with your adhesive of choice.
2. If the edges are thick, Pros-Aide bondo or Cabo patch can be applied with a small brush, Q-tip, or dental spatula to cover them and smoothed with a brush dipped in water or 99% IPA to blend away the edges. Use a blow-dryer to dry it and then powder it because it will be tacky.
3. Pros-Aide can also be applied by itself to help blend away the edges by applying with a piece of stipple sponge or latex makeup sponge. Because Pros-Aide is a water-based acrylic adhesive, if it's left out and exposed to the air the water will evaporate, making the adhesive thicker.
4. Interestingly enough, Duo false eyelash glue also works fairly well as an edge blender, as does liquid latex, though if you use latex to blend or conceal edges you will most likely need to dab the latex with castor sealer in order for the makeup you apply next to match the makeup applied to the rest of the appliance or the skin.

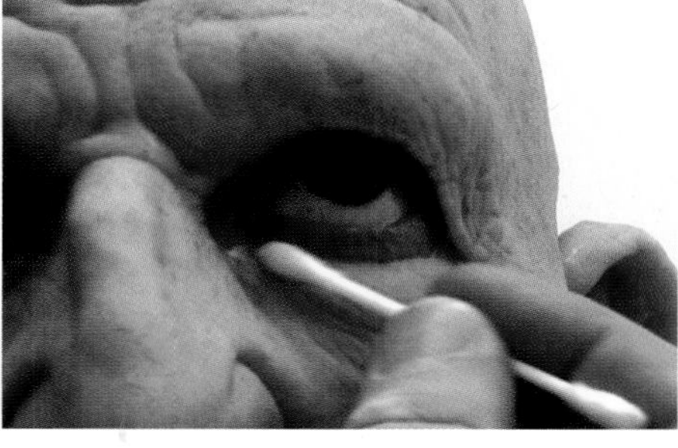

FIGURE 7.40
Apply Pros-Aide bondo with a small brush, Q-tip, or dental spatula to cover the edge, and smooth with a brush dipped in water or 99% IPA to blend away the edge.
Image reproduced by permission of Neill Gorton.

There is really no method I can tell you that will be the be-all and end-all way to conceal edges. Obviously, the best way to hide edges is for the edges to be virtually invisible to begin with and be glued with care. Rushing will betray you. Do not be in a hurry at this stage of the makeup because it will come back to bite you. Redoing the makeup will take far longer than doing it well and doing it right the first time.

However, there is a method of concealing edges that can make your life easier; it involves using the plastic cap material mentioned in the section "Attaching the Appliance." If your edges are made of the cap material (if you've created a GFA with cap material as your encapsulating material), they can be dissolved away with 99% IPA (isopropyl alcohol), witch hazel, or acetone.

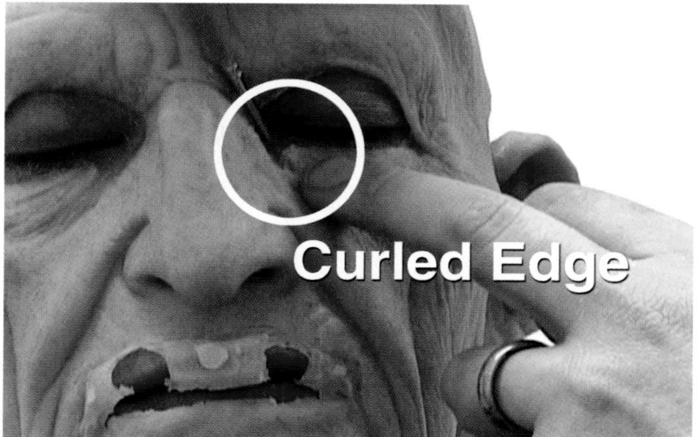

FIGURE 7.41 Edge curled over and stuck; a small brush dipped in thinner will allow it to come back apart and be set right. *Image reproduced by permission of Neill Gorton.*

Now, if the adhesive you are using is a silicone adhesive such as Telesis or Snappy G, your appliance edges can be worked and reworked with a small brush dipped in Telesis thinner. The thinner will slightly swell the silicone edge, popping it out and allowing you to press the edge back into its proper position. This works very well if an edge has curled over on itself and stuck together; the thinner will allow it to come back apart and be set right. Then you can proceed to complete the application and blend all the edges invisibly.

Applying Pros-Aide along edges can be done with a Q-tip or cotton swab, but you must be careful not to let the adhesive begin to dry or you will risk getting fibers from the cotton tip embedded in the adhesive. There are a number of small brushes that can be purchased in bulk that will allow you to do the same thing without the risk of errant fibers getting caught.

APPLYING THE MAKEUP

The foundation you use for your appliance will largely be decided by the material the appliance is made of.

Foam Latex

If your makeup appliance is made of foam latex, a good choice for coloring after application is rubber mask greasepaint (RMGP); Graftobian, Kryolan, and Mehron each make RMGP. RMGP is best applied by sponge and by stippling the color over the entire prosthetic. If RMGP is used to color the appliance only and not for the rest of the makeup, the following should be done:

1. The greasepaint should be stippled over the edge of the appliance and onto the immediately surrounding skin and blended with your fingers, sponge,

or brush to blend with the makeup used for the rest of the face or other body parts.

2. RMGP should be powdered, pressing in as much powder as the greasepaint will absorb and then lightly brushing off the excess with a powder brush. RMGP may require periodic powdering to prevent shine.
3. To help the makeup look more natural and help conceal the edge between the appliance and the skin, stipple additional colors (these can be RMGP or crème makeup) to add variation to the base color. Using a stipple sponge or piece of latex sponge applicator, rubber sponge, or piece of sea sponge, apply a shade that is three or four times darker than the base color, and then powder.
   - Next, stipple a color that is three or four shades lighter than the base, and powder.
   - If you are working on a face, apply a crème pink or red (rouge)—if appropriate to the character—to the cheeks. Then powder. Do the same for the nose, if needed.

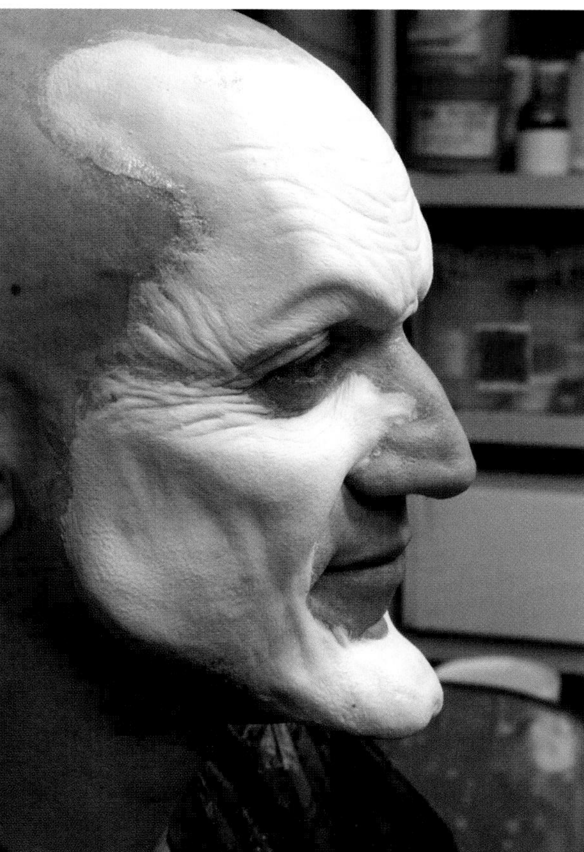

FIGURE 7.42 Frank Ippolito's foam latex Joker makeup ready for painting on Frank Langley. *Image reproduced by permission of Frank Ippolito.*

Much of this will depend on lighting conditions for the makeup and whether it is for the stage or the screen. Often what looks good under makeup lighting will look quite different under stage or shooting lights or even sunlight. If appliance edges are still visible, apply some detailed stippling with a small pointed brush or piece of stipple sponge.

- Where the edge is visible as a result of shadows, use a lighter stipple to counteract them.
- Use a dark stipple to offset highlights.

Crème foundations such as the ones available from Ben Nye seem to work just fine with foam latex also and can be applied in the same manner as RMGP.

NOTE

Foam latex can be airbrushed or painted using a spatter technique and any of the alcohol-activated palettes just as easily (if not more so) as with RMGP or crèmes.

FIGURE 7.43
Frank's finished foam latex makeup on Frank Langley.
Image reproduced by permission of Frank Ippolito.

FIGURE 7.44
Franks Ippolito and Langley; Monsterpalooza, 2012.
Image reproduced by permission of Frank Ippolito.

Gelatin

When applying makeup on gelatin, you first need to seal it, if it hasn't already been made as part of a GFA, with the G (for *gel*) being gelatin. If you apply makeup directly onto gelatin, the color will be absorbed into gelatin instead of sitting on top; depending on what you are using to color the appliance, you could also begin to dissolve the gelatin if you aren't careful. You can use a number of materials as a sealer, including plastic cap material, Kryolan Fixier spray (spray a small amount into a cup along the edge of the cup, and then brush it on), WM Creations' Shiny Sealer or Soft Sealer, Premiere Products' Blue Marble Se-Lr, Green Marble Se-Lr, BJB SC-115 acrylic sealer, or the like.

Once the gelatin is properly sealed, makeup can be applied normally; RMGP is not recommended. You can use crème foundation color and makeup sponges, but I recommend using one of the alcohol-activated color palettes—Skin Illustrator, Sta-Color, Reel Creations, etc.

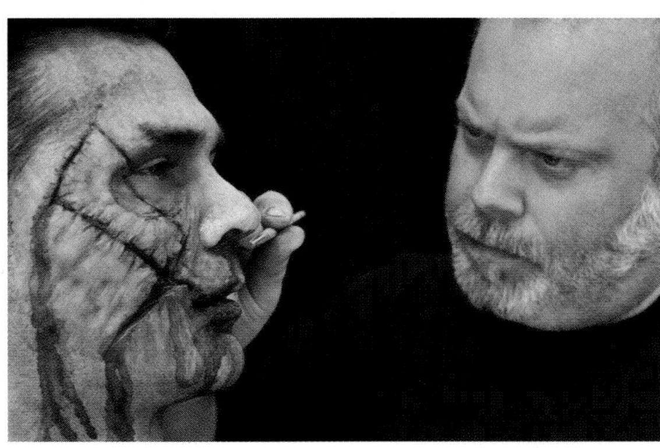

FIGURE 7.45
Tom Lauten of Nimba Creations painting gelatin appliance on Graham Hay.
Image reproduced by permission of Tom & Siobhan Lauten, Nimba Creations.

Almost without exception, the appliances you will be putting on will have been pigmented at least basically with a foundation color at the time of casting them in their molds. So your task at this stage will be to finish the job, and this can be done quite nicely by spattering numerous layers of transparent color from one

TIP
Gelatin can be blended neatly with warm witch hazel to dissolve, blend, and smooth rough edges.

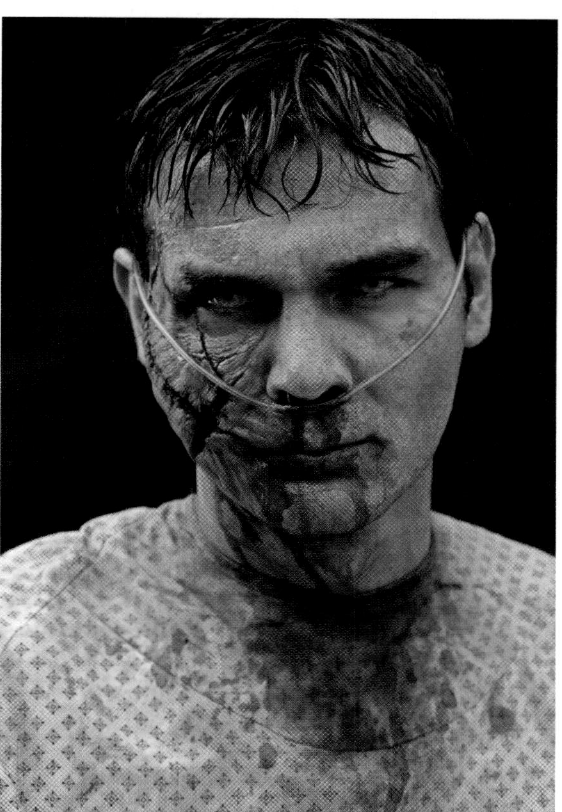

FIGURE 7.46 Graham Hay; gelatin appliance by Nimba Creations. *Image reproduced by permission of Tom & Siobhan Lauten, Nimba Creations.*

or more palettes, 99% IPA, and a few cut-down chip brushes.

If your appliance edges are well made and the appliance is placed properly at the beginning of the application, you are less likely to need to make corrections later.

Cold Foam

Makeup should be applied to cold foam in the same way as for gelatin or foam latex; it should be sealed first and the sealer allowed to dry fully. Remember that urethane foam is moisture sensitive and, even after having fully cured, might wrinkle slightly when exposed to moisture in a makeup foundation or even the sealer, particularly if it is water based. RMGP, PAX crème foundation, or alcohol color palettes can all be used to color cold foam. Follow the preceding steps to apply makeup to your cold foam appliance.

Silicone

If your silicone appliance has been painted already, as described in Chapter 6, your makeup needs for the appliance should be minimal after application. If you were not the one who painted the appliance, it would be beneficial to have a color chart showing what was used. If not, you must eyeball it and mix your best match with a Skin Illustrator palette or something similar. Remember that with silicone it is important to maintain translucency of the material; that's one of the reasons why silicone is used as a prosthetic material. Work with light color application of whatever makeup you use, and build up layers of depth to blend from the appliance to the skin.

REMOVING THE APPLIANCE

If handled deftly, an appliance should be reusable, no matter what material it was cast with. Even foam latex can see multiple applications if the removal is gentle and the appliance is properly cleaned and stored, though more often than not foam latex won't survive the removal. At best the appliance will hold up, but there will be significant edge damage that will need attention if the makeup is to be reusable.

No matter what the appliance is made of, you should never attempt to simply pull it off. Depending on the adhesive used to apply the prosthetic, one of two things will happen: The appliance will tear and come off in chunks, or the appliance will come off with chunks of the wearer's face still attached to it. Either way, it will be uncomfortable, if not downright excruciating, so always use the appropriate adhesive remover to first loosen the edges and then proceed.

Materials

Q-tips	Small cups
Misc. makeup brushes (for adhesive remover)	
Pros-Aide remover	99% IPA
Telesis Super Solv	Ben Nye Bond Off! or Remove-It-All
Isopropyl myristate	Sponges
Cloth towels	Cotton pads

Removers

There are a number of adhesive removers available, depending on which adhesive you use, though many of them will work well with different adhesives. If you have used spirit gum, spirit gum remover or mastic remover generally works better than some other removers. Residual stickiness can be removed by either applying more of the spirit gum remover or using isopropyl myristate with a cloth, sponge, or cotton pad.

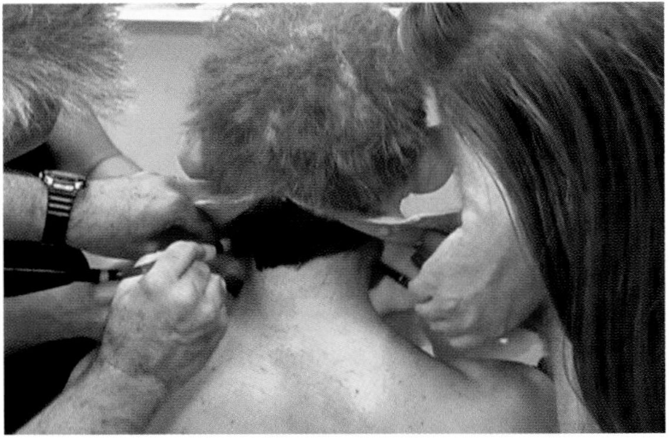

FIGURE 7.47
Insert brush bristles between appliance and skin, gently moving the brush to increase the opening.
Image reproduced by permission of Mark Alfrey.

Technique

Before starting, make sure you have everything at hand that you will need for the removal; it is more than likely that your performer has been wearing the prosthetic for a long time and is more than ready for the appliance or appliances to come off. The trick is to work efficiently and carefully, particularly around the eyes. The last thing you want is to accidentally get remover where it should not be.

1. Dip a fairly firm-bristled brush into the remover (Telesis Super Solv or Ben Nye Bond Off! works well with most adhesives), and gently begin to insert the brush bristles between the edge of the appliance and the skin, moving the brush softly to increase the size of the opening.
2. As the remover dissolves the adhesive, gently start to lift the appliance as you go, continuing to apply more of the remover either with the brush or with a Q-tip or other type of applicator.
3. Try to avoid letting the appliance flop over onto itself, adhesive to adhesive, because it will be difficult to separate and could rip or tear. If the

appliance is large, another pair of hands might be useful to hold it out of your way as you work.

4. When the appliance has been removed, place it on its form until you are able to clean it properly for storage.
5. With Q-tips, cloth, or cotton pads, use isopropyl myristate or more of the adhesive remover to gently wipe off the remaining adhesive residue from the skin. The skin can be quite sensitive to irritation, especially if the performer has been in prosthetics regularly. Simply repeat step 5 until the skin is no longer sticky.

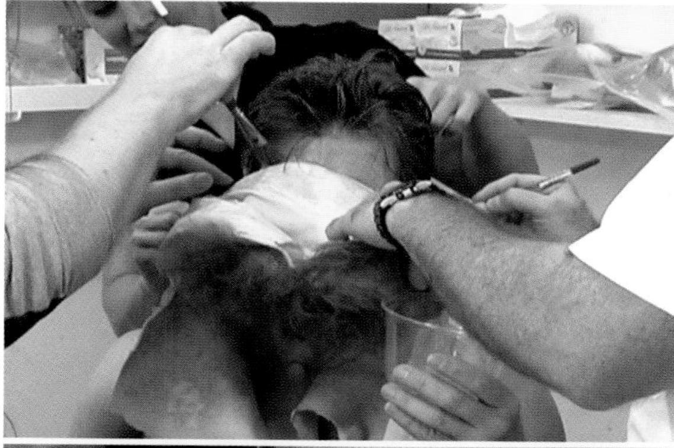

FIGURE 7.48
As the remover dissolves the adhesive, gently lift the appliance, applying more remover with brush or Q-tip.
Image reproduced by permission of Mark Alfrey.

SKIN CARE

I've said before that it's never about the makeup; it's always about the performance. That includes post performance. If my actor is worried that his or her skin is getting more and more irritated and becomes consciously aware of discomfort, in and out of the makeup, I am not doing my job well enough. Making sure I've done everything I can to leave my subject's skin clean and feeling good will ensure that skin care is one less thing the actor has to think about and he or she can concentrate on the performance. Skin care is part of the job description.

The first step in skin care is preventive: skin preparation. Do you recall my anecdote from the beginning of this chapter about the actor who played the Cowardly Lion in a production of The Wiz? Premiere Products' Top Guard is a methacrylate-based, nonoily skin preparation and surface primer that reduces skin irritation. It also increases the adhesion of prosthetic appliances *as well as* making it easier to remove them. This one product alone can make a makeup artist's post-makeup routine a relative breeze.

1. Once the adhesive residue and remover are fully removed from the skin, gently wipe the skin with isopropyl myristate using a soft cloth. This is an extra measure as a safeguard to clean the skin.
2. Apply a dedicated skin cleanser, such as Ben Nye Hydra Cleanse or Premiere Products' Telesis Brisk, which can be sprayed and wiped off with a soft cloth or cotton pad. Hydra Cleanse is a gentle oil-free skin cleanser, and Brisk is a skin cleanser with a peppermint oil fragrance and tea tree oil that acts also as an antiseptic, analgesic, and astringent.
3. There is no one single product choice; this is a personal preference, and you might have skin care products (cleansers, lotions, and conditioners)

already in mind that you prefer. The important thing to keep in mind is comfort. Buzzwords to look for in products are as follows:

- Emollient
- Moisturize
- Condition
- Soothing
- Refresh

Many actors have their own routine for skin care and so their own products, but it is a good idea to be involved because their skin is the foundation for our work. If the actor's skin becomes irritated, it is in your best interests and the actor's to make certain that the skin is clean before and after makeup. Since it is our responsibility to restore skin to its original state when we are finished, keep a variety of cleansers, toners, emollients, and moisturizers at hand.

CLEANING AND STORING THE APPLIANCE

Whatever you do to clean the appliance and remove the adhesive residue and buildup, it is important that it not be sticky or greasy (oily). If it is sticky, it will be hard to manage, it could tear if it sticks to the mold form, and it won't feel clean. It also means that there is still adhesive, and adding more adhesive will add to a buildup, causing the appliance to be ill fitting.

If the appliance is oily, adhesive will not stick to it, and the appliance will not hold well after application. In addition, if the appliance is going to be reused (which is why you're cleaning it in the first place), there is likely to be a buildup on its surface where edges are concealed. Carefully work off the Pros-Aide bondo, Duo, or whatever was used to conceal the edges. Any number of tools could be useful for this task, including toothpicks, dental spatulas, or eyelash brushes. This could take some time to do as well.

Once the appliance is clean and free of adhesive and remover, powder it and store it in an airtight baggie on a mold form so that it will hold its shape until it is ready to be reapplied.

CHAPTER SUMMARY

In this chapter you learned about:

- The three basic skin types
- Pre-appliance skin care
- Various adhesives
- Materials needed for appliance application
- Application and painting techniques
- Blending appliance edges
- Applying makeup to various appliance materials
- Removing and cleaning prosthetic appliances
- Post-removal skin care
- Storing appliances

CHAPTER 8

Hair and Wigs

Key Points

- Types and varieties of hair
- Tools and materials for postiche boardwork
- Wigs
- Hair attachment
- Laid-on hair
- Ventilating hair
- Punching hair

INTRODUCTION

When the book *Wig Making and Styling: A Complete Guide for Theatre and Film* was released in 2010 (Focal Press), written by Martha Ruskai and Allison Lowery, I considered having only these words for Chapter 8: *See Martha and Allison's Book*. It needs to be in every makeup artist's reference library.

Numerous wonderful sources of in-depth information are readily available, so there is no need to reinvent the wheel for this book. Just as something as small and simple as a nose can transform a familiar face into something new and almost unrecognizable, the same can be said of hair for suggesting a particular time period, personality, or age. Merely changing one's hair color and length can often be enough to render that individual immediately unrecognizable to friends.

FIGURE 8.1
Brian Walker Smith, "before" (left) and "after" (right).
Photos by author.

TYPES AND VARIETIES OF HAIR

When creating postiche for a character makeup, various types of hair are often used: human hair, animal hair, and synthetic hair. You might think that hair is hair, but there are very clear differences in hair textures, in addition to the obvious color variations. Of the human hair used for postiche, there are *European* and *Asian*. European hair is the most expensive because it offers the widest variety of natural colors and has a mild texture. Asian hair is less expensive and coarser than European hair and sometimes does not last long, but it's readily available and can also be found in a variety of colors.[1]

Yak hair is frequently used in postiche work, and because of its coarseness, it is particularly suited for moustache or beard work. It is naturally black, gray, or off-white and can be artificially colored. *Angora goat hair* (mohair) is a very soft hair used predominantly for fantasy character work. It colors very well, but it can be quite expensive. *Sheep's wool* (crepe wool/crepe hair) is sold in braided ropes that can be easily straightened and used for a variety of postiche, but it's used quite often for hand-laid (laid-on) hair work such as beards and moustaches. It is relatively inexpensive and available in a broad range of colors. *Synthetic hair* is quite versatile and can be permanently curled, which is something that cannot be achieved with real hair. However, synthetic hair does not last as long as the real hair.

Tools and Materials for Postiche

There are several tools and materials that are essential for postiche boardwork if you are going to do any of the work yourself.

- *Drawing mats and drawing brushes*—These two devices are designed to hold hair in place while you work to prevent wasting any hair by keeping it under control. When hair is placed between the brushes or mats, the longest hairs can be drawn out first.
- *Net foundation*—Foundation comes in different varieties and is used by wigmakers for ventilating hair (hand tying); fine, flesh-colored nylon or silk lace is used for street wear, film, television, and studio work, and heavier, flesh-colored nylon lace is used for theater, although often fine lace is used to front wigs for theater as well.
- *Ventilating needle*—Also called *knotting hooks*, ventilating needles come in different sizes, all of them quite small; the size will depend on the number of hairs required in each knot. Size 00 is the finest needle and used for finishing edges, drawing one hair at a time. Sizes 01 and 02 are used for main fill areas, drawing two or three hairs at a time. Larger needles can be used for drawing even more hair for areas where more hair is required without showing the hairline. A ventilating needle is actually a very tiny fish hook and is quite sharp and should be treated carefully so as not to accidentally hook yourself or someone else.
- *Blocks*—These include *wooden blocks, malleable blocks*, and *beard blocks/chin blocks*. Wooden blocks are solid, head-shaped forms for making wigs. A malleable block is head shaped but soft and covered with canvas; these are usually used for dressing wigs. Beard/chin blocks can be made of either solid wood or soft canvas; these are chin shaped to facilitate beard work.

FIGURE 8.2
Drawing mat.
Photo by author.

Wig Measurement & Information

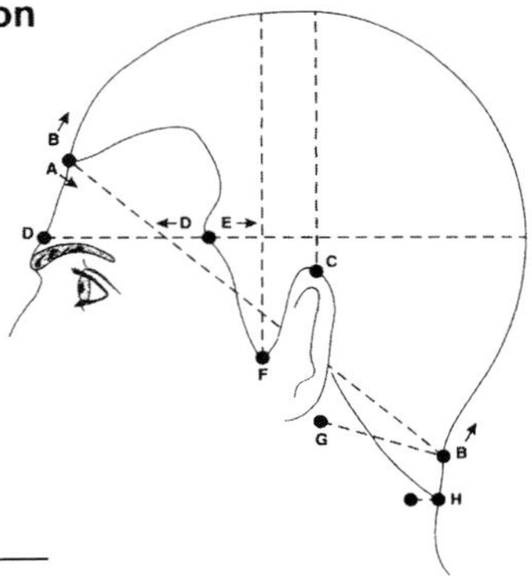

NOTE: Add 1/2" to 1" to measurements if performer's hair reaches center of back or longer,OR is at least shoulder-length and thick.

A. Around the head (hairline) ____________

B. Over the top (hairline to nape) ____________

C. Ear to ear (over the top) ____________

D. Temple to temple (front) ____________

E. Temple to temple (back) ____________

F. Sideburn to sideburn (over the top) ____________

G. Bottom of ear to bottom of ear (back, over nape) ____________

H. Nape (back, bottom of hairline on neck) ____________

Hair information:

Color number: Human ____________ Synthetic ____________

Highlights: Human ____________ Synthetic ____________

Texture: ______________________________
(thick, fine, curly...)

Length: ______________________________
(top of shoulders, center of back, crew cut...)

Other Notes:

FIGURE 8.3
Wig measurement form.
Illustration reproduced by permission of Martha Ruskai.

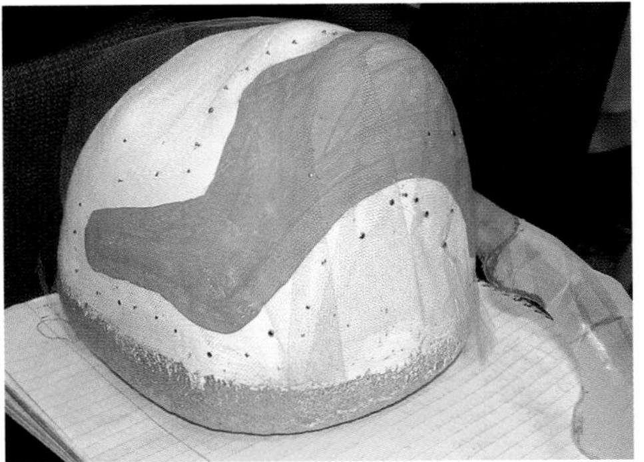

FIGURE 8.4
Chin block.
Photo by author.

WIGS

If a wig has had any handwork done to it, or if it is completely handmade, it is going to be more valuable than one without. In general, there are also some excellent machine-made wigs. If the foundation is handmade, the hair knotted into it is most likely going to be human hair. Synthetic hair is less likely to hold its knot in the lace foundation. The reasons for knowing what type of wig you have is so that it can be cleaned without being damaged and you can determine the possibilities for dressing it.

There are two choices for cleaning a wig: shampoo and water or dry cleaning with industrial chemicals. Human hair, whether hand ventilated or wefted (sewn), needs to be dry cleaned. Machine-wefted hair can be shampooed as synthetic hair (which has most likely been machine wefted). A combination wig, such as machine-wefted and hand-tied wig, must get a shampoo wash.[2]

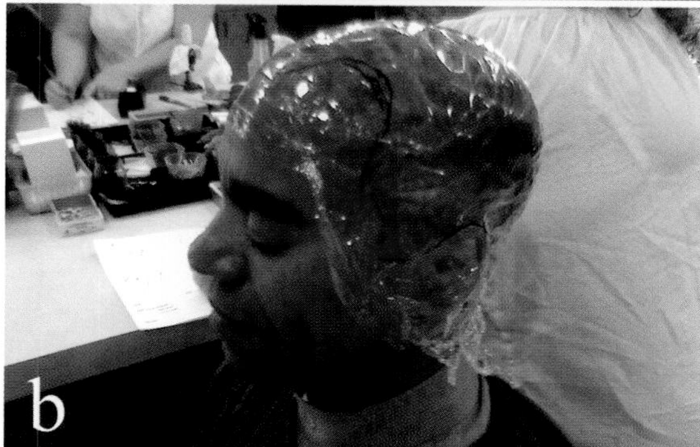

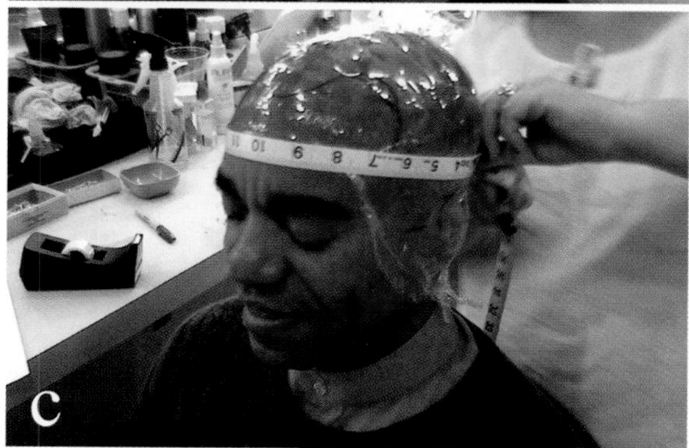

FIGURE 8.5
(a) Wig measurements; Man of La Mancha (2009) Diana Ben Kiki, Leonard Barrett, Jr., Rod Zuniga and author; (b) Wig outline on plastic wrap; and (c) Measuring head circumference.
Photos by author.

Weft Wigs

Simple weft wigs come in different sizes and are relatively inexpensive, mass-produced wigs that are good for crowd scenes. These wigs use machine-made hair wefts that are either synthetic or real hair that has been acid reduced (to facilitate styling). A synthetic wig cannot have its style changed, although a reduced hair wig can be styled with limitations.[3]

A stretch weft wig is designed to fit most people; these are the kind of wigs most often

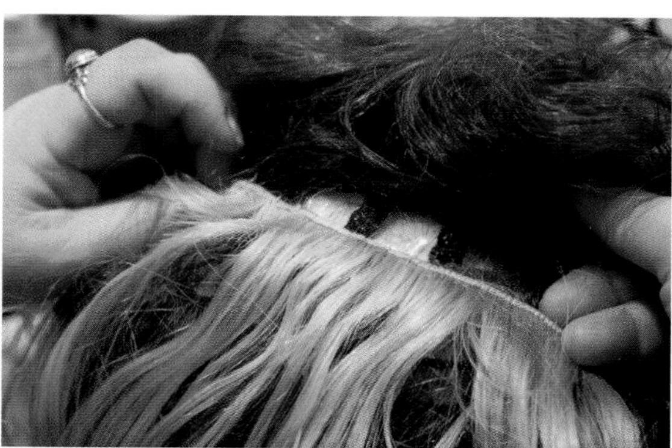

FIGURE 8.6
Hair weft being added to existing wig.
Photo by author.

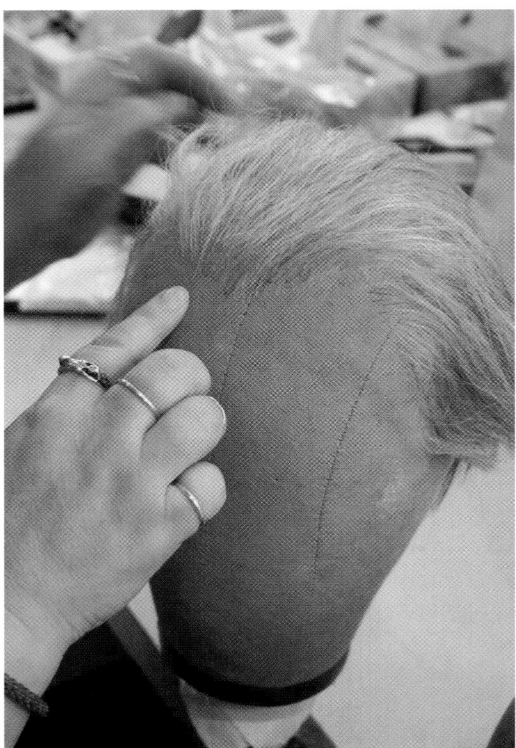

FIGURE 8.7
Hand-tied hair appears to be growing directly out of scalp.
Photo by author.

found in costume shops for Halloween, are cheap, and are mostly synthetic hair, although reduced hair stretch wigs do exist. These wigs could be suitable for a crowd scene but probably won't fool anyone up close. On the other hand, because they're so inexpensive (especially compared to hand-knotted wigs), they can come in handy when push comes to shove. I'd call these "last resort" wigs.

Another type of weft wig is more expensive: fashion weft stretch wigs. These are also known as combination wigs because the tops of these wigs have a large area of hand-tied, drawn-through parting-style work.[4]

This makes the hair appear to be growing directly out of the scalp. These are stretch wigs designed to fit most people, are medium to expensive in price, and are made in a variety of hairstyles and colors.

These weft wigs are easy to care for and wear, but there are disadvantages, which are as follows:

- They're heavy to wear.
- They fade easily in strong light.
- They have a short lifespan compared with hand-knotted real hair wigs.

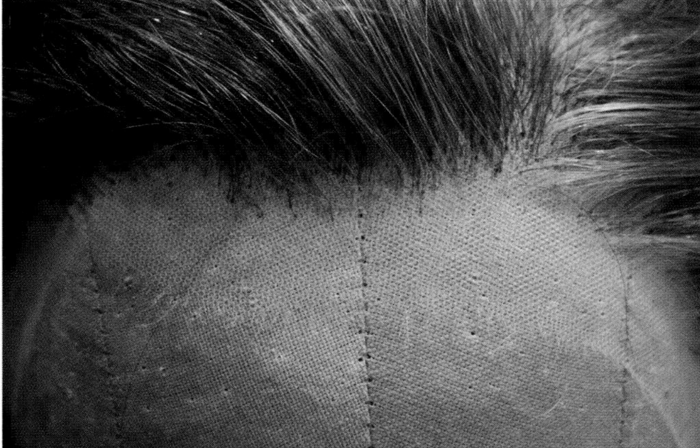

FIGURE 8.8
Lace on hand-tied wig is so fine that it becomes invisible to all but closest scrutiny.
Photo by author.

Knotted Wigs

Hand-knotted wigs are almost always made to order from specific measurements and can be quite expensive. Unless you have a money tree in your backyard, these are not Halloween wigs. They are the real deal, and they look and fit fantastic. These are fully custom wigs that are available in varying weight, color, length, and quality. Being custom wigs, knotted wigs can have hand-sewn foundations or machine-sewn vegetable (veg) net foundations with a *galloon* (silk lace ribbon) base; they can also have a hair lace front that will allow the wigmaker to knot an actual hairline for theatrical use. The lace is so fine that with makeup it becomes invisible to all but the closest scrutiny. Even then it can be barely perceptible.

Hand-knotted wigs can have a very long life if well cared for. For stage and screen, hand-knotted lace wigs are what principal cast members wear. In researching wigs and postiche for this book, I've learned a great deal about the craft from Diana Ben-Kiki, hair and wig mistress for the Denver Center for the Performing Arts. She and her work are amazing, and I'm sure glad I know her.

Hair Attachment

There are essentially six ways to attach hair—actually seven, but six of them do not involve a medical procedure:

1. To weave the hair on weaving silks to create a weft.
2. To knot the hair onto a lace net foundation.
3. To plant (lay) the hair into wax (I've never done this, but have into latex).
4. To punch graft the living hair root into the scalp. This is a medical (surgical) procedure and should *never* be tried by anyone without MD at the end of his or her name. *This is not a practical theatrical application of hair and should not be attempted as such.*
5. To punch hair into a silicone, gelatin, cold foam, or foam latex appliance with a hair-punching needle.
6. To bind and sew hair (real or synthetic) to growing hair; this is called *hair extensions*.
7. To hand lay hair onto the face (or elsewhere) and secure with adhesive such as spirit gum, Pros-Aide, or Telesis 5.

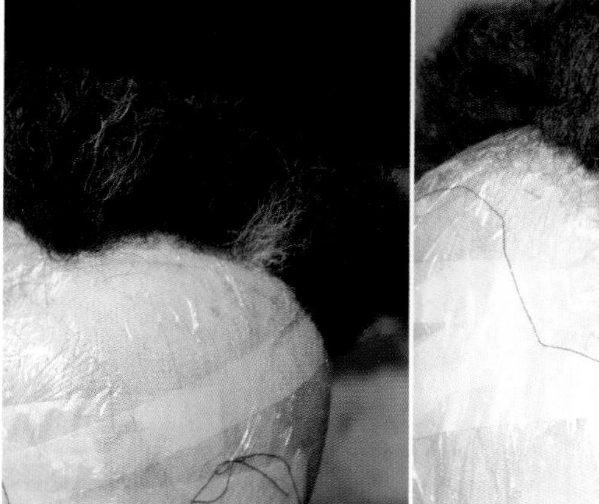
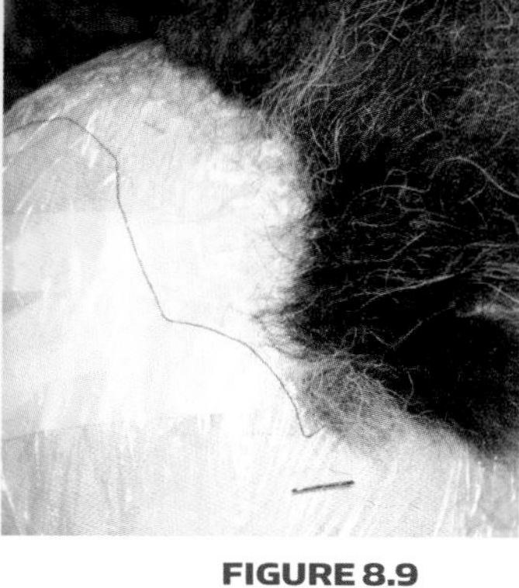

FIGURE 8.9
Laying crepe wool into latex on lace for theatrical wig.
Wig and photo by author.

In this chapter, we'll look at numbers 2, 5, and 7.

Preparation for a Wig

There are several steps for getting a head ready to wear a wig, including large elastic bands (called Alice bands in the United Kingdom), hairpins, combs (including a rattail comb), and a wig cap.

FOR SHORT HAIR

- Take a section of your subject's own hair from the front center hairline and braid it backward into a small tight plait (braid) if possible and secure with a hairpin or two.
- Place a large elastic hair band over the head to the neck, then comb the rest of the hair back and away from the face.

- Bring the elastic band up and around the head to hold the hair back.
- Put a wig cap over the hair; if there is any excess, tuck it in to hide it.

FOR MEDIUM HAIR

- Just as with short hair, take a section of your subject's own hair from the front center hairline and braid it backward into a small tight plait (braid) if possible and secure with a hairpin or two.
- Divide the hair into small sections and pin-curl each section flat to the head, using crossed hairpins to hold the curls in place. To make the pin-curls, twist the hair around two of your fingers.
- Place a large elastic band around the head and over as many of the sections as you can.
- Put a wig cap over the hair and tuck in any excess.

FOR LONGER HAIR

- Take a section of your subject's own hair from the front center hairline and braid it backward into a small tight plait (braid) if possible and secure with a hairpin or two.
- Make a ponytail and hold the hair tightly at the base with a small elastic band.
- Roll the ponytail into a flat chignon, or bun, and secure it firmly with hairpins.
- Use a large elastic band to keep short hairs in check, particularly those at the back of the neck.
- Put a wig cap on the subject, being sure to tuck in any excess.

Obviously these steps are useless if the makeup you are creating requires your subject to be in a bald cap as part of the makeup. (Bald cap application is described in detail in Chapter 9.) So if your subject is in a bald cap, why do you need a wig? Perhaps the character is going bald but still has hair—perhaps an "outer rim" or "comb-over," or perhaps the hairline is receding or the hair is simply getting thinner. For whatever reason, there is visible scalp and hair; hence, there is the need for a wig—and not just any wig. A wig for any of these situations requires a hand-ventilated lace wig. In the case of a bald cap and lace wig, it is important to know where the imagined hairline would be before wig placement. But I digress.

How do you place a wig onto someone's head? Funny you should ask.

How to Put on a Wig

Before the wig can be placed on your subject, it is important to know where the center front of the wig is.

- Standing behind your subject, place the center front of the wig onto the forehead just below the hairline.
- Carefully set the wig down onto the head and gently shift it into place.

- Use the sides of the wig by the ears as a hand-hold to adjust the wig, making sure that it's properly placed—centered and even.
- Secure the wig with hairpins, medium pins along the front hairline and large pins toward the back. Until you get adjusted to the feel of a pin pushing through the wig cap nylon mesh, ease your hand under the wig at the spot where you are placing a pin, push until the pin touches your hand, and then remove your hand and gently push the pin into the hair (pin-curl). If pinned properly, the wig should be secure and not come off until you take it off.

To remove the wig, first remove all the hairpins, and then take the back nape of the wig in both your hands and carefully lift the wig up and forward. To store it until the next application, place it on a wig form or malleable wig block.

How to Put on a Lace Wig

Okay, so your makeup requires a lace wig or, to be more exact, a lace-front wig. Your subject could have a full bald cap, full-head cowl, or a forehead extension that covers the head to about the midline of the head. How do you apply a lace or lace-front wig? If your subject is in full bald cap or full-head cowl, the job of applying the wig is relatively simple. I'll describe that first.

1. Place the wig on your subject's head in the normal way. The lace wig should go on before makeup has been applied, because the lace must be carefully glued in place. Spirit gum can be used, as well as Pros-Aide, Beta Bond, or silicone adhesive.
2. Make sure that the wig is seated properly and then apply the adhesive *thinly* along the hairline under the lace and down the temples to the ears on both sides. If you are using Pros-Aide, let the adhesive get tacky; if you are using Telesis 5, you can press the lace into the fresh adhesive. Use a damp makeup sponge to press the lace down firmly to the head. When the adhesive is dry, lightly powder to remove tackiness and then apply makeup over the hair lace.

FIGURE 8.10 Leonard Barrett, Jr.; Miguel de Cervantes; *Man of La Mancha* (2009). *Wig, prosthetic nose and photo by author. Application by Kamala Quintana.*

Removal of a lace wig takes the kind of care and finesse needed to remove a prosthetic appliance that you plan to use again.

1. Dip a medium flat brush into some Super Solv (gel or liquid) or Pros-Aide remover and gently brush along the glued hairline of the lace.
2. When the adhesive becomes soft, carefully begin to lift the lace edge with the brush or a pair of tweezers.
3. When the hairline lifts without resistance, lift the nape of the wig at the back and pull it up and forward, with the lace coming off last.

4. Clean the lace carefully to remove all traces of adhesive from it. You can use more of the adhesive remover or acetone.
5. When you're done, place the wig on a wig form for storage until it is ready to be worn again.

FIGURE 8.11
Leonard Barrett, Jr.; Don Quixote; *Man of La Mancha* (2009); wig, beard, and moustache applied onstage by Leonard Barrett, Jr. during performance.
Wig, nose, and photo by author.

BEARDS, MUSTACHES, AND EYEBROWS

There are really just two ways to apply hair to the face: by hand or by applying a knotted lace piece. Beards, moustaches, and eyebrows can be easily glued to the face as ready-made appliances but can be less comfortable than hand-laid hair simply because the hair is knotted into a lace foundation that is then glued in place. Although fronting lace—which is what most tied beard, moustache, and eyebrows are ventilated into—is very fine and lightweight, it has very little flexibility and might have the ability to hamper a performance by inhibiting movement. If that is the case, hand-laid hair might be preferable. All considerations must be weighed around the performance. Even when using a lace beard piece, the edge should be hand laid to blend hair into a more realistic look.

FIGURE 8.12
Lace beard; hand-laid blend on cheeks. Applied by John Blake.
Photo by author.

Laid-On Facial Hair

Hand-laid hair is difficult to match on a daily basis and takes considerably longer to do than applying a lace piece. For that reason, it is not often used in many screen productions. Hand-laid hair is still used fairly extensively in some circles—theater and low-budget shows—although it does appear to be lessening. It's not hard to do, but it is time consuming, and lest it becomes a lost art, I'm going to do my part to describe how to do it. Paul Thompson of the Makeup Designory does a terrific job describing and showing the process step by step in his book, *Character Make-up*, and so does master wigmaker Patsy Baker in her book, *Wigs and Make-up for Theatre Television and Film*.

I've had mixed results (more bad than good, really) laying on real hair versus crepe wool. The problem with real hair is threefold: Crimping it is critical because facial hair does not grow straight; real hair is expensive, far more expensive than crepe wool; and real hair is not particularly fond of any kind of adhesive. Facial hair is not usually straight, either, and real hair would need to be kinked rather substantially to be believable.

FIGURE 8.13
Hand-laid crepe beard (pre-trimming). By Alison Chilen and author on Brian Landis Folkins.
Photo by author.

FIGURE 8.14
Crepe hair/crepe wool.
Photo by author.

Crepe Wool (Hair)

Crepe wool is ordinarily sold by the yard, but at most places, you can buy it in whatever length you want; they'll just cut it to order. The wool is braided; so when it is straightened, it will almost double in length. To hand-lay hair, you'll need the following:

- Adhesive
- Various colors of crepe wool
- Scissors
- Drawing mats
- Hackle
- Rattail comb
- Adhesive remover
- Setting powder

There are a few ways to straighten the crepe before you lay it on the face. It can be dampened slightly and ironed (on the wool steam setting) or held in front of a clothes steamer or even a boiling tea kettle. Either of the last two options comes with this caveat: Watch your fingers! I've found that placing a section of the crepe wool into a bowl of water and microwaving it for a minute or so will take the curl right out of it. Then, the wool needs to be dried before it can be separated. The straighter the crepe wool, the easier it is to work with, but completely straight facial hair doesn't look realistic when applied to the face, the exception being Asian facial hair, which is often quite straight. For a character makeup of African ancestry, you might want to forego straightening the crepe at all, because the facial hair tends to be quite curly.

PREPARATION

1. Unravel some crepe wool from the braid but be careful not to pull too far and tangle the hair and strings. Cut away the string from the braid.
2. The goal is to remove most of the curl from the crepe hair, but not all; keep about 30–40% of the curl.
3. Put the cut length of hair in a microwave-safe bowl of water and nuke it for about a minute; keep an eye on it to make sure you don't lose too much curl.
4. If you are going to mix hair to get a specific color, repeat step 3 for each color you intend to mix.
5. When the hair is dry (you can pat it almost completely dry in a towel), pull the straightened braid of crepe hair apart by gently pulling one end while holding the other end. You could use a wide-toothed comb but that tends to waste a lot of hair.
6. As you pull, the hair should separate into 6- to 8-inch length (15–20 cm). Now is when you should mix in other colors if necessary.

7. Pull several strands of each color and put them together until you have a pile of hairs the color you want. From here, continue to pull the hair apart, put it back into a bundle, and repeat until you have a bundle of crepe hair that looks fluffy and even. If you are not going to use the hair right away or have more than you will need immediately, you can wrap any excess hair in a paper towel, tape the roll, and put it in a plastic zipper bag.
8. The next step, if you have one, is to run the hair through a hackle.

If you've never used one before, get some Band-Aids® and antiseptic and keep them close. A hair hackle looks like a small medieval torture device but is actually used to detangle hair. When it's not in use, a cover should be placed over the hackle pins to prevent accidental impalement. I put a big chunk of Styrofoam over mine.

9. Clamp or tape the hackle to the edge of a table or other work surface. Slowly and carefully place a small amount of hair about 1 inch (2.5 cm) into the hackle. Hold the hair firmly and pull it toward you through the pins. Repeat this process a few times, adding an inch or so more hair as you pull it through the hackle.
10. Now repeat this process with the other end of the bunch of hair you just pulled through the hackle.
11. Do this with all the hair you will be laying on. As hair is pulled through the hackle, short hairs and tangled wads of hair will build up in the pins. When the buildup of crud hair begins to interfere with your hackling, carefully remove the hair buildup and set it aside. You can pull and separate that hair later to put through the hackle again.
12. Cutting or trimming the crepe hair before laying it on is critical to a good application, as is how and where you hold the hair. The amount of hair sticking out from your hand as you hold it in your fingers is directly related to how thick the hair will be when applied. The more the hair is sticking out, the thinner the application (note how the hair fans out, away from your fingers).

FIGURE 8.15 Hair hackle. Cover it to avoid blood loss. *Photos by author.*

The closer the end of the hair is to your fingers, the thicker it will be. Be careful, because with facial hair, there should be a little daylight visible between the hairs, not an impenetrable carpet. Hair will be thickest under the chin and getting thinner as you go toward the side edges on the cheeks, where the hair will be the thinnest.

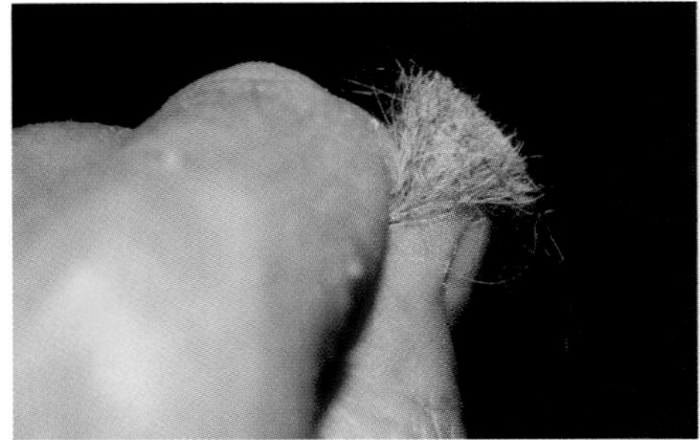
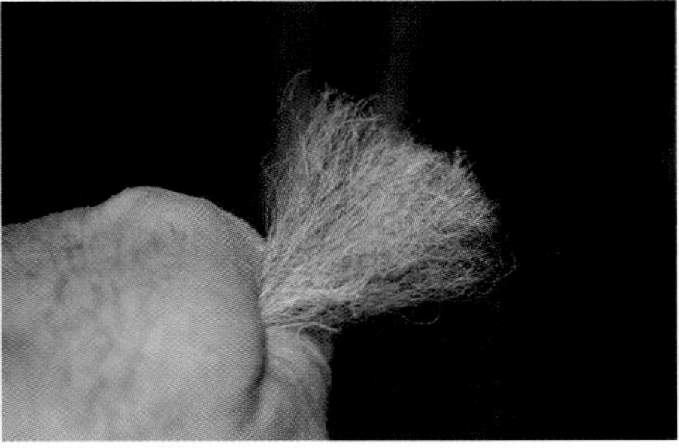

FIGURE 8.16
Amount of hair sticking out from hand as you hold it is directly related to how thick hair will be when applied.
Photos by author.

FIGURE 8.17
Face is broken into sections for laying hair by hand, with fore-most sections applied last.
Illustration by author.

13. The hair ends should be cut at an angle that will mimic the direction the hair should be growing in. Be careful when cutting so that clippings will not fall into the hair and get caught.

When laying hair by hand, the idea is to work in sections, with the hair furthest back and underneath being applied first and the foremost or top most hair being laid on last. With that in mind, you need a plan. The hair can't simply go on. For a full beard and moustache application, the hair will be applied in 15 or 16 sections.

APPLICATION

Hand-laying hair is not a particularly difficult skill to master, relative to some other aspects of special makeup effects, but it does take repetition to become good at it. And this is definitely a skill to be good at. I mentioned before that hand-laying hair is becoming a lost art, but there's no reason that it should disappear. It's your makeup that the hair is going to be part of, so you should be the one putting the hair on. Enough said. It's time to apply the hair.

FIGURE 8.18
Crepe wool pulled through hackle.
Photo by author.

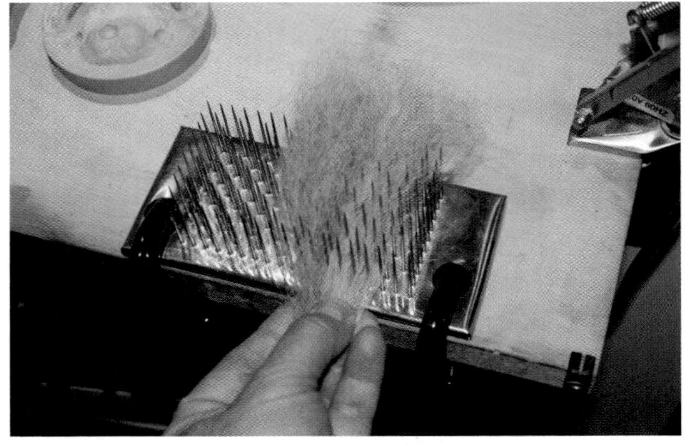

1. Do a position test before applying adhesive by holding the hair up to your subject's face, under the chin, because under the chin will be the first section to fill.
2. The hair under the chin should appear to grow somewhat forward, so the hair ends should be cut to make sure the application of the hair will be in the right direction.

NOTE

Don't use too much hair, and you want the hair to stand on end, with only the ends of the hair stuck into the adhesive.

Now that you know where adhesive will go first, mix some Telesis 5 (thinned 1:1 with Telesis Thinner) or Pros-Aide. Your choice; crepe hair will adhere well with either of these adhesives. Just remember that Pros-Aide needs to dry (clear) before you apply the hair.

3. Once you've applied the adhesive, gently press the ends of the crepe hair into it and hold until it's dry. Telesis dries pretty quickly—even more quickly when it's thinned. If necessary you can use the back of an applicator swab to press the hair into the adhesive.
4. When the adhesive is completely dry, use the tail end of a rattail comb to pick through the hair and remove any hair that isn't glued down. There will be some. The resulting hair glued in this section should be pretty thin.
5. The next section will go right in front of the last one. Comb through it and hold it the way you held the last bunch of hair. Combing will make sure the hairs are going in the right direction and will also remove any small, extraneous hairs.
6. Apply adhesive to the next area, being careful not to get adhesive in the first section of hair. Press the hair into the adhesive and hold until it's dry. Make sure the hairs look like they're growing out of the skin and not just lying on the surface.
7. When the adhesive is dry, pick or comb gently through the hair to remove loose ones.
8. Continue this process through each section, back to front, bottom to top, until all the hair has been applied.

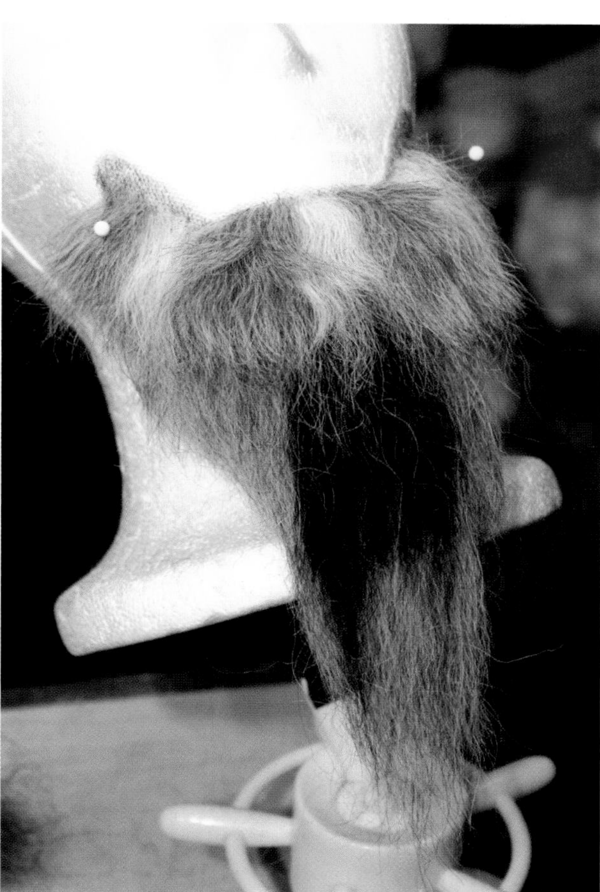

FIGURE 8.19
Hand-laid crepe beard in latex; Man of La Mancha (2010).
Beard and photo by author.

Once the all hair has been laid on, it must be neatly trimmed into a normal beard. Begin with the moustache and trim the hair back to the edge of the upper lip. Then trim the hair over the corners of the mouth in a downward direction (cutting away from the nose) with the scissors almost parallel to the skin.

Continue to trim, forming the shape of the beard along the edges; use a comb to lift sections of hair and continue to keep the scissors parallel to the skin beneath the hair you're cutting to avoid lopping off too much hair. When you've finished trimming and shaping the beard and moustache, use a pair of tweezers to pick off stray bits of hair from the beard and the skin.

If you have a lifecast of your actor's face, it is possible to create a hand-laid beard that can be used multiple times. In the same way that you would create a bald cap from scratch on a plastic bald cap form, you can build up latex on your subject's lifecast, too, provided that it has been sealed to make removal of the latex easy.

Another option is to use Baldiez or Super Baldiez in place of latex; the beard may not have the durability/longevity of a latex-backed appliance but you'd have the benefit (if necessary) of being able to see "skin" through the hair, if laid on sparsely enough.

FIGURE 8.20
Hair being laid on for a moustache. Work from the outside in, from the outside corner of the mouth toward the nose.
Photos by author.

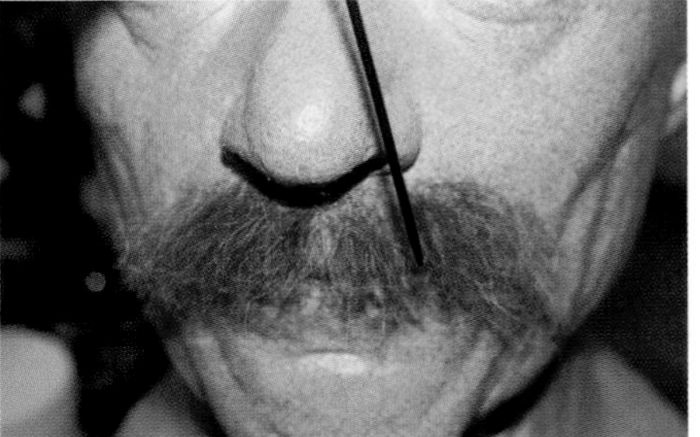

FIGURE 8.21
Press hair into adhesive and hold until it's dry (left); use tail end of rattail comb to pick through hair and remove any that isn't glued down (right).
Photos by author.

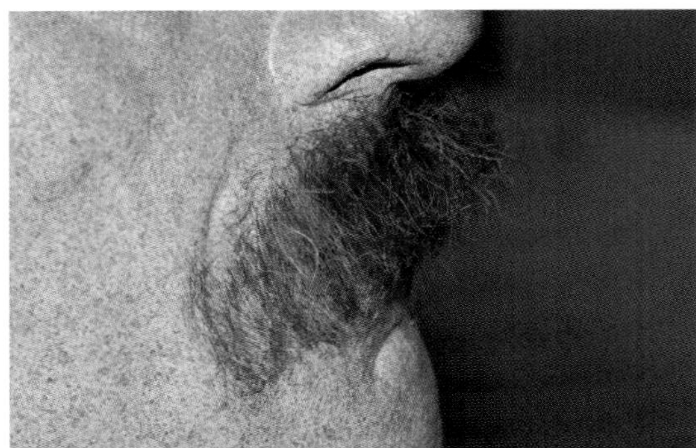

FIGURE 8.22
When done properly, crepe hair should appear to be growing out of skin.
Photo by author.

1. With a pencil, draw a pencil line for the outline of the beard and moustache.
2. With a small piece of sponge, stipple a thin layer of latex over the beard/moustache area. When the first layer is dry, repeat, building up as many as three layers of latex to provide a good base.
3. When you are ready to apply the hair, stipple another layer of latex over the first section, then immediately press the hair ends into the latex. Just as with the Telesis, hold the hair still until the latex is dry and then carefully pick out loose hairs.
4. Repeat for the next section, and the next, and the next until you've created the new piece, picking out loose hairs before moving on to each new section of hair.

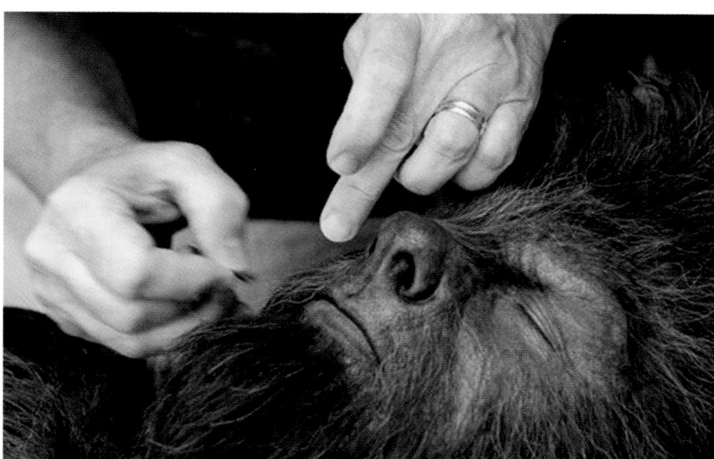

FIGURE 8.23
Dave Elsey laying hair; Benicio Del Toro; The Wolfman (2010).
Image reproduced by permission of David Elsey.

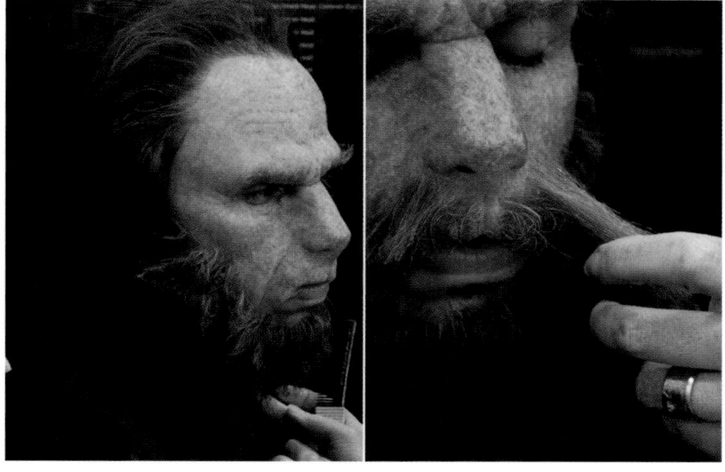

FIGURE 8.24
Dominie till laying hair with lace pieces on Marcel banks; IMATS LA, 2011.
Photos by author.

5. Trim the beard as before and you're ready to remove the new piece from the lifecast.
6. Powder the exposed edge and carefully lift off the beard, powdering the back so that the latex doesn't stick to itself. If you need to trim the latex, try to keep the blending edge as thin as possible. When you glue the hair appliance onto your subject's face, you might find it necessary to add thin hairs along the top edge of the moustache and beard to help conceal the edge. The bottom edge under the chin and upper lip should not be visible.

To remove the hand-laid beard and moustache, use the appropriate adhesive remover, being careful not to get any in your subject's mouth and work in small sections just as you did to apply the hair. Brush on a small amount of remover along the top edge of the beard or moustache and, as the solvent loosens the adhesive, gently pull the hair off and continue. When all the hair has been removed, cleanse the skin and apply a moisturizer to the skin.

Eyebrows can also be hand laid using crepe hair or yak hair, or human hair, but again if you are going to use human hair for eyebrows, I think the best way is to ventilate the real hair into fronting lace. One method for applying crepe eyebrows is to attach the crepe to the skin just above the natural eyebrows and comb the crepe down into the natural hair *or* glue the crepe directly onto the natural brows. However, you might find it necessary to completely cover the natural eyebrows. The consideration here is, will the eyebrows have to match up over several shooting days? In addition, how long will it take to do it every time? If speed and repetition are the order of the day, then by all means, ventilated eyebrows are the way to go. It still might be necessary to block to the original eyebrows, however. This is all essentially moot, of course, if your subject is wearing prosthetics in which eyebrows become part of the makeup. Then, the eyebrows will most likely be ventilated pieces or punched.

I learned a nifty procedure at IMATS 2011 in Los Angeles courtesy of New Zealand makeup effects master Dominie Till. If I were to write a book called *The Women of Special Makeup Effects*, there would definitely be a chapter devoted to her. Her hair and makeup work is second to none.

As you might correctly surmise, hand-laying hair can be a tedious and time-consuming endeavor and potentially mind numbingly boring for your actor. What Dominie showed was how to use the alcohol-soluble vinyl cap plastic material called Super Baldiez to create hair appliances that can be applied to an actor in a fraction of the time it would take to hand lay that same hair onto an actor. It still takes a substantial amount of time to prep and pre-lay the hair into thin sheets of Super Baldiez, but your actor won't be fighting narcolepsy in your makeup chair while you do it. The application then takes a fraction of the time it would take otherwise.

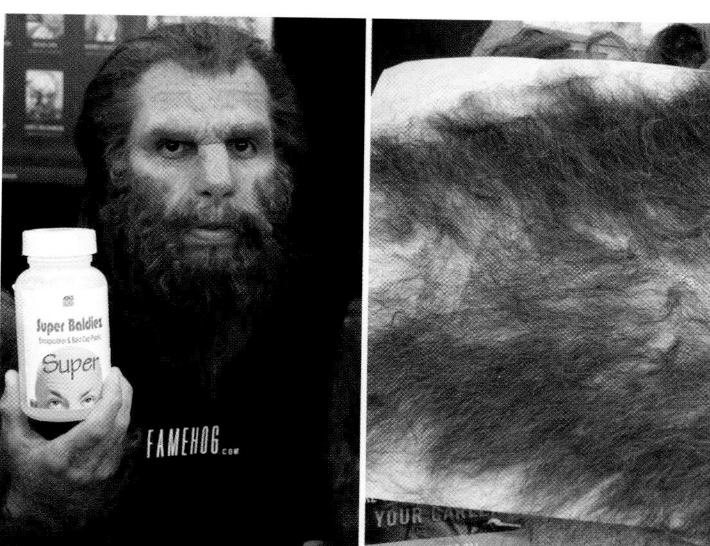

FIGURE 8.25
Pre-laid hair and Super Baldiez; by Dominie Till.
Photos by author.

Dominie's model for her IMATS demo was Marcel Banks, whose name many of you may recognize from Season 1 (2011) of The SyFy Channel's hit TV show *Face-Off*; you definitely won't recognize his face here, although you may recognize the tattoos...

If you want to give this a whirl yourself, you'll need the following:

- Hair (synthetic, human, yak, crepe, etc)
- Adhesive (Telesis, Pros-Aide, Beta Bond, etc.)
- Super Baldiez
- 99% Isopropyl alcohol
- Epoxy Parfilm
- Wax paper or disposable palette paper
- Sponge cut into small squares
- Airbrush foundation

FIGURE 8.26
Dominie, Jason Hamer setting pre-laid appliance; Marcel Banks.
Photo by author.

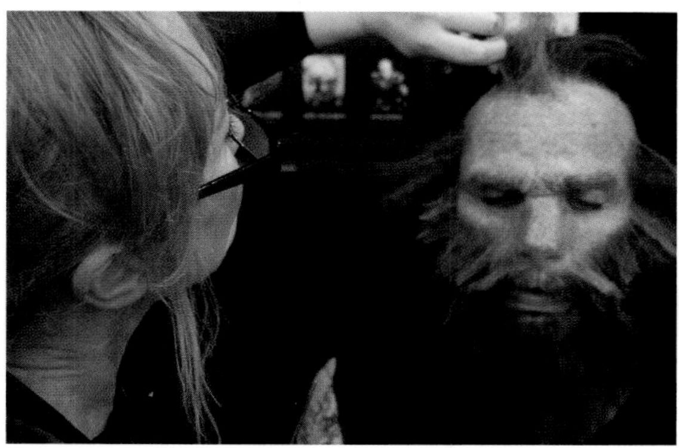

FIGURE 8.27
Dominie till laying hair into Baldiez; Marcel Banks.
Photo by author.

FIGURE 8.28
Dominie Till applying Telesis to Marcel Banks (left); Dominie adjusting pre-laid hair; Marcel Banks (right).
Photos by author.

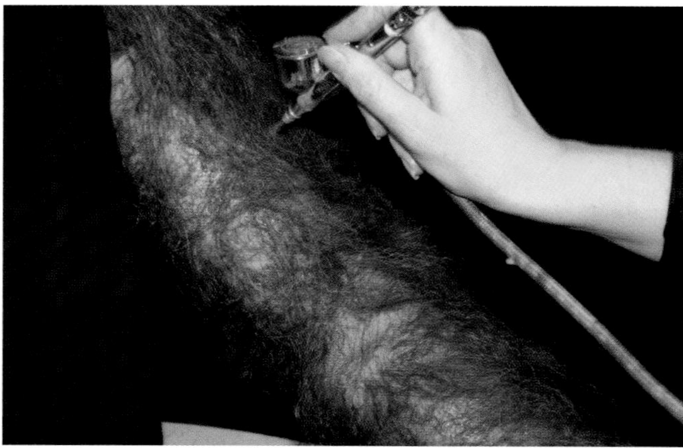

FIGURE 8.29
Dominie Till lightly airbrushing foundation to knock back shine.
Photo by author.

1. Brush a layer of full-strength or very slightly thinned Super Baldiez onto a sheet of wax paper or palette paper in the shape of your appliance. You may want to have an outline of the shape drawn on the other side of the paper that can be seen through it. Release the paper with Epoxy Parfilm just to be on the safe side.
2. Prep the hair.
3. When the first layer of Baldiez is dried, use a piece of sponge to stipple Baldiez onto a small section of the dry Baldiez, and lay a section of hair into the wet Baldiez.
4. Continue this until you've laid hair into the entire Baldiez appliance.
5. To apply, clean the skin and apply adhesive; carefully attach the Baldiez appliance at one end, and using slight tension, press the appliance down against the skin.

TIP

Blocking eyebrows with Telesis: Telesis is great for gluing hair down flat. Brush a tiny bit of full-strength Telesis into your subject's eyebrows, pressing the hair down flat as you brush. Full-strength adhesive is not as runny as thinned adhesive, but still be careful so none drips near your subject's eyes. When the glue is dry, powder and apply a skin-safe silicone such as Alcone's 3rd Degree, Smooth-On's Skin Tite, or Mould Life's Sculpt Gel. Silicone can be smoothed with 99% alcohol while the silicone is still uncured; once the silicone has begun to kick—that is, while it is still soft but has begun to form a skin—a small piece of plastic wrap can be laid on top of the silicone and the edges pressed smooth and invisible. Once the silicone has fully cured, the plastic wrap can be carefully removed and the edges will be seamless. No eyebrows!

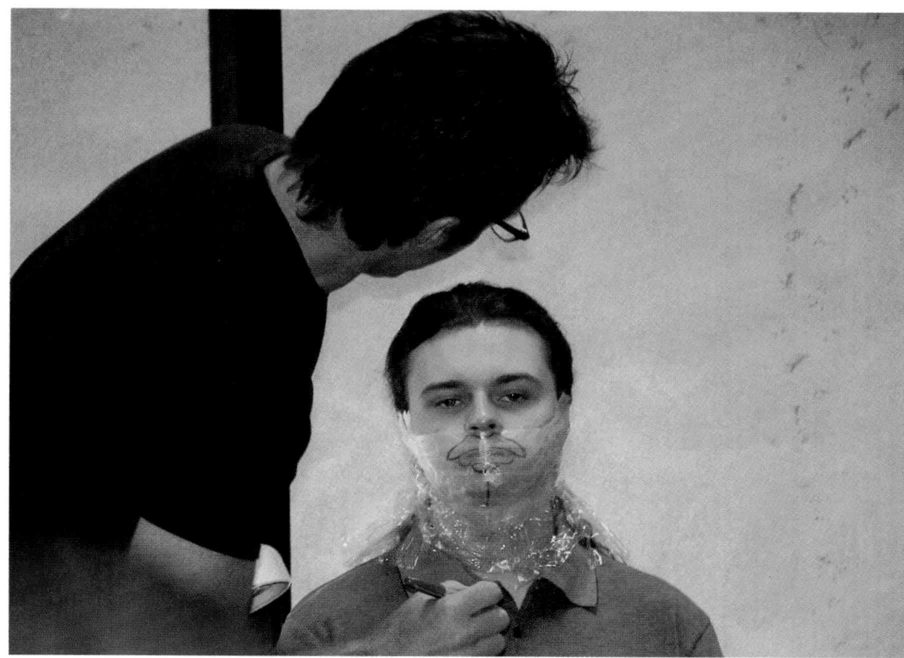

FIGURE 8.30
John blake creating beard template with plastic wrap, tape, marker.
Photo by author.

Rough Baldiez edges can be blended with 99% IPA. To eliminate shine of Baldiez, lightly airbrush foundation through hair.

VENTILATING HAIR

Hand-knotting, or ventilating, hair is a skill not easily acquired but one that if mastered could find you in rather high demand. Only the best and finest wigs and hairpieces are completely hand ventilated. Even machine-ventilated pieces that can be purchased from any number of makeup effects suppliers are better than the best wefted ones. (I've never seen a wefted beard or moustache; only wigs.)

The first step in ventilating a beard, moustache, or eyebrow is to have the proper tools and materials on hand, not the least of which is a good lighted magnifier. Even a Young Turk with 20/20 vision will go wonky in the head trying to focus on individual hairs through a 1-millimeter hole in fronting lace and then tie a knot in it with a microscopic fishhook on a stick.

But before ventilation can logically begin, you need to have a pattern for a hair appliance to create. Right? Right.

Using a piece of clear plastic wrap, place it over your subject's face, being careful not to obstruct breathing, and shape it to conform to your subject's facial structure. Once the plastic wrap is in place, proceed to cover it with pieces of

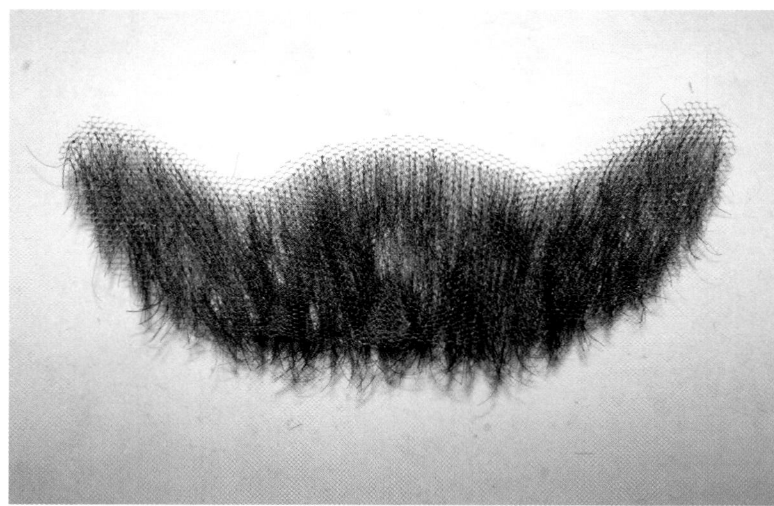

FIGURE 8.31
Commercially ventilated beard.
Photo by author.

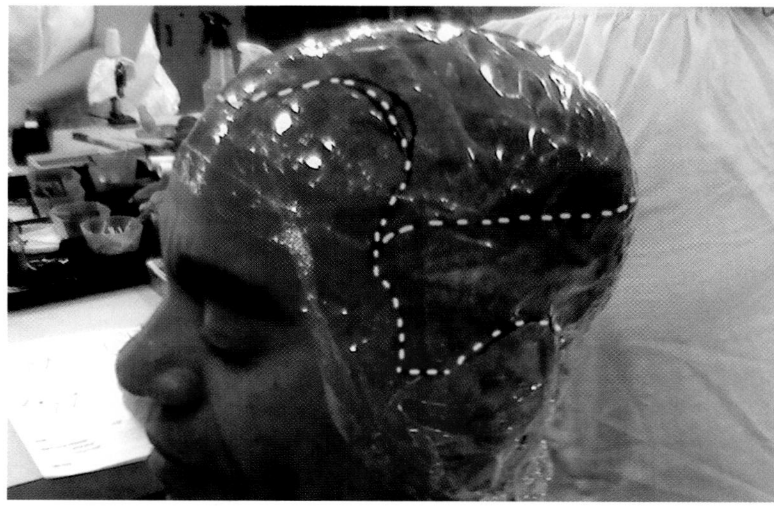

FIGURE 8.32
Outline of wigs; Man of La Mancha.
Photo by author.

Scotch tape; the form will become somewhat rigid and will hold its shape. Then, you can draw on the tape the shape of the beard and/or moustache you will create. This pattern can then be cut out with scissors and placed on a chin block or a cast of your subject's face. A piece of fronting lace or foundation (opera) lace can then be laid on top of the pattern. This can be done on the head for creating a wig that will be ventilated, or as in the photos below, to hand lay hair.

There are different types of netting used for wig making, beards, and moustaches. Veg net, caul net, and power net are too heavy for beard or moustache work and are best for making wig foundations. Veg net has the smallest

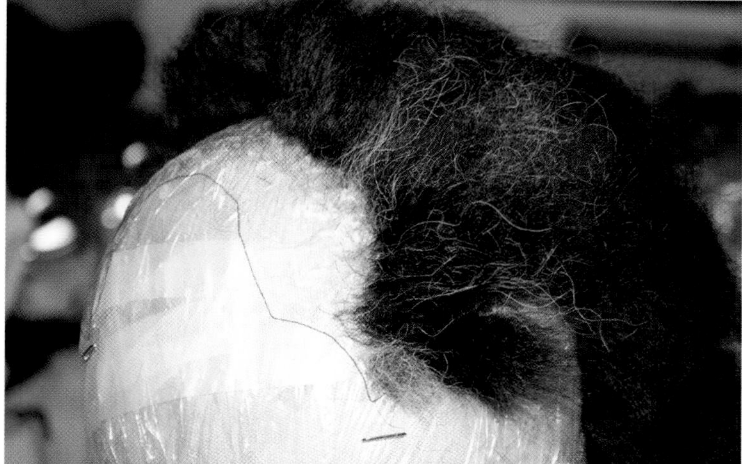

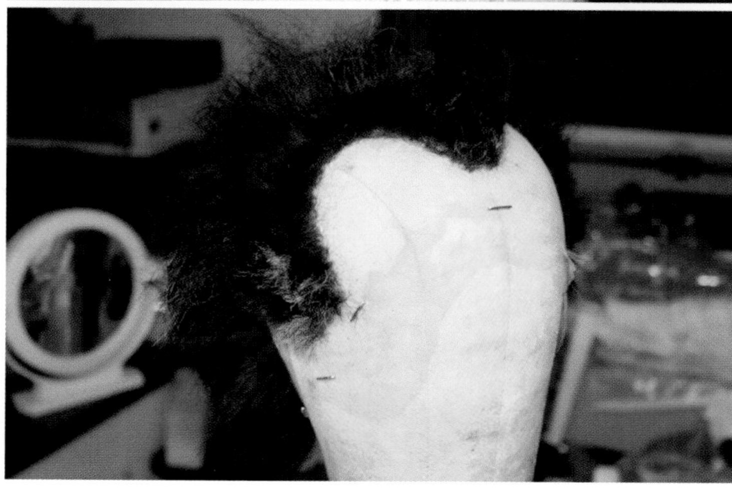

FIGURE 8.33
Crepe wool for Cervantes wig (top); build in progress (middle); and Cervantes wig, *Man of La Mancha* finished but untrimmed (bottom). *Wig and photo by author.*

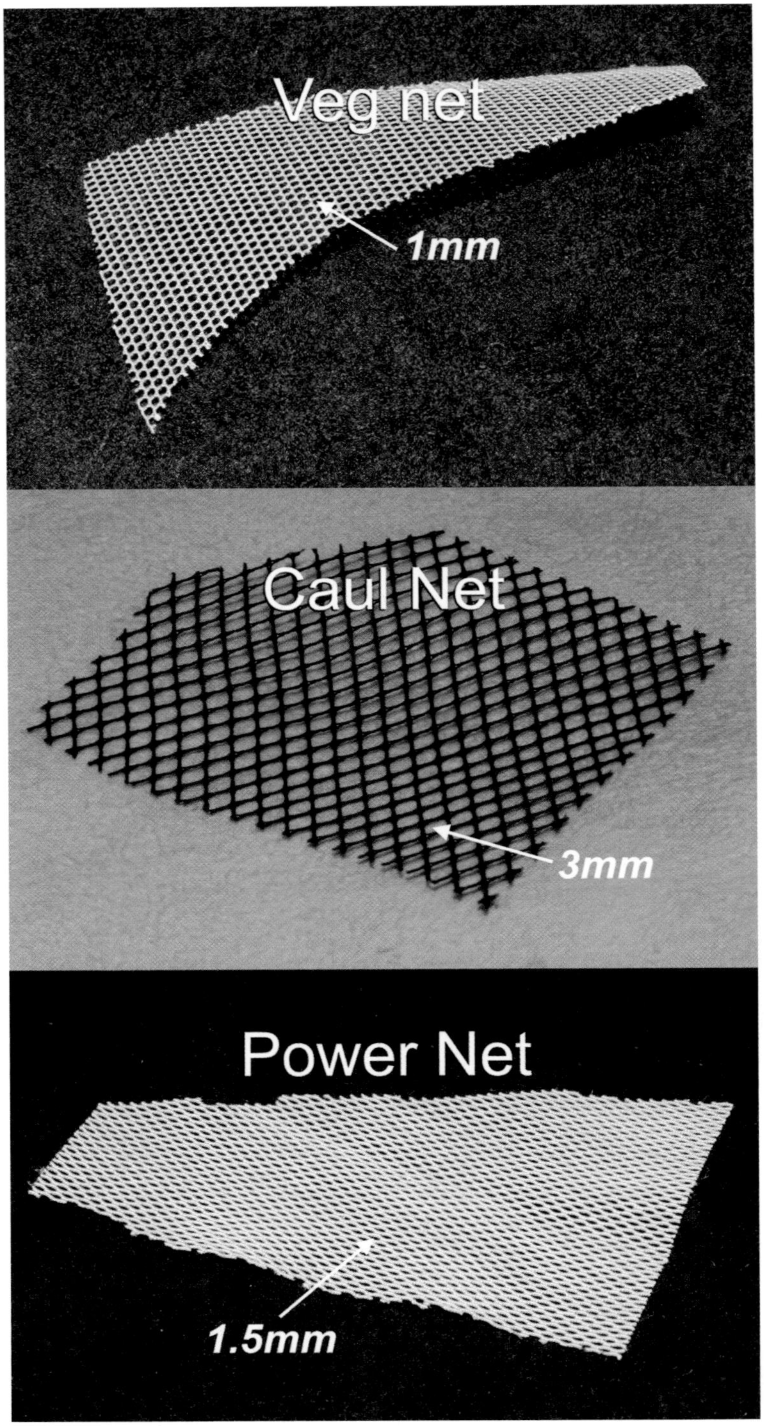

FIGURE 8.34
Veg net, caul net, and power net.
Photos by the author.

holes but does not stretch in any direction. Caul net has the largest holes and stretches horizontally but not much vertically. Power net has small holes and stretches considerably in all directions.

Foundation or opera lace and fronting lace are the two varieties best suited for beard and moustache work. Foundation or opera lace has small holes but very little stretch in any direction. Fronting lace is about half the weight of foundation or opera lace and is virtually invisible when applied to the skin as a foundation for a beard or moustache. Because it is so delicate, it is a bit more flexible in stretch than foundation or opera lace but is more apt to tear as well.

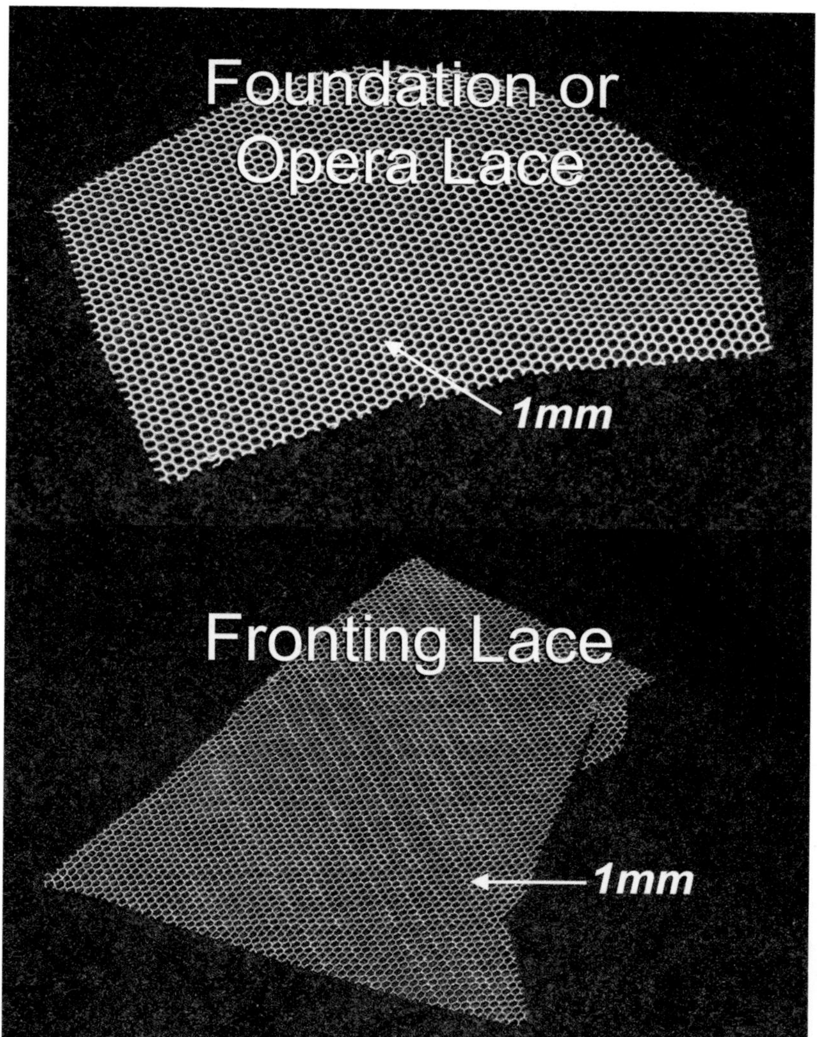

FIGURE 8.35
Foundation/opera lace and fronting lace are good for beard and moustache ventilating.
Photo by the author.

The lace should be at least 1 inch (2.5 centimeter) longer than the pattern; it will be trimmed later. The pattern should be pinned down with dressmaker pins (on a malleable block) or with transparent tape if you're using a cast of your subject or if you're using a plaster or wood chin block. Position the lace so that the holes are running in a vertical pattern.

1. Place a pin in the top center of the lace, about 0.25 inch (6 millimeters) from the edge of the pattern.
2. Put another pin in the bottom center of the lace, opposite to the top pin, pulling slightly to eliminate any slack in the lace.
3. Do the same for the left and right sides of the lace.
4. Fill in the perimeter of the lace with pins placed no more than 0.25–0.5 inches (6–12 millimeters) apart.

Ventilating needles come in several sizes, beginning with the smallest: #00. The bigger the number, the larger the needle. The #00 will grab one hair at a time, whereas #1 or #2 will snag several hairs at a time. As you might suspect, knotting several hairs at once will result in a larger knot, so the larger needles are only to be used where the knots will be covered by subsequent layers of hair. For a moustache, you probably don't want to pull more than two or three hairs at a time, and for edges, a needle that will pull only single hairs should be used.

Preparation

Knowing which end of the hair is the tip and which end is the root is more important for tying wigs than for facial hair, but if you hold a single strand and run your fingers along the shaft you can (usually) tell which end is which. The hair shaft should feel smooth going toward the tip and rough toward the root because of the cuticle direction.

Some hair is coarser than others and it's easier to tell which end is which. Even when I know which end is which, I have trouble telling the difference; I guess my fingertips just aren't that sensitive anymore.

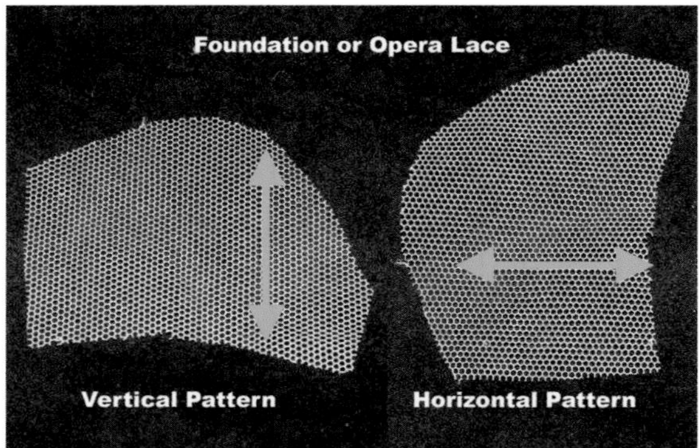

FIGURE 8.36
Ventilate with lace pattern running vertically.
Photo by author.

I am going to assume you will practice hair tying for a while before you attempt to ventilate a moustache, beard, or wig. Learning how to ventilate on a real piece is likely to be a recipe for disaster. Practice first! It is not as easy as it sounds, I promise. Before you can begin ventilating hair, you will need a few things, not to mention the hair you'll be tying:

Drawing mats
Canvas head block
Pins
Ventilating handle and needle(s)
Foundation lace

Technique

Okay, you've already pinned a piece of practice foundation lace onto a malleable head block, just as described a few paragraphs ago. Now it's time to prepare the hair in the drawing mats. Drawing mats resemble really large pet brushes without handles.

1. Lay one side of the drawing mats (they come in pairs) on a surface in front of you with the bent teeth facing *away* from you.
2. Next, put a small amount of hair on the mat with about 2–2.5 inches (5–6.5 centimeters) of the root end toward you, hanging over the edge of the mat.
3. Put the other mat on top of the first mat also with the teeth facing away from you, and press down on the mats so that the teeth are meshed together, with the hair between them.
4. Now you will be able to *draw* the amount of hair you want from the mats, hence their name. Wow!
5. If you haven't done so already, put a ventilating needle into the handle and then practice holding the way you hold a pencil or pen, rolling the needle's hook toward you and away from you. Then, find a safe place for the needle to rest so it won't roll off your work surface and break. I use one of my brush holders.
6. If you have a wig clamp with which to mount your canvas block, use it; otherwise you can hold the block in your lap or support it on your work surface with rolled towels to keep it from rolling. However you work, you are almost certainly going to need a lighted magnifier to see what you're doing and not strain your eyes.
7. Pull a small amount of hair from the mats and about 2 inches from the root end of the hair, bend it into a loop called the *turnover* and pinch the loop between your thumb and index finger.

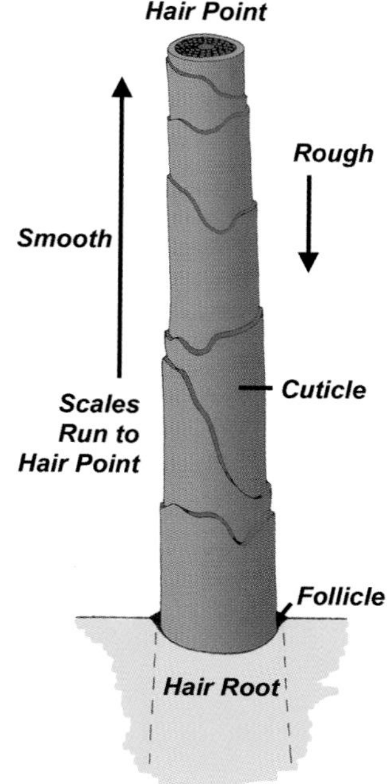

FIGURE 8.37
Hair shaft.
Illustration by author.

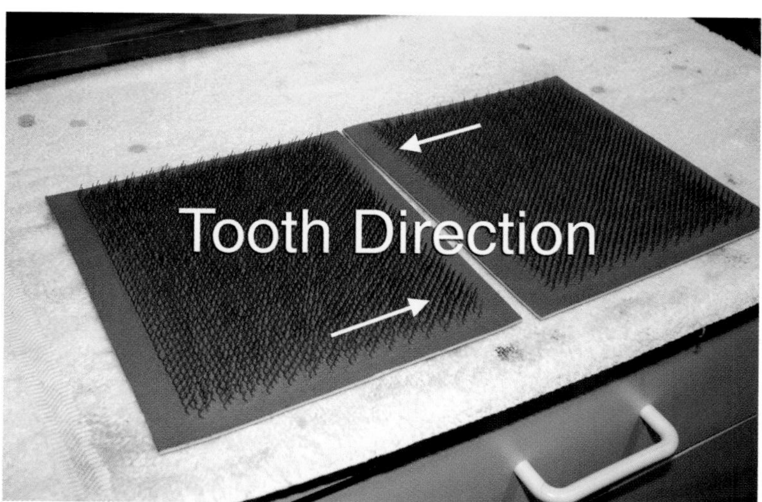

FIGURE 8.38
Place drawing mat with teeth facing away.
Photo by author.

FIGURE 8.39
Put small amount of hair on mat with 2 inches hanging beyond edge.
Photo by author.

FIGURE 8.40
Hair between drawing mats.
Photo by author.

For a skill like this, I am ambidextrous, so it wouldn't matter which hand the hair was in for me, but you should hold the turnover in whichever hand will not be your needle hand.

8. With the needle in your hand, slip it through a hole in the lace mesh, passing under the separating fiber and coming out/up through the next hole. Catch a few hairs (which will depend on the size of the needle) from the loop and pull them out just a bit. Moving both hands together, pull the hair back through the holes and out the original hole; be careful not to catch the hook on the lace. If you roll the needle slightly in a counterclockwise direction while also lifting the needle slightly upward against the lace, the needle hook and hair will slide out without becoming caught. Yes, this is easier said than done, but to become good at anything takes practice. Fortunately, this task gets easier quickly. If I can do it, so can you. *You must keep even tension between both hands so that the hair doesn't go slack and slip off the hook!* It will also take practice to find just the right amount of force for the tension.
9. Pull the hook back enough to comfortably be clear of the lace but not so far as to pull the short (root) end of the hair out of the loop between your fingers.
10. With the loop of hair attached to the needle, move the needle forward so that the hair catches in the neck; roll the hook away from you so that the hair wraps around the neck of the needle. Using both hands together to maintain tension, pull the hair and needle toward you, rotating the needle so that the hair is caught by the hook.
11. Turn the needle clockwise; keep the turnover hand still and pull the hooked hair back through the loop of hair that is still on the needle. Pull it all the way so that the hair comes free of the turnover hand. If you maintain tension with both hands, the knot will tighten on the lace. Always pull with the needle hand in the direction you want the hair to lay.

Practice, practice, practice! It's a relatively easy skill to develop. It is not relatively difficult for an artist like you to master, but it is time consuming and potentially

FIGURE 8.41
Pull small amount of hair from mats; 2 inches from root end of hair, bend into loop called turnover, and pinch loop between your thumb and index finger.
Photo by author.

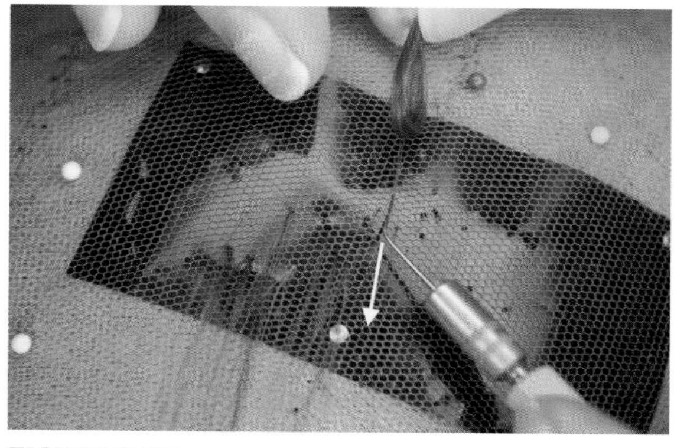

FIGURE 8.42
Pulling a few hairs with ventilating needle from turnover through lace.
Photo by author.

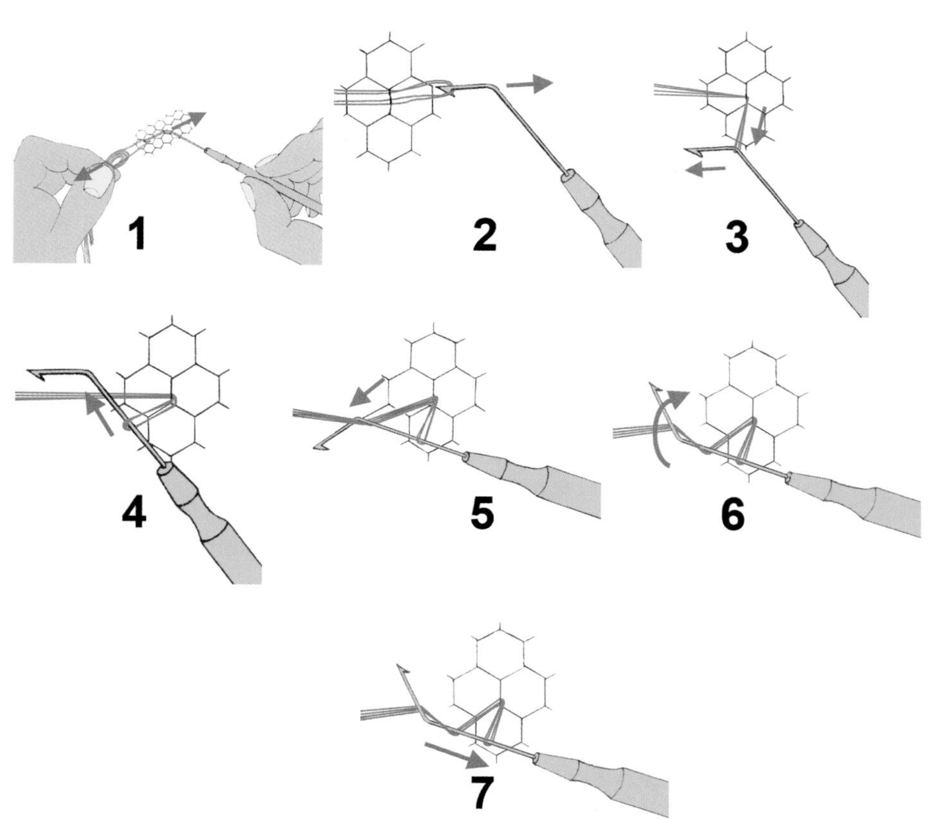

FIGURE 8.43
Hair-ventilating sequence.
Illustrations by author.

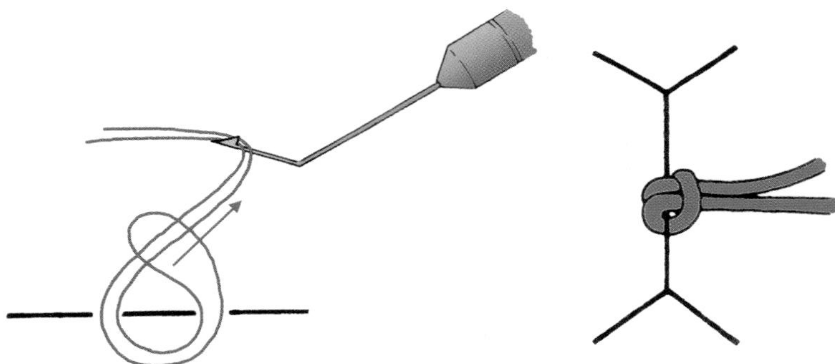

FIGURE 8.44
Final step; pull hair through loop to form knot in hair.
Illustrations by author.

monotonous. This is most definitely a repetitive-motion activity, so I strongly suggest taking regular breaks and developing a therapeutic routine to alleviate stress and tension in your wrists and hands. Listen to music.

PUNCHING HAIR

Punching in hair by hand is no less tedious than hand ventilating a lace foundation piece, but it is considerably easier in that there is no lace through which to maneuver an angled needle with a hook at the end. So, what is hair punching?

Hair punching involves taking individual strands of hair and pushing them into foam latex, silicone, gelatin, and so on. Hair punching is *not* to be done on an actual person; this technique is reserved solely for prosthetic appliances, masks, or dummies. The actual technique itself does not differ fundamentally from ventilating hair into lace; the difference is that you're not tying knots but planting hairs into a material's surface. You still want to create a mixture of hair colors to create a more natural look just as for hand-ventilating or hand-laying hair. You can even use a ventilating handle for the punching needle.

You can purchase hair-punching needles and holders from various suppliers (see the appendix at the back of this book), but it is also quite easy to make your own, much more inexpensively (no offense to retailers!). I find it easiest to hold a sewing needle with a pair of pliers and cut off part of the eye at an angle with a Dremel cutting wheel, creating a *U* or a *V*, and with the same tool, sharpen the edges to points. If the needle is a long one, you might want to shorten it a bit to give it a bit little of rigidity when you push the needle into the surface to which you are adding hair.

Technique

Do you recall that there is a pattern to follow when hand laying facial hair? Do you also recall that there is a pattern to follow for ventilating hair? Well, there is for punching hair, too, with the front hairline being the last to go in. Otherwise,

already punched hairs will be in the way when you put in more; the needle must be inserted at the angle at which you want the hair to lie or else you'll have a head of hair standing on end, straight up.

To save yourself a considerable amount of time, however, consider hand laying the body of the hair (if it's on a head) with adhesive and only punching the hairline at an inch or so (2.5 centimeters) beyond.

1. Pull a small amount of hair from the drawing mats (they'll come in handy here, too); about 2 inches (5 centimeters) from the root end of the hair, bend it into a loop and hold it between your thumb and index finger.
2. Holding the needle in your other hand, snag a hair or five and simply inject the needle into the surface, just deep enough for the hairs to remain embedded. Angle the needle to give the hair a "growing" direction.
3. As you move closer to the outer hairline, switch to a lighter hair color. You can also angle the hair direction slightly to help blend lines so the hair "growth" appears to be more random. By the time you reach the hairline, you should be punching only one hair at a time because only one hair grows out of each follicle. For this, you will also need to be snagging each hair very near the end so it will be punched into the surface, leaving only a single hair strand sticking out.
4. If you feel that there are too many hairs making up your hairline, you can pull hair out (and punch it back in) to give you the best look.

Can you do facial hair by punching? Sure. What about beard stubble? Yes. Ordinarily, for beard stubble, you need to use real hair or crepe hair cut into very tiny pieces, the size of shaved whiskers, and attached with adhesive to achieve the unshaved look. Before describing the punched stubble technique, here's how to do that. This can be done to an appliance, mask, or dummy or directly onto an actor's face. No poking or stabbing is involved.

1. Make sure the surface is clean; if the skin beneath the stubble will be visible, use transparent liquid makeup, preferably alcohol-based foundation and color such as Temptu, WM Creations, or Skin Illustrator. (You might use whatever you choose so long as it is not an oil-based makeup; that will inhibit the adhesive from working properly.)
2. Choose the hair color or colors you want to use, cut tiny pieces onto a flat surface you can control, such as a piece of palette paper.
3. Working in small sections at a time so you don't waste adhesive, cover a small area with adhesive. (Pros-Aide is great for doing this; it dries sticky and is clear when dry, so you know when it's okay to apply the hair.)
4. Use a dry rouge brush or similar brush; you probably won't want to use a good brush for this, or at least not one you'll use for rouge or other makeup again, because it'll be full of tiny bits of hair. Dab the brush into the cut hair. The brush will be a surprisingly effective pickup tool. Carefully transfer the hair to the face. Spread the hairs evenly to avoid clumps that will look fake. A second brush would be good for this.

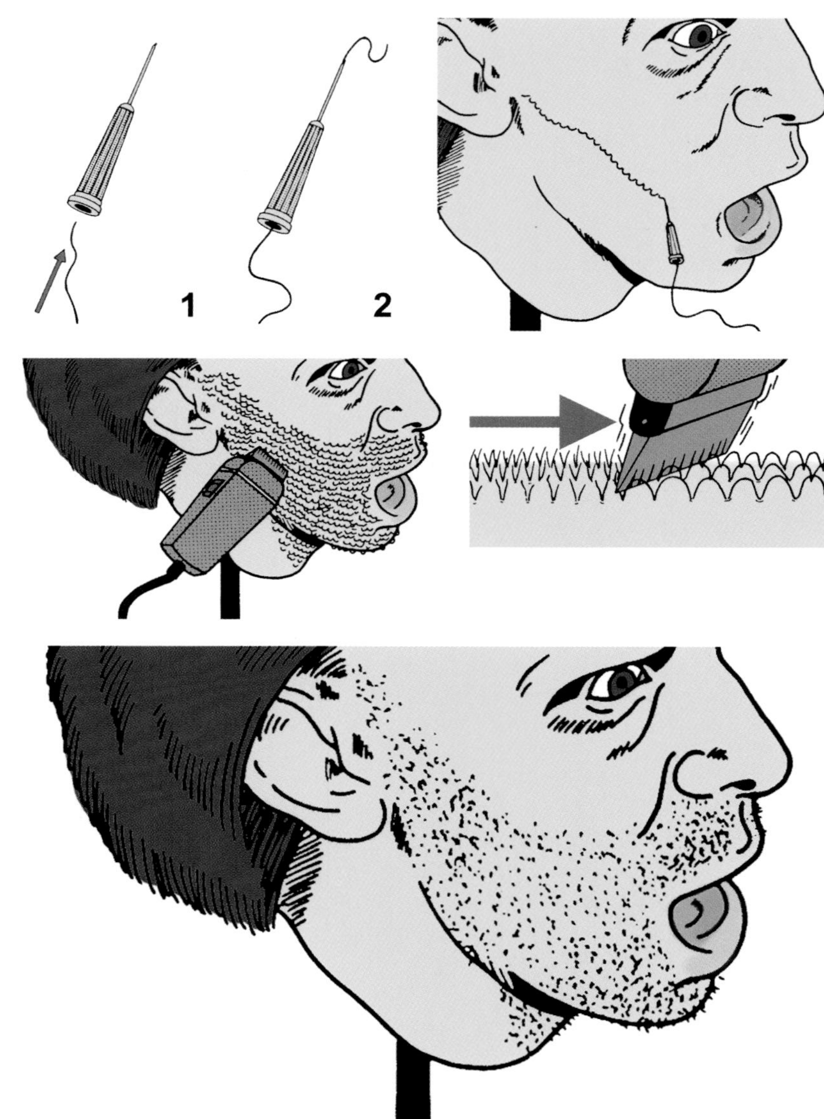

FIGURE 8.45
Punching stubble into dummy head.
Images reproduced by permission of Tom Savini.

This might not be the best way to do beard stubble, but if it doesn't have to read believably in a tight close-up, it will be fine. This technique should also read well in almost every theater environment, from intimate to substantial.

In his outstanding "how-to" book *Grand Illusions II*, Tom Savini talks about threading a hypodermic needle with a long strand of hair and punching it in loops into the face or facial part of an appliance, until the entire area of beard growth is punched. Then either insert small, sharp scissors into each loop (this could take a while) and cut them individually or take hair clippers or an electric

beard trimmer and shave off the tops of the loops, leaving the face with beard stubble just like the real thing! Brilliant!

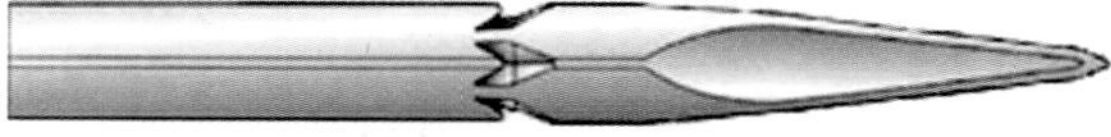

FIGURE 8.46
Crown punching needle cross-section.
Illustration provided by Lars Carlsson.

In addition to the punching needles described above, there is a class of needles used extensively in doll making, called *rooting*, *felting* needles, or *crown* needles. These needles differ from traditional punching needles in that they are multisided with barbs.

When you use a crown needle to punch hair, you don't snag one or two hairs at a time and punch individually; with crown needles, your hand and wrist work like a sewing machine in a rapid up and down motion into a thick weft of hair, moving the location of the needle slightly with each downward motion into your mask or appliance. The barbs on the needle grab hairs and insert them much more quickly than the traditional method. You may not catch a hair with every punch, but because of the rapid motion of your hand and needle, you can populate a surface more quickly.

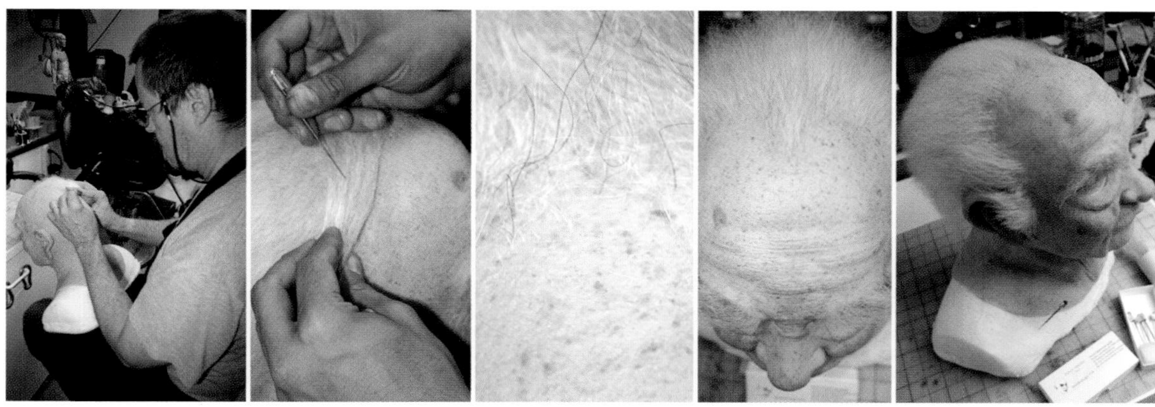

FIGURE 8.47
Full-head silicone mask; crepe wool punched with crown rooting needles.
Mask and photos by author.

Another method that I will discuss in a bit more detail in the next chapter is using an electrostatic flocking device. You can use real hair, not just flocking, and you can use it on a real person, not just masks, dummies, and prosthetics. The drawback is that electrostatic flocking guns (they look nothing like a gun, per se) are rather expensive to purchase and are somewhat difficult to find for rental (see the appendix at the back of this book).

A company in Lawrence, Massachusetts, called National Fiber Technology (NFT), specializes in the manufacture of custom-made hair, wigs, and fur fabrics for the entertainment industry, including TV commercials, theme parks, movies, theater, opera, taxidermists, special effects, costumes, mascots, museums, and ballet. And, though much of what NFT makes and sells could be considered the domain of costumers and wardrobe people, there's definitely an overlap area that spills over into the realm of makeup effects and hair and makeup. NFT is a terrific resource that has saved my bacon more than once. Put them on speed dial.

CHAPTER SUMMARY

From this chapter, you should now have a better understanding of the following:

- The types and varieties of hair
- The tools and materials needed to create postiche
- Wefted wigs and knotted wigs
- Laying on hair
- Ventilating hair
- Punching hair

Endnotes

1 Patsy Baker, *Wigs & Makeup for Theatre, Film, and Television* (Butterworth-Heinemann, 1993).

2 Ibid.

3 Ibid.

4 Ibid.

CHAPTER 9

Animatronics

Key Points

- History
- Design philosophy
- Technology
- Components
- Construction
- Operation
- Application

INTRODUCTION

I'm about as far removed from being a mechanical engineer as you can get. But when I held my first servo and saw how it moved when a joystick on an R/C (radio controlled) transmitter moved back and forth, I totally got it! It makes sense. As a visual learner, I can read about things all day long, but it isn't until I can touch it—see it in my hands—that the light bulb really comes on.

FIGURE 9.1
Gary Willett's My Animatronic Project.
Image reproduced by permission of Gary Willett.

When I decided to add a chapter on animatronics, I realized after many discussions with Chris Clarke that it needed to focus more on "principles of designing" and "techniques of the mind" in approaching *how* to begin the complex journey from conceptualization to a moving, working creature effect, as opposed to trying to tell you every nut, bolt, servo, and Dremel bit to use. He and I agreed that this would be the best use of the paper it's printed on. To quote Chris, "Many roads lead to Rome, but as long as you're on one of them, it doesn't matter which." I hope this section helps train your mind to discover your own road, as self-discovery is the key to great design.[1]

NOTE

As I mentioned in the Preface, in many ways, this is like a cookbook. Inside are "recipes" you can follow or modify and adapt to suit your taste to whip up your own creative masterpiece. Chapter 8 is sorta like that, but not as much of a step-by-step as the other chapters. Same with this chapter. Every recipe will be different, but the essential ingredients will, for the most part, be the same. For example, the steps—the recipe—to make an infant's eyes blink will be very different from the recipe to make a head turn or a tentacle grasp, even though most of the same ingredients—the servos and controller—may be used for each of those actions.

Therefore, this chapter is a primer; a list of animatronics ingredients, not recipes. You'll make up your own recipes. While I hope the information presented is informative regarding the design and construction of an animatronic puppet, there's no actual step-by-step process. There are numerous images, diagrams, and descriptions that should go a long way toward helping you understand the process well enough to take a crack at it yourself. If you really want to explore further on your own beyond what is presented here, I suggest the DVDs *Movie Animatronics Vols. 1 and 2* by Daniel E Tirinnanzi, *My Animatronic Project* by Gary Willett, and the books *Affordable Animatronics Vols. 1 and 2* by Harry Lapping, Robert Van Deest, and Jim Litchko or even Dick Smith's *Advanced Professional Makeup Course.*

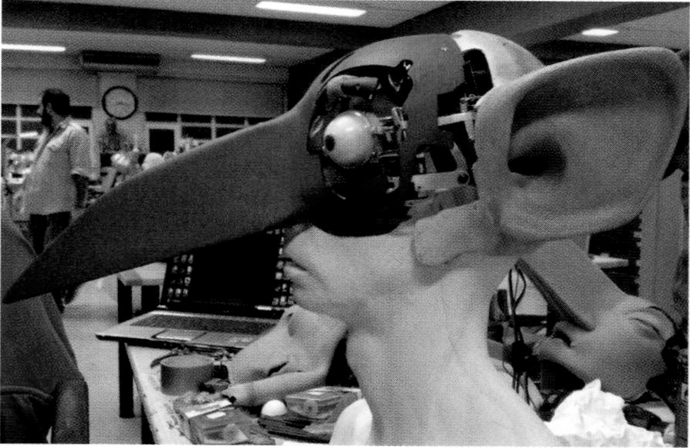
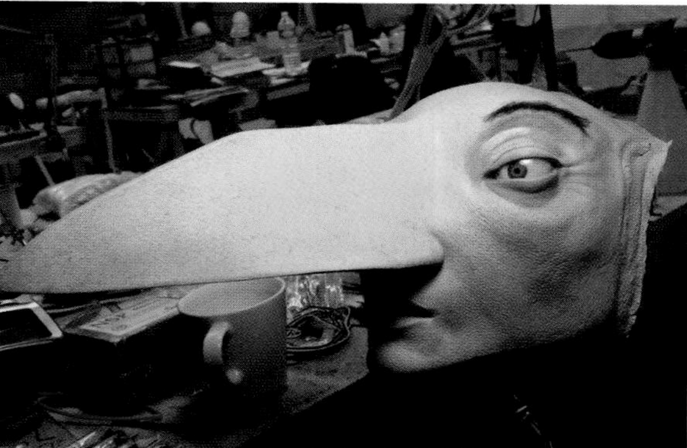

FIGURE 9.2
Animatronic mechanism; *Gainsbourg: A Heroic Life.*
Image reproduced by permission of Chris Clarke.

I'd be amazed to learn of anyone reading this book who has not at least heard of animatronics to some degree.

These animated, electronic mechanical puppets can be programmed via computer to move in a predetermined way, or can be remotely controlled by a radio controller (or controllers), or by manually controlled devices to provide real-time animation. The actuation of specific puppet movements can be manipulated with electric motors, pneumatic cylinders, hydraulic cylinders, and/or cable-driven mechanisms. The type of mechanism employed is usually mandated by the character parameters—size, agility; specific movement requirements—speed, range of motion; and the project constraints—time, budget.

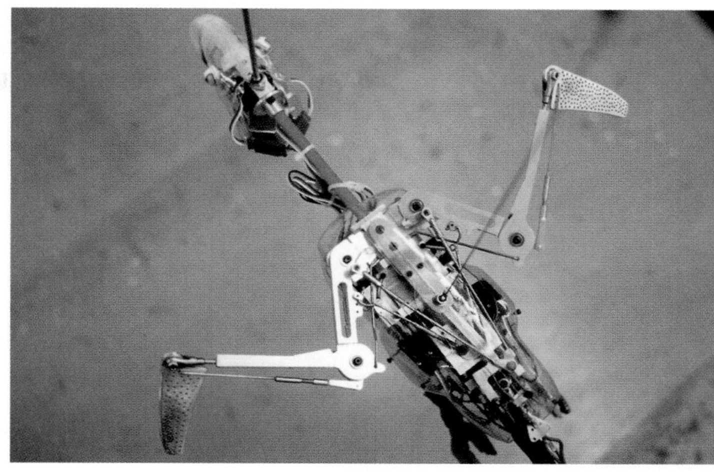

FIGURE 9.3 Disney's *102 Dalmatians* flying parrot mech. *Image reproduced by permission of Chris Clarke.*

Animatronics began to gain broad public appeal largely as a result of *The Enchanted Tiki Room*, which opened at Disneyland in 1963. *Audio-Animatronics*, to be concise. Audio-Animatronics is the registered trademark of Walt Disney Imagineering and works off of prerecorded moves and sounds. At some point in the past, the word "audio" was dropped, and the term "animatronics" became a generic name for similar mechanical devices created by other companies over the years and has come to define a category of special effects. So why is there a chapter about animatronics in a book about creating special makeup effects? I refer you to back to Chapter 1: *Within the industry, there is some confusion about boundaries; when do special makeup effects stop being makeup, per se, and become special effects* (*which includes puppetry and animatronics*) *or the domain of prop designers? Is a severed head made from a lifecast of the lead actor's head and whose eyes blink and neck bleeds a makeup effect, special effect, or a prop?* The correct answer is "yes."

Animatronics have come to be widely used in film and television productions and are primarily used to perform actions on camera for one of the following reasons: The action involves a creature that does not exist; the action is too dangerous or expensive to use real humans or animals; or the action could never happen with a living person or animal.

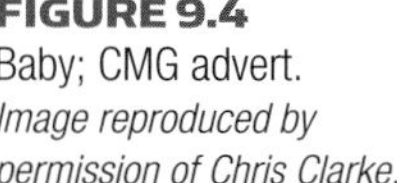

FIGURE 9.4 Baby; CMG advert. *Image reproduced by permission of Chris Clarke.*

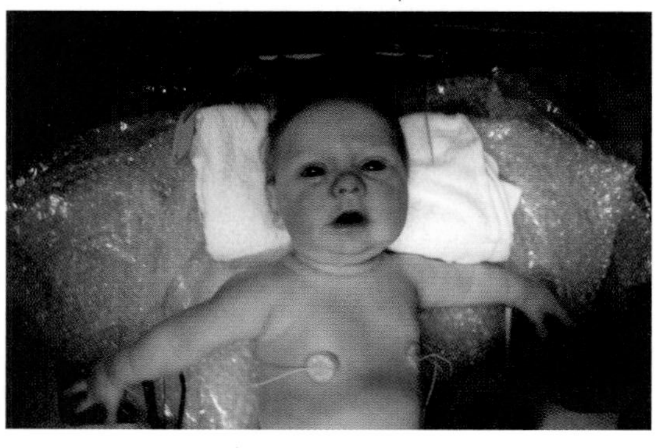

However, film quality animatronics can come at a pretty high price, beyond the budget of many. "So, Todd," you're probably wondering, "Why not just use CGI instead of animatronics? Wouldn't it be cheaper? That's a valid question, and it is the subject of much heated debate in the industry and has drawn some battle lines between many VFX artists, MUFX artists, and SFX artists. First, both can be quite costly (when done right), and I believe anything worth doing is worth doing well and doing right. Cost is a relative thing also, but—and you may find this somewhat surprising—animatronics are substantially *less* expensive than CGI. You read that correctly. Second, ask an actor which he or she'd prefer to act with and react to: A life-size Velociraptor puppet or a tennis ball on the end of a C-stand? Real is real.

CHRISTOPHER CLARKE

Chris was raised in the northwest of England and spent much of his youth trying to replicate special effects he'd seen. By washing cars on weekends—*many* cars—Chris earned enough to buy an AGFA MovieZoom10 8-mm film camera he'd seen in a secondhand photo shop and then spent all his time in the garage shooting models, miniatures, in-camera composites, and animating figures. In his school metalwork class, Chris figured out the gearing, so he could splice together two Bell and Howell projectors he'd bought and turn them into a working optical printer.

A self-taught metalworker and mechanical engineer, Chris wisely decided to turn his hobby into a career and worked on building sets before becoming the head of metalwork/engineering for Tussauds Art Workshops. After the refit of Tussaud's *Chamber of Horrors*, Chris moved over to ARTEM Visual Effects and has lived in London ever since. His first Head of Department gig was on *Resident Evil*. Some 40 films and countless television and advertising jobs later, Chris still loves what he does, and it shows in the level of his work. He's had the good fortune to work for the likes of DDT, Jim Henson's Creature Shop, Neil Scanlan Studios, Animated Extras, CFX, CNFX, EffektStudion, alongside ADI on AVP, Millennium Effects, and Neil Corbould SFX. His credits include *War Horse*, *Doctor Who*, *The Brothers Grimm*, *Sahara, Resident Evil* and *Harry Potter, and* the *Prizoner of Azkaban*.

FIGURE 9.5
Chris Clarke working on walrus mech.
Image reproduced by permission of Chris Clarke.

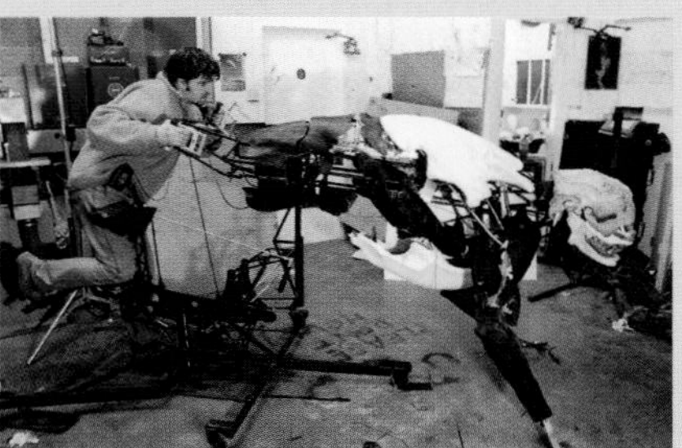

FIGURE 9.6
Chris operating *Resident Evil* Licker mech.
Image reproduced by permission of Chris Clarke.

Before I get into the technology of animatronics, here's a brief discourse about what a robot is and what is an animatronic. First of all, the word "robot" was coined by Czech writer Karel čapek in his play *R.U.R.* (*Rossum's Universal Robots*), published in 1920.[2] A robot is a mechanical device that can perform tasks on

its own, or with guidance. An animatronic is a mechanical device that can perform tasks on its own or with guidance. What is the difference? Is there one? Does it really matter? For the purposes of this book, there really isn't a significant difference at the core of how robots or animatronics actually work; they can be preprogrammed or have guided operation in real time. But, I've never heard anyone refer to an industrial robot in a manufacturing environment as an "animatronic." So, let's call mechanical devices that are used for creating character performances "animatronics" or even puppets and call those mechanical devices used to replace human effort (though they may not resemble real people in any way) "robots."

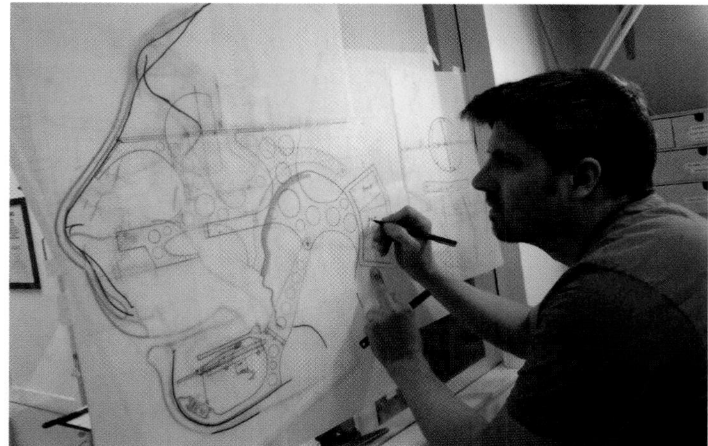

FIGURE 9.7
Chris designing workings of lion mech for ING advert.
Image reproduced by permission of Chris Clarke.

Chris Clarke shared some of his design philosophy with me: "The first thing to remember is, there's no real textbook way of doing any of this. If it works, it works. Don't be too guided and restricted by what's gone before. My rule is, always work from the skin backwards! Never work from the servo forwards. With the premise for the project firmly in mind, look at the skin or sculpt and morph it in your mind and see the expressions forming (squinting when you look helps.) A face, or whatever it is, should not just move with the prerequisite actions that are listed in "what happens when you smile/frown/look a bit angry." It should move as a whole. It amazes me that although when you look happy, every single muscle in your face moves—with the exception of the forehead—yet I've seen guys accredit this monumental and extreme show of personal joy and inner harmony to just a paddle pulling the mouth corners out! So, study faces, anatomy, how people move, but be careful not to stare, as that can get you into trouble on the train to work!"

NOTE

A paddle is a small piece of the underskeleton, such as an eyebrow, that is attached to the skin and is controlled by a dedicated servo that subtly moves certain parts of the puppet like an eyebrow or a mouth corner and is somewhat paddle shaped, hence its name.

Chris goes on, saying, "So, with this desired end result firmly in your mind, the next rule is 'never lose sight of it!' It's so easy to do this during the translation into a mechanism, and you end up with something that moves like a, well, mechanism. I try never to have a pivot point within the paddle area unless it's

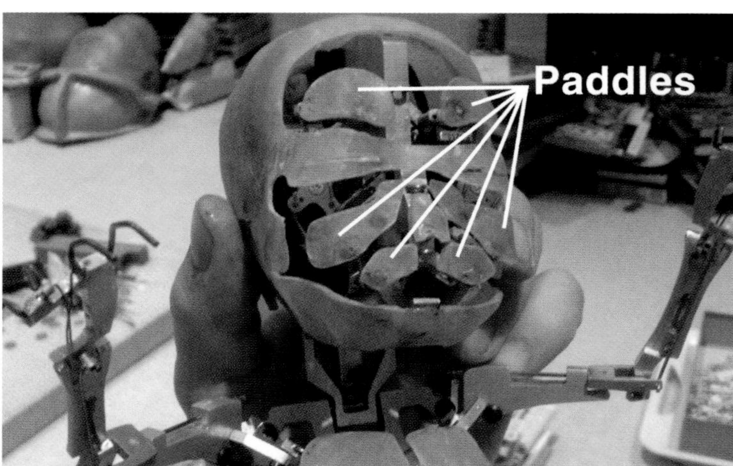

FIGURE 9.8
Infant mech showing paddles of underskeleton.
Image reproduced by permission of Chris Clarke.

a floating one that is itself connected to still another pivot, otherwise you end up with a dead area and nothing gives the illusion away like a dead spot. Go into every job with 'organic' as your keyword and you won't go wrong.

I try always to mechanize a creature to move generically the way that creature moves, so the mechanism itself moves in the manner of that creature. For example, take the way a human arm works; you'd instinctively put a pivot straight out sideways from the shoulder and hang an arm from it, but this would be wrong! When you walk and look down, you'll notice your arms swing in front of you at about a 20°–25° angle, not parallel to each other. The reason for this is that an arm's primary function is to put food in your mouth, and if you curl your arm forward, you'll find it takes your hand to your face, not to your ear. All movements can be accredited to evolutionary common sense; find that reason and then work out your pivot centers and axis to accommodate it."

TIP
Always work from the skin backwards, not from the servo forward. Design from the outside inward.[3]

FIGURE 9.9
Infant mech showing paddles of underskeleton.
Images reproduced by permission of Chris Clarke.

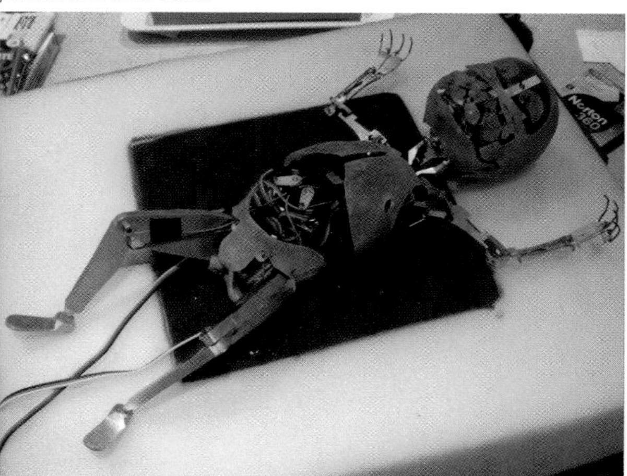

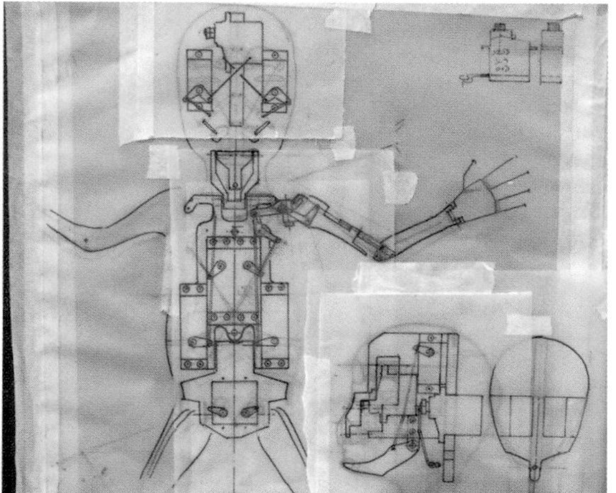

TECHNOLOGY

The technology used in creating animatronics, like most technology, continues to change and evolve to keep up with the trends and needs of the industry. Parts and mechanisms are getting stronger and smaller; advances in medical prosthetic technology are propelling advances in entertainment animatronics, and this shrinking technology is creating the ability to fit more parts into the same amount of space—actuators (motors) for individual fingers in a hand, for example, or a mouth with the ability for the lips to purse when the mouth pronounces a "B," "P," or "W" sound. (*Note*: An actuator is a mechanical device for moving or controlling a puppet mechanism or system.)

There are four areas of concentration we'll look at for animatronics:

- Mechanical
- Electronic
- Structural
- Surface

Mechanical

It includes everything from basic gears to sophisticated hydraulics as well as pneumatics. Even Legos and K'nex!

SERVOS

A servo—by most accounts the workhorse device of animatronics—is an electromechanical motor/device with an output shaft that can be positioned remotely into specific angular positions by sending the servo a coded signal. As that signal changes, the angular position of the shaft changes. For example, servos are used in radio-controlled aircraft to position control surfaces like flaps, ailerons, elevators, and rudders. They are also used in puppets to cause mouths to open and close, eyes to blink, look up, down and side-to-side, and to make heads turn. The motors can be very small, have built-in circuitry, and are very powerful for their size. A pretty basic servo such as this one of mine, a Futaba S3003 has 44 inches/ounces of torque, which is pretty powerful for its size. It also draws power proportional to the mechanical load. A lightly loaded servo, therefore, doesn't consume much energy. Each of the servos used for animatronics contains:

- A direct current (DC) electric motor
- Gears with an output shaft
- A position-sensing mechanism
- Control circuitry, and
- Horn or arm that attaches to the spline (output shaft)

FIGURE 9.10
Small MKS servo.
Photo by author.

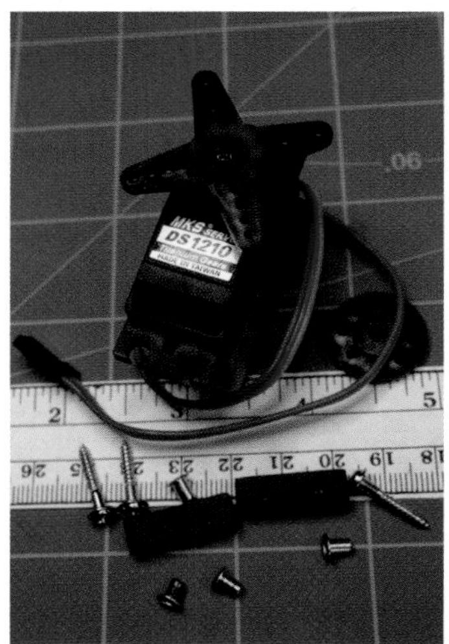

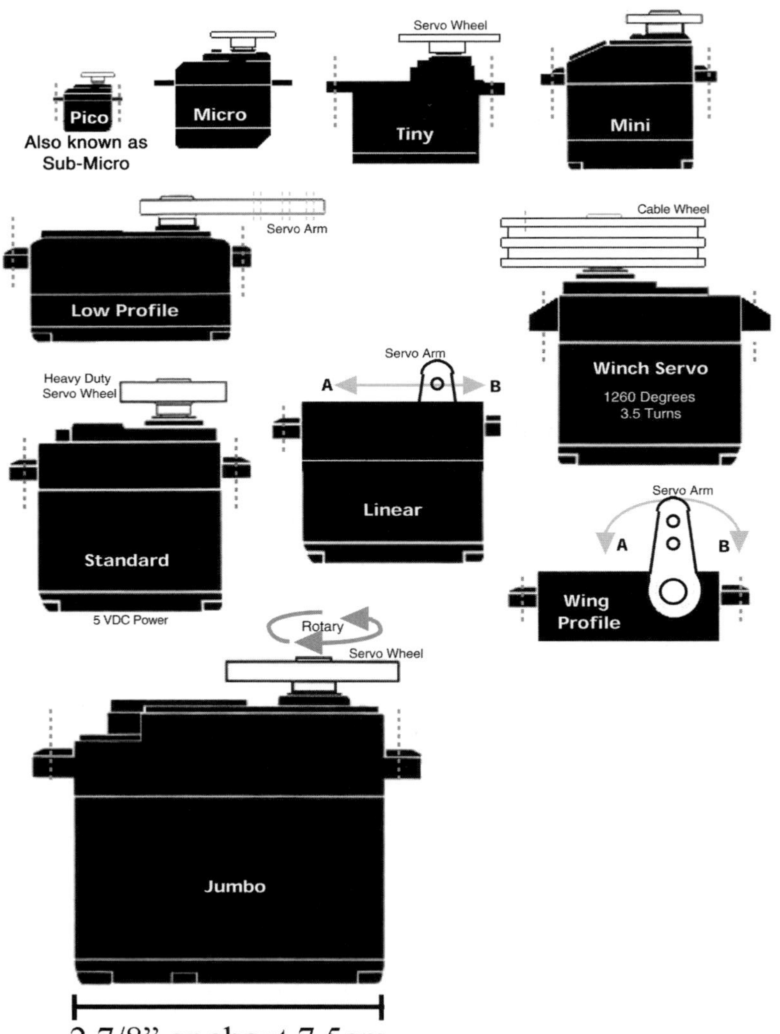

FIGURE 9.11
Different servos.
Illustration reproduced by permission of Robert Van Deest and Harry Lapping.

How does a servo work? ALL servos have a three-wire connector—one (RED) carrying positive DC voltage, usually 5 to 6 V; one (BLACK or BROWN) for the voltage ground (return path for the DC), and the third (YELLOW, ORANGE, or WHITE) carrying the signal from and to the transmitter. The transmitter talks to the servo through the signal wire by means of simple, brief on/off electrical pulses, known as PWM or pulse width modulation. The width of the pulse (duration) determines the movement of the servo.

The servo motor has control circuits and a potentiometer (if you have a stereo system at home and the volume knob is one you rotate to increase or decrease the volume, *which* is a potentiometer)—also known simply as a *pot*, that is connected to the

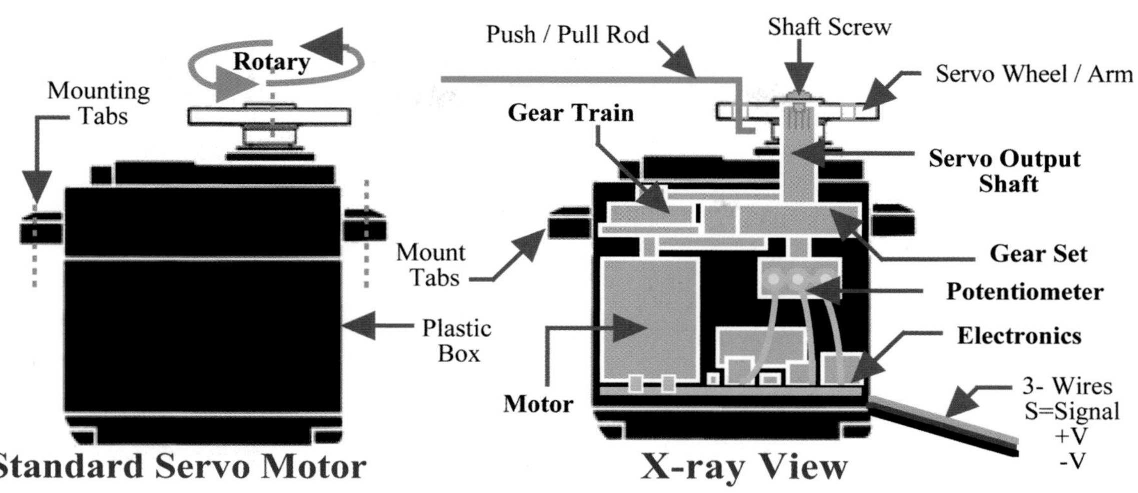

FIGURE 9.12
Servo workings.
Illustration reproduced by permission of Robert Van Deest and Harry Lapping.

output shaft, also known as the *spline*. The pot allows the servo's control circuitry to tell what the current angle (position) of the servo motor is. If the shaft is at the correct angle, then the motor will stop; if the angle is not correct, the motor will continue to turn the shaft in the right direction until the correct angle is reached.

The shaft output of each servo is capable of traveling somewhere in the neighborhood of 180° (though probably it's closer to 210°). It really depends on the manufacturer. Anyway, a normal servo controls angular motion between 0° and 180°. There is a mechanical stop built into the servo's main output gear that prevents turning any further. The amount of juice applied to the servo motor is proportional to the distance it needs to travel, that is, the number of degrees the shaft needs to turn. So, if the shaft needs to rotate fully, the motor will run at full speed; if it only needs to rotate partially, the motor will run at a slower speed. This is what's known as proportional control. How great or small the angle of rotation of the servo is determined by the duration of the electric pulse (PWM signal). Servos are manufactured to expect a pulse every 0.02 seconds (20 milliseconds), and the length of that pulse will determine how far the motor turns the shaft. For example, a 1.5-millisecond pulse will make the servo rotate the shaft from 0° to 90° (this is called *neutral*). A shorter pulse will result in a turn closer to 0°, and a pulse longer than 1.5 milliseconds will turn the shaft closer to 180°. Is this making any sense yet? Take a look at this drawing:

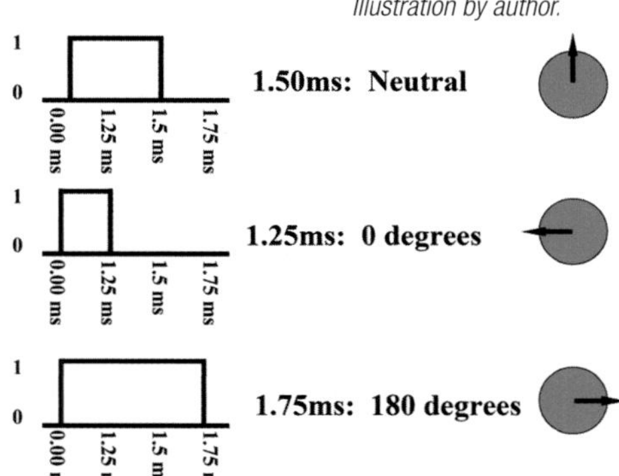

FIGURE 9.13
Pulse code graphic.
Illustration by author.

Put a little simpler perhaps, the controlling intelligence of the servo, in this case the puppeteer—or you—indicates to the servo (via the radio transmitter) the position that the output shaft *should have*. The position-sensing mechanism in the servo tells the servo what position the shaft *currently is in*. The control circuitry of the servo recognizes the difference between the *desired* position and the *current* position and engages the servo's electric motor to make the correction. If the difference in position is large, the motor moves rapidly to the correct position; if the difference is small, the adjustment is more subtle. As for the puppeteer, all he knows is that he moved a joystick, and the mouth of his puppet opened and will stay open until he moves the joystick again.

Most servos need a power supply between 4.8 volts and 6.0 volts; the higher the voltage, the faster the servo will move and the more torque it will have. For those of you unfamiliar with the term, *torque* refers to the force required to make an object turn around an axis, like loosening or tightening a nut on a bolt. It is that pushing or pulling the handle of a wrench connected to a nut or bolt that produces the torque (turning force) that loosens or tightens the nut or bolt.

Back at the beginning of this section, I said that a Futaba S3003 servo has 44 ounces/inches of torque. I also said that's quite a lot for its size. (That servo will move a load weighing almost 3 pounds.) And you're wondering, "why the heck should I care about this? IT'S MATH! *I HATE MATH*!!" I know, I know. And it's algebra, to boot. And physics! But you've got to know if the servo you just spent $30 on will work repeatedly on the jaw you need to open and close and spent the last 3 days fabricating. I'd want to know.

Now, a servo is a geared system. The DC electric motor in the servo turns gears that rotate the shaft. How do we determine the torque of a given motor in a geared system? Let me back up a little first. Imagine that you have a pulley with a 1-inch radius (that would be a 2-inch diameter) and a wire attached to it holding a 1-ounce weight hanging down off the end of it; it would produce 1 inch/ounce of torque on the pulley shaft (the axis). In physics math lingo, it becomes this: $T = F \times d = 1$ ounce $\times$ 1 inch = 1 inch/ounce, where T is torque, F is force (the force applied perpendicular to the axis, which in this instance is weight), and d is distance. Does your head hurt? Mine does.

FIGURE 9.14
Torque drawing 1.
Illustration by author.

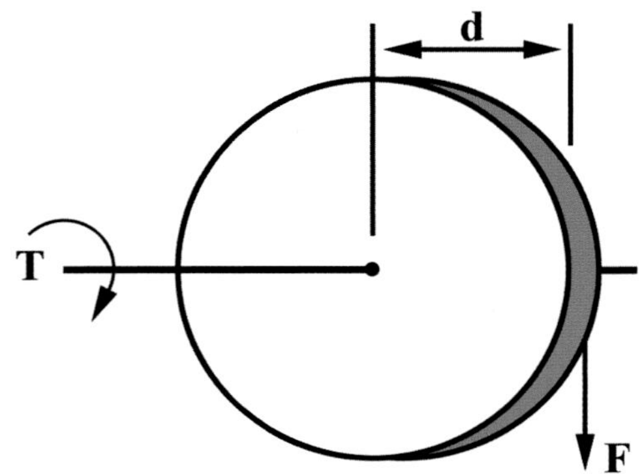

FIGURE 9.15
Torque drawing 2.
Illustration by author.

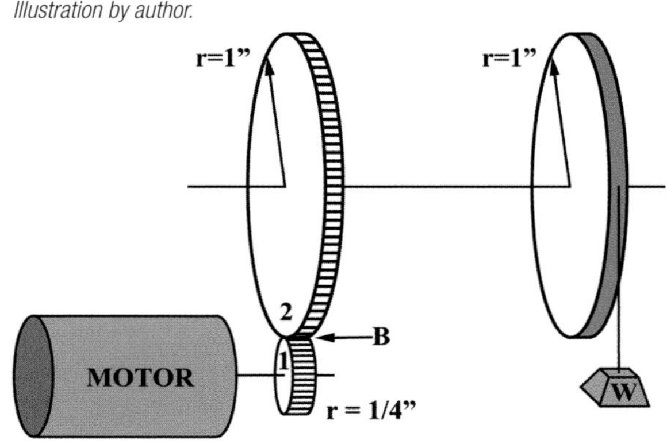

So, to figure out the torque of a motor in a geared system like a servo, we've still got our formula T = F × d = 1 ounce × 1 inch = 1 ounce/inch.

Look at the last drawing. The amount of torque remains constant along the shaft, so at the big gear (gear #2), there is still 1 ounce/inch of torque trying to turn it. What is the force at point B where the two gears meet? Well, we can use a second version of our torque equation: F = T ÷ d = (1 ounce/inch) ÷ (1 inch) = 1 ounce, where F, T, and d are still the same.

Since the gear teeth meet at point B, the force at point B where they meet is pushing on the smaller gear (#1) with that same 1 ounce force. Since we'll ignore friction between the gears (that's getting into physics, and if I went there you'd probably just toss this book in the rubbish and go see if McDonald's is hiring), the force remains constant across the contact surface where the gears are touching.

Okay. The torque on the motor shaft is T = F × d = (1 ounce) × (¼ inch) = ¼ ounce/inch. (The radius of the small gear is ¼ inch, remember? Its in the drawing.) So there is ¼ ounce/inch of torque trying to twist the motor, so the motor must be twisting with ¼ ounce/inch of torque to oppose it. If we look this from the servo's point of view, its torque of ¼ ounce/inch is magnified to 1 ounce/inch at the pulley. Sa-weet! (*Note:* ¼ ounce/inch or even 1 ounce/inch of torque is a very, very small amount. Even most submicro servos are rated with at least 11 ounces/inches of torque).

FIGURE 9.16
Mech head from *Planet of the Dead* episode of *Doctor Who*; Millennium Studios, 2009.
Photo by author.

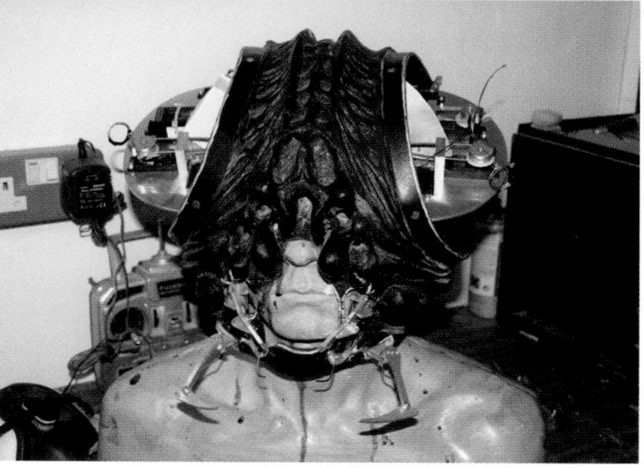

Now its unlikely that you'll EVER actually need to use this information because the amount of inch/ounce torque is written right on the boxes the servos come in, but you won't be able to say I didn't at least give you the information. And if you ever do need it, it's here and you won't have to waste time to Google it. There are supplier listings for servos and all sorts of animatronic goodies in the appendix on the companion website.

Math and physics aside, how do you know what 44 ounces/inches of torque means? Imagine a servo arm 1 inch long; that arm attached to your servo would be able to produce 44 ounces of push or pull at the end of the servo arm before stalling or 2.75 pounds of force (16 ounces = 1 pound). An arm ½inch long would produce twice that amount of force; an arm 2 inches long would produce half that force, and so on. Does it make more sense yet?

ADDITIONAL TERMINOLOGY

Coreless motor—This refers to the armature of the motor, that is, the power-producing component of the motor. A conventional servo motor has a steel core armature wrapped with wire that spins inside the magnets. In a coreless design, the armature uses a thin wire mesh that forms a cup that spins around the outside of the magnets, thereby eliminating the heavy steel core. This design results in smoother operation and faster response time.

Indirect drive—This refers to the potentiometer inside the servo. The final output shaft (the part that the horn/arm attaches to) has to be supported not only near the end of the shaft but also deep inside the servo case. Indirect drive is when the final output shaft is not dependent on the potentiometer for support inside the gear box. Normally, a bushing or bearing supports the load. Direct drive is when the potentiometer plays a supporting role in holding the output shaft in place. Most submicro servos are direct drive since they are limited on space and don't have room for an extra bushing or bearing.

FIGURE 9.17
Sixty degrees of rotation and amount of torque. *Illustration reproduced by permission of Robert Van Deest and Harry Lapping.*

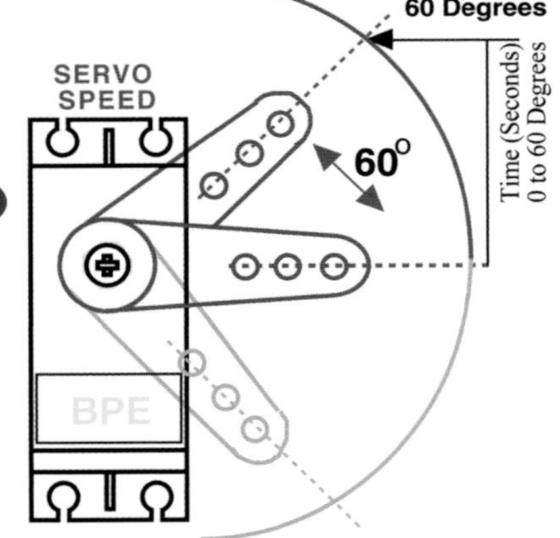

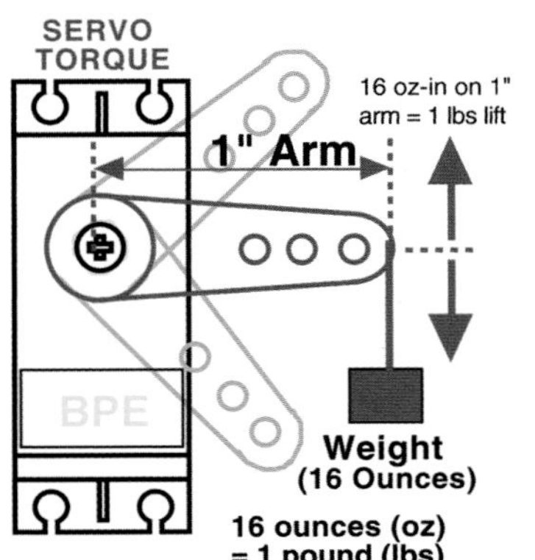

Spline—This is the output shaft of the servo. The shaft (spline) is what you attach the servo horns or arms to. Standard Hitec servo splines have 24 teeth; standard Futaba servo splines have 25 teeth.

Transit time—This is the amount of time it takes for the servo to move a set amount, usually rated at 60°. Example: A servo with at transit time of .19 seconds to 60° would mean that is takes the servo nearly one-third of a second to rotate 60°.

Torque—This is the maximum power, or force, the servo can produce. It is normally rated in ounces/inches. This means that the servo can move this set amount with a 1″ arm attached to the output shaft or spline. Example: A servo with a torque rating of 130 ounces/inches can move that amount with a 1-inch arm or slightly over 8 pounds. To convert ounces/inches to pounds of force, divide this rating by 16 (because there are 16 ounces in a pound). Example: 130/16 = 8.125 (which is in pounds).

Three- or five-psole Motors—This refers to the commutator in the motor. (A commutator is a rotary electrical switch that periodically reverses the current between the rotor and the external circuit.) The commutator is where the brushes make contact with the armature. The more motor poles, the smoother and more accurate the servo will operate. Most servos have either three- or five-pole commutators.

Nylon gears—Nylon gears are most common in servos. They are extremely smooth with little or no wear factors. They are also very lightweight. If your application calls for long duration but not jarring motion, nylon gears are a top choice.

Karbonite gears—Karbonite gears are relatively new to the market. They offer almost five times the strength of nylon gears and also better wear resistance. Cycle times of well over 300,000 have been observed with these gears with virtually no wear. Servos with these gears are more expensive but what you get in durability is more than equaled.

Metal gears—Metal gears have been around quite a while, and they offer unparalleled strength. In applications that are jarred around, metal gears really shine. There are two cons to metal gears, weight, and wear. First, metal gears are much heavier than both nylon and karbonite gears. Second, metal gears wear several times that of nylon gears. How quickly depends on the loads that you place on the servo. They will eventually develop a slight play or slop in the gear train that will be transferred to the spline. It will not be much, but accuracy will be lost at some point.

Monster servo—an ultra-high-torque servo with up to 1,600 ounces/inches of torque (there are 16 ounces in 1 pound, if you get the picture; these puppies are strong!).

Submicro servo—As you might guess, very small, in the neighborhood of 3 grams. These servos are great for tiny actuators in animatronic mechanisms that need to be quick and very light, but they are not very powerful, at only about 5 ounces/inches of torque. A submicro servo can easily sit within the diameter of a US quarter.

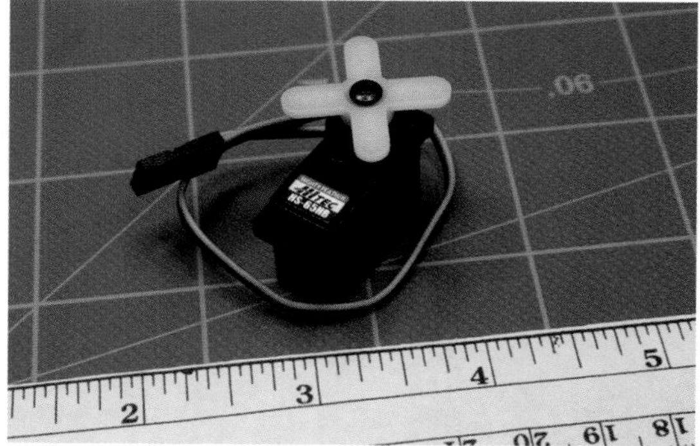

FIGURE 9.18
HiTec submicro servo.
Photo by the author.

Servo motors can be used for a number of motion functions, including rotary, vertical, horizontal, push, or pull. Servos can be either analog or digital too. What's the difference between an analog servo and a digital one? Well, at the user end—*our* end—they're controlled the same way. The way they differ is in how the servo is controlled by it circuitry: The motor of an analog servo receives a signal from the circuit board (amplifier) 30 times a second or at 30 Hz. This signal allows the circuit board to update the motor position. Digital servos use a higher-frequency amplifier that can update the motor position faster—receiving a signal 300 times a second (300 Hz) versus 30 times a second. Ten times faster. By updating the motor position more frequently, the servo can deliver its full torque capability from the very first movement and also increase the holding power of the servo. There are really only two downsides to choosing digital servos over analog ones: cost and power. Digital servos are more expensive and require higher starting currents, so make sure your batteries can handle the load. Digital servos can also be programmed for direction of rotation, starting points, center points, and end points. This can be useful when you need two servos moving in opposition to one another on the same channel (the servos are attached to a Y harness). I'll explain this in more detail later on.

FIGURE 9.19
Neill Gorton contemplates work still to be completed on mech head that shoots two days hence; *Planet of the Dead* episode; Doctor Who, 2009. *Photo by author.*

MOTION CONTROL

Being able to run your servo, being able to make the shaft turn, doesn't really do you any good unless it is attached to something you want it to move. Say you want the ears on an animatronic dog's head to move. You can't just attach the shaft of the servo to the ear and expect very good results or any results at all. To control the motion, you will need cables, push/pull rods, ball and socket joints, clevis joints, pulleys, wheels, cable guides and supports, mechanical linkages, and so on. Not all of these things at once, but some of them; it depends on the motion you want to control. Oh man, the fun is just getting started! I'll get into this in the design section, but in order to know what type of control to create, you have to decide what you want the movement to be and then work backward to design the mechanism. Getting back to the dog's ear, we could do several things. Most dogs' ears relax and flop a bit, but when they're alerted to something, they perk up quickly and turn toward a sound to locate it. That's simplistic, but how would we accomplish those two separate movements? Two ears standing at attention and turning? How many servos do you think it would take? I'm going to just let that question simmer for a while and you can think about it.

When an animal of any kind moves, be it a mammal, reptile, bird, or fish, there are a great many subtle, extra movements that happen along with the obvious ones. The jaw muscles (temporalis), for example, attach along the jaw bone, run up beneath the cheek bone, and fan out and attach to the side of the skull, so when you chew and even when you talk, there's a pulse in your temple area. Its not an obvious motion, so most wouldn't bother with it, but its within a group of actions Chris Clarke calls, "Things You Don't Notice Unless They're Not There." Your subconscious notices when things don't quite look right. Expending just a little more time and effort to cover just a few of those simple additions can really elevate an animatronic to a whole different level of believability. Chris had muscle paddles dotted all over the Joey puppet (Chris would call Joey a mechanism) from *War Horse* and the life it added to the face made the extra few days work well worth it. If you've seen the film, you know what I mean; you can't tell the difference between the shots of real Joey and mechanism Joey. The movements are flawless. Chris watched many horse clips on YouTube and took copious notes when they visited the stables for the movies horses, and the two things he noticed were (1) the group of muscles at the mouth corners went absolutely crazy when the horses chewed (and they chewed all the time) and (2) the muscles on the bridge of the nose behind the nostrils flexed whenever the horse smelled anything (which they do all the time). So, he incorporated paddle groups for all of those muscles and programmed them on the sticks for jaw, jaw skew, as well as the outer nostril controls. It was well worth the effort.

The next of the four main categories of animatronics development is as described in the following sections.

FIGURE 9.20
Joey mech; *War Horse*. *Image reproduced by permission of Chris Clarke.*

Electronic

The electrical control system needed to operate the animatronic puppet. We're building remote-controlled toys, essentially. All of the servos in your puppet will be manipulated by some sort of remote control transmitter, also known as a telemetry device. Really large, complicated puppets may require multiple devices to accommodate the number of channels needed to run many servos and so on. The juice to run your RC controller (transmitter) and the receiver and the servos will be provided by batteries (most likely).

These controllers can be radio controlled—wireless; they can be hardwire controllers or stand-alone controllers—circuit boards that are preprogrammed to control a repetitive motion, such as a waving zombie hand in your annual Halloween yard display. Only the radio controllers and hardwire controllers can be either preprogrammed to run independently or manually controlled by an operator. There can even be light, sound, and motion sensors that will trigger control movements.

In order for the servos to be controlled, there needs to be a transmitter that sends the signal to the servo and a receiver to get the signal from the transmitter and relay it to the servo. But because these are radio signals, they are controlled (in the United States) by the Federal Communications Commission (FCC) under strict guidelines. However, the FCC ceased requiring a license for operating R/C transmitters in 1983. Transmitters like my Futaba 6EX–2.4-GHz transmitter is part of a six-channel FASST radio control system. What's that mean? Other 2.4-GHz systems hold firm to one or two frequencies, increasing the potential for interference—which is why using other transmitters designed for controlling RC aircraft cannot effectively be used for animatronics. The frequency of Futaba-2.4-GHz FASST (Futaba Advanced Spread Spectrum Technology) shifts hundreds of times per second, so there are no signal conflicts or interruptions.

This will also keep the FCC at bay because other RC transmitters are designed for either surface devices or aircraft; because of the constant shifting of frequencies of the Futaba 2.4-GHz system that distinction is nullified. I don't want to make this a commercial for Futaba, although they are one of only a handful of servo makers; there are other RC transmitters available that also have shifting frequencies or spread spectrum technology. Spektrum also makes 2.4-GHz transmitters that offer spread spectrum technology.

Any time you're working with electronics and mechanical devices, there is the potential for mishap. Granted, it is less likely to pose an extreme threat as working with hydraulics, for example, but it is never wrong to err on the side of caution. You should all be familiar with Murphy's Law: *If something can go wrong, it will*. One of my mottos is *Safety First, Last, and Always*. Always understand the elements you will be working with and the environment where you will be working with them.

DMX CONTROLLERS

Developed initially as a standard for digital control of stage lighting and effects, DMX (for **D**igital **M**ultiple**X**) control has become the primary method for linking not only lighting controllers and lighting dimmer packs but also more advance lighting fixtures and special effects devices such as fog machines and moving lights.[4] That includes animatronics. However, because of the nature of DMX control—it has no error detection or correction—it should *never* be used to control dangerous devices such as pyrotechnics. But you can control just about anything else. The current state of DMX is DMX512, meaning it is capable of controlling 512 channels, far more than most animatronics will need, although you can combine daisy chain DMX controllers together to form even more channels.

NOTE

DMX should NEVER be used to control dangerous devices such as pyrotechnics. It's a good way to possibly meet your maker or to accidentally help someone else meet theirs.

The way DMX works is this: each of the 512 channels has an ID—1 through 512, and each ID is capable of attaining a value between 0 and 255, where (for us) 0 is OFF and 255 is ON FULL and the other numbers relate to a value somewhere in between, although the operator (puppeteer) will see a slider on a controller, and the device being controlled will interpret the values based on its function.

DMX only conveys control information, not power.

Clearly, DMX would be overkill to control a rat that needed to have wiggly whiskers and nose, a moving tail, and a slight head turn. But for larger, more complicated puppets, including whole environments, DMX could be a godsend.

In addition to DMX and RC transmitters, there are numerous programmable controller boards and computer-based controllers—stand-alone controllers. One of the leading manufacturers of programmable controller boards is

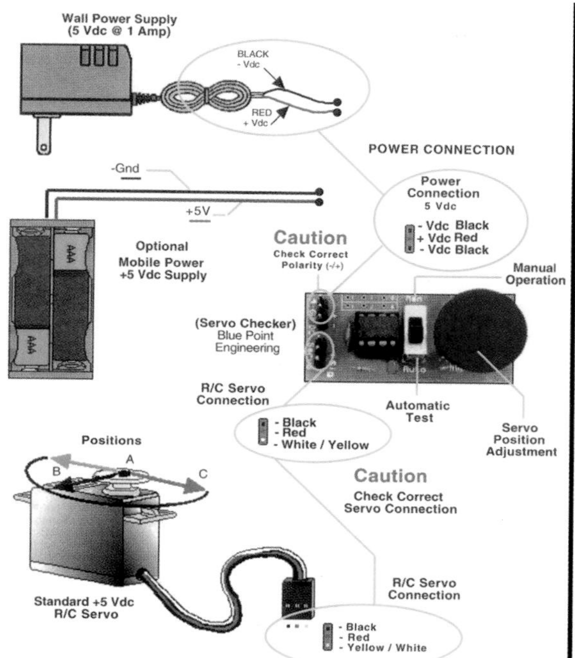

Servo Checker

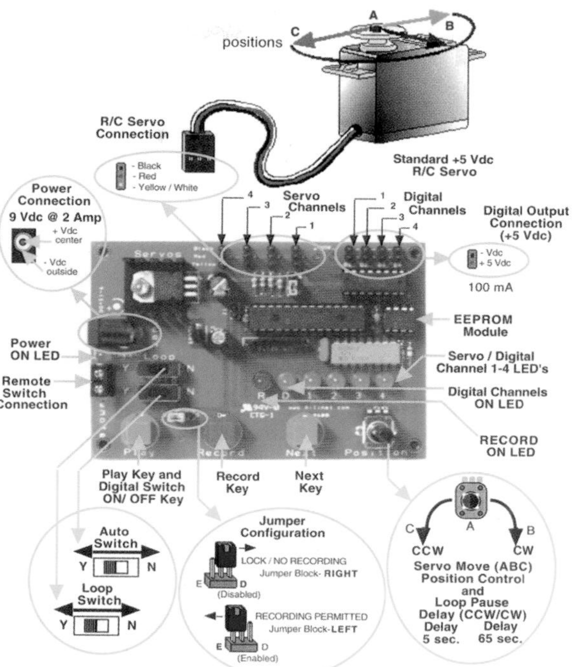

Wizard Board

FIGURE 9.21 Blue Point Engineering Servo Checker (L); Wizard Board (R). *Images reproduced by permission of Robert Van Deest and Harry Lapping.*

in Colorado—Blue Point Engineering—supplying professional imagineers and designers in animatronics, robotics, haunted amusement attractions, technology applications, and electronic media arts.

A programmable controller board is really a sophisticated circuit board designed—in this instance—for animatronics control. These Wizard Boards—as they're called by my pals Robert Van Deest and Harry Lapping of Blue Point Engineering in Longmont, Colorado (though Harry lives back East)—are produced in a number of different configurations and have the capability of controlling multiple channels of servo, motor motion, digital outputs, LED, and sound control features. These controller boards are lower powered (7–12 volts DC), self-contained boards that can be easily programmed by the end user (you or me) without the need for a computer to perform any of the following functions:

- Operating multiple channels of servo motor motion and travel movements;
- Activating DC motors in clockwise and counterclockwise rotation and to emulate servo control;
- Activating mechanical or solid state relays onboard and off-board that can be connected to other external devices for control, such as DC or AC lights, LEDs, special effects devices (like a fog machine), mechanical devices, pumps, pneumatics, solenoids, and so on.
- Digitally recording high-quality audio and playback of that audio via a solid state recording chip.

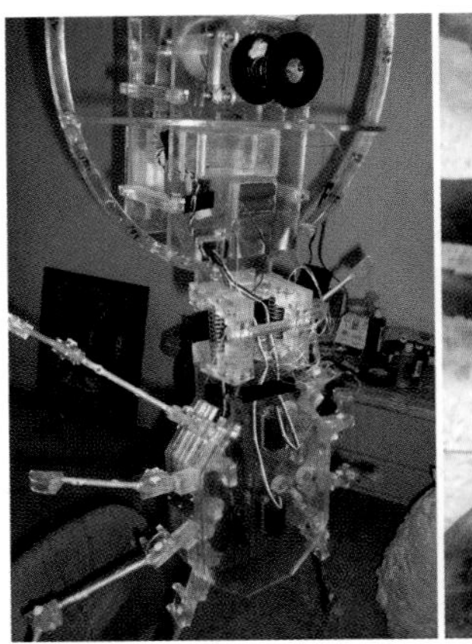
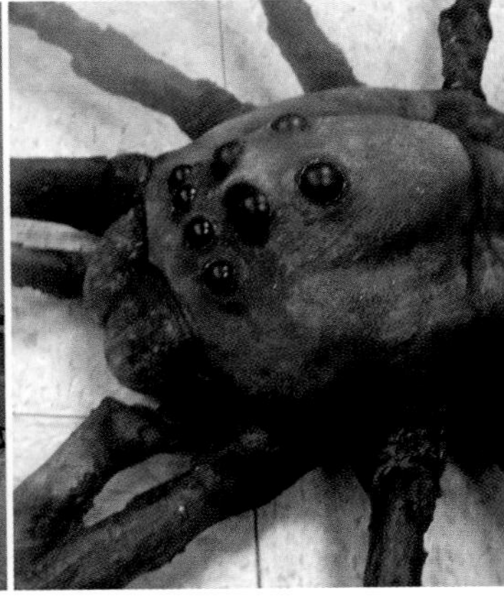

FIGURE 9.22
Student thesis project—giant spider mech.
Images reproduced by permission of Kevon Ward.

Once these boards have been programmed with the above functions, they can be configured to control these devices via remote sensors, trigger devices, or wireless RF signals. The boards can also be set up to run automatically, replaying the programmed routine, or to loop the recorded routine with a user-defined time delay created by an onboard potentiometer. Multiple boards can even be linked together and activated as a single operating system.

Users can program the control routines one channel at a time in real time by means of a set of programming switches, buttons, jumper pins, and potentiometer and LED status lights. The recording sessions are built channel by channel, and during recording, the previously recorded channels are replayed to aid in the synchronization of the channel currently being programmed. The program routine is recorded to an onboard RAM chip called an EEprom. The EEproms can be rerecorded over numerous times or the user can select individual channels to be reprogrammed independently. The chips can be removed, copied to blank EEproms to produce identical programs, or archived.

Other types of programmable controller boards can do the same things as the wizard boards but can be triggered by sound (making it a true audio-animatronic device) or even by proximity sensors (that are not part of the circuit board). Autotalk controller boards, for example, work one of two ways. The programmed functions are in response to a prerecorded audio track or the programmed functions can respond to live audio via a microphone. If the animatronic is a character puppet, the puppeteer's voice will trigger the prerecorded motions of the puppet to engage.

WALDO

The term refers to a Robert Heinlein character in a short story of the same name published in *Astounding* magazine in 1942. Waldo Farthingwaite-Jones was born a weakling, unable even to lift his head up to drink or to hold a spoon. Far from destroying him, this channeled his intellect, and his family's money, into the development of the device patented as "Waldo F. Jones' Synchronous Reduplicating Pantograph." Wearing a glove and harness, Waldo could control a much more powerful mechanical hand simply by moving his hand and fingers. This and other technologies he develops make him a rich man, rich enough to build a home in space.[5]

Years later, NASA scientists nicknamed some of their early telemetry systems Waldo, and when the telemetry devices were developed, Waldo is what they were called. Oddly enough, the name was never trademarked in relation to telemetry devices; Waldo has since been trademarked by The Character Shop to distinguish its brand of ergonomic-gonio-kineti-telemetric input devices for controlling its puppets and animatronics. Ergonomic because it's engineered to fit a puppeteer's or performer's body (and/or head and/or face) and comfortably allow a wide range of physical freedom. Goniometric and kinetimetric because it measures the angle (gonio) and movement (kineti) of the wearer's joints and limbs. And telemetric because the movement data are measured and sent via remote control. In simpler terms, a Waldo is an electromechanical rig that is worn and makes a puppet (whether actually three-dimensional or a CGI "electronic puppet") mimic the wearer's movements.[6]

POWERING THE ELECTRONICS

In order for any of these things to work, they need power, and the size of the power supply needs to be factored into the equation so that everything will fit. Having room for all the servos and applicable mechanisms, but not the batteries well, that's not good, right?

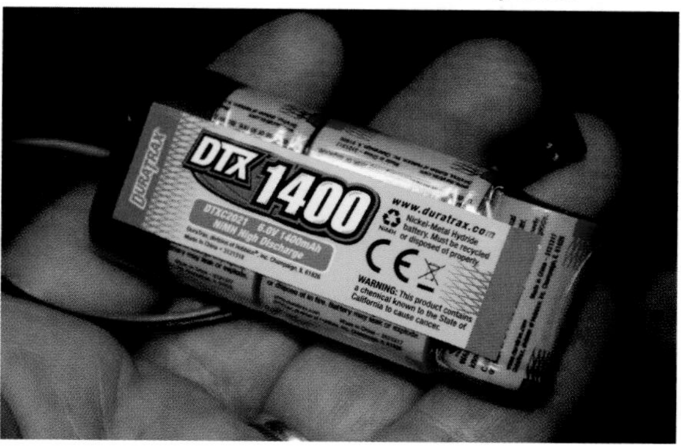

FIGURE 9.23
Six-volt R/C battery pack.
Photo by author.

Servo power is defined as the amount of DC voltage needed to operate a servo without damage. Servos operate from 4.5 to 6.0 volts DC. At the higher voltage, servos have a tendency to be faster and potentially stronger, but will heat up faster when stalled or in a holding position with stress force against the servo output shaft. Some servo controllers need a separate power source from the control source in order to deliver the higher 6.0 volts DC. The electric current drain (number of amps needed) depends on the torque being put out by the servo motor and can be in excess of 1 amp if the servo stalls under load. Its a good idea to calculate 1 amp per servo when calculating the power supply for most servos.[7]

BASIC ELECTRONICS PRIMER

You may or may not be the least bit interested in how electricity works, but for some of you, after reading this, a lightbulb may go on (please excuse the pun—I couldn't help it).

There are three basic units in electricity, which are voltage (V), current (I), and resistance (r). Voltage is measured in *volts*, current is measured in *amps* (short form for amperes), and resistance is measured in *ohms*. I learned this plumbing analogy to help me understand. It goes like this: Voltage is equivalent to the water pressure, the current is equivalent to the flow rate, and the resistance is like the pipe size. In a formula, the current (I) equals the voltage (V) divided by the resistance (r), or $I = V \div r$.

Applying the plumbing analogy, let's say you have a pressurized tank of water with a garden hose attached for watering your lawn. If the pressure in the tank is increased, more water will come out of the hose, as will increasing the diameter of the hose (as well as all the fittings). This is like increasing the voltage (more tank pressure) and decreasing the resistance (increasing the hose diameter). Electrical power is measured in watts; in an electrical system, *power* (P) is equal to voltage times current or $P = V \times I$. It's like this: take the hose and point it at a waterwheel like one that would turn a millwheel. You can increase the power generated by the waterwheel in two ways—(1) If you increase the pressure of the water coming out of the hose, it hits the waterwheel with a lot more force and the wheel turns faster, generating more power and (2) if you increase the flow rate, the waterwheel turns faster because of the weight of the extra water hitting it.

Putting this into an electrical system, increasing either the current or the voltage will result in higher power. Let's say you have a 6-volt light bulb hooked up to a 6-volt battery, and the power output of the light bulb is 100 watts. Using our equation, we can calculate how much current in amps would be required to get 100 watts out of this 6-volt bulb.

You know that **P** = 100 W and **V** = 6 V. So, you can rearrange the equation to solve for **I** and substitute in the numbers. Its more math, I know, but I hope this is helpful to someone.

The next category of animatronics development is structural.

Structural

All of the above stuff needs something to be anchored to and to control. The exterior skin or fur also needs some kind of frame to help give the animatronic its shape. This is usually done by making a plastic, metal, or composite framework, sometimes actually resembling a skeleton. But beyond serving the function of giving the animatronic puppet its shape, this underskull or underskeleton also provides the necessary surface to attach servo mounting brackets and other hardware so that the movement functions will be able to take place unhindered. The servos can't just sit loose inside the belly of the beast or rattle around in the head! They must be secured to something so that they can do their job.

Both the skin thickness and the softness are integral parts of the mechanism. So, much movement can be lost if a skin is either too thick, too soft, or both. I've been told that a good thickness is ¼ inch (6 millimeters) on average, with the skin being thinner around eye areas. Chris Clarke likes to have input during the coring stage—creating the underskull front the mold of the sculpt—and would even prefer to do it himself, especially on a face. He tells me that only the mechanic (the puppeteer) is aware of how he plans to move the face, where the fatty parts are needed, where the thinner, wrinkly areas will be most suitable, and so on. Chris believes that for a skin to be successful, it needs to be advised on by the person who's going to move it. As ever, observation of how things move in real life is key to gaining the experience necessary to be able to effectively judge the coring stage, and how thick or thin the skin will be.

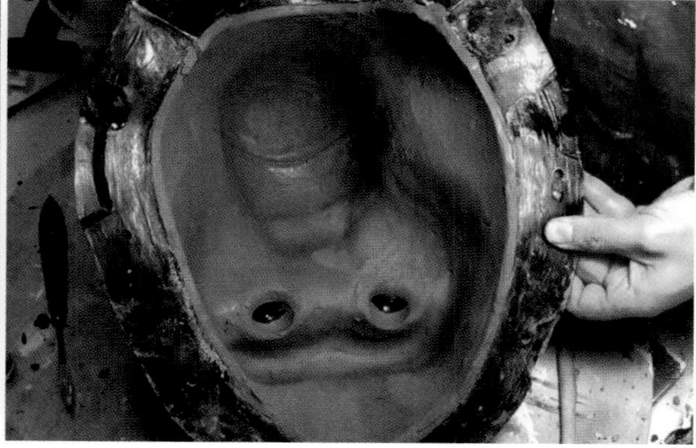

FIGURE 9.24
Adding ¼ inch of clay that represents skin depth (L); Defining skin depth of underskull (R).
Images reproduced by permission of Daniel E Tirinnanzi.

FIGURE 9.25
Making fiberglass underskull (L); demolding underskull (R).
Images reproduced by permission of Daniel E Tirinnanzi.

Typically, the underskeleton—or under*skull* as is often the case—is fabricated out of a structurally sound, lightweight material—graphite, for example. However, thin fiberglass is often used. Developments in materials such as syntactic dough—an epoxy dough—now allow for even lighter, stronger underskeletal pieces to be constructed. Depending on the size of your animatronic creation, the weight of your underskeleton needs only to be light enough for the servos you've chosen to efficiently move it and the outer skin (and hair/fur, etc.) that is attached to it.

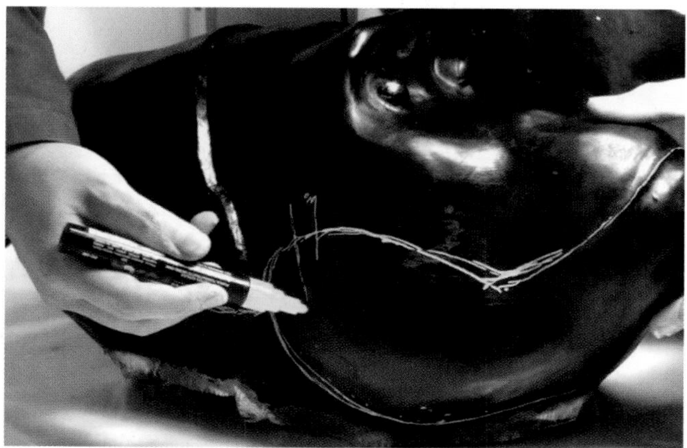

FIGURE 9.26
Defining how jaw will be hinged and separated.
Images reproduced by permission of Daniel E Tirinnanzi.

What performance characteristics you intend to endow upon your puppet will determine how your underskull or underskeleton is constructed. This will require ample thought and design on your part, because not only will the underskeleton help inform the outer shape of your puppet, it will also support the structure that holds your servos, receiver, batteries, and other surface control mechanisms.

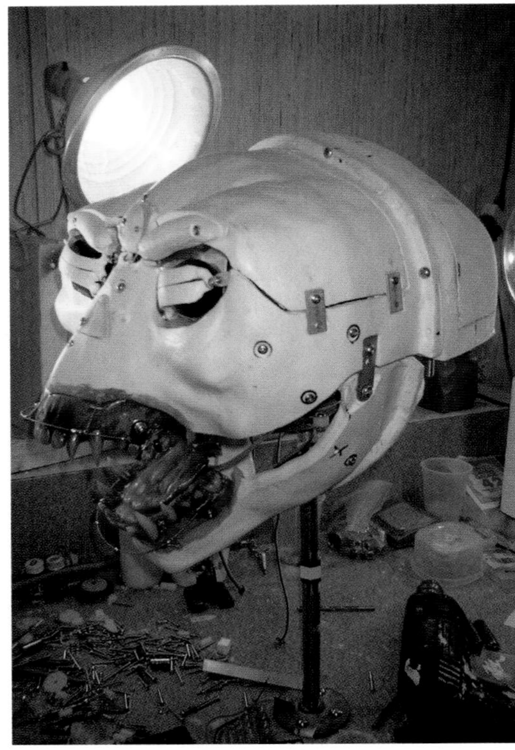

FIGURE 9.27
Gary Willett creature mech.
Image reproduced by permission of Gary Willett.

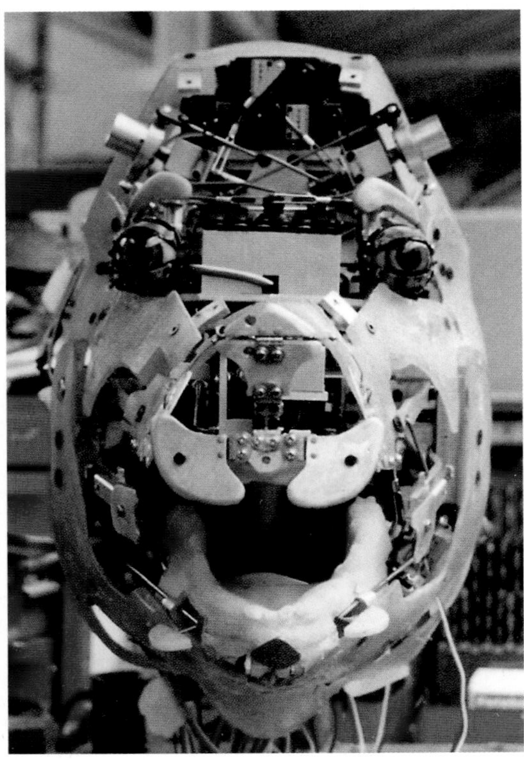

FIGURE 9.28
Napoleon mech; Animal Farm; Jim Henson's Creature Shop.
Image reproduced by permission of Chris Clarke.

Once the components are assembled, it's time to test and make sure that the movement is accurate and all control surfaces are working properly. Once that is confirmed, the outer skin can be dressed onto the puppet.

Surface

The outer surface, or skin, of your puppet can be made from any of numerous materials that will be determined by the look of the puppet—it may be covered in fur, or it may require humanlike skin or even scales, if your puppet is a dragon. The point is that the material needs to be puppet—appropriate as well as movement appropriate. If the skin is to fit over an area of high repetitive motion, the material must be flexible enough and strong enough to withstand the abuse. It must also be created and attached in such a way as to be maintainable and repairable if (and when) the need arises. And it will eventually.

FIGURE 9.29
Joey underskeleton; *War Horse.*
Image reproduced by permission of Chris Clarke.

Because of the underlying mechanics—the servos and other control devices (cables, joints, push rods, etc.)—the skin's overall weight needs to be taken into account (as does the underskeleton, the servos themselves, the other control devices, and their mounting hardware). While silicone moves the most closely like real skin, it is considerably heavier than urethane rubber, latex rubber, or foam latex and is (in most cases) stronger and more resilient (will last longer too).

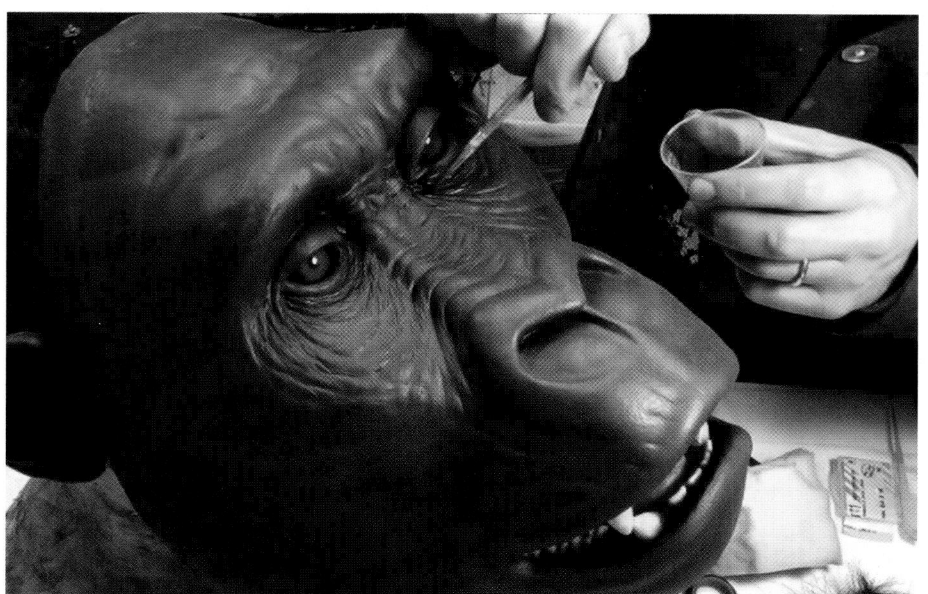

FIGURE 9.30
Final mech skin paint.
Image reproduced by permission of Daniel E Tirinnanzi.

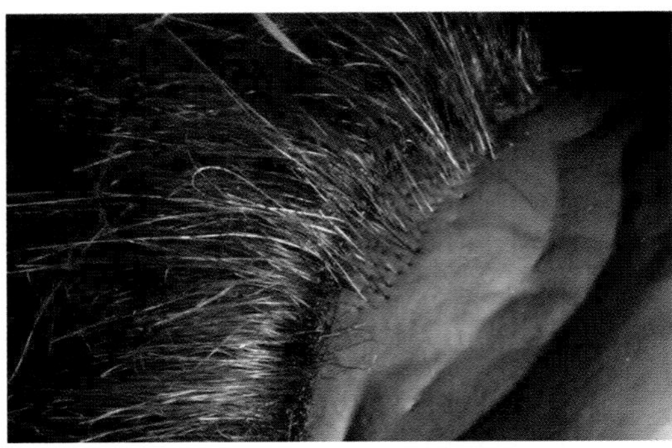

FIGURE 9.31
Punching hair into silicone.
Image reproduced by permission of Daniel E Tirinnanzi.

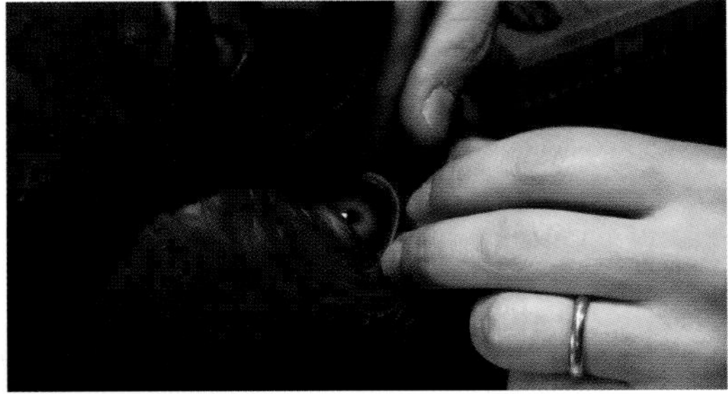

FIGURE 9.32
Gluing silicone eyelid to eyelid mechanism.
Image reproduced by permission of Daniel E Tirinnanzi.

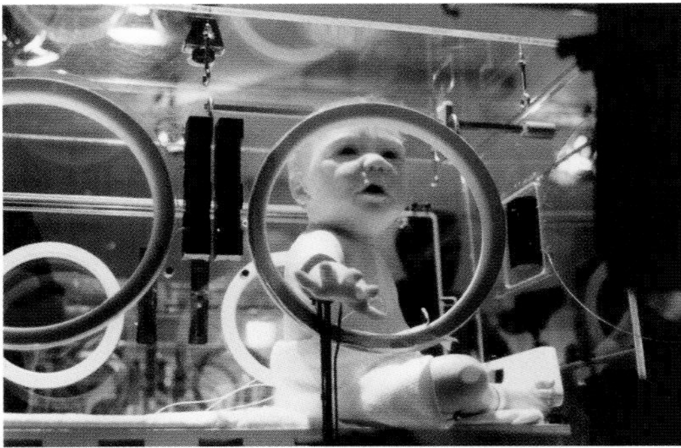

FIGURE 9.33
CMG mech baby.
Image reproduced by permission of Chris Clarke.

Because of all this, there are some considerations to take into account when dealing with the sculpt for an animatronic. There are so many stages in the completion of a creature effect, and if just one of them is allowed to go awry, then the whole thing will likely fail. So, keep your eye on the ball and don't be afraid to discuss your requirements with each department. Here are some suggestions from Chris Clarke:

The mouth—The mouth ought to be sculpted as closed as possible, with it open just enough to sculpt the lip return inside the mouth. If it's sculpted open more than that, when you try and close it there's absolutely nowhere for the excess skin to go, it'll just bulge out sideways like you've tried to shove a whole baguette in sideways! A skin can be stretched, but not compressed.[8]

The eyes—It's good form that once the sculpt has been completed and everyone is happy with it, signed off on it and are "Oooohing" and "Ahhhing" you skill as a sculptor, add just a little more lid to the eyes to close them slightly. Trying to blink a fully open eye sometimes produces funny shapes and nothing stops the "Oooohing" and "Ahhhing" like funny shapes. And not good funny. Try adding to the top lid something like one-third or one-fourth of the eye opening. So, if the aperture of the open eye is about 3/8 inch (10 millimeters), close the upper lid 1/8 inch (2.5–3 millimeters). Try it and see if you like it, but do experiment and come up with what works for you.[9]

Expression—If you have a sculpt of a creature that looks like he's about to rip your face off, then angry is pretty much all that that creature is ever going to look. A sculpt has to suit a certain premise if the script and storyboards dictates that your creature "looks at the damsel with sympathetic eyes and then becomes enraged," a sculpt of a creature that looks inherently angry is going to give you problems when the 1st AD says, "Okay people, moving on to the sympathetic shot." All the cable pulling and paddle twisting in the world won't help, so from design, you must go for either (1) a neutral sculpt somewhere between sympathetic and angry (but nearer the calmer end of the spectrum) or (2) consider two separate creature puppets if the expressions needed are too extreme to manage with one face.[10]

If a full range of expressions is required, adding very subtle frown or laugh lines into the sculpt can often be a good compromise; you'll find that a subtle crease worked by a paddle will deepen, but can also pull flat if stretched. This can help sell different looks and is worth a little experimentation.[11]

OPERATION

The talented people that control the animatronic figure—the artist who makes it move—are called puppeteers because that is really what an animatronic device is—an electronic/mechanical puppet, albeit a potentially rather sophisticated one.

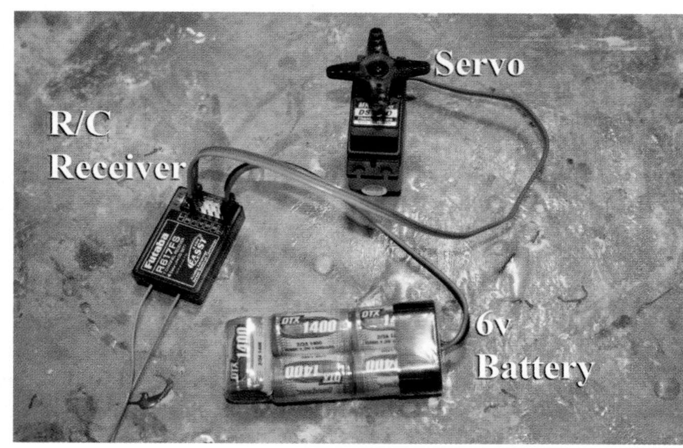

FIGURE 9.34
CMG mech baby.
Image reproduced by permission of Chris Clarke.

Depending on the level of complexity required for the movement of your puppet, it may be as simple as a plug-n-play Halloween display or toys like Furby or require the expertise of several operators each with a multichannel RC controller or a single operator wearing a Waldo or some other type of sophisticated telemetry device.

The servos controlling individual functions of your animatronic must be connected to the receiver channel corresponding to the channel controlling movement on the RC controller; it will be either a simple switch or a joystick on a slider that will allow for incremental motion. The switch will turn on or off any movement by the servo that will travel the full range of its motion.

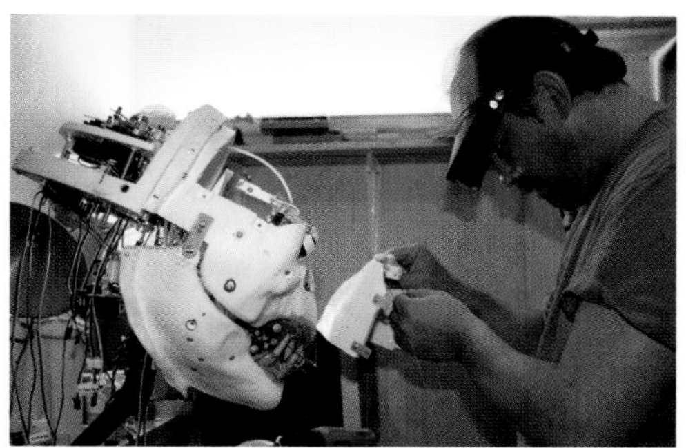

FIGURE 9.35
Gary Willett making adjustment to mech.
Image reproduced by permission of Gary Willett.

Having said at the beginning of this chapter that it was only going to be a primer of animatronics and not a specific *How To* of an animatronic project, I think it would be remiss of me not to show stages of a specific project and how it illustrates why there is no set formula that can be used for creating an animatronic puppet—beyond what has already been explained in this chapter.

You can see in these images from Gary Willett and Daniel E Tirinnanzi their different approaches to somewhat similar creature projects.

FIGURE 9.36
Daniel E Tirinnanzi airbrushing gums of mech.
Image reproduced by permission of Daniel E Tirinnanzi.

Ask any sculptor what their animatronic pet peeve is and they'll likely tell you it's how some "mechy" changed the shape of the core they're working with, thereby losing the original sculpted form entirely. As far as anyone should be concerned, the sculpt is Gospel and as such should not be altered; it is your initial data point that all other data are set to. Finding techniques to keep

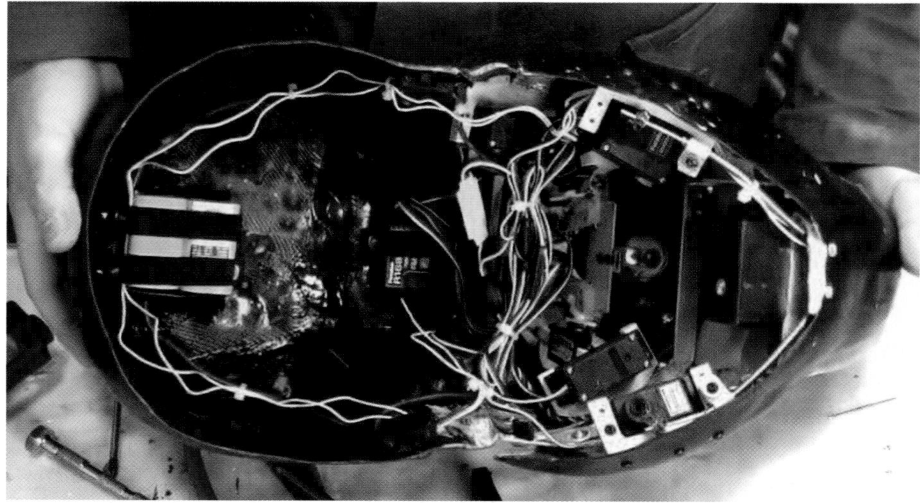

FIGURE 9.37
Workings of gorilla mech.
Image reproduced by permission of Daniel E Tirinnanzi.

reference of the core's form during the cutting it up into paddles stage is critical. Three methods are as follows[12]:

- *Vacuum forming*—If the shape allows it, take a clear plastic form off the face part of the core you're working with, and once you've drawn your paddle shapes on it, place the clear form on the core and drill two small holes per paddle through both the form and the core so that once cut free, each one can be screwed into its respective position on the inside of the form. Then, once the mech is built and the pickup points for each paddle on the puppet are built in place and set to their neutral position (DON'T FORGET TO DO THAT!!), the reference form can simply be offered up, add a few careful dabs of superglue, adlock, devweld, or similar acrylic-based glue applied to temporarily hold them in their correct positions, and you can then carefully remove all the screws from the vac-formed piece and lift it clear leaving all your paddles in their respective neutral settings for you to carefully attach properly.
- *Straight lining and dots*—Using a bendy ruler and a marker pen, draw three lines projecting from a center point (dot) in the middle of each paddle you've drawn on the core, making sure that each line crosses onto either a center dot on an adjacent paddle or onto a dot on a section of the core that doesn't move (are you following this?) On each paddle, write the distance between each paddle's center dot and the dots they project to next to each line that projects to it (still with me?). When setting the paddles, you can use your eye to line up the lines and use calipers or a ruler to measure the center point distances to triangulate the paddles into their correct positions. There's a bit of a knack to this, but it works.
- *Tabs*—With a Dremel tool, you can cut all of the paddles clear off the core but leave three thin tabs per paddle that keep the paddle connected—joining it to the adjacent paddles and/or core so that the whole thing stays

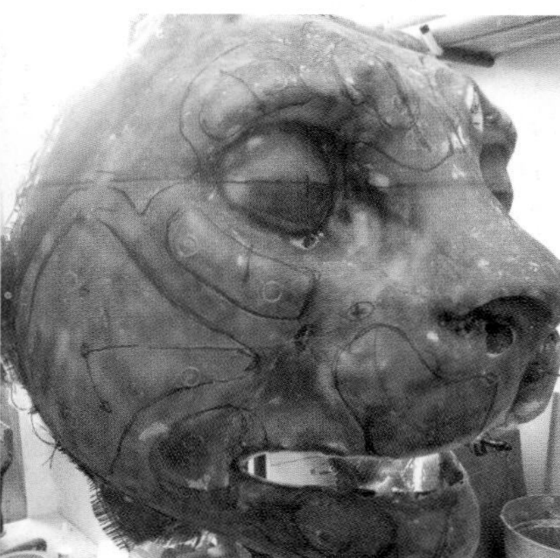

FIGURE 9.38
ING lion mech showing straight lining and dots (R); eye mech (L).
Images reproduced by permission of Chris Clarke.

together as a kind of mesh. This is good because once the waste parts of the core are removed, you can see through it to see how the core is fitting to the mech. Then, once the paddles are afixed, it's a simple job to touch the Dremel to each tab to cut it free, and if you are able to hold a vacuum nozzle next to where you're cutting, it'll keep the dust it makes out of the mechanics.

Depending on what an animatronic is being built for, the usability and ease of use should be considered. If it's for a movie, then building a creature that takes a day to set up and tear down probably isn't going to be workable unless its unavoidable. Chris Clarke says, "I've noticed in my 21 years doing this that (people are) far more impressed when you're set up and ready to shoot before the DOP's finished lighting and that you've de-rigged and cleared set before they've even finished moving the camera to the next shot, these impressions are far more enduring and can secure you the next job that production is working on!" When he worked on *Animal Farm* for Jim Henson's Creature Shop several years ago, Chris noticed that the best moving creatures of the 13 they'd all built for it were the horses; they used a simple three-rod parallel linkage for the gross body movements. They were quick to make, with very direct control, and were eminently organic in their operation. It looks simple and as a principle it is, but its about where the pivot centers are that is crucial; the way people will be seeing the puppet on camera—the way it looks on screen and the way it moves during the take is paramount, not how technical and clever it looks. Find the *best* way to make the creature work, not the most impressive-looking way. You won't regret that decision, and the production will eventually thank you for it.[13]

FIGURE 9.39
Napoleon and friend; Animal Farm; Jim Henson's Creature Shop.
Image reproduced by permission of Chris Clarke.

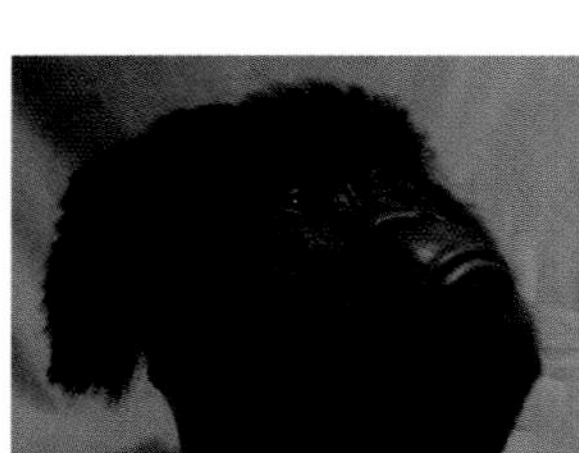
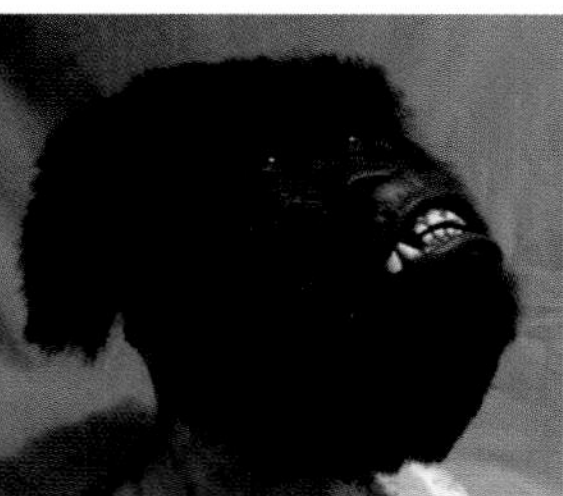

FIGURE 9.40
Misc. facial positions of finished gorilla mech.
Images reproduced by permission of Daniel E Tirinnanzi.

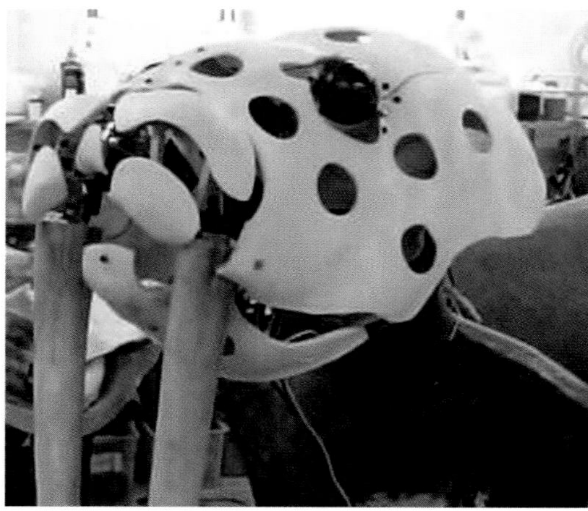

FIGURE 9.41
Walrus underskull (L); Walrus on set waiting for the director to call 'Action!' (R).
Images reproduced by permission of Chris Clarke.

Bottom Line: If a close up creature moves well and is realistic finishwise, then only a foolish person would ignore the chance to use it and save the production money.

CHAPTER SUMMARY

- This chapter describes the history and design philosophy of animatronics.
- You learned about servos and their operation/function.
- You were introduced to electronics and puppet control.
- You learned about creating the understructure of an animatronic.
- You were given insight into the operation of an animatronic puppet.

Endnotes

1 Christopher Clarke, 2012.

2 Zunt, Dominik. "Who did actually invent the word "robot" and what does it mean?" The Karel Čapek website.

3 Christopher Clarke, 2012.

4 http://en.wikipedia.org/wiki/DMX512#DMX_in_practice.

5 http://en.wikipedia.org/wiki/Waldo_(short_story).

6 http://www.character-shop.com/waldo.html.

7 http://www.bpesolutions.com/bpemanuals/Servo.Info.pdf; Harry Lapping and Robert Van Deest, 2007.

8 Christopher Clarke, 2012.

9 Christopher Clarke, 2012.

10 Christopher Clarke, 2012.

11 Christopher Clarke, 2012.

12 Christopher Clarke.

13 Christopher Clarke, 2012.

CHAPTER 10

Other Makeup Effects

Key Points

- Making silicone and resin eyes
- Making Pros-Aide bondo or Cabo patch, aka TPA (thickened Pros-Aide)
- Uses of plastic bald cap material
- How to make and apply a bald cap
- Simple buildup of ears and nose
- Tuplast
- Sculpting with nose and scar wax
- Making rigid collodion scars
- Airbrush stipple
- Brush spatter/stipple
- 3D transfers
- Stencil tattoos, printed tattoos, and paint accents
- Electrostatic hair flocking
- Applying wrinkle/age stipple
- Creating trauma, wounds, and bruises
- How to create a nosebleed on demand
- Creating burns, blisters, and skin diseases
- Using skin-safe silicone and gelatin for direct buildup

INTRODUCTION

In addition to the prosthetics covered throughout this book, there are other materials that can be used both alone and in conjunction with prosthetic appliances. Just as a wig can be used without any other makeup or makeup effects, a rigid collodion (RC) scar, airbrush tattoo, or any of the items described in the Objectives can be used separately or in combination to create character and creature makeup that is still considered special makeup effects. Some of the items and techniques that are the focus of this chapter have been mentioned in the earlier chapters of this book—for example, *bondo*.

MAKING SILICONE EYES

By Matt Singer

The Shape of the Eye

When ocular prosthetists make custom prostheses, the prosthetics they make are never round. They are created from an impression of the eye socket, and the cornea of the eye has an apex approximately 3 millimeter high to create an optical lens that makes the eye look alive, not doll-like. For FX purposes, you might not even have the room for a complete ball in the prosthetic or head you are manufacturing, so having flexibility with the shape can be liberating. For this tutorial, I'll make a standard ocular prosthetic shape.

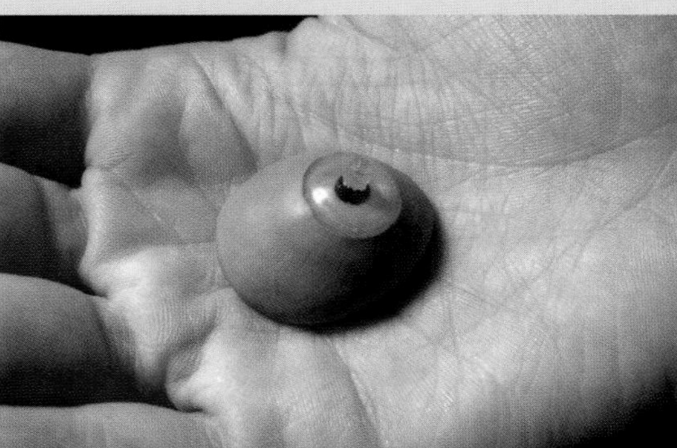

FIGURE 10.1
Master shape of eye with iris button.
Image reproduced by permission of Matt Singer.

To create the master shape, use a sulfur-free, firm, oil clay. The firmer, the better; you need to sculpt a fairly smooth surface. We'll be using platinum silicones to fabricate the eye. The posterior (back) side of the eye we will be making will be relatively concave. The surfaces don't have to be perfect, you'll be able to sand the surfaces of the mold to improve the surface quality later.

Iris Buttons: Iris buttons are clear domes available in different diameters. They have a stem at the apex that allows the button to be registered in the same location after the mold is manufactured. You can purchase them through Factor II. Although they will not be a part of the final silicone eye, they are essential for reproducing a realistic cornea with optical quality. The average human iris is 12 millimeter, but every eye is different. It's best to take a measurement of the iris to ensure a good likeness. You should purchase at least one of each size; 10, 10.5, 11, 11.5, 12, 12.5, and 13 millimeter. Once you determine the iris diameter, you'll grind the stem with a Dremel tool to about 2 millimeter. Take the iris button and add it to your clay master. It should be located closer to the nasal corner of the master, and not directly in the center. The clay should meet the button gradually so that there is not an abrupt change of shape. It should look like it's part of the form. Spray with matte Crystal Clear acrylic spray. Let it dry. Now, you have your master.

Making the Mold

Making the mold is simple. I recommend a less-porous stone-like Die-Keen. (You can get these through a number of dental supply companies or directly from the manufacturer.) You can also use Ultracal 30. Use a piece of rubber matting material from the hardware store and cut a piece that is 1" wide and 10" long. Make a circle and hot glue to a table surface.

FIGURE 10.2
(1) Glue form to flat surface; (2) fill mold with dental stone; (3) put master eye shape into mold; (4) cut keys into mold.
Image reproduced by permission of Matt Singer.

Release the stem of the button with a little petroleum jelly. You can add a little clay around the base of the stem to give a little wiggle room for getting it out later. Mix the stone and pour to the top of the rubber matting.

Wait until the stone begins to thicken and submerge your master shape to the leading edge as demonstrated.

Let it set until hard. Remove the matting and carve three negative keys with carving tools or a Dremel.

Release the stone with petroleum jelly and wrap with 3"-wide and 10"-long rubber matting and hot glue down around the stone.

FIGURE 10.3
(1) Mold ready for additional stone; (2) filled mold; (3) completed mold.
Image reproduced by permission of Matt Singer.

Mix stone and brush onto all surfaces and pour to the top of the rubber matting. When cured, carefully pry open your mold and clean out the clay with alcohol or EnSolve. Carefully pry off the iris button. You can fill any air bubbles with additional stone.

Creating the Scleral Core

The sclera is the white portion of the eye. When ocularists make acrylic eyes, they usually place the iris button back into the mold and fill the mold with white acrylic. The acrylic is polymerized in a pressure cooker and removed from the mold. The ocularist will them grind the surface of the acrylic master by eye with a hand tool to accommodate the clear acrylic, to help facilitate the clear cornea region and the shiny optical surface of the eye. The grinding of the acrylic provides additional space so that when the eye is polished or adjusted, the paint will not be affected. I've invented a different technique that requires no grinding of the silicone and provides a more exacting negative space.

Instead of grinding, we'll core the anterior surface of the mold with clay using a Pasta Maker set to represent the thickness of the clear region of the eye and set the iris button back in the mold to create a flat painting surface for the iris.

Coring the Mold

Before coring, I recommend sanding both the anterior and posterior surfaces with a fine grit sand paper to improve the surfaces.

FIGURE 10.4
Sanding before coring.
Image reproduced by permission of Matt Singer.

Set the Pasta Maker to a thickness of about a 1/6" to 1/8" and place a piece of Kleen Klay (a soft sulfur-free clay) in the shape of a worm into the rollers. The clay should come out as a flat even piece.

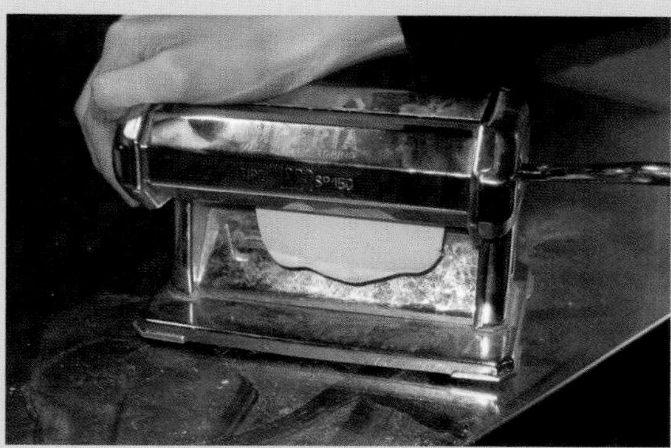

FIGURE 10.5
Kleen Clay in pasta maker.
Image reproduced by permission of Matt Singer.

Press the clay into the negative space of the anterior mold covering the surface. Trim the excess clay.

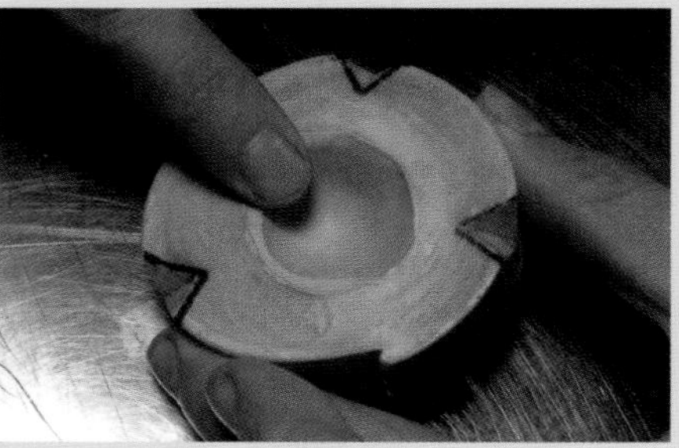

FIGURE 10.6
Clay being pressed into mold (L); graduating edge of clay (R).
Image reproduced by permission of Matt Singer.

Once the clay is trimmed, take your finger and graduate the edge of the clay to a knife-like edge around the circumference of the negative space. Take a tool and find the hole under the clay created by the stem of the button. Cut a circle slightly smaller than the button diameter. This area will receive the iris button.

FIGURE 10.7
Making room for iris button.
Image reproduced by permission of Matt Singer.

Preparing the Button

Now we'll create the circular canvas for our iris painting. For this, we'll use tinted silicone painted onto the flat side of that iris button. This silicone will transfer to the surface of the sclera. Using "P125" from Silicones Inc., weigh out 3 gram and catalyze. A platinum dispersion called "588" by Silicones Inc. is a platinum catalyst dispersed in alcohol that we will put in a small spray bottle. This spray bottle will enable us to spray the surface of our silicone and substantially accelerate the cure. I use Factor II intrinsic silicone pigments to tint my silicone for all the painting. I prefer to use a medium gray background when I paint eyes, since the edge of the eye or "limbus" is usually gray and by having a gray background, you can paint just shy of the edge to create an even limbus. Tint the silicone by mixing a little white and black pigment. You want it fairly opaque. Next, brush the silicone onto the surface of the button and let the silicone level itself.

FIGURE 10.8
Painting back of button.
Image reproduced by permission of Matt Singer.

Spray the surface from about 6" away, and let the alcohol flash off for a few seconds and place in a craft oven or toaster oven at 250°F (121°C) for about 10 minutes. To keep the button upright and prevent the silicone from sliding over the edge, press the button into a small mound of Kleen Klay on a metal palette or flat oven tray. I really like those two-part silicone putties to make custom stands and rigs for things I do. You might try making a reusable silicone stand for this purpose. Remove from the oven and test the surface with a tool to assure that the surface is completely set. If it's still not set, spray again and place in the oven for a few more minutes. A really thick surface will take longer to cure.

Placing the Button

Take your painted button with stem down, and press back into its original position in the mold. Be careful not to delaminate the silicone from the surface of the button. Add clay around the button if necessary.

FIGURE 10.9
Smoothing clay around button.
Image reproduced by permission of Matt Singer.

You don't want the clay to hang over the silicone surface, so clean any clay off with a tool. And smooth the edge with a silicone tool. Don't get too much clay on the button or else it will not stick well to the sclera. Use a little alcohol to clean the surface if necessary. I don't recommend using a solvent to smooth the clay; it tends to be messy. Now you have cored the negative. Release the outer stone surfaces as well as the posterior mold surface with a liquid dish soap. Make sure the surface is not visibly wet.

FIGURE 10.10
Releasing mold.
Image reproduced by permission of Matt Singer.

Casting the Scleral Core

Weigh out 5 gram of "P-45" and catalyze (10:1 mix ratio). Tint with white silicone pigment and evacuate in a vacuum chamber. A vacuum chamber is essential for doing quality silicone work especially when casting optically clear pieces. You can buy the components from Factor II. Once evacuated, carefully decant into the negative and pore some onto the posterior surface as well. Carefully close your mold and clamp with a small C-Clamp.

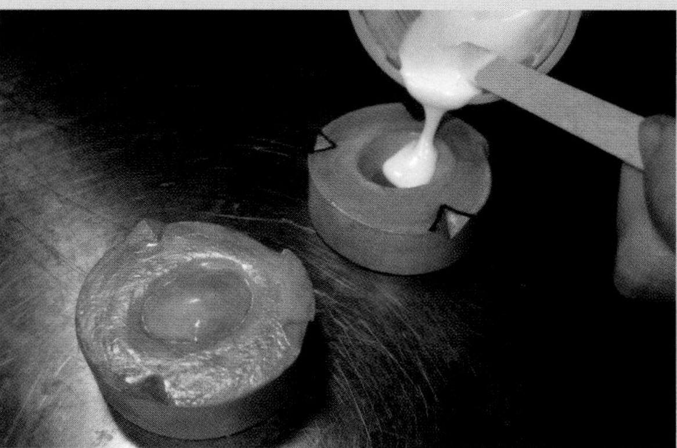

FIGURE 10.11
Filling mold halves.
Image reproduced by permission of Matt Singer.

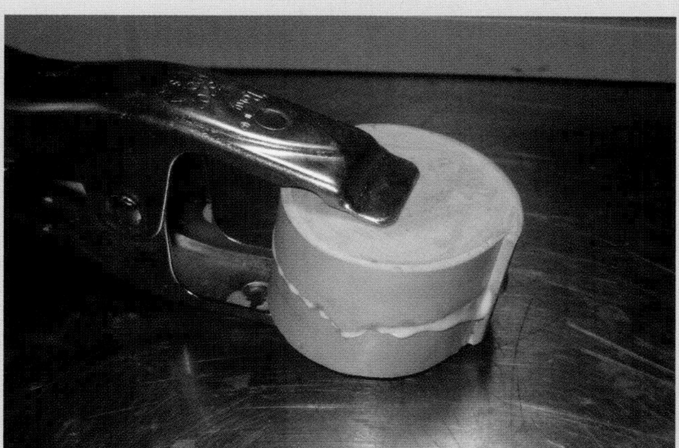

FIGURE 10.12
Clamp tightly.
Image reproduced by permission of Matt Singer.

I use a little two-part putty to create a custom, self-standing, clamp for making eyes. Place in an oven for 40 minutes at 200°F (93°C).

Trimming and Prepping the Scleral Core

Durometer is the term used to measure firmness of a material. When a silicone is firm or of a high durometer, you can actually grind the surface or the edge to shape it with a red acrylic wheel available through "Dedeco" and a Dremel. You can also use this same wheel to erase seams on different silicones, assuming that the durometer is high. It will not work well for low durometer or soft silicones.

Pry the mold apart and marvel at your expertise. Clean the surface of the silicone with alcohol and a paper towel. Trim the flashing with cuticle scissors and carefully grind the seam. Don't be over zealous, just remove the seam.

FIGURE 10.13
Demolded eye.
Image reproduced by permission of Matt Singer.

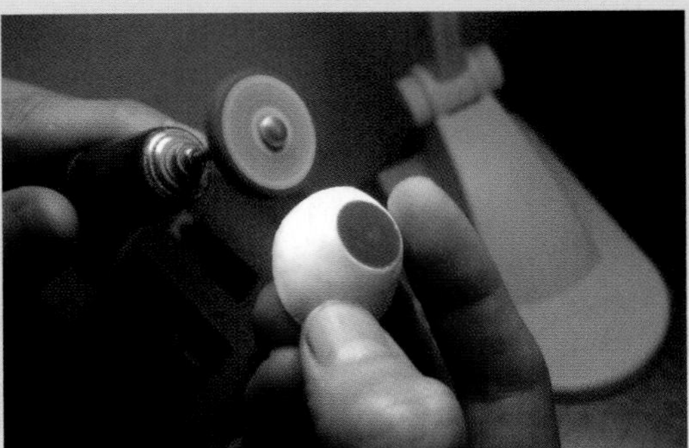

FIGURE 10.14
Grinding seam.
Image reproduced by permission of Matt Singer.

FIGURE 10.15
Iris button hole in negative.
Image reproduced by permission of Matt Singer.

Prepping Your Mold before Painting

You will need to fill the hole created by the stem of the iris button.

FIGURE 10.16
Filling button hole.
Image reproduced by permission of Matt Singer.

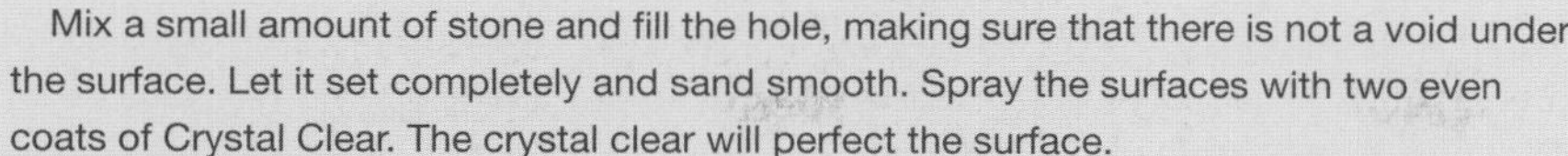

Mix a small amount of stone and fill the hole, making sure that there is not a void under the surface. Let it set completely and sand smooth. Spray the surfaces with two even coats of Crystal Clear. The crystal clear will perfect the surface.

Painting the Eye

To paint in silicone, we will make our own silicone paint that we can cure quickly between layers. To create our silicone paint medium, we will use P-125 by Silicones Inc. Mix 5 gram of P-125 and catalyze (10:1 mix ratio). Evacuate the silicone using a vacuum. Silicone pigments available through Factor II will serve as the pigment to tint the silicone.

FIGURE 10.17
Mixing thickened silicone.
Image reproduced by permission of Matt Singer.

To clean your brush, I use a solvent called "EnSolve" from "Enviro Tech." It is great for cleaning brushes and dispersing silicone. It is a great replacement for zylene or toluene. You should also purchase some thixotropic agent for platinum silicone available at Factor II, Silicones Inc. or Smooth-On. "Thixo" is used to instantly thicken a silicone so that it will not slump or displace. It is essential for creating the striations without fear of the paint moving out of place. Place your prepared silicone core piece back onto the posterior portion of the mold. Take some paint base and mix with appropriate color that will match the color of the striations you are trying to create. For a blue or green eye, I use white striations, and for a brown eye, I use black. Add a drop of thixotropic agent and mix. Brush away from the center toward the edge of the iris just shy of the edge so as to create a gray edge.

FIGURE 10.18
Adding striations to iris (L); adding color to iris (R).
Image reproduced by permission of Matt Singer.

Brush technique is essential for creating an even and a radial look. You can take a pin to further add the depth and detail of the striations. Once you are satisfied, spray with the 588 and let flash off for 10 seconds and place in oven set at 250°C for a few minutes. Check with probe tool to determine whether the material is set enough as to not disturb. Don't over cure. Once our anatomy is done, we can add washes of color without the addition of thixo to paint the eye. Set each paint layer with 588 and cure in the oven for a few minutes.

To create the pupil, I make a pupil sheet I can use over and over again. To do this, tint P125 with black pigment and brush a thin even layer onto the back of a metal make-up palette or another metal surface. It is important to make the sheet as thin as possible. You do not want a thick pupil. Be sure to release the metal surface with a little dish soap before applying the silicone. Spray with 588 and place in an oven until cured. Once cured, carefully peel off the silicone and place onto a soft surface like a magazine and punch out an iris using leather punches.

FIGURE 10.19
Punching pupils.
Image reproduced by permission of Matt Singer.

Leather punches are readily available. Iris sizes vary. The average is 2.5 to 4 millimeter. Add a little paint base to the center of your iris and place the iris onto the wet silicone. Spray with 588 and cure. Before adding veins, I seal the scleral core to the surface of the posterior mold, so that it will not change position when the clear part is processed.

FIGURE 10.20
Sealing core to posterior mold.
Image reproduced by permission of Matt Singer.

Take the paint base and brush a thin untinted layer over the entire silicone core excluding the iris and go a little past the edge to seal to the mold. Spray 588 and cure. To make veins, use red cotton thread and, with a tweezers, pull fibers from the thread and place on a paper towel. The threads will stick to the towel so that they do not blow away. Brush a thin layer of clear paint base over the surface of the sclera and carefully set the veins. You can manipulate their position with your brush.

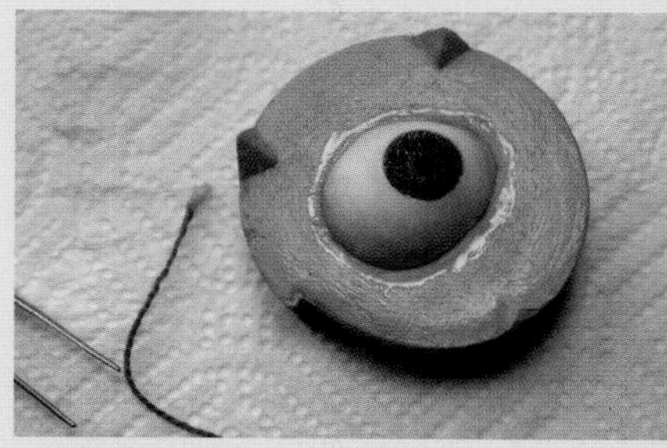
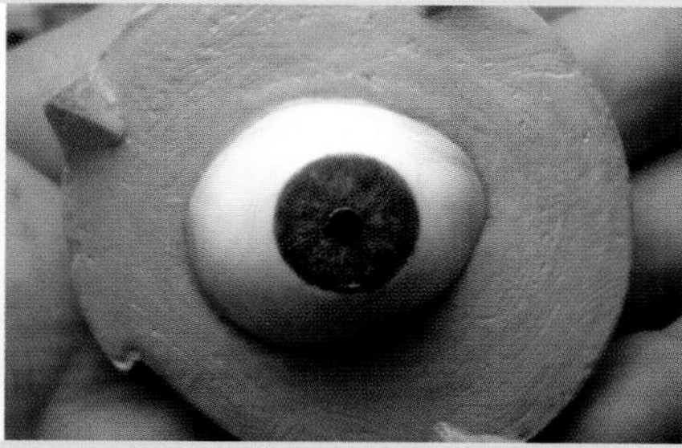

FIGURE 10.21
Adding veins to sclera.
Image reproduced by permission of Matt Singer.

Spray with 588 and cure. Finally, to create the pinkish corners of the eye, I mix tin and red pigment in paint base and tint the corners. As always spray with 588 and cure. You are now ready to process the clear.

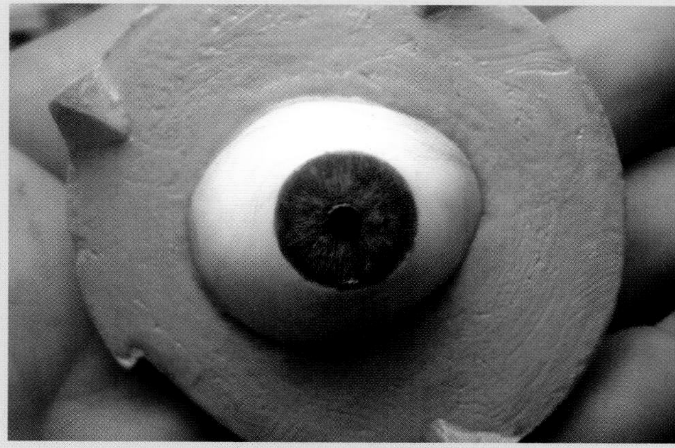

FIGURE 10.22
Final paint job; ready for clear layer.
Image reproduced by permission of Matt Singer.

Processing the Optical Silicone

To cast the clear portion of the eye, we will use an optically clear silicone from Silicones Inc. called WC 575. Release the anterior surface of the mold with dish soap and let it dry. Mix 5 gram of 575 and catalyze (10:1 mix ratio). Degas and pour slowly into the anterior portion of the mold. Slowly submerge the posterior side of the mold with painted silicone core and clamp slowly as to not create bubbles. Let cure without the addition of heat to avoid bubbles. Cure time is approximately 6 hours.

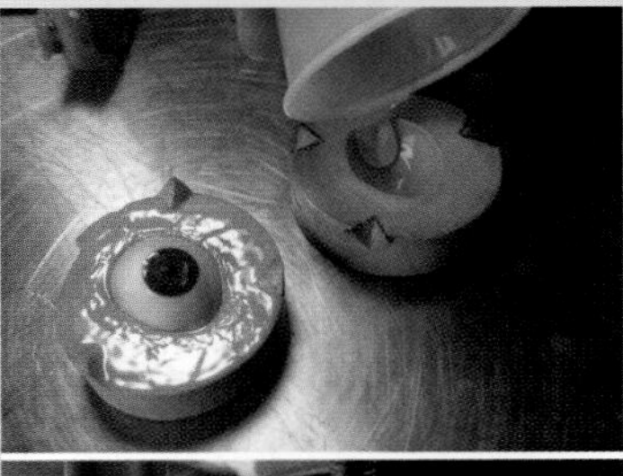

FIGURE 10.23
Pouring optical silicone into mold (top); mold clamped shut. Now we wait (bottom).
Image reproduced by permission of Matt Singer.

Trimming and Polishing the Silicone Eye

Carefully remove the eye from the mold. Trim the flashing and grind the edge with an acrylic grinding wheel. Be careful not to be too aggressive—you don't want to delaminate the clear silicone from the surface of the sclera.

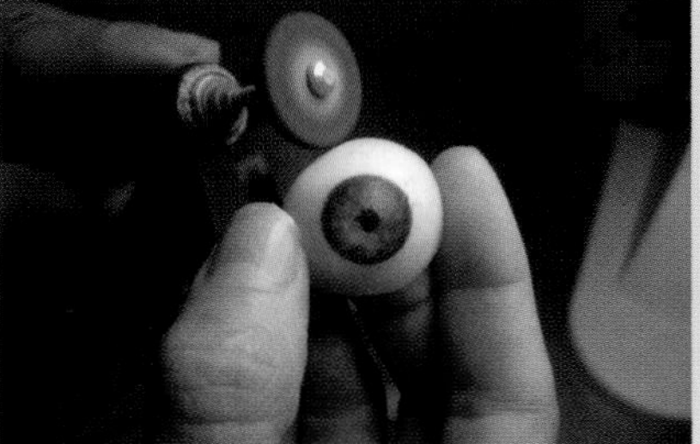

FIGURE 10.24
Trimming demolded eye (top); grinding edge (bottom).
Image reproduced by permission of Matt Singer.

A silicone primer available from Factor II can be brushed onto the silicone core before casting the clear to prevent any delamination. Make sure it is a primer designed for platinum silicones. Once you are satisfied with edge, you are now ready to add the polish coat. I make a little rig for polishing, I call the "polish stand." You can simply push pins through a polyethylene dram cup if you don't want to make such a rig. Push three to four push pins through the cup to impale the posterior side of the silicone eye, suspending it. This will allow you to paint your polish over the edge of the eye.

Mix and catalyze 2 gram of 575 and evacuate. Brush a thin layer of 575 over the surface and around the edge. Don't use too much to avoid dripping. Baby the polish and place in oven at 225°C for 10–15 minutes. Remove the eye and revel in your achievement!

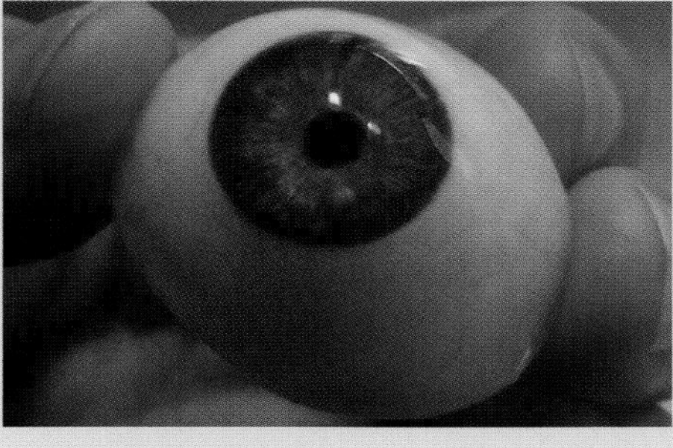

FIGURE 10.25
Thin surface layer of 575 (top); finished eye (bottom).
Image reproduced by permission of Matt Singer.

You can clean the eye with alcohol when it gets dusty or dirty. Do not use any other solvent.

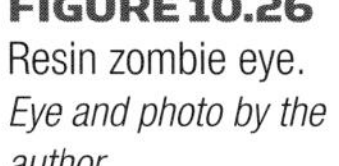

FIGURE 10.26
Resin zombie eye.
Eye and photo by the author.

RESIN EYES

You can approach making acrylic or resin eyes in much the same way as Matt Singer's tutorial describes, substituting silicone for the dental stone used for the molds, or you can make silicone molds of acrylic spheres and attempt to model your own eyes, corneal bulge and all… or shell out a few bucks and pick up a copy of Ken Banks' *Eyes Made Easy* DVD and premade mold kit. The premade molds and guides make the process eminently simpler to fabricate eyes for any manner of prop heads and display busts… Thank you, Ken!

FIGURE 10.27
(1) Basics of mold kit—inner mold, outer mold, ¼" #20 bolt and eye plate; (2) black resin in inner mold; (3) ¼" #20 bolt and eye plate inserted into inner mold; finished inner eye core piece; notice recessed pupil and pre-printed iris.
Photos by the author.

The best way to cast your own eyes is with the aide of a pressure pot; when you pour the resin into the inner mold and insert (the released) bolt and eye plate, put the mold into a pressure pot and pressurize to 40–45 psi until the resin is cured to ensure a bubble-free cast. Do the same for the outer mold and the clear resin; bubbles will be much more noticeable in the clear resin if you do not do this. For the zombie eye above (Figure 10.26), I didn't care, because it is a zombie eye with decomposing gas bubbles.

If you'd like to make your own iris prints instead of hand painting, the diameter of the iris for these molds is ½" (13 millimeter).

FIGURE 10.28
Pros-Aide drying on iris plane (top); iris glued in place (bottom).
Photo by the author.

FIGURE 10.29
Finished creature eye.
Photo by the author.

BONDO

Not to be mistaken for its polyester resin car repair namesake from the Bondo Corporation, our *bondo* is a versatile material made from mixing Pros-Aide and Cab-O-Sil (a trademark of the Cabot Corporation), hence its other name *Cabo patch*. It is also known in some circles as TPA or Thickened Pros-Aide. It is called bondo because it is used in much the same way auto body shops use it to repair dings and dents in cars. By mixing Pros-Aide adhesive and Cab-O-Sil together until you have a paste, either thin or thick, you can fill holes in prosthetics caused by defects during the casting process or during seaming; you can also use it to blend off thick edges during application. When the bondo is still wet, the edges can be further smoothed using a brush dipped in water or 99% alcohol.

Cab-O-Sil is fumed silica (silica being the second most common mineral in the world) used as a thickener in food products such as ketchup, pharmaceuticals, and cosmetics. Fumed silica is nontoxic when ingested, but prolonged exposure by inhalation can result in silicosis, which is the most common occupational lung disease worldwide. Fumed silica is very fine and care should be taken to minimize its dust when mixing with Pros-Aide.

FIGURE 10.30 Mixing Pros-Aide in Sunbeam mixer. *Photo by the author.*

The best way is to pour Pros-Aide (I am very fond of Graftobian's answer to Pros-Aide—*Pro Adhesive*) into a mixing bowl and stir with a mixer on its lowest speed all day and let the water evaporate slowing, leaving a bowl full of thickened Pros-Aide. The resulting prosthetics made with this bondo will shrink less and be softer than bondo made with Cab-O-Sil. I use an old Sunbeam mixer on its lowest setting.

Bondo has also become an industry standard for creating durable, waterproof 3D prosthetic transfers, applied in a similar fashion to temporary tattoo transfers. In fact, Christien Tinsley won a 2007 Technical Achievement Academy Award for developing the process (Tinsley Transfers). Christien was also nominated in 2004 (Oscar for Best Achievement in Makeup, shared with Keith VanderLaan) for Mel Gibson's *The Passion of the Christ*, which used his 3D transfers extensively. I'll get into the specifics of making your own 3D transfers in a later section of this chapter, using both bondo and silicone. You can even use gelatin.

CAP MATERIAL

Cap material comes in two varieties: acetone-based plastic (vinyl) and water-based plastic (vinyl). Michael Davy Film & TV Makeup makes and sells a water-based cap plastic called Water-Melon that can be dissolved with alcohol; Mould Life, in the United Kingdom, makes acetone-based and alcohol-soluble cap material that is also available in the United States under the names Baldiez and Super Baldiez. This stuff has become an industry standard as well.

FIGURE 10.31
The late Richard Snell (L) applying custom silicone bald cap; IMATS LA, 2004. *Photo by the author.*

Plastic cap material can be used for a variety of applications, not the least of which is making bald caps; hence the name. It can also be used to seal molds or sculpture before molding and as an encapsulating layer for gel-filled appliances (GFAs). Cap material is an excellent encapsulating material for silicone GFAs because the edges can so easily be blended off instead of fighting them. Silicone will not dissolve away once it is cured, but the cap material will, with either 99% IPA or acetone, the less acetone comes in direct contact with skin, the better.

Cap plastic can also be used to make thin appliances to cover eyebrows or to make other small prosthetic appliances such as eye bags or built-up ears instead of using slush or slip latex. The most prominent use of cap plastic today is as a skin for GFAs. It is a part of one of the biggest technical innovations in MUFX in years.

Bald Caps

Bald caps are a specialty in and of themselves, and for a long time demonstrating that you could apply one was a requirement for membership into any of the makeup guilds. From start to finish, the application of a bald cap, including makeup, can take an hour or longer, easily. Bald caps can be made generically and fit just about anyone or they can be completely custom made for a specific head. Generic caps are usually made from either latex or vinyl, whereas custom jobs can be foam latex or even silicone. The late Richard Snell (*AI, How the Grinch Stole Christmas, Pirates of the Caribbean* (2 and 3)), who showed me how to apply a bald cap, was great at it and could put a bald cap on someone with hair down to her waist and make it look as though she'd shaved her head. I don't have a photo of that, unfortunately, but I do have one taken by one of my former students at the International Makeup Artist Trade Show (IMATS), in Pasadena, California, in 2004. It shows Richard applying one of the custom silicone caps he was known for. He was an amazing guy.

Making a Bald Cap

You can certainly buy ready-made bald caps that are quite good. There are several choices of premade caps. Michael Davy Film & TV Makeup sells WaterMelon® caps. Woochie® caps are ones I've used a lot; they're latex, and Kryolan sells Glatzan L caps. But where's the fun in buying something premade?

The first thing you need to have before you can make your own bald cap is something to make the cap on. You can purchase a plastic bald cap head form made of polyethylene from Alcone for about $35 (£19), see Appendix C for contact details. Or you can try your hand at making your own bald cap form from one of the full-head lifecasts you no doubt have by now. You know you want to!

For material, Kryolan makes an acetone-based vinyl cap plastic called Glatzan L and Glatzan L matte, and I already mentioned Baldiez and Super Baldiez and Michael Davy's Water-Melon. You can also use slip latex, balloon latex, mold latex, or Pliatex mold rubber (which is latex) or you could try stippling on silicone that has had a thixotropic agent added to it so that it won't be runny. Or, you can sculpt and mold a custom silicone cap. I'd hold off on this last one until you feel really comfortable working with silicones and with mold making. Foam latex bald caps are also commonly used. Keep in mind that if you make a latex cap, you will not be able to use platinum silicone such as Alcone 3rd Degree or Smooth-On Skin-Tite to create any kind of build-up effects or wounds, or if you are doing a platinum silicone lifecast with Smooth-On's Body Double or Mould Life's Life Form because latex will inhibit the cure of platinum silicone and leave you with a gooey mess.

I make almost all of my bald caps out of Baldiez or Super Baldiez, unless it's for a lifecast, then I will use less-expensive latex.

MATERIALS

Polyethylene bald cap head form
Misc. rubber sponges
Petroleum jelly
Plastic wrap
Sharpie marker
China marker
1-inch chip brushes
Latex rubber or cap plastic
Powder and brush
Clear tape
Scissors
Eyebrow pencil
Tweezers

There are three ways to approach making your own bald caps: (1) make a one-size-fits-all cap, (2) make a custom stippled cap for a specific individual, and (3) a sculpted, cast foam latex or silicone cap. I'll describe how to make a custom cap for a specific head and then describe the actual cap process, which is the same for the second type of cap. Cast foam latex and silicone caps are jobs that require sculpting and mold making and, in the case of foam latex, an oven heat cure.

The steps are as follows:

1. With a roll of cling wrap, wrap the plastic fairly tight around your subject's head (the part with hair on it) and then cover the plastic wrap with the clear tape. Use small pieces that will be easier to manage (you did trim the plastic off from the rest of the roll, right?). The tape will make the shell you are creating rigid enough to be manageable.
2. When the tape has been applied, draw an outline of your subject's hairline all the way around, adding about ½ inch (1.25 cm).
3. Carefully lift off the shell and trim it with scissors along the drawn line.
4. Place the shell on the plastic head form and trace the edge with the china marker.

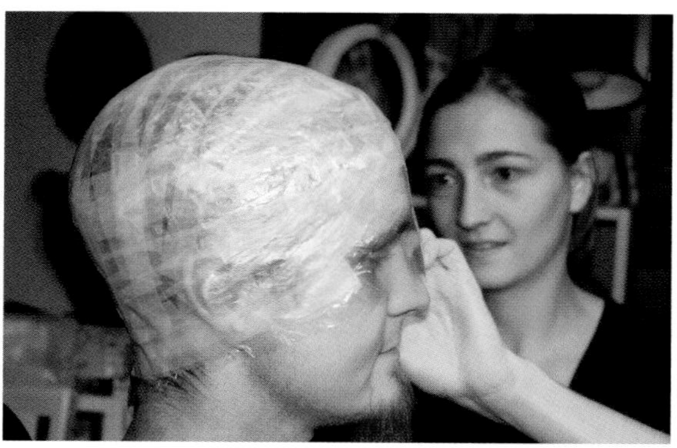

FIGURE 10.32
Measuring for custom bald cap with plastic wrap, tape, and marker.
Photo by the author.

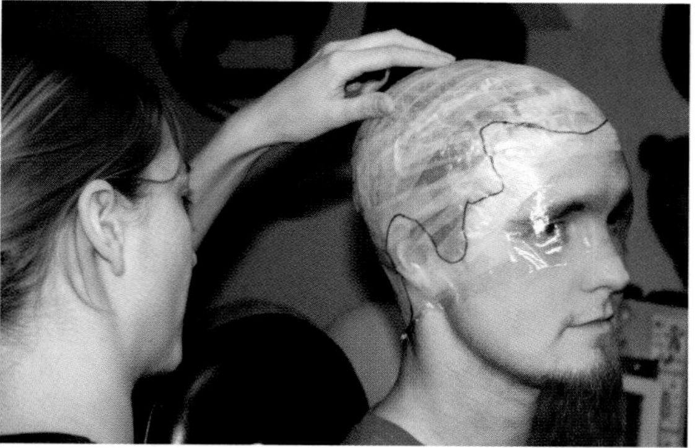

FIGURE 10.33
When tape applied, draw outline of subject's hairline, adding ½" (1.25 cm).
Photo by the author.

The following steps are the same even if you are making a generic one-size-fits-all bald cap.

NOTE

If you are going to make a bald cap using acetone-based plastic cap material, make sure you have good ventilation, wear a respirator, or both.

FIGURE 10.34
Place shell on plastic head form and trace edge with china marker.
Photo by the author.

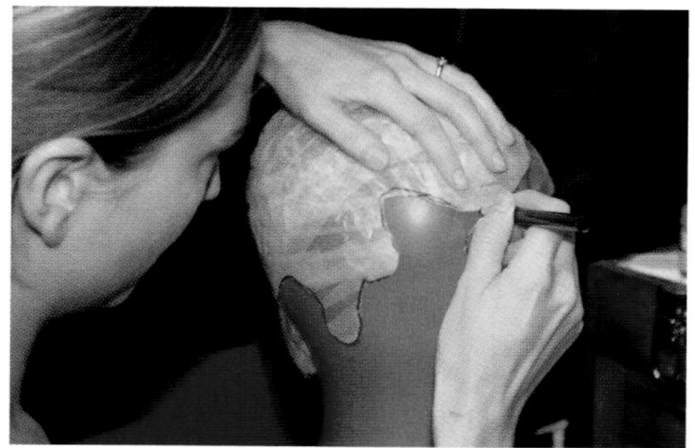

5. Remove the clear shell and rub a very light layer of petroleum jelly on the surface of the head.
6. Pour a small to moderate amount of the bald cap material of your choice (cap plastic or latex) into a small shallow cup and stipple a thin layer over the cap area on the plastic head with a piece of rubber sponge.
7. When the first layer is dry, stipple on another layer over the first one; repeat this step until you have five thin layers.

If you made a vinyl cap, it can be powdered and removed when the final layer is completely dry; if the cap is latex, let it sit for 24 hours to fully cure. Otherwise, it could tear because it is thin and weak. Powder both the outside and the inside, being very careful not to let the edges roll, because the material, both vinyl and latex, will stick to itself and could be difficult to separate.

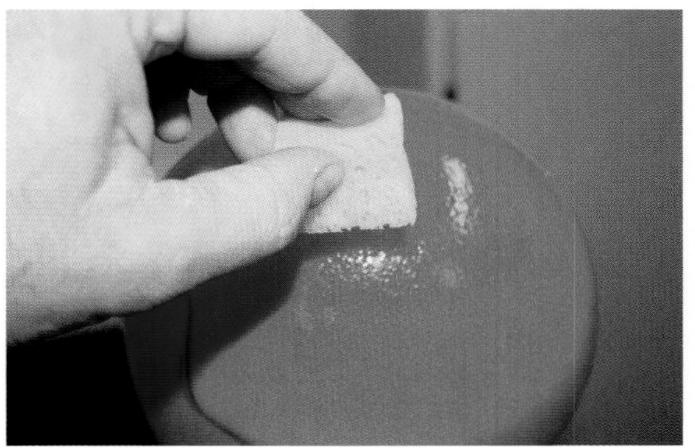

FIGURE 10.35
Stippling latex or bald cap plastic onto head form.
Photo by the author.

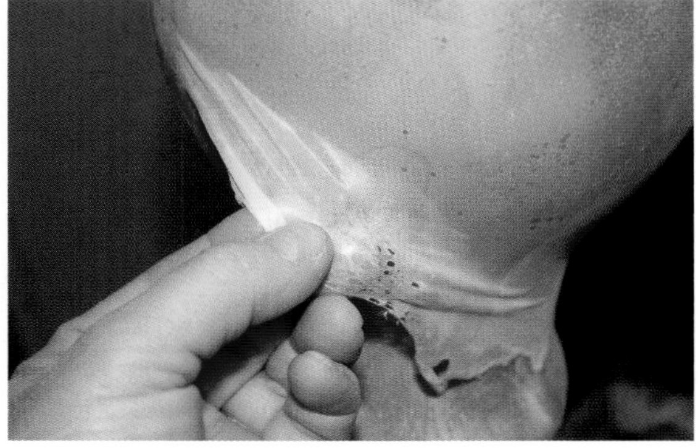

FIGURE 10.36
Powder cap as you remove it from form to prevent edges from sticking.
Photo by the author.

Applying a Bald Cap

Applying a bald cap is not as easy as making one, but like many aspects of this field, applying a bald cap is not necessarily difficult, but it requires a little patience and some concentration to do it well. The more hair you have to deal with flattening down, the longer it may take you to apply the bald cap.

1. Have your subject sit comfortably in a chair that is at a height at which it will be comfortable for you to work. Your subject should wear a loose-collared shirt or a robe that will give you good access to the neck.
2. The next step is to flatten your subject's hair as flat as possible to her head. The longer or thicker the hair, the more difficult this will be to accomplish. However, there are a few things you can try:
   Simply wetting the hair with water might be good enough for applying a bald cap before lifecasting, but it's not always good for a cap that will be part of a makeup. Whatever you use on the hair, make sure it's not a greasy product that will interfere with the adhesive you use or with the bald cap itself. Some hair gels have alcohol in them, which will begin to dissolve a vinyl bald cap and throw off your whole makeup. A product called Gafquat, which is a copolymer widely used in hairstyling products and is soluble in both water and alcohol, is frequently used to flatten the hair for a bald cap application. When it dries, it forms a film that will hold the hair firmly in place. Richard Snell used to literally glue the hair down with Telesis 5 silicone adhesive: a rather expensive and time consuming way to ensure that the hair would lie flat and stay in place, but it sure did work!

NOTE

If you are using a bald cap made with Super Baldiez—which is alcohol soluble—do not use a hair gel with alcohol in it to flatten the hair. Your cap will disintegrate.

NOTE
MUA Michael Mosher applies bald caps using no product in the hair at all. His DVD is listed in Appendix E

3. Make sure the inside of the bald cap is clean—no powder residue to hamper the adhesion. A bit of alcohol on a cotton pad will wipe away any excess powder; if you're using a vinyl cap, be careful because alcohol can easily damage the cap. It won't affect a rubber cap.
4. A cap that is a bit small is preferable to one that's too large, because it will not fit the crown of the head properly or lie correctly against the nape of the neck. A cap that is too small will result in stretching the skin like a bad facelift if you try to make it fit, so try to have one that will fit well without a lot of effort.
5. Make sure that your subject's face is clean, especially around the perimeter of the hairline. Clean the skin with an astringent or with 99% IPA.
6. Ask your subject to help with the initial placement if you are unable to stretch the cap sufficiently yourself to get it onto the head.
7. With your subject holding a finger on the front edge of the cap, position it so that there are no wrinkles.
8. Pros-Aide is a good adhesive. It works best as a contact cement, with the adhesive applied to both surfaces, skin and cap, and allowed to dry before pressing them together.
9. Start at the front of the bald cap. Apply adhesive to the forehead (center) and to the underside of the bald cap in about a 2-inch (5 cm) strip; allow both surfaces to dry (clear) and then press the cap to the forehead. This will serve as an anchor as you glue the back of the neck.
10. Fold back the bottom of the bald cap and apply some adhesive; tilt your subject's head back slightly and apply adhesive to the back of your subject's neck.
11. With your subject's head still tilted back slightly, pull the cap down and press the cap to the skin. This will ensure a tight fit and no wrinkles once your subject's head is straightened again.
12. Next, pick a side and stretch the cap into position over the ear; with the eyebrow pencil, make a mark above the ear and draw down just behind the ear, following the curve of the helix—the outer flap of the ear.
    This drawn line is where you will make a cut to place the cap around the ear. You will most likely need to do some trimming to fit the cap cleanly behind the ear.
13. Apply adhesive about ½-inch (1 cm) wide to the skin behind the ear and down along the hairline to where the cap is attached to the neck and to the cap; when both surfaces are dry, have your subject's head tilt a bit toward the side you've just glued, then pull the cap into place and press it to the skin behind the ear down to the neck.

FIGURE 10.37
Ask subject to help with initial placement onto head.
Photo by the author.

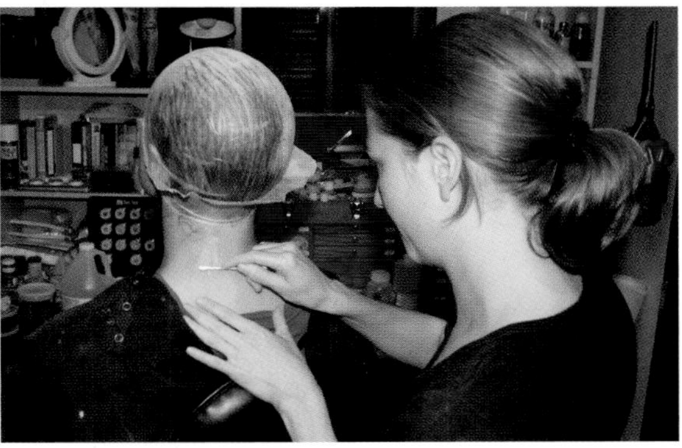

FIGURE 10.38
Fold back bottom of bald cap and apply adhesive; tilt subject's head back slightly and apply adhesive on back of subject's neck.
Photo by the author.

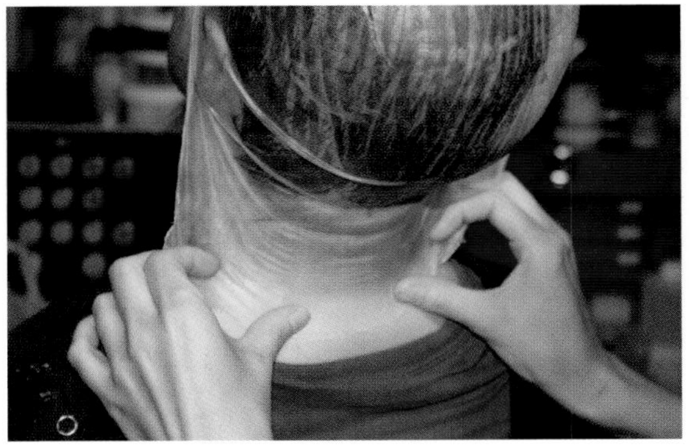

FIGURE 10.39
With the subject's head still tilted back, pull cap down and press to skin. This will ensure tight fit and no wrinkles.
Photo by the author.

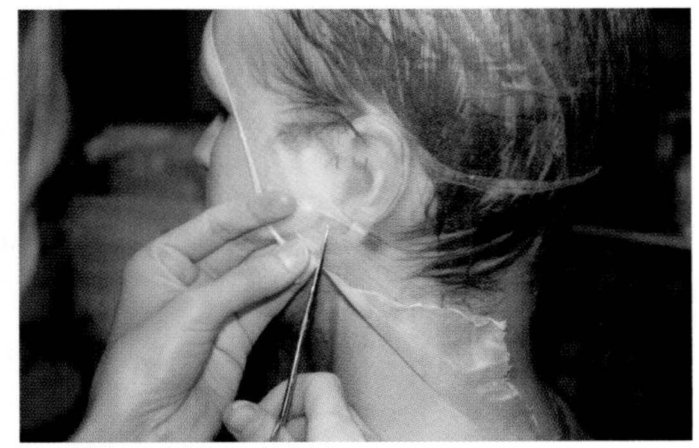

FIGURE 10.40
Pick a side and stretch cap into position over ear; with eyebrow pencil, make mark above ear and draw down just behind ear, following curve of helix (outer flap of ear).
Photo by the author.

14. Next, affix the cap in front of the ear by applying glue from the skin at the top of the ear, down in front of the ear, and around the sideburn to where the cap is attached on the forehead. Apply the glue along the hairline about ½ inch (1 cm) wide. When the glue is dry, pull the cap down and forward to remove any wrinkles, then press the cap to the skin.
15. Repeat Steps 12–14 on the other side of the head.

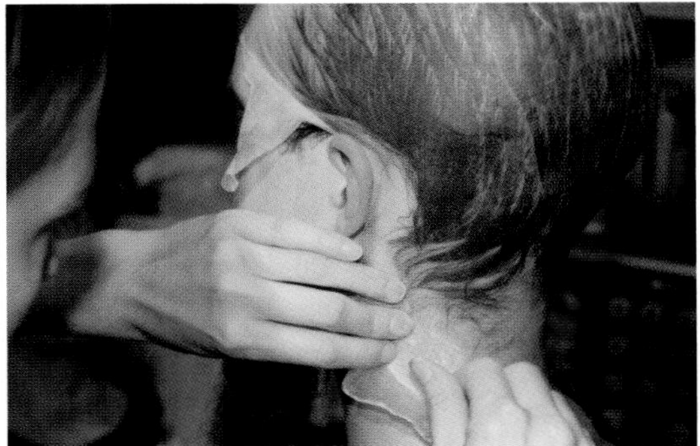

FIGURE 10.41
When both surfaces dry, have subject's head tilt toward side just glued, then pull cap into place and press to skin behind ear down to neck.
Photo by the author.

Once the cap has been applied, it must be trimmed of loose and rolled edges. With a good pair of tweezers, lift up the edges that need trimming and cut away the excess, then lay the cap smoothly back into the adhesive. Do this all the way around the cap; don't cut perfect straight lines—vary the cut so the edges will be easier to blend.

Blending the bald cap edges can be done by one of the four ways: naphtha, acetone, 99% IPA, or bondo (Cabo patch). Naphtha, essentially lighter fluid, will dissolve the edges of a latex cap, but it's a bit harsh on the skin and can cause irritation. If your edges are thick, you'll destroy the bald cap before you can thin the edges enough to matter. Mineral Spirit will also dissolve latex, but the same caveat applies.

Acetone won't dissolve latex, but it'll go through vinyl cap material like nobody's business. It's also likely to cause some skin irritation, so you might want to use 99% IPA on a vinyl cap. It also works very well dissolving edges. For a latex cap, though, what is the other option? Oh, yes. Bondo. Of course, you remember that bondo is a mixture of Cab-O-Sil (fumed silica) and Pros-Aide adhesive, or thickened by mixing to evaporate the moisture.

If you can't get the edge down to the level of the skin, build *up* to the level of the edge. You don't want to apply the bondo to the cap but to the skin and fill the gap between the skin and the cap. Smooth UP to the edge, *not* from the edge down to the skin.

You can apply the bondo with a small dental spatula or palette knife or even with a small brush. A piece of damp sponge can be used to further blend and texture the bondo to match the skin and the cap. When the bondo has dried, stipple a layer or two of latex over the edges all the way around the cap onto the cap and the skin, using the same kind of sponge you used to make the cap. When the latex is dry, powder it. Now it's ready to paint as described in Chapters 6 and 7.

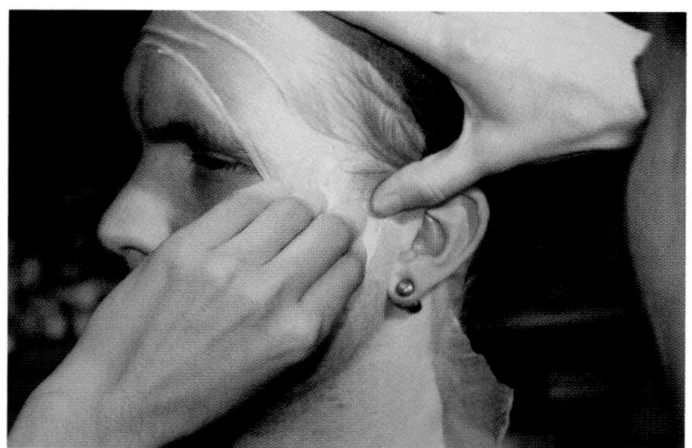

FIGURE 10.42
When glue is dry, pull cap down and forward to remove any wrinkles, and then press cap to skin.
Photo by the author.

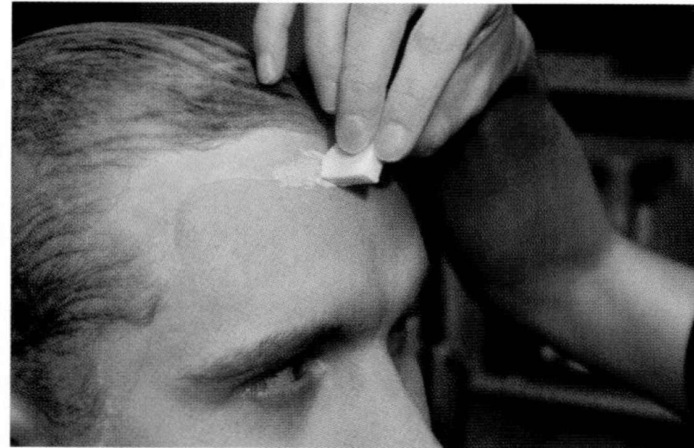

FIGURE 10.43
Apply bondo to blend cap edges.
Photos by the author.

BUILDING UP EARS AND NOSE

This is not rocket science but prosthetics at about their most primitive. Even so, the results can be very good. Full, over-the-ear appliances can be made by building up layers of latex rubber or plastic cap material (or both) onto a positive of the ear.

FIGURE 10.44
Positives for *Bat Boy* latex build-up ears.
Photo by the author.

It is important when building each layer to be cognizant of the edge thickness because it will have to be blended to seal the illusion of reality. How many layers will you need? At least six and perhaps 10 or 12, depending on the needed rigidity of the appliance. When I made rather large ears a few years ago for a production of *Bat Boy: The Musical*, I think there were 10 thin layers of latex plus a very thin foam insert up into the pointy helix to hold the ear upright and still be very light. I have since done another production of *Bat Boy: The Musical*, but the process hasn't changed.

For a nose, instead of a positive, you'll need a negative; you could use a positive, I suppose, but the reason a positive works for an ear and not so much for a nose is that the ears don't really have much texture detail, whereas noses often do. Try it both ways and see which you prefer and which looks better. In either instance, blending off the edges and matching the coloration will be the deal breakers.

Before starting any of these tasks, give the positives and the negatives a release of a very thin layer of petroleum jelly to ensure an easier removal of the appliance.

TUPLAST

Tuplast is a liquid plastic material from Kryolan. It comes in a tube and can be useful in creating small flexible cuts, scars, blisters, and so on. It can be applied to the skin directly from the tube and can be sculpted on a piece of glass or placed into a stone plate mold that has been sealed and released with a very thin coat of petroleum jelly or vegetable oil. Or you can use a small silicone mold in the same way, but you really don't need to release it; I'd still give it a thin coat of Epoxy Parfilm. If you intend to apply Tuplast directly to the skin (it is actually pretty decent for creating some burn effects and for creating raised scars), I suggest a barrier layer of PPI's Top Guard or Pros-Aide to make adhesion and removal of the Tuplast easier. Kryolan also makes a remover called Old Skin Plast Remover that will facilitate removing the Tuplast.

FIGURE 10.45
Tuplast from Kryolan.
Photo by the author.

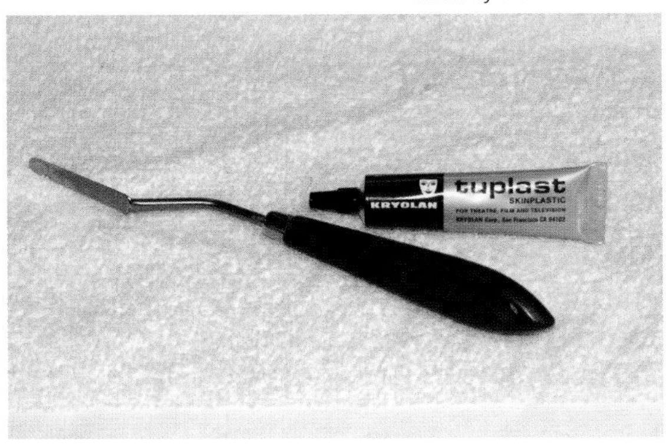

Tuplast is not my favorite material to work with, but probably only because I've had very few occasions to use it, but you should know what's available in the marketplace. Your kit ought to have a little bit of everything in it; you never know when something could come in handy at just the right time. A lot of material is available for creating the same type of makeup effects that can be done with Tuplast, such as gelatin or skin-safe silicone, which I find much easier to work with and apply.

NOSE AND SCAR WAX

More for theatrical use than for film and television applications, nose and scar wax (also Derma Wax, Naturo Plasto Mortician's Wax, Bone Simulation Wax, Nose Putty, etc.) is primarily for facial applications to the bony parts of the face: nose, cheeks, chin, and so on. In many ways, theater can be more forgiving than film or television, mostly because in theater we see everything in a wide shot. Unless a character makeup is being seen in an intimate theater setting where the audience is mere feet away from the performers, lighting and distance can help sell a makeup effect that would not fly in a close-up on screen.

When it comes to subtle facial changes, nothing can alter someone's face as dramatically as the nose. An upturn or downturn of the tip or a bump on the bridge can often change a person's face enough to make them literally become someone else.

Working with nose wax is not difficult, but like all makeup effects, it should not be rushed or your results could suffer. Be patient and work diligently. You should definitely experiment with this material because, as with everything else, proficiency comes with practice. Once you have a design in mind, whether it is a new nose, a puffy eye, or some sort of horrific wound, the less material you need to use, the better; it will be easier to shape and blend.

Materials

Nose and scar wax
Clear latex
Castor sealer or plastic sealer
Petroleum jelly
Small palette knife or dental spatula
Applicators (Q-tips, small brushes)
Stipple sponge
99% IPA or astringent
Rubber makeup sponges (triangles)
Pros-Aide
Cotton balls
K-Y lubricant

- 99% IPA or astringent is for cleaning the skin before application.
- K-Y is for your fingers so that the wax won't stick to you and make application difficult—*if* you're using your fingers for application. It can also be used to help smooth and blend the wax edges.
- Applicators are for applying Pros-Aide.
- Pros-Aide is to provide a surface for the cotton fibers (only a few!) to adhere to.
- Cotton balls are to provide a few fibers for the wax to grab; dab the cotton into dry Pros-Aide, then pick off most of the cotton, leaving only a few fibers.

- Clear latex can be used as a sealer over the wax, as can plastic sealer. Your choice. If you use latex, castor sealer will help makeup adhere better and blend well. Makeup or paints can go directly over plastic sealer.
- Rubber sponges can be used to stipple latex or plastic sealer over the wax.
- The stipple sponge can be used to create skin texture if needed.

RIGID COLLODION

RC is a solution of nitrocellulose in acetone, sometimes with the addition of alcohols. For makeup effects, it is used to create indented scars on the skin. When the acetone evaporates, it pulls and puckers the skin, creating very realistic-looking scars. Michael Davy Film & TV Makeup makes a tinted RC called Collodacolor that comes in translucent red, blue, and yellow.

NOTE

RC will peel off when you're done; that's because the top layer of dead epidermal skin cells (our bodies continually slough off dead skin cells) has released from the skin, not because the collodion has let go. The collodion will peel off and the skin will be fine if it's for a 1-day use; wait a few days for the skin to properly regenerate before using the RC in the same spot. If you reapply to the same spot before the skin has had time to regenerate, peeling off the collodion will peel off living cells and that can cause damage to the skin. Even removing with nail polish remover can be abrasive to the skin (because of the acetone). Actor Tom Berenger had collodion scars on his face in *Platoon*, and part of his daily wrap ritual was peeling it off—against the advice of his makeup artist. Doing this week after week created real lesions on his face that lasted for quite some time.

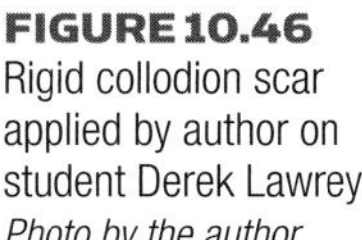

FIGURE 10.46 Rigid collodion scar applied by author on student Derek Lawrey. *Photo by the author.*

Before applying RC, make sure the skin is clean so the RC will stay on the skin without beginning to peel up at the edges. If applied well, RC should stay on the skin for quite some time. After the skin has been cleaned with alcohol or astringent, apply a thin layer of either Top Guard or Pros-Aide to help the RC adhere to the skin better (and come off easier). Pros-Aide might be preferable because of its flexibility when dry. After the RC has been applied over the adhesive where you want the scar to be, let it dry; the skin around it will pucker as the RC shrinks from the evaporation of the acetone. For best results, stretch the skin the way you would for stippling latex, then apply the collodion; hold until dry and then release. The scar effect will be more pronounced where you are able to stretch the skin first. Then stipple a thin layer of Pros-Aide over the RC to encapsulate it. Powder the adhesive to remove its stickiness. Powdering will also remove some of the shininess of the RC.

STENCILS

Stencils are a great way to add both accent and detail to a character or creature makeup. Stencils for all sorts of tattoos are available from Temptu and other sources, as well as stencils for creating shapes and patterns to mimic alien skin textures. Zazzo's Character Troupe templates designed by Brad Look are a great series of stencils that can be used for both beauty and alien character makeups.

FIGURE 10.47 Traditional tattoo sleeve design (L); MUFX tattoo design (R).
Images reproduced by permission of Rob Riffey, Brian Adams.

Tattoos and Character/Creature Textures

Of course, you can always try your hand at original tattoo artwork by tracing your design onto newsprint using an inkblot pencil—*A Bottle of Ink in a Pencil*. This will result in a temporary tattoo similar to those you can get through Reel Creations, Temptu, or Tinsley Transfers. You will most likely need or want to augment the tattoos with additional color from a source such as Skin Illustrator® palettes. For the best way to create your own temporary tattoos, see the accompanying sidebar.

TEMPORARY TATTOOS AND TATTOO COVER

by Aeni Domme

Whether it is a design you've drawn beforehand or drawn directly on the skin, you can easily create your own temporary tattoos.

Like any artwork, copying and using someone else's design without permission is a "No No," so give credit where credit is due and avoid potential problems down the road.

Marker/Pen Transfers

This method is much like what actual tattoo artists used to do before better techniques and materials came along. Either way, this method continues to work for makeup artists of different skill levels. This technique works for smaller tattoos and not back pieces or sleeves.

Materials:

1. Design (tracing or freehand)
2. Tracing paper
3. Bic pen, thin Sharpie, or Staedtler marker
4. Alcohol (70%, 91%, and 99%)

5. Clear deodorant
6. Alcohol-activated pigments (Reel Creations, Skin Illustrator, Temptu Dura, Stacolors, etc.)
7. Sealer (Green or Blue Marble Slr, Blue Aqua Sealer, Final Seal, etc.)

FIGURE 10.48
Tracing design onto water transfer paer.
Image reproduced by permission of Aeni Domme.

Take the design you'd like to use and begin tracing the design on transfer paper using either a Bic pen or a thin Sharpie (which will transfer as brown). When finished and ready to apply, clean the skin area you will be applying to with 70% alcohol—you can find this at any drug store or pharmacy. Apply the clear deodorant to the skin liberally—if you miss a spot, the design won't transfer in that area and you'll need to hand paint it! Take the design and apply it to the skin pressing down firmly. You can lift the corners to see if the ink has transferred. If not, press it down again and wait. If it didn't work, you may not have applied enough deodorant, used a pen that may not transfer (such as Micron pens), or waited too long from drawing to applying. You can draw a design a few hours to approximately a day or two in advance, but not weeks!

Now that the transfer's on the skin, you can paint with your inks and 99% alcohol to line it. If you mess up or need your lines to be thinner, use a flat brush with 91% or 99% alcohol. When finished with the outline, you can airbrush a layer of sealer (I prefer Green or Blue Marble Slr from Premiere Products). If you'd like to color the tattoo, you can do it now in layers, for example, paint, sealer, paint, sealer. When fully finished, you can powder with a color powder and puff or airbrush a very thin layer of skin tone foundation over it.

FIGURE 10.49
Finished transfer.
Image reproduced by permission of Aeni Domme.

Alternate Marker Method

You might like the idea of doing a marker transfer and not having to paint or do outlines. If so, I will share a little trick that I discovered one day.

Black sharpie = brown ink
Staedtler black = black ink
Bic Markers = their color

I personally think this method looks best with black and gray tattoos. You begin tracing the design with the Staedtler marker as it is the darkest black. *You must do this step first or else the black will not be dark enough*! I then use the black sharpie (I prefer the fine pen) to do shading. The design may look like one big dark blob on the transfer paper at this point but just wait until you transfer it! You transfer it the same way as with the marker/pen transfer, using clear deodorant. With more prep in doing the transfer drawing, you now can seal it and be done!

Stencils

Airbrushing a tattoo with stencils is one of the fastest methods for creating temporary tattoos. You can make your own stencils with a variety of media—paper, cardboard, or clear acetate—to name a few. To cut a stencil you will need either an xacto knife and a self-healing mat to cut on or an electric stencil cutter. There are numerous tutorials online that show you how to cut stencils, so we won't go into that here. There are also many premade stencils available online.

FIGURE 10.50
Airbrushing with tattoo stencil.
Image reproduced by permission of Aeni Domme.

Materials:

1. Stencil
2. Alcohol pigments
3. Alcohol (70%, 99%)
4. Airbrush
5. Stencil Tac (Temptu's Stencil Tac is made for the skin)

Clean the skin with 70% alcohol. Next, you place the stencil onto the skin. Depending on the size and intricacy of the stencil, you may want to pre-spray the stencil with Stencil Tac. Now, you select your color and begin airbrushing! Make sure not to paint the design too opaque or else it will look fake. Remove the stencil when you are finished airbrushing. If you have any overspray, clean it off with 99% alcohol. Now, you can begin airbrushing or hand painting color into the tattoo. When finished, you can either spray a flesh tone foundation over the tattoo or use a colored powder with a puff.

FIGURE 10.51
Nearly finished tattoo; needs some cleanup.
Image reproduced by permission of Aeni Domme.

Tattoo Water Transfers

I like tattoo transfers; they can be a bit more time consuming but are inexpensive to make and look the most realistic when finished. The downside is that these are essentially Pros-Aide transfers and can start to look dirty quickly with fabric that rubs against it.

You will need:

1. A design
2. Tattoo transfer paper
3. A (color) laser printer
4. Pros-Aide
5. An airbrush
6. Water
7. Cotton balls

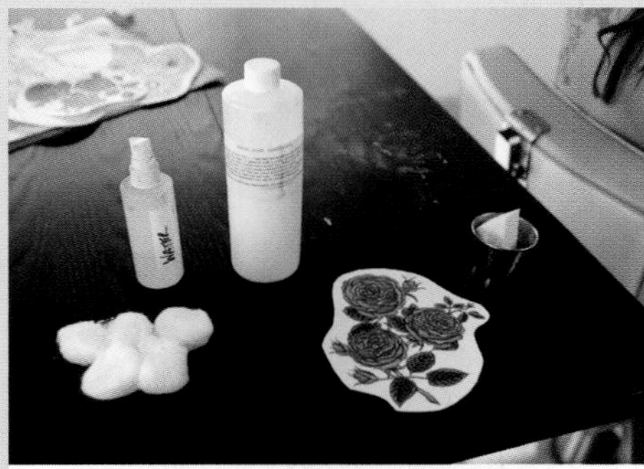

FIGURE 10.52
Temporary tattoo on transfer paper ready to transfer (top); coat transfer with light coating of Pros-Aide (bottom).
Image reproduced by permission of Aeni Domme.

The transfer paper is sold in large sheets about 20 × 26 inches (approximately 50 × 66 cm), so for printing purposes, you will need to precut sheets to fit the printer (8.5 × 11 or 11 × 17 inches, or 21.6 × 27.9 and 27.9 × 43.2 cm). If you do not have a laser printer, you can take the precut paper to print shops that do have one. Just be sure to bring your image documents with you on a CD or USB drive. The cost is minimal—a little more than $1 for an 11" × 17" B&W print at most copy centers in the United States! Color will be a little more.

Now coat the transfer with Pros-Aide. If you're doing this in advance or for resale, I advise coating the transfer with Pros-Aide through an airbrush in thin layers and allowing it to dry. [*Note*: If you airbrush Pros-Aide, clean your airbrush quickly!] When fully dried and lightly powder, so it's no longer tacky to the touch, you can take the acetate that comes along with the transfer paper (this is the same transfer paper and acetate we use for making Pros-Aide transfers), cut the designs apart and staple or tape the acetate and transfer paper together. If you are on set and in a hurry, you can coat the paper with Pros-Aide using a latex sponge (a brush can leave bristles behind). Depending on how long the transfer should last, you can apply 1–3 thin coats of Pros-Aide. Don't worry about leaving stroke marks behind as they won't be seen when the transfer is applied. Just make sure that the entire design is coated.

The next important step is to shave the area you'll be applying the transfer to. Vellus hairs can trap air and create air bubbles (which can be tedious to pop later—use a safety pin). It will be easier to remove the transfer later if there's no hair there! After shaving, clean the skin with 70% alcohol. Yes, it may sting a little.

Now you're ready to apply the transfer. Have your water and cotton balls ready (powder puffs work well too). Position the transfer carefully and lay it onto the skin. Starting from the center, rub a wet cotton ball or powder puff up and down (or side to side) and work your way to one side of the transfer. When fully saturated (about 30 seconds), lift the paper (or if it's a large piece, tear it off—it'll tear easily). Repeat going toward the other side. This method is the best way to avoid having air pockets and tears! If you are applying a large back piece, have the model lie down on a comfortable surface and work in small sections. Tear off pieces of the wet paper as you go.

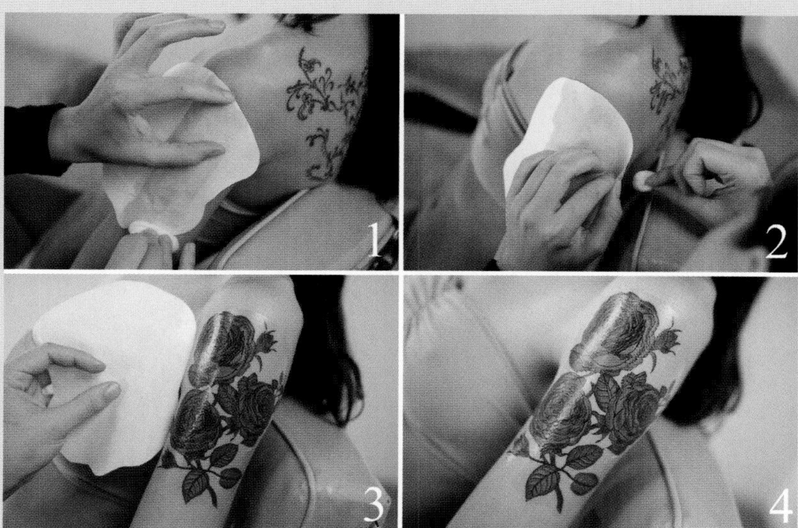

FIGURE 10.53
(1) Position transfer onto skin; (2) apply wet cotton pad or towel to transfer paper; (3) carefully peel off transfer paper; (4) finished temp tattoo; add matte finish.
Images reproduced by permission of Aeni Domme.

Finally you can blend the edges off with 99% alcohol. Take some flesh-toned airbrush foundation or inks and airbrush it over the tattoo. These will matte the shine down considerably—better than powder alone. Before the talent gets dressed, dust with colorless powder and a good powder brush so that the clothes don't stick.
If you have a line tattoo that needs to be filled in, you can hand paint or airbrush with inks.

Tattoo Cover-up Techniques

Tattoo covering has become an often requested and used technique by many artists. Knowing how to do it and using what products you have on hand will be an excellent talent to keep in your back pocket. Depending on how colored and dark the tattoo is will greatly decide on your cover-up technique and product. With more practice under your belt, you'll be glad to have this talent.

There are many different brands you can buy and use to cover a tattoo ranging from theatrical to beauty suppliers such as Sephora. Ben Nye, Mehron, CoverFX, Dermablend, Dermacolor, and ColorTration all have specific lines for covering. Highly pigmented concealers and foundations can also be used—Makeup Forever, RCMA, and Revlon Colorstay are a few brands. More durable solutions are alcohol inks—Skin Illustrator, Reel Creations Inks, Temptu Dura, OCC Inks, Bluebird Inks, and so forth.

Depending on where the tattoo is going to be, I'll either hand paint or airbrush alcohol inks or PAX. The thing to remember about these techniques is that if you go too heavy, or build up product too fast, the result will crepe or wrinkle.

Things you will need:

- Alcohol (70%, 91%, 99%)
- Cotton pads
- Shavers (electric and razor)
- Shaving cream
- Distilled water
- Wax palette
- Sponges (latex, orange, and red rubber)
- Stippling brushes
- Anti-shine
- Aerosol Sunscreen (Neutrogena 100 SPF)
- Thom Suprenant's PAX
- Mel's PAX airbrush thinner
- Alcohol inks (liquid or palette)
- Sealer (Blue Aqua Sealer, Green or Blue Marble Slr, Final Seal, etc.)
- Airbrushes (two or more is ideal if using PAX)
- Compressor that can reach up to 25 psi
- Hairdryer or fan
- Remover (Isopropyl Myristate, Prosaide remover, or SuperSolv Plus)

Step 1—Prep the skin by removing all hair on and around the tattoo. When finished, clean with 70% alcohol to remove any skin oils or lotions. From here is where techniques diverge.

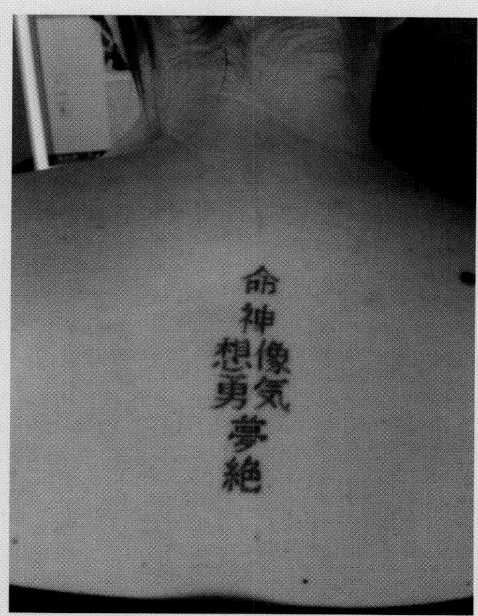

FIGURE 10.54
Before cover.
Image reproduced by permission of Aeni Domme.

Airbrushing with PAX and Inks

Step 2—Mix a red-orange PAX and Mel's thinner in an airbrush. Set the compressor to 10 psi. Before applying onto the talent, test to see if there is any spattering (check the needle, mix the mixture, make sure the gun is not already clogged) or if the mixture is too watery (add more PAX). When the PAX comes out with a fine spray with no spattering, solidly apply the color to the entire tattoo and ½" past its edges. This step blocks out the blue-black used in tattoos and gives you a solid undertone to work with. Let this dry well before proceeding; use this time to clean the airbrush before the Pros-Aide clogs it. Know that when finished with the talent, you'll need to eventually disassemble the airbrush and do a very thorough cleaning with proper airbrush tools.

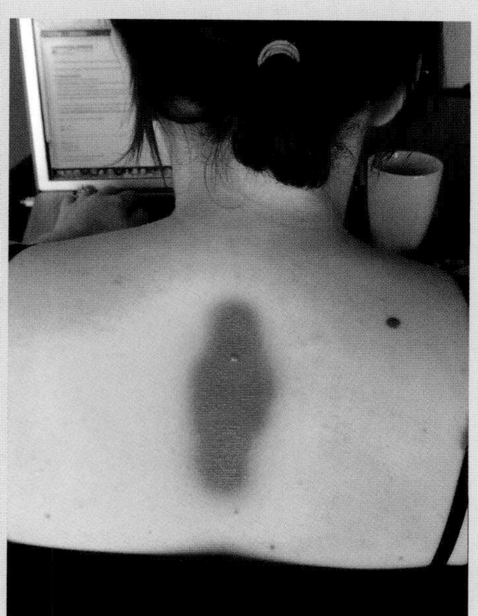

FIGURE 10.55
Red-Orange PAX and Mel's thinner.
Image reproduced by permission of Aeni Domme.

NOTE

Depending on how light the talent's skin tone is and how dark the ink is of the tattoo, you may be able to forego the red-orange step.

Step 3—Now you can use a skin tone PAX to continue and airbrush over the first layer. Try to go from opaque to translucent to begin simulating skin.

Step 4—Use your airbrush (or stipple brush) to add capillaries or freckles to the cover. If still needed, airbrush a flesh tone match. When finished, airbrush a thin layer of sealer over it. Using powder will make the surface *crepe* or buckle.

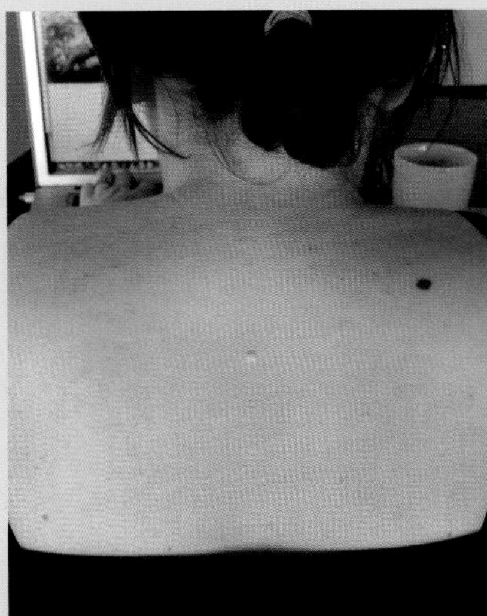

FIGURE 10.56
Flesh tone matched and airbrushed over red-orange.
Image reproduced by permission of Aeni Domme.

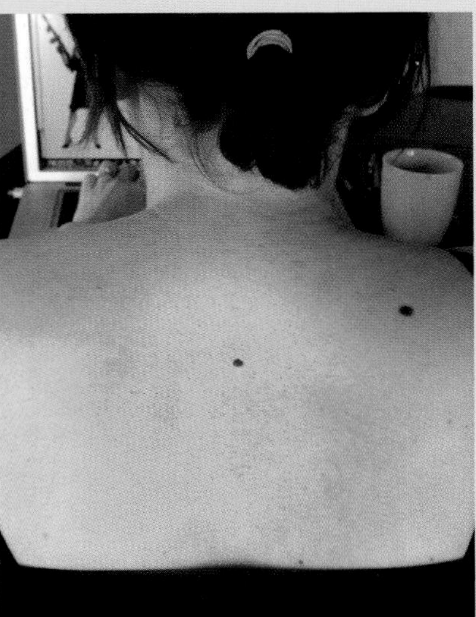

FIGURE 10.57
Flesh tone matched and airbrushed over red-orange.
Image reproduced by permission of Aeni Domme.

Step 5—If the surface looks too shiny, you can use an anti-shine, a silicone, or a water-base foundation airbrushed over it. If the surface looks dry compared to the natural sheen of skin, use sunscreen over it (I like the Neutrogena 100 SPF spray).

Step 6—Remove with either 99% alcohol, isopropyl myristate, Pros-Aide remover, or Super Solv Plus.

Applying by hand follows the same above steps, but with torn makeup sponges, red and orange sponges, and stipple sponges.

Sponge

Just like with covering a tattoo, stencils can also be used with either an airbrush or by hand using a sponging technique. Vittorio Sodano used stencils to sponge paint patterns

on actors in *Apocalypto*, which saved considerable time by not using an airbrush. In using the sponge technique, it is important that the stencil may be flushed with the skin and that the sponge may not be too saturated with color lest it run and seep between the stencil and the skin (which it may do anyway), bleeding all over and ruining the stenciled pattern.

Temptu carries a spray called Stencil Tack that helps hold the stencil against the skin without transferring any of the tackiness to the skin.

Airbrush

An airbrush is a wonderful tool and can create amazing makeup effects in the hands of a skilled user. Airbrushing is not something you can simply become instantly good at; it requires lots of practice and the right equipment: a dual-action airbrush that allows you to control both airflow and the amount of pigment mixing with the air, and a compressor that's quiet, consistent, and allows you to regulate the amount of air pressure from just a few pounds per square inch (psi)—say, 3 psi to at least 10 psi.

More than 10 psi will put almost as much pigment into the air around you as on your subject. You don't want to get a lot of paint or makeup pigment in the air—that's the same air you're breathing, so that's not really good, and you don't want much air pressure when painting around someone's face (eyes, ears, nose, and mouth). Think of sticking your head out the window of a car going 20 mph (32 kph). Airbrushing requires a controlled environment with excellent ventilation. And it's almost imperative that you have more than one airbrush to use so that you aren't stopping and starting frequently to refill the brush, clean it, change color, and so on. If you're working on a show, time is money, and the longer you take, well, you get the picture.

On the other hand, you may only airbrush non-applied pieces, or prop pieces, such as a dead body, in which case the above caveats are less important, though I'd still wear a mask.

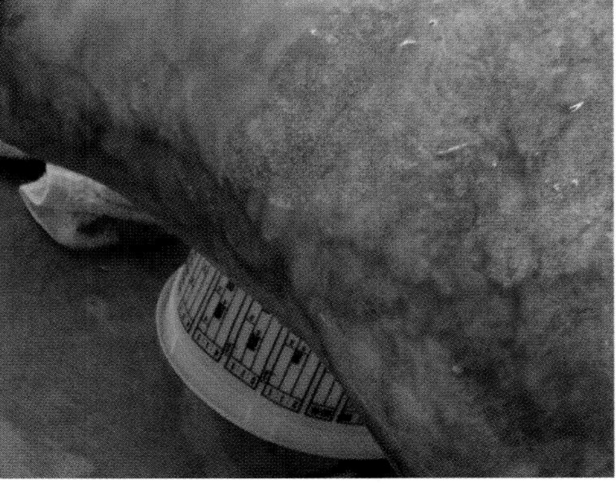

FIGURE 10.58 Thom Floutz airbrushing corpse (L); detail (R). *Photos by author.*

If airbrushing is something you'd like to give a whirl, and I know you do, take a class. There is too much to know about how airbrushes work and what safety precautions you need to know to keep a safe and healthy working environment. You'll find some resources in Appendix E.

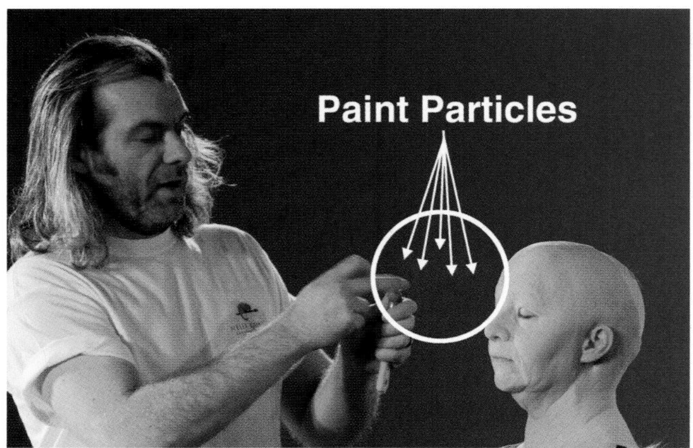

FIGURE 10.59
Neill Gorton painting makeup appliance with cut-down chip brush and spatter technique using Skin Illustrator.
Photo by the author.

SPATTER AND STIPPLE

You can use an airbrush to create a spatter or stipple effect if the pressure is sufficiently low and you remove both the needle cap and nozzle cap of the airbrush. If you're painting directly on someone (or even if you're not), *be careful*, because the needle point is exposed, and airbrush needles are very sharp and pointy. With little air pressure coming from the compressor, you will get even less by not fully pressing down on the trigger; pull back to let the pigment flow and you will get a spatter. The more air you introduce into the mix, the finer the spatter. Trust me when I tell you that this requires a good bit of practice to master. I've been airbrushing since the 1970s, but if I don't do it for a while, sometimes months, it takes a little refreshing to get the feel back.

This effect can also be achieved very effectively using cut down 1-inch chip brushes. It also creates a somewhat more random pattern as well, though I'm sure that point is arguable. By cutting down the brush, lightly swirling it in your color, and then flicking the bristles with your finger, you will flick the pigment.

Moving the brush closer and farther away from your subject and/or using varying pressure will ensure that the randomness of the spatter will continue. Don't forget to move the brush to new areas, too. This technique is discussed in Chapters 6 and 7.

JANE O'KANE

Born and raised in England, Jane O'Kane is another New Zealand transplant. While learning her craft, Jane's first work experience began with the Royal Shakespeare Company where she continued working full-time through 1989, broadening her skills in Makeup and Special Effects. A move to Manchester in 1992 saw Jane working for the Royal Exchange Theatre for the next 3 years. It was within these early stages of her career that Jane was fortunate to train and work alongside some of England's finest wigmakers, adding to her repertoire and providing her with a broad skill base that procured her work in all three areas of Makeup, Hair, and Special Effects.

Since the 1990s, Jane has worked extensively in Film & Television across the globe. Some of her credits include *The Frighteners, Whale Rider, The Warrior's Way, The Grudge, Prince Caspian* and *Aeon Flux*.

FIGURE 10.60
Jane O'Kane.
Image reproduced by permission of Jane O'Kane.

FIGURE 10.61
30 Days of Night makeup and full scleral contacts.
Image reproduced by permission of Cristina Patterson.

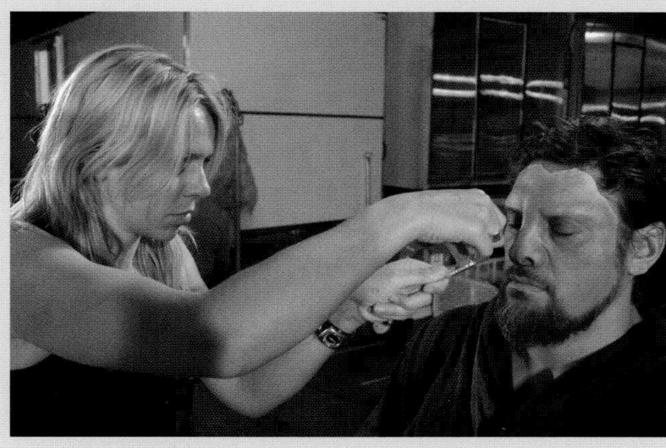

FIGURE 10.62
Jane flicking paint onto foam piece on Stunt Centaur (Shane Dawson); *The Chronicles of Narnia: Prince Caspian*—with KNB.
Image reproduced by permission of Jane O'Kane.

FIGURE 10.63
Jane's handiwork on Geoffrey Rush; *The Warrior's Way*; character makeup/contact lenses/wig/facial hair.
Image reproduced by permission of Jane O'Kane.

FIGURE 10.64 More of Jane's stellar handiwork on "Grandmother" character played by Helen Wong; *The Warrior's Way*. Age makeup and wig (used Attagel and Green Marble Se-Lr to Helen aged 40 years; with Mark Knight).
Image reproduced by permission of Jane O'Kane.

While working with numerous production companies, it was New Zealand's Pacific Renaissance where Jane began in the Television industry with *Hercules* in 1995. A newfound love for New Zealand and a blossoming relationship with Pacific Renaissance, Jane found home. Since 1995 Jane has continued working with Pacific Renaissance for numerous productions; *Jack of All Trades, Cleopatra 2525, Xena, 30 Days of Night* and most recently donning the title of Makeup, Hair, and Prosthetics Designer for *Spartacus: Blood & Sand, Gods of the Arena* and *Vengeance*.

3D PROSTHETIC TRANSFERS

Christien Tinsley's need for time management, ease of application, and continuity in large numbers led to the development of first 2D, then 3D prosthetic transfers, first for the 2001 film *Pearl Harbor* and then for 2003's *Master and Commander: The Far Side of the World*. Prosthetic transfers have been used extensively since on projects such as *The Passion of the Christ, Find Me Guilty, The Cinderella Man, Nip/Tuck, Grey Gardens, Pirates of the Caribbean, The Fallen*, and many more.

Making 3D Transfers

FIGURE 10.65 Neill Gorton painting silicone transfer on Rob Freitas.
Photo by the author.

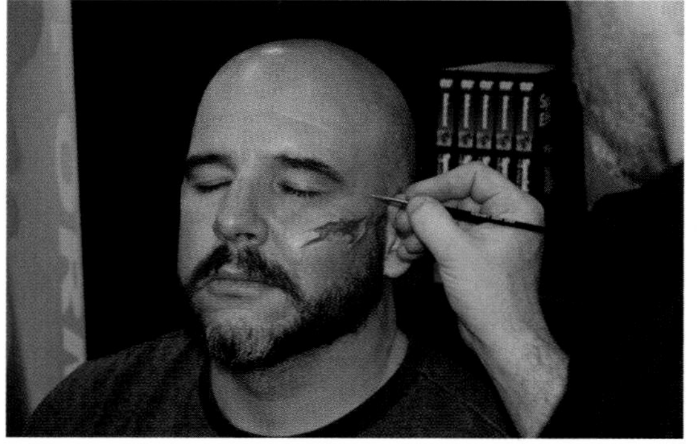

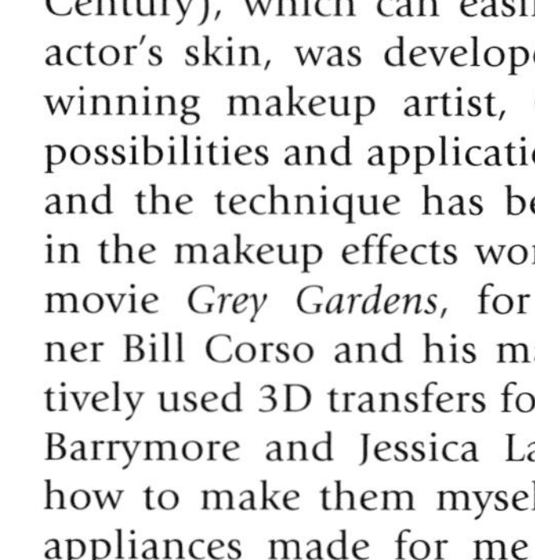

Stab wounds, lacerations, scars, bites, and skin conditions are common 3D makeup effects. A relatively new technique for creating them (early 21st Century), which can easily be transferred to an actor's skin, was developed by Academy Award winning makeup artist, Christien Tinsley. The possibilities and applications are almost endless, and the technique has become widely adopted in the makeup effects world. For the 2009 HBO movie *Grey Gardens*, for example, Oscar winner Bill Corso and his makeup team very effectively used 3D transfers for age makeup on Drew Barrymore and Jessica Lange. Before I learned how to make them myself, I used a number of appliances made for me by Christien and his company Tinsley Transfers for the film *The Enemy God* (2008).

When I returned to the United States from making that movie, I began developing my own bondo, Cab-O-Patch and TPA (Thickened Pros-Aide)—as the material has variously come to be called—to craft my own 3D prosthetic transfer appliances. You can try your own, too. The technical and creative proclivity of this industry only advances by curious experimentation and discovery, so go experiment and discover.

FIGURE 10.66
3D transfers from Tinsley Transfers, Inc., for *The Enemy God*.
Photo by the author.

While 3D transfers can be made using silicone as well, this discussion will be limited to pieces made using Pros-Aide to create a new material affectionately called "bondo" in homage to the brand name product *Bondo*, a polyester filler made by 3M that is used for repairing dings in automobile bodies. The makeup world's bondo has been used for years for seaming and patching tears and holes, but in prosthetic appliances; now it is also used as a material to fabricate prosthetics for stage and screen that are applied like temporary tattoos, using the very same transfer paper.

3D transfers have several benefits over more traditional appliances:

- Translucent appliance material
- Self-adhesive prosthetic
- Very fast and easy to apply
- Edges blend and disappear beautifully
- Coloring and painting is easy
- Transfers accept almost all forms of makeup for coloring
- Appliance edges stay down all day
- They require very little to touch up (if any) during the shoot day or performance
- Move naturally with the skin
- Very effective even when used in and around water

However, no technique is perfect; they do have limitations:

- Cannot/should not be used to cover highly contoured or curved areas such as full nose or ear
- Once the appliance is "touched down" onto the skin during application, it is stuck and difficult to unstick and reposition.
- 3D transfers work best as thin appliances. Sculpts/appliances that are ¼" or less thickness look and work the best. Appliances greater than ⅜"–½" in thickness are generally too thick to work well. They also take a very long time to dry.

That being said, here is a tutorial to begin making your own 3D prosthetic transfers.

3D Prosthetic Bondo, Pros-Aide Transfers or TPA Transfers

These bondo or Pros-Aide transfers (Pros-Aide is the water-based acrylic prosthetic adhesive from which the appliances are made) are becoming more and more used worldwide for a variety of applications by many makeup effects artists such as Joel Harlow, Vittorio Sodano, Christien Tinsley, Matthew Mungle, Kevin Kirkpatrick, Antony McMullen,… and me. Christien was awarded his 2008 Scientific and Technical Academy Award for the development of this process.

These transfers are not only easy to use, but they're also pretty easy to make—once the particular appliance has been sculpted and a flat negative silicone mold has been made—and kept on hand in enough quantity to last for an entire shoot or just to have as a quick out-of-kit application possibility. They really are nothing more than Pros-Aide water-based acrylic adhesive that has been thickened, frozen, thawed, and dried. That's the simple explanation.

FIGURE 10.67
Pros-Aide stirring in Sunbeam mixer.
Photo by the author.

As with almost every process in makeup effects, the Pros-Aide can be thickened in more than one way; the way I was taught is to mix Cab-O-Sil, fumed silica, into the adhesive until it reaches a consistency you find usable, not runny, but not overly thick. However, another way—and I think this is the best method—is to forego the Cab-O-Sil and just use Pros-Aide alone in a mixer on its lowest speed for 8 or 9 hours or until it has reached the thickness you want. I use an old Sunbeam mixer. *Note*: Breathing fumed silica can cause Silicosis, so wear a respirator if you choose to try this method.

Materials

- Silicone mold
- Small (dental) spatula
- Precolored bondo
- Scissors
- Makeup Sealer (Blue Marble, Green Marble, Final Seal, Blue Aqua Sealer, etc.)
- Silicone release (Frekote 1711, Epoxy Parfilm, etc.)
- Transfer paper and silicone-treated acetate
- Krylon Dulling Spray
- Makeup sponges
- Flat straight-edge scraper
- Modeling clay (Monster Clay, Chavant NSP, etc.)
- Q-tips

If you whip it on a high speed, you'll create air bubbles, which you want to avoid; you just want to stir the Pros-Aide. Allowing the Pros-Aide to mix this way allows the water to evaporate without solidifying the adhesive, and you'll wind up with a softer appliance than if you add Cab-O-Sil as a thickener, with less shrinkage of the appliance. As an additional softener, you can add from 5% to 16% DBP (dibutyl phthalate) plasticizer to the Pros-Aide. This can be purchased from a number of makeup effects suppliers, and they're listed in Appendix C. This can be added during the mixing phase or after you've thickened it. You can color the Pros-Aide

with flocking or with a bit of pigment—food coloring, powder, and so forth. Do some experimenting on your own; this industry thrives on innovation and experimentation. I use Createx pure pigment colors and Liquitex Artist Acrylics to tint my bondo.

FIGURE 10.68
Ink beading on silicone-treated side of acetate.
Photo by the author.

You will need a flat silicone plate mold of your sculpted appliance. If you want to try your hand at this, great, though premade molds can be purchased online. I offer them on my website. In addition to needing to have a silicone mold of your appliance, you'll also need temporary tattoo transfer paper, available from several sources, including Alcone, Motion Picture F/X Company, and Nigel's Beauty Emporium. You can also buy the transfer paper together with silicone-treated acetate. The acetate is treated on only one side; to determine which side, make a small mark with a permanent marker (I use a Sharpie) in an area that won't be in contact with the bondo.

The silicone-treated side will cause the marker ink to bead up. Now you're ready to fill the mold. I suggest a light spray release such as Price Driscoll's Ultra 4 Epoxy Parfilm first. All right, *now* you're ready to fill the mold.

Let's presume that you already have a plate mold of the appliance you want to make; we've already covered this kind of mold making earlier in the book, so we don't need to go over it again.

- Put some of the bondo into your silicone mold, being careful to avoid creating air bubbles between the mold surface and the bondo.
- Place a piece of silicone-treated acetate over the bondo (silicone-treated side to the bondo) and carefully squeegee to remove any surface air bubbles.
- Put the mold into the freezer—about an hour and a half—until frozen and then remove the mold. You'll notice that the color has changed slightly.

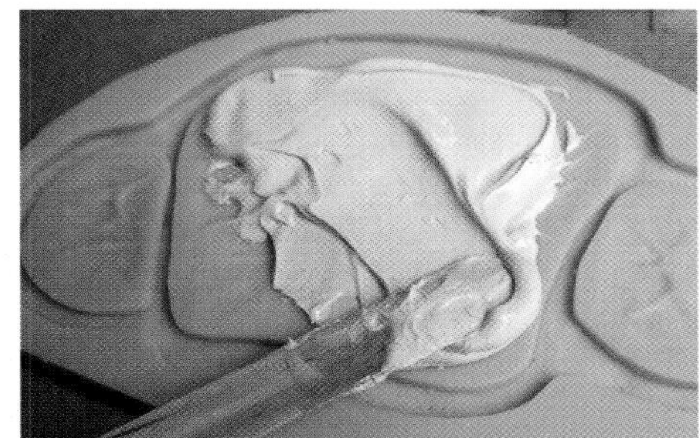
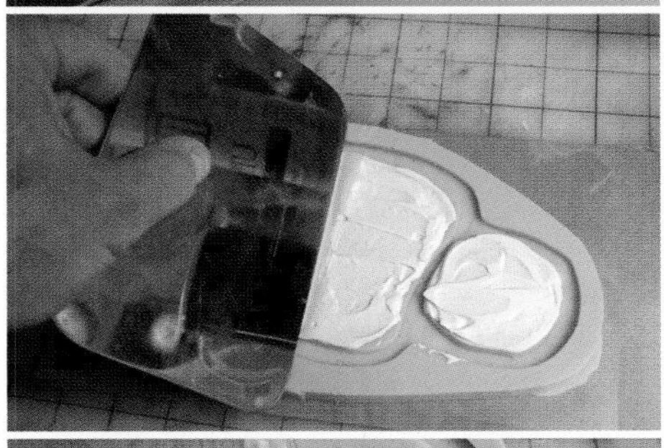
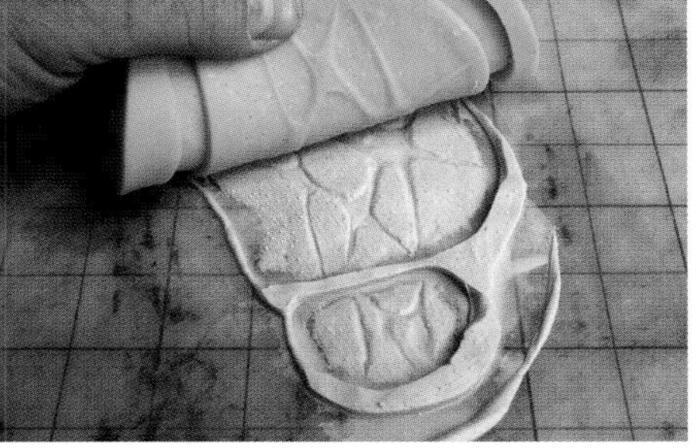

FIGURE 10.69
Spreading TPA (thickened Pros-Aide) into silicone plate mold (top); Squeegee bondo once acetate has been positioned (middle); carefully peel away silicone mold from frozen appliance (bottom).
Photos by the author.

This is what happens: When the adhesive freezes, it polymerizes (becomes plastic) but remains soft and rubbery and still sticky. Why? Near as I can figure, it's because Pros-Aide is a water-based acrylic adhesive; when it freezes, the water is drawn out of the acrylic, allowing it to plasticize and become rubbery. When it thaws, the water begins to evaporate, leaving just the plasticized bondo.

- Carefully remove the frozen appliance from the silicone mold and allow it to thaw and dry; a great way to dry bondo transfers is in a fruit dehydrator. Some people prefer to leave the flashing intact; I remove it while the appliance is still frozen before placing it in the dryer. Peel the mold away from the bondo rather than trying to peel out a frozen appliance.
- Once the appliance is thawed and dry, it can be placed onto the tattoo transfer paper; apply a thin layer of Pros-Aide to the appliance out to the edge of the bondo. One nice thing about Pros-Aide (among many nice things) is that it brushes on white when it is wet, but dries completely clear. Make sure that the adhesive is fully dry before placing it face down onto the transfer paper. The transfer paper is shiny on one side and dull on the other. When the adhesive on your appliance is dry, press it face down onto the shiny side of the transfer paper and then carefully peel off the acetate. If the edges of the appliance start to come up with the acetate, press them back down until they do stick. If they're still sticking to the acetate, here's a trick to try. Take a can of Dust-Off or a similar air-in-a-can product and turn it upside down, directing the long thin nozzle tube at the appliance. Be careful not to freeze yourself! The bondo will instantly refreeze and you can remove the acetate.
- Now you're ready to apply the transfer. The skin should be clean, dry, and absent of any oils, hair, and makeup. Cut the transfer paper close to the edge of the appliance (or appliances) so it will be easier to apply. Place the transfer face down onto the skin and press firmly. Wet the back of the paper with a moist paper towel and hold it in place for about 30 seconds.
- Peel off the transfer paper (carefully) and smooth the transfer gently with some water and let it dry completely. If there are any visible edges, they can be blended off with a small brush or applicator and 99% isopropyl alcohol. On this application, I also blended with a bit of bondo applied with a piece of makeup sponge to further blend edges since there were a couple of places where the edges had flipped over and stuck together.
- Paint the appliance—I used Premier Products' Skin Illustrator palettes (alcohol activated).

FIGURE 10.70
Thin layer of Pros-Aide allowed to dry before pressing appliance onto shiny side of transfer paper (top); peel away acetate before application (bottom). *Photo by the author.*

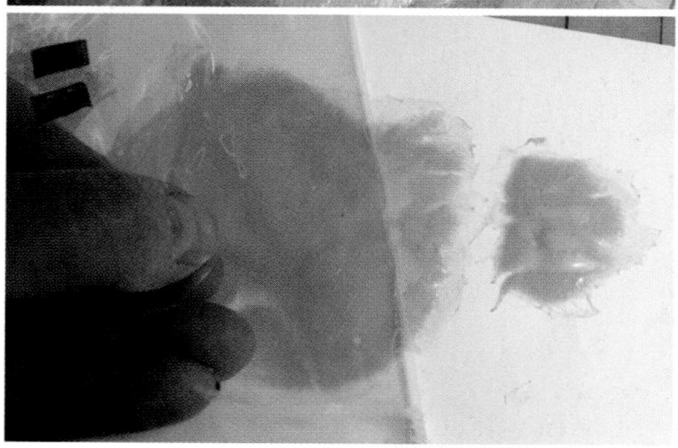

I also added some crepe wool to replace part of the eyebrow and sideburn affected by the prosthetic.

- Seal it with a thin layer of Pros-Aide (let it dry first) and then powder and seal with Ben Nye Final Seal, Reel Creations Blue Aqua Sealer, Graftobian Makeup Setting Spray, Kryolan Fixier Spray or something similar. There are numerous products to choose from.

These prosthetics look terrific on stage and on screen, even in HD. Once they've been applied and sealed, you can even wear them swimming. When you're done, they can be removed with just about any makeup or prosthetic adhesive remover, even with 99% IPA. For the most part, these transfers are for one-time use only.

Matthew Mungle also uses bondo appliances for his award-winning makeup work, but foregoes the transfer paper route. His process is as follows:

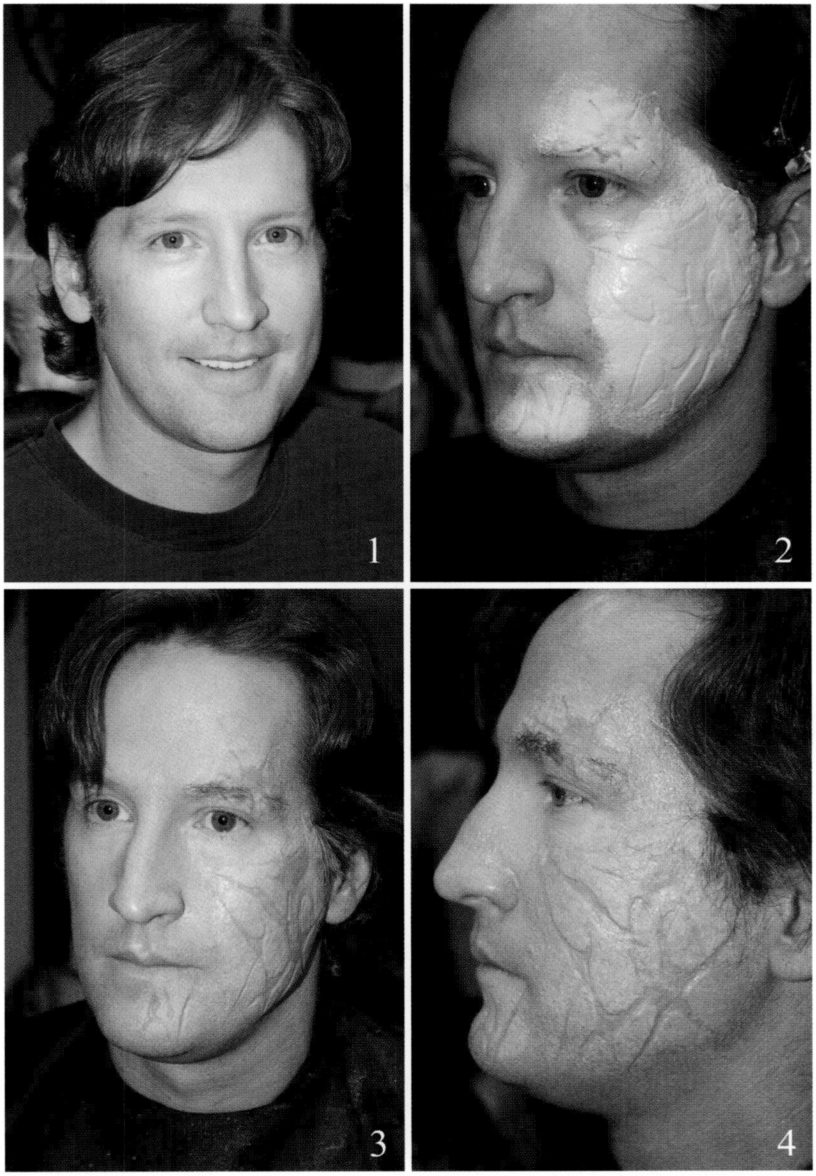

FIGURE 10.71
(1) Student/assistant John Cox "Before"; (2) three pieces in place, ready for paint; (3) painted, blended, with hand-laid hair; (4) finished.
Photos by the author. Makeup appliance inspired by Michael Nickiforek.

1. Two coats W. M. Creations Soft Sealer in silicone mold.
2. Pros-Aide Bondo placed into mold with small spatula. Squeegeed flat and smooth. Dried.
3. One coat of Soft Sealer over dried bondo.

Take some time and try these and other variations. Always remember that there is never one and only one way to do anything in our field.

Removing bondo appliances is easy using Super Solv, Bond Off! or isopropyl myristate dampened on a powder puff, and so on.

NOTE

If you use Baldiez, Super Baldies, W.M. Creations' Soft Sealer, Michael Davy's Water Melon, or any other material to skin your appliance, it is best not to freeze the bondo; let it air dry. If you do want to freeze the bondo to plasticize it, let it fully thaw before attempting to remove it from the mold (or the mold from it); the bondo will come out but will leave the skin in the mold if you try to remove it while still frozen.

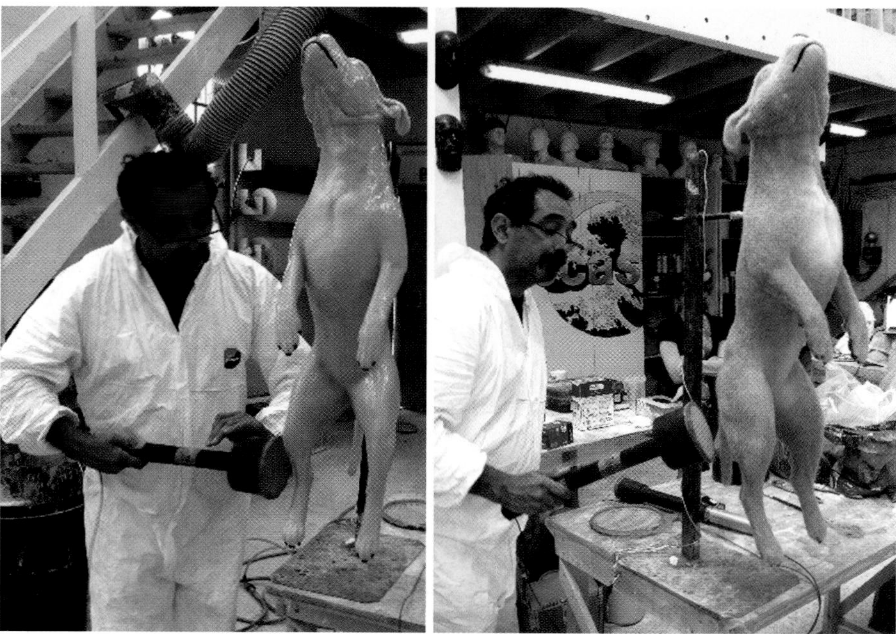

FIGURE 10.72 Esteban Mendoza flocking prop dog corpse; adding flock to wet silicone. *Images reproduced by permission of Esteban Mendoza.*

ELECTROSTATIC FLOCKING

This stuff is cool! I mentioned this process earlier in the book, but it bears repeating here. Outside of Los Angeles, these devices are not very easy to find for makeup use. You might want to consider purchasing one (they're somewhat pricey) and making it available for rental when you are not using it; it is not a tool that is likely to get a lot of regular use unless you also are a mask, costume, prop, or puppet maker, taxidermist, or Furry enthusiast. However, I suspect that having one could inspire lots of uses within the makeup effects craft for both stage and screen. I bought one in London a few years ago and use it now at every opportunity. I even rent it to other artists. It is a kind of like owning a tuxedo—if you have one, you'll find reasons to wear it. Same goes for a flocking wand.

The way it works is as follows: the device is charged with high-voltage electricity, 70 kilovolts, but with very low amperage so that there is no health or safety risk. (Your subject may experience occasional light jolts of electricity, but no more than having someone pop you with a little static electricity after rubbing their feet across the floor.) The principle is that two poles of opposite polarity attract each other and the field lines always hit the surface vertically. So, if a hair (fiber) is charged at one pole, it will fly according to the field lines directly at the opposite pole. Now, presume that the surface at the opposite pole is coated with adhesive; the fiber will embed vertically in the adhesive. The flocking wand should be no more than about 8–12 inches (20–30 centimeters) from the subject.

This does not work well against a latex rubber skin, as rubber is non conductive; the flocking will go everywhere. Trust me. Even with a conductive receiver surface, do this in a closed room wearing goggles and a dust mask and good ventilation.

Varying lengths of flocking material can be used to simulate bottom and top hairs, and depending on the adhesive used, low pressure compressed air can be used to direct hairs in a particular direction or pattern to mimic the reality of growth patterns.

When flocking, Esteban Mendoza suggests holding the applicator 10–60 millimeter, or ½"–2½" away from the target, that way the flock doesn't get "sleepy" on the way to the figure and decide to have a rest; by holding the flocking gun very close, you have a better chance of the flock spearing straight into the glue rather than landing flat.

One fairly obvious note of caution: during application, which should occur in brief stages when applied directly to a subject's face and head, keep your subject's eyes closed and have her hold breath for a moment, since the flocking can and will enter the eyes, nose, and mouth if they're open during application.

FIGURE 10.73
Tiger head flocked with 2, 3, 4, 6, and 10 millimeter flock and punched to blend.
Image reproduced by permission of Esteban Mendoza.

FIGURE 10.74
Adding different hair after bald cap application using electrostatic flocking instead of wig.
Photo by the author.

WRINKLE (AGE) STIPPLE

This is an easy way to age someone either subtly or dramatically. There are also a variety of methods for creating age-simulating wrinkles. However, trying to age someone in their late teens to late 20s might be ineffective with this technique because for it to work well there needs to be some stretch and pliability to the skin. Young skin is often too firm and taut to stretch enough for the stipple technique to be very noticeable. However, combined with more traditional makeup techniques of highlight and shadow, and with prosthetics, aging can be convincingly achieved, particularly for stage or background actors.

The most common aging stipple technique involves using latex; it can be done in 16 stages, with each stage involving five steps, or it won't work. Remember that skin stretches perpendicular to the pull of the muscle beneath it. Also, only do those parts of the face that require aging for the particular makeup.

The stages:

1. The eyelid—pull up at the eyebrow. Stipple carefully on the upper eyelid with the eyes closed.
2. The other eyelid—pull up at the eyebrow.
3. Under the eye—pull down and away from the eye.
4. Under the other eye—pull down and toward the center of the face.
5. Temple—pull up above the temple and pull down below to create crow's feet outside the eye.
6. Temple—pull up above the other temple and pull down below to create crow's feet outside the eye.
7. Nasolabial fold—lift area away from center of face or have the subject puff area to be aged.
8. Nasolabial fold (other side)—lift area away from center of face or have subject puff area to be aged.
9. Upper lip—have subject puff entire area to be stippled.
10. Chin—with neck arched, pull the side of the chin away from the center of the face.

NOTE

Latex may have a strong ammonia smell, so be prepared to use a fan of some sort.

11. Chin—with neck arched, pull the other side of the chin away from the center of the face.
12. Cheek—using a large craft stick (tongue depressor), have your subject carefully reach deep into the cheek inside the mouth and push out. This will help tie the nasolabial folds and under-eye areas together.
13. Cheek—have your subject carefully reach deep into the other cheek and push out.

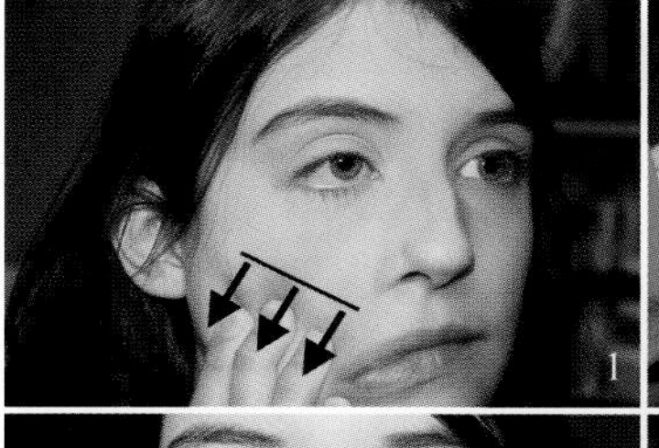

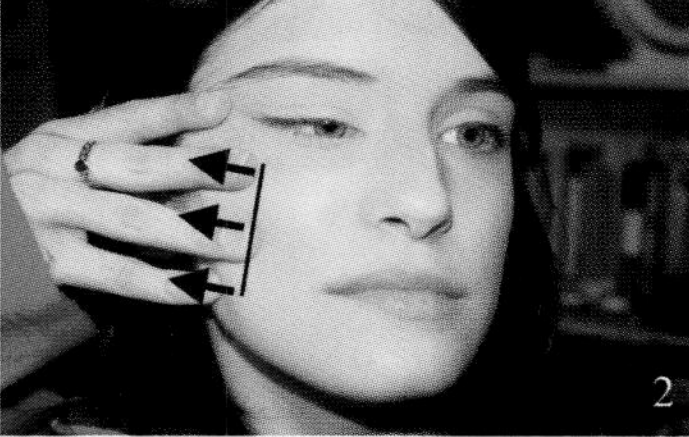

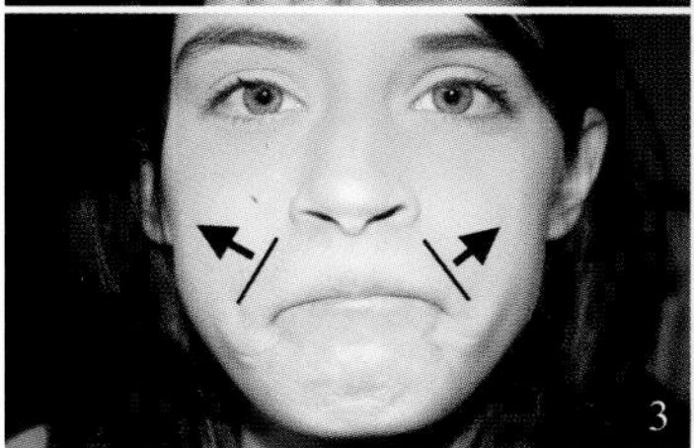

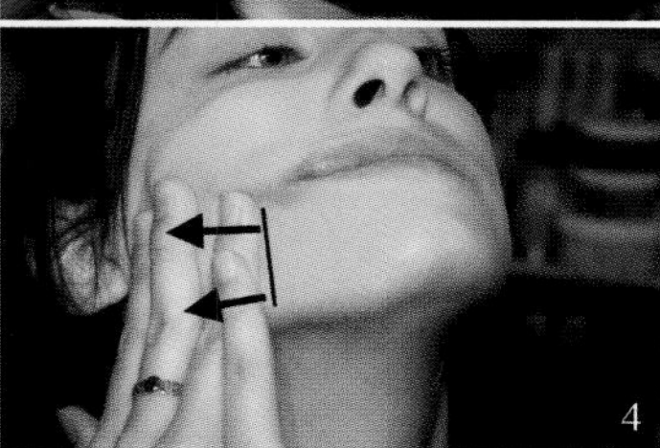

FIGURE 10.75
(1) Under eye—pull down and away from eye; (2) nasolabial fold—lift area away from center of face or have subject puff area to be aged; (3) upper lip—have subject puff entire area to be stippled; (4) chin—with neck arched, pull side of chin away from center of face.
Photos by the author.

14. Neck—begin with the head tilted back to stipple the throat first.
15. Neck—now with the head turned one way.
16. Neck—now with the head turned the other way.

Again, the steps:

1. Stretch the skin.
2. Apply the latex. It does not have to be applied heavily; apply it thinly. Two layers are often enough.
3. Dry the latex.
4. Powder the latex.
5. Release (un-stretch) the skin.

Excess powder should be removed with a small amount of water-soluble lubricant (such as K-Y jelly) on a small brush. To color the latex, you can use RMGP, but it is not absolutely necessary. If you first brush a thin layer of castor sealer over the latex, you can use regular crème colors to paint the latex; if you don't use the castor sealer, the latex will absorb the carrier vehicle of the crème makeup and result in a discoloration of the latex that won't match the rest of the skin.

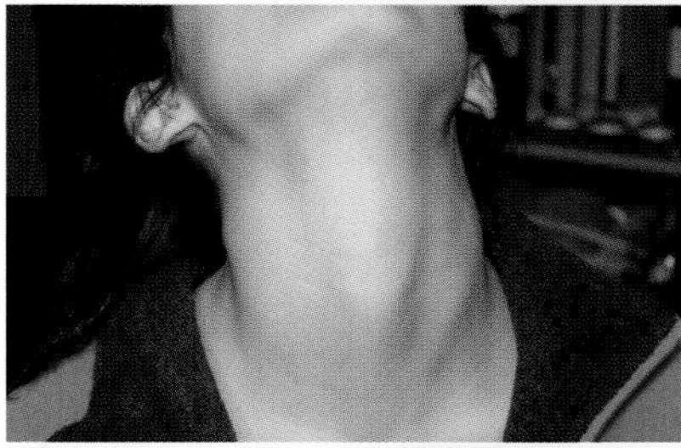

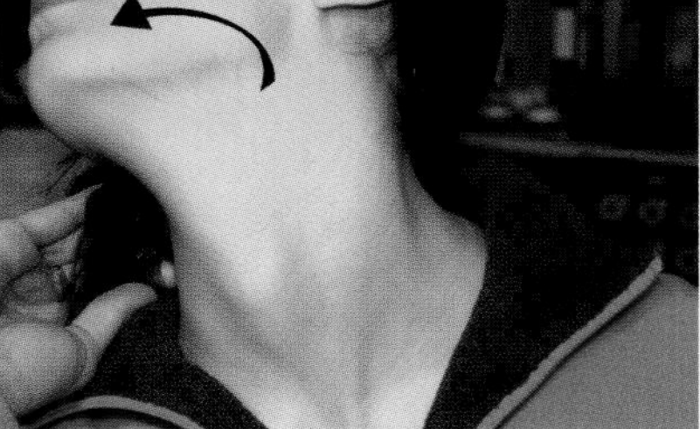

FIGURE 10.76
Cheek—using large craft stick (tongue depressor), have subject carefully reach deep into cheek inside mouth and push out (top); neck—begin with head tilted back to stipple throat first (middle); neck—now with head turned one way, then other (bottom).
Photos by the author.

Latex can be used as a contact adhesive and acts as such. If latex dries on the applicator you are using to add age stipple and dries on the skin, when the two come in contact with one another, they will bond and you will either pull up the latex from your subject's face or your subject will have an applicator stuck to her face.

There are several additional techniques for aging that involve latex and other materials, but I list merely some of them here. These provide more extreme effects, each with its own unique characteristics:

- Latex and tissue
- Latex, tissue, and adhesive
- Latex, cotton, and adhesive
- Latex, cornmeal, wheatgerm, or bran and adhesive
- Green Marble Se-Lr and Attagel

TRAUMA, WOUNDS, AND BRUISES

This is definitely the realm of the well-rounded makeup effects artist but not the focus of this book. So this will be merely a glancing blow. Much of what you'll create to simulate trauma and various wounds is approached from the same direction as much of the work in this book: Know the type of makeup you need to create, research it and gather photos, sculpt it on a cast of the "victim," mold, cast, paint, and apply it. Then add blood, slime, pus, or all the three. For really excellent "how-to" information on this stuff, it is hard to beat Tom Savini's *Grand Illusions* and *Grand Illusions Book II*. Tom's work is as much about special effects as it is makeup effects.

It helps to find reference images for everything you may encounter as a makeup effects artist in terms of wounds you may be asked to create.

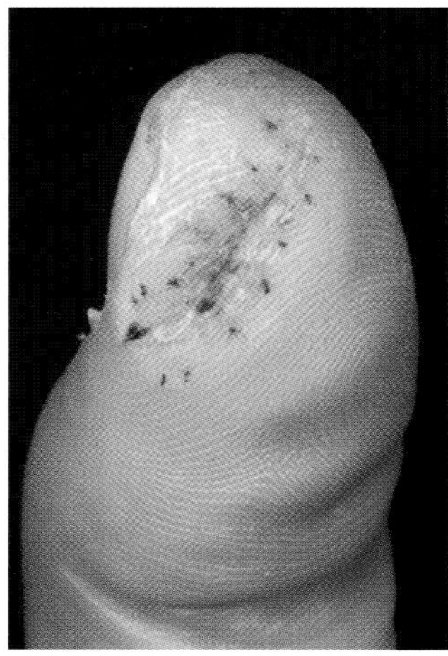

FIGURE 10.77
Author's thumb.
Photo by the author.

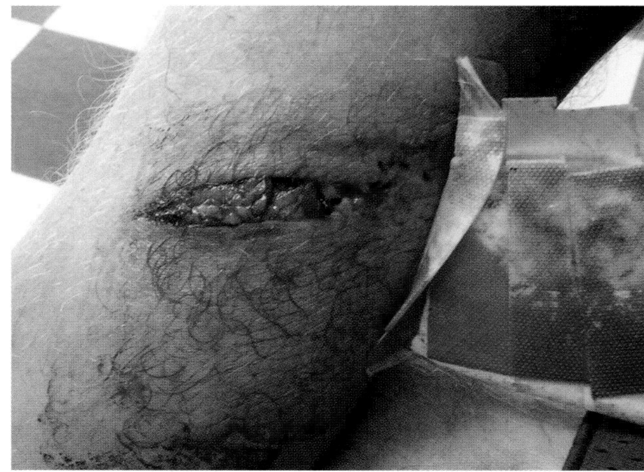

FIGURE 10.78
Calf avulsion.
Image reproduced by permission.

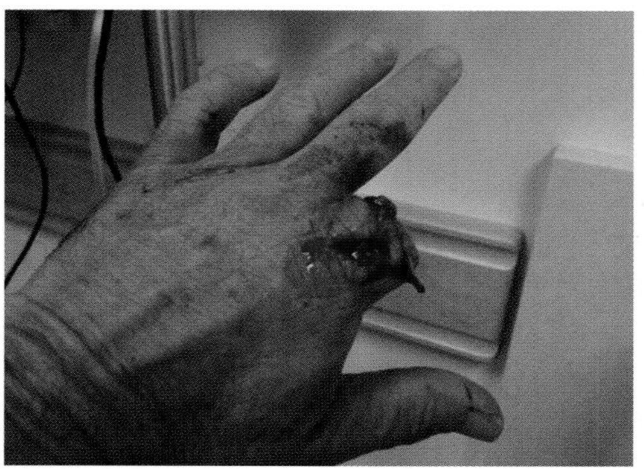

FIGURE 10.79
Gunshot accident.
Image reproduced by permission of Rachel Graham.

FIGURE 10.80
Forensic pathology reference.
Photo by the author.

Bruises

Bruises are the result of internal bleeding, when capillaries near the skin's surface break:

- First is redness as blood spills from the broken vessels.
- Next comes maroon as the blood begins to coagulate, then turns bluish purple over time, maybe even black.
- As the bruise begins to heal, it will change to a brownish green and then to yellow as everything is gradually reabsorbed back into the body.

The Baseball Stitch

Here's one little gem you might get to use one day, the baseball stitch, also known as an autopsy stitch. It is worth knowing so you don't have to think about it if someone asks you to create an autopsy incision and stitch it for a prop or makeup effect. Here's how it works. It is the way most folks lace a shoe, as well.

TIP
Stages of a bruise:
1. Red
2. Maroon/bluish purple/black
3. Brownish green
4. Yellow

Nosebleed on Demand

I'll share one trick I use because it is really effective and quite low tech, as many great effects can be. I wish I could remember who I learned it from so I could give credit where credit is due. This gag requires a piece of porous rubber sponge,

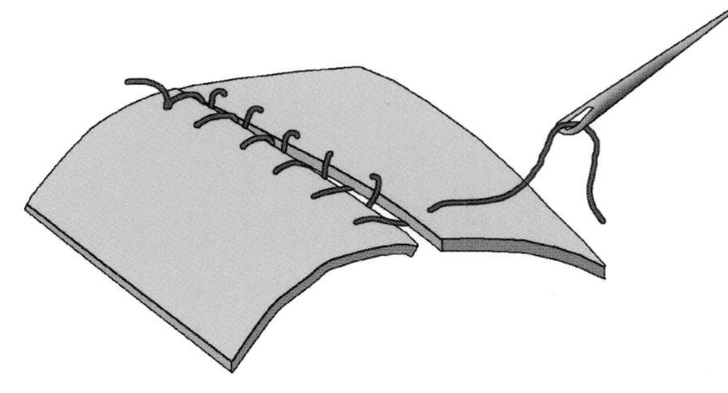

FIGURE 10.81
Baseball or autopsy stitch.
Illustration by the author.

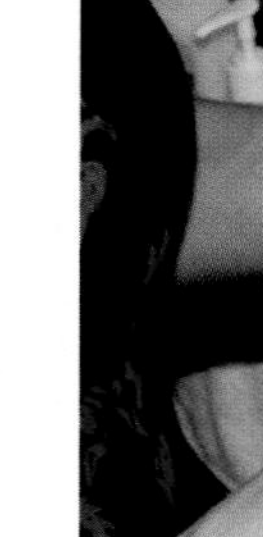

FIGURE 10.82
Small sponge balls for nosebleed-on-command effect.
Photo by the author.

a piece of latex makeup sponge, a pair of tweezers, and some stage blood, and a performer with clear nasal passages.

1. With small, sharp scissors, form each of the sponge pieces into balls about ¼–½ inch (0.5–1 cm).
2. Saturate the porous sponge with stage blood and place it into one of your subject's nostrils with the tweezers, just out of sight. You might want to test first to ensure that the sponge doesn't flare the nostril unnaturally. Clean off any blood with a Q-tip.
3. Place the latex sponge into the other nostril, also out of sight. Make sure it doesn't flare the nostril either. Because the latex sponge is dense, it will prevent your subject from passing air through that nostril.
4. The other nostril has a porous sponge that will allow air through as air forces the blood out.

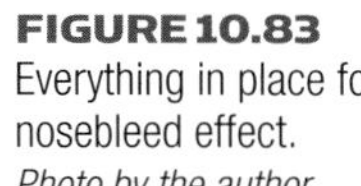

FIGURE 10.83
Everything in place for nosebleed effect.
Photo by the author.

Your performer will need to be a mouth breather for a bit or the effect will be premature. At the appropriate time—say, when your subject gets punched in the face (but not really)—your subject breathes out through the nose; all the air is channeled into one nostril and blood begins to trickle or run out of the nostril, just as if he'd been actually hit.

Of course, keep in mind that breathing out too hard may expel the sponge.

BURNS AND BLISTERS

Tuplast, gelatin, skin-safe silicone (3rd Degree®, Skin Tite®, Sculpt Gel®—see below), and even Old School latex and tissue make great herpes blisters, burn blisters, burns, and any other

FIGURE 10.84
Somebody get a tissue!
Photos by the author.

sort of gross pus-filled lesions you might be called on to create for a character. Again, you need examples from reality for what you are creating. There are forensic books and medical books available as reference with all the pictures you could want and then some. Some of them are listed in Appendix E. Be forewarned that some of the images contained in these books might be quite disturbing to look at and should definitely be kept away from impressionable eyes.

OTHER SKIN CONDITIONS

The best preparation for simulating skin diseases is reference images, unless it's some sort of alien crud that nobody's ever seen before. Go back to Chapter 2 and look at the section on surface anatomy and skin and you might come up with some ideas.

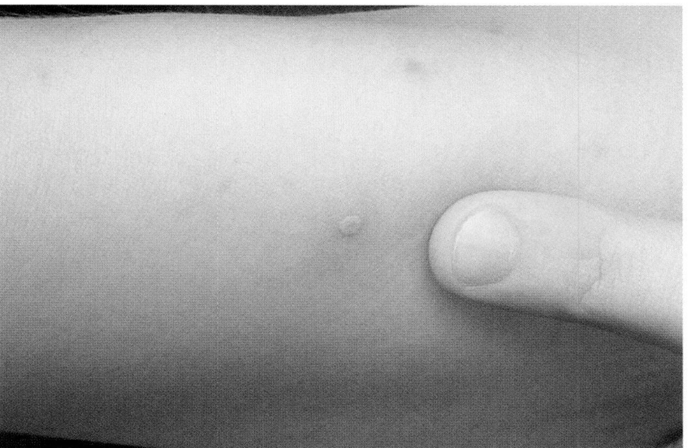

FIGURE 10.85
Chickenpox.
Image reproduced by permission of Wikipedia/GNU Free Documentation License.

SKIN-SAFE SILICONE AND GELATIN

These two materials are absolute essentials for any artist's kit. Skin-safe silicones are two-part (A–B) components that are mixed 1:1 by volume and can be applied directly to the skin, sculpted into a wound, burn, or the like, powdered, and

FIGURE 10.86
Skin-Safe silicone.
Photo by the author.

then painted. These silicones set up in minutes and can feasibly be peeled off and used again later. There are three that I know of on the market currently, from Alcone, Smooth-On, and Mould Life, called 3rd Degree, Skin Tite, and Sculpt Gel, respectively.

Gelatin is easy to use as an out of the kit material. It needs to be heated so that it will melt and can then be applied directly to the skin; make sure that it is not too hot. It will burn if it is heated too much. You can also damage the gelatin itself by too much heat. Warm it just enough for it to melt. Blisters, scars, and so on are easy to create. When the gelatin is set, powder it to remove the stickiness. If you're using gelatin blood, powdering it will remove the glossiness that wet blood would have, so don't powder blood.

TIP

Pick up an electric coffee mug warmer at Target, Brookstone, or wherever you can find one. By keeping your skin, scar, and blood gelatins in small glass jars, you can keep them placed on the warmer and ready to use at a moment's notice. And a coffee mug warmer is a lot easier to schlep around than a microwave.

Before applying gelatin, apply a layer of Top Guard or Pros-Aide as a barrier layer to prevent perspiration from causing the gelatin to loosen. Refer Chapter 6 for more information on working with gelatin.

FIGURE 10.87
Gelatin warming on mug warmer.
Photo by the author.

CHAPTER SUMMARY

After reading this chapter, you should now know more about:

- Making bondo and its use as a prosthetic transfer material
- How to make and apply a bald cap and some other uses for the different types of bald cap plastic material
- Making built-up ears and noses out of latex or plastic cap material
- What Tuplast is
- Using nose and scar wax
- Making scars with rigid collodion
- Tattoo and creature texture stencils
- Why you should take an airbrush class
- How you can stitch a corpse after an autopsy
- Making and using 3D prosthetic transfers
- How to incorporate electrostatic flocking into your work
- Applying latex age stipple
- Collecting reference images for creating trauma, wounds, burns, and skin conditions
- Working out of the kit with skin-safe silicone and gelatin
- Making silicone and resin eyes

Appendix A
Your Kit

You will find discrepancies among makeup artists about what is absolutely essential to have in your kit or at least in your possession. I have kits for different gigs as well as chests, cases, and bags of differing sizes, from countertop oak behemoths to over-the-shoulder canvas on-set bags and everything in between.

Gerstner & Sons of Dayton, Ohio, make well-crafted oak machinist chests that I've found to be excellent units for holding many of the items I use. They are available in numerous sizes and configurations, but they can be quite expensive. Harbor Freight carries a machinist chest that is also oak, versatile, and much less expensive than a Gerstner chest. RCMA used to sell nice makeup cases like these; I'm not sure if they still do or not.

FIGURE A.1
A Gerstner & Sons' machinist chest makes a great makeup storage chest.

Here is a partial list of items you will want to have in your kit; with them you will be armed with the tools to create virtually anything you are asked to create right out of the kit.

- Makeup case
- On-set bag
- Brush holders
- Brush roll
- Misc. makeup brushes
- Triangle sponges
- Orange and red sponges
- Stipple sponges
- Palette knife (plastic and metal)
- Tissues
- Misc. clips
- Velour powder puffs
- Tweezers (several sizes)
- Hand mirror
- Small sharp scissors
- Utility scissors
- Misc. combs
- Misc. hair brushes
- Cotton pads
- Cotton balls
- Q-tips
- Long cotton swabs

FIGURE A.2
Harbor Freight carries a machinist chest that is also oak, versatile, and much less expensive than a Gerstner chest.

FIGURE A.3
Misc. brush holders (these are homemade).

FIGURE A.4
A typical brush roll by Crown Brushes.

- Bald cap head form
- Brush cleaner (Parian Spirit is what I like) and container
- Misc. plastic containers
- 1 and 2 ounces plastic cups for adhesives, etc.
- Hair hackle
- Drawing mats
- Breath mints (seriously; I'm not kidding)
- Hand sanitizer
- Work towels
- Paper mats
- Makeup cape
- Misc. spray bottles
- Misc. hairclips
- Misc. hair bands
- Airbrush and compressor
- Pipe cleaners
- Misc. tooth brushes
- Hair-thinning scissors
- Small blow dryer
- Misc. curling irons
- Misc. flattening/straightening iron
- Disposable lip gloss applicators
- Disposable mascara brushes
- Misc. syringes (without needles)
- Nail clippers
- Setting powder
- Ninety-nine percent isopropyl alcohol
- Silicone adhesive
- Misc. adhesive removers
- Pros-Aide

- Isopropyl myristate
- Blood (fake, of course!)
- Misc. gelatin
- Rigid collodion
- Collodion remover
- Crepe hair (wool)
- Coffee mug warmer
- Makeup sealer
- Plastic cap material
- Latex stipple
- Misc. crème foundations
- Styptic pencil
- Eye drops
- Makeup pencil sharpener
- Disposable razors
- Shaving cream
- Skin moisturizer
- Skin cleanser
- Barrier spray
- Ben Nye® Bond Off!
- Orangewood stick
- Misc. craft sticks
- Toothpicks
- Tuplast
- Skin-safe silicone
- Disposable eyeliner brushes
- Misc. eyebrow pencils
- Alcohol palettes
- Bondo (Pros-Aide® and Cab-O-Sil®)
- Cab-O-Sil®
- Glycerin
- K-Y® lubricant
- Castor sealer
- Latex, vinyl, or nitrile gloves
- Nose and scar wax

Appendix B Recipes

FOAM LATEX

GM Foam/Monster Makers Foam/Burman Foam

A typical batch of foam latex consists of the following:

- 150 grams of high-grade latex base
- 30 grams of foaming agent
- 15 grams of curing agent
- 14 grams of gelling agent

There are other ingredients and quantities that can be added for different foam characteristics, but this is a good place to begin. This operation is time and temperature sensitive as well as humidity sensitive; optimal conditions would be in a room temperature of 69°F–72°F (20.6°C–22°C) with 45%–55% humidity. I am based in Colorado, so I have humidity (rather, the lack of humidity) to contend with, as well as a higher elevation air pressure that also affects what I do. The "optimal" conditions are based on mixing at sea level; I'll show a schedule for both sea level and high altitude, although most of you will probably be working at lower elevations.

Foam latex can be cured in molds made of a variety of materials, including Ultracal 30, dental stone, fiberglass, epoxy, silicone, aluminum, or even steel, and should be only mixed and cured in rooms with good ventilation; foam latex gives off unpleasant and unhealthy fumes.

Weigh the first three components—the latex base, the foaming agent, and the curing agent—and add them to the mixing bowl. It would be great if you have an accurate digital gram scale. Weigh out the gelling agent into a small cup and set it aside. We won't add that until we're almost done mixing. If you're adding pigment, put a few drops of your color into the bowl, too. Then place the mixing bowl into position and you are ready to begin. This first description will be a 12-minute mix. A timer that will count down is a plus, but if you can tell time and count, a clock or a watch will suffice.

1. For first minute, mix ingredients on speed 1.
2. For next 4 minutes, whip ingredients on speed 10. This will froth foam and increase volume (and lower the foam density) in bowl. All mixers run differently, and many conditions can affect how foam will rise in a mixer. Once you understand how foam latex works, you'll be able to adapt to any situation.

Whipping the latex to a high volume lowers the foam's density, which will result in a lighter foam and creates a foam that can be difficult (near impossible) to pour. This foam is more apt to trap air when transferred into molds; this can be especially true when injecting the foam. All three latex manufacturers have a flow enhancer that makes it easier to pour high-volume foam with little or no effect on the gelling process.

What the high-speed mixing does in addition to creating high-volume foam is de-ammoniating the latex. If there is loss of too much ammonia, your foam will gel too quickly; if there is not enough ammonia loss, your foam might not gel at all. It might seem like you need a degree in chemistry to run the foam (it certainly wouldn't hurt), but that is why there is a mixing guideline to follow, so you don't have to know specific pH values and other scientific-type stuff. Simply understanding the function of the ingredients and the stages of the process should be enough information to do some experimentation, such as

- The *foaming agent* is a soap that bonds to the cells of the latex, lowering the surface tension of the latex and allowing it to froth and rise more easily.
- The *curing agent* contains sulfur to help vulcanize—strengthen and add elasticity to—the latex.
- The *gelling agent* creates a reaction that changes the foam from a liquid into a solid.

Okay, back to the process.

3. Now, turn speed down to 4 for 1 minute. This stage will begin to refine foam, breaking up biggest bubbles.
4. Turn speed down to 1 for last 4 minutes to further refine foam. When there are 2 minutes left, begin adding gelling agent and continue mixing until 12 minutes. It is critical that gelling agent be mixed well, and depending on what mixer you use, methods of assuring that gelling agent is sufficiently mixed may vary.
5. At 12 minutes, turn off mixer, remove the bowl, and you are ready to carefully fill molds. Once foam has gelled (you can tell by gently pressing on foam; it should give a little, and bounce back), you can place molds in oven and heat them until foam is fully cured.

NOTE

This recipe is the general one recommended by GM Foam *at sea level*. I suspect Monster Makers and Burman would concur. Check with each manufacturer to be certain.

I have had good results with these times, but I have also had disastrous results with these times; a movie I did recently in Colorado required numerous foam appliances, and the following mixing times worked beautifully every time and has become my high-altitude schedule with a KitchenAid mixer. It is a 9-minute schedule instead of a 12-minute schedule:

09:00 Speed 1
08:00 Speed 10
07:00 Speed 4
05:30 Speed 1
03:00 Speed 1—*add gelling agent*
00:00 Stop

The oven you cure the foam in should be capable of reaching 185°F (85°C). Small molds will most likely need only 2–2½ hours; larger molds might need 3–4 hours. However, if the mold is thin—say, ¼-inch (5 mm) fiberglass—it can be baked at a much lower temperature for a longer period of time—140°F (60°C) for 4–5 hours. Thick gypsum molds will benefit from lower temperatures and longer times; it's less stressful on the molds, and you'll get the added benefit of softer foam (without having to deal with a high-volume, non-pourable foam from the mixing stage). *Monster Makers suggests trying a typical gypsum mold at 140°F (60°C) for 10 hours and comparing the feel of the resulting foam with foam run at a higher temperature for a shorter time using the same mold.*

Once you determine that your foam is fully cured, turn off the oven and let the mold begin to cool. If you try to cool the molds too rapidly, they will crack and break; you do not want to rush the process! When the molds are still warm to touch, you can carefully demold your appliances; they will come out more easily when warm rather than if you let the molds cool completely. Carefully pry the mold halves apart and help remove the appliance with the use of a blunt wooden tool (so you don't scratch the mold's surface detail), powdering as you go to keep the thin foam edges from sticking together.

After you've removed the appliance from the mold, it must be gently washed in warm water containing only a few drops of dishwashing liquid (I use either Ivory or Palmolive soap) to remove any residual sulfur from the curing agent. Repeat this procedure until there is no more visible residue in the water and then rinse until all the soap is gone and gently squeeze out the water; you might want to use two towels to press the appliance between and then allow it to dry completely on the lifecast so that it will maintain its shape. When your appliance is completely dry, it is ready to paint and apply or be stored in an airtight plastic bag for future use.

GELATIN

Just as there are different recipes for foam latex—although I only provided one recipe in this appendix—there are also a number of gelatin recipes. Some include sorbitol, some don't; sorbitol will add to the tear strength of the gelatin. I've seen a recipe that added Elmer's Glue (white school glue), presumably for strength and stability; however, the more glue you use, the less elastic the gelatin will become.

Matthew Mungle's Recipe

- 100 grams sorbitol (liquid)
- 100 grams glycerin
- 20–30 grams 300-bloom gelatin (the higher the bloom, the greater the tear resistance; the gelatin you can buy at your local supermarket has a bloom factor of 250–275)
- Flocking or pigment for internal coloration

PROCEDURE

1. Mix ingredients together in microwave-safe bowl and let sit, preferably overnight.
2. Heat in microwave for approximately 2 minutes, mixing several times. Do not allow mixture to bubble or foam, because that's an indication that it's about to burn. It will change color and leave undesirable bubbles in finished appliance.
3. You can either fill mold and cast appliance or pour gelatin into mold and let it cool and cure for later use. Powder when it's fully set.

Kevin Haney's Recipe

- 21 grams sorbitol (liquid)
- 20 grams glycerin
- 9–11 grams 300 bloom Gelatin

Up to ¼ gram (¼ teaspoon) zinc oxide powder (zinc oxide will cause the opacity of the gelatin, as well as the tear resistance, to increase)

- Flocking or pigment for internal coloration

PROCEDURE

Same as the above procedure.

> **NOTE**
> You can double or triple this formula. Very small or large batches aren't as easy to mix up as a medium-sized one.

Thea's Recipe (FX Warehouse)

- 80 grams sorbitol (⅛ cup)
- 80 grams glycerin (⅛/cup)
- 40 grams 300-bloom gelatin (⅛ cup)
- Up to ½ gram (½ teaspoon) zinc oxide powder

NOTE
The weights are different, but the volumes are actually the same on all three ingredients.

Add flocking to desired effect, about ½ teaspoon or less if mixing colors. Add cosmetic pigment in your choice of flesh color. (You can also use cake makeup ground up finely.)

In a microwave-safe bowl, mix most of the sorbitol and glycerin. Leave a small amount of the sorbitol out so you can mix the zinc oxide into it before adding it all together.

Slowly add the gelatin to the sorbitol and glycerin mixture. Then add the zinc oxide mixed in the small amount of sorbitol and some flocking. If you are adding flesh pigment or red blood pigment (you can use any color), mix the pigment into a small amount of sorbitol before adding to the batch. Heat it in the microwave for another 1 or 2 minutes, stirring frequently, but be careful that it doesn't bubble over the container.

FOAMING GELATIN

Any of the preceding recipes will work for making the base gelatin for a foamed version of gelatin. You will notice that Kevin Haney's recipe is about ½ of the other two, so take that into account.

- 160 grams (¼ cup) glycerin
- 40 grams (⅛ cup) 300-bloom gelatin
- ½ gram (½ teaspoon) zinc oxide
- ½ gram (½ teaspoon) tartaric acid
- ½ gram (½ teaspoon) baking soda

The tartaric acid in Cream of Tartar is what adds volume to egg whites when they're beaten. Baking soda reacts with the heat and the tartaric acid to create carbon dioxide.

1. Mix ingredients together (without tartaric acid and baking soda) in microwave-safe bowl and let sit, preferably overnight.
2. Heat in microwave for approximately 2 minutes, mixing several times. Do not allow mixture to bubble or foam.
3. Add tartaric acid and stir briskly.
4. Add baking soda and stir briskly; let gelatin mixture rise for 30 seconds without stirring, until it stops rising.
5. Stir foamed gelatin to refine it, heating a little if needed.

The foamed gelatin is ready to be poured into a prepared mold.

FOAMED WATER-MELON

This industry thrives on innovation and experimentation, and a recent development by Michael Davy has offered up another use for his Water-Melon cap plastic. It can be foamed to create prosthetic appliances in much the same way as foamed gelatin.

Step 1: Measure out 100 grams of Water-Melon, 10 grams of Dr. Bronner's Pure Castile Soap, and 6 grams of any brand of foam latex gelling agent.

Step 2: Release any surface of your two-part mold that will come in contact with the Water-Melon. Any type of mold will work, be it resin or stone. Use castor oil mixed with 99% IPA as your release and allow to dry. Then powder both halves of the mold. Using Water-Melon in your mold will not contaminate it for future silicone use.

Step 3: Combine the Water-Melon and soap and stir until mixed well. Whip the mixture into froth with an electric mixer's wire whisk attachment for a few minutes. A few drops of water will increase the volume. The longer you whip it, the higher the volume. Once you reach your desired volume, add the gelling agent; reduce the whipping speed and refine the mixture just the way you'd do it for foam latex. You should have plenty of time before the mixture gels.

Step 4: Immediately add the mixture into your released and powdered mold, close the mold, and let it gel. Gel time and the amount of gelling agent you need may require tweaks just like with foam latex. Any leftover material in your mixing bowl should confirm gelation in the mold.

Step 5: Bake for 2 hours on a low setting (100°F; 37.8°C). Cool and open the mold the same way you'd open a foam latex mold. Carefully remove the appliance and powder. Instead of baking, you can open the mold (after gelation) and dehydrate. Dry appliances should spring back when pressed, like foam latex.

Step 6: Application is the same with any Water-Melon appliance; use 99% IPA or denatured alcohol instead of a traditional adhesive like Pros-Aide. The edges will blend away using 99% IPA as well. Foamed Water-Melon pieces are opaque like foam latex (but white), so they will require makeup and paint just like foam latex.

SILICONE FOAM

This process is from my friend and colleague, Matt Singer, who wrote the wonderful step-by-step for making silicone eyes. The following are his words:

What Is a Foam?

Essentially, foam is a liquid with trapped gas regions that create an open cell structure. It is also used to describe solids like foam latex or polyurethane foam with open cells. If you didn't already know, you can't just whip silicone in a mixer and hope to create a silicone foam. I have come up with a way that allows you to create a silicone that has all the attributes of a foam but made of almost any silicone of your choice. For this tutorial, I will describe the process using Smooth-On Dragon Skin platinum silicone.

You can use almost any kind of mold from stone to epoxy as long as the silicone is not inhibited by the mold surface. For this, let's use a mold of prosthetic breasts. Breast prosthetics can be very heavy when constructed of solid silicone. However, the aesthetic superiority of silicone over foam latex also makes it more appealing for film work. Of course, there are other choices to handle such an issue of weight, namely coring the mold and leaving an open space, but you can lose contact with the skin in the areas of the void created by the core, making it more difficult to keep in place and it can also deform in unacceptable ways during performance.

How We Will Create Our Cells

Foam can have large or small cells depending on the degassing of the liquid or how it's whipped. To create our cells, we are going to use small sugar balls called *nonpareils*. Nonpareils are a decorative confection of tiny spheres made with *sugar* and *starch*, traditionally an opaque white but now are available in many colors. The color is not relevant for creating the cell structure of our foam as the spheres will only temporarily be occupying the space. These tiny balls come in different sizes, but I prefer the ones that are 4 mm.

The mold will need to be modified to accommodate the technique. The posterior portion of the mold will need to have a opening about 3 inches in diameter in an inconspicuous place. Release the mold as you would normally do with silicone. We will be creating a silicone skin surface first with the Dragon Skin, by brushing a tinted and slightly more opaque pass. This should be brushed everywhere including the posterior surface. Close the mold before completely cured. Once cured, we will take our sugar balls and completely pack the mold using the opening we created on the posterior side. It's important that the balls are packed very tight so that all the balls are touching one another. Next, we will again use Dragon Skin and add a 50 centistoke (measure of viscosity) diluent (thinner) to make the silicone more pourable. I recommend adding 30%–50% diluent. (If you use silicone oil, leaching may occur in percentages higher than 30%.) Do not accelerate the cure of this silicone. Pour the silicone slowly over the balls exposed at the back of the posterior side. It may take some time until it completely fills the mold around the balls and levels at the top. Once the silicone levels, add more balls so that the balls are clearly exposed from the silicone they are submerged in. Let cure. Once cured, remove the prosthesis and the exposed balls from the back. Find a vessel that the prosthetic can fit inside and be submerged in hot water. Fill the container with hot water and start squeezing to remove the balls that are closer to the posterior surface. Let the prosthesis stand for about 30 minutes and start to squeeze. The hot water will melt the balls and leave perfect cells. Depending on the shape, it can take some time to get them all out, so be patient, and let the water do its job. I get impatient and do a lot of squeezing. If the cells can be seen through the surface skin, make the skin thicker or more opaque. Your prosthetic should be half the weight of a solid silicone prosthesis.

MOULAGE RECIPES (MEDICAL TRAUMA SIMULATIONS)

SIMULATED SKIN

In a large bowl, mix together (2) 13 ounces petroleum jelly, (3) 16 ounces solid cornstarch, and 2–5 tablespoon cocoa powder (depending on color). You don't want it too sticky or too dry. You can start out mixing it with a spatula, but eventually will need to put on rubber gloves and get your hands in it to get it mixed all the way through.

It is easier to clean up with paper towels, first; then wash your hands with soap and water.

If you heat this mixture in a saucepan to about 200°F while mixing occasionally and then letting it cool, you'll find it's similar to Play Doh and will stay pliable for days. Pretty cool stuff. Thanks to Haley Rich of Teen SERT for this and the following blood and sweat recipes.

THIN BLOOD

Mix together 16 ounces of liquid starch with 3 ounces of red food coloring and 1 ounce of yellow food coloring.

MEDIUM BLOOD

Mix 2–5 ounces of Karo Syrup with 10–20 drops of red food coloring, 3–5 drops of blue food coloring, and 5 drops of yellow food coloring.

THICK SLIMY BLOOD

The best coagulated blood is to use blood powder and methylcellulose powder.

SWEAT

People in shock break into cold sweats, which should be simulated. To do this, combine three parts glycerin (available at drug stores) with one part water in a dropper or spray bottle. You can enhance the effect if you apply a thin layer of cold cream before you spray your mixture on the patient. You can also just use a cotton ball dipped into the mixture if you don't have a spray bottle.

Note: Chocolate syrup as an additive to any blood recipe can aid in creating blood that looks real. Most of the time you will need to see the blood in the lighting conditions if you are making blood for on camera work. Ask to see how it looks through the lens and then make the proper adjustments.

BONDO

Mixing up a batch of bondo is about as easy as things get, but you do need to be mindful of working with Cab-O-Sil®; it is extremely light and will get airborne easily.

- Pour Pros-Aide® adhesive into the container you will be using to mix bondo. (Graftobian Pro Adhesive works very well, also, in lieu of Pros-Aide.)
- Carefully spoon a small amount of Cab-O-Sil® from its container into the Pros-Aide®.
- Slowly stir with a small craft stick (popsicle stick) until the Cab-O-Sil® and Pros-Aide® are thoroughly mixed.
- Add more Cab-O-Sil® and stir.
- Repeat until it reaches the thickness that you want.
- Cover to prevent the bondo from drying out.

If you are making bondo for 3D transfer or bondo appliances, you can add flocking or pigment along with the Cab-O-Sil®.

AGE STIPPLE

If you'd like to try your hand at something a little different than simply stretching the skin and stippling on latex, here are a couple of recipes you can try for variety in your repertoire.

Premiere Products

PPI's Green Marble SeLr® is one way to approach subtle aging, but achieving the finished result also requires subtle painting. To turn Green Marble SeLr® into an aging material, you must use the concentrate and not the spray; added to the Green Marble SeLr® is Attagel, a very fine clay powder used as a thixotropic agent in cosmetics.

Ratio (ounce) of Attagel to Green Marble SeLr®:

- 1–3 ounces heavy ager on most skin types
- 1–4 ounces medium to heavy ager
- 1–5 ounces medium to light ager
- 1–6 ounces light ager on most skin types

A 1:6 Attagel:Green Marble SeLr® ratio will work as a fine-line wrinkle texture when used very lightly. Without affecting large wrinkles, this 1:6 formula changes the texture of the skin, which is excellent for subtle, close-up aging. The application technique works the same as with latex for stretch and stipple.

REPAIRS AND QUICK FIXES

Depending on the thickness and placement of the ager, some areas of the face may crack or flake. This usually happens around the mouth, but repairs can be done quickly and easily using any of the following three methods:

- Paint 99% alcohol in the direction of the wrinkles.
- Apply Telesis® thinner and/or acetone (faster) with a brush. Then apply only Green Marble SeLr® (use a brush, sponge, or spray).
- Reapply some of the original ager material.

TEMPORARY PATCHING

This technique is useful when you don't have time to do a thorough repair. Temporary patching media include:

- Oil-free sodium-based moisturizers
- K-Y® jelly
- 99% pure clear aloe.

REMOVAL

The best removal technique to dissolve Green Marble materials involves the use of isopropyl myristate or IPM gel, massaged with the fingers, into the skin. In addition, the finger-massage technique works exceptionally well around the eyes and is more comfortable for the actor.

Pros-Ager

I made up that name (at least I've never seen or heard it anywhere else before), but I didn't make up the formula; it comes from Richard Corson. It's a mixture of Pros-Aide® adhesive, acrylic matte medium (I use Liquitex liquid), and either pure talc or Cab-O-Sil® to thicken the mixture slightly. Too much of either talcum or Cab-O-Sil® will cause the mixture to remain white after it dries. You want it to dry relatively transparently so that it can be used over set foundation for a more natural aging technique.

Try mixing Pros-Aide® and Matte Medium 1:1 by volume. Thinner mixtures will result in finer wrinkles, whereas thicker mixtures will produce thicker, deeper wrinkles. Because Pros-Aide® is part of the solution, it will dry somewhat tacky; so it will need to be powdered.

Dick's Ager

Years ago, makeup pioneer Dick Smith created a latex wrinkle stipple formula that almost everybody has used at one time or another. It's a mixture of high-grade foam latex base, pure talc, pulverized cake makeup foundation, gelatin, and water. Yum! Here's the recipe from Richard Corson and James Glavan's book, *Stage Makeup*:

- 90 grams (100 ml) foam latex base
- 10 grams (5 teaspoons) pure talc U.S.P.

- 6 grams (2 teaspoons) loose powdered cake foundation (or pigmented powder)
- 2 grams (½ teaspoon) Knox® unflavored gelatin (or 300-bloom gelatin if you have it)
- 32 ml (3 teaspoons) boiling distilled water
- Acrylic gel medium (for medium stipple recipe)
- Pliatex Casting Filler from Sculpture House (for heavy stipple)

Once this mixture is prepared, it must be stored in a refrigerator between uses. Because it contains gelatin, it must be heated until it liquefies for application. This recipe can be modified to create a light wrinkle, medium wrinkle, or heavy wrinkle. When you need something that will have a bit more sticking power, mix 1:1 Pros-Aide® and foam latex base.

LIGHT RECIPE

1. Mix talc, powdered foundation, and gelatin in small mixing bowl.
2. Add 3 teaspoons boiling distilled water to the powders. Be sure to use distilled water; some tap water will change the pH of the latex and cause it to curdle. Add 1 teaspoon water *at a time*, stirring after each, until the mixture is smooth.
3. Strain the latex through tulle or cheesecloth to remove lumps.
4. Slowly add the dissolved powder mixture to the latex, stirring quickly to avoid lumps.
5. Pour the mixture into 2 or 3 ounces jars (plastic or glass); label them, including the date.

MEDIUM RECIPE

1. Combine the light recipe with either 60 grams of acrylic gel medium or 50 grams of gel medium and 3 teaspoons of Cab-O-Sil®.
2. Stir small amounts of the light stipple into the gel medium until they are thoroughly mixed.
3. Pour into small jars and label with the date.

HEAVY RECIPE

1. Combine one part medium recipe by volume with one part Sculpture House Pliatex Casting Filler.
2. Pour into jars and label with the date.

These should be refrigerated after pouring into jars and sealed. Application of these formulas follows the same procedures and steps as for regular latex stipple.

H-10

I'm not sure what H-1 through H-9 were like, but H-10 is pretty cool. H-10 is a mixture of Gaf Quat and moustache wax heated and blended, then mixed with

70% isopropyl alcohol (rubbing alcohol); it's used to flatten hair around the hairline for bald cap applications. Here's how to make it.

1. Heat 1 part moustache wax with 1 part Gaf Quat until both are melted. If you use a microwave, be careful not to overheat; the Gaf Quat will bubble and expand. Heat gradually.
2. When both the wax and the Gaf Quat are mixed completely, slowly add 1 part alcohol (all parts are by volume, not weight) until thoroughly mixed.
3. Before the mixture sets up, pour it into a small container with a lid.

The H-10 can then be applied with a small dental spatula, old toothbrush, or your fingers. This stuff will hold hair in place in a typhoon; it'll sure as heck keep hair in place for a bald cap application.

SLIME RECIPES

Recipe 1

Here's how.

1. Pour Elmer's Glue (or similar white glue product) into a large container. If you have a big bottle of glue, you want 4 ounces or ½ cup of glue.
2. Fill the empty glue bottle with water and stir it into the glue (or add ½ cup of water).
3. If desired, add food coloring. Otherwise, the slime will be an opaque white.
4. In a separate, mix one cup (240 ml) of water into the bowl and add 1 teaspoon (5 ml) of borax powder.
5. Slowly stir the glue mixture into the bowl of borax solution.
6. Place the slime that forms into your hands and knead until it feels dry. (Don't worry about the excess water remaining in the bowl.)
7. The more the slime is played with, the firmer and less sticky it will become.
8. Store your slime in a zip-lock bag in the fridge (otherwise it will develop mold).

That's one. Here's another.

The following materials are what you need.

- Borax powder
- Water
- 4 oz (120 ml) glue (e.g., Elmer's white glue)
- Teaspoon
- Bowl
- Jar or measuring cup
- Food coloring (optional)
- Measuring cup

Recipe 2

You can make this nonsticky, edible slime from two easy-to-find ingredients.

"ECTOPLASM" SLIME MATERIALS

You only need two ingredients to make the basic slime, although you can add coloring to make the slime of any combination of colors that you like or to make it glow in the dark.

- 1 teaspoon soluble fiber (e.g., Metamucil psyllium fiber)
- 8 oz (1 cup) water
- Food coloring (optional)
- Glow paint or pigment (optional)

MAKE YOUR "ECTOPLASM"

1. Pour the water and fiber into a large microwave-safe bowl.
2. Microwave the "ectoplasm" on high power for 3 minutes.
3. Stir the ectoplasm. Return it to the microwave and heat it for another 3 minutes.
4. Stir the ectoplasm again and check its consistency. If you want drier ectoplasm, microwave the ectoplasm for another 1 or 2 minutes. Continue checking it and microwaving it until you achieve the desired consistency.
5. Add a drop of food coloring and/or some glow paint, if you'd like. You'll get an interesting effect if you incompletely mix the coloring into the ectoplasm, such as multicolored ectoplasm or ectoplasm slime with glowing streaks.
6. Store your ectoplasm in a sealed baggie to prevent dehydration. The slime will last for a week or longer, as long as you keep it from drying out.

You can buy methylcellulose powder from many sources, but I'm partial to the powder offered by Arnold Goldman and Monster Makers. This is one of the highest molecular weight powders available and capable of creating very thick solutions if required, depending on the powder to water ratio used. Higher molecular weight also means greater value as less powder is needed to achieve gels of any concentration. This is an excellent product for simulating nearly any type of yucky body fluid. Solutions are clear and can be tinted to any shade or color with food or water-based pigments.

PAX PAINT AND PAX MEDIUM

PAX paint has been around for quite a while and is essentially Pros-Aide and artist acrylic paint; it can be used directly on the skin but is best used for painting appliances prior to application. Use good judgment regarding use on someone's skin. To make your own opaque, flexible PAX paint, mix Pros-Aide® and acrylic artist paint (e.g., Liquitex) 1:1. Because it is a mixture of acrylic paint and a strong prosthetic adhesive, it can be somewhat stubborn to remove, so be careful about using it near sensitive areas of skin, such as around the eyes. PAX Paint can be altered and modified for considerable versatility by doing one or more of the following:

- Mix acrylic matte medium with Pros-Aide® to create what is called PAX Medium, a liquid that dries clear and somewhat flat. When PAX Medium is added to PAX Paint in varying amounts, it creates varying layers of transparent color that will aid in creating more realistic skin coloration.
- Add distilled water to make a thinner, more transparent paint. Thinning can be by as much as 24:1 (24 parts water to 1 part PAX Paint). A mixture with this thickness becomes a wash that can add very subtle color tints.
- Thinned PAX Medium can be used as a makeup sealer.
- Adding additional Pros-Aide® (i.e., 2:1) will make the paint stick better, but it will be harder to remove; less adhesive will make a weaker bond and be easier to remove.
- Makeup can be applied over PAX paint; in fact, just about anything (except acetone) can be applied to PAX.

Whether you use PAX Paint, PAX Medium, or both, it dries with a bit of a shine and remains a bit tacky to the touch. It is a good idea to powder it with a translucent setting powder.

Appendix C
Suppliers

9 MM SPECIAL EFFECTS

832 E. Main St., Ste. 4
Medford, OR 97504
Phone: 1-866-826-9696 or 541-608-7412
www.9mmsfx.com
Custom contact lenses

ADMTRONICS

224 Pegasus Ave.
Northvale, NJ 07647
Phone: 201-767-6040
www.admtronics.com
Pros-Aide water-based adhesive

ALCONE COMPANY

5-45 49th Ave.
Long Island City, NY 11101
Phone: 718-361-8373
Fax: 718-729-8296

ALCONE RETAIL STORE NYC

322 West 49th St. (between 8th & 9th Avenues)
New York City, NY 10019
Phone: 212-757-3734
www.alconeco.com
Makeup Technical Tools Instruction

A FOX INTERNATIONAL

G3426 Beecher Rd.
Flint, MI 48532
Phone: 810-732-8861
http://afoxintl.com
Wigs, hair extensions, and accessories

AMERICAN FINE ARTS SUPPLIES

2520 N Ontario Street
Burbank, CA 91504
Phone: 818-848-7593
www.sculptclayandtools.com
Sculpting supply resource built by sculptors, for sculptors, offering everything from clay to wax, armature to tools, sculpting DVDs to modeling stands, and everything in between.

BEN NYE

3655 Lenawee Ave.
Los Angeles, CA 90016
Phone: 310-839-1984
www.bennyemakeup.com
Professional makeup

BJB ENTERPRISES, INC.

14791 Franklin Ave.
Tustin, CA 92780
Phone: 1-714-734-8450
www.bjbenterprises.com
Manufacturer and supplier of thermosetting polyurethane, epoxy, and silicone systems

BLUE POINT ENGINEERING

213 Pikes Peak Place
Longmont, CO 80504
Phone: 1-303-651-3794
www.bpesolutions.com
Hardware, controllers, electronics, mechanics, and construction materials for animatronics

BRICK IN THE YARD MOLD SUPPLY

521 Sterling Dr.
Richardson, TX 75081
Phone: 214-575-5600
http://brickintheyard.com
Mold making, casting, sculpting supplies, and tools

BURMAN INDUSTRIES

13536 Saticoy St.
Van Nuys, CA 91402
Phone: 818-782-9833
http://burmanfoam.com/
Silicones, latex, sculpting, and mold-making supplies

CAISSON LABORATORIES

1740 N Research Park Way
North Logan, UT 84341-1977
Phone: 877-840-0500
http://caissonlabs.com
Sorbitol powder, etc.

CHARLES H. FOX LTD

22 Tavistock St.
Covent Garden
GB-London WC2 E7PY
Phone: +44 207/240 31 11
www.charlesfox.co.uk
Professional makeup supplies

CHEAP CHEMICALS

P.O. Box 480-C
Round Hill, VA 20142-0480
Phone: 540-338-3877
www.cheap-chemicals.com
Cab-O-Sil, sorbitol, zinc oxide

CINEMA SECRETS

4400 Riverside Dr.
Burbank, CA 91505
Phone: 818-846-0431
www.cinemasecrets.com
Professional makeup supplies

COLORADO SCIENTIFIC

95 Lincoln St.
Denver, CO 80223
Phone: 303-777-3777
www.sciencecompany.com
99% isopropyl alcohol, laboratory supplies, containers, scales, etc.

COMPLEAT SCULPTOR, THE

90 Vandam St.
New York, NY 10013
Phone: 212-243-6074
http://sculpt.com/
Mold making, casting, sculpting supplies, and equipment

COMPOSITE STORE, THE

Phone: 1-800-338-1278
www.cstsales.com/
Fiberglass, mold-making products, and epoxy

CROWN BRUSHES

3 North Court St., B354
Crown Point, IN 46307
Phone: 219-791-9930
http://crownbrush.com/
Cosmetic brushes

CHAVANT, INC

5043 Industrial Rd.
Wall Township, NJ 07727-3651
Phone: 1-800-CHAVANT
www.chavant.com
Modeling clay, sculpting tools, and accessories

CROWN BRUSH

http://www.crownbrush.com
3 North Court Street, Suite B354
Crown Point, IN 46307
Phone: 219-791-9930
The leading industry resource for cosmetic and skincare brushes

CUSTOM COLOR CONTACTS

55 W. 49th St.
New York, NY 10020
Phone: 800-598-2020
www.customcontacts.com
Special FX, prosthetic, and cosmetic lenses

CYBERGRAPHIC DESIGNS MAKEUP EFFECTS & SUPPLY CO

3202 Center Dr.
Cleveland, OH 44134
Phone: 440-888-8548
www.getspfx.com
Professional makeup effects supplies

DAPPER CADAVER

7572 San Fernando Road
Sun Valley, CA 91352
Phone: 818-771-0818
www.dappercadaver.com
The finest death related props, Halloween props, haunted house decor, and oddities

DAVIS DENTAL SUPPLY

7347 Ethel Ave.
North Hollywood, CA 91605
Phone: 1-800-842-4203 or 818-765-4994
www.davisdentalsupply.com
Dental molding and casting supplies

DE MEO BROS

129 W. 29th St., 5th Floor
New York, NY 10001
Phone: 212-268-1400
Hair and wig supply, wig lace, wig-making supplies

DIXIE ART SUPPLIES

5440 Mounes Street, Suite 108
New Orleans, LA 70123
Phone: 800-783-2612
www.dixieart.com
Airbrushes and airbrush supplies

THE ENGINEER GUY

1000 Tradeport Blvd., Suite 1003
Atlanta, GA 30354
Phone: 1-404-685-8804
www.theengineerguy.com
Mold making, lifecasting, sculpting supplies and tools, and much more!

ENVIRONMOLDS

18 Bank St.
Summit, NJ 07901
Phone: 1-866-278-6653
www.artmolds.com
www.environmolds.com
Mold making, lifecasting, sculpting supplies, and tools

FACTOR II, INC

P.O. Box 1339
Lakeside, AZ 85929
Phone: 928-537-8387
www.factor2.com
Prosthetic silicone and adhesives, etc.

FANGS F/X, LTD

The Studio, Sheepcote Dell Rd.
Beamond End, Amersham
Bucks HP7 0QS
Phone: +44 (0) 1494 713 807
www.fangsfx.com
Specialized teeth and dental appliances for film and television

FIBERGLASS WAREHOUSE

8250 Commercial St.
La Mesa, CA 91942
Phone: 619-270-9541
www.fiberglasswarehouse.com
Fiberglass, mold-making products, mold release, and epoxy

FIBRE GLAST DEVELOPMENTS CORP

385 Carr Dr.
Brookville, OH 45309
Phone: 1-800-330-6368
www.fibreglast.com
Fiberglass, foam, resins, and reinforcements

FREEDOM OF TEACH

1912 Stanford St.
Alameda, CA 94501
Phone: 510-769-1828
http://freedomofteach.com/
Anatomy figures, DVDs, artist busts, armatures, and wall charts for artists

FRENDS BEAUTY SUPPLY

5270 Laurel Canyon Blvd.
North Hollywood, CA 91607
Phone: 818-769-3834
Cosmetic supplies for FX artists

FUSEFX

2137 Hubbard Cres.
Ottawa, ON
Canada, K1J 6L3
Phone: 613-748-7877
www.fusefx.ca
Platinum silicone painting system

FX WAREHOUSE

2090 S. Nova Rd.
South Daytona, FL 32119
Phone: 386-322-5272
www.fxwarehouse.info *online sales only*
Supplies for FX artists and scenic studios

GEORGE TAUB PRODUCTS & FUSION CO

Phone: 1-800-828-2634
Email: sales@taubdental.com
www.taubdental.com
Minute stain acrylic resin stains

GM FOAM, INC

14956 Delano St.
Van Nuys, CA 91411
Phone: 818-908-1087
www.gmfoam.com
Foam latex and pigments

GRAFTOBIAN

510 Tasman St.
Madison, WI 53714
Phone: 608-222-7849
www.graftobian.com
Professional makeup supplies, makeup effects

GRAPE AND GRANARY, THE

915 Home Ave.
Akron, OH 44310
Phone: 1-800-695-9870
http://thegrape.net
Tartaric acid

HAIRESS CORPORATION

880 Industrial Blvd.
Crown Point, IN 46307
Phone: 219-662-1060
http://hairess.com/
Manufacturer, importer, distributor of hair care products and supplies

HIS & HER HAIR GOODS CO

5525 Wilshire Blvd.
Los Angeles, CA 90036
Phone: 1-800-421-4417
http://hisandher.com/
Hair and wig supply, human hair wigs, tools, and accessories

IASCO

5724 West 36th St.
Minneapolis, MN 55416
Phone: 888-919-0899
www.iasco-tesco.com/oldsite/
Plastics, mold making, casting

JAMESTOWN DISTRIBUTORS

17 Peckham Dr.
Bristol, RI 02809
Phone: 1-800-497-0010 or 401-253-3840
www.jamestowndistributors.com
Fiberglass, adhesives, and epoxy

KAB DENTAL

34842 Mound Rd.
Sterling Heights, MI 48310
Phone: 586-983-2502 or 1-800-422-3520
www.kabdental.com
Dental supplies

K&J MAGNETICS, INC

2110 Ashton Dr., Suite 1A
Jamison, PA 18929
Phone: 1-888-746-7556 or 215-766-8055
www.kjmagnetics.com
Magnets

KEN'S TOOLS

Phone: 951-943-1217
www.drbanksensteinfx.com
www.kenstools.com
Sculpting tools

KOSMETECH CORP

26 Delavan St.
Brooklyn, NY 11231
Phone: 718-858-7000
www.kosmetech.com
Makeup applicators and storage

KRYOLAN

132 Ninth St.
San Francisco, CA 94103
Phone: 415-863-9684
www.kryolan.com
Professional makeup

LAGUNA CLAY

14400 Lomitas Ave.
City of Industry, CA 91746
Phone: 1-800-4-LAGUNA or 626-330-0631
www.lagunaclay.com
Sculpting supplies

LONDON WIGS

Unit 107
156 Blackfriars Rd.
London SE1 8EN U.K.
Phone: 0207 7217095
www.wigslondon.com
Wigs and wig-making supplies

MAC COSMETICS

Phone: 1-800-387-6707
www.maccosmetics.com
Cosmetics, makeup products

MAKE UP MANIA

Headquarters:
4407 Lowell Blvd.
Denver, CO 80211
Phone: 800-711-7182
Make Up Mania @ The Make Up Trailer
182 Allen St.
New York, NY 10002
Phone: 212-380-1090
www.makeupmania.com
Cosmetics, makeup effects products

MAKE UP STORE

Southlands Mall
6205 E. Main St., Suite 101
Aurora, CO 80016
Phone: 303-563-2123
www.makeupstore.se
Cosmetics, makeup products

MASTERPAK

145 E 57th St., 5th Floor
New York, NY 10022
Phone: 1-800-922-5522
www.masterpak-usa.com/
Silicone parchment paper

MEL (MAKEUP & EFFECTS LABORATORIES)

7110 Laurel Canyon Blvd., Building E
North Hollywood, CA 91605
Phone: 818-982-1483
www.elefx.com
All your effects needs including props, costumes, animatronics, vacuum-forming, special effects makeup, miniatures, and more

MILE HI CERAMICS

77 Lipan
Denver, CO 80223
Phone: 303-825-4570
www.milehiceramics.com
WED Clay, ultracal, hydrocal, plaster

MINKE - PROPS

Cecilienstraße 31
D-47051 Duisburg
Phone: +49-(0)203-28101-0
www.minke-props.com
Special effects supplies, electrostatic flocking gun

M. J. GORDON COMPANY

255 North St.
P.O. Box 4441t
Pittsfield, MA 01201
Phone: 413-448-6066
www.mjgordonco.com
Mold release

THE MONSTER MAKERS

15901 Hilliard Rd.
Rear Building
Lakewood, Ohio 44107
Phone: 216-521-7739
www.monstermakers.com
Suppliers of three dimensional special effects materials

MOTION PICTURE F/X COMPANY

2923 Thornton Ave.
Burbank, CA 91504
Phone: 818-563-2366
www.monsterclub.com
Chemicals, dental supplies, latex, silicones, sculpting tools

MOULD LIFE

Tollgate Workshop
Bury Road
Kentford, Suffolk CB8 7PY
Phone: +44(0)1638-750679 (U.K.)
949-923-9583 (U.S.)
www.mouldlife.co.uk
Casting and moulding supplies for special makeup effects

MOUNTAIN ROSE HERBS

P.O. Box 50220
Eugene, OR 97405
Phone: 1-800-879-3337
www.mountainroseherbs.com
Makeup ingredients

MUDSHOP

129 S. San Fernando Blvd.
Burbank, CA 91502
Phone: 818-557-7619
375 W. Broadway #202
New York, NY 10012
Phone: 212-925-9250
www.makeupdesignory.com
Cosmetics, tools, brushes, cases, skin care, books

NAIMIE'S BEAUTY CENTER

12640 Riverside Dr.
Valley Village, CA 91607
Phone: 818-655-9933
www.naimies.com
Cosmetics, tools, and makeup cases

NATIONAL FIBER TECHNOLOGY

300 Canal St.
Lawrence, MA 01840
Phone: 1-800-842-2751
www.nftech.com
Custom-made hair, wigs, and fur fabrics

NIGEL'S BEAUTY EMPORIUM

11252 Magnolia Blvd.
North Hollywood, CA 91601
Phone: 818-760-3902
www.nigelsbeautyemporium.com
Supplier to the beauty, film, television, fashion, and media industries

NIMBA CREATIONS (UK)

Phone: 07516 407539
www.nimbacreations.com
Animatronics, props & prosthetics for film, television and live events

NORCOSTCO

4395 Broadway St.
Denver, CO 80216
Phone: 1-800-220-6928, 303-620-9734
www.norcostco.com
Professional makeup supplies

NOTCUTT

Homewood Farm
Newark Lane
Ripley, Surrey GU23 6DJ
Phone: +44 (0)1483 223311
www.notcutt.co.uk
Mold-making materials and casting resin specialists

PAINT & POWDER COSMETICS/ SWEET B STUDIOS

4116 Walney Road, Suite B
Chantilly, VA 20153
Phone: 703-888-9414
orders@paintandpowderstore.com
www.paintandpowderstore.com
Beauty Naturally and "Effect"ively for a High Definition World

PEARSON DENTAL SUPPLIES CO

Phone: 1-800-535-4535, 818-362-2600
www.pearson-dental.com
Dental molding and casting supplies

PINK HOUSE STUDIOS

35 Bank St.,
St. Albans, VT 05478
Phone: 802-524-7191
www.pinkhouse.com
Lifecasting, mold-making, and casting supplies

PLASTICARE

4211 South Natches Court, Unit K
Englewood, CO 80110
Phone: (303) 781-1171
http://plasticareinc.com/
Mold-making, casting, reinforcement supplies, and equipment

POLYTEK DEVELOPMENT CORP

55 Hilton St.
Easton, PA 18042
Phone: 610-559-8620, 1-800-858-5990
www.polytek.com
Mold-making and casting materials

PREMIERE PRODUCTS, INC.

10312 Norris Ave., Suite C
Pacoima, CA 91331
Phone: 1-818-897-7458
http://www.ppi.cc
Advanced products for the health care, hair replacement, medical, make-up, and special effects industries

PROFESSIONAL VISION CARE ASSOCIATES

14607 Venturea Blvd.
Sherman Oaks, CA 91403
Phone: 1-818-789-3311
http://www.provisioncare.com
Specialty contact lenses for film, television, and the stage

RAY MARSTON WIG STUDIO, LTD

No. 4 Charlotte Rd.
London EC2A 3DH
Phone: 020 7739 3900
www.raymarstonwigs.co.uk
Specialized hair work to the film, television, and theater industry

REEL CREATIONS

7831 Alabama Ave., Suite 21
Canoga Park, CA 91304
Phone: 818-3-GO-REEL (818-346-7335)
www.reelcreations.com
Professional makeup effects supplies

REEL EYE COMPANY, THE

365–367 Watling St.
Radlett, Hertfordshire WD7 7LB
Phone: +44 (0)1923 850207
www.reeleye.co.uk
Special effects contact lenses

REYNOLDS ADVANCED MATERIALS

3920 Grape St.
Denver, CO 80207
Phone: 1-800-603-3080
1-303-399-0202
10856 Vanowen St.
North Hollywood, CA 91605
Phone: 1-800-348-4349
1-818-358-6004
2131 South Harwood St.
Dallas, TX 75215
Phone: 1-800-421-4378
1-214-421-4377
6512 Pinecastle Blvd.
Orlando, FL 32809
1-800-328-8786
1-407-856-6115
5346 East Ave.
Countryside, IL 60525
1-800-477-4457
1-708-354-7825
45 Electric, Ave.
Brighton, MA 02135
1-800-481-9246
1-617-208-0300
www.reynoldsam.com
Mold making, lifecasting, sculpting supplies, and tools

ROYAL & LANGNICKEL

Phone: 800-247-2211
http://www.royalbrush.com/beauty/pro/
A recognized leader in developing, manufacturing, and marketing superior grade art and beauty brushes

SALLY BEAUTY

15091 E. Mississippi Ave.
Aurora, CO 80012
Phone: 303-750-5593
For all locations: www.sallybeauty.com
Professional makeup, hair, and nail supplies

THE SCREAM TEAM

www.screamteam.com
Professional quality foam latex appliances

SCREENFACE

20 Powis Terrace
Westbourne Park Rd.
Notting Hill, London W11 1JH
and:
48 Monmouth St.
Covent Garden
London WC2 9EP
Phone: 020 7221 8289, 020 7836 3955
www.screenface.co.uk
Professional makeup supplies

SCULPTURE HOUSE

405 Skillman Rd.
P.O. Box 69
Skillman, NJ 08558
Phone: 609-466-2986
www.sculpturehouse.com
Professional modeling, molding, and casting supplies

SERVO CITY

Phone: 620-221-0123
www.servocity.com
Radio control accessories and parts

SEPHORA

8505 Park Meadows Center Dr.
Littleton, CO 80124
Phone: 303-799-4800
www.sephora.com
Professional makeup supplies

SILICONES, INC

211 Woodbine St.
P.O. Box 363
High Point, NC 27261
Phone: 336-886-5018
www.silicones-inc.com
Silicone for mold making and prosthetics

SILPAK, INC

470 E. Bonita
Pomona, CA 91767
Phone: 909-625-0056
www.silpak.com
Molding and casting supplies

SMOOTH-ON, INC

2000 Saint John St.
Easton, PA 18042
Phone: 1-800-762-0744
http://www.smooth-on.com/
Silicones, foams, plastics, and urethanes

SPECIAL EFFECTS SUPPLY CORP

543 W. 100 North, Suite 3
Bountiful, UT 84010
Phone: 801-298-9762
www.xmission.com/~spl_efx/
Foams, liquid rubber, and plastics

TEMPTU

26 W. 17th St., Suite 503
New York, NY 10011
Phone: 212-675-4000
www.temptu.com
Cosmetic and special FX makeup and tools

THREEWIT-COOPER

2900 Walnut St.
Denver, CO 80205
Phone: 303-296-1666
Dental impression plaster, lab dental plaster, ultracal, hydrocal

TIRANTI

3 Pipers Court
Berkshire Drive
Thatcham, Berkshire RG19 4ER
and:
27 Warren St.
London W1T 5NB
Phone: +44 (0)845 123 2100
+44 (0)20 7380 0808
www.tiranti.co.uk
Sculptors' tools, materials, and studio equipment

VAN DYKE'S

Orders 1-800-843-3320
Customer Service 1-800-787-3355
www.vandykestaxidemy.com
Glass eyes, animal forms

VARAFORM

U.S. distributors:
Douglass & Sturgess, San Francisco; www.artstuff.com
The Compleat Sculptor, NYC; www.sculpt.com
U.K. distributors:
Bentley Chemicals, Worcestershire; www.bentleychemicals.co.uk
Flint Hire & Supply, London; www.flints.co.uk
Thermoplastic impregnated cotton mesh for mold making

WESTERN SCULPTING SUPPLY

2855 W. 8th Ave.
Denver, CO 80204
Phone: 303-623-4407
www.westernsculptingsupply.com
Sculpting supplies and tools

WILSHIRE WIGS

5241 Craner Ave.
North Hollywood, CA 91601
Phone: 1-800-927-0874 or 818-761-9447
http://wilshirewigs.com/
Wigs, hair extensions, and accessories

WHIP MIX CORPORATION

361 Farmington Ave.
P.O. Box 17183
Louisville, KY 40217
Phone: 1-800-626-5651 or 502-637-1451
www.whipmix.com
Dental molding and casting supplies

WOLFE FACE ART AND FX

224 W. Central Parkway Suite 1020
Altamonte Springs, FL 32714
Toll Free: 877-WOLFEFX
http://www.wolfefx.com
Face art and FX supplies

W.M. CREATIONS, INC

5755 Tujunga Ave.
North Hollywood, CA 91601
Phone: 1-800-454-8339 or 818-763-6692
http://matthewwmungle.com
EZ scar kits, professional specialty cosmetic supplies

ZELLER INTERNATIONAL

Phone: 607-363-2071
http://zeller-int.com/
Makeup effects and special effects, casting, mold-making supplies

Appendix D Conversion Charts

WEIGHT

1 dram (dr)

- = 1.772 grams

1 gram (g)

- = 15.432 grains
- = 0.0353 ounces
- = 0.034 fluid ounces (water)
- = 0.0022 pounds
- = 0.002 pints (water)
- = 0.001 liters (water)
- = 1,000 milligrams
- = 0.001 kilograms

1 ounce (oz)

- = 480 grains
- = 28.35 grams
- = 0.0075 gallons
- = 0.03 quarts
- = 0.06 pints
- = 0.0625 pounds
- = 0.96 fluid ounces (water)

1 pound (lb)

- = 7,000 grains
- = 453.6 grams
- = 16 ounces
- = 0.12 gallons (water)
- = 0.016 cubic feet (water)
- = 0.48 quarts (water)
- = 0.96 pints (water)
- = 15.35 fluid ounces (water)
- = 27.68 cubic inches (water)
- = 453.59 cubic centimeters (water)
- = 453.59 milliliters (water)
- = 453.59 grams
- = 0.454 liters (water)

1 stone

- = 14 pounds

1 hundred weight

- = 100 pounds
- = 45.3592 kilograms

LENGTH

1 millimeters (mm)

- = 0.04 inches

1 centimeters (cm)

- = 0.3937 inches

1 inches (in)

- = 2.54 centimeters

1 feet (ft)

- = 12 inches
- = 30.48 centimeters
- = 0.305 meters

1 yard (yd)

- = 3 feet
- = 36 inches
- = 91.44 centimeters
- = 0.914 meters

1 meter (m)

- = 3.28 feet
- = 39.37 inches
- = 100 centimeters

TEMPERATURE

The United States and Imperial systems measure temperature using the Fahrenheit system. The metric (SI) system originally used the Celsius temperature system but now officially uses the Kelvin temperature system. However, few people aside from brainiacs have switched to the Kelvin system, and the Celsius system is almost always used by most people for nonscientific purposes—unless, of course, you live and work in the United States. The following points compare the Fahrenheit and Celsius systems:

- *The freezing point of water in Fahrenheit is 32°; in Celsius it is 0°.*
- *The boiling point of water in Fahrenheit is 212°; in Celsius it is 100°.*

- *Consequently, the difference between freezing and boiling is 180°F (212–32) or 100°C (100–0). This means that a 180° change in Fahrenheit is equal to a 100° change in Celsius, or more simply, 1.8°F equals 1.0°C.*

This gives rise to the following equations to convert between Celsius and Fahrenheit:

To convert between degrees Fahrenheit (°F) and degrees Celsius (°C), use:

$$°C = (°F - 32) \times 5/9 = (°F - 32)/1.8$$

$$°F = (95 \times °C) + 32 = (1.8 \times °C) + 32°$$

Some common examples are

- Freezing = 0° C, 32° F
- Room temperature = 20° C, 68° F
- Normal body temperature = 37° C, 98.6° F
- A very hot day = 40° C, 104° F
- Boiling point of water = 100° C, 212° F

AREA

1 square foot (sq ft, ft^2)

- = 144 square inches
- = 930 square centimeters

1 square meter (m^2)

- = 10.764 square feet
- = 1,550 square inches
- = 10,000 square centimeters

VOLUME

1 teaspoon (tsp)

- = 5 milliliters
- = 5 cubic centimeters

1 tablespoon (tbs)

- = 3 teaspoons
- = 15 milliliters

1 fluid ounce (fl oz)

- = 6 teaspoons
- = 2 tablespoons
- = 0.0078 gallons
- = 0.031 quarts

- = 29.57 grams (water)
- = 0.0062 pints
- = 0.065 pounds (water)
- = 1.04 ounces (water)
- = 1.8 cubic inches
- = 29.57 cubic centimeters
- = 29.57 milliliters
- = 0.0296 liters

1 cup

- = 48 teaspoons
- = 16 tablespoons
- = 8 fluid ounces
- = 237 milliliters

1 pint (pt)

- = 2.0 cups
- = 0.5679 liters
- = 0.125 gallons
- = 0.5 quarts
- = 1.043 pounds (water)
- = 16.69 ounces (water)
- = 16 fluid ounces
- = 28.875 cubic inches
- = 0.0167 cubic feet
- = 473.18 cubic centimeters
- = 473.18 milliliters
- = 0.473 liters
- = 473.18 grams (water)

1 quart (qt)

- = 2.0 pints
- = 4.0 cups
- = 946.35 milliliters
- = 946.35 cubic centimeters
- = 946.35 grams (water)
- = 0.95 liters
- = 0.25 gallons
- = 2.0 pints
- = 2.085 pounds (water)
- = 33.36 ounces (water)
- = 32 fluid ounces
- = 57.75 cubic inches
- = 0.0334 cubic feet

1 gallon (gal)

- = 4.0 quarts
- = 8.0 pints
- = 16.0 cups
- = 3.785 liters
- = 0.1339 cubic feet
- = 231 cubic inches
- = 8.345 pounds (water)
- = 3,785.4 grams (water)
- = 4 quarts
- = 8 pints
- = 135.52 ounces (water)
- = 128 fluid ounces
- = 3,785.4 cubic centimeters
- = 3,785.4 milliliters

1 Imperial gallon

- = 4.5459 liters
- = 0.1605 cubic feet
- = 277.42 cubic inches
- = 4.845 quarts
- = 1.21 gallons

1 milliliter (ml)

- = 1 cubic centimeters
- = 20 drops (approx.)
- = 0.20 teaspoons
- = 0.061 cubic inches
- = 0.001 liters
- = 1 gram (water)
- = 0.002 pounds (water)
- = 0.0003 gallons

1 liter (l)

- = 1,000 milliliters
- = 1,000 cubic centimeters
- = 1.7598 pints
- = 1.057 quarts
- = 0.264 gallons
- = 203 teaspoons
- = 67.6 tablespoons
- = 35.28 ounces (water)
- = 33.8 fluid ounces
- = 4.23 cups

- = 2.1134 pints
- = 2.205 pounds (water)
- = 61.025 cubic inches
- = 0.0353 cubic feet
- = 1,000 grams (water)
- = 1 kilograms (water)

Measures of volume are different for the two systems due to the Imperial ounce being slightly smaller than the United States equivalent (which affects all multiples of the ounce) and also due to the United Kingdom pint having 20 ounces whereas the United States pint has only 16 ounces.

The sizes of the smaller Imperial measures (teaspoon and tablespoon) are open to interpretation.

CUBIC VOLUME

Volume of a cube:

Width × Length × Height = Cubic volume

$V = 1/3\pi r^2 h$

Volume of a cylinder:

To calculate the volume of a cylinder, we need to know the radius of the circular cross-section of the cylinder; this is the measurement from the center of the circle to the outer edge, or ½ the diameter (outer edge to outer edge). A cylinder with radius r units and height h units has a volume of V cubic units given by $V = \pi r^2 h$; p = 3.142.

Volume of a cone:

$V = 1/3\pi r^2 h$

Volume of a sphere:

$V = 4/3\pi r^3$

1 cubic centimeter (cc, cm^3)

- = 1 milliliter
- = 1 gram (water)
- = 0.061 cubic inches
- = 0.001 quarts
- = 0.002 pints
- = 0.034 fluid ounces

1 cubic inch (cu in, in^3)

- = 16.387 cc (cubic centimeters)
- = 16.387 milliliters
- = 0.0043 gallons

- = 0.017 quarts
- = 0.035 pints
- = 0.036 pounds (water)
- = 0.576 ounces (water)
- = 0.554 fluid ounce
- = 0.00058 cubic feet
- = 0.0164 liters
- = 16.39 grams (water)

1 cubic foot (cu ft, ft^3)

- = 7.481 gallons
- = 29.922 quarts
- = 59.844 pints
- = 62.426 pounds (water)
- = 998.816 ounces (water)
- = 28,355 grams (water)
- = 957.51 fluid ounces
- = 1,728 cubic inches
- = 28.316 liters
- = 28,316 cubic centimeters
- = 28,316 milliliters

1 cubic meter (m^3)

- = 35.314 cubic feet
- = 61,024 cubic inches
- = 1,000 liters

Appendix E Books and Magazines

Anatomy for the Artist, by Sarah Simblet; ISBN 0-7894-8045-X.
The Art and Science of Professional Makeup, by Stan Campbell Place; ISBN 0-87250-361-9.
Atlas of Anatomy, by Giovanni Iazzetti; ISBN-10: 190232840X, ISBN-13: 978-1902328409.
Atlas of Human Anatomy for the Artist, by Stephen Rogers Peck; ISBN-10: 0195030958, ISBN-13: 978-0195030952.
Behind the Mask: The Secrets of Hollywood's Monster Makers, by Mark Salisbury and Alan Hedgcock; ISBN 1-85286-488-5.
Cinefex Magazine; www.cinefex.com/store/subs.html.
The Complete Make-up Artist, by Penny Delamar; ISBN 0-8101-1969-2.
Designing Movie Creatures and Characters, by Richard Rickitt; ISBN-13: 978-0-240-80846-8, ISBN-10: 0-240-80846-0.
Dick Smith's Do-It-Yourself Monster Makeup, by Dick Smith; ASIN B000VJ5U64.
Fangoria Magazine; www.fangoria.com.
Forensic Art and Illustration, by Karen T. Taylor; ISBN 0-8493-8118-5.
Forensic Pathology, by David J. Williams, Anthony J. Ashford, David S. Priday, and Alex S Forrest; ISBN 0-443-05388-X.
Grande *Illusions: A Learn-by-Example Guide to the Art and Technique of Special Make-Up Effects from the Films of Tom Savini*, by Tom Savini; ISBN-10: 0911137009, ISBN-13: 978-0911137002.
Grande Illusions: Book II, by Tom Savini; ISBN-10: 0911137076, ISBN-13: 978-0911137071.
Gray's Anatomy, by Henry Gray; ISBN-10: 0517223651, ISBN-13: 978-0517223659.
Harry's Affordable Animatronics How To Guide, by Harry Lapping, Jim Litchko, and Robert Van Deest; ISBN: 978-097488456-1.
How to Draw the Human Head, by Louise Gordon; ISBN 0-14-046560-X.
Human Proportions for Artists, by Avard T. Fairbanks and Eugene F. Fairbanks; ISBN 0-9725841-1-0.
Kryolan Makeup Manual, by Arnold Langer; ASIN: B000BWPGVA.
The Makeup Artist Handbook, by Gretchen Davis and Mindy Hall; ISBN 978-0-240-809410.
Makeup Artist Magazine; 4018 NE 112th Ave. D-8, Vancouver, WA 98682; http://makeupmag.com/subscribe.htm.

Makeup Designory's Character Makeup, by Paul Thompson; ISBN 0-9749500-0-9, LCCN 2004091103.
Making Faces, Playing God: Identity and the Art of Transformational Makeup, by Thomas Morawetz; ISBN-10: 0292752474, ISBN-13: 978-0292752474.
Men, Makeup & Monsters: Hollywood's Masters of Illusion and FX, by Anthony Timpone; ISBN-10: 0312146787.
The Monster Makers Mask Makers Handbook, by Arnold Goldman; ISBN-10: 0977687007, ISBN-13: 978-0977687008.
The Monster Makers Mask Makers Handbook, by Arnold Goldman; ISBN-10: 0977687007, ISBN-13: 978-0977687008.
The Monstrous Makeup-Manual, by Mike Spatola (2010); http://hauntingconsultant.com.
One Hundred Over 100, by Jim Heynen; ISBN 1-55591-052-1.
The Professional Makeup Artist's Resource Guide, by Shauna Giesbrecht; ISBN 0-9755912-0-7.
The Prop Builder's Molding & Casting Handbook, by Thurston James; ISBN-10: 1558701281, ISBN-13: 978-1558701281.
Special Effects Makeup, by Janus Vinther; ISBN-10: 087830178X, ISBN-13: 978-0878301782.
Special Makeup Effects, by Vincent J-R Kehoe; ISBN-10: 0240800990, ISBN-13: 978-0240800998.
Stage Makeup, by Richard Corson and James Glavan; ISBN-10: 0136061532, ISBN-13: 978-0136061533.
Stage Makeup Step-by-Step, by Rosemary Swinfield; ISBN-10: 155870390X, ISBN-13: 978-1558703902.
Stage Makeup: The Actor's Complete Guide to Today's Techniques and Materials, by Laura Thudium; ISBN-10: 0823088391, ISBN-13: 978-0823088393.
The Technique of the Professional Makeup Artist, by Vincent J-R Kehoe; ISBN-10: 0240802179, ISBN-13: 978-0240802176.
Techniques of Three-Dimensional Makeup, by Lee Baygan; ISBN 0-8230-5260-5, ISBN 0-8230-5261-3.
War Surgery in Afghanistan and Iraq A Series of Cases, 2003-2007, edited by LTC Shawn Christian Nessen, DO, US Army; Dave Edmond Lounsbury, MD, COL, US Army (Ret); Stephen P. Hetz, MD, COL, US Army (Ret); ISBN: 978-0-981822-80-8.
Wig Making and Styling A Complete Guide for Theatre & Film, by Martha Ruskai and Allison Lowery; ISBN: 978-0-240-81320-2.
Wigs & Make-up for Theatre, Television and Film, by Patsy Baker; ISBN 0-7506-0431-X
The Winston Effect: The Art & History of Stan Winston Studio, by Jody Duncan; ISBN-10: 1845761502, ISBN-13: 978-1845761509.
Wisdom, by Andrew Zuckerman; ISBN: 978-0-8109-8359-5 (US); 978-0-8109-8372-4 (UK/Canada).

DVDS AND VIDEOS

Daniel E Tirinnanzi's *Movie Animatronics Building and Radio Controlled Mechanical Mask* (3 Disc Series).
Daniel E Tirinnanzi's *Movie Animatronics (Vol. 2) Building an Advanced Eye Mechanism*, DVD.
Gary Willett's *My Animatronic Project* (4 Disc Series), DVD.
Gil Mosco, *The Special Makeup Effects Artist's Guide to Using GM Foam*, Video.
Graftobian's *HD Makeup 101* with Suzanne Patterson, DVD.
Ken Banks' *Eyes Made Easy (Vol. 1) A Comprehensive Guide to Making Acrylic Human Eyes*, DVD.
Mark Alfrey's *Sculpting the Human Head*, DVD.
Mark Alfrey's *Ultimate Lifecasting*, DVD and Video.
Mark Alfrey's *Sculpting Movie Monsters*, DVD.
Mark Alfrey's *Standard Molds and Castings*, DVD.
Mark Alfrey's *Prosthetic Makeup for Beginners*, DVD.
Mark Alfrey's *Sculpting the Nude Figure*, DVD.
Mark Alfrey's *Sculpting with Water Clay*, DVD
Michael Mosher's *The NEW Bald Cap DVD*, DVD.
Michael Pack's *Bite Me: The Video*, Video.
Neill Gorton Studios' *Creating Character Prosthetics in Silicone* (*Series in 4 Parts*), DVD.
Neill Gorton Studios' *The Art of Silicone Prosthetics* (*2 Disc Series*), DVD.
Neill Gorton Studios' *Lifecasting with Silicones and Alginates* (*Series in 3 Parts*), DVD.

Glossary

2.5D *Two-and-a-half dimensional* is an informal term used to describe visual phenomena that are considered "between" 2D and 3D. This is also called *pseudo-3D*.

3D Three-dimensional; usually a short form for *3D computer graphics.*

3D makeup Dimensional makeup, which includes prosthetic appliances.

3D transfers Small prosthetic appliances that are applied in the same manner as temporary tattoos.

Acetone A solvent. Acetone is the active ingredient in nail polish remover and is also used to make plastics. Acetone is mixable with water, alcohol, ether, and other liquids.

Acrylic A versatile polymer (type of plastic) used in paints, sealers, molds, textiles, etc.

Addition-cure silicone Also known as *platinum-cure silicone*; widely used as a material for making prosthetic appliances. It cures by a self-contained chemical reaction.

Airbrush A small, air-operated tool that sprays various media, including ink and dye but most often paint, by a process of atomization. It is used extensively today for the application of makeup.

Alginate Derived from seaweed and giant kelp, alginate absorbs water quickly and is used extensively as a mold-making material in dentistry, makeup effects and prosthetics, lifecasting, and textiles. It is also used in the food industry as a thickening agent and in various medical products, including burn dressings.

Algislo A product of EnvironMolds, Algislo is an alkaline (base) solution designed to retard the set of alginate, bond set alginate with fresh alginate, and soften freshly set alginate to allow the application of fibers to hold a rigid support mold.

Anaplastology The art and science of restoring a malformed or absent part of the human body through artificial means. An anaplastologist makes prosthetic devices. It is derived from the Greek word *ana* meaning again and *plastos* meaning formed. See also: *Appliance, Prosthetic, Prosthetist.*

Angora hair Also known as *Angora wool*. It is the hair of the Angora goat or of the Angora rabbit.

Animatronics The technology connected with the use of electronics to animate puppets or other figures as for motion pictures.

Anthropometry The study of human body measurement for use in anthropological classification and comparison.

Appliance Another name for a prosthetic device. See also: *Prosthetic*.

Armature In sculpture, a skeletal framework built as a support on which a clay, wax, or plaster figure is constructed.

Articulation 1. The act of properly arranging artificial teeth; 2. the action or manner in which the parts come together at a joint.

Astringent A cosmetic liquid that cleans the skin and constricts the pores.

Attagel A clay mineral used as a thixotropic agent; the active ingredient of fuller's earth. When mixed with PPI's Green Marble Se-Lr,® can be used as stipple ager.

Bald cap A flexible cap, often made of latex or vinyl but can also be made of foam latex or silicone, for creating the appearance of baldness.

Biomechanical engineering *Biomechanics* is mechanics applied to biology; it is the engineering of a living body, especially of the forces exerted by muscles and gravity on the skeletal structure.

Bleeder An escape hole for air trapped inside a mold; it fills with excess casting material as the mold is filled.

Blend line The point at which any prosthetic appliance tapers off into real skin. The blend between appliance and skin must be invisible. Also called the *blending edge*. See also: *Cutting edge*.

Block mold Often a two-piece rubber mold that doesn't need a rigid mother mold due to the thickness of the rubber. Casting material is poured through a sprue hole. See also: *Box mold*.

Boardwork A word used to describe the act of making postiche.

Bondo A mixture of Pros-Aide® water-based acrylic adhesive and Cab-O-Sil® (fumed silica) to create a paste used to blend seams and edges of prosthetic appliances. See also: *Cabo patch*.

Box mold A type of mold made by creating a box form and filling it with mold rubber, covering the model to be reproduced. Box molds can be one or two pieces. One-piece box molds are open faced and used for reproducing objects such as medallions, whereas two-piece box molds can be used to reproduce more complex shapes. See also: *Block mold*.

Breakdown makeup The opposite of beauty makeup.

Brush coat The first, thin coating of material brushed into a mold or onto a sculpture to pick up details before building up reinforcing layers. See also: *Brush-up layer, Detail layer, Print coat*.

Brush-up layer The first coat of material that is applied by brush to pick up detail. See also: *Brush coat, Detail layer, Print coat*.

Buck Another name for the stone positive of a face from a lifecast.

Burlap Bought by the yard or in rolls, burlap is a loose-weave fabric used as a reinforcing material in the outer layers of gypsum molds, making the stone stronger and less susceptible to cracking.

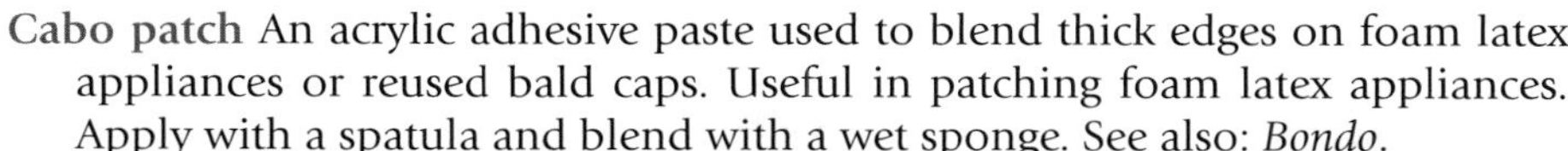

Cabo patch An acrylic adhesive paste used to blend thick edges on foam latex appliances or reused bald caps. Useful in patching foam latex appliances. Apply with a spatula and blend with a wet sponge. See also: *Bondo*.

Cab-O-Sil Untreated fumed silica used as an inert filler to thicken thin liquids. Cab-O-Sil is a registered trademark of the Cabot Corporation.

Capillary action Capillary action is the result of *adhesion and surface tension*. Adhesion of water to the walls of a vessel will cause an upward force on the liquid at the edges and result in a meniscus which turns upward. The surface tension acts to hold the surface intact, so instead of just the edges moving upward, the whole liquid surface is dragged upward.

Case mold A rigid multipiece mold that encases a sculpture when closed and clamped together. A *matrix mold* is a type of case mold.

CGI Computer-generated imagery.

Cholesterol cream A hair-conditioning cream that is an excellent release used on hair in lifecasting, to prevent alginate from sticking to it.

Cold foam Soft or rigid two-part urethane foam that does not require the application of heat to cure. See also: *Poly foam, Soft foam, Urethane*.

Collagen A fibrous structural protein extracted from the bones and connective tissue of animals that when partially hydrolyzed (broken down by water) becomes gelatin.

Collapsible core Collapsible core refers to a mold with an inner core that is designed to come apart as part of the de-molding process to allow easy removal of the cast appliance as well as producing a piece with no outward seams or connecting lines. See also: *Puzzle*

Collodion A solution of nitrocellulose in acetone, sometimes with the addition of alcohols. In makeup, it is used to create scars on the skin. When the acetone evaporates, it pulls and puckers the skin, creating realistic-looking scars.

Condensation-cure silicone Also known as *tin-cure silicone* and *room-temperature vulcanization* or RTV silicone. It is used extensively for mold making but sometimes also used for prosthetics.

Core The interior positive portion of a multipiece mold. If a character makeup requires a full-head cowl, for example, the front and back negative parts of the mold hold the detail of the makeup that will be outward while the interior positive, or core, holds the detail of the head the appliance will be attached to.

Craniofacial implant Usually, titanium anchors surgically implanted to hold medical prostheses in place for individuals with catastrophic injuries, allowing people to improve their quality of life.

Cream time For 1:1 two-part urethane foam, cream time is the working time to mix the liquid before it begins to foam. See also: *Pot life, Working time*.

Critical corner Area where the dividing wall meets the sculpture. It is considered critical because it is an area of the sculpture that is subject to trapping air when the mold is being made.

Crystalline silica A basic component of quartz, soil, sand, granite, and many other minerals. Found in many types of alginate. Respirable crystalline silica is a known carcinogen and can also cause silicosis.

Cure The chemical reaction that causes materials such as silicone, urethane, and Ultracal to set up, or harden.

Cutting edge The cutting edge or *blending edge* of a mold is where the positive and the negative mold parts touch and becomes the thin prosthetic appliance edge that disappears when it is applied.

Cyberscan Method of transcribing a real object into a digital model by accurately measuring it with a laser. Normally used to create a scan of an actor or maquette to produce a 3D copy for sculpting purposes.

Decalcification The loss of calcium or calcium compounds, as from bone or teeth.

Dental acrylic powder Acrylic powder available in various colors; when mixed with a liquid acrylic monomer becomes a plastic liquid used for making false teeth and gums.

Dental impression plaster A very low expansion plaster used for dental impressions; also makes very strong mother mold as a substitute for using plaster bandages.

Dental stone Very hard, low-expansion gypsum for casting dental models. See also: *Die stone.*

Dental tray Plastic upper and lower trays for making dental impressions with dental alginate.

Detail layer The first, thin coating of material brushed into a mold or onto a sculpture to pick up details before building up reinforcing layers. See also: *Brush-up layer, Brush coat, Print coat.*

Die stone Very hard, low-expansion gypsum for casting dental models. See also: *Dental stone.*

Dividing wall A temporary wall made with WED clay or other water clay to create a separation between the front half and the back half of a case mold. See also: *Mold wall.*

Dremel Versatile electric and battery-operated rotary tool used extensively by model makers and sculptors.

Dressing Refers to trimming, curling, and setting postiche—wigs, moustaches, and beards—for a more natural appearance when they are applied.

Drip coat The gypsum stone applied immediately after the brush coat using the remainder of the first batch of stone. Usually built up to a thickness of ½–1 inch. See also: *Splash coat.*

Ectomorphic A human build with little fat or muscle but with long limbs.

Emollient Having the power of softening or relaxing, as a medicinal substance; soothing, especially to the skin.

Endomorphic A squat and fleshy human build.

Epicanthic fold A fold of skin of the upper eyelid that partially covers the inner corner of the eye. Common in many people of Asian descent, American Indians, and American Eskimos.

Ester A compound produced by the reaction between an acid and an alcohol with the elimination of a molecule of water.

Extrinsic coloration External coloration. Appliance materials such as foam latex may be initially colored intrinsically with a base color but are then usually colored extrinsically to add detail and a sense of depth.

Fiberglass A material consisting of extremely fine glass fibers suspended in a polymer resin, used in making various products, such as yarns, fabrics, insulators, and structural objects or parts. An excellent mold material; extremely strong and very lightweight.

Fibonacci series A sequence of numbers named after Leonardo of Pisa, known as Fibonacci; after two starting values, each number is the sum of the two preceding numbers: 0, 1, 1, 2, 3, 5, 8, 13, 21, 34, 55, 89, 144, 233, 377, 610, 987, 1597, 2584, 4181, 6765, 10946, 17711, 28657, 46368, 75025, 121393, ...

Flange A projecting rim, collar, or ring on a mold that gives additional strength, stiffness, or support and provides an area for clamping or bolting mold sections together.

Flashing Excess casting material in a prosthetic mold that is separated from the appliance by the cutting edge of the mold. Also, the area of a mold where overflow collects.

Flocking Usually a synthetic material used for coloring gelatin or silicone prosthetics intrinsically (internally).

Foam latex Very soft, lightweight, spongy material used to create prosthetics. An actor's physical expressions are very easy to project through foam latex. Liquid latex is mixed with various additives and whipped into a foam, then poured or injected into a mold before being placed in an oven to cure. In addition to prosthetic appliances, foam latex is also used to make rubber body suits and skins for animatronic (mechanical) characters.

Forensic Relates to the use of science or technology in the investigation and establishment of facts or evidence.

Forton MG Though technically a gypsum product (Hydrocal is the main ingredient), it is considered a resin casting material because it incorporates plastics and fiberglass.

Foundation Base makeup applied before highlight and shadow. Used to cover or blend blotchy or uneven skin tones.

Fuller's earth Calcium bentonite is known as *fuller's earth,* a term that is also used to refer to *attapulgite. Pascalite* is another commercial name for the calcium bentonite clay. It is used in special effects for simulating explosions. Fine-grained fuller's earth makes a much larger plume than ordinary dirt, suggesting a larger explosion and allowing use of a smaller, safer charge, sometimes only compressed air. It is also used in breakdown makeup to add dirt and smudges.

Fumed silica Silicon dioxide has unique properties and is commonly added to liquids or coatings and solids to improve various properties. Fumed silica is used frequently as a thixotropic additive that, when dispersed into liquids, increases viscosity; when mixed with powders it prevents caking. Cab-O-Sil® is fumed silica.

Galloon A braided silk lace ribbon used to frame a wig foundation.

Gel coat A thick polymer resin coat used in fiberglass fabrication; the gel coat is used as a detail or brush-up layer before applying resin and fiberglass mat or fiberglass cloth as strength layers.

Gelatin Extracted from collagen; when mixed with various ingredients, gelatin is commonly used as a prosthetic appliance material. It is widely considered to be hypoallergenic.

GFA Gel-filled appliance; a silicone gel often encapsulated by a thin envelope of silicone or plastic (vinyl) bald cap material.

Glycerin A colorless, odorless, thick liquid widely used in pharmaceutical formulations; it is a sugar alcohol and is sweet-tasting and of low toxicity. In makeup effects, glycerin is a component of gelatin used for prosthetics. It is also used to simulate tears and sweat because of its viscous nature and low evaporation. It is also found in WED clay and helps it remain moist for longer periods than normal water-based clays.

Gnomatic growth A process that leaves the resultant features of an individual similar to the original. Although our faces undergo enormous growth from youth to adulthood, there is a constancy of appearance; the face of a man remains recognizably the same, regardless of age.

Golden ratio Can be expressed as a mathematical constant, usually denoted by the Greek letter φ (phi). The figure of a golden section illustrates the geometric relationship that defines this constant. Expressed algebraically:

$$\frac{a+b}{a} = \frac{a}{b} = \varphi.$$

This equation has as its unique positive solution the algebraic irrational number:

$$\varphi = \frac{1+\sqrt{5}}{2} \approx 1.6180339887\ldots.$$

Go off To set up. See also: *Kick*.

Green marble Se-Lr Created as a makeup sealer for Premiere Products by Kenny Myers and Richard Snell.

Gypsum A common mineral, hydrated calcium sulfate, used to make Plaster of Paris, Ultracal, Hydrocal, dental stone, etc.

H-10 A material used to flatten hair at the hairline to eliminate the "bump" under a bald cap and to control hair around the ears and at the nape of the neck. Made from a mixture of moustache wax, Gaf Quat, and 70% alcohol. Great for keeping a Mohawk haircut stiff, too.

Hackle A metal plate with rows of pointed needles used to blend or straighten hair. The hackle is clamped to a table with a C-clamp.

Hair lace Very fine, flexible netting material similar to tulle; often made of silk and used for creating wigs and hairpieces. See also: *Wig lace.*

Hair punching The process of adding hairs to a prosthetic appliance one at a time using a special needle, putting it over a strand of hair and pushing it into the surface of the appliance in the direction the hair is "growing."

Hair tying A very tedious process of knotting hairs into wig lace one-by-one with a special needle that resembles a very small, fine fish hook (called a *ventilating needle*). See also: *Ventilating.*

Heptane A petroleum distillate used as a solvent; Bestine® Rubber Cement Thinner is Heptane.

Hexane A petroleum distillate used as a solvent; Hexane is flammable and is a known carcinogen.

Hogger A hogger is a large wire tool—more blade than wire—used for removing large hunks of clay.

HSE Health and Safety Executive, responsible for health and safety regulation in Great Britain; the United Kingdom's equivalent to OSHA in the United States.

Hydraulic Operated, moved or affected by water or other liquid in motion.

Hydrocal A white gypsum plaster.

Hygroscopic Absorbing or attracting moisture from the air.

Hypoallergenic Designed to reduce or minimize the possibility of an allergic response by containing relatively few or no potentially irritating substances.

Incisal Relating to the cutting edges of the incisor and cuspid teeth.

Intrinsic coloration Internal coloration. Often silicone and gelatin appliances are colored intrinsically with different-colored flocking material to more closely mimic the appearance of real human skin.

IPA Isopropyl alcohol.

IPM Isopropyl myristate.

Isopropyl alcohol Also isopropanol; rubbing alcohol. Sometimes sold as isopropyl rubbing alcohol, 70%, and isopropyl rubbing alcohol, 99%, the latter of which is frequently used in makeup effects. See also: *IPA.*

Isopropyl myristate An ester of isopropyl alcohol and myristic acid. Used as an emollient and nongreasy lubricant. Also used in topical medicinal preparations where good skin absorption is needed. An effective makeup remover and Pros-Aide® bondo remover, it is the mildest of the adhesive removers. See also: *IPM.*

Jacket mold A combination mold made with a registered/keyed silicone or urethane rubber interior and a registered/keyed support mold that is registered/keyed to the rubber interior for extremely precise casting; a type of case mold. See also: *Matrix mold.*

Jowls Folds of flesh hanging from the lower jaw in older and overweight people.

Key An indentation or protrusion to aid in precise alignment of mold parts. See also: *Mold key, Registration key.*

Kick Sometimes referred to as *kick time*, the amount of time it takes for a material to begin to set up during its curing phase. Example: "Plat-Sil Gel 10 will kick faster if you apply heat." See also: *Go off.*

Latex As found in nature, the milky sap of Pará rubber trees. Used extensively in creating makeup effects and prosthetics, especially in making foam latex. See also: *Slip latex, Slush latex.*

Laying on hair The process of applying hair by hand (with hair and glue), a small amount at a time, to create a head of hair, eyebrows, moustache, or beard.

Lesion An injury or wound; in pathology, any localized, abnormal structural change in the body.

Lifecasting The process of creating a three-dimensional copy of a living human body or body parts through the use of alginate molding and casting techniques.

Loop Wires or loops are useful for intricate detail work and they don't need much pressure to remove clay from the sculpture. See also: *Wire.*

Maquette French word for scale model, sometimes referred to by the Italian name *bozzetto*. In makeup effects, it is a scale model of a finished sculpture for a character design or makeup. Often used as a guide for a larger sculpture.

Matrix mold A combination mold made with a registered/keyed silicone or urethane rubber interior and a registered/keyed support mold that is registered/keyed to the rubber interior for extremely precise casting. See also: *Jacket mold.*

Maxillofacial prosthetics Prostheses made for patients with acquired, congenital, and developmental defects of the head and neck. Common maxillofacial prosthetics include auricular prostheses (ears), nasal prostheses (noses), and ocular prostheses (eyes). Made by prosthetists and anaplastologists.

Maxillofacial prosthetist A highly specialized physician or technician who helps restore a sense of normalcy to cancer, trauma, and congenital defect patients. There are only about 500 of these specialists in the United States, and they are dedicated to restoring the health and dignity of thousands of people who live with severe facial deformities.

Mech Another name for an animatronic puppet.

Melanin In humans, melanin is the polymeric pigmentation found in our skin and hair. Produced by melanocytes, melanin is the primary determinant of human skin color.

Mesomorphic A human structure that is naturally muscular with a trim waist and that can easily lose and gain fat and muscle weight.

Mold key An indentation or protrusion to aid in precise alignment of mold parts. See also: *Key, Registration key.*

Mold negative In making a casting of a three-dimensional object (the positive), the resulting mold is the opposite or inverse of that object, or a mold negative. See also: *Negative.*

Mold positive The resulting cast of an object when material is put into a negative mold. See also: *Positive.*

Mold wall A temporary water clay wall used to form a divider between the front and back halves of a case mold. See also: *Dividing wall.*

Mother mold The rigid support shell of a soft inner mold.

MSDS Material safety data sheets, required by law on some products. All makeup effects artists should have MSDS sheets available for all materials in their makeup kits and should also be familiar with properties of all materials being used in the workshop.

Negative The mold surface that contains a reverse three-dimensional imprint of the positive sculpture. See also: *Mold negative.*

Nevus The medical term for growths or lesions of the skin commonly known as birthmarks and moles.

New-Baldies The first bald cap plastic to be medically approved; it is completely free from phthalate softeners.

Nitrile Nitrile or nitrile rubber is a synthetic rubber copolymer generally resistant to oil, fuel, and other chemicals. Its resilience makes it the perfect material for disposable lab, cleaning, and examination gloves. These gloves, along with vinyl gloves, are ideal for working with platinum-addition RTV silicone because they will not react negatively with it.

No. 1 Pottery Plaster Made by U.S. Gypsum (USG), this plaster is excellent for mold making and casting.

Occlusal Related to the fitting together of the teeth of the lower jaw with the corresponding teeth of the upper jaw when the jaws are closed. See also: *Occlusion.*

Occlusion Fitting together of the teeth of the lower jaw with the corresponding teeth of the upper jaw when the jaws are closed. See also: *Occlusal.*

Ocularistry The field of designing, fabricating, and fitting artificial eyes and the making of ocular prostheses associated with the appearance or function of human eyes.

Oil clay Oil-based modeling clay; the clay is mixed with oil to prevent it from drying out or shrinking.

Orthotics The field of application and manufacture of devices that support or correct human function. Many professionals use the adjective *orthotic* as a noun, usually to describe a foot-supporting device or shoe insole.

OSHA Occupational Safety and Health Administration, the main federal agency charged with the enforcement of safety and health legislation.

Overflow Excess appliance material in a mold; flashing is added to a mold to allow overflow at someplace to collect without damaging the mold or the casting.

Paddle A paddle is a small piece of the underskeleton, such as an eyebrow, that is attached to the skin and is controlled by a dedicated servo that subtly moves certain parts of the puppet—like an eyebrow, or a mouth corner—and is somewhat paddle-shaped, hence its name.

Parting edge The parting edge or parting line of a mold determines how and where the pieces of a mold will fit together and come apart.

Pax paint Acrylic paint mixed with Pros-Aide adhesive for painting prosthetic appliances.

Phthalate A group of chemicals used in hundreds of products, such as toys, vinyl flooring and wall covering, detergents, lubricating oils, food packaging, pharmaceuticals, blood bags and tubing, and personal care products, such as nail polish, hair sprays, soaps, and shampoos.

Pigmentation Coloration; in skin, it is the coloration by pigment cells called *melanin*. In prosthetics, pigmentation can be achieved by various shades and tints of flocking or by adding solid pigments.

Plaster bandage Plaster of Paris-impregnated cloth bandages used for making support shells for alginate molds.

Plaster of Paris A white gypsum used for mold making and casting that starts as a dry powder that is mixed with water to form a paste that liberates heat and then hardens. Named for a large gypsum deposit found at Montmartre in Paris, France.

Plasticize To render or become plastic. See also: *Polymer, Polymerization*.

Plastiline A type of oil-based modeling clay.

Plate mold In makeup effects, a plate mold is a flat mold with a negative impression, frequently used for making generic wounds or 3D prosthetic transfers. Can be either a one-piece or two-piece mold.

Pneumatic Containing or operated by air or gas under pressure.

Polyfoam Urethane foam that can be either soft or rigid, usually soft, and can be mixed in a 1:1 ratio by either volume or weight. See also: *Cold foam, Soft foam, Urethane.*

Polymer A compound of high molecular weight derived either by the addition of many smaller molecules, as polyethylene, or by the condensation of many smaller molecules with the elimination of water, alcohol, or the like, as nylon. See also: *Plasticize, Polymerization*.

Polymerization The bonding of two or more monomers to form a polymer. See also: *Plasticize, Polymer*.

Positive Any sculpture or model used to create the mold negative. See also: *Mold positive.*

Postiche A French word used to describe any article of hair work, which can be as small as a false eyelash or as large as a wig.

Pot life Term for the working time of a material before it begins to cure. See also: *Working time, Cream time.*

Print coat The first, thin coating of material brushed into a mold or onto a sculpture to pick up details before building up reinforcing layers. See also: *Detail layer, Brush-up layer, Brush coat.*

Pros-Aide A very popular water-based prosthetic adhesive made by ADM Tronics.®

Prosthetic A device, either external or implanted, that substitutes for or supplements a missing or defective part of the body. Also called an *appliance;* used for special makeup effects, the basis of this book. Usually made of silicone, foam latex, or gelatin. See also: *Appliance.*

Prosthetist A professional who makes prosthetic devices. See also: *Anaplastology.*

PSI Pounds per square inch, a measure of pressure.

Pull Term for mask or appliance making using a mold. Each time a prosthetic appliance is removed from a mold, it is known as a *pull.* Well-maintained molds should allow many pulls before breaking down.

Puzzle Mold A mold with an inner core that is designed to come apart as part of the de-molding process to allow easy removal of the cast appliance as well as producing a piece with no outward seams or connecting lines. See also: *collapsible core*

Quik-Tube A cylindrical prefab product manufactured by Quikrete that is well suited to some lifecasting applications.

Rake Rakes are serrated tools used for removing clay efficiently.

Registration key A drilled or carved indentation or a protrusion made of clay, rubber, or resin that is used to precisely align parts of a mold when held together. See also: *Key, Mold key.*

Relative density The ratio of the mass of a solid or liquid to the mass of an equal volume of distilled water at 4 °C (39 °F) or of a gas to an equal volume of air or hydrogen under prescribed conditions of temperature and pressure. See also: *Specific gravity.*

Release agent Release agents are materials that allow you to separate cast objects from molds. There are two categories for most release agents: barrier and reactive or chemically active release agents.

Rigid foam Rigid urethane foam mixed in a 1:1 ratio by either volume or weight. It is available in varying densities.

RTV silicone Most commonly a tin-cure condensation silicone, though there are platinum room-temperature vulcanization (RTV) silicones.

Rubber mask greasepaint RMGP is makeup for use over foam latex and slush latex appliances. Creates washes of color by adding a couple of drops of 99% isopropyl alcohol to the makeup and then applying with a sea sponge for dimensional texture.

Running foam The term for processing a batch of foam latex.

Scraper Also called a steel, these tools are used to smooth out the sketched-in clay that has been raked. See also: *Steel*.

Sculpt Used by makeup effects artists, *sculpt* is just another name for the sculpture.

Sealer Liquids or sprays that are absorbed into porous surfaces to seal against moisture, making the surface essentially no longer porous; they can act as both a seal and a release for some materials.

Seaming Removing and cleaning up surface blemishes and flashing on prosthetic seams.

Servo by most accounts the workhorse device in the world of animatronics—is an electromechanical motor/device with an output shaft that can be positioned remotely into specific angular positions by sending the servo a coded signal.

Shell Support mold; mother mold; the rigid outer part of a matrix mold.

Shim Material, often thin wood or metal, used as a dividing wall in mold making.

Silicosis Sometimes called grinder's disease or potter's rot; a disabling, nonreversible, and sometimes fatal lung disease caused by overexposure to respirable crystalline silica, the second most common mineral on earth.

Slip latex Liquid latex that will air-dry and does not need a heat cure like foam latex. Used most often for making rubber masks. See also: *Latex, Slush latex*.

Slush latex Liquid latex used for build-up appliances or rubber masks. Called *slush* because the latex is poured into a mask mold and sloshed around, forming a skin that will become the mask. See also: *Latex, Slip latex*.

Soft foam Soft urethane foam mixed in a 1:1 ratio by either volume or weight. It is also available in varying densities. See also: *Cold foam, Polyfoam, Urethane*.

Somatotype A term for human body shape and physique type.

Special effects SFX or SPFX in short; traditionally practical or physical effects usually accomplished during live-action shooting. This includes the use of mechanized props, scenery and scale model miniatures, and pyrotechnics.

Specific gravity The ratio of the mass of a solid or liquid to the mass of an equal volume of distilled water at 4°C (39°F) or of a gas to an equal volume of air or hydrogen under prescribed conditions of temperature and pressure. See also: *Relative density*.

Spirit gum Also called as *Mastix*; a natural gum resin commonly used as a theatrical adhesive for lace wigs and beards.

Splash coat The gypsum stone applied immediately after the brush coat using the remainder of the first batch of stone. See also: *Drip coat*.

Sprue In mold making, the passage through which casting material is poured into a mold. The term can also refer to the excess material on a rough casting that solidified in the sprue hole.

Steel Also called a *scraper*, these tools are used to smooth out the sketched-in clay that has been raked. See also: *Scraper*.

Stipple The technique of using small dots to simulate varying degrees of solidity, or shading, such as beard stipple, or lightly applying latex for an aging, wrinkled effect. Usually created with a coarse stipple sponge.

Stipple sponge A rough, open-weave synthetic sponge used for old-age stippling, beard stippling, bruises, and adding a hint of capillary coloring to produce a natural flesh-tone makeup.

Straight makeup Can incorporate corrective makeup and camouflage makeup; it can overlap into beauty and fashion makeup, but its function is to correct and define a person's face, not to change it. Straight makeup, in general, should be understated and imperceptible.

Striae A thin line or band, especially one of several that are parallel or close together; a characteristic stria of contractile tissue. *Striae* is also a medical term for stretch marks on the skin, a form of scarring with a silvery white hue.

Suppurate To produce or discharge fluid, as with severe burns.

Talc-ohol Talcum powder (baby powder) dispersed into a solution with 99% isopropyl alcohol that can be sprayed onto appliances without touching the appliance. The alcohol evaporates almost immediately, leaving behind a fine layer of matte powder.

Telesis Telesis products from Premiere Products (PPI) are a line of adhesives, thinners, removers, solvents, skin preps, and conditioners that are used extensively by medical professionals (maxillofacial prosthetists) and special makeup effects artists.

Terra alba Dried, powdered cured plaster, as an additive to fresh plaster, will cause it to kick, or begin to set, in a fraction of its normal time.

Texture stamp A flexible stamp that is pressed into the clay sculpture to add texture during final detailing.

Thixotropic An example of an application for thixotropic properties is the thickening of silicone, so it won't be runny; it becomes more of a paste. Cab-O-Sil® added to Pros-Aide® adhesive becomes a thixotropic paste that can be used to patch appliance seams and the like.

Tincture of Green Soap Also called as *Green Soap Tincture*; it isn't necessarily green. A medicinal topical detergent used for surgical prep; also an excellent release agent. It contains 30% alcohol.

Tulle A fine, often starched net of silk, rayon, or nylon, used especially for veils, tutus, or gowns.

Ultracal 30 Super-strength gypsum cement recommended where extreme accuracy and greater surface hardness are required. Ultracal 30® has the lowest expansion of any rapid-setting gypsum cement available. Captures very high detail in lifecasting or sculpture.

Undercut Any area of a positive or negative that creates a locking state between the mold and the core.

Urethane Also called as *polyurethane*; a family of rubbers and plastics materials that are used for making molds. Widely known for its tough properties, urethane also refers to soft or rigid foam that is used for casting in molds. See also: *Cold foam, Polyfoam, Soft foam.*

Vascularity Pertaining to vessels or ducts that convey fluids such as blood, lymph, or sap.

Ventilating Hand-tying hair with a ventilating needle into wig lace. See also: *Hair tying.*

Visual effects VFX for short; visual effects usually involve the integration of live action footage with CGI or other elements (such as pyrotechnics or miniatures) to create realistic environments. *Visual effects* predominantly refer to postproduction, whereas special effects refer to on-set mechanical effects.

Vulcanization The process of improving the strength, resiliency, and freedom from stickiness and odor (of rubber, for example) by combining with sulfur or other additives in the presence of heat and pressure.

Water clay A modeling clay suspended in water; like WED clay but without glycerin. Used by sculptors and mold makers.

WED clay A water-based clay great for large sculptures; it has a smooth, fine grain. This clay has been specially formulated to be a very smooth, slow-drying clay for modeling; it stays moist longer because it contains glycerin. It is used primarily by design studios and the entertainment industry for modeling, design, mockup, and tooling. Named for Walter Elias Disney (WED).

Weft As it pertains to hair, a bundle of hair that is sewn together at one end (root end) for easier manipulation during the wig-making process.

Wig block Also called a *malleable*; used for dressing pastiche (wigs and hairpieces).

Wig lace A very fine, flesh-colored, four-way stretch mesh used to blend off hairlines where they meet the skin to give the impression of a natural hairline effect of a wig or hairpiece. See also: *Hair lace.*

Wire Wires or loops are useful for intricate detail work and they don't need much pressure to remove clay from the sculpture. See also: *Loop.*

Witch hazel Used medically as a lotion for treating bruises and insect bites, it is also an effective topical astringent used on the skin prior to applying a prosthetic appliance.

Working time The amount of time to mix, pour, brush, or otherwise apply a material before it begins to kick, or set. See also: *Pot life; Cream time.*

Wrinkle stipple Often made of thin specialty liquid latex that dries nearly transparently; ideal for creating facial wrinkles and crow's feet.

Yak hair Coarse hair often used for makeup effects postiche.

Index

Boldface page numbers refer to figures.

A

abdomen muscles 50–2
acetone 396; plastics 389, 391
Achilles tendon 51
acrylic adhesives 288
Adams, Ansel 29
addition-cured silicones *see* platinum silicone
adhesives: appliance application 285–6; remover 306
Adobe Photoshop 34, 38
Affordable Animatronics Vols. 1 and 2 (Lapping, Deest and Litchko) 344
African ancestry 83–4
age makeup 22, **22**
age spots 62, **63**
aging: distinctions of 75, **76**; facial 77–81, **78**; wrinkle stipple 420–2
aging stipple: Dick's ager 442–3; Green Marble SeLr® 441–2; H-10 443–4; PAX paint 445–6; Pros-Aide® 442
airbrush 409; with PAX and inks 407–8; with tattoo stencil 402–3, **403**
Al-Cote® 150, 171, 172, 259–61
Alfrey, Mark **41, 173, 174, 306, 307**
alginate, lifecasting: bust 123, 125; ears **131**; safety 91, 92; teeth 102–7
Algislo 113, **114**, 134, 135, 139
Alice bands 315
Alpha gypsum 212
Alpine ancestry 82
alternate marker method 402
Amber gels 11
American Anaplastology Association 17
anaplastology 14–17
anatomical planes 66, **67**, 68
ancestry distinctions: Africans 83–4; Asians 84–6; Caucasians 82–3; overview of 81–2; race 81
androgenic hair 65
Angora goat hair 310
animatronics 343–8, **344**
anthropometry 69
appendicular skeleton 44
appliance application techniques: attachment 288–9, 293–7; conforming molds 299–301, **299–301**; edge blending **301**, 301–2, **302**; IPA 287–8; makeup application 302–5; removal 305–7, **306, 307**
appliance casting *see* casting, appliances
arcus senilis 79, 80
area, conversion charts 469
arms: anatomy 49–50; lifecasting 129
Asian ancestry 84–6
Asian facial hair 320
Asian hair 310
Astounding magazine 360
audio-animatronics 345
autopsy stitch 423, **423**
axial skeleton 44, 47

B

baking soda 437
bald cap 109–10; appliance application 295; application 393–6; lifecasting 109–11, **110, 111**; making 390–3; materials and uses 389–90
Band-Aids® 321
Banks, Elizabeth **14**
Barrett, Leonard, Jr. **11**
barrier release agents 171
Barrymore, Drew 21, 412
baseball stitch 423, **423**
Bastard Amber shades 11
beards *see* facial hair
Berger, Howard **46**, 46–7
Beta Bond 288
Beta gypsum 212
biceps 49, **49**
birthmarks 64
Blake, John **329**
bleeders 245
blend cap edges, applying bondo to **396**
blisters 424–5
blocking *see* sculpting
block molds 181, **181**
block, postiche 311
blood recipe 440
bloom factor of gelatin 251
blue filters 11
Blue Point Engineering Servo Checker 359, **359**
body proportions 69–70, **70**
body type *see* somatotype
BondFX 188
bondo 265, 389, 396, 413, 441; removing appliances 418; 3D prosthetic 414
books, resources 475–7
box mold 181
Bray, Stuart 200, **200, 201, 295**
breakdown, sculpture: clay wall building 175–8; fiberglass molds 209–11, **210**; fillers, molds 211; keys, flashing, and cutting edges **174**, 174–5; matrix molds *see* matrix molds; miscellaneous type molds 180–2; negative mold preparation 172–4; overview 169; release agents and sealers 171–2; resin molds 212; silicone rubber molds 186; stone molds 178–80; tools and materials 171; urethane molds 213–15

Browder, Ben **81**
bruise 423
brushed case mold 181
brushes, drawing 311
brush holders **430**
brush technique 384
brush-up mold **178**, 200
burlap 119
Burman foam 433–5
burns 424–5
bust, lifecasting 121–8

C

Cab-O-Sil® 389, 414, 441, 442
café au lait 64
apek, Karel 346
capillary action 234
case mold 181
casting, appliances: cold foam *see* cold foam, appliance casting; dental acrylic *see* teeth, dental acrylic; foam latex *see* foam latex; gelatin *see* gelatin, appliance casting; gel-filled appliance *see* gel-filled appliance; painting 265–9; seaming and patching 263–5; silicone *see* silicone, coloration
caul net **332**, 333
centrifuging 241
Cervantes wig, crepe wool for **331**
CGI *see* computer-generated imagery
Chambers, John **6**
Chan, Jackie **272, 273**
Chaney, Lon 2, **2**, 5, **6**
character design elements 40
chemically active release agents 171
chickenpox **425**
chin block **312**
Chinese ancestry 84
chocolate syrup 440
cholesterol cream 110, 112, 116, 134, 136
Christensen, Hayden **227**
Clarke, Chris 343–4, **345**, 346, 347, 362, **366**, 369, **369, 370**
claustrophobia, feelings of 90
clay: oil 146–7; sulfur 145–6; wall, building in breakdown 175–8; WED 146
Close, Glenn 22, **23**
CMG mech baby **366, 367**
cold foam 213, 305
cold foam, appliance casting: appliance removal 250; gelatin *see* gelatin, appliance casting; materials and quirks 248; mold filling 249–50; mold preparation 248–9; painting 275–6; seaming and patching 265
collagen 250–1
collapsible core molds 215
collodion 399
colored gels 11
combination wig *see* fashion weft stretch wigs
commutator 354
computer-generated imagery (CGI) 1, 345, 346
condensation-cure silicone 106, 182, 204
conforming molds 188, **189**, 236–8
congenital melanocytic nevus 64
contact lenses 54–5, **56–7**; types of 58
contoured molds 188
conversion charts: area 469; cubic volume 472–3; length 468; temperature 468–9; volume 469–72; weight 467–8
coreless motor 354
Corso, Bill 412
cosmetic legs **16**
crack, repairs of 441–2
cranial muscles 47
craniofacial implants 16
Crawford, Michael **283**
creaming 241
crepe wool 310, **320**; application 322–8; preparation 320–2
crown punching needle 341, **341**
cubic volume, conversion charts 472–3
curing agent 243, 434

D

da Vinci, Leonardo 68, **69**
Davy, Michael 438
de-airing/degassing silicone 231
Del Toro, Benicio **226**
De Mille, Agnes 33
demolded appliance **292**
demolded eye **381**; trimming **386**
Densite HS 212
dental acrylic *see* teeth, dental acrylic
dental alginates 103, 131
dental wax **259**
Depp, Johnny 14
DeStephan, Kato 185–6, **185**
Dick's ager 442–3
Digital MultipleX (DMX) controllers 358–60
digital servos 355
Ding, Yi **272**
Dinklage, Peter **286**
direct drive 354
DMX512 358
DMX controllers *see* Digital MultipleX controllers
Dragon Skin 439
drawing brushes 311
drawing mats 311, **311**, 335, **335, 336**
Dyke, Vincent Van **42, 80, 160**, 235, **235**

E

ears: anatomy 53–4, 59, **60**; appliance 164; building up 397; lifecasting 130–2; sculpting 164–6, **164–6**
ectomorphic body type 41, **42, 45**
ectoplasm slime materials 445
edge blending **301**, 301–2, **302**
edge cutting, breakdown of the sculpture 174–5
EEprom 360
electrical control system 357–62
electronic technology, animatronics 357–62
electrostatic flocking 418–19
Elsey, David **34, 81, 226**, 226–7, **227**
endomorphic body type 42
epicanthic fold 84–6
EpoxAcoat RED 291, **291**
epoxy molds 212, **213**
equity theaters 10
Eskimo ancestry 85
European hair 310
extrinsic muscles 47
eye: anatomy 53–4, **54**, 59; resin 387–8; shape of **374**, 374–5
eyebrows *see* facial hair
eyelid mechanism **366**

F

face and neck, lifecasting 107–21
facial aging 77–81, **78**

facial hair 319; chin blocks 311; crepe wool 320–8; laid-on hair 319
facial muscles 48, **48**
facial prostheses 16
facial sculpting: blocking 151–3, **152**; head, face and neck 158, 160–2, **160–2**; refining 153, **154–8**, 155–8; sketching 149, 150
Farrell, Colin **287**
fashion weft stretch wigs 314
FASST *see* Futaba Advanced Spread Spectrum Technology
Federal Communications Commission (FCC) 357, 358
Federal Food, Drug and Cosmetic Act 21
feet, lifecasting 129–30
FGR-95 212
FiberGel, EnvironMolds' 108, 111, 134
fiberglass molds 209–11, **210**
fibonacci series 66
Field, Henry 81–4
fillers, molds 211
film: hair and makeup for 10; makeup effects in 9
five-psole motors 354
flashing 295; breakdown of sculpture **174**, 174–5
flocking 418–19
flood mold 181, **181**
Floutz, Thom 142, **142, 143**
FMG *see* Forton MG
foamed Water-Melon 438
foaming agent 243, 433, 434
foaming gelatin 437
foam latex 15–16, 184, 302–4, **303, 304**; appliance removal 246–7; heat curing 245–6; injector **245**; materials 239; mold filling 244–5; mold preparation 243–4; overview 238–9; painting 273–5; quirks 239–42; recipes 433–5; running 242–3; seaming and patching 264–5
foam stabilizer 245
Forton MG (FMG) 212
foundation 333, **333**
freckles 63, **63**
Freitas, Rob **412**
full body lifecasting: overview 132–3; prone position 133–8; standing position 138–40
full-head silicone mask **341**
Futaba Advanced Spread Spectrum Technology (FASST) 357
Futaba 6EX-2.4-GHz transmitter 357
Futaba-2.4-GHz FASST 357
Futaba S3003 servo 352
FX torso **166**

G

Gaf Quat 443–4
Garbarino, Mark **272**, 272–3
gelatin 15–16, **304**, 304–5, **305**; skin safety 425–6
gelatin, appliance casting: appliance removal 255–7; materials 251–2; mold filling 253–5; overview 250–1; painting 275–6; quirks 252–3; seaming and patching 265
gelatin recipes: foaming gelatin 437; overview 435–7
gel-filled appliance (GFA): encapsulating layer for 390; encapsulators 15; hand filling and removal 234; injection filling 232–3; mold preparation for filling 232; overview 231–2
gelling agent 243, 433, 434
gender, distinctions of 74–5
geometric analysis, body proportions 71, **71–3**
German, Greg **273**
GFA *see* gel-filled appliance
giant spider mech **360**
gluteus maximus 51
glycerin 253
GM foam 433–5
gnomatic growth **76**, 77
Golden Ratio 66, 68–9
gorilla mech **368, 370**; workings of
Gorton, Neill 3–5, **5**, 28, **85**, 101, **160, 161**, 189, **189**, 209, **210**, 263, **295–7, 356, 410, 412**
Graham, Martha 33
Grand Illusions II (Savini) 340
gray glass reinforced plastic (GRP) 216
Green Marble SeLr® 441–2
growth changes 75–7, **76**
GRP *see* gray glass reinforced plastic
gypsum molds *see* stone molds

H

H-10 443–4
hair *see also* wigs: attachment techniques 315; crepe wool 320–8; extensions 315; hackle 321, **321**; laid-on facial 319; punching 338–42; shaft 334, **335**; skin 64; tying 311; types of 65, 310–11; ventilating 329–38
hair-ventilating sequence **337**
hand-drawn tattoo 298
hand-knotted wigs 314, 315
hand-laid crepe beard **319, 323**
hand-laying hair 320, 322, 326
hands: lifecasting 129; sculpting 162–3, **164**
hand-tied hair **314**
hand-tied wig, lace on **314**
Haney, Kevin 436
Hannah, Darryl **283**
Harbor Freight 429, **429**
Hay, Graham **305**
hazardous materials 20
head and neck: muscles **47**, 47–8, **71**; sculpting of head, face and neck 158, 160–2, **160–2**
head and neck, lifecasting: face and neck 107–21; head and shoulders 121–8
Heald, Dustin **29**
health and safety regulations 20
high-consistency silicones 16
Hillard, Brian **298**
Himmell, Jeff **272**
HiTec submicro servo **355**
homemade sculpting tools **145**
Hoskins, Bob **94**
human body 43; skeletal system 44, 45; skeletomuscular system 47–52, **52**
human hair 313
human physiology 31
human skin 16
Hurt, John **282**
Hydrocal 133
hypertrophic scar 65, **66**

I

Ichabod Crane 41
IMATS *see* International Makeup Artist Trade Show
Indian ancestry 85
indirect drive 354
infant mech **348**
infections 19
ING lion mech **369**
Inhibit X 188
integumentary system 43, 44
International Makeup Artist Trade Show (IMATS) 294, 326, 327, 390
intrinsic muscles 47
IPA *see* isopropyl alcohol
Ippolito, Frank **303, 304**
iris button **374**, 375, **378**; hole in negative **382**
isopropyl alcohol (IPA) 287–8, 444

J

jacket mold 200, 216, 217; to brush up core **208**
Japanese ancestry 84–5
Jiffy-Mixer® 108
Joey mech **357**
Jones, Doug **142, 143, 298**
jungle makeup hut **19**

K

karbonite gears 355
Karloff, Boris 5, **6**
Keaton, Michael **13**
Kelly, Chris 43
keloid scar 65–6
keys, breakdown of sculpture 174–5
Kirkpatrick, Kevin 28, **29**, 170
kit, contents 29, 425, 426, 429–31
knotted wigs 314–15
knotting hooks *see* ventilating needle
Kryolan cold foam 248, **248**

L

labeling, products in kit 20
lace beard 319, **319**
lace wig, removal of 317–18
laid-on facial hair 319
Lane, Tami **286**, 286–7, **287**
Lange, Jessica 412
Langley, Frank **303, 304**
lanugo 65
latex 420, 421–2; foam *see* foam latex; liquid 286
Lau, Andy **272**
Lauten, Tom **304**
leather punches 384
legs: anatomy 51; lifecasting 129–30
length, conversion charts 468
lifecasting: bald cap 109–11, **110, 111**; ears 130–2; face and neck 107–21; full body *see* full body lifecasting; hands and arms 129; head and shoulders 121–8; legs and feet 129–30; materials 94–6; overview 96–101; safety 90–3; teeth 101–7
lighting 11–12
light recipe 443
LightWave 3D 33
lion mech **347**
liquid latex 286
liver spots 62
lizard face **166**
long hair, wigs preparation for 316
Lyon, Carl **99, 100**

M

machine-wefted hair 313
magazines, resources 475–7
makeup appliance: adhesives 285–6; cleaning and storing appliance 308; skin care 307–8; skin types 284–5; 3D prosthetic appliances 281
makeup application: cold foam 305; foam latex 302–4, **303, 304**; gelatin **304**, 304–5, **305**; silicone 305
makeup kit 429–31; materials in 29
makeup rooms in theaters 19
malleable block 311
marker transfers 400–2
mastix 285
materials: foam latex 239; lifecasting 94–6; in makeup kit 29; for postiche 310–12; safety 19–20; sculpting 141–2; silicone painting 269–72; tools and 171; used in making theatrical teeth appliances 257
material safety data sheet (MSDS) 20
matrix molds 200, **207**, 214; advantage and disadvantages 208; fiberglass 210, 211
Mauck, Don **284**
Maya 33
Mayor, Rob **296**
McCullagh, Conor **290–3**
McDowell, Roddy **6**
mechanical technology, animatronics: additional terminology 354–5; motion control 356–7; servo **349**, 349–53, **350, 351**
medical-grade adhesives 285
medical trauma simulations 440
Mediterranean ancestry 82
medium hair, wigs preparation for 316
Mendoza, Esteban 418
mesomorphic body type 41–2
metal gears 355
metric conversion *see* conversion charts
Mills, Amy **298–9**
MKS servo **349**
mohair *see* Angora goat hair
MoldGel 122–3
molds 375–6, **375–6**; conforming 236–8; coring 377–8; kit **388**; multipiece **165**; negative 172–4; optical silicone pouring into **386**; releasing **380**
moles 63
Mongolian blue spot 64
monomers 262
Monster Clay 172
Monster Makers foam 433–5
monster makeup 290–3, **290–3**
monster servo 355
Montgomery, Kirk 28
moulage recipes 440
moustaches: crepe wool 320–8; laid-on facial hair 319
MSDS *see* material safety data sheet
MudBox 34, 38, 39
mufx props **299**
multipiece molds **165**
Mungle, Matthew W. 21–4, 28, **165**, 417, 436
Murphy's Law 358
mustaches *see* facial hair
My Animatronic Project (Willett) 344

N

naphtha 396
National Fiber Technology (NFT) 341–2

Neanderthal man **283**
negative 96, **97**, 101
negative mold: making 172–4; for silicone **236**
Neill, Ve **12, 13**, 13–14
net foundation 311
NFT *see* National Fiber Technology
Nicotero, Greg **17**, 17–18
Nobbs, Albert 22, **23**
nonpareils 439
Nordic ancestry 82–3
nose: anatomy 53–4, 59, **60**; building up 397; and scar wax 398–9
nosebleed 423–4, **424**
nylon gears 354

O

Occupational Safety and Health Administration (OSHA) 20
oil clay 146–7
O'Kane, Jane **410**, 410–12
on-set etiquette 26–8
opera lace 333, **333**
optical silicone, processing 385–6
OSHA *see* Occupational Safety and Health Administration

P

paddles stage methods 368–9
painting: eyes 383–5; foam latex 273–5; gelatin and cold foam 275–6; silicone appliances 269–72; teeth, dental acrylic 276–9
palmar aponeurosis 50, 51
paraffin wax 171
partial auricular prosthesis **15**
Parvin, Dave 19, 90, 94–5
pasta maker 377, **377**
patching: foam latex 264–5; gelatin and cold foam 265; silicone appliances 263–4; temporary 442
Patterson, Cristina **53, 56, 57**, 59, **59**
Patterson, Suzanne 12
PAX Medium 445–6
PAX paint 445–6
pen transfers 400–2
petroleum jelly *see* cholesterol cream
Photoshop 34, **35**, 38
phthalates 21
Pierce, Jack 5, **6**
plaster bandage, lifecasting: application of 116; bust 121–2, 126; safety 92–3; uses of 115
plastic cap material 390
plasticizers in products 21
PlastiPaste II **202**, 214
plate mold 181–2, **182**
platinum-cure silicone 93, 107
platinum silicone 106, 182, 186–8, 228, 391; properties of 183–5; skin-safe 92, 299
polishing, silicone eyes 386–7
polyurethane *see* urethane
portfolio, contents 28–9
port wine stain 64
position-sensing mechanism 352
postiche: block 311; tools and materials 310–11
pour mold 181, **181**
Pour Pros-Aide® 441
pour-up mold 200
power net **332**, 333
PPI Premiere Products, Inc. 441–2
pre-laid hair **326**
Premiere Products 441–2
preval sprayer **236**
Price, Wes **74, 78, 82**
professionalism 24–8
programmable controller board 359
Pros-Aide® 110, 265; acrylic matte medium mixing with 446; age stipple 442; airbrush 405; appliance application 286, 288, 293; bondo 389; thin layer of **416**; transfers 414
prosthetics: appliances application 281–2; medical contributions 14–17; transfers *see* 3D transfers
pulse code graphic **351**
pulse width modulation (PWM) 350
punching: hair 338–42; pupils **384**
puppeteers 367
puzzle molds 215
PWM *see* pulse width modulation
Pygram, Wayne **226**

Q

quadriceps femoris muscles 50, **51**

R

race *see* ancestry distinctions
Randall, Tony **5**
RC *see* rigid collodion
recipes: bondo 441; Dick's ager 442–3; foam latex 433–5; gelatin 435–7; Green Marble SeLr® 441–2; H-10 443–4; PAX paint 445–6; Pros-Aide® 442; slime 444–5
red-orange PAX 407, **407**
release agents 171
removal technique 442
removers 306
residual solvents 262
resin eyes 387–8
resin molds 212
resources: books and magazines 475–7; suppliers 447–66
rigid collodion (RC) 399, **399**; scar 374
room temperature vulcanization (RTV) silicone 182, 204, 228, 270
Rooney, Kelly 12
Roscolux color range 11
RTV silicone *see* room temperature vulcanization silicone
Rush, Geoffrey **411**

S

safety: lifecasting 90–3; materials 19–20
Salmon, Jamie 7–8
sartorius 51
scar: features and types 65–6; nose and scar wax 398–9; rigid collodion **399**
Schell, Jordu **42**, 44–5, **44, 62, 144**
Schoonraad, John 93–4, **94**
scleral core: casting 380–1; creation of 376–7; trimming and prepping 381–2
scleral lenses 54, **56**, 58
screen makeup *vs.* stage makeup 8–12
sculpting: breakdown *see* breakdown, sculpture; clay 101, 145–7; ears 164–6, **164–6**; facial sculpting *see* facial sculpting; hands 162–3, **164**; materials 141–2; positive preparation for 143; reference photos 147; teeth 147–8, **149**; tools 143–5, **144, 145**
sealers 172

seaming: foam latex 264–5; gelatin and cold foam 265; silicone appliances 263–4
self-releasing silicone 214
Sells, Toby 265, **265**
servo motors **349**, 349–53, **350, 351**, 355
set etiquette 26–8
sexual dimorphism 74–5
sheep's wool *see* crepe wool
Sheldon, William 41, 42
Shinetsu Silicone Caulk 266, **266**
Shoneberg, Andy **17, 18**
short hair, wigs preparation for 315–16
silicone 182–5, 262; adhesives 288; appliance 305; block mold 190, **191**; gel-filled appliance 15; mixing thickened **383**; platinum 391; prosthesis **15**; seaming and patching 263–4; skin safety 425–6, **426**; types for appliance casting 228
silicone, coloration 228–9; de-airing/degassing 231; materials 230
silicone eyes, making **17**; button placing 379–80; button preparing 378–9; casting scleral core 380–1; creating scleral core 376–7; mold, making 375–6, 377–8; optical processing 385–6; painting 383–5; shape of 374–5; trimming and polishing 386–7
silicone foam 438; creating cells 439; moulage recipes 440
silicone, lifecasting: safety 92–3; teeth **106**, 106–7, **107**
silicone painting 265–9; materials 269–72
silicone rubber molds 186
simulated skin 440
Singer, Matt 387
six-volt R/C battery pack **361**
skeletal system 44, 45
skeletomuscular system: abdomen and lower limbs 50–2; head and neck 47–8; torso and upper limbs 48–50
skin: care 307–8; simulation 425–6, 440; surface anatomy 61–6; types 284–5
Skin Illustrator® palettes 400
Skin Tite 300, **300**
skin tones, matching **23**
slime recipes 444–5
Smith, Dick 2, **2**, **81**, 281, **281**, 442–3
Snell, Richard 390, 393
Snyder, David **272**
Sodano, Vittorio 97–8, **97–8**
Softimage XSI 33
solar lentigo 62
somatotype 41–3
sorbitol 253
spatter 410
Special Lavender category 11
Spencer, Karen **3, 5, 294**
spider veins 63
spirit gum 285
spline 350–1, 354
sponge 408–9
sprues 207
Stage Makeup (Corson and Glavan) 442
stage makeup *vs.* screen makeup 8–12
stencils: airbrush 409; sponge 408–9; tattoos 400, 402
sternocleidomastoid muscle 71
stipple: uses 410; wrinkle stipple 420–2
stipple, age: Dick's ager 442–3; Green Marble SeLr® 441–2; H-10 443–4; PAX paint 445–6; Pros-Aide® 442
stone molds 178–80, 435
Stone, Sharon **39**
stork bite 64
strawberry mark 64
stretch marks **61**, 61–2
stretch weft wig 313
striated muscle 47
structural technology, animatronics 362–4
styrene 211
submicro servo 355
Sugar, Nick 10
sulfur clay 145–6
Super Baldiez 291, 326, **326**
suppliers, contact information 447–66
surface anatomy 52, **60**; eyes, ears, and nose 53–4; mouth 59; skin 61–6
Surprise Pink 11
sweat recipe 440
syntactic dough 212–13
synthetic hair 310, 311
synthetic wig 313

T

tartaric acid 437
tattoos: alternate marker method 402; and character/creature textures 400; cover-up techniques 406; marker/pen transfers 400–2; sponge 408–9; with stencils 402–3; traditional sleeve design **400**; water transfers **404**, 404–6, **405**
technology, animatronics: electronic 357–62; mechanical 349–57; structural 362–4; surface 364–70
teeth: lifecasting 101–7; sculpting 147–8, **149**
teeth, dental acrylic: appliance removal 259–62; materials 257–8; mold filling and appliance removal 258–9; painting 276–9
Telesis 288
Telesis 5 293, 294, 317, 323
television: hair and makeup for 10; makeup effects in 9
temperature, conversion charts 468–9
terminal hair 65
terra alba 114, 115
Teves, Miles 34, **35**, 37–8, **39, 79**
Thea's recipe 436
theaters: hair and makeup for 10; makeup effects for 1; makeup rooms in 19; productions 9
Thickened Pros-Aide (TPA): spreading into silicone plate mold **415**; transfers 414
3D makeup effects, creating for stage 9
3D prosthetic bondo 414
3D transfers: materials 414; overview 412; technique 412–13
3D Studio Max 33
three-psole motors 354
tibialis anterior 51, **52**
tin-cure silicone 106, 107
Tindall, Peter **32, 33**

tin silicone 186–8; properties of 183–5; RTV 228; types of 182–3
Tinsley, Christien 389, 412
Tirinnanzi, Daniel E. **365, 366, 367, 370**
Top Guard 285, 426
torque 352, **352**, 354
torso muscles 48–9, **49**
TPA *see* Thickened Pros-Aide
traditional stage makeup 8, 9
traditional tattoo sleeve design **400**
transit time 354
triceps 49, **50**
trimming, silicone eyes 386–7
Tucker, Christopher **282**, 282–3
tuplast **397**, 397–8
Turi, Joshua 229–30, **229–30**
Tuttle, William 5, **5**

U

Ultracal 30, lifecasting 96–7, 117–19, 127–8, 132–3
underskull, making of 363, **363**
urethane: cold foam, appliance casting *see* cold foam, appliance casting; molds 213–15

V

varicose veins 63
veg net 330–3, **332**
veins: adding to sclera **385**; coloration **271**
vellus hair 65
ventilating hair 338; caul net **332**, 333; Cervantes wig, crepe wool for **331**; drawing mats 335, **335, 336**; foundation/opera lace 333, **333**; hair shaft 334, **335**; hair-ventilating sequence **337**; machine-ventilated pieces 329; power net **332**, 333; veg net 330–3, **332**
ventilating needle 311
ventilation, workspace 18
Venturi-type vacuum pump **231**
vinyl cap, IPA on 396
visual effect 1
volume, conversion charts 469–73
voluntary muscle *see* striated muscle
Vosloo, Arnold 2

W

Wade, Brian 36, **143**
Waldo, telemetry devices 360–1
Walken, Christopher **22**
Walker, Brian **310**
Walter Elias Disney (WED) clay 99, 117, 176, **201**; advantage of 146; for weighing **203**
Wang, Steve **36, 39**, 40, 77–8, 159, **159**
Ware, Colin **227**
water-based acrylic adhesive 416
water-based plastics 389
water transfer paer, tracing design onto **401**
WED clay *see* Walter Elias Disney clay
weft wig 313–14
weight, conversion charts 467–8
wig block 311
Wig Making and Styling: A Complete Guide for Theatre and Film (Ruskai and Lowery) 309
wigs 312; cleaning, ways of 313; knotted wigs 314–15; lace wig 317–18; measurement form **312**; placement **23**, 316–17; postiche tools and materials 310–11; preparation for 315–16; weft wigs 313–14
Wigs and Make-up for Theatre Television and Film (Baker) 319
Willett, Gary **343, 364, 367**
wizard board 359, **359**
wooden blocks 311
workspace 18–19
wreckage installation **7**
wrinkle stipple 420–2

Y

yak hair 310

Z

Zakarian, Louie **229, 230**
ZBrush 34, **34**, 38–9
Zombie **32, 40, 42**